THE RETURN TO
ZION

MATI ALON

Order this book online at www.trafford.com
or email orders@trafford.com

Most Trafford titles are also available at major online book retailers.

Printed in the United States of America.

ISBN: 978-1-4269-6598-2 (sc)
ISBN: 978-1-4269-6600-2 (hc)
ISBN: 978-1-4269-6601-9 (e)

Library of Congress Control Number: 2011907051

Trafford rev. 05/05/2011

 www.trafford.com

North America & international
toll-free: 1 888 232 4444 (USA & Canada)
phone: 250 383 6864 ♦ fax: 812 355 4082

By The Same Author:

The Unavoidable Surgery
Vantage Press
New York, 1983

The Unavoidable Surgery, Second Edition
Trafford Publishing
Victoria, British Columbia, CANADA, 2003

Holocaust and Redemption
Trafford Publishing
Victoria, British Columbia, CANADA, 2003

Coexistence with Hagar's Offspring
Trafford Publishing
Victoria, British Columbia, CANADA, 2007

Not a Vanishing Breed
Trafford Publishing
Victoria, British Columbia, CANADA, 2009

TO MY THREE LOVELY DAUGHTERS: MICHAL,
DORIT AND LIMOR

A Great Thank You To My Two Sons:
The Oldest NIR
The Youngest RAZ
For Their Help with the Computer

"And it came to pass after these things, that God did prove Abraham, and said unto him: 'Abraham'; as and he said: 'Here am I.' And He said:' Take now thy son, thine only son, whom thy lovest, even Isaac, and get thee into the land of Moriah; and offer him there for a burnt-offering upon one of the mountains which I will tell thee of.' And Abraham rose early in the morning, and saddled his ass, and took two of his young men with him, ans Isaac his son; and he cleaved the wood for the burnt-offering, and rose up, and went unto the place of which God had told. On the third day Abraham lifted up his eyes, and saw the place afar off. And Abraham said unto his young men: 'Abide ye here with the ass, and I and the lad will go yonder; and we will worship, and come back to you.' And Abraham took the wood of the burnt-offering, and laid it upon Isaac his son; and he took in his hand the fire and the knife; and they went both of them together. And Isaac spoke unto Abraham his father, and said: 'My father,' and he said: 'Here am I , my son.' And he said: 'Behold the fire and the wood; but where is the lamb for the burnt-offering?' And Abraham said: ' God will provide Himself the lamb for a burnt-offering, my son.' So they went both of them together. And they came to the place which God had told him of: and Abraham built the alter there and laid the wood in order, and bound Isaac his son, and laid him on the alter, upon the wood. And Abraham stretched forth his hand, and took the knife to slay his son. And the angel of the Lord called unto him out of heaven, and said: 'Abraham Abraham', And he said 'Here am I, ' And he said: 'Lay not thy hand upon the lad, neither do thou anything unto him; for now I know that thou art a God-fearing man, seing thou hast not withheld thy son, thine only son, from Me.' And Abraham lifted up his eyes, and looked, and behold behind him a ram, caught in the thicket by his horns. And Abraham went and took the ram, and offered him up for a burnt-offering in the stead of his son. And Abraham called the name of that place Adonai Jireh; as it is said to this day: ' in the mount where the Lord is seen.' And the angel of the Lord called unto Abraham a second time out of heaven, and said: 'By Myself have I sworn, said the Lord, because thou hast done this thing, and hast not withheld thy son, thine only son."

GENESIS 22:1-12

(The two young men watching the ass were: Yishmael, the son of Hagar and Abraham and Eliezer the servant)

"And God said unto Abraham: Let it not be grievous in thy sight because of the lad, and because of thy bondwoman; in all that Sarah saith unto thee; hearken unto her voice for in Isaac shall seed be called to thee."

GENESIS 21:12

"Take heed to thyself lest thou make a covenant with the inhabitants of the land whither thou goest lest they be for a snare in the midst of thee."

Exodus 34: 12

And God said to Moses:" Write this for a memorial in the book, for I will utterly blot out the memory of Amalek from under heaven."

Exodus 17: 8-15

"Remember what Amalek did to you by the way, when you were coming out of Egypt, how he met you by the way and smote your hindmost-all who were feeble-in the rear when you were faint and weary, and feared not God. Therefore, it shall be, when the Lord your God has given you rest from all your enemies round about….you shall blot out the remembrance of Amalek from under heaven."

Deuteronomy 25: 17-19

"And I commanded Joshua at that time, saying: 'Thine eyes have seen all that the Lord your God hath done unto these two kings; so shall the Lord do unto all the kingdoms whither thou goest over. Ye shall not fear them; for the Lord your God, He it is that fighteth for you."

Deuteronomy 3: 21

Contents

1. THE INTIFADA-THE ARAB TERROR

"Recent petrol bomb attacks are further proof that the conflict between us and the Arabs, as expressed in the recent wave of disturbances, does not revolve around a territorial issue. The attack is on our existence."

Yitzhak Shamir, Prime Minister
To Israel Radio on July 7, 1988

For 19 years, from 1948 to 1967, the Palestinian Arabs were under Arab rule; Israel did not hold an inch of the territory they now claim. And instead of pressing their case for independence against the Egyptian, who occupied the Gaza Strip, and the Jordanian kingdom, which ruled them on its West Bank, they turned all their fury against Israel. It is important to remember that Israel is in Judea, Samaria and Gaza not only because it wanted so or planned so, but because the Arabs went to war against Israel and lost it.

Israel has treated the Palestinian Arabs in Judea, Samaria and Gaza better than any other Arab country had ever treated them. Better than Jordan had treated them during the nineteen years of Jordanian occupation. The Palestinian Arabs' standard of living has risen considerably. Their infant mortality rates have declined as a result of the introduction of birth clinics and children vaccinations. The longevity of their elderly had increased substantially due to better food, better hygiene, better doctors, more medicine, modern hospitals.

Better housing, better schools, more universities, more money poured into their municipalities and local governments, etc. They never had it so good before.

When the Israelis freed Judea, Samaria and Gaza from the Jordanian rule there was not a single university in these areas. Since these territories returned to Israel, eight Arab universities and eight Arab colleges were founded.

As already mentioned in my previous book (the Unavoidable Surgery, Vantage Press, New York, 1983, page 159) until December 1987, the Arabs in Eretz Israel, were busy improving their social conditions, their standard of living, their education, and have temporarily and artificially quenched their political ambitions and desires. Once they achieved this goal, on December 1987, they did come up with their political pretensions, their claim for a Palestinian state, at the expense of Israel, of course, even if they had to use force.

Until December 1987, the P.L.O. did the "Job" for them, from outside Israel. On December 1987 they decided to take their fate in their own hands and physically take part in the conflict. It was a big "Palestinian" decision, may be similar to their decision on November 1947, not to accept the UN "partition" plan received by the UN Resolution Number 181. On December 1987, on "Peace Day," the first sign of "Palestinian" Arab civil rebellion started to show up. This Arab show of force intended, mainly, to force Israel to accept an International Peace Conference for the Middle

East, with the participation of P.L.O. representatives. It was also a new phase in the war against the State of Israel, a war going on, at least since the creation of the State of Israel, on May 15, 1948. It was the start of a "War of Independence" from Israeli Occupation, called "Intifada".

Now that their economic situation had substantially improved they decided to satisfy also their political ambitions. Now that their bellies were full and their houses were full, their audacity increased. The Palestinian Arabs are agitating not for civil rights, but rather for national rights; not for an improvement of their "occupation", but rather for the end of the "occupation". They claimed that "good government is no substitute for self government". What the Arabs want now is independence and a Palestinian State, at the expense of Israel and on Israeli soil.

There is nothing surprising or shocking about the refusal of the new generation of Palestinian Arabs to live under the Israeli "Yoke". It was expected. They want independence. They want a Palestinian State. They can have it, but not at the expense of Israel. They can have it across the borders, in the Arab neighboring states.

There is no doubt that the Arab uprising in Judea, Samaria and the Gaza District reflected frustration and despair among the vast majority of the Arab inhabitants in these territories, and their desire for self determination and a political solution. To find a solution to their political ambitions they must go elsewhere, leave the country, because they cannot have it at the expense of another nation. They cannot have it at the expense of Israel.

Something that seemed to have started off as "ordinary" riots has turned, in a relatively very short time, into a fully-fledged Palestinian, Arab war on Israel.

On December 8, 1987, an Israeli truck driving in the Gaza Strip hit two cars. Four Arabs were killed and six Arabs were injured. The next day, masses of people came out into the streets, alleys of the Jabalya refugee camp in a violent demonstration throwing stones and burning tires. The Israeli soldiers were caught by surprise. When their lives were in danger and they understood that the mob was going to tear them apart they opened fire in self defense. A small riot, after the collision between a Jewish truck and an Arab car, broadened to include the entire Palestinian, Arab population in Judea, Samaria and the Gaza Strip. Something that started with no Jewish political ambitions turned into an Arab national movement, called INTIFADA.

The younger Arab Palestinian generation, who were better fed, better educated than their parents, using the Israeli democracy under which they lived for the last two, three decades were seeking a national identity as well as dignity. They also wanted the Israelis off their backs. They were more demanding, more militant than their parents. They shoved their elders aside and became in charge. To Israel they became a dangerous element.

The story relates that a car accident sparked the intifada. The grain of the truth is that the story had no connection to the intifada.

The revolt in the Gaza Strip totally surprised the Israeli security establishment, and they hoped it was a passing phenomenon. At the beginning they did not take it seriously.

The Israelis started to take it more seriously when they realized that it didn't stop but accelerated and turned into a revolt.

The New Arab Revolt is the acceleration of an audacity that has been gaining force for years and the result of a stupid Israeli permissiveness, a result of Israeli negligence, a result of Israeli blindness.

The Palestinian Arab's reaction at the start of their uprising was a mixture of self- confidence, exhilaration and pride. They believed that they "got it made". "We made it.We were much stronger than we had thought we were, the Independent Palestinian State is on its way."

A few days after the up rise erupted in Judea, Samaria and Gaza, the Chief of General Staff Dan Shomron promised the nation over the media that the riots would be over in a few days. A month later the same soothing words came from his boss, Defense Minister Yitzhak Rabin. Two years later they were ridiculed when the uprise, the intifada was still going on.

At the political level two Israeli citizens failed to predict the Palestinian Arabs' uprising, the intifada. Prime Minister Yitzhak Shamir and Defense Minister Yitzhak Rabin. When eventually they woke up, the Palestinian Arabs had already the international media on their side and Israel was on the Defense.

There is no doubt what so ever, that the Shamir-Rabin government fully deserved criticism for being caught by surprise and for taking so long to find the effective measures to handle the new situation.

The Palestinian Arab uprising caught Defense Minister Yitzhak Rabin by surprise and ill-prepared in every respect. The Police and Military Intelligences were also dormant, and did not see it coming. Defense Minister Yitzhak Rabin responded to the breakdown "Public Order" rather than to an undeclared Arab War.

After every Arab terrorist activity against the Jewish population, the Israeli government declared that this was a single phenomenon which involved only very few Arabs who did not represent the majority of the Arab population in Eretz Israel. A very cheap excuse to hide its incompetence to put an end to the Arab Intifada. Since the Arab uprising started the situation in Judea, Samaria and the Gaza Strip fluctuated between calm periods and periods of unrest. Tensions were chronic, constant and increasing, mainly in the refugee camps and among the younger, more militant Palestinian Arabs.

When Col. Richard Henry Meinertzhagen asked a Lebanese constructor in Kuwait, in 1951, "Why do not you Arabs, with all your resources from oil, do something for those wretched refugees from Palestine?" the Lebanese constructor answered:"They are just human rubbish, scum, but a political gold mine." "They" referred to the Arab refugees from the 1948 Arab-Israel war. Then he added:"Good God, do you really think we are going to destroy the finest propaganda we possess? It's a gold mine."

In slightly different language Meinerthagen received identical views from other Arabs too. (Meinertzhagen notes in his Middle East Diary: 1917-1956, Cresset Press, London).

The Arab uprising, the Intifada, had one main purpose: to destroy the State of Israel and establish a Palestinian-Arab state instead.

With a little luck, the Palestinian Arabs' "awakening" will also put an end to the long Israeli hibernation and provoke an Israeli awakening too.

Foreign sources believe that for Israel to sit idle and do nothing, or rather wait and let the Arabs manufacture babies and become a majority is a great mistake and even a great danger to its survival. They also believe that the eruption of the Palestinian Arabs' revolution or Intifada was a blessing for Israel, because it would compel the parties involved to deal with the issue rather than let it hibernate. This is why it is not in the best interest of Israel to end the intifada, but rather keep it glowing. The Palestinian Arabs, if they were smart, could have simply waited patiently, be fruitful and multiply. Multiply until they became a majority and endangered the future of the Jewish State. But, instead, they roused with their intifada and forced Israel into a corner. They forced Israel to make decisions, which Israel had so long postponed. Israel had no choice but to make such a decision, which will remove the threat to its security. For the State of Israel this is a Godsent opportunity.

Israel needed this kind of shock treatment in order to get out of its self-made morass. It was Godsent. Now that the rude awakening is finally happening, it must deal with the issues head on. It can no longer seek shelter under slogans that could barely cope with yesterday's realities. May be it will start thinking more seriously of "transfer".

True, the Intifada for Israel was not a small problem. Many Israelis believe that if the Palestinian Arab uprising will be crushed, it will be worse. Because, then, the Israeli Government might believe that it had already solved the "Palestinian Problem" and sit and do nothing more.

The problem of the Palestinians, and as a matter of fact, also the Israeli problem, will not be solved after the intifada is terminated, but, only after the Last Palestinian Arab has left the country for good.

It is wrong to believe that the PLO did not initiate the Palestinian Arab uprising, but rather it was "on the tail of events, not in the lead of them, and that it was the Islamic fundamentalists who incited the riots and fomenting violence. The intifada did not begin as a sporadic disturbance. It was the result of a very careful and thorough Arab planning.

The uprising, the intifada in the West Bank and the Gaza Strip was planned by Yasser Arafat, long be.fore June 1967. In order to start the uprising Arafat had to have King Hussein and Jordan out of the West Bank and Gaza. This, he realized by increasing the number of borders clashes and infiltrations along the Israeli-Jordanian borders. Arafat heated the borders and contributed to the start of the Six-Day War, in June 1967, and the involvement of Jordan in that war.

Arafat wanted Israel to occupy the West Bank and Gaza rather than Jordan, so he could have a claim on it.

Two victors came out of the Six-Day War: Israel and the PLO. Israel regained its historical lands: Judea, Samaria, Gaza and the Old City of Jerusalem. Arafat, on the other hand, achieved his old dream of chasing Jordan out of the West Bank and Gaza, so that he could use these territories as a base for a Palestinian uprising and a first phase to the conquer of all of Eretz Israel, which he could not realize with Jordan sitting in it.

There is no doubt whatsoever that, sooner or later, the Arabs will use regained territories as a springboard for terrorism or military attacks.

On December 25, 1987 (Tevet 4, 5748) Defense Minister Yitzhak Rabin confirmed that hundreds of people, in Judea, Samaria and Gaza, were detained, following the unrest in the territories but denied that any decision on deportations had yet been made. "We have the legal option of doing so and there is no question that this is a means that we could use," said Rabin.

In an interview to the Jerusalem Post Rabin said that the current tough measures in force would continue "until there is stability. I will not predict, however, when this will be. My message to the inhabitants of the territories is clear: terror and unrest will get you nothing, just more suffering and pain. The only way out of this is at the negotiating table. That no Israeli government has changed the legal status of the territories is absolute proof of our sincerity," he said.

"Our offers of negotiation have gone unanswered," Rabin continued. "In the meantime we have to maintain law and order and we will do so. These past two weeks have been weeks of violence, of road blocks, stones and Molotov cocktails, and the means we will employ will be in direct proportion to the threat."

"I have just enjoyed reminding the BBC that the laws in force in the territories today are laws the British left us. The difference is, however, that when they arrested me, I didn't have recourse to a lawyer within 48 hours," said Rabin.

"Our policies have not changed. We will fight terrorism and unrest, and encourage those elements that want peace. We will close schools that have ceased to fulfill their function as educational institutions and which have been consistent in allowing their children out into the streets," added Rabin.

"We are going after those organizers who have come into the schools, their faces masked, and forced pupils, often against their first will, to riot."

Defense Minister Rabin rejected the criticism that had been leveled against him in the U.S. for reportedly disregarding U.S. advice not to institute a hardline policy.

"I express regret over the loss of life, but our warning went unheeded and the violence continued. Then, rubber bullets and gas were ineffective, leaving us no option but to use the means we did," said Rabin.

"The goal was to minimize casualties and we tried to aim only at the feet."

Rabin denied that most casualties had been children. " Is a 23-years old, or a 19-years old, a child?" asked Rabin.

The Arabs were totally wrong by nurturing the idea that Israel was not capable to absorb casualties and therefore was doomed to disappear soon.

If Defense Minister Yitzhak Rabin as well as Minister of Police, Haim Barlev, in order to restore law and order in the streets, would have given the order to shoot at the militant demonstrator with real bullets, rather than rubber bullets or tear gas, they would have killed twenty to thirty demonstrators and would have stopped the Arab uprising immediately and put an end to their intifada, thus saving many Arab and Jewish lives. Their order should have been:"Shoot to kill." But, unfortunately, these two gentlemen didn't have the stamina to issue such an order. Their order was: "Shoot to maim" and "advertised" it all over, so that the Arabs knew it, and were no longer afraid.

The average Palestinian-Arab may not like the way the Arab uprising against Israel was going on, he may not like Israel's reaction too, yet neither is he willing to do anything to stop it by controlling his violent elements. His silence exposed his approval. Israel cannot be expected to put up with bloodshed, arson and civil disorder. It is Israel's duty to restore law and order in the streets.

One of Israel's reactions should have been the expulsion of those Arabs found guilty. Under the circumstances, it seems to be, relatively, one of the most merciful choice, one of the most moral reactions. More moral than maiming, killing or long detention. Israel is not a free democracy. Israel is a democracy in siege, and a democracy in siege cannot act like a free democracy. An iron fist should have been used to quell the Arab uprising, but for one reason or another, the Israeli government decided to handle the intifada softly, with silken gloves. At the start of the uprising, on December 1987, Israel should have expelled one hundred or two hundred inciters and applied collective punishment and the intifada would have stopped immediately. If the expulsion did not work, Israel should have put up thirty new settlements in Judea, Samaria and Gaza. That would have been a good response to the Arab intifada.

There is a great difference between violent rebellion and non-violent civil disobedience. Non-violent civil disobedience should be suppressed by ample, limited forces. On the other hand, those engaged in violent rebellion are nothing but soldiers engaged in a war, that started in 1948 with the aim of destroying the Jewish state and drive its Jewish population right into the Mediterranean Sea. And these should be exterminated.

If the Israeli government loses this war by allowing the rioters to succeed, it will lose in the streets what it won on the battlefield.

The Arabs decided to try a new tactics. They have decided to confront Israel with civilian resistance, which is more vexing. They tried to imitate the late Mahatma Gandhi from India, who also, in his time, preached for passive resistance, but they, the Arabs were impatient and soon became militant, using stones, Molotov cocktails, knives, sticks, etc.

It is more than clear that the Palestinian Arabs really believed that those street riots will lead them to a Palestinian State at the expense of Israel, and therefore, for them it is a fight to the death. Israel had no choice but to react accordingly.

The Arabs regard Jaffa, Haifa, Acre and the Galilee as occupied territory, no less than Judea, Samaria and Gaza. Therefore, for Israel, territorial concessions and partial withdrawal in Judea, Samaria and Gaza are mortally dangerous. Hence, any Israeli territorial compromise would be a first step towards the dismantling of Israel.

The war against the Arabs was predicted, long ago:

"Ishmael will the Empty Sacred Land, for a long time, and will prevent the Israelites from returning .back to their Land, until such time that the Ishmaelites lose their right."

("Zohar"-Genesis 12, 13, 14, 15,16, 17-Parashat "Lech Lechah")

And the Ishmaelites will succeed to persuade the Gentile world to join them in the war against the Israelites:

"For I will gather all nations against Jerusalem to battle;"
(Zechariah 14:2)

The War between Gog and Magog (Ezekiel:38, 39)-Armageddon-Apocalypse

The danger to the Israelites is expressed in the following sentence:

"Alas! For that day is great,
So that none is like it;
And it is a time of trouble unto Jacob,
But out it shall he be saved."
(Jeremiah 30:7)

Because, the good Lord God will punish these nations:
"And this shall be the plague wherewith the Lord willl smite
All the people that have warred against Jerusalem:"
(Zechariah 14:12)

"Therefore fear thou not, o Jacob My servant, saith the Lord;
Neither be dismayed, O Israel;
And Jacob shall again be quiet and at ease,
And none shall make him afraid.

For I am with thee, saith the Lord, to save thee;
For I will make a full end of all the nations..."
(Jeremiah 30:10, 11)

And Israel will come out victorious.
"And the Lord shall be King over all the earth;
In that day shall the Lord be One, and His name one."
(Zechariah 14:9)

During the first week of the Palestinian-Arab uprising (Intifada), in Judea, Samaria and Gaza, on December 1987, Defense Minister, Yitzhak Rabin, so underestimated its importance, almost ignored it, as to decide not to return from his visit to the United States. A month later, after his return from the US, Rabin issued instructions to confront the uprising with a little greater resoluteness. Statements were issued periodically that it would be suppressed within a matter of days, or weeks at most.

As the uprising continued, Rabin struck a more balanced and realistic note. Rabin, now, predicted that it would go on for some time, and would not end soon. It would turn into a question of who would tire first, the Palestinians or the Israelis. In other words, this was a new version of a war of attrition. It seemed that Israel was displaying more staying power than the Palestinian-Arabs.

Rabin ordered the IDF (Israel Defense Force) to limit itself to the judicious application of only a small portion of the means of violence at its command. This meant that, the means to be adopted to put down the uprising would not include that of a large-scale use of lethal arms against the rioting masses confronting the Israeli army and police. To a large extent, however, the fact that the IDF has continued to rely on the selective use of lethal arms has been the result of a bowing to American pressures.

A more effective means of fighting the intifada would have been the immediate deportation of those caught, bombing down their buildings.

At the beginning of the uprising, Israel had not resorted to it, is because its leaders have bowed to American opposition to expulsion, even if proven terrorists and leaders of the riots.

The decision to limit the IDF's use of lethal force was totally wrong. It postponed the crushing of the uprising and prolonged the agony.

Other recipes to quell the Arab uprising were: large scale arrests and detention of inciters, curfew.

It was a great mistake not to put down the intifada, even by a blood bath, if necessary, right at the beginning, on December 1987. This was one of Israel's greatest mistakes. One pays dear for such a stupid mistake. If such measures have been taken, hundred of Arab and Jewish lives could have been spared. On the other hand, many Israelis believed that by resorting to a blood bath in order to break the intifada would have meant to win the battle but to lose the war. It would have meant winning the battle in the narrow local arena, but losing the world public opinion and the U.S. support in the broader arena.

The P.L.O. is using, very cleverly, the defeatist reactions of the Maarah party, as well as, the differences between the Maarah and the Likud parties, the verbal conflict between these two Israeli parties encouraged the Arabs, in Eretz Israel, to more violent street demonstrations, to more militant riots.

The P.L.O.'s achievements were always directly proportional to their success to distort normal life in Israel.

Critical declarations from "friends", such as Richard Murphy, Assistant to U.S. Secretary of State George Shultz and Paul Bremer, heading the "terror" desk in the U.S. State Department, who declared that the P.L.O. are not terrorists, only worsened the situation.

Richard Murphy suggested that Israel uses rubber bullets and water to disperse Arab demonstrators, same as the South Korean government in Seoul did in dispersing street demonstrations by Korean opposition.

The Moses family from Alfei Manasseh, the mother and the son were killed by an Arab petrol-bomb (Molotov cocktail) thrown at their car and not by a rubber bottle. Besides, the Korean government forces meant only to disperse the opposition's demonstrations, not to kill the opposition. The Arabs are here to kill.

No country in the world likes to be told by another country how to keep law and order in its streets, in its territory.

Also, there is no doubt whatsoever that the U.S. abstention at the UN Security Council on December 1987 only encouraged the Arabs to continue their riots and terror.

By comparing the situation in Israel with the situation in South Korea, the U.S. only shows that it still doesn't grasp the crux of the problem. The U.S. behavior, many believe, is the outcome of a Saudi-Arabian pressure on the U.S. on behalf of the P.L.O.

In spite of the fact that, in every country in the world the police disperses illegal demonstrations and riots by means of the stick, tear gas, and water, the Sikh demonstrations in India, the students' demonstrations in Korea, Basque demonstrations in Spain, are all dispersed by means of the stick. Everybody heard of the Carrot Policy. This is common procedure to keep law and order. Every body is doing.

Rabin the Defense Minister, has caused a great damage to Israel's good reputation, by declaring on television that he is going to use the stick against Arab demonstrations, "to save Arab lives". But Rabin turned to sticks, turned to beatings. But to announce it to the whole world was absolutely ridiculous. This was a very unwise thing to do, unless he meant, like his political boss, Shimon Peres, to invite outside pressure against Israel, in order to undermine Shamir's government.

The late President Ronald Reagan criticized Israel for handling the Arab riots and street demonstrations, on December 1987, a little too rough and defined Israel's self- defense operations as a danger to the World. One sometimes wonders if:

- The U.S. (President Kennedy) involvement in the Cuban crisis in 1962 was not a danger to the world?
- The U.S. (President Truman) involvement in the Korean War in 1952-1953 was not a danger to the world?
- The U.S. (President Nixon) involvement in the Vietnamese War in 1958-1973 was not a danger to the world?
- The U.S. (President Reagan) involvement in the Iraq-Iran war in the Persian Golf in 1987 was not a danger to the world?
- The U.S. (President Bush) involvement in the war in Iraq in was not a danger to the world?
- The U.S. (President Bush Junior) involvement in the war in Iraq in was not a danger to the World? .
- The U.S. State Department, on January 21, 1988 (Shevat 2, 5748), criticized the beating of Palestinians as a method of restoring calm in Judea, Samaria and the Gaza Strip.

"We are disturbed by the adoption of a policy by the government of Israel that calls for beatings as a means to restore or maintain order," said the State Department spokesman Charles Redman.

"We believe that Israel can carry out its responsibility to maintain order in the West Bank and Gaza through the use of humane measures which do not result in additional civilian casualties," said Redman.

When asked whether the U.S. does not view beatings as "more humane than shootings," Redman responded, "We believe both are wrong."

"We also call on the Palestinian inhabitants of the West Bank and Gaza to preserve order and avoid acts of violence," Redman said.

And who is criticizing Israel for mistreating the Arab population in the "occupied" territories, stolen Jewish land?

-Syria, with its president Hafez Assad, who slaughtered thousands of Sunnite Muslims at home?

-Egypt, with its president Hosni Mubarak, whose hands are still full of Israeli blood, men, women and children murdered at Ras Burkah, in the Sinai as well as thousands of Copts killed in Egypt, just because they were Christians.

-Jordan, with its King Hussein, who butchered twenty thousand Palestinians on "Black September" (9. 1970).

-Turkey, who butchered over one and
a half million Armenians?

-The Germans, who killed several million Europeans: Checks, Poles, French, Soviets, Gypsies, as well as Six Million Jews?

-The Soviet Union that killed tens of thousands of Poles, Tatars, and over a million Afghans, the Crimean Tatars, the Volga Germans?

-The United States of America, that wiped out from the surface of the earth the Apaches, the Sioux, the Cheyennes, the Navahos, the Arapahos, the Pequots, the Narragansetts, the Mohicans, the Pokanokets, the Shanees (Sand Creek, Wounded knee, etc.-Kit Carson, (General George Armstrong Custer, etc.)?

As a matter of fact, the United States of America has broken every one of the hundred and forty- seven pacts it made with the Red Indian tribes, or wiped out from the surface of the earth hundreds of villages, including their populations, as well as in Vietnam (Mai Lay, etc.)? And what about Hiroshima and Nagassaki, the Japanese never threatened the American soil proper? And the way they treated their Japanese minority in the United States, the Nisei, during World War II?

And the way they treated their Negroes (Blacks)-the Ku- Kooks Clan?

-Saudi Arabia, that slaughtered six hundred Iranians in Mecca, at the holy shrine of the Kaabah?

-The thousands of Jews burned at the stake during the Spanish Inquisition?

-The thousands of Jews persecuted and killed in all the pogroms and riots in Europe, by Christians?

-The Thousands of Jews persecuted and killed in all the pogroms and riots in the Islamic countries?

These countries want to teach Israel morals, decency, or how to behave?

These countries want to teach Israel how to defend itself when her survival is at stake and after Iranian President Ahmad Il-Najad's declaration that he plans to wipe the State of Israel off the map? With what legal or moral rights? Now when comparing the way the European colonialist countries, like: England, France, Germany, Italy, Spain, etc. have treated their natives and the way the Israelis treat the Palestinian Arabs, unlike most of the European colonialist countries, the Israeli military administration in Judea, Samaria and the Gaza Strip never sentenced an Arab to death and never executed any Arab.

Therefore, all the countries of Europe, Asia and America should first examine their behavior before they start criticizing Israel. The endless explanations and apologies of the Israeli government are needless and damaging its image. There is no need for Israel to feel guilty. There is no need for Israel to justify itself. Let the others look at themselves and stop their preachings. Judea, Samaria and Gaza belonged always to the Israelites. Jewish kings and Jewish prophets have lived there, two thousand years before the Italian navigator Vespucci Amerigo or the Italian Jew Christopher Columbus discovered America. It was never mentioned, neither in the Old Testament nor in the New Testament, or anywhere else that the Good Lord God ever promised the United States of America to the U.S. citizens.

Three hundred and ninety years ago, a very important event in the history of the United States of America occurred. The Mayflower with one hundred and one Pilgrim Fathers on board, left the port of Plymouth, England, on September 16, 1620, crossed the Atlantic Ocean to the New World. On November 21, 1620, the vessel dropped anchor off the site of present-day Provincetown, Massachusets.

How many Americans, today, are aware of it, or how many Americans today remember the dates? Probably, very few.

On the other hand, another very important event in the history of the Jews and in the history of mankind occurred. Three thousand and three hundred years before the Mayflower set sail, the Jews left Egypt. The "Exodus". Every Jew in the world, in the U.S., in the Soviet Union or what was called the Soviet Union, its Sattelites (Russia, the Ukraine, etc.), in China, in Australia, in Canada, in Brasil, etc. knows exactly on what day occurred this exodus, on Nissan 15th. They know exactly what type of bread they ate, the unleavened bread (Matzot) and they commemorate that event every year on the 15th day of the month of Nissan, remembering the oppression of the Israelites by the Egyptians and praying that, with the help of God, "Next Year in Jerusalem".

The British are stuck for many years in Northern Ireland, They cannot solve their own problems and they want to teach Israel how to solve, the so-called, "Palestinian Problem"! The problem, which they have helped to create!

The British were unable to solve their own problem, a problem many years old, the IRA, yet they had the gall to throw simplistic solutions at the Jews and the Arabs, for their even more complex dispute. A problem, the British have created before leaving Palestine, in 1948.

With what legal or moral rights did the British occupy hundreds of years, the Islands of Falkland, the Melvinas, close to shores of Argentina, or Hong Kong, close to the shores of mainland China. Both, thousands kilometers from England, and, yet they are not ashamed to criticize Israel or teach Israel how to handle its affairs!

What are the French still doing in New Caledonia and Dependencies, in the South Pacific Ocean, 875 miles east of Australia, very, very far from France? Why don't the French return these islands to the natives, the legal and natural owners of these islands? And yet, they are not ashamed to criticize Israel!

The unjust White House declaration, on December 1987, after "Peace Day", equaling Israel with the Arab P.L.O., was very insulting to Israel. It was nothing but a prize to the Arab belligerency and an encouragement to the P.L.O. and Palestinians to continue their terror.

If by street demonstrations, the burning of tires and the throwing of stones and Molotov cocktails (Petrol bombs) they can get by and even get a condemnation of Israel at the United Nations Security Council with the U.S. abstention, why not keep the fire of terror glowing?

An unfortunate example of conflict of interests between the United States of America and Israel was, when, on January 5, 1988, the U.S. Ambassador to the United Nations, Herbert Okon, voted against Israel, at the UN Security Council, condemning Israel for the disturbances in Judea, Samaria and the Gaza Strip, on December 1987, and calling for Israel not to expel Arabs from the country.

This was the first time ever, since the establishment of the State of Israel, on May 15, 1948, that the United States of America voted against Israel. Now, that a precedent has been established, this unfortunate phenomenon might repeat itself, and probably more often. No doubt that this unfortunate UN resolution will contribute very little to peace in the Middle East and will only encourage the forces of violence to continue their terror.

On January 1988, UN Security Council unanimously called on Israel to avoid deporting dangerous Palestinian inciters. The United States of America actively supported this resolution by raising its hand for the resolution. A very unjust and unfriendly attitude towards Israel, especially when it came from the U.S. a country with a people that always believed in the Bible, Old and New Testaments, with Founding Fathers' and ancestors' first name were Biblical names, who were more acquainted with the Bible than any other gentile people, and who, probably knew more than others that Eretz Israel is not occupied but is absolutely and entirely the Jewish People's rightful historic patrimony, forever. The United States of America should know more than other people, that Israel's claim to the right and title to the Land, on both sides of the Jordan River is legitimate and just. The United States of America knows very well that Israel is not an occupier in these territories but a rightful possessor. It is therefore, illegitimate, unjust, wrong, to wave in front of Israel's face the Fourth Geneva Convention. It is also unfriendly therefore, to bother Israel with the issue of deportation of Arabs from Judea, Samaria and Gaza. The defense of the Israeli territories of Judea, Samaria and Gaza against hostile elements and militant inciters from both within or without is Israel's own exclusive concern and nobody's business.

It is totally unfair and unacceptable that the Americans, in effect, tell Israel that it can neither shoot, nor beat, nor expel riot organizers. In order to succeed in putting an end to the Arab up rise or intifada, it is essential that Israel applies much more effective punishments. These should include cutting off the electricity and power connections. Cutting off telephones, confiscating driving licenses, to entire villages, to entire neighborhoods, whose residents have been involved in hostilities, and large scale of expulsions of those who are responsible for organizing the continuing resistance.

In dispatches and telephone calls reaching the Foreign Ministry in Israel, on January 1988, Israeli officials in the U.S. continued to sound the alarm about Israel's deteriorating image and slipping status in the U.S.

The Maarah's irresponsible policy and declarations have contributed a lot to this situation.

A split in the U.S. Jewry had encouraged President Reagan's administration to openly distance itself from Israel's actions in Judea, Samaria and Gaza, as well as to support the UN Security Council Resolution calling on Israel not to deport Palestinian Arabs. This wouldn't have happened if the U.S. Jewish Community had shown solid support for Israel.

It is certainly easier for the U.S. administration to differ publicly with Israel when the American Jewry is doing the same.

On January 7, 1988 (Tevet 17, 5748), the editor of the East Jerusalem Arab newspaper El-Fajr, Hanna Siniora, a Christian Arab, generally considered a moderate pro-PLO Palestinian, grabbed the headlines with his plan for an Arab campaign of "non violent civil disobedience" against the "Occupation."

This same Mr. Siniora, on his visit to the U.S. in 1986 (5746), made a public declaration, in the media, supporting Arab terrorism against Israel, and Mr. Hanna Siniora is an Israeli citizen who happens to live in Jerusalem.

Several local Arab leaders in East Jerusalem, Judea, Samaria and Gaza who were

PLO members or PLO supporters, ardent supporters, joined Hanna Siniora in his "Civil Disobedience" campaign against Israel, with the hope that it will turn into the Palestinian equivalent of the "Boston Tea Party".

The Palestinian Arab activists tried to sever contact between the Palestinian Arab population and the Israeli authorities as well as create alternative institutions and services. An alternative Palestinian Arab Administration.

On January 1988, Egyptian Ambassador to Israel, Mohammad Bassiouny told the Nazareth Newspaper As-Sina'ara that the future development of ties between Israel and Egypt "depend on the development of the situation in the West Bank and the Gaza Strip, negative or positive. There exist the possibility of a break in relations, a recall of the Ambassador or the reduction in the Embassy staff. However this is not our objective. Our big objective is to find a just solution to the Palestinian problem. The Israeli-Egyptian peace agreement isn't a separate peace agreement but a first step towards the realization of a comprehensive goal."

Bassiouny later told the Jerusalem Post:" What can I do if there is a negative development in the West Bank and Gaza, like deportation? Nobody can accept it in the world, including Egypt."

On January 10, 1988, Israeli Defense Minister Yitzhak Rabin told the Israeli Cabinet that:"ending the unrest is a complicated and long-drawn-out affair, which cannot be taken care of in a few days. It needs more time."

The PLO jumped on the Band Wagon, trying to make political capital out of Israel's temporary inferior position, as Israel tries to contain the rioting in Judea, Samaria and Gaza.

On January 13, 1988 (Tevet 23, 5748), Yasser Arafat, head of the PLO, offered to bring and end to the Arab riots if Israel starts negotiation with the PLO. Israel rejected his "kind" offer.

In an interview with the New York Times and the Washington Post, on January 21-23, 1988, Rabin said: "The uprising was spontaneous and not a result of outside PLO incitement. The PLO had been as surprised by the outbreak of riots as had Israel."

Defense Minister Rabin told on January 24, 1988, to the Israeli Cabinet: "The Palestinian Arabs have succeeded in elevating the issue to the international level. You can restore order by the use of force, but force only is no help in attaining a political solution to what is basically a political problem."

On February 3, 1988, following a meeting of the inner Cabinet, Yitzhak Rabin said: "Settlers in the West Bank and Gaza are 'a burden' on the defense establishment." This was an irresponsible declaration, a shocking when it comes out from the mouth of a Israeli Defense Minister, when the fact of the matter is that the Gush Emunim settlements in Judea, Samaria and Gaza rested primarily on security considerations and assuring the indivisibility of Eretz Israel, which belongs to the Jews.

The Gush Emunim motivation is sacred, because it will prevent any future Israeli government from ceding any portion of Judea, Samaria and Gaza to the Arab invaders for some piece of paper. The settlements, a constantly growing Jewish presence right in their midst will teach the local Palestinian Arabs that their hope for an Arab Palestinian State in Judea, Samaria and Gaza, at the expense of Israel is nothing but an illusion, a dream, a wishful thinking. Coming up with declarations, such as President George W. Bush did, like: "Two States, side by side. A Palestinian-Arab State and Israel, side by side" is detrimental to Israel. George W. Bush wants to chop one more portion of Israeli soil and give it to the Arabs. A prize for their belligerency, a prize for their terror? This is not a clever idea from a President who claims that he is fighting terror. This is why his idea of the Road Map is not a clever idea.

The same Yitzhak Rabin once said, that every settlement is very important to the defense of the country because it is an integral part of the country's defense plan, the "Regional Defense" ("Haganah Merchavit"), that can hold the enemy for a few hours or a few days before the IDF arrives. Every settlement is like a fortress, a Magino Line of Israel, the yes of Israel. It can break a surprise enemy attack or free the IDF, thus enabling it to operate in other fronts.

The settlers occupying the various settlements in Judea, Samaria and Gaza are fulfilling a sacred national mission with governmental approval. Very dedicated, loyal men and women. They are not public order disturbers or law-breakers and deserve full governmental protection like the rest of the population of Israel. They should not be exposed to the Arab intifada without protection. If the government of Israel cannot provide them with ample protection, it is only natural and fair that they be allowed to protect themselves.

The Arab militant riots, the burning of tires, the tossing of stones and Molotov Cocktails (Petrol Bombs)at Jewish civilians,at Jewish Police Officers, at Jewish vehicles and military personnel, who happened to pass by brought many Israelis back to rational reasoning and to the realization that coexistence with the Arabs was a silly idea, impractical, impossible and out of the question. Two completely different people with total different languages, different religions, different mentalities with mutual suspicion and with a high cultural and ethnic wall between them cannot live together in the same country will never be able to live together in the same country. "Not even side by side".

Keffiyah-clad youth threw stones and clashed with the Israeli police and border police until they were dispersed by tear gas or gravel stone cannons.

A stone is a very dangerous weapon. Many Israeli civilians and soldiers have been injured and even killed by stones. David killed Goliath with a stone. Stone throwers and Molotov Cocktails throwers should be punished severely.

In spite of the Arab uprising and the Israeli suffering from it, it is very astonishing to see that most the Israelis understand that the Arabs are permitted to walk freely and safely in

Jewish neighborhoods without fear or any body harassing them. On the other hand, ninety five percent of the Israelis do not consider it safe to walk in the Arab neighborhoods. Yet, thousands Arabs from East Jerusalem, the West Bank and Gaza work in Israel every day. Yet, there is no one Jew who will risk his life and work in the West Bank or Gaza without police or military escort. For an Israeli to walk in an Arab neighborhood is like walking in Indian country. Walking in a lawless and fearful place. A country where behind every tree or rock might be an ambush or an Arab sniper waiting for him, a country where the Israeli must carry a gun. And this in spite of the fact that the country belonged to the Israelis, thousands of years before these "Indians" invaded Eretz Israel, or appeared in the arena. On January 14, 1988 (Tevet 24, 5748), in New York, the UN Security Council called on Israel to end its deportation of Palestinians Arabs and to allow the return of the four Arabs expelled the day before.

The resolution was adopted by a vote of 14-0, with the U.S. abstaining. A week earlier, the U.S. voted in favor of a Security Council resolution calling upon Israel not to deport Palestinians. Speaking before the votes were taken, Embassador Netanyahu accused the council of gross imbalance and disregard of the real situation in the territories. The resolution was fundamentally imbalanced and one-sided, without a word of context," said Netanyahu.

"These resolutions hinder the process of restoring tranquility and security, the Council is now acting in collusion with, and on behalf of the inciters of riot and bloodshed." The P.L.O. were quite smart and knew well the importance of the world public opinion and the news media, a tool, which they learned to use, to promote their interests. The P.L.O. knew also, how to change their old long image of master terrorists, killers, and bad guys and in relatively a very short time turned to be the good guys, while the Israelis became the bad guys.

The objective of the intifada is a separate Palestinian Arab state in Judea, Samaria and the Gaza Strip, by casting Israel in an unfavorable moral situation and smearing it in the eyes of the world.

During the Palestinian-Arab up rise, during the intifada, the international media has been so biased and unfair towards Israel. They went out of their way in covering happenings in Israel in detail, neglecting almost completely the butcher, the poisonous gas and chemical warfare that has been going on for years between Iran and Iraq, which in fact has legalized the use of land-to-land missiles and the use of poisonous gas and killing chemicals against civilians.

The world has not seen such devotion, professional devotion, in covering the killing of thousands of Kurds in Iraq, by the Iraqis, with poisionous gas. The international news media covered very quietly the death of tens of thousands of Ethiopians by starvation. Neither did they cover, in such details the riots in Sweto, South Africa, in 1976, when in less than two months over six hundred blacks were killed cold bloodedly.

But we have read and watched and heard how keen and zealous were the news media in covering the Israeli police, who tried to disperse an Arab mob and their violent demonstrations, with sticks, high water pressure and rubber slugs, in order to restore law and order in the streets of Israel. Rubber slugs, high water pressure and sticks, in order to avoid casualties!

The international news media were more than happy to show on colored screens "black or white", distorted pictures showing half- truths. Showing Israeli troops, armed to their teeth, chasing poor, innocent, defenseless women and children who did really no harm at all but throw stones, axes, burning tires, nails, Molotov-Cocktails and other similar "toys" at the Israeli "occupying" forces.

The cold-blooded use of children by the adults, sending children to the streets to throw rocks at the Israelis, turning them into cannon fodder is deplorable. And where are the human rights of these children? And where are their parents? Hiding in the house? Hiding in the kitchen? The fathers were afraid to come out.

Israeli officials have been taken aback by the vehemence of the international reaction to the new situation caused by the Arab uprising in Judea, Samaria and the Gaza Strip. The Israeli Foreign Ministry had received several appeals from Israeli embassies and consulates abroad that were worried about Israel's deteriorating image.

A team was set up to deal with the criticism aimed at Jerusalem, which the ministry's director-general Yossi Beilin described as the worst since the bombing of Beirut in 1982.

The team's task was to ensure that the Israeli ambassadors and consuls overseas are kept up to date with information. Yet, however, it was difficult to fight the TV pictures of the violence in Judea, Samaria and the Gaza Strip, which were hampering Israel's efforts to convince the world that the Palestinian-Arab demonstrators are being shot only when Israeli soldiers' lives are at risk. It was also difficult to fight the widespread distortion of the facts by the international news media.

True, all these years Israel had lousy public relations. Yet, many Israelis believe that no matter how good of a public relations Israel may have, the deep-rooted anti-Semitism in the world would neutralize it. And David Bar-Illan brings very solid proofs every weekend in his column "Eye on the Media," in the Jerusalem Post. In his weekly column (on Fridays) in the Jerusalem Post, David Bar-Illan represents very vividly the anti-Israeli, anti-Jewish biased CNN, BBC and ARTE networks.

The foreign vicious, anti-Semitic media is crying and shedding crocodile tears or the "young Palestinian mother" whose children are threatened by Israelis and who is prevented from buying "the things her young baby might need," but not of the Jewish family whose baby's skull was fractured by young Palestinian-Arab rock-throwers.

The foreign anti-Semitic media is telling the world of the "martyrdom" of Palestinian- Arab boys shot dead by Israeli soldiers, but not of the Jewish mother's anguish when her daughter was stabbed to death while waiting for her school bus, in the bus stop, right across the street from her home.

The write and show on TV how the Israelis with their rubber and plastic bullets "shatter Palestinian-Arab bones, perforate, perforate their stomachs, paralyze and maim..."

We, don't hear about what rocks thrown at cars traveling at 90 kilometers per hour on the highways of Israel, do to Jewish faces. Of how cinder blocks or bricks dropped from Arab roofs crush Jewish heads, or of how a bus forcibly driven over a cliff mangles and burns sixteen Jews and wounds and maims forty others-on the road to Jerusalem.

The international news media were not there when the Arab villagers blocked the highways, the roads, with huge rocks, burning tires, broken glass, junk, garbage, etc. The international media were not there when the Arab mob stoned the Israeli police or army arrived at the scene to enforce law and order. They didn't see the steel bars, the iron rods, the sticks, the bottles, cans and rocks thrown at the police, or the spittings and insulting remarks made at them. The international news media arrived at the scene when the Israeli forces were engaged in dispersing the mob, a task that requires, obviously, the use of force. Tear gas, beatings, arrests, etc. The international news media arrived at the scene when the Israeli forces were implementing law and order and only this phase was covered by them and shown all over the world. It gave a very biased and distorted picture, because it didn't show the reason for the use of force. It didn't show the previous phases. This totally distorted coverage was, unfortunately for

Israel, adverse publicity and did a great damage to Israel's good reputation and international stature.

Nowhere among the twisted presentation of facts there is even a murmur of sympathy for the Jewish people. For what they have suffered during the generations and continue to suffer day after day. Nowhere is there recognition or admittance of the danger to Israel posed by surrounding Arab States and Palestinian Arab terrorism. Relationship toward the Jews and Israel has been characterized, for ages, by malice and vicious hatred, with no rational reason whatsoever.

Arabs throwing stones or Molotov-cocktails, or burning tires are attraction for the cameras of the television crews, on the other hand, the victims of Arab violence are rarely shown. The selective news coverage of the Arab uprising created a false impression that the Israelis are unjust and that the Arab cause is right, which is a tremendous distortion in concept.

CBS's 48 Hours was very impressive in its fairness. Two scenes left a great impression on everybody.

One scene showed an Arab, face covered with a headdress, advancing without fear on an Israeli soldier, with a stick in his hand. The Israeli soldier retreated. The Israeli soldier retreated because he was following orders and violating strict military orders will get him involved in a court-martial. The orders were very specific: Shoot only if your life is in danger. How could he prove that his life was in danger from just a stick? Therefore, the soldier avoided a confrontation. The Arab advanced without fear because he knew also that the Israeli soldier's orders were not to shoot. The Arab knew that the soldier will prefer not to get involved in a court martial and will retreat. The soldier will also retreat because of the TV cameras around. This situation was totally demoralizing to the Israeli soldiers. The Israeli soldiers were subjected to insults and slander by ideologues that denounced them for defending themselves, ideologues who disputed their right to defend themselves.

The second CBS scene showed a TV correspondent interviewing a group of Arabs. The correspondent asked the Arabs if the troubles with the Israelis could be solved by Israel leaving Gaza, Judea and Samaria. The answer was flat "NO". The Arabs added that Israel couldn't exist. They said that all the land from the Mediterranean Sea to the Jordan River is Arab land. In effect, they were repeating very clearly the PLO Charter that says that all Jews who came to Palestine after 1917 had to leave. It is legal duty of the Government of Israel to keep law and order in the country. Therefore, it is also its duty to censor and supervise the movement of the international media personnel in its territories. In order to secure the national interests of the State of Israel, Israel should limit the activities of the foreign correspondents in areas of unrest or combat zones, if they seem detrimental.

Under the hospice of democracy some foreign correspondents are abusing their rights and are meddling constantly in one of Israel's most sensitive areas, in its security, as if they were some kind of international supervisors to watch Israel's behavior. Some of them have taken the liberty to act like Israel's moral keepers. As if Israel was operating in a surgery room or a Clean Room, in a sterile environment. Others are trying, very hard to prove that Israel is a dictatorship and racist.

During the U.S. military operations in the island of Granada, the U.S. military authorities forbade any U.S. or foreign correspondent to enter the combat zone or take pictures.

During the British military operations in the islands of Faulkland (the Malvinas) the British military authorities forbade any British or foreign correspondent to enter the combat zone or take pictures. Not to mention the Soviets in Afghanistan.

To show on the international TV screens hysterical Arab women crying in the streets and the Arab mob throwing rocks at the Israeli armed forces might be very photogenic, but without mentioning the cause and reason for acts like these, is to show only part of the story, is distortion of the truth and a big lie.

In several cases the mere presence of the news media encouraged the Arab demonstrators to become more violent. The presence of the correspondents, the TV personnel, was stimulant.

The world had learned about the Arab uprising, the intifada, from the television, which showed daily fights between Arab citizens and Israeli soldiers, chasing them. It was not clear enough that a third party was involved too. The third party was the Jewish Israeli citizen, driving on the roads, he was the main victim of the intifada, the main target.

The international news media ignored and didn't show the burning of the Moses family from Alfei Manasseh, when their car was hit by a Palestinian-Arab Molotov- Cocktail. The media didn't show the burning of Mrs. Weiss and her three children on the Egged bus, passing through Jericho. For one reason or another, the television ignored it. Their bus was also hit by a Palestinian Molotov-Cocktail, which killed all the four of them. The television didn't show the eight-months- old baby who was hit by a stone that penetrated their car and hit her head. She is still in critical condition, in the intensive care unit.

A decision by the Maryland Court of Appeals on June 1993 failed to get the attention it deserved. The court upheld the conviction of an eighteen-year-old Maurice Ford involved in a rock throwing incident on the Capital Beltline, near Washington D.C.

The incident occurred in 1990, when Ford and two other students threw rocks at passing cars. One rock hit fifteen-year-old Destiny Morris, fracturing her skull. She is expected to function at an intelligence level no higher than that of a fourth-grader.

The contrast between Ford's conviction in the world's greatest democracy, the United States of America, and the glorification of the stone-throwers of the intifada is striking. The Palestinian-Arab stone throwers are glorified not only in the Islamic World, but also in the West (Europe, America, etc.) as well. For almost six years now, the media-ignoring the thousands of civilian injuries, some fatal-have celebrated these youths as heroic revolutionaries and martyrs,

No one seems to question the cynical and cruel exploitation of the Palestinian children who were encouraged to risk their lives.

The stone-throwers are, after all, the Palestinian version of the Iranian children sent by Ayatollah Khomeini to run over minefields with plastic keys to heaven in their pockets, during the Iraq-Iran War.

The Arabs were known to be experts in using, once and again, the strategy of "Victory through Victimization." The PLO did it in Lebanon, in 1982, when they provoked a war. Heaped up the deads and called the media. The West Bankers, the Palestinian Arabs did the same, and were very successful with their telegenic intifada. The Arab youngsters who threw rocks at the Israeli soldiers were extremely photogenic on the U.S. television screens. Anybody who sees these pictures on television and does not know the context of these confrontations or the history behind them is very likely to sympathize with the Palestinians, the "underdogs."

Sometimes, the Israeli news media was also one sided, totally unfair, biased, when a Palestinian-Arab rock blew out the brain of a Jewish, newly wed, young man, in Kalandiyah, Jerusalem, it was published in the bottom of the page, in small letters. On the other hand, when a Palestinian-Arab girl was hit in the eye by a rubber bullet, during an Arab violent demonstration, down town Ramallah, north of Jerusalem, it made headlines in the Jewish newspapers.

The Israeli news media, being part of the international news media, was not different. In several cases it was very pro-Arab, pro-Palestinian, in general, and was siding with the left, many times, disturbing and even damaging Israel's national interests.

The international new media had succeeded to change the image of the IDF, Israel's Defense Forces, to fascists, and they never bothered to broadcast the paragraphs of the PLO Charter, which advocate the extermination of the State of Israel and its Jewish population.

The news media, foreign and local, did a "very good" job in creating an atmosphere of panic and chaos.

The prolongation of the intifada war and the decision to permit foreign television to operate freely and undisturbed in this new battlefield caused Israel a great damage. The IDF spokesman, who should have been all the time in close contact with the foreign correspondents and whose task was to explain Israel's position on the new situation to the news media and the world public opinion, was very unprofessional, very inefficient, and made every possible mistake. This new situation was handled by him very clumsily. This resulted in the Arabs becoming the good guys; the "underdogs"; and the Israelis became the bad guys.

There were certain military operations that should have been closed to both local and foreign correspondents and the areas declared "Military Zones".

Every normal, free, open, society, would have acted like this in order to protect itself and its interests. To permit the news media, local or foreign, to cover cases like this was totally insane, unless, for some sreason or other, somebody meant to sacrifice the interest and security of Israel for the sake of "democracy". Many Israelis wonder why the Israeli censor permit damaging information reach the press.

On the other hand, the Israeli liberals and left believed that the Israeli leaders were wrong in accusing the media of acting irresponsibly in their coverage of the violent incidents during the Arab uprising in Judea, Samaria and the Gaza Strip. Such accusations they said reveal a common misconception about the role of the press in modern society and their responsibility to give the public, Israeli and international, all the information necessary to shape an opinion on the issue. But, by bringing to the international public only part of the information, without a full explanation of the background, the media brought to the public only part of the information, which made the information totally distorted and half the truth is sometimes worse than a lie.

In general it is the media's responsibility to bring to the public, full, true, relevant facts and complete pictures of the situation and not only portions of it, besides, in time of war, sometimes, the media must be restrained, censored, when it is in the best interest of the state. After establishing its accuracy it is the duty of the media to publish information it acquires. The public's right to know ends only where there is clear danger to the national security and when it is in the best of the national interest. In spite of its democratic instincts, a country that is in the midst of a national crisis, cannot afford the luxury of the presence of the news media. Therefore, their entrance to certain crucial areas should have been temporarily restricted. The instincts of survival are stronger than the instincts of democracy. Even the British in Faulkland (Malvinas) and the Americans in Granada had forbidden the news media from approaching the combat zones. Are the British and Americans, therefore, less democratic than the Israelis? Democracy is flexible enough to accommodate almost every shade of political opinion that accepts the rule of the game. Those who would destroy democracy must be barred from using it.

Sometimes, also, U.S. Radio and Television stations like: ABC, CBS and NBC or the British BBC, would hire the services of local, Israeli, newsmen, who were more than happy to "moonlight" for an extra buck.

During the intifada, Japanese television crews in Gaza were caught staging a rock-throwing assault on passing jeeps. They, even, paid more than the German crews, in Judea and Samaria.

In Judea and Samaria, American networks would pay Arab women to demonstrate and yell anti-Israeli and anti-American slogans. The minute the cameras stopped rolling, the women would stop shrieking and calmly stand in line to collect their fees.

Another American Television crew was accused by the Israeli police of paying Arab boys to set tires on fire for the cameras.

An American television crew was caught paying Arab children to burn tires. Many television producers practiced deception.

Far more harmful to Israel and to the truth were the exercises in distortion, omission, bias, and vindictiveness, which characterized the news reporting from Israel by foreign television crews. Reuters headlined a story:"Killing of Palestinians by Israelis continues." They all adopted the Arab story and totally ignored the Israeli version.

The CNN Television turned leaders of one of the world's most murderous terrorist organizations into beloved martyrs, victims of Israeli "brutality".

The television news networks in America have painted a very nasty picture of Israel, which caused a widespread sense of unease among American Jews. The excessive coverage of the uprising was extremely damaging to Israel. The coverage was out of proportion. The local Israeli and the international press, have contributed substantially to the pollution of the atmosphere. It was heart breaking to see the media coverage, which Israel was receiving in the United States. It was a distorted, slanted image that was transmitted into every American home, devoided of historical and legal perspective, and one that suffered from "the Sin of Omission" in that it neglected to address the dreadful political dilemma that Israel was facing.

All over the world, from Dakar in Senegal to Dacca in Bangladesh, massive disturbances, with the same pattern of stone throwing, tires burning and petrol bombs (Molotov-Cocktails) occurred. Civil disorders in Punjab India, Armenia and Tibet, which were bloodier, did not receive half as much media coverage as the Arab uprising, the intifada.

Naturally, the Israelis were understandably indignant that television screens, all over the world, showed an exaggerated number of hours of intifada.

At the height of the intifada over 600 foreign reporters, who did not reside in Israel descended on Israel to cover the intifada, which was the hottest story in journalism. Not all of them were qualified journalists or knew the area and the mentality of its people. On the other hand the 250 local foreign press corps was highly qualified, had a thorough knowledge of the area and the mentality of its people and we usually fair and unbiased. These reporters knew the history of the Middle East and that it did not start on December 9, 1987.

For the PLO it was a great time. They never had it so good. They were capitalizing on the demonstrations and riots. They were getting broad coverage abroad and their prestige had never been so high.

"Hasbarah", which means in Hebrew: information, propaganda, explanation, has an important role. It can help policy but it cannot replace policy. It is a very important tool to smoothen policy, but if it is in the wrong hands it becomes damaging, harmful.

It shouldn't be difficult to expose the Arabs' lies and distortions in their sophisticated and expensive propaganda.

For years, the Israeli propaganda (Hasbarah) was on the defense. This, because it was run by "fossiles from the stone age" who "heated" their seats in the Israeli Foreign Office for "ages", and who did not realize that only active, offensive diplomacy had a chance to succeed.

There have been numerous expressions of criticism of the way Israel's case is exposed before an uncomprehending, uncaring, sometimes hostile, sometimes inflicted with traditional anti-Semitism, non-Israeli audience with notoriously short memories.

The most reasonable thing to do was to establish immediately a Ministry of Information to fight the successful Arab propaganda. If Israel does not act quickly things could erode increasingly under the Arab propaganda campaign', which in turn, can cause Israel a great damage.

The Israeli public was watching carefully the international conscience, to see, how they would react to the genocide committed by the Iraqis against their Kurds minority, in the north, using poison gas.

The international conscience, expressed by the international news media didn't utter a sound. The world conscience fell asleep. The West, the East and the Third World became blind, deaf and mute. They all ignored the thousands of Kurds exterminated by the Iraqi gas, as well as the tens of thousands of refugees crossing the borders into Turkey. The news media didn't "see" it, as it was busy covering the 1988 Olympic Games, in Seoul, South Korea. Also, the great politicians of the world, who, usually, have an opinion about every topic and a ready answer to every problem, became suddenly mute.

The Kurds, prior to World War I, had a country, called Kurdistan. Kurdistan was stolen from them and divided among Iraq, Iran, Turkey, Syria, and the U.S.S.R. And according to the Treaty of Sevres, concluded by the allies with Turkey, in 1920, the Kurds were promised an independent state. This promise was never kept. Since, they were slaughtered gradually by their five new masters. The Iraqis were the first to introduce the poison gas. Same as they did with the Iranians. In both cases the world's conscience didn't move.

Here we have a nation, the Kurds, who had a country, a political entity, a language, a history, a nation that didn't use terror, that was torn to pieces and nobody gave a damn. The world conscience kept sleeping peacefully.

Yet, the world conscience went out of its way to give the Palestinian Arabs, who never had a country, never had a political entity, never had a history, not only political self determination, but a new state, and at the expense of the State of Israel.

The Iraqis burned down towns inhabited by the Kurds, wiped out completely hundreds of Kurd villages, while the world stood by watching, without finding it necessary to interfere.

Yet, when a house of an Arab terrorist is torn down, the world's conscience suddenly wakes up from its long hibernation to denounce Israel for its "atrocities". The world moral suddenly becomes vivid, hyperactive, to criticize Israel for brutality against the Palestinian-Arabs. It seemes, that the only reason for this discriminate behavior, is the fact that everybody is reluctant to criticize an oil supplier, especially when he is also an excellent weapon buyer.

The world's conscience and moral were also missing when Estonia, Latvia and Lithuania were under the Soviet yoke, or the freedom of Afghanistan, the three million Soviet Jews or the six thousand Syrian Jews!

Many are inclined to believe that the world's conscience and the international moral and justice are selective, very selective. To criticize Israel's defense performance or advise Israel how to defend itself is totally unfair, because its Israeli necks that were on the block.

Where were the defenders of human rights when Syria crushed an insurrection in the city of Chama, killing 20,000 people? Did the world protest? Did the U.S. protest? Where were the news media? Were there sanctions against Syria? Nobody said a word. Everybody kept silent.

LE QUOTIDIEN DE PARIS
Friday, February 12, 1988
OPINION
The Twelve against Israel

I admit to having been extremely shocked-and I am not the only one, by the hostile position taken by the Foreign Ministers of the EEC, twelve against the Jewish State.

To condemn the "repression" which the Israeli security forces are exercising in Gaza and in Judea-Samaria, and to "demand " that Israel put an end to this immediately, is very easy for diplomats and senior officials whom no one is threatening, whose countries are at peace, and whose existence is not under dispute.

What frightening incomprehension! Is it so difficult to muster the minimum effort necessary to realize what mortal danger hangs over Israel, over every man, woman and child of this country, which is permanently exposed to forces of destruction that have vowed to annihilate her?

Are these European personages who are the spokesmen of a continent which has had the good fortune of not experiencing war for 60 years, ignorant of the fact that Israel-a rock battered by waves of hatred- has never known real peace since its rebirth in 1948?

Do we have to recall the terrible pogroms in Jerusalem of the infamous Grand Mufti Haj Amin Al-Husseini, the war criminal, accomplice of Adolf Hitler and Himmler? Is the fact not known that, after the decision of the United Nations to partition Palestine under the British Mandate into a Jewish state and an Arab state (although the Jews were gravely disadvantaged by this partition they nevertheless accepted it). Six Arab armies invaded the territory allocated to Israel? Where it not for the extraordinary response of the Haganah and the Irgun, that the State could have been annihilated even as it was born? It is precisely this aim which has been followed with maniacal stubbornness throughout the years by Yasser Arafat's PLO and the terrorist leaders Dr. George Habash, Naief Hawatmeh, etc. with unceasing aggression, assassinations and criminal outrages.

All this, which is as clear as the light of day, seems to have escaped our European hierarchy. For them, and for the media, which seems to be playing a somewhat suspect role in this drama, the Jew deserves interest only if he is being beaten, humiliated and pursued. Ah, how one loves the Jews when the Holocaust and the Final Solution are evoked, in order to put on, at little cost, a humanist face! But when the modern, proud Israeli, dominant and sure of himself, dares to defend himself, to react, giving back as good as he gets, then the tone changes! The only role for the Jew is to be a victim. Three considerations seem to me indisputable. Firstly, those responsible for the troubles in Gaza and the West Bank are, for the most part pushing very young fanatical demonstrators and women into the front ranks of the riots, while they themselves stay prudently under cover. This is to make it possible for the duly "informed" (misinformed) "universal conscience" to be able to condemn the repression without qualms.

Furthermore, this agitation-with its media aura is extremely well orchestrated by the terrorist organization, a major factor in international subversion, whose charter states as it aim the destruction of Israel and the expulsion of all the Jews who arrived in, or were born in Palestine in the past half century.

Finally, Moscow, which finances and arms the PLO, hopes to exploit the unrest in the Middle East, and the unfathomable gullibility of the Europeans, in order to re-establish a foothold in this region of the world, and under the pretext of an international conference- to force the Jewish State to appear before an Aeropause composed of its worst enemies.

By taking sides with those who wish to destroy the so-called "Zionist entity", namely the only democratic State in this region of the world, the Twelve are abandoning (That's the least one can say) their normal role and are committing a grave injustice.

Jacques Soustelle, former French Government Minister and member of the French Academy.

A new phase in the intifada started when the Palestinian-Arabs were ordered by the PLO to quit working for the Israelis and the Israeli authorities and resign from public offices, as well as, stop all businesses with Jews. A few Arab Police Officers, working for the Israeli Police have been murdered by the Arabs, after refusing to follow these orders, for fear of losing their jobs, their livelihood, their tenure and their pension. Their self-inflicted several strikes, closing stores, etc. have caused them loss of income and a lot of damages.

The Unified National leadership of the Uprising directed the Intifada by means of leaflets distributed all over the West Bank and Gaza.

Leaflet No. 8 called for "escalating the struggle toward civil disobedience," and encouraged a boycott of the Israeli military administration and Israeli goods. It called for the return to the soil. It suggested cultivating agricultural plots near homes and growing poultry, vegetables and fruits as well as other basic needs. The leaflet also called on Palestinians to increase home production of bread and dairy products, as well as conserve water to meet possible water cut-offs by the Israelis.

Leaflet No. 9 called for Palestinian Arab factories to work at "full steam" in order to provide alternatives to Israeli products.

Leaflet No. 10 called for acts of civil rebellion organizing popular committees, opening shops and gas stations according to hours set up by local committees; non-payment of taxes; It also urged the return of pupils to schools and colleges.

All the leaflets were signed by the "Unified National Leadership of the Uprising."

Communique number 10 issued by the PLO to Palestinian-Arabs in the territories called for the resignation of local members of the Jordanian parliament and of Arab policemen, and urged actions against Jewish settlers, "collaborators" and backers of Jordan.

The communiqué also called for the fiercest clashes with the IDF troops on March 21, 1988, the twentieth anniversary of the IDF raid on Palestinian-Arab bases in Karameh, Jordan. The contents were also reported in part over Radio Monte Carlo. The communiqué urged the Arab policemen to resign immediately and Jordanian parliament members in the territories to step down and return to the ranks of the people, otherwise they will have no place on our land. The message withdrew an earlier call for resignation of all Arab employees of the Civil Administration. The communiqué urged Palestinian-Arabs to boycott Israeli goods when Arab alternatives are available, and provide material and moral support for communities under curfew. The Palestinian-Arabs should refuse to pay taxes and continue their commercial strikes while opening shops for only three hours a day.

On October 6, 1988 (Tishrei 25, 5749), two West Bank residents-Mustafa Abu Bakr, the Mukhtar of Bidya and Yusuf Za'rur from Anin village, were slain in Umm el-Fahem, because of their cooperation with the Israeli authorities.

Inhabitants of the West Bank and the Gaza Strip, collaborating with Israel, have been killed in the past too, but this is the first time an appointed mukhtar has been slain. It is also the first time that a West Bank inhabitant has been killed on the other side of the Green Line, inside Israel, on suspicion of collaborating with Israel.

This event in the West Bank was interpreted by the Palestinian Arabs as a warning to all Palestinian-Arabs in the territories whoever dared cooperate with Israel or with Israelis may be killed.

The PLO ordered their followers and sympathizers in Judea, Samaria and the Gaza Strip to strike, close their stores, close their businesses, not to show up at work, but didn't find it necessary to give them alternative means of living: salary, food stamps, anything to feed their many children. Soon, the Palestinian-Arabs realized that the fact is that they were utterly dependent on jobs in Israel. On licenses, permits and other documents issued by Israeli military authorities, which had imposed tough measures to subdue civil disobedience.

A large majority of Palestinian-Arabs participated in the strikes conducted by the PLO. The PLO organizers succeeded to force these strikes upon the majority of the Palestinian-Arabs, in Judea, Samaria and the Gaza Strip.

The aim of the "United Leadership" of the intifada was to destroy every economic and social Arab enterprise. Few dared to ignore these strikes for fear of being executed. They wanted to cause chaos in the Arab sector, hardship and anger, thus increase the amount of hatred to the Israelis. It seemed that the "United leadership" of the intifada planned to turn the Palestinian-Arab towns and villages of Judea, Samaria and Gaza into more refugee camps.

The Arabs were torn by violent disagreement and lack of organization and discipline. The leadership in Judea, Samaria and Gaza lost control over a new breed of street militant activists, who imposed their own rule. Gangs of masked Arab youths went on killing, stabbing, beating to death, suspected collaborators, extorting contributions from the population, for the intifada. The PLO intimidated their own community and killed more Arabs than Israelis and to justify this slaughter they called their victims "collaborators" Ninety five per cent of these "collaborators " had nothing to do with Israelis. A full two-thirds of over 1000 Palestinian-Arabs executed by Arabs for "collaborating" had no contact with the Israeli authorities at all. Yet, they were tortured and eliminated for reasons known only to their killers.

So, having no other choice, the Palestinian-Arabs started to bite into their savings, and when the savings were exhausted they started to feel the economic pressure, the misery, which they brought upon themselves. They soon became sick and tired of the situation, and after six months of intifada they were worn out and wished they should have never started it. The uprising did not bring them any tangible results. They understood very quickly that all their gain was headlines. They also understood that they did not have the slightest chance to create a "Palestinian State" at the expense of Israel, because Israel will never give up territories bequeathed by their forefathers and promised to them by the good Lord God, which makes the "Road Map" nil. They already have twenty-two Arab, Moslem states and it should suffice. They can be greedy but not at the expense of others.

At the beginning of the Arab uprising, at the beginning of the intifada, Arab male adults didn't participate directly in these riots, because they were afraid that when caught, sentenced and sent to prison, they could lose their jobs, their tenure and their pension. Therefore, what they did was to send out to the streets women and children, while they directed the riots and demonstrations against Israel from inside their houses, without having to expose themselves. The Israeli police had to fight women and children, and therefore, it was only natural that they were more careful and reserved.

Appearing before the Israeli National Television, on the night of March 9, 1988, Israeli Defense Minister, Yitzhak Rabin, admitted on the "Mabat Shenee" program that he didn't have an answer to the new challenge. Rabin also added that over half the Israeli Military Forces were busy chasing women and kids.

This situation has already been dragging on too long and caused the State of Israel substantial damage. Defense Minister Yitzhak Rabin showed incompetence, lack of imagination, complete failure and should have been fired from his office immediately.

On the other hand, if Mr. Rabin didn't want to put an end to this situation and preferred for one reason or another to drag it, so as to draw the attention of the international public, thus, invite outside pressure on Prime Minister Yitzhak Shamir and force him to attend the International Middle East Conference and give up Israeli territories. If this version is true, Rabin and Peres were playing dirty politics, very dirty, very vicious and very dangerous. Rabin and Peres were representing the Left. Shamir represented the Right.

The Arab boy with a slingshot and stones in his hands, chased by the Israeli soldier, with tear gas and a rifle, shooting rubber rounds, will always get more sympathy from the news media, in spite of the fact that the Israeli soldier is serving a right cause while the Arab boy is serving a terrorist organization. As a matter of fact, Israel is in a state of war, since its inception in 1948. In war the media must yield its ssprivileges to the demands of survival. As vital as freedom of speech may be to democracy, it is not more important than life itself. It is only normal that in time of war the media must be censored for the safety of the nation.

Since the start of the Palestinian-Arab uprising, the intifada, in Judea, Samaria and Gaza, Israel had suffered a serious erosion of support.

By letting the Israeli soldiers, with heavy military boots, to chase Arab teen agers and youngsters at their early twenties with light Jim, shoes Defense Minister Yitzhak Rabin brought on the IDF (Israel Defense Forces) not only a catastrophe but also insult and shame. Had he given the orders, at the very outset of the up rise to open fire, to shoot at those who were disturbing the public peace, the IDF would not have been so ridiculed. Israel has the full right, in fact its her duty, its her obligation to put an end to these riots and restore law and order, and protect peaceful Arabs from their militant Shabab (Youth) or Shbibah (the younger wing of the PLO). Rabin declared that it has always been like this and the Israelis must learn to live with it. Defense Minister Rabin handled the

Palestinian-Arab waves of violence very clumsily, and therefore should have been dismissed from office.

The Israeli soldiers' hands were "handcuffed" by orders from their superiors. This rendered them hesitant and reluctant to get too much involved. For fear of reacted so slowly to Arab provocations. This is why they were unsuccessful in putting down the intifada.

From day to day the IDF showed more and more restraint while the Arabs dared more and more to thssrow stones on the Israeli soldiers. The Arabs didn't even bother to run away. They kept standing there and smiled at the soldiers, as they knew very well that the soldiers are not permitted to shoot, that the army had orders not to shoot. The Israeli public couldn't take it any more. Rabin was depressing any initiative of a soldier or a police officer in the field, threatening him with arrest.

Speculators believe that, as soon as the Palestinian-Arabs will feel that the international media and the Arab countries are backing them, they might dig out their fire-arms from under the floor tiles and start an open rebellion against Israel. Defense Minister Yitzhak Rabin (Maarah, Alignment, Labor) could not afford to endanger the Maarah's good relation with Arab population in a year of general elections. Not when he needed the Arab votes, their fourteen mandates (seats in the Knesset). This was the reason why Mr. Rabin didn't advocate an abrupt, radical solution. This is why Mr. Rabin handled the situation easy and soft, and dragged it so long, so as not to anger his Arab voters and lose their "Indispensable Votes."

The other reason was, according to some speculators, to give ample time to the international news media to take enough photos of the riots and demonstrators, which will make the world believe that Israel couldn't handle the situation, thus inviting international pressure on the Israeli Government and force her to attend an international conference of Peace in the Middle East, where she will be forced to make territorial concessions to the Arabs. Defense Minister Yitzhak Rabin and his colleague Foreign Minister Shimon Peres were both from the Maarah Party, both leftists. By avoiding the use of real bullets and refusing to shoot at the Arab rebels, which would have stopped the Arab rebels immediately they were acting against the best interest of Israel. They prolonged the agony and were directly responsible for the outside pressure on Israel to give up more lands to the Arabs.

Prime Minister Yitzhak Shamir's great mistake was, not to fire these two gentlemen from the Cabinet and replace them with members of his own Likud Party.

The National Unity Government was divided on the issue, politically. It was paralyzed and therefore, useless and should have been dismantled.

The Maarah leaders admitted very clearly and very openly, that they did invite U.S. involvement but denied of having invited U.S. pressure.

An Israeli show of hesitation only encourages the Arab uprising. An Israeli show of weakness only increases the Arab rebellion.

When the Palestinian-Arabs started their uprising they expected to drag along all the Arab countries. They believed that eventually the Arab countries will be carried away and join their "fight for freedom". But Egypt and Syria still remember the end results of the Yom Kippur War (October 1973). Egypt remembers well the siege of their Third Army by the Israelis as well as the Israeli tanks closing on their capital, Cairo. Syria still remembers the Israeli tanks on the Beirut-Damascus road. Beirut in the hands of the Israelis and Damascus within the range of the Israeli cannons, Both Egypt and Syria are still licking their wounds. Besides, Syria will not budge without Egypt, and Egypt's hands were tied up by the Camp David Peace Accord. Iraq and Iran are busy exterminating each other in a long bloody war that started in 1981, when Iraqi troops invaded the Iranian region of Horamshar. Lebanon is trying to put order in its chaos. Saudi-Arabia is busy making money selling oil and hates to be bothered, Jordan didn't forget the Six-Day War (June 1967), in which it lost all "her" territories west of the Jordan River.

The Palestinian-Arabs were very naïve to believe that with burning tires, stones and terror they could beat Israel. Again, once more, same as in 1948, the Palestinian Arabs made a terrible mistake by relying on their flesh and blood brethren, the Arab countries, who didn't make a move on their behalf, for fear of losing another war. The Arab countries were realistic. The only way for the Palestinian-Arabs to get their "freedom", if they really want it so much, is by moving to the neighboring Arab countries and making it their home for good and leave Israel alone. Leave Israel to the Israelis. Israel doesn't belong to them, Israel never belonged to them, and whoever told them the opposite was nothing but a professional liar. A Charltan.And with this lie they have been living a whole century, one hundred years. With this lie they went to bed, with this lie they went to war and died and with this lie they have been trying to deprive the Israelis from their land.

It was totally shocking and unbelievable to see that women and children were throwing deadly rocks and Molotov-Cocktails and aiming slingshots with metal objects at Israeli soldiers, school-buses, and civilians, with the intend to kill and maim. What a civilized people places women and children on the front line against soldiers?

On "Peace Day" (December 9, 1987), the Israeli Arabs, that's the Arabs carrying Israeli passports, "supported" the Palestinian-Arabs, from Judea, Samaria and the Gaza Strip (the West Bank), in their fight against what they called "Israeli occupation". Israeli Arabs from Nazareth, Jaffa, Lod, Abu-Gosh, Wadi-Arah, Um-il-Fachem, Haifa, etc., and even the "loyal" Druz, participated in the several, militant street demonstrations and riots.

At the beginning of the Intifada, getting more of the economic pie seemed to come before politics. Most of the Israeli Arabs were busy looking after their personal profits, but later, like their brethren in Judea, Samaria and the Gaza Strip, they were also carried away.

The Israeli Arabs believed that in spite of the fact that they were Israeli citizens they were not losing their "loyalty" to the State of Israel if they were only exercising their democratic prerogative to manifest collective pain and concern over what had been happening to their brethren, the Palestinian Arabs in Judea, Samaria and the Gaza Strip.

Most of the Arab Moslem population in Judea, Samaria and the Gaza Strip, and a significant number of Israeli Arabs are unquestionably antagonistic to Israel and its existence as a Jewish state and continue to harbor the burning hostility to Israel, mostly as an expression of their Palestinian-PLO identity. The Israeli Arabs couldn't hide their deep sympathy with the cause of their brethren in Judea, Samaria and the Gaza Strip. The Israeli Arabs couldn't hide their support of the Arab rebels in Judea, Samaria and the Gaza Strip. It started with sending truckloads of food and clothing to Judea, Samaria and the Gaza Strip as well as large monetary contributions, and slowly, but gradually, became more and more involved. Many were caught by the Israeli police or even worse, caught throwing stones and Molotov-Cocktails.

The one-day strike of the Israeli-Arab community on Monday, December 21, 1987, turned violent, came as a shock to Jewish Israel who did not expect such behavior from their fellow citizens. It was also quite a shock to the Israeli Arabs, at least to many of them who feared that the Arabs might have gone a little too far, may have overstepped a very dangerous red line in the relations with Jewish majority and with Israel's ruling establishment.

Shocks like these, however, can be very useful in the life of a nation, in focusing attention on neglect or disputed areas of public policy, which are urgently in need of such attention.

There were clear signs that the Arab uprising, the Intifada, was creeping across the Green Line into Israel proper. There were also clear signs that the Jewish population in Israel, already fed up with the "game", might be tempted to take retaliatory action if the present trend continues and if the government of Israel fails to adopt firm measures for dealing with the "nationalistic actions of the Israeli Arab extremists."

So far, the Israelis have shown restrain, but there could come a time when their elected representatives will be unable to convince them anymore, to let the security forces deal with these incidents.

The fact is that the Israeli Arabs who are citizens of the State of Israel, whose allegiance and loyalty should be first to the State, are great sympathizers of the PLO, those who are trying to destroy Israel. In the past the Israeli Arabs understood very clearly that despite their sympathy for their brethren across the borders and in Judea, Samaria and the Gaza Strip, identifying openly with the PLO was dangerous. Israeli Arab's affinity for their Palestinian brethren in Judea, Samaria and the Gaza Strip is not something that was born with the Intifada. It was always there, but its expression was muted. The Palestinian- Arabs just couldn't cut their umbilical cord with their Palestinian brethren in Judea, Samaria and the Gaza Strip.

An Israeli-Arab from Haifa, Israel, an academician, in an interview, told a reporter that: "I have no conflict of interest because I am a Palestinian who feels the sufferings of my people in the territories and want them to have the right of self-determination, but who, as an Israeli citizen sees his future in Israel and wants the same privileges as those enjoyed by Jewish citizens."

The reporter then asked him:" If a Palestinian state existed along side with Israel would you go and live there?"

The Arab answered: "No, absolutely no,"

Why should he? He could keep living in Israel and one day wake up and ask to slice Israel again, for a third Arab state, within Israel and at the expense of Israel. Very "clever"!

The Israeli-Arabs enjoy their Israeli citizenship and its shelter, but do not want to accept any obligation or make any sacrifices. They refuse to take the oath of allegiance and openly support the Palestinian Arab's political aspirations at the expense of Israel.

The "Palestinian" identity of the Israeli-Arabs had gradually but constantly increased, especially since the intifada, thus, increasing, daily, the contradiction between their identity as Palestinian-Arabs and their identity as Israelis. Their loyalty to Israel was no longer trustworthy

The hightened emotional identification of the Israeli-Arabs with their Palestinian brethren in Judea, Samaria and the Gaza Strip and against the IDF, with whom they have been in violent confrontation, has emphasized the naivety of the thesis that the Israeli-Arabs would, in time, serve as a bridge to peace with the Palestinian-Arabs and the surrounding Arab world.

Yet, in spite of the fact that the Israeli-Arabs have clearly identified themselves with the side of their Palestinian kinsmen and their intifada, their actual behavior in support of their feelings has been quite restrained, though one hundred and fifty hostile acts committed in Israel during the first three months of the intifada could be attributed to Israeli-Arabs. The Israeli-Arabs have realized that they had much to lose by physically joining the intifada. The Israeli-Arabs response to the intifada has made it possible to distinguish more clearly where they stand in regard to the Israeli-Palestinian conflict. Israel has definitely ascertained that the Israeli-Arabs are clearly hostile to Israel. They have provided legitimate cause and ample proof for Israel to regard them as potentially dangerous element in the Arab-Israeli conflict, especially in the case of the outbreak of another war. Showing so much devotion and loyalty to their Palestinian brethren in Judea, Samaria and the Gaza Strip and spending so much energy to draw public attention to their identification with the cause of the Palestinians and the Intifada, they can expect very little sympathy from the general public in Israel.

Not that the Israeli-Arabs, bearing Israeli passport or Israeli citizenship, had ever shown any special loyalty, minimum loyalty, to their country, the State of Israel, where they live and make a living. During the fifty years of Israel's existence, they have never raised the Israeli flag over their buildings, or public buildings, during the State's national holidays.

Yet, during the intifada, the Palestinian-Arab uprising they had the courage, the chutzpah, the nerves to raise the PLO flag over their private buildings and have shown whole hearted support and loyalty to the PLO and to their brethren in Judea, Samaria and the Gaza Strip or what the Arabs and many others call the "West Bank".

The Israeli-Arabs sent them, to the Palestinian-Arabs, truckloads of care packages and even joined their violent, illegal street demonstrations.

Needless to mention that the Israeli-Arabs have prospered in the State of Israel, for the last fifty years and were enjoying the highest standard of living in the area. Many of them bought new houses, new cars, new stores, even in the big cities of Jerusalem, Tel-Aviv, Haifa, etc.

The doors of all Israeli universities were open for them and the State of Israel was spending a fortune on their education.

They used to carry tins of water, buckets of water from remote wells in the mountains to their houses, for centuries. Israel has installed water taps in their houses, electricity, gas, televisions, roads, schools and other necessary public houses, which they never had before, neither during the British Mandate, nor during the Turkish occupation. Yet, these Israeli-Arabs refuse to serve in the Israeli military service and defend "their" homeland.

Therefore the Camp David Autonomy Plan is not really for the Arabs of the West Bank. These seek independence from Israel, total independence and the establishment of a separate Palestinian-Arab State, at least in the first phase.

It is the Israeli-Arabs who look forward, also as a first phase, to autonomy, in the areas where they have demographic majority already, in Israel. Like in Wadi-Arah, the Galilee, etc. Later, they will probably, declare, unilaterally, annexation to the newly established Palestinian-Arab State. This could easily generate several additional Palestinian-Arab states. What the Arabs are asking now is their second state, the first being Jordan. Then, it will be the Galilee's turn.

There are several signs that even Israeli-Arabs have joined, overtly, the Palestinian-Arab struggle against the State of Israel This means nothing less than betraying "their" country, Israel and will have to be dealt with accordingly. Israel cannot permit a fifth column in its midst.

The Israeli-Arabs backed up their Palestinian-Arab brethren in Judea, Samaria and the Gaza Strip, one hundred per cent, from the very beginning of their uprising. The first thing to do was to organize a one-day strike in solidarity with the Palestinian-Arab rebellion and in protest against the Israeli government's "iron-fist" policy there.

"We want to shock the government and the people of Israel into realizing what is happening. We cannot, for one moment, think that liberal and broad-minded people accept with equanimity the brutal tactics that have been adopted by the security forces in the territories," said Nimer Murkos, head of the Kfar Yassif council in Galilee and member of the National Committee of Arab local councils.

Members of the Rakah Party (Communist) and the radical Sons of the Village Movement and distributed leaflets in Arab towns and villages calling on the residents to protest against the Israeli violence and support the residents of the territories "in their fight for liberty and independence."

The National Committee of Arab Local Councils declared: "We also call on the Israeli government to rethink its present policies and work towards a peaceful solution under the auspices of a UN-sponsored international peace conference." Said Nimer Murkos.

The continued existence of the council should be considered as a threat to the security of Israel and declared illegal.

The Israeli Arabs, carrying Israeli passports, "promise" that after the establishment of the "Palestinian State" in the West Bank their whole concept will change and they will be able to feel at home in Israel. This is another big Arab lie, because right after the "Palestinian" state is established, the very next day, they will start planning their next step-the taking over of the State of Israel or more parts of it, like Jaffa, Haifa, Lod, Ramle, Acre, etc. thus following to the letter the Tunisian late president, Habib Bourgiba's advise of the "Salami" system. As soon as the "Palestinian State" is created, the "Palestinian" in the Galilee, Jaffa, Haifa, Lod, Ramle, Acre, etc. will demand annexation to the newly born "Palestinian State." A new uprising, a new "Palestinian" intifada will probably start immediately, or a few years later, this time the Israeli-Arabs will seek to join their brethren. Sooner or later it will become a new "casus belli", an endless blackmail, and a big headache.

The Israeli consensus was very insistent on the fact that the PLO was Israel's implacable enemy, Therefore, in a state of on-going war with that enemy, any association with the PLO- and declared support for it- must be considered as treason. High-Treason.

The Israeli Arab's behavior, attitude and feelings during the intifada of their brethren in Judea, Samaria and the Gaza Strip could be defined only as a national Arab opposition within Israel, in alliance with the state's external enemies, plotting to destroy Israel.

The Israeli-Arabs cannot be citizens of Israel, enjoying equal rights with the Jewish majority and at the same time express, to the extreme, their identification with the PLO.

It is naïve to believe that the Israeli-Arabs are torn between their loyalty to the Arab nation and their loyalty to the Jewish State. The Israeli-Arabs are masquerading as loyal Israeli citizens. The fact is that they are Arabs and their hearts and minds are with the Arab nation and would betray Israel when the first opportunity occurs. Most of the Israeli-Arabs are so far gone in their hatred for Israel that they will never be loyal to Israel. This attitude of the Israeli-Arabs proves beyond the shadow of a doubt, that most of the Israeli-Arabs are clearly disloyal to the State of Israel all the time and were potentially subversive and extremely dangerous in a situation of on-going war between Israel and the Arab World, and therefore, should not be trusted. A Jewish Israel, with so many hostile Arab countries surrounding it, cannot tolerate the risk of an organized Arab national entity in its midst. Before tending the seeds of "Palestinian" irredentism, Israeli-Arabs better realize that even Israel's democracy has its limit. This is why the Israeli-Arabs must be prevented from forming political bodies.

On January 1988, when four Palestinian-Arab master terrorists, who where personally responsible for the stoning, kidnapping and killing of Israeli soldiers and civilians and who led violent riots and demonstrations in the streets of Israel were brought to court, tried and expelled from Israel. The International Red Cross Organization interfered in their favor by criticizing and denouncing Israel. In fact they raised hell. This same International Red Cross Organization didn't budge a finger when, during World War II, the Germans slaughtered Six Million Jews in Europe. What hypocrites!

In an interview to the Saudi-Arabian newspaper "Il-shark-il-awsat", Haled Il Hassan, a chief PLO ideologist, declared, that the December 1987 Arab rebellion against Israel started, because Arafat's promise that the Reagan-Gorbachev summit meeting in Washington, on December 1987, will find a solution to their "problem", was not kept. Reagan and Gorbachev didn't discuss even the Middle East. In despair and to draw attention, they started the "Peace Day" rebellion, without having the slightest chance to get anywhere. The immediate result was a little turmoil, headlines and the loss of human lives.

The Israeli control of another people is an unnecessary evil, which should be discontinued, as soon as possible.

The Palestinian-Arabs had aspirations, political aspirations, which grew violent. Aspirations, which if Israel doesn't deal with it urgently, aspirations, which if Israel ignores it or overlooks it, Israel will most probably, pay a penalty, a heavy penalty. Aspirations, which must be dealt with, not by means of concessions, at the expense of Israel, but by means of sending the Palestinian-Arabs across the border. Otherwise, Israel will have to choose between Judaism or Democracy and Democracy or Judaism.

The Israelis believe that living in Israel implies a decision to live in a Jewish State, not necessarily a democratic state. This definition is a national consensus in Israel.

Coexistence with over a million Palestinian-Arabs has shaken Israel, morally and politically. Getting used to a status quo or being addicted to a status quo is very dangerous to Israel, because, meanwhile, during this hibernation, the quantity, the number of the Palestinian-Arabs increase substantially and shakes the balance of demography in the area in favor of the Arabs. The losers for this delay in action are the Israelis, the Jews. To allow the Arab breed quietly in the "Greenhouse" of coexistence is extremely dangerous to Israel's survival.

Since December 1987, when the Palestinian-Arab current wave of violence started, both the number of terrorist acts and the use of firearms, in Judea, Samaria and the Gaza Strip decreased substantially. This doesn't mean that the Arabs do not have firearms. It means only that they haven't decided yet to use it, for tactical reasons. But, when they will think that the time is ripe, they will not hesitate to use it against the Israelis. Therefore, to keep these Arabs within its borders is very unwise, to keep a Quisling, a fifth Column, within its borders is very unwise as it endangers Israel's own survival. Therefore, their transfer should be considered by the Israeli Government, in all earnest, seriously and urgently. The Palestinian-Arab uprising, the intifada, in a way, was quite beneficial to the State of Israel as it woke her up from a long sleep and shattered the long-standing complacency of the Israeli Right and the academic illusions of the Left. Old-New ideas started running in the heads of the people, the Israelis, ranging from transfer, population displacement and annexation to direct talk with the Palestinian-Arabs, Some Israelis, mainly from the Left, had such heretic ideas as unilateral withdrawal. The Arab uprising helped stop the long stalemate, which is destructive to Israel, and pushed Israel to some efficient actions.

Politically, the Palestinian-Arab uprising, the Palestinian-Arab intifada was a blessing to both the Arabs and the Jews. Because it raised the "Palestinian" problem from somewhere near the bottom of the agenda, to somewhere near the top. It forced both parties to consider the matter as top urgent, top priority. It forced the parties to find a solution. It broke the status quo. It forced the Israelis to consider the matter more seriously. From a real-politic point of view the Palestinian-Arab uprising presents an opportunity for truth. For too long, too many Israelis as well as the Israeli Government, have denied, or intellectually and emotionally deflected, the brute fact that the Palestinian-Arabs are a danger to the Jewish State. Danger to its survival and that something has to be done before it is too late.

What the Arabs wanted was that Israel retreats to the June 1967 borders called by Abba Eban the "Auschwitz borders". And this they want only as a first step towards a total Israeli withdrawal from the "occupied" territories, including Jerusalem, Wishful thinking!

All those who believe that there is already a general-Israeli agreement on most of the land and that the conflict is only over a certain small area, are completely wrong. The conflict is over Haifa, Jaffa, the Galilee, Jerusalem, Lod, Ramleh, Beer-Sheva, Acre, etc. The fact of the matter is that the conflict is over the whole land, the whole country. They want the whole lot. They are for the whole "Bank". The Arabs want a Palestinian State from the Mediterranean Sea to the Jordan River. It is not a matter of giving up a little here or a little there. It is also not a matter of making small compromises. The Arabs are and have been, always, for the whole lot. They went for the whole "Bank". They are after the whole country of Israel. This makes it, not a struggle for territories, but rather a struggle for life, for survival.

New slogans appeared in Judea, Samaria and the Gaza Strip: "Jaffa before Jerusalem." The PLO is not satisfied with the West Bank. The PLO wants the whole country, the State of Israel.

"We shall take from the Israelis whatever we can get now and the rest we shall take later."

Yasser Arafat

The PLO with Yasser Arafat as its head is divided into the following departments:

Fatah: Internal Security- Military Operations- Force 17
Palestine Communist Party
Palestine Liberation Front
Democratic Front for the Liberation of Palestine (Nayef Hawatmeh)
Popular Front for the Liberation of Palestine (Dr. George Habash)
Arafat's Political Adviser
Commander of Occupied Territories
Lebanon Commander
South Lebanon Commander

There is no comparison between the Palestinian-Arab conflict and the Blacks and Whites in America. The Middle East Israeli-Arab conflict is totally different from the problem of the American Blacks. American Blacks demand equality with the American Whites. They do not want to destroy the "White Government" and the US Constitution and set up a new Black Republic.

This is not the case in the Middle East. All Arabs, even the most moderate ones want to replace Israel by an Arab-Palestinian State. The question is only one of method. The moderates have now adopted the piecemeal method for the dismemberment of the Jewish State. They agree to do it by stages. They want Israel to withdraw to the 1967 borders as stage one; to the 1947 borders as stage two; and then to replace it completely with an Arab state, where they claim, they will permit Jews to be tolerated as a minority.

The Palestinian-Arabs of the West Bank and the Gaza Strip are living in their homes. On the other hand, those living in the refugee camps and abroad are those who fled in 1948 from Jaffa, Haifa, Lod, Ramleh, Jerusalem, etc. and demand to go back to their "homes", that's in Israel proper. Arafat in his Charter promised to bring them back to their homes. That's why; if he wants to keep his promise to the refugees he must have control of all of Israel.

It had been the policy of most of the Arab World to keep the refugees in the refugee camps as an open sore and a political weapon against Israel. One should go down to Gaza and Samaria and see how people live in refugee camps. A third generation is living under intolerable conditions. Yet, neither the world community nor the rich Arab Oil community gives a damn about them. So far they haven't contributed a cent for their relief. The Palestinian-Arabs will not accept a state without Jerusalem as its capital. For Israel it means that the Arabs insist that Israel will give away part of Jerusalem in the First phase. Of course Israel will never accept this Arab precondition.

It seems that in spite of the fact that the PLO still advocates terror as a tool to achieve its goal their main stream has begun thinking also politically, more than they have done in the past may be it is a sign of maturity. It seems that they have become more pragmatic and realistic. But, this is merely a temporary change of tactics, a change of strategy. They haven't given up their ideology of exterminating Israel.

Formerly, and in their charter, the Arab and the PLO positions called for the destruction of Israel, and they claimed it loudly, bluntly, without fear or shame. However, they have learned from past experience that this goal is unattainable. Therefore, temporarily, they geared their policies to more moderate goals, always bearing in mind the destruction of Israel.

Arafat threatens that if Israel retains the West Bank and Gaza he will escalate the uprising to greater extremes with the hope that the surrounding Arab countries will not be able to refrain from counter reaction. Arab intends to drive them into an all out war against Israel.

Syria had never given up its attempt to hold the Palestinian-Arabs under its control, a main reason for distrust between Syria and the PLO. Despite their "esteem" for each other, Assad and Arafat had shared interests in the Palestinian uprising in Judea, Samaria and Gaza and in terrorist attacks in Israel.

There is not a single Palestinian-Arab who is ready to negotiate with Israel on "territories for peace". Yet, they are ready to talk on "all the territories (including Jerusalem) for peace." They want the whole country of Israel as well as the right of all the Palestinians in the world, including the refugees, to return to their homes in Jaffa, Haifa, Acco (Acre), Lod, Ramleh, Jerusalem, etc. which means, adding three more million Arabs into the country and rendering the situation worse. They also want, of course, all the Jews out.

This only can mean that there is no goodwill on the part of the Arabs. They donot want to hear of compromise, therefore there is no solution. No political solution. Therefore, considering all the possible aspects of the situation, the only way out from this dilemma is, that Israel stops "playing" and takes a more firm and decisive stand.

Unfortunately for Israel, the Likud and the Maarah and Kadimah fail to address themselves to the real challenges facing the country and their platforms are frivolous and unrealistic. The real issue is how to get rid of two and half million Arabs within its territories. Two and a half million Arabs who do not belong there. Therefore, the policy of the Likud: autonomy and the policy of the Maarah: Territories for Peace, are both dangerous and courting disaster.

The Likud's autonomy was designed for an interim period and will eventually develop into an independent Arab-Palestinian state. Even so, it doesn't seem that the Arabs will accept it. Therefore, this Likud proposal is unrealistic and dangerous.

The National Unity Government was working very "efficiently", the "harmony" between these two parties, the Likud and the Maarah was scary. The Prime Minister Yitzhak Shamir (Likud) had his own policy and his Foreign Minister Moshe Arens (Likud) had his own policy, the Defense Minister Yitzhak Rabin (Maarah) had his own policy and Finance Minister Shimon Peres (Maarah) had his own policy. With a system like this the country can be torn apart.

Foreign Minister Moshe Arens (Likud) declared openly over the international news media that Israel shouldn't remain stubborn like a stone wall, because things have changed, and therefore, Israel has to consider the national needs of the Palestinian-Arabs. A very clear sign that Israel might be willing to yield to Arab demands. A very clumsy, unfortunate declaration. On the other hand, Defense Minister Yitzhak Rabin (Maarah) tried to buy from the PLO, through the Palestinians, the end of their uprising, intifada, and is ready to pay for it a very expensive political price, which included a promise that soon Israel will be ready to enter in a dialogue with the Palestinians on the issue of the "Final Solution" of Judea, Samaria and Gaza.

Now, every body understands that the "Final Solution" means "the Relinquish of Territories."

One Government , four foreign policies. What a sad situation!

Israeli Cabinet Ministers were making political statements, which did not always belong to their portfolio something not done in any other country, something unheard of. Something that is against the best interest of Israel. One Minister infringing in the other Minister's territory which shows only readiness for a binational state, where the majority and the minority live together. Everybody knows for sure that the minority will soon become the majority, within a few decades. This knowledge causes unrest and even nightmares. Israel was surprised and angry to the European Parliament's unprecedented condemnation on March 1, 1988 (Adar 21, 5748), which harshly attacked Israel's policy in Judea, Samaria and the Gaza Strip and which expressed "solidarity with all Palestinians living in what are now intolerable conditions,"

The body representing parliamentarians from twelve EC countries refused to ratify three trade protocols within Israel, which added insult to injury.

The condemnation was a grave distortion of reality, which showed a basic lack of understanding of the situationThe protocols would also have provided Israel with seventy seven million US Dollars in European Investment Bank loans.

On the month of May 1988, the Israeli public was astound to hear that their Chief-of –Staff, General Dan Shomron, declaring that the great part of the tension in the country was caused by the Jewish settlers, in Judea, Samaria and the Gaza Strip, that's by Gush Emunim. What a distortion! What an irresponsible declaration1, and made by the Israeli Chief-of-Staff, over the radio and the Television, in public!

Dr. Mubarak Awad, an Arab, a US citizen, preaches for passive, non-violent struggle against Israel, until it collapses.

Faress Buchafah, a Palestinian-Arab, also with US citizenship, head of the ADC (Arab Discrimination Committee) in America Public Relation Office, Washington,D.C.also, like Dr. Mubarak Awad, is also a "vegeterian" who preaches "non-violence". He declared in public that he "hates" violence or militancy and pledges to "peacefully" fight Israel until it collapses and until the establishment of a Palestinian-Arab state. AIPAC, the Israeli lobby in Washington D.C. is warning that Faress Buchafah is dangerous.

Another very dangerous person is the leader of the Islamic Movement in Israel, Sheich Abdallah Nimer Darwish, from Kafar Kassem. Sheich Abdallah Nimer Darwish is a citizen of Israel, an Islamic zealot who seriously believes he is a prophet and wants to see the whole world become Moslem. In his youth he was a follower of Nasser (Egyptian President) and a Communist. He was also an etheist and believed that religion is opium for the fools. Tens of thousands of Moslem fanatics are his followers. How this coincides with being a Moslem? Only Darwish knows! His house was for years a base for terror activities. His basement was an arsenal. He was caught, sentenced and sent to jail (1981-1984). After his release he became more careful and speaks of "peace" and "non-violence" and "freedom" to the Palestinian-Arabs.

Mahmoud Darwish, in his last song, suggested that the leaving Israelis, the leaving Jews should not leave alone, but take with them their deads from the cemeteries. What a distorted brain! Their goal is not an Arab-Palestinian state, side by side with Israel but another Moslem state instead of Israel. Therefore, the Arabs are not serious customers to be considered seriously.

The increase of the extremists, maximalists and fundamentalists influence on the Palestinian-Arabs in the territories has been accompanied by the emergence of the mosque as a political center, as inciters center, a shelter for terrorists and a weapons' storage. One thousand out of four thousand of the students in the University of Najah in Nablus (Shechem) were booked in, or even charged, for actively participating in the Intifada, in the war against Israel.

The Arabs opened a new war against Israel, by setting fires. During the three days, the 15th, the 16th and 17th of May 1988, the Israeli Fire Brigade have been called to extinguish one thousand and one hundred and fifty fires, and the total loss was 55-100 million Sheqels, that's about 62 million US Dollars.

On September 1989 (Elul 5749), the Palestinian-Arabs set fire to the Mount Carmel National Park, near Haifa, one of the most beautiful and rare woods in Israel. The fire ravaged the Park. The arson destroyed eight thousand Dunams (one thousand and six hundred acres) of forest and bush land. The Mount Carmel National Park contained also the "hai Bar" biblical animal sanctuary. Twenty-two rare animals died in the blaze. The sanctuary's thirty-three fallow deers were the only ones in the entire world. One of them died in the blaze. The blaze occurred during what would normally be the mating season of the deer. The panic of the animals would prevent them from mating that year.

The fires gave every body in Israel a bitter feeling towards the Arabs. It showed that their struggle was against barbarians. The Arabs, claim it's their land. If this was true, how could they treat it like this? People, who have no feelings to trees and animals, have no feelings to human being either. Those who do not love the trees of Eretz Israel and burn it, admit that Eretz Israel doesn't mean for them anything, doesn't belong to them and that they have no part in it.

For years, burning forests in Israel by the Arabs had been standard routine. As soon as the summer started some of the new forests that the country of Israel had, were set on fire. Fires do not start, usualy, alone they are caused by human beings.

The Arabs set the fires in the summer so that the Israelis, the Jews believe that it's the heat or the sun that started the fires. This has been going on for several years. Since June 1967, and even before the Palestinian-Arabs' uprising started, the number of fires had grown substantially. To this the Arabs have added also the burning of Jewish plantations, the cutting of trees, blowing water pipes, telephone poles, electric poles, blocking roads, etc. The number of forests, the number of trees, are scarce in Israel. Therefore, the Israelis look upon the burning of trees very seriously and very severely, as it takes over a decade to grow a tree.

By burning down forests, woods, plantations, orange groves, Olive groves, vineyards, the Arabs have decided to render the State of Israel into ashes. Something like this you cannot forgive. Something like this you do not fight with rubber bullets or tear gas. Something like this you do not fight with politeness, justice or democracy. Such phenomena needs a treatment of the jungle, there you have to fight like an animal, because you deal with animals.

These Arab sabotage acts rendered the lives of the Israeli settlers miserable. If Israel reached a situation like this, only one person could be blamed for it, Defense Minister Yitzhak Rabin, who was too soft and mellow.

Many wars have been conducted in the name of peace and for the sake of peace. The Palestinian-Arabs also claim that their intifada is in the name of peace.

On October 1988, from Tunis, Yasser Arafat addressed the Israeli public over the media, ordering them to vote for parties belonging to the "Camp of Peace". By this he meant for the Maarah and the other Left parties. Arafat added a threat that if Shamir is elected premier and not Shimon Peres the PLO will resort to fire arms, thus dictating the outcome of the November general elections in Israel. In order to clarify his intentions the PLO attacked with Molotov-Cocktails, on October 30th, 1988, two days before the elections, a number 961 Egged bus, loaded with civilians, coming from Tiberias and going to Jerusalem, passing through Jericho. Mrs. Weiss from Jerusalem, with her three little boys, ages 3 years, 9 years, and 10 months were burned to death. Several other passengers were severely wounded. This, Arafat did in the name of peace, for the sake of peace.

The Mayor of Jerusalem, Teddy Kollek, called, on November 10, 1988, (Kislev 1, 5749) on the Mufti of Jerusalem to denounce the recent firebomb attack, which killed the Jerusalem mother, Mrs. Weiss, and her three children in Jericho and seriously injured another woman in Wadi Joz (Jerusalem) on her way to vote. In a long and angry letter, Kollek the Mayor rebuked Sheich Sa'ad e-Din el-Alami, the Mufti of Jerusalem and head of the Supreme Moslem Council, for statements that he reportedly made abroad about the Israeli Defense Forces (IDF) soldiers torturing and burning Palestinian-Arabs alive.

These statements were "groundless" and "intended to incite", Kollek wrote. "You know that things like that are not said by reasonable people. It seems to me that you are abusing the Israeli democracy, which allows each person to speak freely."

Our first duty was to condemn the shocking crime committed by young Arabs, whose victims were a Jewish mother and her three children, who were burned alive." Kollek said, "it is very strange that I didn't hear or read any denunciation from you and your colleagues about that".

Saddam Hussein (Iraq), Hafez Assad (Syria), Yasser Arafat and Muamar Kaddafi (Lybia) have already violated with their behavior every Koranic precept. Terror is specifically precluded. Yet, there has been no Islamic condemnation of terrorism. Not a single imam has ever preached a sermon denouncing their terror. Not a single Rayess (president) ever denounced the behavior of these four gentlemen.Not a single Malek (king) ever denounced their atrocities. There seems to be very little genuine Islamic outrage at their behavior.

The "covenant" between Adolf Hitler and the Mufti of Jerusalem, Haj Amin al-Husseini was signed before the establishment of the State of Israel, during World War II. The massacre of the whole Jewish community in Hebron occurred in 1929, long before the establishment of the State of Israel, and without the provocation of a long period of Jewish occupation. Therefore, the Palestinian-Arab argument that their conflict with the Israelis, with the Jews, is because the establishment of the State of Israel and because of the Israeli "occupation" of the West Bank and Gaza is nothing but a big lie, same as the rest of their arguments.

The Korean War (1950-1953) lasted three years. The United States of America could have stayed out of it, but it decided to get involved. General Douglas MacArthur could have ended the war much earlier. He requested permission to cross the Yalu River and attack the Communist bases in Manchuria. MacArthur's request was flatly rejected. His strategy was conflicting with the policies established by his civilian and military superiors and he was relieved from his command in 1951 by President Harry Truman and replaced by General Matthew Ridgway. Both MacArthur and Ridgway could have crushed the Communists, North Koreans and Chinese in a relatively much shorter time. But, unfortunately, not the generals ran the war, the politicians ran the war and at a very high cost. The US suffered 157,530 casualties and with a total of 34,000 deaths. What is more ridiculous is, that in 1988 the United States of America still had 40,000 US soldiers there, guarding the South Koreans from an attack from the North.

The Vietnam War (1958-1973) lasted fifteen years. The United States of America could have stayed out of it, but it decided to get involved. The US supported the corrupt regime of President Ngo Dinh Diem and started pouring military personnel and weapon into South Vietnam. US General William C. Westmoreland could have crushed the Communists, North Vietnamese, in a relatively short time, but again, as in Korea, he did not have a free hand, and again as in Korea, the politicians in Washington ran the war.

Similarly, the intifada, the Palestinian-Arab uprising could have been crushed in 24 hours, by the Israeli army, if politics would not intervene. But, again, as in Korea and Vietnam, the politicians in Jerusalem ran the show and not the generals in the field.

The real problem facing Yitzhak Rabin is not only how to find and remove the leadership of the uprising, but also to cope with a grass root civil rebellion, which is nothing but another phase in the old long struggle against Israel and the Arab endeavor to exterminate it.

Same as a few years ago, in the US, with the "Vietnam Syndrome", in Israel, the Left has introduced the defeatist "Intifada Sindrom". Jordan has crushed such an uprising in a couple of days. Remember "Black September"? Rabin admitted that he couldn't handle it. Why wasn't he fired immediately by Premier Shamir? Again Politics!

During the term of the weak National Unity Government the Arabs have learned to use and abuse the Israeli democracy. Israel lost its deterrent capabilities. The Arabs were no longer afraid of the Israelis. Thus Israel lost the central component of her security conception; because of a lousy Minister of Defense.

Doubts about Yitzhak Rabin's capability to function under stress were raised as early as 1974 when his appointment as Prime Minister was being considered. In an extraordinary act, Ezer Weizman, who had served under Rabin as Chief of operations went to Prime Minister Golda Meir, to warn her against accepting Rabin as her successer?

Ezer Weizman disclosed important information about Rabin's state of health prior to the Six-Day War on June 1967 and his collapse. Many Israelis believe that in spite of the fact that he served his country well and faithfully at earlier stages of his career, today, the greatest service he could render to his people and country would be to resign.

"The IDF has not provided suitable answers to the problem of terror in the area. This situation has the effect of bringing war closer because it diminishes Israel's deterrent power among the Arab states." – Ariel (Arik) Sharon, on a tour to Kfar Tabor on March 27, 1988.

Israeli traffic was attacked. Buses full of Israeli passengers were burned with Molotov-Cocktails. The Arab mob was throwing stones as well as Molotov-Cocktails. Thousands of acres of fine forestry were burned. Jewish Children were kidnapped, raped and murdered. Old and young people were stabbed in the middle of the streets in broad day- light. Soldiers were kidnapped and murdered, and all the Defense Minister was doing was to call for restraint and prudence.

The military policy of Defense Minister Yitzhak Rabin in dealing with the Arab uprising had been very disappointing. Much more was expected from an ex-Chief-of-Staff. Two years of incessant Arab violence without being able to put an end to it shows a complete failure. So it's the insecurity of Jewish life in Judea, Samaria and the Gaza Strip, for which, Rabin is personally responsible and must shoulder the blame.

Aharon Peretz, 16, was the first settler to be stabbed since the Palestinian-Arab uprising started in the territories, that's, since December 1987. Aharon Peretz was stabbed in the back on March 3, 1988 (Adar 14, 5748), near Beit-Hadassah in Hebron, by an unidentified Palestinian Arab.

The Jewish settlers in Judea, Samaria and the Gaza Strip have not received ample protection from the IDF during the first year of the intifada. Speculations are that if Yitzhak Shamir keeps backing Yitzhak Rabin and his policy, he is going to have to accept the inevitability of clashes between the IDF and the settlers.

The Jewish settlers, determined to stay in Judea, Samaria and the Gaza Strip were demanding and very rightfully their right to have the same level of personal security as those living within the Green Line, Tel-Aviv, Haifa, etc. Unfortunately, during the Arab uprising, they didn't enjoy that security. Of course this was, no doubt, the Government responsibility.

The Maarah Party and its leaders (Peres, Rabin, etc.) openly declared that they were against the establishment of settlements in Judea, Samaria and the Gaza Strip, and never hid their intentions to give away these territories to the Arabs.

During the phiscal year 1989, the government's budget didn't include funds for the settlements in Judea, Samaria and the Gaza Strip, to help and fortify existing settlements and establish new settlements. This is, no doubt, a great neglect, because it curtails the right of the Israeli settlers anywhere in Eretz-Israel. The settlements in Judea, Samaria and the Gaza Strip should have been top priority.

"Rabin should have been fired months ago for failing to put an end to the uprising."

Ariel (Arik) Sharon
In Jerusalem's Katamon neighborhood
October 24, 1988

Because of Rabin's "vegetarian" way of handling the intifada there is a great possibility that history will record that Arab children beat the famous IDF with rocks and a few Molotov-cocktails and founded a Palestinian-Arab state! This is a shame!

In critical times like these, that Israel still had internal and external security problems unsolved, to have Ariel Sharon acting as Minister of Industry and Commerce, was a criminal waste. Sharon could have been a much better and more efficient Defense Minister. Especially when Yitzhak Rabin admitted in public that he had no military answer to the Palestinian-Arab uprising, and declared that only a political solution is possible. Rabin declared publicly that the IDF couldn't handle the intifada, all it could is decrease it but not crush it. To expose such a military top secret, such classified material, and by the Defense Minister is extremely dangerous. This could only encourage the enemy to keep pressing. Rabin was absolutely incompetent and Sharon should have replaced him immediately. In any other normal country the Defense Minister would have resigned immediately for such incompetence and negligence. General Ariel Sharon crushed the Palestinian terror in the Gaza Strip in 1972 in a week's time. Yitzhak Rabin should have learned from Sharon how to do it. If Rabin couldn't quell the intifada, he should have resigned from office of Defense Minister and let Sharon do it. "What man is here that is fearful and faint-hearted? Let him go and return unto his house, lest his brethren's heart melt as his heart." To crush the intifada, to break the uprising, firm and unorthodox measures should have been applied, immediately. Israel should have taken more preemptive measures, such as preventing them, the Arabs, from entering Israel, deportation and capital punishment, same as the British did during their mandate. Deflecting Rabin's reminder on November 6, 1988, that the Kahan commission, which investigated the 1982 Sabra and Shatilah massacre, had disqualified Sharon as Defense Minister, Sharon said: "I was not disqualified for service as Defense Minister forever. What was I really held responsible for? The fact that Christians killed Palestinians didn't make any less of an expert on security matters, and didn't make some one else any more of an expert. I paid heavily because Christians killed Palestinians, but, it should be mentioned that Palestinians kill and injure Jews throughout Israel every day, and for that, no one is the top echelons of the Defense establishment has paid to this day. I would call this situation the responsibility of those who shirk responsibility."

The Arabs were the ones that started the intifada. They hit the Israelis, military or civilians, wherever they could lay hands on. It is quite difficult to predict where or when their next hit will be. They have the backing of the entire Arab population in Eretz Israel, that's Israel, and the territories of Judea, Samaria and the Gaza. It will be naïve or even ignorance to believe that only a minority is supporting and cooperating with the PLO and its subsidiaries. The whole Arab population in Eretz Israel is either PLO members or ardent PLO supporters. Therefore, collective punishment should be efficient. It might not sound so popular but it will be sure efficient and practical. If not every individual Arab is physically involved in the intifada, they all participate in it, directly or indirectly, by supplying them with hiding places, shelters, room and board, etc. before and after their attacks.

There are many efficient ways to put an end to the Arab "uprising":

Bulldoze or bomb the houses of those people who throw stones or Molotov-Cocktails. If they happen to be minors destroy their parents' houses, then deport the whole family. Stop Arab work in Israel. Let them get jobs elsewhere.

Declare Judea, Samaria and the Gaza Strip military zones and out of bounds for the news Media.Close all hostile, inciting Arab newspapers, mainly published in East Jerusalem.Flood Judea, Samaria and the Gaza Strip with Jewish settlements.

Urban renewal projects can also be very helpful in putting an end to the Arab "uprising".

The Engineering Corps chooses a straight line, crossing the problematic Arab city, from north to south or from east to west. Then destroy all houses on both sides of the straight lines, with the formal pretext that a new road is being constructed, of course for the benefit of the city.

The British did it, in Jaffa, in 1936, during the Arab uprising. They destroyed a big part of Jaffa's Kasba and old city. 237 houses were destroyed. The British repeated this system in other cities too. This

is is a fair sample of the methods adopted by the British for subduing an urban area which has got completely out of hand and where every form of law and order ceased to exist, and provides an excellent illustration of means of reducing a recalcitrant urban area by the most human and democratic means.

During the Arab revolt in Palestine (1936-1939), the British also brought artillery pieces and shelled the villages and towns from where the Arab terrorists came and the villages or towns to where they fled.

Unfortunately, the politically paralyzed Jewish National Government could not provide an answer to this "complex" problem. It is totally untrue that the intifada cannot be stopped by means of military repression, as the Defense Minister Yitzhak Rabin claimed, while the cry in the country was for a complete, drastic, revision of the security policy that will make Judea, Samaria and the Gaza Strip safe for Jews also. Harsher measures must be taken against Arab terrorists and a more aggressive stance against Arab instigators. It must be made crystal clear to the Palestinian-Arabs that Jewish blood is very expensive. That if they stick to terror more Arab houses will be demolished or sealed and their inhabitants deported. Unorthodox, radical, unconventional measures should be used, day and night, to confront the Palestinian-Arab terror, and without mercy or feeling of guilt. The intifada must be wiped out without delay, before it becomes routine and gets out of control or worse becomes a habit.

Degradation of IDF soldiers should not be permitted. IDF soldiers should have the full backing and support of their superiors to do whatever is necessary without the threat of a court martial.

Israel should start an offensive against the Arab leaders, located mainly in East Jerusalm, Ramallah, Nablus and Tulkarem. These leaders are behind all the riots, the leaflets, the transfer of funds for terror activities, etc. These leaders should be captured, deported and their houses destroyed.

There was a guiding hand behind the Arab riots. It made sure that by 8:30 in the morning, Arabic translations of the Hebrew press, including the afternoon papers, showing the impact of the Arab riots on Israel's national psychology, were distributed in thousands of copies in almost every village and town throughout the territories.

Somehow, inexplicably, the Defense Minister, Yitzhak Rabin and the security forces misread the situation. Instead of silencing the mosques from which messages of indescribable hatred were being spewed forth by teenagers who had been given microphones by compliant imams, or ensuring that the Arab printing presses churning out calls for "death to the Jews and their Palestinian lackeys" were shut down, the IDF and the Israeli Border Police lashed out blindly at an amorphous, invisible enemy. This ugly confrontation could have been averted, stopped, if the Israeli authorities had taken their duties and policies more seriously, especially when the Arabs are openly struggling to get Israel out of the territories.

Confrontations and wars are unpleasant. It goes against the grain, for Jews especially, to pit soldiers against civilians. But that is no reason to raise your hands in surrender and let the enemy have his way with you.

If turmoil should erupt among the Arabs of Galilee will anybody advocate giving up the Galilee, too? Where does Israel then draw the line?

A nation is forced sometimes to do also unpleasant things in order to defend itself and to avoid catastrophe.

The human and democratic way in which the Palestinian-Arabs were treated in Judea, Samaria and the Gaza Strip during their uprising is a good example of a Defense Minister's misjudgment. This is not exactly the time to be kind, understanding and generous, in retaliation to stones and Molotov-Cocktails. This is the time to make a quick reassessment of the limits of democracy in times of stress, in times of danger, danger to the Israeli democracy, danger to Israel's survival.

Since the intifada's very beginning there have been constant attempts by several educated Palestinian-Arabs, in Judea, Samaria and the Gaza Strip to "work" on the Israeli public opinion and get their support and sympathy. They appealed to the Israeli conscience with hints that a Israeli unilateral withdrawal from the territories will finally put an end to the long Arab-Israeli conflict in the area, but in the same time there was a parallel attempt to induce a sense of war-weariness in Israel by creating the impression that the Palestinians will never give up. They tried to impact those elements that could get Israel out of Judea, Samaria and the Gaza Strip. The Arabs were not smart enough and failed to manipulate Israeli public opinion. The Palestinian-Arab uprising turned a much larger proportion of Israelis in the Middle towards the hawkish position rather than the dovish position. Most Israelis believe that the Arab riots have encroached upon areas of freedom and security and threatens their survival. It hasn't ended only because of the weak Israeli Government policy showing the Arabs compassion and understanding.

The intifada must be contained immediately because a long intifada is eroding both the IDF operational capability and its effectiveness as a deterrent. The fact that troops are tied up in an attempt to keep the intifada under control, for such a long time, seriously disrupts vital routine training.

The Palestinian-Arab uprising strengthened the spirit and conviction of the Jewish settlers in Judea, Samaria and the Gaza Strip and their decision to stay forever. The daily Arab violence, the daily Jewish casualties, had made the Isrealis think differently.

During the intifada several Israelis in the streets were approached to feel their reaction:

"We, Israelis, have been living with these Arabs much more than forty years, almost for a century. They do not love us. We do not love them. They do not want to live with us and we do not want to live with them. In spite of what some Israeli leaders declare privately or publicly, the majority of the Israelis hate the idea of coexistence with the Arabs. We do not want to depend on their work, which is known as lousy work. They come to work when they decide to take a break from the riots or run out of stones, bottles, and tires. We do not need their services, we can serve ourselves. We are not that lazy. We do not want the Arabs to cook for us our meals, in our restaurants or hotels and we do not want as well, Arab waiters to carry our meals from the kitchen to our tables, while spitting their venom into our food, which we have to eat. We do not want to see the deep hate in his eyes when he serves us. We do not want to mingle with them. We do not want our culture to mingle with their culture. During the years, which we have lived with them, or rather were compelled to live with them, due to very unfortunate circumstances, there was no love between us. No sex between us. No mutual understanding, no mutual interests. They have been nothing but trouble, a pain in the neck. Therefore, it is time to separate. We want them out - out of our way, out of our sight. We want them on the other side of the fence, on the other side of the border, where they belong. This is how most of the Israelis feel. Because of the ongoing intifada it seems that the hope of coexistence with the Arabs dimmed, even among the Israeli doves. Freedom and independence are not only objective conditions, but also a state of mind. With the Arabs around, harassing, there is no peace of mind, there is no freedom, and there is no independence. The idea that two nations can share the same territory or sovereignty is doomed, because duality was never written into the very essence and texture of Eretz Israel, that's Greater Israel. Eretz Israel is the holy land, the land of the Bible, the land of one history, one tongue, one society, one recollection, one national passion, one identity, one religion. Therefore, any coexistence structure is bound to fail.

Speulations are that if the Syrians carried out a military offensive against Israel Israel would destroy them easily, inspite of their missiles. The same goes with any other Arab country that dares launch a military attack against Israel, alone or together. Therefore, the Palestinian-Arab outbreak, the intifada suits them better. Indeed, they find it an ideal solution, a permanent solution. It damages Israel at no cost, or very little cost to themselves and it spoils Israel's image and reputation in the eyes of the world. Presenting the Arabs as the long-suffering underdogs.That's how they think. That's how the Arabs think. After their reconciliation both superpowers, the United States and the Soviet Union were no longer prepared to tolerate or subsidies regional conflicts. It appears that the superpowers are determined not to permit local conflicts to drag them into global confrontation. The Soviets under Gorbachev had concluded that dangerous flashpoints of tension should be resolved, neutralized, or at least quarantined so that they don't spill over into areas where the superpowers have vital interests. The superpowers will do their utmost to protect themselves from being dragged into direct confrontation as a result of a regional conflict.

Most people hate violence. Jews hate violence. In general, a Jew will go to any length to prevent war, even if it is at the expense of his vital interests. An excellent proof is the return of the whole of Sinai to Egypt. Even when Israel tried to put down the Palestinian-Arab uprise, it never descended to the level of brutality of their Arab neighbors. This is why Israel found it so difficult to put an end to the Arab uprising. In 1970, the Palestinian-Arabs have tried some sort of uprising in Jordan. Thousands of Palestinians were machine gunned by the Jordanian army. The World's news media was hibernating then and was not in uproar, nor was the UN Security Council. The Israeli army could have done the same, may be better, but it did not. Yitzhak Rabin was trying to accomplish his task with minmum loss of human lives. This was another reason why Israel found it difficult to end the uprising. Under Yitzhak Rabin as Defense Minister, the Arab uprising dragged until it gave birth to the declaration of independence in Algiers. The intifada could have and should have ended long ago.

Israel could have and should have taken drastic measures to suppress the Arab intifada in the first day of its inception. The "trouble" is that the Israeli society is basically democratic and believe in certain moral and legal standards as well as in the sanctity of human life. Therefore couldn't shoot at random.

The Israelis cannot do what the French paratroopers did in Algiers, the Green berets did in May Lay or what the Indian army did in Sri Lanka (Ceylon), the Soviet army In Afghanistan and the Germans did in Europe, during World War II British atrocities committed against the Palestinian-Arabs, in 1938. In retaliation to the assassination of the British Governor in Palestine, Sir Andrews. The British exiled the members of the Arab High Committee in Palestine to the Seychelles Island in the Indian Oean. The British were not satisfied yet and pushed several Arabs into minefields and half ruined the city of Jenin. The Israelis, cannot do what the Indian army did in Sri Lanka (Ceylon), the Soviet army in Afghanistan and the German's did in Europe, during World War II. This is why it will take a little longer to end the Arab uprising.

Israel could not compete with the Soviet cruelties in Warsaw (Poland) and Budapest (Hungary), in 1956 or in Prague (Czechoslovakia). Israel could not compete with Red China cruelties against the people of Tibet or the bloodbath against the Chinese Students in Beijing's Tiananem Square on June 4, 1989. Israel could not compete with the cruelties of the Roumanians against the Hungarians in Timisoare, Transylvania, on December 1989. In Algeria, the Arab uprising lasted only one day, because the Algerian army slaughtered 400 Algerians In one day. In Israel the intifada is already lasting over Six years because the Israelis didn't use yet such drastic measures.

Even ex US secretary of State, Dr. Henry Kissinger, suggested that Israel puts an end to the Palestinian-Arab uprising, the intifada, as soon as possible, even if necessary, by force, mercilessly.

Speaking at a meeting with senior infantry officers and defense reporters, on March 31, 1988, (Nissan 13,5748), Chief Infantry Officer, Tat-Aluf (Brigadier General) Shmuel Arad declared that there was no absolute military solution to the current intifada, in Judea, Samaria and the Gaza Strip, because the people of Israel will not allow it.

Israel must replace immediately its Defense Minister Yitzhak Rabin (Maarah), who failed to suppress the Palestinian-Arab uprising, by somebody like Ariel Sharon(Likud) and Suppress the Palestinian-Arab uprising within a weak or so. But Prime Minister Yitzhak Shamir (Likud) preferred that somebody from the Maarah Party would do this job and no matter how long it takes, because Sh0amir wanted to avoid another demonstration of four hundred thousand people at Kikar Malchei Israel (The Kings of Israel Square-Kikar Rabin) in Tel-Aviv, led by the Maarah Party against his government, if the uprising was supressed by a Defense Minister from the Likud Party. Shamir still remembered vividly the demonstration at Kikar Malchei Israel (Now Kikar Rabin), organized by the Maarah against ex-Prime Minister Menachem Begin, during the War of Lebanon, in 1982.Israel knows from her past experience that a long war invites outside pressure. The long "War of Attrition" in 1970-1971 produced the "Roger's Plan". The Yom Kippur War in 1973 invited US-Soviet pressure. The long War of Lebanon, in 1982 produced the "Reagan Plan". Similarly, the long Palestinian-Arab uprising, the long intifada drag produced outside pressure: US pressure and European Community (EC) pressure. All these pressures against Israel are nothing but more amunition to the PLO, more hope to the Palestinian-Arabs, more encouragement to the intifada to keep pushing, Israel out of the West Bank. And all of these pressures are exirted upon Israel by some of her "best friends". For an Israeli Defense Minister or Chief-of-Staff to utter phrases like: "There is no military solution to the intifada. Only a political arrangement can stop it!", and over the radio and television, means, paving the road for a Palestinian-Arab state and for Israel's total defeat. And in a time when the most important weapon is to have cool nerves. Tremendously irresponsible declarations. Treacherous declarations. Reasons for Israel's troubles are many. The bad example, which the Israeli politicians are giving with their behavior and irresponsible statements over the media. The classified, top secret material which is exposed to the public, and to the enemy. All these are very damaging to the Israeli war efforts and to her security. It only encourages the intifadists to persevere. What also encouraged the Palestinian-Arabs and their intifada and increased its longevity was: the Israeli democracy, the open communication and free media, the Israeli leadership crisis, the division in the Israeli society on the issue, the Israeli Left, that with its irresponsible semantics helped split the Israeli society and blurred the image of Israel in the World.

The life span of the Palestinian-Arab uprising, the intifada, was also prolonged by the US decision to open a dialogue with the PLO.

All these encouraged the momentum of the Arab uprising and kept it alive The Arab intifada is still going on because of the impotence of the Israeli politicians who did not give the Green light to the forces in the field. Because the Israeli Defence Forces, the IDF, did not receive yet the order from the politicians, the Cabinet, the Prime Minister the

Defense Minister, to crush it. Once they get the order they will probably do it very efficiently and in very short time.

Speculations are, that the Israeli Government didn't order the IDF to crush the intifada, because, the Israeli Government was, for one reason or another, interested in the continuation of this situation.

On August 18, 1988 (Elul 5, 5748), the Red Cross declared that holding the Palestinian-Arab terrorists in "Ketziot" detention center was violating international humanitarian law.

This same Red Cross didn't condemn the detention of millions of Jews in the concentration camps in Europe, during World War II. A typical interference in a sovereign country's internal affairs with a strong smell of Anti-Semitism. The International Committee of the Red Cross was, in fact, mute, silent and mostly inact as Jews by the millions were being pushed to their death by the Germans. A full scale slaughter of the Jews was going on in Europe, yet, the Red Cross did nothing to stop it, nothing to pressure the Germans by publicizing the facts or at least raise an alarm about their mass slaughter. The Red Cross people answered that they were afraid not to jeopardize their chance to assist prisoners of war in the hands of the Germans of the Third Reich. It was a phony excuse.

Between September and December 1987, nine members of the Syrian Jewish Community were detained without charges. What did Amnesty International do about it? Where was the Red Cross? They did nothing to free the Jewish detainees.

On August 25, 1988 (Elul 12, 5748), at the Arab village of Yatta, south of Hebron, in Judea, Saadi Hazaza, 32, was dragged from his house before dawn by ten masked Arabs who attacked Hazaza with axes, knives and iron bars, in a nearby field. Villagers reported that Hazaza's stomach and throat had been slashed and his skull cracked. Hazaza was assassinated for collaborating with Israel.

Members of PLO Executive Committee as of January 1989:

Yasser Arafat (Abu Ammar)- Fatah, Chairman of the Executive Committee, Head of the Military Department, Commander-in-Chief of Revolutionary Forces and Chairman of Fatah's Central Committee.

Farouk Kaddoumi- Fatah, Head of the Political Department and member of Fatah's Central Committee.

Mahmud Abbas (Abu Mazan)-Fatah, Head of the National Department and member of Fatah's Central Committee.

Yasser Abed Rabbo (Abu Bashir)-Democratic Front of the Liberation of Palestine (DFLP), Head of the Propaganda and Information Department and Deputy-Secretary-General of the DFLP

Abdel Rahim Ahmed- Arab Liberation Front (ALF), Head of the Popular Organization Department and Secretary General of the ALF.

Mohammad Zaidan Abbas (Abul Abbas)-Palestine Liberation Front (PLF), without portfolio and Head of the two PLF factions loyal to Arafat.

Suleiman Najab-Revolutionary Palestinian Communist Party (RPCP), Head of the Social Affairs Department and Secretary General of the RPCP.

Jamal Surani, Independent, Secretary General of the Executive Committee and Head of the Organizations Department.

Ilia Huri (Abu Mahar)-Independent, without portfolio, considered the Christian representative on the Executive Committee.

Muhammed Hassan Milham (Abu A'Ala), Independent, Head of the Occupied Homeland Department and the Higher Education Department.

Abdel Razek Yahia (Abu Anas)-Independent, Head of the Economic Department and the Senior PLO representative in Jordan.

Yaweed Yacoub Hussain (Abu Tufiq)- Independent, Chairman of the Board of Directors of the Palestinian National Fund (PNF).

Abdullah Hurani-Independent, Head of the Cultural Affairs Department.

Mahmoud Darwish-Independent, Chairman of the Supreme Council for Education, Propaganda and Heritage. A famous Palestinian Poet.

Rabin's patient approach of grinding down the Arab uprising with economic and administrative pressures only failed. Rabin's cool reaction to the intifada didn't help to contain the Palestinian-Arab uprising. Patience and perseverance were not enough. Force and determination were needed. Rabin just didn't have it. Rabin naively believed that he has the whole time in the World to crush the Arab intifada. Rabin was totally wrong. Because there was very good reason to believe that America would soon try to force Israel into talks with the Arabs and the PLO, or even worse, the US might, even impose a solution on Israel, a solution not to the best interest of Israel. To carry out its policy the US might even recruit the Soviet Union and Western Europe or even apply economic and other pressures on Israel.

In 1989, the Palestinian-Arab terror has intensified. Both Yitzhak Rabin and Haim Barlev did not react accordingly. Very few Israelis understood their policy or may be their tactics. It looked as if Defense Minister Rabin was trying to imitate Russian General Kutuzov's army retreat from French Napoleon Bonaparte during the French-Russian War in 1812, as suggested by French Marechal Jean Bernadotte who became later King Charles XIV of Sweden. Rabin's decision to play the weaker party was feeding the Arabs' aggressive line and kept the intifada alive.

Shamir's hands were tied by coalition agreement, which gave the Maarah full freedom in their operations, and prevented the Prime Minister Shamir from interfering, for fear of breaking the fragile coalition and losing the majority in the Knesset.

The Israeli public held the whole Cabinet responsible for the incompetence to handle the situation. Not only Rabin was responsible for this situation, but Prime Minister Yitzhak Shamir as well. The whole Israeli Cabinet was sitting idly, doing nothing for months to change this situation. Outwardly it looked as if they were at loss and lost control.

Most of the Israelis are very disturbed by the persistence and increased violence of the intifada, especially as it crossed already the Green Line, into Israel proper, as well as at the use of fire-arms and perhaps more by the failure of the Defense Minister Yitzhak Rabin to put down the prolonged intifada.

Something had changed in the Palestinian-Arabs' politics. Something had changed in their mentality. Unlike in 1948, for the first time in many years, the Arabs in Judea, Samaria and the Gaza Strip are leading a struggle, all by themselves, without the help of the Egyptians, Syrians or Jordanians armies.

The following is Arafat's declaration in Saudi Arabia, which was published in the New York Times, on January 19, 1989:

"He who thinks of terminating the intifada before it had reached its goal will get from me ten rounds in his chest."

In the Israeli Cabinet meeting, on January 1989, Prime Minister Yitzhak Shamir admitted that Israel failed, so far, to suppress the Palestinian Arab uprising, the intifada, and that the intifada was already dragging too long and emphasizing that the intifada must be suppressed soon, without delay and even by force. The Palestinian-Arab intifada must be met head-on with force, if necessary, that will both overwhelm and deter. Everybody in Israel, except the Left, understood that the unrest must be confronted immediately, if necessary, with drastic, radical, measures. And it is the political echelon's responsibility to order the Israeli troops to restore civic order. It seems that the IDF is cramped by legal constraints. It seems that the laws governing IDF actions against the intifada were restricting its capacity to take quick and effective measures to quell the Arab uprising.

During the British Mandate in Palestine, Eretz Israel, the British dealt with the Arab terror during the years 1936-1939 with a strong hand. Terrorists were hung. Their leaders were exiled. The slightest Arab resistance to the British authorities was met with collective punishment, property confiscation and immediate expulsion.

In spite of the fact that the Palestinian-Arab uprising was still going on, and even became rougher, just a few days before the Moslem feast of Ramadan started, on April 1989, Defense Minister Yitzhak Rabin ordered the release of four hundred Palestinian-Arab intifada prisoners, as a good will gesture. Defense Minister Yitzhak Rabin released four hundred able-bodied men, four hundred terrorists, thus increasing the manpower of the enemy camp. There is no doubt, whatsoever, that these released prisoners will join their six hundred brethren from Ahmad Jibreel's faction, who were also previously released in another Israeli gesture and are fully active in the intifada.

Most of the Israelis believe that this was an act of cowardice, irrational and beyond comprehension. Their question was: "On whose side is Rabin? It was a great sin to release 1150 terrorists in return for 3 Israeli soldiers. But much greater sin was to let 600 of them to remain in the country, in Israel proper.

These 600 were the nucleus of the Arab uprising or Palestinian-Arab intifada that started on December 9, 1987.

As soon as the Palestinian-Arab intifada started, these 600 Arab terrorists should have been arrested immediately or expelled from the country. But, Defense Minister Rabin said that he could not violate a deal made with Ahmad Jibreel. This same deal included also a paragraph, which read specifically that these 600 terrorists be allowed to stay and live in Eretz Israel, only, if they stay away from terror activities and will never be involved in activities undermining the security and safety of the State of Israel.

For Mr. Rabin, not to break a deal with a master-murderer like Ahmad Jibreel seemed to be more important than the safety and security of his fellow citizens.

The Israeli authorities had in their hands a list of forty-three leaders of the Palestinian-Arabs uprising, the intifada in Judea, Samaria and the Gaza Strip, the top leaders were: Faissal Husseini, Raduan Abu Ayesh, Simean Houri, Hassan Abd-il Rabu, Ednan Shalalde, Taher Shaludi, Zuheir Abd-il-Hadi, Abu Tarek, Sari Nusseiba, Izzat Ghasawi and Hamdi Samadi. Many Israelis still wonder why the "Great Intifador", Faissal Husseini, the nephew of the "Great Mufti of Jerusalem" and the son of Abdul Kader Al-Husseini, the Arab gang leader, who was killed in action on the Castel, near Jerusalem, in 1948, hasn't been deported yet. These Arab leaders haven't been arrested or called in for interrogation, probably because of American pressure. The same reason why Israel couldn't crush the intifada. Many Israelis also wonder why the PLO sponsored daily newspapers are still being published, "legally", in Jerusalem.

The terrorist PLO bases were operating a few yards, a few meters from the Israeli Department of Justice, in Salah-el-Din Street, in Jerusalem, under the nose of the Israeli Police. Of course the Israeli Government knew it, but did not do anything to stop it. Again, probably of American pressure.

Three Israeli soldiers: Zecharia Baumel, Zvi Feldman, and Yehuda Katz were captured at Sultan Yaakub, in 1982, by a pro-Syrian terrorist group, and had not been heard of since. These three have been held in total violation of international law, with neither the Red Cross nor any other international body allowed to visit them. The Syrians have not even acknowledged their existence. Two more Israeli soldiers: Rahamim Alscheich and Yossi Fink were captured in 1986 by the Hizbullah. Pilot-Navigator Ron Arad was also captured by the Hizbullah, in 1986, when his plane fell in Lebanon.

It was, therefore, very odd to hear that, when US ambassador to Lebanon, Ryan Crocker was asked by the press if there existed a possibility of exchanging Arab prisoners held by Israel with these Israeli soldiers and with other western hostages held by the Arabs? Crocker replied that the US "wants to see the hostages, held by the Arabs, released unconditioanally." On the other hand, it is no secret at all that US pressure was exerted on Israrel to release Palestinian and Shiite prisoners in exchange for the Western hostages. The seven Israeli soldiers were not included.

Israel still remembers that, in 1985, it was forced to release 300 Shiite prisoners in return for the release of TWA passengers hijacked to Beirut, without receiving back its own prisoners, One must be naïve to believe that Israel will repeat its mistake. It would be nothing short of tragic were the Israeli Government to release anyone, in a deal, which does not include the return of all seven Israeli prisoners now in the hands of the Arabs.

1n March 1991, Muhamad Jawal Ramniyan, Iran's Charge D'Affaires in Beirut declared that the release of Sheikh Abdul Karim Obeidi, held in Israel, "would be very important in winning the release of Western hostages in Lebanon." On April 2, 1991, another prominent Hizbullah leader, Abbas Mousawi declared that, Sheikh Obeid must be released unconditionally, before any possibility of exchanging Israeli prisoners can be taken under consideration. This can only happen because the Western policies of appeasement towards terrorist-sponsoring governments, mainly Syria and Iran.

The Western governments, mainly France, have been trying to make separate back-door deals with the kidnappers and have paid them huge sums in ransom, and preferred to play along with the cynical pretense that the terrorists were independent, and to accept Syrian and Iranian denials of involvement. To complete this Orwellian charade, they ended each deal by expressing their gratitude for Syria's president, Hafez el-Assad, the terrorists' Godfather.

The day after November 29, 1947 (UN Resolution on the partition of Palestine into two states: A Jewish State and an Arab State), Palestinian Arabs stabbed Asher Lazzar, the Ha'Aretz newspaper Correspondent, a Jew, near Cinema Rex, downtown Jerusalem. This, to avoid the establishment of a Jewish State.

On May 1989, forty-two years later, two hundred feet from there, downtown Jerusalem, Nidhal Abdul Razek Zalum, a Moslem from Ramallah (A city north of Jerusalem) stabbed and killed two innocent, ninety years old Jews, waiting in a bus-stop. This, to "encourage" the establishment of a new Palestinian-Arab State, "Side by Side the Jewish State." According to the moral standards of most of the UN members, these two ninety-years old Jews were criminals, "occupiers", but, Nidhal abdul Razek Zalum was "innocent and underdog".

If more proof is needed to show and convince that peaceful coexistence of Israeli Jews and Palestinian Arabs under the same political roof is impossible, the discovery of the body of the kidnapped Israeli paratrooper, Avi Saportas, on May 1989 supplied it. Avi Saporta was murdered by Arab terrorists. The Israelis were outraged. There is very little doubt that the Arabs will have to pay dear for this act of violence.

On June 29, 1989 (Sivan 26, 5749), the Israeli authorities deported eight Arab residents of Judea, Samaria and the Gaza Strip. Only two of them had exhausted the appeals procedure by turning to the High Court of Justice and being turned down. All eight of them were PLO terrorists, brought to trial for their active part in the Arab intifada and convicted. The figures in the group were: Mohamad al-Labadi and Radwan Ziyada, both active in Judea and Samaria Labor Unions and supporters of the Democratic Front of Liberation of Palestine. Two others were also from Judea and Samaria, Akef Hamdallah and Taysir Nasrallah.

The deportees from Gaza were: Nabil Tamuz, Riyad Ajur, Muhamad Amduh and Atta Abu Kirsh

Thirteen others who have received deportation orders on August 1988 were expelled on January 1, 1989.

During the years 1967-1977, 1,180 Palestinians were deported. Nine were deported in 1978. One Palestinian in 1979 and three in 1980. During 1981-1985, no Palestinian Arab was deported. During 1986-1987, 45 Palestinian-Arabs were deported, and since the beginning of the Arab uprising, the intifada, in December 1987, 45 Palestinian-Arabs were deported.

The George W. Bush Administration was furious at the expulsions and reacted nervously and angrily. US officials stressed that they had specifically appealed to Israel for no more deportation. The Americans stated that these expulsions hindered their efforts to win Arab support for the Israeli peace initiative. More American pressure on Israel.

Bulgaria has expelled over 300,000 Turks in recent months. Rumania had removed two million Hungarians and Germans from its territory, without much of an international uproar. But when Israel deported one Arab it caused a big stir.

UN Secretary-General Javier Perez de Cuellar said that he is "greatly dismayed" by the expulsions, he called it "a clear violation " of the Fourth Geneva Convention and of "Lebanese Sovereignty". The deportees were flown to Lebanon.

Javier Perez De Cuellar appealed to Israel to "rescind the deportation order and allow the deportees to return to their homes and families."

No one ever mentioned that these were master terrorists. It didn't bother Javier Perez De Cuellar or the Bush Administration that these were Master Murderers engaged in hostile activities against Israel, and committed to its destruction.

Javier Perez De Cuellar didn't call upon the Bulgarian Government to promptly allow the Turks to return to their homes in Bulgaria.

Foreign Observers concluded that the bilateral relationship between Israel and the Arabs could be damaged if the deportation policy is not changed. The Foreign Observers just didn't know that there was no relationship between Israel and the Arabs, for several years.

If Israel's American friends object to Israel's deportation policy, they should first set an example, by emptying their own Indian reservations and return its inhabitants to the land from which they were expelled or release the prisoners in Guentanamo.

No judgment of Israel's punishment or preemptive system, like deportation, etc. is fair without the proper analysis of the causes and the conflicting interests between Arabs and Jews. Israeli citizens are being harassed, stabbed and killed by Arab terrorists, for several years. Therefore, there is no wonder if its legislators have placed a slightly heavier weight on the protection of its citizens from the Arab terrorists. Israel should not be judged by US standards. Israeli Judiciary process is different from that in the US or elsewhere. This should not be strange, as the US or any other country has never faced a situation like this.

On August 25, 1988 (Elul 12, 5748), Israel defended its policy of deportation, appealing for US understanding of the unusual situation, which necessitated unusual measures to quell the Palestinian-Arab uprising. In fact there was no policy of deportation, neither did it become a norm, Deportation was used only when it was absolutely necessary to react when the security situation became grave and difficult and in order to quell the violence in the territories. Israel submitted to the US the following "talking points":

1. As our two countries share an interest in containing terrorism and extremism, Israel expects and needs US understanding for unusual measures taken only under equally unusual circumstances.
2. These measures are taken in the face of increasing violence and incitement to violence, and have proved to be relatively effective in combating chaos and lawlessness.
3. According to authoritative Legal experts, expulsions in individual cases are compatible with the provisions of Israeli, Jordanian and international law. This interpretation was confirmed by the Supreme Court of Israel.
4. Israel is, and has been, making every effort to contain these measures to the necessary minimum and to extreme cases only. The steps are weighed case by case and each person will have, as in the past, the right to request review by the Supreme Court.
5. Members of the European Community were very quick in denouncing Israel for deporting Arab terrorists and murderers of innocent civilians, but totally ignore their own arms deals with Arab countries, like Iraq, Syria and Libya, which harbor terrorists and deal with terrorists.

On August 25, 1988 (Elul 12, 5748), Aluf-Mishne (colonel) G. a Brigade Commander was accused of killing a fleeing Palestinian demonstrator who threw stones at Israeli soldiers as well as Molotov-Cocktails, in the village of Bani Naim. The Israeli colonel was severely reprimanded by Deputy Chief-of-Staff Ehud Barak, after being found guilty of illegal use of his weapon and improper interpretation of 0the guidelines for opening fire. A serious punishment for a senior officer. General Barak made a terrible mistake.

This and similar other cases lowered substantially the moral of the soldiers who avoided shooting lest they get involved or even court martialed.

On October 5, 1988, a military court of appeals sent four soldiers of the Giveati Brigade back to jail pending their trial on charges of manslaughter, although the court said that the four soldiers may have not dealt the fatal blows that killed the Arab. In addition, the court warned soldiers against excessive use of force in the "administrative" territories.

Soldiers who were convicted of brutalities were sentenced. After which they were careful and reluctant to pull the trigger even in dangerous situations. The gap between the orders the soldiers were supposed to carry out and the norms of behavior demanded from them in court was annoying and confusing. The moral and legal limitations placed on the soldiers were terribly difficult.

General Amram Mitznah, member of kibbutz Ein-Gev (Maarah), who was in charge of the Central Command, that included also Judea and Samaria, since the intifada started on December 1987, for over nineteen months, was personally responsible for carrying his superiors' policy. General Amram Mitznah failed to crush the Arab uprising because he didn't understand the material he was working against, because he wasn't tough enough, because he was too delicate and liberal towards the Arabs. In the middle of 1989, when Mitznah felt that he will soon be required to use tougher means to break the Arab uprising, which was against his "morals", he requested a one year leave of absence, with the pretext that he wanted to go and finish his education.

This is the second time that General Mitznah is behaving unusual. The previous time was when during the War of Lebanon, in 1982, he suggested that the then Defense Minister Ariel (Arik) Sharon, who was doing an excellent job, should resign. Amram Mitznah was praised by his superiors, Rabin and Shomron, as well as the US administration. To many Israelis Mitznah's performance will remain inexcusable.

Many believe that the Palestinian-Arabs were totally wrong if they thought that by violence they could achieve their political objectives. There is no doubt that, if need be, the Israelis would increase the severity of the steps taken to combat Arab violence and the Palestinian-Arabs will face a crackdown on continued violence in the territories and in Israel. The Arabs are mistaken again. The Israelis are not the Crusaders. The Israelis are here to stay. The Crusaders didn't fight with their backs to the sea. They had their homes in Europe, where they could always retreat. The Israelis are fighting with their backs to the sea. They do not have another country ready to receive them. Eretz Israel is their only home. Therefore, they will fight like lions and drive the Arabs out. This time the Arabs will have to pay an extremely heavy toll for their misjudgment.

The Jews, the Israelis, are making a terrible mistake by minimizing their war against the Arabs into a fight against terror only. The national conflict with the Arabs is total and should be fought in several fronts, in several sectors. Israel must realize that it is not really fighting only terror, but also trying to control the seeds of incipient civil rebellion, which are expressing themselves increasingly in the streets of Israel, not only with burned tires, Molotov-Cocktails, stones and kitchen-knives. Guns are being pulled far more often, and many more Arabs are carrying guns. In the heart of the Palestinian-Arabs ideology is not democracy but revolution, which is to replace the "Zionist Invasion", and also prepare the Moslem World towards global power and spiritual fulfillment. It is this transcending vision, which highlights Arab messianic yearning. The fate of the Palestinian-Arab uprising, if it will fade out or turn into a Palestinian-Arab state, depends only on the Israeli Government. The Arab uprising cannot harm a determined Israeli Government with a strong conviction. One thing is sure, that without Israeli consent all the attempts to apply pressure are doomed to failure, if Jerusalem refuses to budge. It depends only on Israel's will, strength and determination, on whether Judea, Samaria and the Gaza Strip, which belong to Israel, and are vital to maintaining its security, will remain Israeli territory or not.

There is absolutely no doubt that the United States is aware of the fact that an independent Palestinian state in Judea, Samaria and the Gaza Strip means the insertion of PLO's Soviet-trained military apparatus into the heart of these territories which will pose a considerable danger to both Israel and Jordan.

In spite of the fact that the PLO is still continuing its terror, the Israeli forces have shown little initiative to stop it. Is it because it doesn't want to antagonize its future partner to the negotiation table? Or is it a result of some kind of coordination with the U.S.A?

It was clear and obvious, for the last few decades, as far as Israel's freedom to react to Arab terror was concerned, that its hands were tied, tied by American handcuffs.

Israel could not act freely because Uncle Sam's "big eyes" were constantly watching and monitoring Israel's behavior. Because of economical and military obligations to the United States, Israel was not sovereign, independent or free to act according to its heart wish, or according to its own logic. So long as the Arab terror exists Israel should not tie the hands of its defense forces while the Arabs remain free to act without any moral reservations. Many people believe that the United States of America was indirectly supporting the Arab uprising, the intifada, from its inception. This, in order to get Arab sympathy and promote US interests in the Middle East. This, they did by forcing (Three billion dollars yearly grant to Israel) to force her to restrain, be patient, act in prudent manner, make concessions, compromise, etc.

Since several years the Israeli Government noticed that some members of the UNRWA personnel in the Middle East, with the pretext of humanitarian aid, were closely cooperating with the Arabs and their different terror organizations. Hiring Arab help (never Jewish help): workers, drivers, etc., supplying them with UNRWA ID cards, with which they can cross borders without Israeli permits.

These UNRWA personnel were spying for the Arabs, passing orders and information, smuggling weapons, leaflets, etc. even during the curfews. Hiding "wanted" terrorists, smuggling narcotics, etc.

All these instead of doing their jobs of helping the Arab refugees, the poor and the sick, for which they were hired and/or sent to the Middle East.

The intifada that started on December 1987 is not an uprising. It is a war, an all out war, the seventh war between Israel and the Arab World. It is nothing but a direct continuation to the six previous wars (1948-1956-1967-1970-1973-1982). In spite of the fact that the means and the tools are different, the goal is the same, and the goal is the destruction of the State of Israel. Though, it seems so, the intifada is really not a "national uprising" of an oppressed people, but rather a war that is handled according to the concepts and principles of "National Wars" of revolutionary movements, by a smiting force supported and protected by a civilian population. The intifada is not a struggle of a national minority for self-determination, but a war of the whole Arab World, with the Palestinian-Arabs acting as the pioneer foot-soldiers supported behind by twenty Arab sovereign states who have a common obsession to put an end to the one and only Jewish state and replace it by another Arabic state.

This is not a conflict between a Palestinian-Arab state and the Israelis, but between the Arab nations, all the Arab nations and the Jewish nation.

Many believe that the intifada really didn't start on December 1987, but on April 1, 1920. Haj Amin Al Husseini (later the Mufti of Jerusalem) led a huge demonstration of Arabs to Nabi Mussah, a Sheikh tomb, south of Jericho. According to Islamic tradition the burial place of the Jewish prophet Moses. There, in Nabi Mussah, Haj Amin Al Husseini raised the flag of revolution against the British occupiers and the Jewish settlers. In Nabi Mussah he started the pogroms against the infidels, the war against Jews, the slaughter of Jews. That is where the Arab uprising started. That is when the Arab intifada started.

Though the intifada seemed like a rebellion, the truth is that it was nothing but the continuation of the Arab-Israeli conflict in a different façade. It is the continuation of the cruel and vicious Moslem Jihad, the "holy" Moslem war against the infidels, against the Jews. This is not a struggle for freedom. This is a struggle to totally and completely exterminate the Jews and the State of Israel, because they are not Moslems, and, therefore, "do not belong to the region."

The Arab uprising, the intifada didn't start on December 1987 in Israel. It started many years ago, in Beirut, in Cairo, in Alexandria, in Damascus, in Halab, in Baghdad (June 1, 1941), in Fez, etc. where the Jews were stoned by the Arab mob constantly. The Jews didn't have there trees, forests or cars, but they had synagogues, which the Arab mob burned down. This, in addition to pogroms, the murder of Jews, the raping of Jewish girls and women, the kidnapping of Jewish children and converting them into Islam, burning of Jewish stores, etc.

This Arab behavior made the Jews leave the Arab countries as quick as they could. These remote, but very vivid memories drive the Israelis to break the Arab uprising with iron fists. The Arab intifada just doesn't have a chance to succeed. The Israelis will never let it happen.

The war against the intifada, the Arab uprising is not a war against a small number of terrorists but a national confrontation between two peoples for the same piece of land.

The Palestinian-Arab's uprising, the intifada, represents nothing more and nothing less than the opening of a new front and a new set of tactics, a new strategy in the war that the Arabs have been waging to destroy anything that smells Jewish, since April 1, 1920.

The purpose of the intifada was to win the world public opinion and affect a political change, which will lead to a Palestinian-Arab state.

It was wrong on the part of Israel not to label the intifada a war, and consider all the Palestinian-Arabs in Judea, Samaria and the Gaza

Strip as, either PLO members, or PLO supporters, or PLO supporters and collaborators with Israel's bitter enemies. The identification of the Palestinian-Arabs from the West Bank and Gaza with the PLO can only strengthen Israel's long claim that the population of the West Bank and Gaza are not exactly innocent civilians, because the intifada is not only the breaking of law and order, that should have been dealt with by the police, but rather a continuation of the one-hundred-year Arab-Jewish war, by different means. It will be, therefore, totally irrational on the part of Israel to make territorial concessions to a seemingly innocent population, which insists on being represented by a terrorist organization that seeks the destruction of Israel.

Arafat's aide, in Tunis, Khalil Al-Wazir, told the Kuwaiti Al-Watan newspaper that: "The position of the Palestinian Arabs is clear, and it rejects any initiative that does not include a clear, true recognition of its right to self-determination, freedom and independence, and to set up an independent Arab state."

Bassam Abu Sharif, a leader of George Habash's Popular Front and a senior advisor to PLO leader, Yasser Arafat declared that: "No third party will be allowed to make use of Palestinian sacrifices."

When the Government of Tunisia offered to host the PLO leadership after its retreat from Lebanon, late in 1982, it did not have failed to realize the meaning of that policy. For that policy meant clearly that Tunisian territory could not only be used for spreading Palestinian propaganda, but also for the bloody prosecution of terrorism. They must also have realized that from that moment their territory became target to Israeli retaliation

In April 16, 1988, the PLO military chief Abu Jihad also known as Khalil Al-Wazir was killed by an Israeli commando raid in his home in Tunis.

The shock, the mourning, the near-hysterical worship on the part of the Palestinian-Arabs in the wake of Khalil Al-Wazir's (Abu Jihad) assassination in Tunis was not surprising in Israel. The outpouring of Palestinian Arab grief shared also by Israeli-Arabs, was an open expression of solidarity and identification with Abu Jihad's extremism and the PLO terror policy.

Following his record of murders and assassination of innocent civilians, men, women and children is ample proof that Yasser Arafat and his number one man, Abu Jihad or Khalil Al-Wazir do not seek political compromise or solution but blood, Jewish blood. What is mostly ridiculous and completely unfair was, that his death was defined as "murder" and "assassination", as if by killing him a crime had been committed.

The Arab's reaction, and this includes also the Israeli-Arabs, to Abu Jihad's death, was only proof to those who have deceived themselves about peace-loving intentions of the Arabs, how wrong they were.

The Western condemnation of Abu Jihad's killing reflected the amount of its moral degeneration and way of thinking, as well as, its political double standards. The West, which refuses to acknowledge the strong contradiction between its lip service to a democratic Israel "with secure borders" and its support of a PLO state between Israel and Jordan.

A West, which had long placed trade, oil and the Arab Market as its top priorities rather than justice and fairness. A West that must be very careful to understand and respect the Arabs's feelings as well as their weaknesses even if it is at the expense of another people.

An assassin who set behind the desk and sent his units to kill innocent, unarmed people, a master murderer, became an acknowledged national hero, a martyr, almost a saint in the Arab World.

In the eve of Israel's Independence Day in 1988, a group of Israeli-Arab notables had offered condolences to the Supreme Moslem Council in East Jerusalem for the death of Abu Jihad in Tunis. A member of his group later told Israel's Television's Hebrew program that Abu Jihad, Khalil Al-Wazir was a great Palestinian Leader.

It is a very great mistake on the part of the Israeli-Arabs to think that the freedom of expression granted to them as citizens of a democratic country includes the right to preach terrorism against it. It is also very unfortunate that there still exist many Israeli-Arab leaders who have not yet drawn the obvious moral and conclusion from the tragic history of their own people.

Leaflet number 14, issued on April 20, 1988 (Iyar 3, 5748), by the "Unified National Leadership of the Uprising", was dedicated to the "leader, teacher, symbol and martyr, Khalil Al-Wazir, also called Abu Jihad." The leaflet called on Palestinian-Arabs to step up attacks on the Israeli "occupiers" to avenge the death of Abu Jihad, killed in Tunis by a Israeli commando unit.

The Americans were naïve to believe that the intifada would fade away by itself, without an Israeli incision. Yasser Arafat needed the intifada because it was also the cause of substantial Arab financial contributions and a huge source of income. It was also supported by the Soviet Block and was an excellent pressure on the US public opinion and administration to abandon their refusal to the establishment of a Palestinian-Arab state.

The religious Arab activists have moved from a parochial passivity to a militant activism, from breaking windows in local restaurants, which served wine and whiskey, to open confrontation with Israeli troops. What encouraged them to do so was the mild reaction of the IDF.

The "Islamic Jihad", whose main headquarters was in Amman, the capital of Jordan, is a Sunnite fanatic Moslem fundamentalist movement trying to imitate or compete with their Sheeite brethrens, the Hizbullah, who receive their orders directly from Teheran. Same as the Hizbullah they claim that they are working for the Great Islamic Revolution and swear to let the intifada fire glow ten years.

The Islamic Jihad is an extremely religious Movement. Their ideologists were Haj Amin Al-Husseini, the late Mufti of Jerusalem and Adolf Hitler's friend. The Az Il-Din el-Kassam from Haifa. Gazi Abdel Kader Al-Husseini, from Jordan, the son of the gangster leader Abdel Kader Al-Husseini, who was killed in 1948, in the Castel, on the road to Jerusalem and brother of Faisal Husseini from Jerusalem, Sheikh Assead Bayood Al-Tamimi, the Mufti of Hebron and Iran's Ayatollah Khomeini (a Sheeite Moslem) supporter.

The leader of the Islamic Jihad is Jaber Amer. The Islamic Jihad has become very active during the recent years. Their main weapon is the knife and their battle cry is "Allahu Akbar" (God is greater), this they shout before stabbing their victims. In 1989, they started using firearms too. They are very militant, extremely fanatic and religious zealots.

They have been carrying several suicidal missions, which they believe will be rewarded, later, in heaven.

It was members of the Islamic Jihad who killed King Abdallah of Jordan. It was members of the Islamic Jihad who killed Egyptian President Anwar Sadat, in Cairo.

On May 3, 1989, they killed two old people waiting for the bus, in Jaffa road, in Jerusalem. Two Jews. Mr. Kalman Vardi and Mr. Nissim Levi. Two senior citizens, two lawyers. A few months earlier they kidnapped the Israeli soldier, Avi Saporta and killed him. They also kidnapped another Israeli Soldier, Ilan Saadoon who hasn't been found yet. They tossed hand grenades from a driving car into a group of Giveati soldiers near the Kotel (The Wailing Wall-The Western Wall). On July 1989, an Islamic Jihad member turned the steering wheel of a 405 Egged bus going to Jerusalem and drove it into a steep ravine, killing sixteen of its passengers. On

September 1989 the Islamic Jihad set fire to the Carmel Woods, in Haifa, and burned thousands of acres, full of trees, animals, etc. They were the one's who killed a Yeshiva student, Aharon Gross, in Hebron.

The Islamic Jihad movement operates in all the Arab countries as well as in Israel. They cooperate with Yasser Arafat's Fatah. They have very good relations with Ahmad Jibreel and even use his radio broadcasting station in Syria. The Islamic Jihad also cooperated with Sabri Al-Bannah, also known as Abu Nidal. They are very ambitious, irrational and very dangerous, and are outlawed in Israel.

The Religious Front, which includes the Chamas or Islamic Movement and the Islamic Jihad, Moslem fundamentalists, do not accept a Palestinian state with 1967 borders. Their appetite is much bigger than that. But, temporarily they will take anything. Any territory that Israel will relinquish, and no matter how small it be. Exactly the same policy as their opponents and competitors, the PLO.

As soon as they will be in power they will continue their struggle to "free" the rest, that's: Jaffa, Acre, Haifa, Nazareth, Jerusalem, etc.

Since the elections in the Arab sector there has been a constant increase in support of the extreme religious front, Chamas, etc. at the expense of the PLO. It is very likely, that with time, the Islamic Jihad fundamentalists will become the majority among the Palestinian-Arabs and later even among the Israeli-Arabs. For Israel it can mean only more troubles.

The Jabalya refugee camp was one of the breeding spots for Islamic fundamentalism in Gaza, and a home of the Chamas leader Muhamad Shartaha, who ordered the kidnap-murders of at least two Israeli soldiers, Avi Saporta and Ilan Saadoon, in 1989.

On May 22, 1989, the IDF spokesman announced the arrest of 250 Chamas activists, including its leader Sheikh Ahmed Yassin.

Israel's image and relations with some of the nations in the world may suffer from the intifada but those who really suffer are those who started the uprising, the Palestinian-Arabs, in Judea Samaria and the Gaza Strip. Most of the fatalities were theirs. Its their shops, their businesses, their hotels their restaurants, that have been closed by their self inflicting strikes. It's the Arab economy that suffered great losses.

The presence of the Islamic fundamentalism in Judea, Samaria and the Gaza Strip is a much greater threat to the Palestinian-Arab population than to the Israelis. They have executed many more Arabs than Jews. To be ruled by the whim of the leaderless mob, day and night, and harassed by Arab "ninjas" had rendered their lives miserable.

It was known for decades that in the Arab World, in the Middle East, the Arabs have always solved their political differences by means of assassinations. This had become their standard procedure. Hundred of Arabs have been killed by their Arab brethren for not following the PLO's or Chamas orders to the letter.

Jordan was undergoing a severe economic crisis in 1990. Discontent was spreading all over the Hashemite Kingdom, fundamentalism and radicalism was on the rise. The majority of its population, the Palestinians considered Yasser Arafat and Sadam Hussein as their leaders and not King Hussein. King Hussein admitted that he was deeply concerned about the rising influence of the PLO and fundamentalists in the territories of Judea, Samaria and Gaza.

All the Arab leaders were very well aware of the fact that in the next war Israel could push the combats into their territories or see to it that it takes place in Judea, Samaria and the Gaza Strip, very heavy Arab populated areas, who will have to absorb the Arab blows as well as the Arab missiles. This alone should cause the Arab countries to give up the idea of invading Israel. True, the fighting in hostile Judea, Samaria and the Gaza Strip can be difficult, because there is no doubt that the Arab population in Judea, Samaria and the Gaza Strip will not sit idle this time but try to cause troubles and help the Arab invading forces. Obviossusly, this will cost them very dear, very expensive and might turn Judea, Samaria and the Gaza Strip into another Lebanon. In time of war Israel could use the Palestinian-Arabs in Judea, Samaria and the Gaza Strip as a buffer, as a shield or even as hostages. Should an Arab uprising occur in the event of a war, they will simply have to be deported. Israel could defend deportation if it could show a clear security connection.

On November 23, 1989 (Heshvan 25, 5750), in the Shechem (Nablus) Casbah, an Arab woman, suspected of being an informer and a prostitute was carried out by the "Red Eagle" gang, in broad daylight before dozens of onlookers and was shot in the head six times. Thousands of Casbah residents streamed the area, and, for half an hour, women spat at the body, and many kicked her in the head. The poor woman wasn't brought to justice, wasn't allowed to defend herself. This is how Arab justice works.

If the Bir Zeit students, the "Red Eagles", the "Black Panthers", or any other group tried to pull this sort of stuff in Damascus, Amman, Cairo or Baghdad, they would receive a much rougher handling than the one they are getting in Israel.

The hypocrisy of the UN Security Council decision to send Observers to "protect" the Arab population of Judea, Samaria and the Gaza Strip is outrageous. The hundreds of PLO crimes have never received UN attention. Certain Arab despotic regimes have repeatedly committed crimes against humanity, yet, never received UN or even media attention. Other countries, faced with much lesser threats, have reacted much worse, and yet, only Israel is singled out for blame. This is pure evidence of the double standard of the World Community when it comes to deal with Israel.

Israel's image, as a free, democratic country, has taken a severe battering since the beginning of the Palestinian-Arab uprising on December 1987. The decline in the popularity of Israel was entirely the responsibility of the Defense Minister Yitzhak Rabin, the local press and the foreign press.

The effect of the Arab uprising, the intifada, was an overall shift to the right coupled with aparalysis and confusion on the part of the Israeli Left. From 1977 on, the Maarah has consistently been losing the votes of young Israelis, soldiers and veteran Maarah voters who believe in a more activist approach to the Arab uprising issue. They also expected to see consistency from their leaders, not the zig-zag they have been offering the last two years, from December 1987 and on.

The Palestinian-Arab uprising, the intifada should not be countered or dealt with by political actions, but only by the application of force. The techniques of counter-violence should have been left to the military.

Israel must restore law and order and persuade the Arabs that they can gain nothing by violence. Israel should not start any diplomatic effort as long as the Arab riots in Judea, Samaria and the Gaza Strip continue. Beginning negotiations with the Arabs while the uprising is still going on would be interpreted as an Israeli weakness.

The Israeli public considers both the Maarah and the Likud parties incapable of handling the Arab uprising and accuse these two parties for dragging the issue of solving it too long. By demonstrating inconsistency and helplessness in decision-making, the National Unity Government is increasingly seen in the public mind as being "dragged along the mercy of events," rather than taking appropriate action to control the course of events.

The Israeli public feels that because of the present National Unity Government, Israel is losing its integrity and credibility. The public in Israel blames the two major parties, the Maarah and the Likud for the situation.

On October 21, 1990 (Heshvan 2, 5751), two men and a woman, on their way to work, were killed and a twelve years old boy on his way to school was wounded, in Bakah, Jerusalem, by an Arab brick layer, with a knife.

The next day, two more Jews were wounded by Arab workers in the street, in Neve-Yaakov (Jerusalem) and in Gan Ha'Atzmaut (Independence Park), all in Jerusalem.

One way to stop these unfortunate phenomena is by issuing a governmental decree, a law, which will prohibit the use of Arab workers by Jews. Every Israeli contractor or businessman that hires Arab help, his license should be revoked and his business closed. This could decrease substantially the number of Jews killed in the streets of Israel. It will provide work for young Israelis who ended their military service as well as to the Soviet Jews, newly arrived in Israel.

Jews were slaughtered in the streets of Israel and the leadership was completely at loss. Premier Yitzhak Shamir was afraid to order "Shoot to Kill" in order to save Jewish lives. The Israelis, the Jewish population in Israel was eager for some better leadership, but, there was none.

Most Israelis agree that during the National Unity Government, as well as during Yitzhak Shamir's right wing (Likud) Government the security situation in Israel sharply deteriorated.

The majority of the Arabs in Israel and the territories are full of fanatic hatred that are ready to indiscriminately stab any Israeli Jew they meet in the street.

During the first three years of intifada, tens of Israeli cars have been burned by the Palestinian-Arabs and ninety Israelis were killed. The Israeli population started to lose patience and ask questions. How many more Israelis have to be stabbed to death before the Israeli Government decides to do something about it? Or may be the Americans are also here involved and wouldn't let the Israelis to react?

The Arab minority was stabbing the Jewish majority in the streets of Israel, freely, without fear, because they knew very well that the Jewish soldiers and the Jewish police had orders:"not to shoot".

In those days "there was no king in Israel" (Judges 18:1-19:1).

According to Jordanian law, which is still valid in Judea and Samaria, Israel could have charged the Arab population of Judea and Samaria for all the expenses Israel had in order to fight the intifada.

The Arabs have been using very often the "hit and run" system to kill Jews. Arab cars were driving in full speed into Jewish crowds or gatherings, like bus stops, "trempiyadahs" (Soldiers hitch-hiking stops), etc. trying to kill those who were waiting in line for the bus.

Arab trucks, semi-trailers, heavy cars, were running in full speed into Jewish private cars, causing "head on collisions", killing its content and speeding away. But the National Unity Government (Likud and Maarah) was completely helpless, impotent, and did not do anything to stop these phenomena.

Israelis still remember the Arab attacks on Israeli traffic since the establishment of the state, and before:

The attack on the Eilat bus in Maaleh Ha'Akrabim in the 50's

The attack on the bus on the beach road, near the Country Club, in 1978.

The attack on the 405 Egged bus on the road to Jerusalem.

The attack on the # 300 Egged bus near Gaza.

The attack on the # 18 Egged bus in Jerusalem Etc.

The PLO had partially achieved their goal. The Jewish population in Israel had been terrorized by the intifada and felt helpless. Every Arab was regarded as a potential assassin. The Israeli Government, for political reasons, haven't done anything or have done very little to avoid this situation. Therefore, the Israeli citizens felt unsafe in their own country, in their own streets.

During the years 1987-1990, the first three intifada years, Defense Minister Yitzhak Rabin together with the Chief-of-Staff General Dan Shomron, succeeded to lower the fame and reputation of the IDF to a degree, which encouraged the Palestinian-Arabs to become more and more militant, believing that the IDF was weak.

It is totally unfair to blame the IDF as untrained, ineffective in fighting intifada type terror, which exploits the "soft belly" of a democratic society. There are few equals in fighting terror. Had the IDF only been given the "Green Light" to do so by the politicians. There isn't the slightest doubt that the intifada could have been quenched easily and immediately, had the IDF shot down several Palestinian Arab rioters in the first few days of the intifada. This is exactly how similar uprisings were put down in Cairo, Amman, Algeria, etc. But the Shamir-Rabin Government refused to give such an order. They obviously had their reasons, though they became very unpopular for that.

After failing to quell the intifada, army personnel and politicians, including Rabin and Peres, began "singing" a new chant in a rising, wonderfully coordinated orchestra. "Only a political solution can work," they warbled. "There is no other way," they claimed. They didn't even try a military solution.

It was inconceivable and unbelievable that military officers could advocate giving away their nation's most precious resource, its land, for any reason. It was also shocking to hear the Israeli officers attack and demonize their own citizens as fanatical "settlers" who were "inciting the Arabs" because they were living in the historically Jewish Judea, Samaria and Hebron. It was shocking to hear these Leftist officers and their feckless assertion that there was "no alternative" to rewarding defeated Arabs with Israeli land, water and holy places. In any other nation, in any other country a military officer who displayed such lack of patriotism would have very short military career. Similarly an officer who declares in public that the IDF doesn't have a military solution to curb the Arab uprising and that the only solution for the Arab intifada is political was releasing a top military secret to the enemy, even if this declaration is far from being true. In any other country such officers would be court-martial and if the Prime Minister, the Defense Minister or the Chief-of-Staff come out with declarations like these, they would be immediately impeached and removed from office, because he is a danger to his country.

The image of Shamir, the Prime Minister, among the young Israelis, is that of a guardian of a status quo-ante, which they do not like. US administration fears that the situation in the ...territories of Judea, Samaria and Gaza has the potential of undermining broader American interests in the region.

Israelis believe that Arafat is afraid that the intifada may die out suddenly, the same way it started. Arafat is also very much afraid that what has been so far a civil or popular rebellion may turn into an armed revolt, and he is doing everything he can to avoid it. This, because Arafat knows very well that the moment firearms are used, the Palestinian-Arabs will lose their greatest advantage, the world's sympathy. The fact that they avoided from using firearms turned them into the underdogs and gave them an image of a Palestinian David fighting an Israeli Goliat, besides, an armed revolt against the Israelis would be quashed immediately by the IDF, causing a substantial amount of casualties. Mainly among the Palestinian-Arabs, and may push also the Israelis to start a massive expulsion of Arabs from Eretz Israel. Arafat knows very well that Israel could handle such a revolt very efficiently, since the IDF is trained to fight armed soldiers rather than unarmed civilians. This is why Arafat ordered the Palestinian-Arabs, through the leaflets published by the "United Leadership of the Uprising in the Territories", to refrain from using firearms and to try to maintain internal unity at all cost.

The PLO was a great business, worth at least $6-10 billion. Arafat personally controlled most of the budget. Members of the PLO executives drew monthly salaries of over $100,000. All the Arab states, particularly Saudi Arabia and the Gulf Emirates, have always financed the Palestinian terror groups generously.

Negotiations alone will not put an end to the uprising. Only a flexible combination of force and policy can stop it and bring the Arabs to the negotiating table. Only a defeat in the Yom Kippur War brought Sadat to Jerusalem.

Former security officers such as ex-Mossad operative Rafi Eitan and former director of the General Security Services Yosef Harmelin openly expressed their defeatist opinions that Israel has no alternative but to learn to live with terror and murderous attacks. A very disheartening advice. Eitan and Harmelin were both totally wrong. The Israelis do not have to live with the Arab terror and should get rid of it as soon as possible.

In Leaflet number 65, issued on Sunday, December 2, 1990 (Kislev 15, 5751), by the "Unified National Leadership of the Uprising," composed of the PLO, the Chamas, etc. declared that the Arabs might use in their war against Israel any arms available, including firearms. This is another step up of their war against the Israelis. So far they did not dare use firearms. So far they used only rocks (stones), Molotov-Cocktails, daggers and knives. On December 2, 1990, the Arabs realized after three years of Intifada, that stone throwing didn't get them anywhere. It didn't change the Israeli policy. Not enough Jewish blood was spilled to force the Israelis to change their policy. More Jewish blood must be spilled. The Arabs decided to step up terror. Terrorism is usually directed towards reaching political ends. By using Fear, Panic and Hysteria, the Arabs believed they can force some kind of policy change, and they resorted to the use of firearms. They started also to poison the Gerber baby food bottles. This was a new phase of terror.

On January 1991, the PLO, Arafat suffered a terrible blow when Palestinian, apparently working for PLO dissident Abu Nidal, assassinated in Tunis, Abu Iyad, the PLO's No. 2 leader, and Abu Hol, its Chief of Internal Security.

Portraying the Palestinian Arabs as virtuous is hypocrisy. Not only have the Palestinian-Arabs kidnapped Israeli citizens and murdered them viciously, but they have also murdered their own people at the slightest suspicion of their collaboration with the Israeli authorities, and without even verifying if it was true.

The very same day that James Baker, the US Secretary of State arrived in Jerusalem the "big heroes" have slaughtered four Jewish women in the middle of Hanteke Street, in Kiryat Yovel, Jerusalem, when these four ladies were waiting for the bus, near the senior citizens home of Nofim, across the street from the "Monster Park". The Arab did it using a kitchen knife, and these bastards are asking for a fair trial!

After a series of attacks on Israeli soldiers and civilians Ariel (Aric) Sharon, the " hard-line" Housing Minister accused the Israeli Government of poor leadership. "Israeli citizens are now asked to stand against knives, just as they had to stand up against Scud missiles-perplexed and without response."

The increased violence and calls for separation between Jews and Arabs, coming from both the right and the left, might end the so-called status quo between the two communities, Jewish and Arab. The increased violence also revived the discussion over the meaning of Zionism and Jewish Labor and the debate over Arab employment in Israel. The Israeli public accused the Israeli businessmen for hiring Arab labor, which, they believed was the key issue of the Arab violence. The illegal presence of an Arab alien population in the heart of Israel during the day, and more so during the night, was the recipe for more troubles. Arab employment in Israel was directly responsible for the loss of Jewish lives and deterioration of internal security. When Arab labor is removed and replaced by Jewish unemployed, the operations of the Israeli businessmen will no longer be plagued by endless strikes called by the different leaders of the intifada.

Government officials in Israel believe that mass unemployment among the Palestinian-Arabs would only add to the already explosive situation. Other Israelis believe that if the situation is already explosive, Palestinian unemployment couldn't hurt much. Many Israelis believe that due to the Arab militant behavior there is no point to meetings between Jews and Arabs and that the only solution is to separate the Arabs from the Jews. This without differentiating between Palestinian-Arabs and Israeli-Arabs.

By stabbing Jews, Palestinians are rapidly changing the remaining Israeli doves into hawks and increase among them the conviction that there is nothing to talk about or deal with the Arabs.

Most of the Israelis are frustrated by the government's inability to stop the violence, probably because of US pressure. They found, that self-defense is their only and most effective alternative and there has been a surge in gun-licenses applications over the last year. Wall posters urging the boycott of firms using Arab workers appeared in Jerusalem promising that the list of offending businesses would soon be published. Stores employing Arabs received warning notices asking them to lay-off their Arab workers. To keep the violence at a minimum, Israel should separate the actual and potential terrorists from the rest of the Palestinian population. The second phase would be to re-arrest all the prisoners released during the deal with Abu Nidal and Ahmad Jibreel.

In May 1991, the Palestinian-Arabs started using firearms. The Israeli soldiers couldn't do much because their hands were handcuffed by stupid orders, not to shoot. The Israeli Likud government continued its chronic negligence. Its complacency, or may be, for some reason, it was the Israeli government's interest that the intifada continues.

In June 1991, the Israelis made another concession to the Arabs by releasing 400 Arab prisoners, a few days before the Moslem holiday of Eed el-Adchah. There is very little doubt that these released Arab prisoners will go back to their old trade, which put them in prison, that's stabbing Jews in the streets of Israel.

But, this time it was not Yitzhak Rabin from the Maarah who released them. This time it was Moshe Arens (Mishka) from the Likud.

One wonders how many concessions did the Arabs do to the Israelis for the last hundred years? None. Again this is, probably, the result of US pressure or Israeli stupidity. Israel reinforcing the intifada forces? This is ridiculous!

These 400 Arab released prisoners will, no doubt, also join their 1250 brethrens released from prison, with the deal with Jibreel and the 1220 brethren released on the Moslem holiday of Eed Al-Fiter, to increase the terror in the streets of Israel or abroad. Making concessions to the Arabs by releasing hundreds of terrorists and sending them to the Israeli streets to continue their terror is an unforgivable mistake.

The Israeli society has paid a price for this zealous protection of human rights, individual freedom and privacy.

The Israeli settlers in Judea, Samaria and the Gaza Strip rightfully believed that they had a government protection against Arab attacks, but were soon disappointed. They realized that government protection was not ample and that they had to protect themselves.

On one hand, the Israeli public concluded that by protecting Ofra and Tekoah, in Judea, Samaria and the Gaza Strip, the cities of Haifa, Tel Aviv, etc. are also protected.

The Arab uprising, the intifada that started on December 1987 with throwing stones, the burning of tires and the stabbing changed phases after three years of intifada. In 1991, the Arab terrorist started using Firearms, automatic rifles, etc. Defense Minister Yitzhak Rabin declared in 1988, that the Arabs were very clever for not using firearms, because if they did, Israel had a very effective answer to that. Yet, when the Arabs did start using firearms, in 1991, Israel didn't seem to have an effective answer to that. On December 9, 1991, four years after the intifada started, Israel had already 98 people killed of whom 13 were soldiers. 1400 civilians wounded and 3400 soldiers wounded, a very heavy toll, and Israel still did not use its effective answer to the problem.

On Tuesday March 17, 1992 (Adar II, 12, 5752) a bomb explosion leveled the Israeli Embassy in Buenos Aires, killing 28 people and injuring 240. Eight of the dead were embassy personnel

The pro-Iranian Islamic Jihad group claimed responsibility for the bombing. Argentine's President Carlos Menem declared that:

"I want to tell those anti-Semites that we have in Argentina, the pro-Nazis and coup-mongers, that this bombing, instead of weakening, will strengthen our ties with Israel."

President Menem invited the CIA and the Mossad to participate in the investigations and efforts to locate those responsible for the high human toll.

Two weeks earlier, a bomb killed Ehud Sadan, Chief Security Officer in the Israeli Embassy in Ankara, Turkey.

The Islamic Jihad faction, which claimed responsibility for the attack on Israel's Embassy in Buenos Aires, was headed by Fatthi Shqaqi of Gaza, who was expelled from the country a few years ago on charges of terrorist activities and supported financially and logistically by Teheran.

By May 1992, the number of Israeli citizens killed by Arabs reached the figure of 113. No terrorist organization has committed more heinous crimes than Arafat's Fatah, nor has it changed its modus operandi since the PLO's ballyhooed renunciation of terrorism.

Prime Minister Yitzhak Shamir and Defense Minister Moshe Arens also failed to stop the Palestinian Arab intifada. This time, they didn't have the excuse that their hands were tied by a coalition with the Labor (Maarah) Party, because the Labor (Maarah) party was in opposition and Shamir and Arens were heading a pure Likud-right wing government. Same as their predecessors, Peres and Rabin, as far as the intifada is concerned, Shamir and Arens were total failures.

It is imperative that an Israeli voice of reason be projected so that the world can better perceive the harsh realities, which Israel faces in balancing her need for survival.

It seems that the contradictory voices that came from the Arab camp meant only that the Arabs have made certain tactical shift, not enough to convince Israel of their sincerity to make peace. Today, when an Arab thinks of a dialog between Israel and the Arabs, he doesn't think of the Camp David Accord. What he is thinking about is nothing less than another Arab state, in Judea, Samaria and the Gaza Strip at the expense of Israeli territory.

Lately, the PLO had been signaling readiness to negotiate with Israel, but, of course, on their terms: an international conference, a Palestinian State and the return of the Palestinian refugees. They are still dreaming. They are still far from realistic approach, which Israel could find acceptable. This is why Israel cannot take them seriously. Peace between Israel and the Arabs is remote because the Arab extremists will not tolerate negotiations between Israel and the Arabs and will prevent reaching any realistic solution. Several decades of ample evidence prove that the Arabs were not about to start facing reality in a civilized manner. There will be no peace until such time as a Palestinian leadership is ready to face reality and to forgo those dreams and wishful thinkings that can never be realized. No matter what anybody said, the territories of Judea, Samaria and Gaza are vital to Israel's security, and therefore, cannot be negotiable.

Less than two months of rock-throwing accomplished more than the Arab world, with all its military might, was able to do in twenty years and everyone knows this," said Maher Abu Khater, editor of the Al-Fajr English-language weekly.

"The mood in the streets is that if two months of protests gets America to press Shamir for a Palestinian self-rule, then four months will bring a UN force and a year will see Israel pulling out in disgust as it did from Lebanon," he added.

In order to "keep out of troubles" and stop "provoking" the Arabs, and in order to avoid the Arab's Molotov-Cocktails and rocks, the Shamir administration came up with a very unwise idea, the idea of the "bypassing roads" ("Kvish Okef").

The Likud Government started actually the construction of the "bypassing roads". The bypassing Hebron road, the bypassing Deheisheh (refugee camp) road, etc. A very unwise thing to do because the Arabs saw in it cowardice and the beginning of Israeli capitulation. It showed a weak

Israeli leadership, lack of vision, lack of conviction. A very wrong Israeli reaction to the Arab intifada. The "bypass roads" was a very unclever idea, because on these "bypass roads" the Israeli vehicles became an excellent target for the Arab snipers.

As soon as the Israelis have finished constructing their "bypass roads", the Arabs started planting along these roads olive trees and build buildings. Arab illegal buildings pop up like mushrooms. The Israeli government, unfortunately, doesn't react at all, or reacts very softly and slowly to this new phenomenon. A very dangerous situation, in the long run, which must be dealt with much more firmly. This wrong policy of the Likud government, of constructing alternative "bypass roads", bypassing the Arab populated areas, cost Israel a fortune. The Arabs could get the wrong feeling that the Israelis are retreating. It could also give the Arabs the feeling of success and encourage them to keep pushing until the last Israeli is out of the country. It could give the Arabs the wrong impression that they were the real owners of the Land.

The Israelis, the Jews should keep driving through the Arab populated areas in the territories, lest the Arabs will get the wrong idea that the land also belongs to them. According to the Oslo Agreement the autonomy is for the people, not for the land. To give the Arabs a little more freedom to handle their municipalities and local administration under Israeli sovereignty. The land remains Israeli property. Therefore, the bypass roads are very foolish, unwise idea and a waste of money as well as against the best interest of Israel.

"In the days of Yitzhak (Jael), the highways ceased,
And the travelers walked through byways.
The rulers ceased in Israel, they ceased..."

JUDGES 5: 6-7

The truth is that since the Middle of 1990 the Palestinian intifada was attracting much less world attention than before. Eastern Europe became more attractive to the news media. It was the Palestinian themselves that contributed to this new situation. More and more terror was used by the PLO activists against their own people. The intifada just didn't hurt Israel enough, either militarily, economically or politically, to end its "occupation" in Judea, Samaria and the Gaza Strip. The Palestinian Arabs have proved nothing so far by the point of the dagger. Yes, they proved that they were nothing but assassins.

The following letter was sent to The Jerusalem Post, on August 23, 1991, (Elul 13, 5751):

TERRORIST STATES

Sir-We are American victims of terrorism. The most important people in our lives died on December 21, 1988, in the bombing of a Pan Am 103. Of course we want to see the hostages, American, European and Israeli, freed. We know better than most, the barbaric nature of their captors. We also know that at times it is necessary for a nation to deal with odious characters in order to save lives. But we fear that in the deals that are being struck, too much may be given to the terrorists and their sponsors.

Current event show with stunning clarity that Syria and Iran control terrorist activity in the Middle East. Shadowy hostage-holders do not act without the approval of their sponsors. Neither do shadowy bombers. Yet, these two terrorist nations are receiving elaborate praise for having their surrogates release two hostages after years of captivity and for having fed the others and not beaten them too often. On the other hand, Israel is being blamed for prolonging the crisis. This strikes us monstrous.

All credible evidence indicates that Iran paid for the Pan Am bombing and the operation was planned by Syria's Popular Front for Liberation of Palestine/General Command. These two terrorist nations may now be forgiven for their crime, or more likely the Pan Am 103 investigation will be allowed to fade away inconclusively. We cannot forget what happened, but most Americans have very short memories and our politicians count on that.

Then, there is the matter of who is to be released in the swap. In 1979, Israel released Hafez Dalkemoni, who had originally been arrested for a bombing in Israel, in a prisoner exchange. Dalkemoni went on to become a top agent of the PFLP/GC and was arrested in Germany in the fall of 1988 for planning the operation, which ultimately resulted in the Pan Am bombing. He now sits in a German jail. Will he soon be turned loose to kill again?

The Bush administration has never regarded terrorism as a serious problem, even when large numbers of Americans are killed. Once the flight profile hostage issue is out of the way, President Bush will be only too happy to cut all manner of deals with Syria and Iran.

JOHN ROOT
Husband of Hanne-Marie Root, age 26
Port Jervis, N. Y.
DANIEL AND SUSAN COHN
Parents of Theodora Cohen age 20

In December 1991, in retaliation of the murder of an Israeli citizen from Kfar Darom, by Arab terrorists, the Israeli government announced its intention to deport twelve terrorist leaders and inciters. One of the most effective measures to fight the intifada was deportation. The deportation of dangerous elements within the Palestinian-Arab population in Judea, Samaria and the Gaza Strip is sometimes necessary to reduce tension in the region. The Israeli government was well aware of the fact that the US Ambassador to the United Nations, Thomas Pickering, together with the Moroccan Ambassador and the PLO representative had drafted the UN resolution to denounce Israel for its intention to deport 12 terrorists.

To defend its decision to side with the Arabs, the Bush Administration came up with the false accusation that the Israeli government was violating the Fourth Geneva Convention.

The Fourth Geneva Convention doesn't apply to the "Occupied Territories", because Judea, Samaria and the Gaza Strip were always natural Jewish territories; same as it doesn't apply on the freed French territories of Alsace-Lorraine.

This unfortunate US act only confirms, once more, the US stand in the Arab-Israeli conflict, that Judea, Samaria and the Gaza Strip, freed by the IDF in June 1967, from Jordanian and Egyptian occupations were Arab territories and should be returned to the Arabs. This is also why the United States of America is not fit to act as an unbiased, objective arbitrator in the Middle East conflict.

There is not the slightest sign that the intifada succeeded to recruit ample international or local forces to dislodge Israel from Judea, Samaria and the Gaza Strip against its will. Also there is not the slightest sign that the intifada brought the Arabs closer to their goal. On the contrary, Israel had become stronger and stronger than ever before.

The Palestinian-Arab intifada had so far a "great success." Arab families lost their jobs and income, businesses collapsed, schools were closed for months; houses were demolished by Israeli counter-measures. Molotov-Cocktails and stones stimulated Jews to counter attack. Arab families lost their loved-ones, some were killed by the Israelis during the Arab riots and militant demonstrations, but most, over one thousand, were executed by their Arab brethren, for "collaborating" with the Jews. Thousands of Arabs emigrated to Jordan, Saudi Arabia, the Gulf Emirates, wherever they could find work. This is the real "success" of the intifada. While the Palestinian State remained wishful thinking and will, probably never realize.

The general impression is that many of the Arabs of Judea, Samaria and the Gaza Strip are already sick and tired of the intifada. After quite a long experience they must have realized that it is only bringing them more and more losses and sufferings, as well as great deterioration in their economic condition, and understand that violence will get them nowhere, making matters worse. Yet, they are afraid to admit it in public for fear of the street gangs and for fear of the PLO who have taken over the towns and villages of Judea, Samaria and the Gaza Strip, and go around killing Arabs and destroying their properties with the pretext of getting rid of the "collaborators."

Yasser Arafat's "Fatah" and Abu Nidal's "Revolutionary Fatah" have been feuding for years. The feud culminated with the assassination of Arafat's right-hand man, Abu Iyyad by an Abu Nidal "mole" in PLO headquarters in Tunis. In June and July 1992, two major PLO figures have been assassinated, one in Paris, the other in Lebanon, and in what seemed to be a retaliatory action. Two leading terrorists of the rival Abu Nidal group have been murdered. One victim was Walid Khaled, Abu Nidal's top aide and official spokesman who was killed in Beirut, in July 23, 1992, who was rumored to have been involved in the Munich Olympics massacre in 1972.

The intifada have achieved nothing tangible for the Palestinian-Arabs. Their economy was ruined. Intra-Arab murders exceeded casualties inflicted to them by the IDF. A whole generation is losing its chance for a decent education. The Palestinian-Arab society is more divided than ever. A total dissatisfaction of the local Palestinian-Arab population in the territories with the results of the intifada, which caused them great frustration, pessimism and depression, and a growth for fundementalism.

International observers believe that the PLO are getting impatient, even desperate as they finally understood that they can never realize their national aspirations by force. Adding to this the change in the policies of the Soviet Union. Also, Gorbachev has told the Arabs that time is ripe for negotiations, and that the Soviet Union can no longer subsidize the Arab wars.

In order to avoid more bloodshed in the area the Arabs must become more reasonable and forsake their old dream that by exerting more pressure or increase their violence they could force Israel to commit itself to the establishment of an Arab-Palestinian State. The Palestinian-Arabs have been cheated again by their so-called leaders and are repeating their mistakes. Their mistake is their first uprising in 1936-1939, their mistake in 1947 of rejecting the UN Resolution 181 (the Partition), and now with their seeond uprising, the intifada (December 1987-1993). Therefore, the Palestinian-Arabs will have to pay a high price, a heavy toll, for their mistakes, and for harassing another people.

The Palestinian-Arabs should stop dreaming and wake up. They will never get a "Palestinian State" on Israeli soil at Israel's expense, because Israel will never permit it. Because the whole of Eretz Israel belongs to the people of Israel from time immemorial, from the dawn of history.

The Palestinian-Arabs should start looking for other venues, instead of losing precious time. Their only chance and future, that's if they want to avoid losing more lives, is to emigrate and seek refuge in one of the twenty two Arab countries or elsewhere. Those Arabs who cannot accept Jewish sovereignty in Israel and actively resist should be expelled immediately. If the Palestinian-Arabs will continue to be led by the PLO and their old extremist ways, they will be heading for a disaster. Jews can be killed by terror, but Jews cannot be subdued by terror. It is very unlikely that the issue will be determined by that "war of attrition-the intifada". Israel must win this war, and quickly. The intifada is a war that the Israelis must win; otherwise it will follow them to the shores of the Mediterranean Sea.

The Palestinian-Arab national movement was the first to insist on receiving one hundred percent of their claim, grotesquely denying the UN Resolution 181, the partition plan, and grotesquely under estimating the strength of Zionism and Israel, in spite of the fact of losing six wars and hundreds of battles against the Jews. The Palestinian-Arabs have paid very dearly for their error and miscalculations. Yet, they still "stick to their guns" and follow the same path. If they think that stubbornness and perseverance will bring them victory they are tremendously wrong.

It has been known that the Arabs have an 80-year record of repeated rejections of any compromise with the Jews in the Middle East. The Arabs are fanatically against the idea of a sovereign Jewish presence in the Middle East. The Arab refugee problem and the subsequent suffering were the direct product of the Arab's rejection of the UN partition proposal for the establishment of a Jewish and Arab state in Western Eretz Israel (Palestine), and their attempt to throttle the newborn Jewish state.

In pursuing their own national interests, their expertise is manifested in nothing so much as self-destruction. The Arabs keep missing every chance that comes their way, and after having missed it, demand that it be presented again, as if the world owed them something. When the UN offered them half of Palestine for an independent state they rejected the plan, insisting on "all or nothing". When the signing of armistice agreement summoned them to seek peaceful coexistence with the established Jewish state, they committed themselves to Israel's extermination by terror and refused. When presented with a plan for autonomy as a transitional arrangement to a final negotiated solution based on Resolution 242, they refused again and insisted on immediate self-determination or nothing. The Arabs have always been their own worst enemies. The Palestinian-Arabs have been the biggest losers from the wars in the region, because they reside on land that acts as a buffer between the Arab armies and Israel. Therefore, only if they leave the West Bank and the Gaza Strip, they will no longer be the cause or victims of war.

The failure to recognize ones limit may place everything that has been so far achieved, in jeopardy. There is no lack of examples of what may happen in the absence of restraint or when one is blind and cannot see the difference between "aspiration" and "reality". A most striking example is the great mistake the Arabs made in 1948, by rejecting the UN Partition Plan of Eretz Israel (Palestine).

To better control the intifada or even try to eliminate it, the IDF had founded special units like, the "Cherry" or "Samson" also called the "Mistaerabin" who are disguised as Arabs, speak Arabic fluently and operate in the Arab cities and villages in Judea, Samaria and the Gaza Strip. These Mistaerabin have been very successful in catching many "wanted" and in bringing panic among the Arabs in the areas they function.

Arafat's PLO subsidiaries, like the Black Panthers or the Red Eagles, or the Hamas and the Islamic Jihad were frightened. The Mistaerabin together with the different Sayarot forced the Arabs keep a low profile. Many militant Arabs surrendered, preferring the Israeli jail rather than potential death at the hands of the Israeli commandoes.

The Palestinian-Arabs needed the intifada to find out that the Jews cannot be beaten or driven out of

the region and that they, the Arabs, have no military option.

The 1936-1939 riots, during the British Mandate of Palestine, began on April 19, 1936, in Jaffa, with the stabbing to death eleven unarmed Jews and wounding of scores of others.

The next day seven more Jews were murdered in Jaffa. An Arab mob attacked a Jewish village near Tel Aviv, and disturbances broke out throughout the country. The Arabs soon declared a general strike, and within a few days, six thousands Jewish refugees from vulnerable communities sought shelter in Tel Aviv. The United Palestine Appeal (predecessor of the UJA) announced a drive for an emergency fund for terror victims.

For the next three years, the Arabs of Palestine (who refused to be called "Palestinians" then, only the Jews were known as Palestinians) were led by the Jerusalem Mufti Haj Amin Al-Husseini, who was also known as a Nazi-collaborators and a Hitler associate, and the acknowledged hero of today's PLO.

During the three years of the revolt, the Arabs killed more than six hundred Jews and three thousands Arabs. Another two thousands Arabs were killed by the British seeurity forces.

Same as in 1987 intifada, what began as mob violence developed into organized actions. Armed Arab gangs attacked Jewish settlements, public transportation, civilian vehicles and British police on an almost daily basis. Forests were burned, businesses torched, trains derailed, cars stoned. Arab neighborhoods flattened by British Bulldozers, whole towns were placed under curfew. July 26, 1936, the day cited as the elimination of the great Zionist terror campaign, was not unusual. Arab terrorists ambushing a Jewish civilian convoy proceeding from Jerusalem to Tel Aviv near Bab-el-Wad (Shaar Hagai), were engaged by British troops assisted by RAF planes. Twelve of the Arab terrorists were killed. In Jaffa, the British authorities were preparing barricades in anticipation of the observance of the 100th day of Arab general strike. Several Jewish settlements, including Kfar Sabah, a northern suburb of Tel Aviv. were attacked by armed Arab bands. A routine day in the British-ruled Palestine.

On July 25, 1938, more than two years after the Great Arab revolt began, more than five hundred Jews had been killed and thousands wounded. Life in Palestine was intolerable, unbearable.

The following is a letter to the editor of The Jerusalem Post:

Sir,- The presentation of a "Tolerance Award" by a Jerusalem-based group ostensibly dedicated to non-violence, to the woman who defended an Arab terrorist after he stabbed two Jewish schoolchildren in Mahaneh Yehuda, Jerusalem, once again graphically illustrates that in a Jewish state, which has "tolerated" an Arab uprising against its citizens for almost five years, "the patients are running the asylum."

Aside from disregard for sensitivities of countless families in Israel whose loved ones have been murdered or injured through similar acts of terror-what sort of perverted logic dictates it is Israelis who must constantly show tolerance and forgiveness? Coexistence is a two-way street; It would therefore behooved the Arab world to have just how sincerely they desire peaceful relations with Jews in Israel, by tendering their recognition in a Tolerance Award to this Jewish woman who put her body on the line to save one of their own.

Clearly, however, unlike Israel, Arab nations do not feel the need to genuflect before the world, and indeed have made the perpetration of terror against Jews a badge of honor.

The treaty the Prophet Muhammad made with the Koreish Tribe, from which the Arabs later renegaded, does not encourage the Israelis to strike any deal with the Arabs. The Israelis just cannot trust the Arabs.

2. JONATHAN POLLARD

On March 4, 1987 Jonathan Pollard was sentenced to life imprisonment and his wife Anne was sentenced to five years.

According to foreign sources, shortly after Jay Pollard was sentenced to life imprisonment, after pleading guilty to spying for Israel, Richard Cheney, Congressman of Wyoming, and other members of the House Intelligence Committee received a top secret high level classified briefing from the Central Intelligence Agency.

Cheney emerged from that closed-door session and told reporters that he did not believe that Jonathan Pollard was part of any unauthorized Israeli operation.

"I don't think it was a rogue operation", he said on March 5, 1987, "I think it was a major very successful penetration of the U.S. government and our intelligence agencies by the Israeli government." He said that such behavior "doesn't behoove an ally," adding: "I don't think we have heard the last of it."

Cheney, like other members of the House panel, had been informed of the exact kind of top-secret information compromised by Pollard. The Congressman was very angry.

"On the other hand", he said, "Israel pleads a special relationship with the United States, and on the other hand, they run a major intelligence operation against us. There isn't much they couldn't get if they asked for it, but they chose not to do it that way, and I think the Israeli government ought to know, that some of us are deeply concerned about that kind of conduct."

Yet, Cheney, even in his deep anger and frustration, still insisted that the U.S. should not retaliate against Israel by cutting economic and military aid. "It wouldn't be in our national interest to significantly reduce the levels because the Israelis made a dumb mistake," he added.

Richard Cheney was appointed Secretary of Defense by President George Bush in 1989, to succeed Frank Carlucci.

If from the information received from Jonathan Pollard it was clear, beyond the shadow of a doubt, that Israel's security or survival were not at stake, then Jonathan Pollard was either mistaken, or misled, or greedy, or used.

Speculation are, that Pollard did not consider himself traitor to his country, the United States of America, or endangering its security, by passing information to Israel, He felt that as a Jew, he must help Israel stay strong, so she can always overcome her enemies. Also Pollard was angry, mad, that Israel didn't receive this information through the regular diplomatic channels.

Arab PLO military positions, anywhere, in the Middle East, or in Tunisia, is very important to the security of Israel and the United States of America, a best friend of Israel, is expected to pass this information to Israel, as soon as possible.

As reported by the U.S. media, information on China, passed by Pollard to Israel, does not really help, in any shape or form, the security of Israel.

True, if the United States of America was hiding important information from Israel, there are diplomatic ways of approaching the U.S. Government and persuade her to pass this information.

Pollard's Affair reminds the readers of the Lavon Affair in 1960-1961. Since the Lavon Affair, spying in a friendly country became illegal in Israel.

On the other hand, passing information on Arab, PLO, and military positions, or on China, to Israel, is not endangering at all, in any way, the security of the U.S.

Jonathan Pollard passed information to Israel, a country known to be friendly to the U.S.

There is no chance whatsoever that Israel will pass these information to America's enemies, which are also her enemies.

Pollard spied for a friend and ally, which will never betray the United States of America by giving any secrets to be used against her. One of Pollard's operators was Israeli citizen Raphi Eithan. Raphi Eithan worked for over thirty years in the Israeli Intelligence. Highly intelligent, very clever, very smart, very shrewd, very capable.

It was Raphi Eithan who discovered the Soviet spy, Dr. Israel Ber, one of Ben-Gurion's top advisers. Raphi Eithan also participated in the kidnapping of Adolf Eichmann from Argentina and flying him over to Israel, for trial.

It is well known in the Intelligence and Government circles that Raphi Eithan saved many Israeli lives and also several American lives.

As soon as Jonathan Pollard was discovered, Raphi Eithan took the blame on himself and admitted that it was he who planted Jonathan Pollard as an Israeli spy in the U.S., thus violating the Israeli law, and resigned from office. Another Israeli involved is Air Force Colonel Aviem Sellah, an excellent pilot. Sellah was one of those who planned the air raid which levelled down the Iraqi nuclear reactor at Baghdad, "Operation Ozirak".

Colonel Aviem Sellah was directly responsible to the passing of very important information to the United States of America. Top-secret information on the Soviet MIG-21, the Missile SA-6, etc.

Colonel Aviem Sellah was personally involved in air battles over the Suez Canal, in 1970 and on July 30, 1970 he shot down MIG-21's flown by Soviet pilots. Conclusions of these air battles were sent over to the U.S., immediately.

It is also known that the balance of intelligence information passed from the U.S. to Israel and vice versa, is in favor of Israel.

Speculators believe that there are probably several CIA agents operating in Israel proper and in the West Bank. There are several "Pollards" operating in Israel, using the most recent, sophisticated electronic devices, not counting the US spy satellites, which can read every Israeli newspaper headline, at night, or detect the slightest Israeli military move, and, transmit it, in a fraction of a second, to the Pentagon, in Washington.

As soon as Jonathan Pollard was caught spying for Israel, the Israeli Government, immediately, without giving itself ample time to investigate the matter, declared that it didn't know anything about it. The political branch denied that it had anything to do with it. The ruling "triumvirate", Shamir-Peres-Rabin, declared that those who initiated the Pollard spy operation were "rogues".

The ruling "Troyke", Shamir-Peres-Rabin, declared that it was a clandestine operation executed by a group of individuals (Raphi Eithan, Aviem Sellah, Joseph Yagur, Ilan Ravid, Irit Arb, etc.) who had no permission or authority to do it. They also added that the ministerial level was not aware of the fact. This panicky, stuttering explanation is ridiculous and childish and very difficult to believe. Nobody in Israel will accept the thesis that the military can plant a spy in the U.S. without the knowledge of the political branch and first receiving its approval.

Only few Israelis will accept the version that it was a supervision negligence of the ministerial level over the Intelligence.

Such a lack of coordination between the military and the political branch? Not in Israel! Even if the ministerial level didn't know what the military branch performed, the political branch is still responsible, ministerial responsibility. Even if Colonel Sellah did something on his own, without receiving permission from his superiors, his superiors are still responsible. The Defense Minister has a ministerial responsibility over Colonel Sellah. If Colonel Aviem Sellah did it on his own, which is very difficult to believe, no matter how professionally good the man is, he is to be punished. On the other hand, if he did it by orders from his superiors, his superiors must bear the consequences.

In 1969, Alfred Praunknacht, a Swiss Engineer, not Jewish, not even a gentile, a Christian, stole two hundred thousands drawings, plans, documents, describing the French Mirage engine, and gave them to Israel. His motivation was ideological. He intended to help. He wanted to save the Jewish people, the Israelis from another holocaust, this time from an Arab Holocaust.

On the other hand Jonathan Pollard, a Jew, did what he did, primarily for money, to raise his standard of living, and only then, may be, for Zionism, or, may be for other reasons, as some speculators believe.

The question remains, not who recruited Jonathan Pollard for Israel? But who recruited Jonathan Pollard against Israel? Pollard didn't spy for Israel, Pollard spied against Israel! If it is true, there is not a single document, which Pollard passed to the Israelis, in Washington, that is worth the damage he caused to Israel and to the Jewish Community in the U.S. There is a feeling, in Israel, not without substantial reason, that there is somebody in Washington, who is after Israel, for one reason or another, and who used Pollard to trap, to "catch" Israel, to disgrace Israel, and may be also the Jewish Community in the U.S. There are some questions to be asked: How could a small clerk, like Jonathan Pollard, in the Navy Intelligence, have access to classified, top secret material? How could a small clerk in the U.S. Navy Intelligence with a low salary, travel abroad, twice a year, without drawing the attention of his superiors and raising their suspicion? How could it be, that after he was discovered, a suspect, didn't take the minimum necessary precaution, and activated his wife Anne to make several phone calls, mentioning places, etc., when, as a professional spy, he should have known that his phone was bugged? One also wonders how did his U.S. detectives permit Pollard to contact the Israeli Embassy Security Officer? More than that, how did they permit his wife reach the Israeli Embassy gates?

Speculations are that somebody, in Washington, have used him to jeoperdize the long excellent, U.S.-Israeli relations as well as the long, excellent relations between the Jewish Community in the U.S. and the administration.

There is a strong feeling in Israel, that somebody, up high, in the Pentagon, through the Justice Department has a very strong urge to smear Israel's reputation in the U.S.and has even gone out of proportion to do it. They have even brought up names like the Rosenbergs, in spite of the fact that Israel had nothing to do with the Rosenbergs, beside the fact that they happened to be Jewish, but so were also:Albert Einstein, Robert Oppenheimer, Edward Teller, Howard Temin, Major-General Salomon from Port Jackson, South Carolina and others. Speculations are, that one of their reasons is, probably, the fact that they would have liked Israel to back up from the "Lavi" project and would do anything and everything, by hook or by crook, to realize it. By shoving, by pushing Israel into the corner and putting her on the defense.

Most likely, Aviem Sellah did not operate on his own, and without receiving orders from his superiors, who were satisfied with his work and promoted Sellah from the rank of Colonel to the rank of General, and giving him command over "Tel-Nof", one of the greatest air bases in the country. Public opinion forced Aviem Sellah to give up the command over "Tel-Nof" and resign.

Again, as after the Yom Kippur War, in 1973, and as a result of the conclusions of the Agranat Commission, the military had to be the scapegoat for the politicians' mistakes.

The argument, which, some Israelis use, that the U.S. help to Israel, is in return for services the U.S. received from Israel in the area is ridiculous, or that because Israel is a U.S. strategic asset in the area, is wrong, totally wrong and irrelevant. The U.S.-Israeli relations are not based on materialistic interests at all. They are based on something much bigger than that. Also, the Jewish vote in America is only five per cent of the votes and no longer indispensable. Both parties, the Republican and the Democrat, could probably live without it.

The main supporters of Israel in the United States of America are: the Right, who believes that Israel is the main U.S. strategic asset in the Middle East; The Liberals, who consider Israel as a Democracy in the spirit and style of the U.S., political tradition: The American Jewish Community.

The Jews of the United States of America are zealot patriots of the U.S. and also great supporters and protectors of the State of Israel, for religious-Zionist reasons, and it is totally unfair, immoral and wrong to shake their long good reputation in the United States.

Pollard's verdict put the whole Jewish Community in the U.S. on alert, on the defense. One of the most influential ethnic group in the U.S., living in one of the most Democratic-Liberal countries in the world, with of the highest social standards and one of the most beautiful constitutions, is in distress, uneasy, because one man, Jonathan Pollard. And this is easily detected by its reaction. Hundreds of apologetic articles, written by Jews, showing reluctance to Pollard's behavior and even criticizing Israel, without even bothering to check if the allegations against Israel are true. The Jewish Community in the U.S. is kind of worried, lest it should also be accused of disloyalty to the U.S. of America.

The American Jewish community's primary concern in the Pollard affair is the fear of anti-Semitism repercussions and the so-called "dual loyalty" issue. The American Jewry is also concerned about the reaction of the other ethnic groups in the United States to Pollard's affair. True, Americans of other ethnic groups and religious groups have occasionally been subjected to the "dual loyalty" issue, but they never took it seriously as the Jews. They were never worried as the Jews are.

Sympathy to Israel suddenly became a burden. It is not so comfortable anymore to be pro-Israeli, openly, or defend Israel's case. It is not so comfortable these days to be Jewish in America.

The Jewish community in the United States, in spite of its denial, is even a little hysterical. It sent over to Israel, immediately, representative members of the President's Conference, headed by its chairman, Mr. Morris Abrams, to coordinate with the Government of Israel, moves, to appease the U.S. administration.

On the other hand, the American Jewry deny categorically that they are ever reacting because their "Galutic status", insecurity or "minority fear". They claim that their first and foremost concern is the future of the U.S.-Israeli relations.

There is no doubt that the Pollard affair could deteriorate the U.S.-Israeli relations.

In spite of the fact that they are "unhappy with Israel" and feel annoyed, it is not true that they are ashamed to back Israel in the Pollard case, on the contrary, the American Jewry had sent, immediately emissaries, members of the President's Conference and members of the World Jewish Congress to help Israel out of this unfortunate situation. Which proves that they are not shying away and did not decrease their political support for Israel.

The American Jewry admit also, that they are not blind at all and that they, like all the Jews in the Diasporas, understand very well, that in a certain constellation of happenings, in certain external circumstances, a new wave of violent anti-Semitism is not impossible. But right now, they feel "at home" and not in exile. The United States of America is still far from being an intolerable exile, like Russia or Syria.

The following is a letter to the editor published in The Jerusalem Post on April 17, 1987 (Nissan 18, 5747):

ANTI-SEMITISM IS ALIVE AND WELL IN THE U.S.

Sir,-I should like to respond to the article of March 18, by Henry Siegman, the executive Director of the American Jewish Congress.

Mr. Siegman stated that:"contrary to the Israeli views, Jews feel at home and secure in America." Where in the U.S. do you live Mr. Siegman? You must feel secure in your ghetto. Is it New York, Los Angeles, Skokie? I'll bet Mr. Siegman's friends are mostly Jewish; his professional associates of the same persuasion. He must belong to a Jewish country club, and of course is an active member of the Conference of Christians and Jews in his area. His higher socio-economic gentile friends respect him, and all is well in his pluralistic society.

As a successful middle-aged businessman, I can personally attest to the fact that, in America, a deep-seated hatred of the Jews is alive and well. Of course, any such evaluation is subjective at best; however, my perspectives are tempered by empirical reality. My looks and my name belie my heritage, so the day seldom passes when I am not witness to some form of ant-Jewish slur. It is, in fact, as common as a discussion of the weather. We must not be "trembling Jews in the shtetl", but as Jews and Americans, we have a marvelous capacity for self-delusion.

Mr. Pollard spent his formative years in South Bend, Indiana, the heartland of America. I suspect his ardent Zionism and his subsequent activities on behalf of Israel were in no small part tempered by his treatment as a Jew in that not-so-delightful mid-western city. I too live in a mid-western, mid-central city.

On March 20, the St. Paul Minnesota, "Pioneer Press Dispatch" (the only daily in the city), published a letter to the editor calling for the execution of the Pollards (with reference to the fate of the Rosenbergs), and for the cancel of the $ 3 billion earmarked for Israel this year to balance its budget.

That a large daily circulation newspaper owned and controlled by a huge corporation would willingly disseminate such a letter should give Mr, Siegman cause to reflect.

Adrian I. Warren, St. Paul Minnesota.

The Israeli citizen received this news with great surprise. Not hysterically, not in panic, but worried.

The Israeli citizen believes that he has the full right, not only to serve long reserve terms in the military; all his life, and pay the highest taxes in the world, but also to know how Israel got mixed up in such a mess and who are the individuals who got her involved in such a dirty conflict with the friendly U.S. Administration.

The Israeli citizen wants the full story revealed and those involved punished. He will not accept shoving things under the carpet, not this time. This had gone too far. The Israeli citizen will not accept hushing the matter up or a cover up.

The average Israeli citizen or rather the majority of the Israelis believe that action like this against the United States of America is abhorrent and those involved should be brought to trial.

The Israeli citizen feels that his government lacks comprehension of the outrage Pollard had caused in Washington. He also feels that something is lacking in the government's decisions making.

American support is extremely critical for Israel because the friendship of the United States of America is the greatest security of Israel. Losing that friendship is what endangers the security and welfare of Israel.

Usually, for an American Jew, conscientious wise, there shouldn't be any conflict of interest between his loyalty to his country, the United States of America and his love for Zion, that's for Israel. Jonathan Pollard's great love for Zion, or, rather, for money? This problem hasn't been, yet, strongly resolved, brought him in conflict with the U.S. Law.

Legally the Pollards have been found guilty and sentenced, and, very rightfully, the Court, the Judges, didn't have to consider Pollard's motivation.

But, unfortunately, Jonathan Pollard came forth with very solid evidence that the U.S. was hiding important information from one of its best friends, from Israel, which, if they were not brought up to the attention of Israel, immediately, and answers were not found to it, would endanger the survival of Israel, in fact, its very existence.

It seems that Jonathan Pollard had no difficulties to convince the Israeli Intelligence authorities on the seriousness of the matter, which means that the information was crucial, even critical.

Therefore, the Israelis had no choice, but to take the calculated risk of a breach with the U.S., because its very survival was at stake. The proofs represented by Jonathan Pollard were that, either Israel loses the United States of America as a friend of Israel or Israel loses its very existence.

As a matter of fact, Israel was completely astonished by the information received from Jonathan Pollard.

Here are only few examples of the information received by Pollard:

-Pakistan's efforts to produce an Islamic Atom Bomb.

-Soviet arms supplies to the Arab countries at war with Israel.

-Gas, Nerve Gas, Chemical and Biological Warfares purchased from West Germany which, with the missiles received from the Soviet Union, the Arab countries can hit the Israeli centers and cause a lot of casualties.

-Movement of the Soviet Fleet in the Mediterranean Sea,

-Lybian air defense system.

-PLO plans for future operations against Israel.

-The U.S. Spy Satellites gathered information on Syrian and Egyptian military movements and positions.

And the United States of America never bothered to pass such important information to Israel, its friend. The United States of America didn't find it necessary to draw the attention of Israel on such important matters.

Therefore, this is not enough reason for Israel to have spies in the United States? And this is only part of the Information received from Pollard!

Also, considering the well known attitude of the U.S. Secretary of Defense, Casper Weinberger, who has never been too fond of Israel, towards the "Lavi " project, which he fought against, from its inception, and the selling of sophisticated arms (Hawks, etc.) to Arab countries, like Saudi-Arabia, Egypt, Syria, etc. (to Egypt before and after the Peace Accord with Israel). Israel suspected that Weinberger was hiding important information from her.

A U.S. Congressional Committee should be appointed to investigate, who is responsible for denying important information from Israel, in spite of the U.S.-Israeli Treaty of passing information to each other, and in spite of promises, from several U.S. Presidents, past and present, about the U.S. commitment to the safety and security of the State of Israel. Thus endangering its existence. These are people to be punished too, if this is true.

This is, probably, why Israel was forced to act the way she did. Operations like these were condoned by a great American General and Politician, Alexander Hague.

When asked if the U.S. is spying on its friends, General Alexander Hague, Commander-in-Chief of the NATO forces in Europe and the first Secretary of State in the Reagan administration, replied: : "I hope so", because he thought that the U.S. should know, not only what is going on among its enemies, but, also, what is going on among its friends, and if a Superpower, like the U.S. believes that it must gather information on its friends, more so Israel, who is at war with her Arab neighbors for forty years.

Whenever its survival was at stake, Israel took the initiative, because it couldn't take chances, even if its operations were not so popular in the short range. This is why they broke the U.S. and Canadian arms embargo, in 1948. This is why they stole five French missile-boats from Cherbourg, under General De Gaulle's nose. This is why they landed troups at the Entebbe airport. This is why they were involved in the Uranium Affair. This is they Levelled the Nuclear Reactor in Baghdad. This is why they raided the PLO Headquarters in Tunisia. This is why they "Knocked Out" the Soviet Ground-to-Air missiles batteries in Syria, etc. In cases like these Israel must act swiftly, before it becomes too late.

One should understand the sensitivity of Israel to its security, especially after the Holocaust in Europe, during World War II. A small vulnerable country, surrounded, or rather almost besieged by hostile Arab countries, who are at war with Israel for forty years and who are just waiting, at the corner, for an opportunity to overrun her.

This is why Israel had no choice but to take calculated risk.

Therefore Jonathan Pollard's reaction is a typical example of how should a conscientious Jew behave, when his people are in danger, when Israel is in danger, in order to avoid the loss of more lives, in order to avoid another holocaust. This is a typical example of how should a responsible Jew or gentile act when any human life is in danger, be it Jewish, Christian, Moslem, or whatever.

But if Pollard demanded money for his services, which means that he acted, not out of altruism, ideology, religion, Zionism or humanitarian reason but out of greediness, the love of money, it makes Pollard a regular spy, a professional spy and not a hero, and no matter what important information he gave Israel. All this remains to be seen. If the security of Israel only was Pollard's motivation and not money, as some speculators believe, his deed might deprive him from his U.S. citizenship, but it is certainly an honorable entry ticket to an Israeli citizenship. It might not be compatible, may be, for U.S. standards but it is excellent for Israeli standards. He just didn't pass the test for dual citizenship but he sure did pass the test for Israeli citizenship.

Usually, in most of the cases, when spies are caught, after "sitting" a while, they are exchanged and returned to their native countries. The Pollards' native country is the U.S. More than that, Israel doesn't hold U.S. spies and if by chance, one is caught, which is very rare, close to nil, he is released immediately and returned to the U.S. because the U.S. and Israel are friends and not enemies. The Pollard's case was a single exception. the first, and hopefully the last.

A secret service today is indispensable to an independent country, and once in a while secret services make mistakes. The British MI-5 and MI-6 make mistakes, the French Suretee makes mistakes, the U.S, CIA makes mistakes and the Israeli secret services make mistakes. Only the Soviet KGB does not make mistakes!

The Israeli secret services made mistakes: When they arrested Mr. Jules Amster, in Haifa, tortured him, then found him innocent-When they executed Meir Tubiyanski for spying against Israel, then found him innocent-When they bombed the U.S. Information Centers in Cairo and Alexandria, Egypt (The "Essek Bish" or the "blunder"), in 1954, When they sent Eli Cohen, the last time, to Damascus, Syria, sent him to his death and didn't see the "hand writing on the wall" (Mid-Sixties), etc. etc.

Mistakes are inevitable, unavoidable. But, mistakes in the secret services are not always transgress, felony or crime. Most of the time they are work accidents, which happen, and such is the case with Jonathan Pollard. Yes, if a wise country doesn't want to weaken its secret services it should never deal with its mistakes in public. This means that internally, Israel should pursue its investigations into this mess to the limit, but externally it should proceed with dignity and insistence on its sovereign independence.

Therefore, the decision of the Israeli Government to fully cooperate with the U.S. Criminal Investigation people was absolutely right but permitting the interrogation of Israeli citizens by a foreign country's officials was wrong and unprecedented nature and should cause concern, because, such an attitude is, obviously, against the best interests of Israel and hurting its sovereignty. Sovereign nations do not expose sensitive Intelligence informations and operations to the scrutiny of a foreign country.

No wonder that the average Israeli citizen felt insulted by his government behavior. It proved to him that the whole process of decision-making in the Israeli Government was far from being mature.

On the other hand, the big problem is, when the Secret Services, without their superiors' permission, take the liberty, feel free, to make decisions and act, in matters concerning life and death. And when they make a mistake or fail, protect themselves with artificially fabricated lies, false stories, to their superiors, to the Courts and even to the Cabinet, and turn this into a system, which repeats itself again and again and even become standard routine, that's when they start to become dangerous to their own country.

True, it is an unfortunate misunderstanding, but it is a misunderstanding between friends and not between foes.

The Government of Israel appointed the Tzur-Rotenshtreich Committee to investigate the matter and make its recommendations. The Eban Parliamentary Investigation Committee also investigated the matter.

On May 1987, after a very thorough investigation, thousands of hours of work, hundreds of meetings, interviews, several dozens of people, going through three thousands pages of secret material, the Abba Eban Parliamentary Investigation Committee came up with the conclusion that the governing quartet at the time, Shimon Peres, Yitzhak Rabin, Yitzhak

Shamir and Moshe Arens are guilty, but found Shimon Peres and Yitzhak Rabin were personally responsible for the Pollard Affair.

A Parliamentary Committee of Inquiry, headed by Abba Eban, declared that: "the Minister of Defense, Rabin, did not fulfill the obligation of Ministerial responsibility", and made very similar determinations about Shimon Peres and other ministers.

Abba Eban's Committee, or rather the Knesset's subcommittee, blamed, mainly, Shimon Peres and Yitzhak Rabin. The Committee, also, accused the Defense Minister Yitzhak Rabin, for creating an atmosphere and machinery, which would have warned him and enabled him to know if things were happening which compromised the nation"s international relations or security. Eban's Committee accused Rabin for total lack of vigilance, complete lack of supervision and laxity.

This was a very strong and courageous line, as Abba Eban belonged to the same party Shimon Peres and Yitzhak Rabin belonged, that is the Maarah Party.

At the same time, another panel, the Tzur-Rotenshtreich Investigation Committee, acting totally independently, reached the same conclusions.

On May 1987, the Tzur-Rotenshtreich Investigation Committee, appointed by the Israeli Government, came out with a similar verdict, that is, that the whole "National Unity Government" was guilty.

Dr. Eliahu Ben Elissar, the ranking Likud member of the Eban Committee, insisted that Shimon Peres lied to the subcommittee, back in November 1985, when he reported that Pollard had represented himself as sent by the U.S. undercover agency. The two other Likud members, Ehud Olmert and David Magen, backed Ben Elissar.

In an interview to the press, on June 1987, Abba Eban declared:

"Although it is very mysterious: eight days after the capture of Pollard, a Prime Minister (Shimon Peres) doesn't know the exact circumstances in which Pollard was engaged. It's pretty slovenly, I must say."

In his testimony before the Eban Committee, Peres stated that Pollard had presented himself to the Israelis as an emissary working for the CIA. Peres repeated that story to the Israeli Cabinet and to U.S. Secretary of State George Shultz. The Committee disclosed that there was not a grain of truth in Peres' statement.

All the six members of the Eban Committee, three from the Likud Party (Dr. Eliahu Ben Elissar, Ehud Olmert, David Magen) and three from the Maarah Party (Abba Eban, Simcha Dinitz, Micha Harish), agreed that Shimon Peres was "First among equals and his responsibility was greater."

These six members also agreed that, a Defense Minister, for fourteen months, while the Pollard operation was in progress, Yitzhak Rabin, had prolonged opportunity to assess the phenomenon that should necessarily have caused him concern. Rabin should have warned Rafi Eitan of the dangers involved in his activity, and ordered him to stop it.

The conclusions of the two committees, but especially of the committee chaired by Eban,

Infuriated both Peres and Rabin and completely unbalanced them diplomatically and politically. Peres and Rabin were furious because they knew better than anybody else that they were guilty.

No doubt that Abba Eban's political stand in the Maarah Party became shaky, and even in danger. Peres and Rabin will be after him to get him, as in Israel, party members are tied by their loyalty to party headquarters. The only alleviation really is the change of the system, so that the party member still has a chance of survival even if the party boss doesn't like him.

The Eban Subcommittee introduced, for the first time, the concept of individual ministerial responsibility, which is a great contribution to Israel's constitutional development.

Unfortunately, the Labor leaders, Shimon Peres and Yitzhak Rabin, used the meeting of the Maarah Party Central Committee, on Committee's, on May 28, 1987, to settle accounts with Abba Eban, for his Sub-committee's Report on the Pollard's affair. Eban had received a vicious public tonguelashing from the Party leader, Shimon Peres. The vituperation rained down on him by the man whom, by his lights, he had bent over backwards to protect.

Both Peres and Rabin mocked ridiculed the Eban's Sub-Committee Report, in public, they called him "traitor", that the Party was convening to give its backing to leaders criticized by the Knesset Sub-Committee. Eban replied that he wouldn't "retreat" or "fold" in the face of the "forceful onslaught" against him. He claimed that he had "the full right to differ with leaders with power and responsibility" and added that he had not invested all the hard work on his committee's report "in order to be someone else's echo".

"Political movements are not the supreme expression of tolerance."

"This meeting contradicts the assumption that we have no problem with tolerance and freedom."

"If Peres was only capable of a single expression of humility in any respect...if he didn't insist on a zero per cent of responsibility..."

During all his speech Eban was greeted by boos from the crowd, from his Party colleagues. A well orchestrated crowd. What a shame!

Many Americans and Israelis believed that the punishment of "Life Imprisonment" was too harsh for somebody who spied for a friendly country like Israel. After all the Pollards didn't steal nuclear, classified, top secret material and handed it over to the Soviet Union, a hostile country, an enemy country.

On the other hand, one doesn't spy on a friendly country like the U.S. that gives Israel a yearly three billion dollars in economical aid, unless it really jeopardized and endangered the security and survival of Israel.

According to Pollard, the whole affair started by Casper Weinberger's refusal to fulfill a memorandum of understanding that provided for full exchanges of intelligence information. Pollard claimed that he acted to rectify this situation.

Secretary of Defense Weinberger exaggerated when he declared that this was the "worst case of espionage in 200 years," and that it "upset the balance of power in the Middle East and would cause war."

Weinberger's extremely critical pronouncements helped create a climate, which led to the severe punishment to the Pollards.

A member of the prosecution team admitted that Jonathan Pollard had not damaged the security of the U.S.

Everybody agrees that Jonathan Pollard was a spy, caught in action and therefore deserves punishment. What is debatable is the amount of punishment, bearing in mind that Pollard spied for a friendly country, like Israel and not for America's enemies.

The following persons: Philby, McLean, Burgess, Blunt, Walker and Longtree spied for their country's enemies, yet they received much lighter sentences than Pollard.

The great question is whether anti-Semitism or vendetta against Israel was not involved in the decision of the judges?

Jonathan Jay Pollard, who is serving a life sentence in the U.S. is a hero, if he did it for helping preserve the security of Israel, but if he did it for money, he is no hero. From Israeli sources, the money paid to Pollard was for personal expenses. Many believe that the maximum punishment was a personal vendetta to punish Israel through Jonathan Pollard.

If what Jonathan Pollard claimed was true, than it is the Secretary of Defense, Casper Weinberger, who was acting against the best interests of the U.S. by denying crucial information from the State of Israel. Because he was acting contrary to an exchange of information agreement, signed by the U.S. President, trying to weaken Israel, one of the best U.S. ally, one of the most trustworthy ally in the Middle East, thereby harming the security of the U.S. itself.

If it is true what Jonathan Pollard claimed that the Secretary of Defense, Casper Weinberger, denied Israel the access to certain very important intelligence information, the Secretary of Defense was abusing his "higher authority", and this should be taken under consideration to reduce his punishment.

What would have angered the Reagan administration was the fact that while the trial was still going on Raphi Eithan and Aviem Sellah were given much publicized promotions. A very clumsy timing. They may have been perfectly qualified, but it was not the right time.

In Israel, in the United States of America, and probably elsewhere too, the case of Jonathan Pollard excited many, especially people who had a juridical approach and who understood that there is an issue of public integrity.

Colonel Aviem Sellah was forced to leave the Air force and couldn't get a job. The U.S. Administration ordered all American firms to refuse to make business with any company that hires Colonel Aviem Sellah.

Pollard was sent to Springfield, Missouri, where he spent his first year in jail. This jail is for people who committed murders, rapes, burglaries, etc. Many of them are psychopaths and mentally retarded. Pollard was held there in solitary confinement and naked. He was insulted and beaten by his jailers, for no reason at all. They tried to shake him out of balance, break him, degrade him and distort his human image. Pollard was treated in Springfield, Missouri like an animal, like a beast.   At the request of Lee Hamilton, Congressman from Indiana, Pollard was transferred to Marion, Illinois, one of the toughest and best-guarded prisons in the United States, and where some of the worst criminals are held.

In 1992 (5752) the ex-Secretary of Defense Casper Weinberger was accused of lying to the Congress, when testifying on the issue of "Irangate."

The Attorney General would be using a certain 1,700 pages booklet, Casper Weinberger's personal diary. This diary revealed that the ex-Secretary of Defense and the President were involved in a deal with Iraq.

Foreign observers believe that the ex-Secretary of Defense was afraid of Pollard and wanted to get rid of him because Pollard was aware of highly classified material proving the U.S. Administration's military cooperation with Iraqi President Saddam Hussein, strengthening his chemical, biological, and even nuclear capability.

Something that was extremely dangerous to Israel's survival. In order to avoid another holocaust he decided to reveal this secret to the Israeli Government.

Casper Weinberger sent the Judges a document defining Pollard's behavior as "High Treason". When Pollard appealed to the U.S. judges Silverman and Ginzburg, they rejected his appeal.

There is a strong feeling that Jonathan Pollard was punished out of all proportion to American law. There remain three more questions that are screaming for answers:

1. What information did Jonathan Pollard give Israel that was being withheld by US Intelligence in spite of the 1983 US/Israel Exchange of Intelligence Agreement?

2. Why did the U.S. Government renege on its promise of leniency if Jonathan Pollard agreed to a plea bargain?

3. What was in Casper Weinberger's secret memo to the Judge that resulted in only Jonathan being given a life sentence without possibility of parole-something not even given to those who spied for the former Soviet Union?

To those who are familiar with World History, Judge Robinson's harsh sentencing of Jonathan Pollard was no surprise. By just turning back to the end of the 19th century to find similarities with the infamous Dreyfus case, with former Secretary of Defense, Casper Weinberger, as Esterhazy. Judge Williams of the Federal Appellate Court made it quite clear when he gave vent to his emotions at the unjust decision.

"The same gas which the Germans used to murder our European brethren could just be easily used today by the Arabs to exterminate the Jewish population of Israel. Was I really expected to just let history repeat itself without doing anything to protect our people from such calamity? Granted, I broke the law, but, to tell you the truth, I had rather be rotting in prison than sitting Shiva for the hundreds of thousands of Israelis who could have died because of my cowardice. Have the fires of the concentration camps grown so cold that people have forgotten that six million Jews were butchered while the world looked on in silence? I just could not walk away from the intelligence embargo (lifted in 1985) and pretend that it didn't exist. I had to act," said Pollard.

Jonathan Pollard acknowledged that he broke the American law and expressed regret that he did not find a legal way for passing the life-saving information to Israel. But when confronted with the possibility that his failure to act could result in a physical catastrophe of potentially devastating proportions, Pollard acted instinctively in defense of the Jewish people. There is no doubt that if these were his calculations and logic Pollard was legally wrong but morally right in what he did. Naturally, what should be taken under consideration? In terms of mitigating his sentence, is the consequence of his actions. Especially when it didn't harm the American people or their Government.   Pollard knew for sure that the material he transmitted to Israel could not cause injury to the United States of America.

Judge Stephen Williams of the D.C. Court of Appeals called the Pollard case "a fundamental miscarriage of Justice."

Lawrence Korb, a key assistant of Casper Weinberger, wrote that Weinberger's "visceral dislike of Israel" contributed to the excessiveness of Pollard's sentence.

One of the appellate judges during the September 10, 1991, hearing exclaimed: "How can it be justified that the Secretary of Defense uses the term 'treason' in a case in which the Government could not and did not charge treason?"

In 1992, the American Jewish Community leadership started to change its attitude towards Jonathan Pollard. It seemed that the problem of dual loyalties didn't bother them anymore. They became more understanding and more supportive.

It seemed that they finally realized when Pollard encountered a conflict between the interests of the U.S. and that of Israel, which certainly endangered the survival of the State of Israel and even threatened to become another holocaust for Israel and its Jews, Pollard felt that he couldn't remain silent and take under his conscience another holocaust to his people, and preferred to intervene, this time, in favor of Israel, the underdog, and especially when it didn't hurt the U.S. at all.

A full-page ad in Friday's (October 23, 1992) New York Times, signed by a broad coalition of hundreds of American Rabbis, called on U.S. President George Bush to commute the life sentence of Jonathan Pollard. A weak before, the U.S. Supreme Court refused to hear his petition to retract his guilt plea and stand trial. The U.S. Supreme Court decision confirmed that Jonathan Pollard should rot in his cell in Marion, Illinois until he dies.

Presidential clemency is now the only option open to Pollard.

The New York Times ad, representing a cross-section of more than 560 Rabbis from all four movements, was the first major public statement of support for clemency for Pollard. The signators included the heads of National Rabbinic Organizations of the Orthodox, Conservative, Reform and Constructionist movements.

The ad reads, in part, "We in no way condone acts of espionage. We nonetheless call upon you, Mr. President, to recognize that the lifetime sentence imposed upon Jonathan Pollard is unduly harsh and grossly inconsistent with the punishment given to other Americans convicted of similar and even worse crimes."

Major Jewish Community Relations Organizations have not come out in support of clemency for Pollard. "This is not a Jewish issue, and this ad does not make it one," said Philip Baum, a leader of the AJC and chairman of the National Jewish Community Relations Advisory Council's committee on Pollard. "I don't know of anything in this case that demands a response from the Jewish Community."

Rabbi Avi Weiss, national president of Amcha, which organized the ad and a long-time Pollard supporter, said that Philip Baum's position only shows how out of touch the leadership of U.S. Jewish organizations is with the grass roots. "There is a tremendous chasm between these elite organizations and the people. This ad proves that Pollard's case, and the commutation of his sentence to time served, is a priority issue on the American Jewish scene. This has nothing to do with dual loyalty. Pollard was tried as an American, but convicted as a Jew."

Many believe that the excessiveness of Pollard's sentence is a perversion of American justice.

At the beginning of 1994 Aldrich Ames, head of the CIA Counter Espionage, was found to be a Russian spy. It was he who claimed that Jonathan Pollard spied for Israel, that passed the information to the Soviet Union, which caused the death of several US agents stationed in Moscow, which was found to be a lie. This he did in order to draw the attention away from him. In order to save his own skin.

On April 1994, President Bill Clinton rejected the request for pardon to Jonathan Pollard. The President explained his reasons for making that decision:

"After personally reviewing the Jonathan Pollard matter, I have decided to deny his application for executive clemency." Clinton said in a statement issued by the White House, "My decision is based on the grave nature of this offence and the considerable damage that this action caused our nation,"

Clinton said that Pollard committed "one of the most serious crimes against our country-placing national secrets of the U.S. in hands of another country. The enormity of Mr. Pollard's crime, the harm his actions caused our country, and the need to deter every person who might even consider such actions, warrant his continued incarceration," said Clinton.

In order to pardon Jonathan Pollard, Clinton would have to ignore strong opposition to a pardon from Justice Department prosecutors, the Defense Department, the CIA and the U.S. Intelligence agencies, plus advice from Attorney-General Janet Reno to deny Pollard's plea. Public passions and official sensitivities were further aggravated by the arrest of Aldrich Ames, accused of being a top KGB mole in the CIA.

On April 28, 1994 (Iyar 17, 5754), Aldrich Ames, the highest-ranking CIA employee ever caught spying, was sentenced to life in prison.

What Jonathan Pollard did was to pass crucial information to a friendly country, the State of Israel, because the U.S. was withholding critical defense information from Israel after Iraq's nuclear facility was bombed, and Pollard believed his actions were necessary to prevent another Holocaust. The events of the Gulf War tend to confirm his claim.

As New York Daily News columnist Sidney Zion has put it. "The moment Pollard was arrested in 1985, the CIA agent Aldrich Ames, who was a Soviet spy, started spreading the news that Pollard's information to Israel was delivered by a mole in the Mossad to the Soviet Union. He convinced Casper Weinberger, then Secretary of Defense, that Pollard was the worst spy in American history. Weinberger delivered a 46-page secret memorandum to Pollard's sentencing judge that practically demanded a life sentence."

The U.S. Intelligence Community, of course, is refusing to admit error. Having exhibited unpardonable incompetence in the Ames case-one of the worst cases of treason in American history, which cost the lives of, at least, 10 U.S. agents-it is refusing to exonerate Pollard. Such conduct is not unusual in bureaucracies, particularly those, who can shroud themselves in secrecy. Nor is it uncommon for intelligence agencies to sacrifice lives to preserve their reputation.

But Pollard's motives are not relevant as the simple fact that he spied not for America' enemies, but for one of its closest allies. Israel.

At no time in American history has anyone convicted of such a crime received a life sentence. What makes Pollard's life sentence particularly outrageous is that the U.S. Justice Department promised him that in exchange for a guilty plea and the waiving of a trial, it would only ask for no more than "substantial sentence." Up to that time, no spy who worked for an ally received a sentence of more than 10 years.

So far it was possible to treat the Pollard's case, as no more than an example of arbitrary injustice, which proves that life can be unfair. But now the case has become a major blot on the reputation of the U.S. and an indictment of American humanism and sense of justice. It raises the possibility that even in the World's greatest Democracy, deliberate cruelty and senseless oppression can become Government policy.

The unfairness of the Pollard case is so palpable that it defies understanding. It is clear now that Pollard could not have done the U.S. any harm, and that the suspicion that his actions did damage to the American interests was based on false information planted by the Soviet spy Ames Aldrich.

But above all, it is President Bill Clinton who should understand that every day Pollard stays in jail erodes America's reputation as a country with heart, and its credibility as a bastion of fairness and a just society.

The Pentagon has been making accusations against Israelis for "spying behind its lines."

Why would Israel need to spy in the U.S.? if it could buy almost everything from the U.S. legally. Besides, Israel, since its inception in 1948, had been a respectable Partner to the U.S. in many most classified projects and had been contributing for many years very generously to the U.S. in Research and Development in many fields. The first Soviet MIG-21 the U.S. obtained from Israel.

The Pentagon accused Israel for showing special interest in the nuclear field. Unfortunately, the Pentagon had forgotten to mention that the U.S. had adopted two extremely remarkable scientists: Dr. Shai Feldman from the University of Tel Aviv who is now with Harvard and Professor Moshe Rosen from the Nuclear Plant in Dimona and the University of Ben-Gurion, who is heading the Department of Materials at John Hopkins.

The U.S. had also adopted many other scientists, like: Professor Marcel Kalfish from the Hebrew University in Jerusalem who works for the Navy Laboratories. Dr. Yuval Carmel, one of the most brilliant brains from Rafael who works for the Research And Development department of the University of Maryland. Prof. Amnon Yariv, an expert in Electro-Optics who works for CALTEC. Prof. Peretz Friedman and Prof. Moshe Rubinshtein, both in the field of Aeraunotics. Prof. Yossef Rom from the

Technion, in Haifa, who works for NASA and the U.S. Army, an expert in the technology of missile acceleration.

The Pentagon had also forgotten to mention the US-Israeli partnership in the Lavi (Pratt and Whitney) projects as well as in the Hetz Ground-to-Air missile, still going on successfully. Then there is the great Israeli Colony of first class scientists at the Silicon Valley in California.

The U.S. had also adopted first class Israeli musicians like: Isaac Perlman and Pinhas Zukerman, Gil Shaham, etc.

America is defending itself from the Israeli urge of survival!

The Pentagon had mentioned the "ethnic" relation Israel had in the U.S., meaning the American Jewry, pointing at Jonathan Pollard as an example.

The Jewish Community in America will do a great mistake to disregard or ignore such charges, because it could then leave every Jew in America or Israel a potential danger to the U.S.

Again, Pollard was arrested as an American, but was sentenced as a Jew, just like the French Jew, Alfred Dreyfus, in France.

Jonathan Pollard has been "Buried Alive" in federal prisons under unfounded exaggerated accusations for reasons that have nothing to do with his crime and everything to do with politics. Anti-Semitism does not require facts or performance on which to base their slurs.

3. THE ARAB-ISRAELI CONFLICT

Statistics show that fifty years from now, in the year 2050 the Arab population in Israel will become a majority. Therefore, the Arab population in and outside Israel will be smart in doing nothing but sit quietly and wait and avoid another war with the Israelis, which they can lose. In the year 2050, when the sArabs become a majority in the democratic State of Israel, Israel will become an Arab State. The Jews in the Arab State will be loyal to the country where they live and active in helping build and strengthen it.

Meanwhile, the Jews of the United States (and the Western World) integrated in an affluent society and assimilated by intermarriage will lose their identity and uniqueness, thus, contribute less and less to the United States. The United States becomes weaker and weaker, the Arabs become stronger, may be even a Superpower (Together with their brethren in the Arab World and the Arab Oil).

The United States must be out of its wits to let this happen. For the United States, a strong Jewish State of Israel is a strong ally, an asset, while an Arab "State of Israel" is a big problem. A Palestinian-Arab state in the West Bank will only expedite the realization of this scenario.

To get peace the Arabs must realize that they must give up their repeated trials to oust the Israelis from their land. They must give up their old plan to rob the Hebrews' homeland and must recognize and accept the viability and existence of the State of Israel.

A Palestinian state, side by side with Israel, means a terrorist state on the border of Israel. It means insecurity to the citizens of Israel, it means constant troubles for Israel. More bloodshed for many more years.

Now, when the whole world is fighting terror, Israel should be the last one to encourage theestablishment of a Palestinian state beside it, and on Israeli soil.

Therefore, the idea of two states, a Palestinian state beside the State of Israel, in Judea, Samaria and the Gaza Strip, on Israeli soil, at the expense of Israel, is a great mistake. It is also a major violation of the Almighty's will, it is a great sin.

This is why the "Road Map" Plan should be discarded and never implemented.

The Arabs declared, several times, that they would stop their Intifadah, the slaughter of Innocent people, only when the "Israelis put an end to their occupation of our territories."

The fact of the matter is that these territories really belonged to the Israelis. The truth is that the Arab invaders were occupying illigaly Israeli land.

Therefore, be it popular or not, Israel must liquidate the Arab population from its territories, the sooner the better. An Arab population displacement is imperative. The Arabs must leave. They must go back to their natural and normal environment, their countries of origin. This is an unavoidable surgery. This is a must. This is the core and crux of the whole problem. This is the only practical solution. Any other solution is impractical and is a merry-go-round full of problems from here to eternity. Any other solution is impossible, lengthy and won't last. The Arabs must evacuate Israel and return the land of

Israel to the Israelites. Under President Bill Clinton, the Secretary of State Ms, Madeleine Albright made several trips to the Middle East trying to bring peace between the parties, the Arabs and the Jews, but with very little progress. The Arabs expected her to bring them an Arab State, but in vain. Because the Arabs were stubborn. They did not want to budge towards a compromise. They were joking on Albright trips and chanted in Arabic :"Ya Madeleine, ya Madeleine, Zay Ma Ruchtee, Zay Ma Jetee" (Madeleine, Madeleine, same as you went same as you came."). "You came back with no results for the Arabs."

4. WHO IS A JEW?

It is clear to every thinking individual that the question of "Who is Jew?" is closely connected to the question of "What is a Jew?" This, in turn leads to the definition of Jews and Judaism, and from there the question of what are the tasks and role of the State of Israel in Jewish history, past, present and future. The answer to this question is that the State of Israel has two tasks: the survival of the Jews and the revival of Judaism.

For several thousand years the identity of a Jew was never disputed, the criteria for Jewish status were always very clear.

"Who is a Jew?" has turned into one of the most dividing issues in Jewish history. Unfortunately, the "Who is a Jew?" issue threatened to disrupt the cohesion of the Jewish nation in Israel and throughout the diaspora.

Here is one of the oldest people on earth suddenly checking its own identity.

On March 19, 1970, under the "Law of Return", the Government of Israel defined a Jew "as one born to a Jewish mother or one who has converted." The new law didn't specify any standards of conversion. The movement to amend the law intends to add the four words: "According to the Halacha," or in Hebrew, add one word: "Ka'Halacha." That is, the law should emphacize that "a Jew is one born to a Jewish mother or one who has converted according to the Halacha."

For the past 4000 years of Jewish existence there has been one, very clearly defined process, whereby a non-Jew becomes a Jew. The practical details of this process were defined in the Code of Jewish Law, the Laws of Moses or the Halacha. The traditional, historic and halachaic criteria prevailed all these years. The amendment in 1970 with the exclusion of the word "Ka'Halacha" changed the traditional status quo and became the cause of the arguments between the Religious and Orthodox versus the Reforms, Conservatives and Reconstructionists, mainly American Jews.

It is inconceivable that a matter as serious and profound as conversion to Judaism should not be defined precisely, without any doubts, and should possess no standard at all by which to measure its authenticity, and most ridiculous is the fact that, a gentile who did not undergo the proper conversion, that's according to the Halacha, is defined by the Government of Israel as a Jew.

Each and every Jew, without reservation, Orthodox, Reform, Conservative, Reconstructionist, Secular Atheist or whatever, is recognized by the Government of Israel as one hundred per cent Jew. Therefore, the continuously espoused argument that the amended Law of Return would mean the disenfranchisement of Jews who are members of the Reform, Conservative, Reconstructionist Movements, is completely wrong.

Unofficial estimates put the number of Reform Rabbis who perform intermarriages without a "conversion" at over five hundred. A significant number of these Rabbis even perform intermarriages in a Christian church, side by side with the priest or minister.

In spite of the fact that for some it may make no difference if a Jew converts according to the Halacha or not, yet, for many, even those who are not "observant", even the secularists. This question is of vital importance. For a large percentage of Jews, 4000 years of Jewish tradition for which countless of Jews gave their lives, is something worth holding to. You just do not dump 4000 years of tradition; You just do not have the right to break a chain of 4000 years of history. Yet, the amendments of March 19, 1970, disregards what for many Jews is a crucial priority and leads to falsely believe that this or that individual is a universally accepted Jew, when he is not. This amendment is also an injustice to the gentile. Because, having undergone non-Halachaic "conversion", by mistake, many Gentiles sincerely believe that they are now Jews and have become part of the Jewish people. Obviously they will be very disappointed and angry when they find out that they are not. This can be rectified by undergoing an Halachaic conversion.

If the Halachaic conversion were not observed over the generation the Jews would have become a divided people. There is no greater threat to the unity and future survival of the Jewish people than the acceptance into its midst of non-Jews under the guise of converts,

Therefore, the action that conversion to Judaism requires no standards is utterly false and dangerously wrong. Giyur, conversion, must be according to the Laws of Moses, according to the Halacha, and Halacha is only one.

The problem "Who is a Jew?" has been bothering the people of Israel since the days of Ezrah. Ezrah preferred to send away, back home, all the foreign women and their children rather than establish special conversion courts.

The State of Israel met with the problem, for the first time, in 1958, when the Minister of Interior, Israel Bar-Yehudah (Achdut Avodah) introduced an ordinance establishing the fact that: "Anyone who declares, in good faith, that he was Jewish will be registered as Jewish."

The National Religious Party (NRP) rejected the definition and quit the Cabinet.

Ex-Prime Minister David Ben-Gurion consulted the issue with seventy Jewish scholars, all over the world. He asked their opinion on the matter. Only forty-five answered, most of them advocated the Orthodox definition, that's the definition of the Halacha (the Laws of Moses). Several even belonged to the Reform and conservative denominations.

The Israeli Government, then, refused to endorse Bar-Yehudah's version and the NRP returned to the Cabinet.

The Amendment to the "Law of Return" also known as "Who is a Jew?" has been on the religious parties' agenda for several years. They have tried to amend the Law several times but failed. They couldn't recruit a majority in the Knesset for their proposal. What the religious parties wanted was to add only four words: "According to the Halacha." The existing law read:"A Jew is one who was born to a Jewish mother or was converted (Giyur), and wanted to amend it, so that it will read: "A Jews is one who was born to a Jewish mother or was converted according to the Halacha and is not member of another religion."

On December 10, 1987 (Kislev 20, 5748), in Jerusalem, the Zionist Congress called for "complete equality for all streams within Judaism" which would give their Rabbis in Israel the "legal right to perform all life-cyclic events and other rabbinical functions."

The resolution was passed by 291 votes, with 271 against, at the closing of the Congress, which was also to elect a new World Zionist Organization Executives.

The resolution on religious equality was supported by the Labor block, which included the Maarah, Mapam, the Confederation of United Zionists and the Reform and Conservative Zionist organizations. It was opposed by the Likud and the Mizrahi.

Prime Minister Yizhak Shamir addressed the closing session and said: "it was inconceivable to question the legitimacy of any Jew, whether he belonged to the Reform, Conservative or Orthodox stream. They are all equal as Jews in our eyes and in the eyes of Israeli Law."

Referring to conversions performed abroad, outside Israel, Shamir added that a solution in this problem should be sought "through consultations, tolerance and understanding, based on Jewish unity and solidarity." This formula appeared to exclude legislative solutions, such as the proposed change in the "Law of Return."

On December 1987 (kislev 5748), Ashkenazi Chief Rabbi Avraham Shapiro spoke at the World Zionist Congress, in Jerusalem and said: " No Rabbi, not even an Orthodox Rabbi, has the right to bring individuals, who are not wanted, into the Jewish People. It is a moral problem."

Rabbi Shapiro continued by saying that he believes that "non-Orthodox had a perfect right to bring whomever they feel like into their own synagogues and to pray with whomever they pleased." But, he added," it is not fair to say that they are bringing them into the Jewish people. It is not fair not to the Jewish People and not to the non-Jews."

"In Israel ", he added, " this is such an insignificant problem, and it is not worth creating a problem of it. It is also not worth creating a division among the Jews over this issue, because only four or five people a year fall into the category of non-Orthodox converts coming from abroad. In these few cases, in Israel, the Reform, Conservative and Reconstructionist movements," he suggested, "should give in and refer such converts to the Orthodox Rabbinate. This is basically an American problem."

It is no secret at all that the Maarah had cultivated its ties with the Reform movement since the late of the 1970s, and an ideological link merged between them on a number of issues, particularly the "peace process", in addition, the Maarah managed to keep its promise to oppose efforts to change the "Law of Return"even though it could jeoperdize its position with the Orthodox parties.

There was a strong opposition to the attempt to amend the "Law of Return" from the secular Maarah, and more so, from the Left parties. These reluctant to endorse this amendment for fear of a conflict with the Reform and Conservative denominations in the U.S. Jewry. The Reform and Conservative denominations in Israel is small, minute, infinitisimal.

Reform and Conservative Jews in America, U.S. citizens, wanted to dictate, by remote control, the political shape of the Knesset in Israel. By what right? After all the Orthodox in Israel have gained their political power by living in Israel and through very democratic elections.

If the Reforms and Conservatives in America are really such big Zionist and hate to see the Orthodox dominancy in Israel, all they have to do is cross the Atlantic ocean and go live in Israel and establish a majority. Israel after all is a democratic country and respects the decision of the majority and abides by the decision of the majority. Meanwhile what the Reform and Conservative Jews in America are doing is enjoying the "fleshpot" of the U.S. and couldn't give up this cosy, comfortable life, while the Orthodox, and mostly religious Jews from Brooklyn, Boroughpark and elsewhere in the United States, Britain, Canada, etc. are settling in the Israeli frontiers and fighting the Molotov-Cocktails, stones and bullets of the Palestinian-Arab intifadah, and made Israel their permanent home.

The issue reappeared again, when, in 1970, Major Benjamin Shalit and Scottish wife, Anne, won their appeal at the Supreme Court, in Jerusalem, against the Minister of Interior, who refused to register her and their two children as Jews.

The Supreme Court ordered the Ministry of Interior to register Mrs. Shalit and her two children as Jews.

The religious parties couldn't accept an "instant" conversion of a gentile by a Reform Rabbi. The National Religious Party (NRP) threatened to end the coalition with the Mapai. To appease the NRP, they amended the law to read:"A Jew is one who was born to a Jewish mother or was converted (Giyur), and is not member of another religion." But still refused to add the four words: "according to the Halacha." After the word "converted". It was an anoying compromise but kept the NRP in the coalition with Mapai (Maarah).

Helen Zeidman, member of a kibbutz in the south of Israel, was converted by a Reform Rabbi, which was not recognized in Israel. Ms. Zeidman agreed to be converted again by an Orthodox Rabbi, according to the Halacha.

Ms. Susan Miller was converted to Judaism by a Reform Rabbi, in Colorado, U.S.A. She then moved to Israel and applied for registration as a Jewess. The Minister of Interior, Rabbi Yitzhak Peretz, refused to recognize her conversion and demanded that she converts again by an Orthodox Rabbi, according to the Halacha, before he can approve her registration. Ms.Miller refused and appealed to the Supreme Court in Jerusalem. She won the case, The Supreme Court ordered the Ministry of Interior to register Ms. Miller as a Jewess. The Minister of Interior, Rabbi Yitzhak Peretz refused, and in order to avoid contempt of Court, resigned from office. Ms. Miller was registered as a Jewess and returned to the U.S.

The new law did not stipulate that "conversion" had to be performed in accordance with the Halacha. It still left the issue open. Obviously, the religious parties were not satisfied and kept pushing to get the amendment.

North American Jews urged Prime Minister Yitzhak Shamir to block the amendment. Seven leading U.S. and Canadian Jews have sent a letter to the Prime Minister of Israel urging him to forestall any change in the "Law of Return". The signers warned that if the "Law of Return" would be amended, as Orthodox legislaters wished, there would be "a terrible schism in the Jewish people." Shamir was asked to consider the negative impact on Diaspora communities of any change in the status quo.

This letter was sent to Prime Minister Shamir sometime during the second part of 1987. Similar requests by North American Jewish leaders have arrived Israel several times, addressed also to previous Israeli governments. The American Jewry, the Reform, Conservative and Reconstructionst Jews concerned about the religious monopoly that the Orthodox Jews had in Israel. Rabbi Alexander Schindler, head of the Reform Jewry in America had warned Israel that the amendment of the "Law of Return" and the definition of "Who is a Jew?" would, probably break the solidarity between Israel and its American Diaspora,

Leaders of American fundraising and federation establishment, met in New Orleans, on November 17, 1988, and demanded categorically that Israel remove the "Who is a Jew?" issue from its political agenda.

Israel's Ambassador to Washington, Moshe Arad, in a rare move intended to influence decision-making in Jerusalem, said in a cable to Prime Minister Yitzhak Shamir and Foreign Minister Shimon Peres, which was received in Jerusalem, on November 17, 1988 (Kislev 8, 5749): I implore you to discuss and reassess the grave repercussions which the Law would have on the relations between Israel and the Jewish community, and, as a direct consequence, the ramifications on our standing in the U.S."

Shoshanah Cardin, former president of the Council of Jewish Federation in North America and head of the delegation of American Jewish organizational officials, who flew to Israel to try to persuade Prime Minister Shamir to abandon the plan to amend the "Law of Return", declared on November 21, 1988 (Kislev 12, 5749), at Ben-Gurion Airport, that the problem of defining "Who is a Jew" is not political, but religious and spiritual and, therefore, should be resolved by the religious, not the political leadership.

"The Prime Minister and other Israeli politicians must be made to realize that this is very serious matter," Ms. Cardin said. "it is liable to split the Jewish people."

The delegation arrived in Israel, immediately after the week-long CJF General Assembly in New Orleans and included Stanley Horowitz, President and Director-General of rhe United Jewish Appeal in the U.S.A.; Morton Kornreich, UJA National- Chairman; Martin Stein, Chairman of the UJA board of Governers; Carmi Schwartz, CJF Executive- Director; and Peter Hess, Executive-Director of the United Israel Appeal of Canada.

"We are one people, and must remain so," Cardin said, adding that changing the "Law of Return" could "seriously affect" the Jewish Agency and other pro-Israeli organizations.

The World Zionist Executive declared that it opposed the attempt of the Israeli Government to amend the "Law of Return", and, at the same time, "rejected all threats regarding the mobilization of funds for the benefit of Israel and the Jewish people" and "dissociated itself from the rethoric of Jewish organizations issuing threats regarding their links with the State of Israel" over the matter.

In a statement issued after it met in Jerusalem, the Executive noted that the Government-Jewish Agency-World Zionist Organization covenant requires consultation among the three before the Government takes any decision regarding the "Law of Return".

It called on "all the Jews of the World to express absolute solidarity" with Israel and to continue providing "traditional and ongoing support."

Some American-Jewish leaders warned that amending the "Law of Return" might bring a profoundly negative effect. Thy also said that they were afraid that the unity of the Jewish people would be dissipated and our people, the Jews, would be torn apart by anger and resentment.

The Reform and Conservative Jews in the U.S.A., or at least their leaders, claim, that the change in the definition of "Who is a Jew?' would cause a deep rift between Israel and the Diaspora and therefore recommend not to amend the "Law of Return" They believe that changing the status quo on "Who is a Jew?" would spark a widespread rebellion in the ranks of the fun-raising establishments (the UJA, the CJF, etc.) in the U.S. and will cut their contributions to Israel as well as their political support.

The Chairman of the Jewish Agency Board of Governors, Mendel Kaplan, warned, on November 24, 1988 (Kislev 15, 5749) that passage of the amendment would create the "greatest division we have ever seen in the Jewish World."

In letters sent to Shamir, Jewish Agency Chairman, Simcha Dinitz stressed that "amending the Law could lead to a split in the Jewish people."

The following was published in The Jerusalem Post on January 6, 1989:

To the Editor of the Jerusalem Post,

Sir-A recent article stated that three Jewish communities, Atlanta, Boston and Pittsburgh, threaten to re-evaluate their donations to Israel, should the (unseemly, obnoxious) "Who is a Jew?" amendment to the "Law of Return" become statutory. Such press publicity could not have been timed more propitiously to aid and abet Arafat in his evil designs, while simultaneously wounding, the morale of a solitary, heroic Israel let down by the world for the n'th time. If any group or individual anywhere is considering denial of funds, which is their right: what is advantageous to the PLO are related public announcements.

Before such financial decisions are concluded, perhaps individuals concerned might consider: the effort to rebuild the nation, beginning with the Russian-Jewish pioneers of the 1880s; the Holocaust survivors, who needed Israel, and those who make Aliyah today; the families of all heroes living and dead, in all of the wars, since 1948; and the Jewish youth in uniform who live in imminent danger now. Finally, we may ponder on Israel's values to each of us, as a healthy, financially and militarily secure, self-confident nation, inspiring us all as our spiritual and solely a matter of dollars and cents. There is something we can give to Israel at no cost: moral support.

MARTIN H. SABLE
Editorial Coordinator
Wisconsin Coalition for Israel
Milwaukee, Wisconsin.

Many American Jews do not even know the difference between Shass and Degel Hatorah, or between the "Law of Return" and the Rabbinical Courts of Law, yet, when the issue "Who is a Jew?" came up, they reacted with spontaneous outcry at the prospect as they see it-as they see it- of becoming disenfranchised as Jews.

Answering JIA Chairman Trevor Chinn's speculations that "a change in 'the Law of

Return' can significantly affect the unity of the Jewish people." Shamir said that: "the first principle on which the new government will stand is the unity of the entire Jewish people."

Shamir also added that: "there is no question whatsoever of disputing the legitimacy of any Jew outside Israel, and the dispute concerns only olim (immigrants) who were converted to Judaism by a Court that is not recognized by the Israeli Rabbinate."

The State of Israel has its intention of getting involved in disputes among the various religious streams in our people. All are considered parts of the Jewish people.

The Government has no preference for one group and does not exclude others."

Members of the United Jewish Appeal delegation from the United States, representing all three Jewish streams, declared, in Jerusalem, that passage of the "Who is a Jew?" amendment would drastically reduce the chances of the different streams, resolving differences that threatens to prevent members of one movement from marrying members of another. The amendment threatens to divide the Diaspora Jewry, mainly the U.S. Jewry, irretrievable and prevent them from marrying each other, they said.

The Reform and Conservative movements claim to represent the majority of American Jews. The Orthodox Jews in America reject their claim.

The Reform and Conservative leaders claim that they represent the majority of the American Jews. How do they know? Are the Jews in America democratically organized? Do they have elections? Were their leaders voted into office or mainly appointed? Do 360,000 members of Hadassah (Women's Zionist Organization of America) elect their leaders? Was Rabbi Alexander Schindler elected?

Everybody knows that the answer is negative. The word "election" has never been on their agenda. Therefore, how can they claim that they represent the majority of the Jews in America?

The heads of three American Orthodoxy's most prestigious groups arrived in Israel on November 1988, to argue against amending the "Law of Return". On the other hand, another distinguished American Orthodox leader, Rabbi Aharon Soloveitchik who also arrived in Israel, has come out wholeheartedly in favor of such an amendment.

The three opposing Rabbis were: Rabbi Max Schreier, President of the Rabbinical Council of America (RCA); Rabbi Louis Bernstein, President of Young Israel; and Rabbi Yehezkel Lookstein, President of American Mizrahi-argue that despite their deep commitment to conversion (Giyur) according to the Halacha, a change in the "Law of Return" at this time would cause a deep rift in the World Jewry.

However, Rabbi Aharon Soloveitchik, head of the Brisk Yeshiva in Chicago, said he was shocked to hear that the RCA had called for removing the issue from the political agenda. It was "incomprehensible that such a statement be made without consulting the membership," he said.

Aharon Soloveitchik is mentor of Yeshiva University's Isaac Elhanan Yeshiva.

In a public statement issued in Chicago, Rabbi Soloveitchik said that "the proposed amendment is of utmost importance for the preservation of Judaism throughout the world, and there can be no compromise on this issue."

When the Rebbe of Belz, Yissachar Dov Rokach, was approached on the matter, he replied that he believes that "this is a Reform attempt to bring its struggle to the Land of Israel, which is a shame."

Tremendous pressures were exirted on Israel against the changing of the "Law of Return". Five powerful Jewish senators, Israel's main supporters in the U.S. Senate, have warned the Israeli Ambassador Moshe Arad that changing the 'Law of Return" will have grave consequences on the relations between Israel and the Jews of America and on the political and economic support of the U.S. Congress and Administration to Israel.

Senator Rudy Boschwitz (Republican-Minnesota), Howard Metzenbaum (Democrat-Ohio), Alan Spector (Republican-Pennsylvania), Frank Lautenberg (Democrat-New Jersey) and Carl Levin (Democrat-Michigan) told Ambassador Arad to convey to the Israeli Government their concern about "the situation, which is both dangerous and ridiculous."

"Non-Jewish Congressmen were flying to Israel to defend the interests of their Jewish constituents," they said, "They might soon adopt anti-Israeli positions to protect, they will say, their Jewish electorate."

Deputy Secretary of State, John Whitehead, told Jerusalem Mayor Teddy Kollek, in Washington, on November 1988, that American Jews are undergoing a trauma caused by the Israeli coalition negotiations concerning the "Law of Return". He noted that good relations between the two countries very much depend on the existence of a common front between Israel and the American Jewish Community.

The Reform and Conservative movements in the U.S. Jewry denounced the "blackmail demands of the extremist non-Zionist Orthodox parties" in Israel. Are these U.S. movements not using "blackmail" against Israel? Are they not interfering in Israeli politics?

Minister without portfolio Avner Shaki (NRP) commented that these American Jews who flew to Israel to protest the issue of "Who is a Jew?" were just a bunch of "Reform Millionaires". He added emphatically, "I do not understand what these people have against the Israeli Law? They can keep conversion (Giyur) the way they do now in the U.S. If they don't live here, they should not tell me what to do."

Some people in Israel are disgusted with the fact that a totally religious issue such as "Who is a Jew?" is introduced into the political arena. A religious issue by which, a secular Government is either formed or toppled.

They also claim that there is no need for a Secular Government in Israel to deal with this Halachaic issue, and that it would be best if the issue is left for the Chief Rabbinate in Jerusalem.

Those who are against the amendment, in Israel, claiming that: "the amendment just isn't worth the price." They feel that the Reform and Conservative Jews in the Diaspora will weaken their identification with the State of Israel and also weaken their Jewish identity. This could lead to more intermarriages and assimilations, they believe.

From facts and figures received by Israeli Government statistics, during the year ending on December 1988, only 160 U.S. Jews per month moved to Israel. 105 were Orthodox Jews, the rest, 55, were Conservative and Reform Jews, of which only three were converted by non-Orthodox Rabbis in the U.S.

But the number of prospective convert-Olim is irrelevant. This is a matter of principle. Either we want Judaism to survive, therefore, we must live according to the Torah and stick to the Halacha or we want Judaism to die completely or turn into some Androgynous form, then we should live the Reform way.

If we decide that we want to remain original Jews, true Jews, as per our ancient tradition, and follow our ancestral path, then we should not permit "hocus-pocus" or "instant" conversion. To enter the Jewish faith quasi-conversions is not enough.

Conversion according to the Halacha is a normal, easy, standard procedure. All the Ethiopian Jews who reached Israel the last seven years have undergone it. And so did most of the Russian and Ukraine Jews.

The idea of amending the "Law of Return" in Israel has created an outpouring of anger and frustration on part of the American Jews. The U.S. Jewish leadership was caught between its constituents and the Israeli politics. The whole matter does not involve only three to ten converts a year, who want to settle in Israel, as some people believe. This is, rather, a matter of principle. Should a conversion (Giyur) be conducted according the Laws of Moses, the Halacha, as has been for the last four thousand years or according to "American-Reform Style"?

Those who want it the "American-Reform Style" are not serious, irresponsible and not loyal to their Jewish heritage.

The Reform Jews in America claim that the Orthodox Rabbis do not hold the true keys to the Jewish heritage and identity.

Who then is holding it?

The Reform Rabbis who perform "instant" conversions (Giyur), not according to the Jewish Halacha?

The Reform Rabbis who performed mixed marriages, together with the Catholic Priest or the Protestant Minister?

They are holding the true keys to Jewish heritage and identity.

A most important issue like this should not be left open. A crucial topic like this should not remain vague. It must be very clear and precise. The amendment must be performed for the benefit of Judaism and this is worth any price.

The pressure against the change in the "Law of Return" came mainly from American Jewish leaders who were either themselves married to non-Jews or who had family members who were married to non-Jews, all converted by Reform Rabbis. They just don't want to be reminded that they have "Goyim" (Gentile) in their family.

The Reform movement, the Conservative movement as well as the Reconstructionist movement, without any consultation, adopted rules, which were partially unacceptable to basic Judaism, to original Judaism and to Jewish tradition. Also unacceptable to the Jews in Israel and the rest of the World, who are loyal to the Orthodox Movement. It is inconceivable that anybody should be able to do what he wants and interprets the Jewish Halacha as he wants regarding the entry of Gentiles into the Jewish faith.

The Reform congregations are poor innocent sheep that were led astray and know very little about the issue of "Who is a Jew?"

Many expressed concern that if the "Law of Return" is amended it will have a negative effect on the immigration from the U.S., from the Soviet Union and from other Diaspora, because they believe that some of the immigrants going to Israel are not exactly "Jews according to the Halacha."

This assessment is not accurate because it has been found that the Diaspora Jews are not making Aliyah to Israel mainly because of two reasons: economical and security. Fear from unemployment, the lack of housing and fear from the fact that they or their children will have to serve in the military. The possibility that the Knesset will amend the "Law of Return" and introduce conversion according to the Halacha only, is only an additional excuse.

The majority of the United States Jews and the Jews of the rest of the world identify completely with the State of Israel and its problems, whatever they are. Only a small group in the Diaspora, mainly in the U.S.want to dictate to State Israel on ideology, religion, politics, etc., with a hint or a threat, that if Israel doesn't "behave" or comply with their demands they might stop all contributions and political support.

This small group claims that it is representing the majority of the Jews in America, which is far from being true. Is this not blackmail?

Israel is a democracy and decides on matters of ideology, religion, politics, etc., without outside pressure or "advice".

The U.S. and other Jewish communities in the world, on the merit of charity work for Israel, contributions, etc., cannot expect to decide or change Israel's laws, policies or habits.

The prevailing view in the U.S. Jewry is that the Diaspora Jews will continue to give Israel no matter what, after all the Israelis are their brothers and sisters and the Israelis know what is best for them.

One of the major Jewish immigrant groups, in the last few decades, were the Orthodox and Ultra-Orthodox, not the Reforms or Conservatives. The leaders of the Reforms and Conservatives, in America and elsewhere, have been neglecting the issue of Aliyah to Eretz Israel. Had they decided to commit themselves more to Israel, by actual immigration, moving to Israel and making it their home, may be they could have avoided the development of current argument of "Who is a Jew?"

On an average basis, over half the world Jewry is assimilated. That is why the amendment in the "Law of Return" ("Who is a Jew?") is indispensable and urgent.

The Likud Party is totally convinced that sticking to the plan of Greater Israel (Israel Ha' Shlemah) requires, and justifies, the enactment of the "Who is a Jew?" amendment even in disregard of warnings by the Israeli Ambassador to the U.S. and by American Jewish leaders, that it could result in the alienation of the U.S. Jewry and the U.S. from Israel.

The State of Israel is the state of the Jewish people, in all its pluralistic diversity and no matter where they live.

All Israelis, all Jews, even the most Haredi (Ultra Religious) factions would agree that the severance of Reconstructionist, Conservative and Reform Jewry from the body of the Jewish people, the body of the Jewish nation, would be inconceivable.

After the new Likud-Maarah coalition was formed and a new National Unity Government was established the "threat" to change the "Law of Return" has been taken off the agenda temporarily, as well as the crisis predicted. The immediate pressure for a resolution has been lifted, temporarily. But it is more than certain that the "Law of Return" will become an issue once again. A permanent solution must be found soon which will preserve the Jewish nation and keep it eternal, as was promised by the Good Lord God.

A consensus with which the Jewish people, the Jewish nation can live must be the goal. For which the Liberal factions within the Jewish community, that's the Reform, the Conservative and Reconstructionist movements must be willing to abide by the traditional Jewish Law, the Halacha (The Laws of Moses).

The Liberal factions within the Jewish community must be willing to reqire converts to follow the traditional guidelines for conversion. That is the Halacha, same as the Orthodox Jews. Leaders from all streams of Judaism must accept the Orthodox way of conversion.

"Who is a Jew?" is a very important issue that cannot be ignored or postponed for a long time. The issue cannot be circumvented. It must be dealt with in a thorough and responsible way. In the Jewish way. Yet, another important issue is the issue of who will remain Jewish in the generations ahead? This is also an important challenge that Israel has to face.

5. NOVEMBER 1988 GENERAL ELECTIONS

Speaking to the annual convention of the Israel Institute of Accountants, in Jerualem, on November 1988, three weeks safter the general elections, in Israel, Vice-Premier and Foreign Minister Shimon Peres said that, now, he was convinced for the need for direct elections for the post of prime-minister, and a sharp rise for a party to gain Knesset representation, as urgently needed first steps in electoral reform.

The introduction of direct voting for the premiership would give the prime minister the power he currently lacked, while a higher vote threshold would cut the number of small parties. Thus, he said, would be reflected in an effective government. The present system, said Peres, did not allow the formation of a government that could make tough decisions.

One wonders, if Shimon Peres would have won the elections, would he also crticize the present Israeli electoral system and urges an overhaul of that system? The answer is obvious. Now that he lost the elections, every thing is wrong.

Shimon Peres also criticized the religious parties, who, he said, did not vote in the Knesset, on the basis of political philosophies, but rather on the basis of religious considerations.

Again, one wonders how could Peres read the minds of the religious voters? Did Mr. Shimon Peres really forget that right after the elections of 1988, he himself led intensive negotiations with all the religious parties, trying to form a coalition with them, with the intent to undermine Yitzhak

Shamir, who won the elections, promising the religious parties everything, but failed.

The current system guarantees a gradual depreciation in the quality of the members of Knesset, because they are not responsible to the citizens, but to their parties and the party leadership. According to the present system, the citizens, the voters, cannot elect directly their own member of Knesset. Therefore, there is no accountability and there is no way to rectify mistakes by not re-electing the incompetent members.

Many Israelis believe that it is the system that is the source of political fragmentation, and that a change of the present electoral system is indispensable. A change of the damaging electoral system in Israel is, therefore, very urgent. This, to avoid the phenomenon of fifteen parties running in the elections and also to avoid ties. It is believed that the passage of the electoral reform bill, direct elections, would have been the beginning of responsible and responsive government.

On the other hand, to change the existing proportional representaion election system in Israel, as suggested by some members of the Hiloni/Secular parties is impractical, because it will reduce substantially, or may be even, eliminate completely the influence and the political power of the religious parties, and therefore, is not in their best interest, nor in the best interest of Israel. Many believe that the pure proportional system makes for so many complications, but still, Israel has to have some form of proportional representation.

The main purpose for changing the existing electoral system in Israel is to create a direct personal link between the Member of Knesset and thosewho put him in office, that's the voters, so that the MK will have to assume responsibility to serve, and a personal obligation to voters who meet him face to face.

Those who believe in changing the present election system in Israel claim that precious time is wasted after each election and each coalition crisis, and the small parties enjoy too much leverage, as was the case after the November 1988 elections.

Some Israelis believe that Israel has to go over to a new governmental system, a new election system, whereby the prime minister is elected directly, on a separate ticket. If he wins over fifty per cent of the votes, nationwide, he would be empowered to form his own cabinet, and would not require the initial vote of confidence in the Knesset for his cabinet, as is required today. Also, half of the Knesset seats will be allocated on a constituency basis and the others on a national basis. It is believed that such a system will make for stronger, more stable government.

The results of the elections showed very clearly a great tendency towards religion. The political leaders of the so-called secular parties must realize that the people desire Judaism. If, by chance, these leaders, by planning to institute direct elections seam to suppress the nation's desire to go back to religion, the people will most probably find another way to express themselves and fill up their spiritual needs, not necessarily always democratic. Any attempt to try to silence the religious voice will boomerang hardly.

The Israeli voter, unlike the American, has no way of dividing his vote to express the combination of hard-headedness he expects from the Likud with the sensitivity he expects from the Maarah. This is why many Israelis would have loved to adopt the American system of presidential elections and the checks and balances system.

The November 1988 elections could not have come at a worse time for the Maarah.Yitzhak Shamir had been prime minister for the last two years and had been in constant conflict with Shimon Peres. Peres was far from being popular. People "hated" Peres because his obstinacy in insisting on going to the International Conference. Then comes the Intifadah, the Palestinian uprising, and Yitzhak Rabin declares over the air, on Radio and Television, that he cannot cope with it. Thousands are thrown out of work and their Union; the Histadrut doesn't budge a finger to defend their interests. Hvrat Ha'Ovdim goes broke and so is Kupat Holim, the Sick Fund.

Inspite of all this, the Maarah came out only one Seat less than the Likud. This is something beyond comprehension. Unbelievable! This can be explained only in one way. Many of the conservative old-timers, out of habit, keep voting for the Maarah.

The secularists, members of his own party, the Maarah, have accused Peres of violating the principles of the party and the spirit of its platform. "The damage Peres did cannot be undone," they said, and added "he has supplied Mr. Shamir with what ever justification the Likud leader needed to knuckle under to Orthodox, even against his better judgement.

That the out going and future premier is not too happy to do so is plain enough. For he can readily appreciate the disastrous impact which the passage of the promised "Who is a Jew" legislation, in whichever form is, likely to have on world Jewry."

Shimon Peres has led his party, the Maarah, to four electoral defeats: In 1977, 1981, 1984 and 1988. There must have been something in the chemistry between the majority of the electorates and between Shimon Peres, who made him vitually unelectable. There is just no chemistry between them.

True, Uzi Baram had democratized the Maarah party, and except for a few top-level nominations the rest of the members have to be elcted into office. The result of this was that the Maarah party became more democratic than before, but it lost the elections to the Likud.

Disappointed from the results of the elections, disappointed from the Maarah's present leadership: Shimon Peres and Yitzhak Rabin, who couldn't win the election, the Maarah Party Secretary-General Uzi Baram characteristically straightforward, conceded that the Maarah will have to change its leadership before the next elections.

"There is no doubt that a change of personalities must take place," he said. "It may not happen immediately, but it will happen before the next elections. I think we'll know more in a week or two about whether it will happen in the short term."

But, Secretary-General Uzi Baram could be mistaken. Uzi Baram had very eager intentions to replace Shimon Peres as head of the Maarah Party. But Peres "wasn't born yesterday" and when it comes to political survival, Peres is second to none. Inspite of his loss in the elections Peres navigated skillfully Maarah's political boat and has reasserted himself, at least temporarily, as the unrivalled leader of his party. Peres was only "a hair's breadth" from forming a coalition with the left and Religious-Orthodox parties. Members of the Maarah believed that to try and topple Peres now, will not succeed, It might succeed, may be, in some future date.

There was no doubt that the violent events in Judea, Samaria and Gaza during the eleven months prior to the elections to the Twelfth Knesset had an impact on the results of the election. Many Israelis had become more realistic and moved to the right. There is no doubt that the Palestinian uprising was an important in the Israeli voters' decisions. The Israelis were already sick and tired of the continued anarchy and lawlessness, of woman and childrenkilled on the roads, of stones and Molotov-Cocktails. After forty years of independence they thought they deserved a little more security and peace of mind.

Like most people, the Israelis were not happy of the intervention of other nations in their internal affairs, especially when they told them how to vote, and no matter how friendly these "advisers" were.

During the November 1988 elections in Israel, the United States of America, the U.S.S.R., Egypt, Jordan and the PLO sided openly with the Maarah and even campaigned for the Maarah. If ever, the Americans, the Europeans, the President of Egypt, the King of Jordan or Arafat, expected to persuade the Israeli voters, they were totally wrong.

Right after the elections, a respectable member of the Maarah Party (Labor), ex- member of Knesset, Rabbi Menachem Hacohen, bluntly accused the Orthodox parties with the following words:

-It frightens me, as a religious Jew, to see the type of person who voted for Shass and Chabad, kisses the mezzuza, but goes to watch a football game on Shabbat,

-Their years in the Government and the coalition have simply earned them money. Shabbat desecration has increased, and hatred of the religious by the secular has grown.

-They don't deal with Jewish education. In education their only achievement has been to ensure the evasion from military service.

Any way, their dovishness stems from their hartred of the State of Israel. Shach would certainly agree to give away territory: He'd give away the entire state-gladly!

-Rabbi Eliezer Shach is a dove and Rabbi Ovadiah Yossef has a record of favouring territorial concessions for the sake of peace.

-David Ben Gurion, even Menachem Begin, never visited graves, as Shimon Peres went to the Baba Sali's grave.

-There has been steady erosion and the winners have been the anti-Zionist parties: Shass, Agudah and Degel Hatorah.

-They know who their supporters are and they will never antagonize them by going with Labor on the basis of territory for peace, just as they never come out really strongly against football games on the Shabbat.

-They would go with any body to get money for their yeshivas.

-I will be worried even more if the Alignment (Maarah) was in a position to set up an alliance with the Ultra-Orthodox, which would corrupt our society.

-I was appaled at the way Rabbi Ovadiah Yossef criss-crossed the country by helicopter with his curses and blessings. It was the most primitive appeal to superstition.

A religious Rabbi full of venom against the Orthodox! What a shame.

On November 21, 1988, that's Kislev 12, 5749 the twelfth Knesset convened for its first session. President Chaim Herzog opened the first session of the newly elected twelfth Knesset. President Herzog called on the one hundred and twenty Knesset members to cherish the dignity of the House and warned them that if they showed disrespect for their own institution, "your own prestige as members of the Knesset will be impaired, as well as the prestige of our democratic system in the eyes of the public."

The President added that Israel's democracy must not be taken for granted, "History has known many democratic regims that collapsed in times of crisis." He called on the nation to "obey the precept of tolerance" and warned that "we dare not accusing ourselves to a cheap and violent form of public and political debate characterized by slander and abusive language." Herzog said that parlimentarians dared not be oblivious to the growing concern over the future character and course of the State.

"There is concern lest we lose the Zionist content of our renewed nationhood in our ancestral land. There is concern regarding the freedom of the individual and his rights in the State. There is concern regarding the unity of the Jewish people."

In a reference to mounting anti-Arab feeling, he said: We must denounce attempts to whip up feelings against the minorities among us, without distinction between the law-abiding and the violators of the law. The injunction to respect minority rights occurs thirty-six times in the Bible," he reminded the Knesset. The founding fathers of Israel "repeatedly emphacized that the State would be judged by its relationship to its Arab-minority."

President Herzog then called on Yair Sprinzak ("Moledet"), the oldest (76 years old) member of the House, to make his declaration of loyalty and chair the session.

Yair Sprinzak, son of the late Yosef Sprizak (Mapai), the Speaker of the first Knesset in 1948-1952, conducted the first session of the twelfth Knesset very gracefully by expounding his political philosophy. Some of the Maarah members of the Knesset, like Michael Zohar, Haim Ramon, Rafi Edri, Ariye "Lova" Eliav, Moshe Shahal and Avraham Burg, as well as all the Left parties and the Arab parties' members, constantly disturbed his speech. What was to have been a festive inauguration of the newly elected legislature was marred by the deliberate, intentional, well-planned shameful disturbance of the Arab and Left-wing members of the Knesset who protested noisily. Shulamit Aloni, Yossi Sarid, Ran Cohen, Daddi Zucker, Avrum Burg, Ariye "Lova" Eliav, Abdul-Wahab Darawsha and Muhammad Miari staged a demonstrative, mini-walkout to the sides and isles of the chamber. It was clear that they set out deliberately to spoil what should have been a dignified ceremonial occasion. The silly left-wing behavior was completely out of place.

The next step was the pledge of allegiance. The chairman MK Yair Sprinzak instructed the members of Knesset that all they should say as they were called to pledge allegiance was:"I do pledge". A hush came over the chamber as the roll call started. Three names were called by alphabetical order and it seemed that all went well. Then came the turn of Mapam's Haim "Jumas" Oron who sprang to his feet and shouted: "I pledge to keep the laws of the State of Israel and to fight against racism." He read his declaration from a prepared piece of paper. "That is not the proper form. You, Mr. MK, have not pledged allegiance," countered Sprinzak.

And thus it went on, through the CRM, Mapam, DFPE, PLP, and Arab Democratic Party lists, with each MK making his pledge to combat racism.

Then came the turn of Avraham (Avrum) Burg, the son of Joseph Burg, ex-Minister of Interior and ex-Head of the NRP. Avrum Burg, one of the two skull-capped Maarah members rose to say:"I pledge to remain faithful to the Torah, which commands us to refrain from oppressing the stranger, for we our selves were strangers in Egypt!" But that formulation, too, was ruled out of order.

The roll call over, Sprinzak moved on to the next business of the House, that's the election of the Speaker.

Ronni Milo (Likud) rose to propose Dov Shilansky. There was consternation in the Maarah, and first Shachal and then Edri tried to forstall a vote. When Sprinzak asked if there were more proposals, the Maarah said they had no other candidate. As Edri again sought to delay a vote, and the House seemed to become close to ungovernable, Moshe Nissim, the Finance Minister requested permission to mount the podium. The left, he said, amid absolute silence, had shamed the Knesset. How would the country's youth judge what had happened in this session?

It was quite legal to vote for a Speaker. If Sprinzak truly respected the Knesset's honour he had no choice but to call the vote without further ado and more scandals.

At this point, Maarah's David Libai stood up to propose that Shlomo Hillel be Speaker for another term. But he was outvoted.

At first, the left-wing members of Knesset together with the Arab members of the Knesset planned to boycott the session, but then, they changed their minds and turned up to ensure their right to vote for a Speaker. Their use of the declaration of allegiance formula for political protest statements was childish and undignified. It showed bad taste and immature politicians. They came with their "tails between their legs" begging for the right to repeat their declarations of allegiance, this time, properly. Without the pledge of allegiance they are not members of Knesset, and therefore, do not have the right to vote or to take part in the election of the new Speaker for the House. They also made it impossible for the Maarah to obtain a postponement of the vote.

Dov Shilansky of the Likud was elected Speaker of the twelfth Knesset by 64 to 55. He was supported by the entire right wing and Orthodox block after a failed last-minute attempt by the Maarah's Moshe Shachal and Rafi Edri to postpone the election of a Speaker.

Everybody agreed that the twelvth Knesset had an undignified start.

Two days later, fifty residents of the Yemin Orde religious youth Aliyah village, near Haifa, presented President Herzog with a petition signed by five hundred and thirty two pupils, immigrants from sixteen countries, who were dismayed by the MK's behavior in the Knesset.

Reading from the parchment, Ayah Brachah of Maalot said that Jewish youth were determined to change the "reprehensible norms" that had taken root in the Knesset. "Education does not end in the classroom teaching about democracy. We are watching you (MKs) and we expect something better.

You degraded our flag."

President Herzog praised the pupils for their initiative and suggested that if there were a system of direct elections, such shameful spectacles would not be repeated. Perhaps, he said, some good would eventually come of the disgrace in the Knesset.

Bet Hanassi, the President's House has received numerous calls from citizens protesting against the MKs' behavior. Herzog said he was sure the majority of the country's citizens, young and old, shared the pupils' "disgust" at the MKs' disruptions. Soon before the MKs began shouting and walking out, over a speech by Acting Speaker, Yair Sprinzak of Moledet, Herzog had advised them to honour the Knesset, if they showed disrespect for it, he warned, their "own prestige would be impaired, as would the prestige of our democratic system."

Most of the Israelis in the Knesset and at home were ashamed of the foreign dignitaries who occupied the balcony and the whole world that were following this "circus" on television.

After the elections of November 1988, to the twelfth Knesset, Ariel (Arik) Sharon played a key role in coalition talks, prior to the formation of the new Government headed by Yitzhak Shamir. Sharon had special relationship with the Orthodox (Haredi) leaders. Sharon was the most qualified person in the Likud Party to handle negotiation with the Orthodox. Sharon had also a previous experience of coalition talks, when he initiated the combination of the Gahal Party and the Liberal Party to form the Likud Party, several years ago.

The problem ahead will probably be, among others, coping with a world granting increasing recognition to the PLO, more terror and more intifadah. Bush coming to term with the Soviets, misunderstanding with the Diaspora, economic mess encouraged by the Histadrut and the Maarah, more strikes, etc. Life will not be easy for the next Premier, whoever he may be.

The Likud and the right never defined the Religious-Orthodox parties as non-Zionist. Yet, when they were wealing and dealing with the Orthodox parties with the intention to form a narrow coalition with them, this, inspite of the fact that Yitzhak Shamir and the Likud party received the President's mandate to form the Government, suddenly the Orthodox parties became "Kosher" for the Maarah, suddenly they were no longer non-Zionist.

The increasing involvement of the Orthodox parties in the Israeli politics and the affars of state will gradually bring them closer to the Secularists. The differences between the two parties will derease, the gap will narrow and suspicion will diminish or even vanish. They will get to know each other better. Contribute to each other. Influence each other. Both the Secularists and the Orthodox will benefit from it.

History sometimes repeats itself. It is quite possible that, if Yitzhak Shamir came up with a suitable offer to Yitzhak Rabin, Yitzhak Rabin and his "hawkish" supporters in the Maarah will desert the Maarah, form a new party, as the late General Moshe Dayan did, and join a coalition under the Likud, for Rabin is no less a pragmatist than Peres.

Because of the political manipulation of the Maarah, trying to steal away some Haredi (Orthodox) parties (like Agudat Yisrael, etc.) from the

Likud, Shamir couldn't form his Government in 21 days and needed some more time. President Herzog extended his mandate and gave Shamir 21 additioal days.

The regular Israeli citizen rightfully suspected that the long political negotiations and bargaining between the different parties trying to form a new Government were no longer about ideas, but about jobs.

On Wednesday, November 30, 1988 (Kislev 21, 5749), the Maarah Bureau rejected its top leadership's (Shimon Peres and Yitzhak Rabin) bid for broad-Government negotiations with the Likud. The majority of the Bureau was not prepared to sacrifice the party's identity by forming coalition with the Likud. They preferred to stay in opposition to the Likud-Right-Religious narrow coalition and hold the option for a future political alternative open.

The President of Israel is the apolitical head of state and represents the sovereignty of the state and its mission on this earth and history. He is also responsible for the unity of the Jewish people. The President of Israel lacks executive power, which is in the hands of the prime minister and the Government.

Inspite of the fact that the President of Israel does not interfere in Political matters, President Herzog made it an exception when he requested Shimon Peres to go back to his party the Maarah, and ask them to change their decision of November 30 and try to form a coalition with the Likud, because, that is what the Israeli voter really wanted (40:39).

President Herzog was also worried about the current situation (economy, unemployment, Arab uprising, etc.) and believed that in order to cope with the situation the country needed badly a stable National Unity Government like the one it had before the elections of November 1st.

Contemplating a tie, a hung Parliament (Knesset), the President decided to intervene. Therefore, it was President Herzog who revived the atmosphere of negotiations between the Likud and the Maarah, after the "compliments" they gave each other during the elections campaign.

Though the president considers himself the spokesman for Israel's higher interests, the Israelis still remember Herzog's Maarah background, and some may suspect him that he is depriving the Likud of the fruits of victory by calling for a change in the "rules".

Deputy Prime Minister David Levi was persistently for the establishment of National Unity Government like many others, he belived that only abroad coalition can cope with problems Israel was facing. Levi was disgusted of the humiliation that the large parties have inflicted upon themselves by courting the small parties mainly the Ultra-Orthodox (Haredi) parties.

David Levi was appointed to lead the Likud negotiation team with other parties, but when Shamir refused to commit into accepting Levi's request for the Foreign Affairs portfolio, Levi reportedly telephoned Rabbi Ovadiah Yossef, the political patron of Shass and warned him that Shamir's promises are not to be trusted.

Levi insisted that a few days earlier Shamir promised him the Foreign Ministry folio. Naturally, this scandalous incident caused a deep rift between Levi and Shamir.

It will not be the first time in history that when a large party like the Maarah loses power it breaks up into pieces never to recover again. The risk of Dissolution of the Maarah party through the loss of power to opposition is as great as joining a coalition with the Likud, or, under the Likud. If the Maarah will decide to form a coalition Government with the Likud it will be as a result of the unprecedented interference of President Herzog, who, thus, saved the Maarah Party from degenerating on the opposition benches.

At a meeting of Maarah's "Sareinu", the forum of Maarah ministers, Defense Minister Yitzhak Rabin angrily accused a new member of the Knesset, Yossi Beilin (Maarah), for making a deal with Agudat Yisrael and signing a document with Rabbi Shmuel Halpert, MK (Agudah), by which, under certain conditions, the Agudah will be ready to back the Maarah Party. According to Rabin, the agreement with the Agudah was signed behind the backs of the Maarah's ministers, and while Yitzhak Shamir was having his coalition talks with the endorsement of President Herzog. An underhand attempt to interfere with Shamir's coalition talks. This agreement with the Agudah was concealed from the Maarah Party Bureau, which only hours earlier had rejected Rabin's plea to go with Shamir (Likud). Beilin's agreement with the Agudah persuaded bureau members to vote against a broad Government Some of them still had the illusion that the Maarah could demand that Shimon Peres be allowed to share the premiership with Yitzhak Shamir. Another Rotation.

The description "Peres's Poodle", attached by Rabin in an early morning radio interview to MK Yossi Beilin, showed the grudge that Rabin still hold for Peres, as well as an expression of the enmity that still existed between the Maarah's two divided ideological camps, the camp of Rabin and the camp of Peres. Beilin was Peres's aid at the Prime Minister's office during the years 1984-1986 and at the Foreign Ministery during the years 1986-1988.

Rabin also detested Yossi Beilin because he represented the ideological left wing of the party, the super doves, which prefer talks with the PLO to negotiations with the Likud.

But less than twenty four hours after Rabin's accusation of Beilin, meaning Peres, he and Peres could be seen in close conference on the proper strategies needed to win over the Central Committee. Birds of feather stick together; both Peres and Rabin knew well that if they didn't hang together they would hang separately. They needed each other in the coalition government. They need each other in the opposition where Uzi Baram, Mota Gur and others are waiting them in the "corner".

Opposition will bring a major revolution in the Maarah, and can also spark the long awaited ideological battle between Peres and Rabin.

On December 8, 1988 (Kislev 29, 5749), the Maarah's Central Committee voted for entering negotiations with the Likud on forming a broad government, according to the proposal by Party Chairman Shimon Peres and the number 2 man in the Maarah, Defense Minister Yitzhak Rabin. This was also a vote of confidence in Peres and Rabin and nullified the Party Bureau's vote of November 30, 1988 (Kislev 21, 5749).

After the vote, Secretary-General Uzi Baram called joining a broad coalition with the Likud "running amok with no reason into a government headed by Yitzhak Shamir. The argument is not for joining or not joining the government, but between hope and despair, between accepting Maarah's certain decline and the belief that it can be an alternative.

What good did the previous national unity government, in the years 1986 and 1987 do? The Maarah will become a permanent satellite of the Likud, like the National Religious Party and like the General Zionists (Liberals), and we saw what became of them," Said Baram.

On the other hand, Shamir was pleased with the Maarah's decision, because it opens the way to the broad-based government that he wanted since the election, as it will bring the country a quiet and stable economy with the minimum amounts of strikes and the cooperation of the Histadrut, the Union.

Speculators believe that it is very important for the survival of the Maarah that they grab hold of the Finance portfolio so as to save Koor, Kupat Holim, Hevrat Ha'Ovdim, and the Kibbutzim, from financial disaster. It is vital for the future of the Maarah that these institutions be resuscitated and preserved.

If the Maarah will eventually join the Likud in a coalition with the substantial amount of debts they (the Maarah) have to cover, it will be wise if they do not take the Treasury Folio, because, it will be obvious that they do it for party interests rather than national interests and will have to pay for it dear during the next elections, in 1992.

"The Likud Can" was the slogan of the Likud Party in the election campaign, which meant, that, the Likud can handle the political situation, the Likud can handle the outside pressure, the Likud can handle the security problems, the Likud can handle the Palestinian-Arab uprising, the Likud can crush the Arab Intifadah, the Likud can take care of the bad economy, the Likud can take care of the heavy unemployment, the Likud can take care of the problem "Who is a Jew", the Likud can take care of all these alone, without the help of the Maarah, without the support of the Labor.

The Israeli public believed, trusted the Likud promises and gave it its vote. The Likud has been given the majority. The Likud won the election. The Likud had the opportunity to carry out its promises, to carry out its policies, together with the right block and the religious block as partners, in a "narrow" coalition.

Finally, after so many years the Likud have become independent from the Maarah and can carry out its plans, its ideology, its platform. But instead, the Likud had suddenly, for no reason whatsoever, lost it self-confidence. The Likud have "chickened out", afraid to act alone, and sought very eagerly the partnership with the Maarah. Mr. Yitzhak Shamir, the out going Premier and the future Premier seeks to form a large coalition with the Maarah, very similar to the National Unity Government which he presently heads with all the defects and heart brakes. This inspite of the bad experience he just had with the Maarah, for four years. Yitzhak Shamir was afraid to face the problems ahead, alone, without the Maarah on his side.

Yitzhak Shamir got the "Height Fear" which reminds of Premier Menachem Begin, when he reached power on May 1977, had the "Dayan Syndrom" when he appointed General Moshe Dayan (Maarah) Foreign Minister. Gave up the Foreign Ministry to an ex-member of the Maarah, his greatest competitors.

Shamir needed the 'broad coalition" with the Maarah so that he could withstand better the outside pressure from the Reforms and Conservatives in the U.S.A. when trying to implement the amendment of the Law of Return, that's "Who is a Jew?" and also to nutralize the Union, the

Histadrut and avoid series of Labor strikes and increase in salary demands which could bring back the inflation chaos. Likud sources said that Yitzhak Shamir was convinced that only broad government could withstand international pressure to negotiate with the PLO. Shamir believed that a narrow right-wing government could face constant pressure, with "the entire world" supporting the large opposition led by the Maarah. The same sources said that Shamir was also worried by the recent statements made by Rabbi Eliezer Shach, who welcomed the U.S. decision to talk to the PLO because it could help avoid blood-shed. Shamir feared that under pressure, Degel Hatorah and Shass, who consider Rabbi Shach a spiritual leader, might bolt his government and transfer their allegiance to the Maarah. Shamir was resolved to keep Shimon Peres out of the Foreign Office, where his diplomatic statements, contradicting the Likud policies would be damaging.

Shamir's main goal in working hard for National Unity Government, to show the world that the Israeli public is united, speaks with one voice and is determined to fight the idea of an independent Palestinian-Arab state on its territories. Also to show the world that it cannot profit from the Arabs at Israel's expense.

What expedited the positive conclusion of the broad coalition negotiations between the Likud and the Maarah was the fact that the Maarah accepted the Likud's conditions:

1. The Maarah will not receive the Foreign Ministry and will not interfere in matters of foreign affairs
2. Israel will resist the establishment of an additional Palestinian-Arab in the Gaza Strip and the territories between Israel and Jordan, that's Judea and Samaria or the West Bank
3. Israel will not negotiate with the PLO.

Three necessary tools with which Shamir and Arens will be able to oppose, on behalf of the two great parties, the Likud and the Maarah, any foreign policy that is dangerous to the interests of Israel. Tools with which Israel could speak outwardly, to the world, with one voice.

It was difficult to explain how a party (Maarah) that advocates negotiations with the PLO joins a government that its platform rejects any negotiations with PLO. The broad government is also based on a compromise between the Likud and the Maarah.

The common denominator rather than the dividing prevailed and brought the parties together.

Judging from Isreal's past experience, the continuation of a so-called National Unity Government between two major opposing parties,the Likud and the Maarah is admittedly a bad choice. It is a formula for continued governmental paralysis. But, as some Israelis believe, that sort of bad is infinitely better than the alternative of a Likud led coalition with the right and the religious.

Same as all the Israeli governments didn't know what to do with the military victories and wasted them, so, it seems, the Likud party's will to govern is inferior to its capability to win the election.

When finally the opportunity arrived, instead of grasping it with two hands and rule the country it preferred to rehabilitate the losing Maarah, its old rival. A totally irrational attitude derived from some kind of inferiority complex towards the Maarah.

The Maarah had no choice but to join Shamir's government. If they stayed outside, with the debts they had, they would be ruined. Therefore, the Maarah had no choice but to consent to exchange its peace plan for a mess of economic-aid pottage for curing Histadrut industries and enterprises.

The few days of uncertainty, when it was not clear yet whether the Maarah will or will not join Shamir's government, showed exactly what would happen to the party if they stayed outside. Instead of preparing an alternative to the Likud, they quarreled with each other on internal alternatives, they were busy with internal intrigues, trying to undermine each other, which climaxed with the resignation of the Secretary General Uzi Baram, who opposed Peres's decision to join Shamir's coalition.

Apart from the extremely heavy debts and the questions of national policy the Maarah had serious reasons to prefer Shamir's government.

In this new situation the National Unity Government continues to survive. After All, a lot of people are happy with this arrangement. Peres can continue to present himself as a man of peace and talk all he likes abroad about how he is fighting for it, if only the Likud.Meanwhile he needs to do nothing, concede nothing. For Peres, Unity Government is the best bargain. It assures his continued leadership of the Maarah and Postpones the Showdown with Rabin, his strongest competitor.

Yitzhak Shamir, at first, created the impression of being ready to give the Religious Party everything they demanded-to win their support to get the President to name him to form a government: then after receiving the mandate from the President to form a government Shamir did everything in his power to draw the Maarah into a broad coalition. It was his prerogative.

Shamir might have sacrificed his credibility with the Religious, but Shamir will be seventy-seven years old in the next elections, in 1992 and it is very likely that he will not run again.Likud campaign managers were worried that the Likud might lose the next elections if the party fulfilled its agreement and promises to the religious parties, because, after all, the majority of the Likud supporters are secularists and not religious.

Many in Israel believed, mainly the secularists that during the coalition negotiations, the religious parties, separately and collectively, exaggerated in their demands on matters of principle, in hard cash and in ministerial seats. It was believed that their demands were far beyond what their limited strength justified. After all the four religious parties won only fifteen per cent of the vote, their stable proportion in previous votes up to the 1981 election.

"It has taken a long time," stated a secular Israeli, "but the important thing is that we have a broad government and have not given in to religious blackmail."

Certain people in Israel have accused the religious parties for extortion, blackmailing and selling their political support to those who pay more. At least everybody acknowledged that the religious parties were using these monies to maintain existing schools, building new Yeshivot, on education. With these monies they support orphanages, homes for the elderlies, philanthropic institutions, etc. So what is wrong with this?

Other parties are also doing it. That's politics. Only they do not make contributions to philanthropic institutions. They make contributions to their own pockets.

"We have been tricked and we have been cheated. The religious sector has always been discriminated against and it seems that it always will be," said an Orthodox man when he saw on television Shamir's broad coalition government. It should not surprise anyone that the religious parties which worked hard prior and during the elections for their principles have settled so soberly for their bread-and-butter, day-to-day interests. Politicians learn very quickly not to bear grudges. Politicians also learn very quickly not to count on promises given by other politicians. They know very well that after the elections, first thing to do is, to salvage whatever they could from the wreckage.

The religious parties understood that it is more efficient to sit inside than stay outside. It is a vital stake in sitting inside, so that they can watch over the religious status quo.

The religious parties also understood that since the amendment to the Law of Return has small prospect to receive a majority in this Knesset their task was, at least, to hold the big parties, the Likud and the Maarah, to their promises with regard to the Enabling Law (Hasmacha) whereby all coversions conducted abroad receive the endorsement of the rabbinate in Israel.

The religious parties understood that they have to join the coalition also for the sake of observing that the budgets on religious matters remain in their former levels and are not reduced.

Both the Likud and the Maarah feel more comfortable having the religious parties inside the coalition than wandering around free, outside, cold and hungry.

It is a lie to claim that the religious parties tried to play the two big parties, the Likud and the Maarah, off against each other. For that, the two big parties didn't need any help.

Israel that wants to save its bad "socialitic" economy, finally realized that it could be done only by adopting a western capitalistic type of economy and by encouraging free enterprize. Therefore, one sometimes wonders if by nominating Shimon Peres as Finance minister, Shamir didn't make a terrible mistake. Shimon Peres, who was born and raised in the socialistic school that brought complete bankruptcy to the economy of the country as well as over one hundred thousand people unemployed.

The new broad government will have to handle two important, top priority issues: the impressive PLO successful propaganda offensive in the area of foreign policy and the economic recession with the great unemployment. It will be a hindrance and obstacle to the required amendment of the Law of Return (Who is a Jew). The worse thing that the Maarah can do in the new Shamir's government is block the "Who is a Jew" amendment, that's kill it. To most Israelis this is something unforgivable. To survive, the Maarah had to accept the inevitable. In reurn for continued economic aid to its hard-pressed institutions and enterprises it had to give up its foreign policy initiatives. In teaming with Shamir and the Likud, Peres has irrevocably blurred Maarah's ideological distinction. Ideologically the Maarah had degenerated completely. It seemed that the whole Labour movement had reached the end of the road. The Maarah is dead and living in the Unity Government.

In the Maarah no one really believed Shimon Peres that the party did not lose the local elections. Several members in the Maarah denounced his attempt to sweep this defeat under the carpet. Responsible members in the Maarah took this defeat as a vote of no-confidense in the Maarah. Several Maarah members saw the handwriting on the wall several weaks before the election, though not imagining the full extent of the defeat. They blamed the Maarah ministers, mainly Peres and Rabin for the defeat. The cause, they believed, was entering the coalition government.

They believed that the Maarah ministers yielded to vested-interest groups, such as the Kibbutzim, the Moshavim, the Histadrut, Kupat Holim, Koor, Sollel Boneh, etc. who wanted to install Peres in the Treasury, expecting him to pay out their enormous debts.

The Maarah had reconciled itself to Likud policy, accepting the Likud's foreign affairs and defense policy in return for money.

To ignore the political meaning of the results of the 1989 municipal elections would be a great mistake for the Maarah. The Israeli citizen is very politically conscientious. Life made him a "political animal". Therefore, inspite of the fact that the elections were for the local governments there is no doubt that the Israeli voter took into consideration his political affiliation as well. This, in addition to his liking to a particular candidate in his town.

The Israeli citizen still feels that the Maarah Party is guilty for the nation's difficulties and can no longer fathom its behaviour and the personal examples of its leaders.

The Likud had another convincing victory. The Israelis, as we have seen time and again, want Likud.

The Maarah admitted that the Likud has just won a resounding vote of confidence. The results reflected a strong pro-Likud sentiment, which was sweeping the country. The voters were not only interested in garbage collection, sewage removal, and sanitation or sidewalks cleanliness. The voter was interested in ending the intifada, in getting rid of the Arabs, in the future of his children.

One should also admit that the Likud chalked up these successes despite low voter turnout. Had there been a higher turnout, its performance would have been much more impressive.

The municipal election victory deepened Likud's roots in the people. Shamir's government is strong and stands on two legs-central and local.

The results of the municipal elections with an almost landslide victoty of the Likud was not accidental. It reflected the Israelis thinking, the Israelis logic. The Likud was turning into Israel's main rulling party, same as the Mapai-Maarah was for several decades.

During the elections, in Israel and in the U.S., on November 1988, in general, a peaceful atmosphere prevailed over the planet Earth.

The U.S. economy "seemed" fine, though no longer competitive (Japan flooded the world market with cheaper products: Mazda, Toyota, Honda, Subaru, Sony, Sanyo, Nikon, etc.).

Same as Japan, China started flooding the World markets with cheap merchandize The Soviets were out of Afghanistan, hopefully for good and not to return. An ideal détente between the two Superpowers. The U.S. and the Soviets were "destroying" their missiles. In the Persian Gulf Iraq and Iran recently signed a cease-fire agreement. Angola, Namibia Cyprus and Cambodia finally became quiet. Morocco and the Polysario have come to an agreement.

Yet, tension still prevailed in several places: Northern Ireland, South Africa, Spain (the Basque), South America, Sari-Lanka and the Middle East.

A poll on the eve of the National Democratic Convention in Atlanta, Georgia, showed a strong support for the creation of a Palestinian homeland in Judea, Samaria and the Gaza Strip. Over 70 percent of the 4,000 delegates were in favor of "giving the Palestinians a homeland in the West Bank and Gaza," Forty percent of the 4,000 delegates were in favor of cutting aid to Israel. This is exactly Jesse Jackson's proposition.

On September 1988, in Baltimore, Democratic presidential candidate Michael Dukakis has flatly endorsed Israel's "undivided control of Jerusalem" and has pledged to move the U.S. Embassy there. "I can only state", said Dukakis, "what I think has been traditional American policy on this issue, and that is that we accept the determination of the host country as to what their capital is."

Mr. Dukakis also added that: "I don't support an international conference that is designed to impose a settlement on Israel'

George and Barbara Bush, the Republican Party, made more than a token effort to get the American Jews to cross over from their support of Michael Dukakis and the Democrates. The Republicans knew well enough that the road to the American Jewish vote ran through Jerusalem.

There couldn't be any significant movement in the Middle Eastern diplomacy during the period before the elections in the U.S. and Israel. Politically everything froze. A pre-election paralysis prevailed.

Politics is the drive to power, and in order to reach this goal certain compromises, sometimes, must be made, ideological compromises, moral compromises are sometimes unavoidable.

In order to receive the president's nod when the time comes to form the next government, both the Likud and the Maarah felt that they needed more votes than those of their supporters. Both the Likud and the Maarah worked to secure also support of the floating votes.

In politics, during all the generations, people had changed their ideology and even crossed lines. Which is legitimate. But, if somebody changed his mind or crossed lines in return for money or bribery, this is corruption and illegal.

Some Knesset members were prepared to change party in return for political favors. Naturally a corrupt practice.

Corrupt and unfair, because they were elected to the Knesset not individually but according to their place on a party list. They did not "own" their seat and therefore should not be allowed to sell it. This practice has exposed the shortcomings of the system. An overhaul of the system will serve to reduce such abuses.

There is a large gap between party platform and government policy. Even if a party does win the election, it can only govern with a coalition of other parties, and then the coalition, not the platform dictates the government policy.

In Israel's first eight Knesset elections, the issue was to whom Labor- or its Mapai antecedent-would have to take into the government coalition it would form. There were never any thoughts that the Right might force Labor into the Opposition.

The election of 1977, which brought Menahem Begin and the Likud to power, was decided by a few seats. The same was true of the 1981 election, in which the Likud had a 1-3 vote majority coalition in Knesset seats between the two camps.

Usually, a change in government occurs when the majority of the voters believe that the existing government is incompetent. The reaction to such an incompetent government is "Kick the bums out!"

This is exactly what happened in 1977, when the Likud replaced the Maarah.

The victory of the Likud ended the Labor hegemony of more than half a century (that period includes Labor-Mapai's control of the pre-State Zionist institutions)

The 1977 political upheaval was one of the most welcomed things to happen to the Israelis and Israeli history.

Finally, after twenty-nine years in opposition, on May 15, 1977, the Likud Party headed by Menahem Begin won the general elections and formed a government. It was the first time since the establishment of Israel, on May 14, 1948, that the Mapai/Maarah Party could'nt form a government.

Ezer Weizmann, the nephew of the first president of Israel, Chaim Weizmann was invited, on December 1969, to join the Likud Party. Ezer Weizmann headed the election campaign of the Likud Party and the Likud Party came out victorious. The first time in twenty-nine years.

Mapai/Maarah were in power for twenty-nine years, since the foundation of State of Israel, and many more years prior to that, and did not permit access to anybody who belonged to the Likud (Herouth) Party, to high government office, so that the Likud did not have a chance to train a cadre ready for this day and capable to take over all the top government offices. To avoid administrative chaos, Menahem Begin, the Likud, kept the Maarah members in their positions.

The Likud higher administrative echelons, like Cabinet Ministers, members of Knesset, Ambassadors, etc. were good, competent people, but in the level of governmental heads of Departments, public administration, Chairman in Board of Directors, etc., the Likud had a noticeable shortage of manpower. Therefore, the Likud had to allow into its ranks even people who were not from the Likud "Fighting Family" (members of Etzel and Lehi, who fought the British out of the country), like: Ezer Weizmann, Professor Shaveh, Michael Bruno, etc. The deficiency, the lack in manpower was sometimes discouraging.

The Clerical positions in the National Government, Local Government (Municipality, City Hall), Histadrut, Post Offices, etc., were filled with members of the Maarah Party. The Likud just couldn't replace them. The Likud didn't have a candidate to the Presidency and came up with Professor Shaveh, somebody who lived in Paris and nobody in Israel ever heard of him. Yitzhak Navon, from the Maarah, was chosen. The Likud put Simcha Ehrlich, Yitzhak Modai and Moshe Nissim, all three from the Liberal Party, as Finance Ministers, because they didn't have a candidate. They put Menahem Savidor from the Liberal Party as Chairman of the

Knesset. The Likud didn't have a serious candidate to head the National Bank of Israel. Michael Bruno, not a member of the Likud was chosen. They didn't have a candidate to the Chairmanship of the Knesset and Shlomo Hillel from the Maarah was chosen. At this and lower levels, the human resource of the Likud was poor. So they kept using the "good" services of the Maarah. The Likud had over fifty percent of the votes and couldn't staff the important positions. The Likud had people without the adequate training, without the adequate experience, incompetent, and this was one of their greatest failures.

On May 1977, Time Magazine informed its readers that Israel had just elected a "war-monger" as Prime Minister. This "war-monger" was Menahem Begin. Time Magazine was not alone to express displeasure to the result of the Israeli elections.

There is absolutely no reason for panic or hysteria over the Likud bloc's victory (World Affaire, Newsweek, May 30, 1977).

The Likud's members are normal, down-to-earth people. Menahem Begin is a most intelligent, honest, wise and straightforward person. He is not a terrorist but a freedom fighter and founding father that chased the British out of the Land of Israel just as Americans, like George Washington, once chased them from America.

The Israelis, like other democratic peoples, have the right to run their politics freely and without outside interference. After eight terms of Labor Party rule and a couple of "Water-Gates" of their own, the Israeli wanted a change and got it.

The policy of the Likud Block is very clear: Israel will not give any land that is given title to, in the Bible.

Unfortunately, the Labor/Maarah Party didn't have the courage to take such a stand. Rather, it presented plans that would never work.

The U.S.-Israeli relations will continue to be as good as they have been or even better.

Hopefully, as a friendly gesture to the New Israeli Government, the U.S. will, finally, move its

Embassy from Tel-Aviv to Jerusalem, the Capital, as promised.

Menahem Begin supported the Sepharadim, the downtrodden Jews from Arab countries who were ignored by the Mapai/Maarah/Labor Party, which governed modern Israel for its first decades, and were considered second-rate citizens.

The victory in 1977 of the Likud, which was riding a tide of Sephardi resentment at playing "Second Israel" to the Ashkenazis' "First", marked the turning point in the Sephardi self-image. It was then Prime Minister Menahem Begin who sharpened this resentment by referring to the kibbutzniks as millionaires with swimming pools-clearly settling them apart from the residents of the neighboring, economicall-distressed towns.

When the Likud won the elections, the first time, in 1977, the Maarah were in a shock, they felt deceived. Somebody has stolen away "Their State". There was an "evolution" in the laws of nature. They just couldn't believe this could happen. It was probably some kind of an accident. For the Maarah it was a nightmare. They hoped it is temporary and that they will soon gain back their power. But it was wishful thinking, because the Likud had also very deep roots in this country (Israel) and wouldn't give up easily. Their roots were: the Bible, the philosophy of Greater Israel (Eretz Israel Ha'shlemah) and the philosophy of Zeev Zabotinsky. The Israelis were already tired of the Socialists and their system of Government and needed a change. For them twenty-nine years of socialism was more than enough.prior to the elections of November 1988 (Heshvan5749) in Israel, and since the establishment of the State of Israel, in 1948, it was for the first time that the Maarah Party couldn't bribe its voters before the elections. The Treasury, this time, was in the hands of the Likud Party, and Minister Moshe Nissim was handling the Treasury in a very responsible way.

As the November 1988 elections were approaching in Israel, voters were sharply divided over the issue of "Transfer" or "Population Displacement", over the future of Judea, Samaria and the Gaza Strip, the so-called "Occupied Territories" and the Jewish settlements there and over the idea of continued Israeli administration of the Palestinian-Arab population,

According to the latest poll conducted by the Continuing Survey, which was founded in 1967 by the Israeli Institute of Applied Social Research and the Smart Family Foundation Communications Institute of the Hebrew University in Jerusalem, the attitudes towards the territories related to political ideology. The electorate, was as sharply divided by these issues as it was along lines of age and ethnicity. Hawkish attitudes identify supporters of the Right (Likud, Hatechiyah, Religious parties, Kach) as strongly as did their youth (under 45) and their father's country of origin (Afro-Asian). By the same token, the dovishness of Left-leaning voters (Labor, Mapam, CRM) was as sure an indication of their plans for voting behavior, as was their age (over 45) and Western origin.

While the population as a whole splitted almost evenly on issues, such as whether to continue Jewish settlements (Hitnahalut) in the territories, and whether to return at least some part of the West Bank in exchange for Peace, analysis of those reporting their voting intentions in late June 1988, revealed that fully 80 per cent of the hawks, on both issues, supported the Likud and its satellites and 80 per cent of the doves supported Labor.

Support for the two blocs divided almost as sharply on whether to bring the Arabs to leave the territories. Some 60 per cent of those intending to vote Likud and other Right parties chose the "Transfer" option in reply to questions on how to maintain a Jewish and democratic state if the occupation continues, Only 30 per cent chose this option among intending voters of the Left. The option of relinquishing the territories to maintain a Jewish and democratic state was chosen by over half of the Left-leaning voters and by only 10 per cent of those on the Right.

Supporters of the Satellite parties on each side were more unanimous in their options that supporters of the two-dominent parties, but this difference were mere marked in the Left.

While ethnicity was powerfully related to political inclinations, it did not overpower the influence of ideology. Taken together, both ethnicity and ideology appear about equally influential on the feeling of the "closeness" to one of the camps. For example, among voters of Sephardi origin (born in Africa or Asia or whose father was born there), 80 per cent of the hawkish majority felt close to parties of the Right, but less than half of the Sephardim with dovish views felt close to the Right. On the other hand, more than 80 per cent of the dovish Ashkenazim (born in Eastern Europe, in the West or their fathers were born there) felt close to the Left parties, compared with less than half of the Ashkenazim with hawkish views.

The National UnityGovernment, in Israel, with its built-in stalemate, established after the election tie in 1984, was a weak government, with very little achievements. The two parties forming the coalition, the Likud and the Maarah, with their totally different ideologies and platforms, were too clumsy and couldn't manipulate. A government that broke in disfunctioning.

The greatest failure of the Unity Government, which ruled Israel from 1984 until 1988, was the fact that, not a single settlement was founded, in Israel, during these four years. Unfortunately for Israel, the Likud yielded to the Maarah policy and dictate. The National Unity Government was detrimental to Israel and its image in the world. In 1988 most of the Israelis felt that they were approaching the moment of truth with regard to the main issue in the national debate during the last forty years: territories and the Arab population of Eretz Israel. "Territories for Peace."

To be able to handle such important issues Israel needs a strong government capable of taking policy and executing it.The National Unity Government that ruled Israel during the period 1984-1988 could not handle such a heavy burden. Therefore, only one of the two big parties should be empowered by the public to lead the country.Those who knew the Maarah Party know also that there are some exceptional people there. But their influence on what is going on in their higher echelons are close to nil.

The two main parties forming the coalition in the Unity Government, the Likud and the Maarah, made it. They succeeded to survive together, as full partners, a whole term, for years, from 1984 until 1988. This, in spite of the obstacles and differences. True, there was never real love between the two partners, yet managed to live together and shared equally responsibilities as well as failures and successes.

Unfortunately they had only one success. Stopping the inflation. True, something very important and shouldn't be underestimated.

On the other hand their failures were many. The five main failures were:

-The retreat from Lebanon without receiving anything tangible in return.

- Total freeze in settlements.

-Heavy unemployment.

-Loss of Tabah.

-The long drag of the Intifadah, that caused the Palestinian Declaration in Algeria.

The agreement between the Likud and the Maarah gave the two parties equal power and equal representation. No one of them could act without his partner's consent. Programs were carried out only if they had the approval of the two parties. Others were rejected or neglected because they did not receive the approval of both partners.

The inflations were put under control because the two parties wanted it.

The Israeli Defense Forces pulled out from Lebanon because the two parties agreed to it,

Neither party could spend a single shekel on either old settlements or new setlements without his partner's consent.

Heavy Unemployment existed because it was the agreed policy of the two parties.

Tabah was lost because they both agreed to International Arbitration.

The kibbutzim and Moshavim that were in the "red" didn't receive financial aid because it was the policy of the two parties, both the Likud and the Maarah.

The National Sewage System was neglected because the two parties decided that it was not yet top priority. This caused later, in 1988, the Polio epidemic.

The National Health Service collapsed because it was the policy of the two parties.

Old roads were neglected, new roads were not built. This, because the two parties decided that it was not urgent. The number of car accidents in Israel is, percentage wise, one of the greatest in the world. For every soldier killed in action, three are killed in car accidents. The Unity Government did absolutely nothing to correct the situation. Israel didn't participate in the International peace Conference because the Likud Party refused right decisions.Israel had nothing to gain in such a conference.

The Galilee and the Negev were neglected because it was Government policy, the Unity Government.

The way this election campaign was handled mainly by smearing the facts and distorting the truth.

"all the successes are ours. All the failures are yours."

"It was Shimon Peres who stopped the inflation. It was the Maarah that brought back the IDF from Lebanon, inspite of the resistance from the Likud."

Two big lies.

The fact of the matter is that the inflation was controlled and the economy stabilized due to the responsible contribution of the two parties. The Likud and the Maarah. The cooperation between Finance Minister Yitzhak Modai and the Secretary General of the Histadrut, Yisrael Kessar. Modai froze prices. Kessar froze salaries. The combination of these two elements stopped the inflation and not Shimon Peres.

Similarly, the Maarah alone didn't bring the Israeli soldiers back from Lebanon. The Likud withdrew their resistance and agreed to their return. Again, the cooperation of the two parties, the Likud and the Maarah brought back the Israeli soldiers from Lebanon.

The main issues in the 1988 general elections campaign were: Judea, Samaria, the Gaza Strip and the Arab intifadah. Other matters of the moment, such as heavy unemployment, the agriculture and health crises, the economy, immigration, education, social services, the mounting number of death on Israel's roads, etc. had been pushed aside. Postponed for a later date.

Neither the Likud nor the Maarah had an Answer to the heavy unemployment and the mass of lay-offs. So, the issue of unemployment was kept pending, was hushed during the campaign by both parties. A crucial issue was shoved under the carpet. Nobody mentioned it. Not even the news media. The Unity Government, same as all previous Israeli Governments, failed to deregulate the economy, liberalize trade and privatize government owned enterprises. It seemed that the great two parties didn't find it necessary to come up with a program of radical reforms. This could cost them many voices.

On October 5, 1988 (Tishrei 24, 5749), the Central Knesset Elections Committee, by an overwhelming majority disqualified Meir Kahane's Kach Party from contesting in (November 1, 1988) Knesset elections. Twenty-Eight members of the CKEC voted to bar Kach as a racist party; five voted against disqualification and three abstained. Supreme Court Justice, Eliezer Goldberg voted with the majority on the racism issue and also disqualified the Kach Party.

The juggernaut pushing Kach off the electoral stage centred on the two biggest parties, the Likud and the Maarah, who were supported by the Liberal and Leftist lists. The five votes against disqualification all came from delegates representing religious factions; Kach itself; Shass; the National Religious Party; and Poale Aguda. The Tehiyah or Hatechiyah provided the three abstentions.

The Central Knesset Elections Committee based its verdict on an existing law, passed in the Knesset disqualifying lists that reject the existence of the State of Israel as a Jewish State, or advance racist platforms, or reject the democratic nature of the State. It was the latter two counts that the CKEC acted on October 5, 1988. Meir Kahane was labeled a racist.

Rabbi Meir Kahane, head of the Kach Party was open, blunt and frank about the need of transferring the Arabs from Eretz Israel to the Arab neighboring countries. On the other hand, the other Right Wing parties, the Likud and the Tehiyah did not have the courage to speak up openly. They spoke of "autonomy" and "coexistence". Probably, because they feared the reaction of the world public opinion and the U.S. Administration.

Unlike Meir Kahane and his Kach Party, the other Right Wing parties, like the Likud and the Tehiyah mumbled: "Autonomy", "Coexistence", but are afraid to mention the word "Transfer", "The Unavoidable Surgery", the only practical solution to the Israeli-Arab conflict. On the other hand, the Moledet Party does mention, "Transfer" but only for the Arabs in the West Bank and the Gaza Strip, not for the Israeli Arabs, who, eventually, are more dangerous to Israel.

To call Rabbi Meir Kahane and the Kach Party "racist" was wrong and very unfair. Rabbi Kahane and his Party were not racist. They didn't hate the Arabs because of their religion, or the color of their skin. They hated the Arabs because they were Israel's enemies. Because they killed and still kill Jews and plan to exterminate the State of Israel. Because of Security reasons.

It is the Likud, whose strength, like that of Kach, is greatest in the development towns and poor urban suburbs, that stands to gain from the disqualification of Kach, if ratified at the Supreme Court.

An election fought without Kach could also benefit the Ultra-Orthodox parties and perhaps even the National Religious Party under its new hawkish and predominantly non-European, non establishment leadership.

Yet, in spite of the fact that the religious parties can only benefit from the disqualification of Kahane and his Kach Party, they all voted against his disqualification. On the other hand, the Likud joined the Maarah and the Left to disqualify Kahane.

The Likud sank to the level of Shimon Peres, What a shame! Everybody was astounded from the behavior of the Likud. It was something unbelievable, something unexpected.

The Likud was afraid that Kahane might receive many votes from members of the Likud Party. Many believed that if Kach won the appeal at the Supreme Court the Likud would lose many votes to Kach, mainly because of this behavior. On the other hand, if Kach loses the appeal the Likud will probably, also lose votes to the other right wing and religious parties, such as Shass, Moledet, Tzomet, Tehiyah, etc.

Those who ran out of arguments pick on Kahane's "Style" and "tactics". His political opponents criticized his style. Some "delicate souls" and "vegetarians" believe that: Kahane's main mistake was his inability to distinguish between tactics and strategy.

When you deal with a dangerous enemy like the PLO and the Palestinians, who have terrorized not only Israel, but the whole world, any style is legal. Any system is "Kosher". And what about the Palestinians' style? What about their Molotov cocktails (Petrol bomb)? What about their stones (rocks)? What about their terror? What about the cold blood murder of the boy Daniel Katz from Haifa? What about the Cold blooded murder of the boy Rami Haba from Eilon Moreh? What about the burning of half of the Moses family from Alfei-Menashe? Does the Kahane's style really matter? Or his goal to get rid of Israel's enemies? And what is wrong with it?

Kach councel Aharon Papo argued before the Supreme Court of Jerusalem that the 1985 law under which the Central Knesset Elections Committee barred the list from competing in the elections is "legal monster". He also said that Kach is neither anti-democratic nor racist, the counts under which the ban was invoked.

Kach's Arab policies are motivated only by the concern for security and for life, according to the Halacha. Papo also argued that the 1985 law was unconstitutional. "There is no precedent in the Western democracies for a law that limits either the right to vote for any party the citizen choses, or the right to be elected on any platform that can gain the voters' support." Then Papo added that:"Therefore, Kach is a legitimate party. It has not been banned. How, therefore, can it be barred from competing in the elections?'

Papo told the Court: "Kach is in favor of democracy. If there are anti-democratic parties in the Knesset, they are the Communists, who advocate the dictatorship of the proletariat:

The Progressive list for Peace, espousing the philosophy of the PLO terrorists: Mapam, which still sticks to Marxist ideas. Kach is not racist and has no biological objections to Arabs. Kach is being discriminated against by interested parties."

Jerusalem, October 18, 1988, "kach is clearly racist in aim and action," a five-man bench of the Supreme Court ruled unanimously. Thus rejecting the party's Appeal.

"The party's systematic encouragement of hatred against Arabs, its calls for the violent denial of their rights, and the consistent scorn and humiliation it has heaped upon them, are reminiscent of the worst experiences that suffered by the Jewish people itself. These hints of racism, and at any price. Kach's own acts and utterances against Israeli Arabs were themselves anti-democratic.

All these reasons are quite sufficient to support the conclusion that Kach incites to racism." Ruled Supreme Court President, Chief-Justice Meir Shamgar, who wrote the decision with Justices Dov Levin, Shlomo Levin, Moshe Bejski and Menahem Elon, concurring.

The bench, thus, rejecting the definition of racism that Kach's councel, Aharon Papo, had offered. Racism as it is understood in criminal law went further than philosophy of biological superiority.

The Supreme Court ruling prevented Kahane from running for the twelfth Knesset, on November 1988.

One of the few members of Knesset who had a potential idea of how to solve the Arab-Israeli conflict was accused of being a "fascist', a "racist" and incompatible, and was "thrown" out of the Knesset.

Prime Minister Yitzhak Shamir (Likud), expressed satisfaction at the Court's ruling on Kach, saying: "democracy must defend itself." Tzomet leader Refael Eitan condemned the Kach decision as "undemocratic" saying: If you disagree with a party's views, you should convince voters to support it. Tomorrow there may be a political coalition in favor banning either parties".

Maarah Party Secretary-General Uzi Baream called the decision "a declaration that Israel will not lend a hand to racism."

Israel is a democratic country where there exist the freedom of thinking, the freedom of speech and the freedom of expression, and no matter how distorted they be. Therefore, banning Rabbi Meir Kahane from the Knesset was totally unjust and this because he suggested to transfer the Palestinian Arabs to Jordan.

In defense of democracy and the right of every person to express his views, a very clever man once said: "I might disagree with his opinion but I shall fight for his right to express it."

As of 1970, the NRP abandoned its traditional strategy and gave the issue of the eventual annexation of Judea, Samaria and Gaza and their settlement by Israelis, top priority.

In 1977 the NRP's stand on that issue ended its historical alliance with Mapai-Maarah for partnership with the Likud.

During the first eight elections to the Knesset the alternatives available to the NRP were either to cooperate with Mapai-Maarah Party or stay out of the government, for its right wing opposition (Herout- Gahal-Likud) was too small to form an alternative coalition government.

The results of the vote taken in the National Religious Party, in April 1988 (Iyar 5748), showed that Avner Shaki, the Sephardi religious fundamentalist and political hardliner became the number one on its list of candidates for the forthcoming Knesset elections on November 1988 (Heshvan 5749) in place of Ashkenazi Zevulun Hammer.

On October 6, 1988, in Jerusalem, the Central Knesset Elections Committee (CKEC) rejected the request of the two right-wing parties, the Likud and the Tehiya, to bar the Progressive List for Peace Party (PLP) from contesting the November 1 elections.

The PLP case against disqualification was supported by the Labor-Alignment (Maarah) Party and by all the Liberal and Left parties.

Justice Eliezer Goldberg cast the deciding vote, against disqualification.

The PLP Party, headed by Mr. Mohammed Miari, the PLP Arab member of Knesset, negates Zionism and identifies with the enemies of Israel.

Mohammed Miari advocates negotiation with the PLO and the establishment of a Palestinian State in the West Bank, that's, in Jewish Judea, Samaria and the Gaza Strip.

Therefore, the PLP is an imminent danger to the security of the State of Israel. Justice Eliezer Goldberg declared that the PLP did not seek to liquidate the State of Israel. He also added that the burden of proof rested with the Likud and the Tehiya, whose arguments had fallen short. He also said that the PLP did not constitute a real or an anticipated threat of a magnitude justifying its disqualification. "I believe the state must tolerate views not palatable to the majority," he said.

Jerusalem, October 18, 1988. By a 3-2 majority, the Supreme Court decded to uphold the Central Election Committee's decision not to disqualify the Progressive List for Peace from participation in the November 1 elections.

Supreme Court President Meir Shamgar, Justice Moshe Bejski and justice Shlomo Levin voted in the PLP's favor while Deputy President Menahem Elon and Judge Dov Levin supported the appeal against the CKEC decision, which was submitted by the Likud, Agudat Israel and the National Religious Party (Mafdal, NRP).

A spokesman for the National Religious Party declared that the Supreme Court's ruling against Kahane and in favor of the PLP amounted to a lack of public justice. Kahane out and Muhammed Miari in, is ridiculous!

In defense of democracy, the Central Knesset Elections Committee as well as the Supreme Court had curbed the importance of democratic right to vote for a certain political party. In defense of democracy they might have also jeopardized the security of Israel.

With the years, the Israeli Arab electoral-power has grown and so has the temptation to use it. A very worrying phenomenon is the new bad habit of the Jewish political parties to flirt after the Arab vote, and this includes almost all the Jewish parties. The Arab vote has become very attractive in the Jewish sector, especially before and during elections time. Everybody wants to ride on the "Arab Horse". The forteen seats that the Arabs have in the Knesset will be the "steelyard" in every future coalition, and will decide the fate of the Jews in Israel. The greatest "joke" is that the Arabs will decide who will the Israeli Prime Minister be. They might even decide the issue "who is a Jew?" What a "laugh". This is ridiculous, even tragic. Unless something drastic and radical is done about the "Israeli democracy", and before it is too late, the "Arab Horse" might turn into a "Trojan horse". This is also the result of the "coexistence".

In the 1984 elections, the Maarah had received massive support in the Arab section. The Arab section usually voted according to Hamulah (family clan) considerations rather than ideological principles. But with time, attitudes have changed; with it changed also the political thinking of the Israeli Arabs. It matured. The Arabs in 1988 were already concerned with major political issues, such as the Palestinian question, the Palestinian State, etc. Only 68% of the 250,000 Israeli Arabs and Druse who were eligible to vote in 1984 actually exercised their right. In 1988 the number of Israeli Arabs eligible voters were 300,000, and the way they cast their ballots could be crucial in deciding which party should form the government. Obviously both parties, the Likud and the Maarah were aware of the potentially decisive role of the Arab sector. A very tragic situation. The Arabs would decide the way, shape and form of the Jewish state.

The estimated political power of the Israeli Arabs in the November 1988 general elections is forteen and a half seat in the Knesset. This they will get from three hundred and twenty thousands Israeli Arabs. These figures donot include the Arabs of Judea, Samaria and the Gaza Strip who donot have a voting right. Since the present, eleventh Knesset was elected in 1984. The number of Arab votes has increased by thirty thousands. All the political parties are competing over the Arab vote. The previous elections to the eleventh Knesset brought to the Knesset seven Arab members. The Maarah headed by Shimon Peres received twenty nine per cent of the Arab vote. On November 1988 it is expected that the Israeli Arabs will have forteen and a half seats in the Knesset, which, if used smartly can change the balance of power in favor of the Arabs and Arab interests.

The PLO also regarded the Israeli Arabs as an important element and a factor with a significant role to play. Any party, small or big, in the Arab sector, would happily welcome a PLO endorsement.

Abdul Wahab Darouche MK, Former Maarah MK, at present heading the newly-formed "Arab Democratic Party" declared: "The PLO is part of the political map in the Middle East and as the representative of the Palestinian people it is not cut off from what is happening in Israel. It wants to influence the election and strengthen the moderate and the left-wing elements in Israel, and will also call on Israeli Arabs to participate and not boycott the elections."

The Maarah affiliated companies had a deficit of eight billion sheqels, which equal to five billion U.S. dollars. Therefore, they were very eager to win these elections, so that they could raise taxes or print more money to cover their deficit. Regardless of the fact that such an action will bring back inflation to the country.

A week before the November 1, 1988 general elections, Israel witnessed a whole aggregation of Histadrut unions trying to hold the government to last minute ransom, by demanding a raise in salary. The list included doctors in government hospitals, who threatened a five-day "warning" strike; engineers, technicians, academics, in the public sector; high-school teachers as well as the bank tellers. The Histadrut, a tool of the Maarah has been put to work again, probably to influence, one way or another, the outcome of the elections.

During the election campaign most of the parties have mentioned very vaguely important problems, basic issues, such as the urgent need to increase immigration (Aliyah), the urgent need to decrease emigration (Yeridah), encouraging great families, developing new industries and forming new woking places in order to overcome the heavy unemployment, augment construction of housing projects, to produce more housing for great families and young coupes, the establishment of more Jewish settlements in the West Bank, putting an end to the plague of road accidents, etc.

Not a single party mentioned the word Zionism, the corner stones, the foundation of the State of Israel.

The Israelis have enjoyed during the years 1986-1988 economic stability, though, at the expense of rising unemployment. This could have been achieved only under a Likud-Maarah government who had almost total control over both the Histadrut and the Manufacturers Association (the major Israeli industrial companies were united in a single bargaining unit called the Manufacturers Association).

As a politician, Finance Minister Moshe Nissim knew very well the limits of his freedom to maneuver. Election fear kept him from taking such unpopular steps as devaluation. This, in spite of the fact that the Bank of Israel's head, Governor Michael Bruno, together with the bank heads, have tried to convince the Finance Minister about the pressing need to squeeze in flation down to a single digit figure.

Obviously, the Bank of Israel could not consider political aspects. The Bank of Israel considers only economical criteria. Yet, not even Nissim could afford the luxury to risk his neck in making the changes advised by Michael Bruno, before a general election. Reducing the inflation rates before an election was beyond Nissim's power.

Mr. Nissim backed by Prime Minister Yitzhak Shamir has proven to be an excellent guardian of the state treasury. He faced down many strikes for higher wages, by different sectors, without giving in. Nissim had the highest approval rating of any cabinet member-unheard of for a finance minister. This because the Israelis in general are responsible people and understand that the economy of the country must be healed and Nissim is the man to do it. The Israeli public appreciated the tough, unpopular decisions; Nissim had made to hold the budget down.

During the election campaign neither of the big parties, the Likud or the Maarah, or any other party ever mentioned the sick phenomenon that Israel's scientists and engineers are leaving the country, that one thousand and six hundred Israeli professors live in the U.S.,that thirty four thousand engineers and scientists from Israel moved to the U.S. That more funds have to be allocated to higher education, to the Universities. More money has to be allocated also to solve the health problem and hospital crisis. Yet, nobody talked about these important issues or suggested how to solve it.

In spite of the fact that Israel was facing an economic recession, yet, hardly anybody mentioned this serious fact during the campaign. It was hushed and shoved under the carpet by all parties, without exception.

Arafat was trying to deceive the Israeli voters with the false illusion that the Israeli-Palestinian peace is on the threshold. All they have to do is vote for Shimon Peres and the Maarah.

Obviously, this was only a trick. Only the naïve voters can "buy" it. Arafat never meant to make peace with Israel. He spoke with peace but really meant war. Arafat is very cunning. Very dangerous.

One wonders why Arafat wants Shimon Peres to be Israel's next premier!

Peace with the Arabs is nothing but wishful thinking, a mirage, at least at this stage. It is obvious and very clear that the Arabs are answering with diplomatic tricks and meaningless slogans, in order to conceal their real intention to liquidate Israel by stages.

The following excerp is from the Maarah campaign broadcast:

"The present policy of occupation forces Israeli and Palestinian societies into close and daily contact with each other. Despite the hostility between our two peoples, a large and growing network of economic, institutional and even social and cultural ties has developed between the Israelis and the Palestinian Arabs over the past twenty-one years. This process may eventually produce an integrated society in which the economic issues, will become the dominant element.

"In our view, once the Palestinians become, de facto, the larger element of a mixed society, the ability of Israel's political institutions to maintain the unity and integrity of the Jewish community in Eretz Israel will be severely challenged. Lebanon, for example, shows us what happens to a state in which an ethnic group has lost the social and economic weight, which once sustained its political power.

"Our democratic values will be threatened if we continue to maintain our rule over the Palestinians against their will. They must be encouraged to develop their social, economic and cultural ties among themselves, within their own society, rather than with the Israelis.

"We must give them territory of reasonable size, continuous to the extend that geography permits, within borders that are consistent with Israel's security needs, and which contain the bulk of the Palestinian-Arab population. This territory should be separated from Israel by an international border.

"Regulated economic contact between our two nations could enhance the development of peaeeful relations, but the essential advantage to us of such border is that we can close if we feel the need to. The Allon plan provides the basic geographic outline for such settlement.

"Jordan, however, has shown that it is not prepared to take the part of the Palestinians.Therefore, we are now willing to consider the establishment of a sovereign Palestinian state, on condition that the Palestinians recognize Israel, renounce any future territorial claims upon us, and accept our security concerns.

"We will, of course, insist that this future state be demilitarized and we will hold it responsible, as we hold states responsible, for outrages against our territory and our citizens launched from its soil. We reserve the right to decide whether we are faced with military or terrorist threat from the Palestinian-Arabs and will not hesitate to respond accordingly."

The following excerpt is from the Likud Campaign broadcast:

"While security has always been a concern of our party in formulating our policy regarding Judea, Samaria and Gaza, a more fundamental interest has been our desire to assure Jewish settlement and sovereignty over the complete Land of Israel. We represent the large number of Israelis for whom theses values are paramount.

"Nevertheless, we realize that our interest in Jewish sovereignty over the complete of Israel is tempered by other lasting interests. We cannot ignore that an alien people lives in organized communities within the Land of Israel.

"It forms no part of our conception of the Zionist ideal to rule over these people perpetuity against their will. These people will not leave their homes voluntarily. Our humanistic principles-over which, our political opponents enjoy no monopoly- will not permit us to cast them out forcibly from their homes, as some advocate.

"Since we concede that we have no desire to rule over the Palestinian Arabs, we would be content for them to rule themselves, provided that they recognize Israel and acknowledge our security concerns.

"We donot claim jurisdiction over their persons, their private property or their communal property in the towns and villages where they live. Therefore, we are prepared to hand over the villages and municipal areas where the Palestinan Arabs actually dwell or form to Palestinian Arabs jurisdiction.

"We stipulate, however, that the lines of demarcation between Palestinian Arabs and Israel need not always follow the municipal boundaries inherited from the previous regime, since we lay claim to all those parts of the Land of Israel where Palestinian Arabs do not actually reside or farm.

"We promise not to interfere in any way in the areas which we acknowledge should be under Palestinian Arab jurisdiction. Moreover we do not care whether they chose to define themselves as a sovereignty, or they chose to govern themselves, or how they arrange their relations with other nations abroad or whom they admit into the areas under their jurisdiction. But we will insist that the security arrangements we stipulate be preserved.

"Certain arrangements will have to be made to govern the relations between the Palestinian Arabs and the Israelis. Palestinian Arab territory will not be contiguous and the Palestinian Arabs will need to have the right access through Israeli territory. We are prepared to grant such access on the basis of reciprocity."

The clarity with which the two major contending parties, the Likud and the Maarah, outlined their positions, presentate the electorate with a clear and genuine choice, to vote Likud or to vote Maarah.

These two parties differed sharply over what constituted a settlement acceptable to Israel. This became the issue over which the elections were fought.

The Israeli electorate was given the option to decide on their own destiny. They were being asked to decide what policy to sdopt with regards to the Palestinian Arabs. The people, not the politicians, would make that choice, and then they would have to bear the consequences.

In the elections of November 1988, the Israeli had to make a very crucial decision. The decision of whether he should give away part of the land over which he has ancient rights anchored in the Holy Scriptures, in exchange for a peace of paper, or he should stick to guns and fight for it.

Most of the Israeli voters were deeply committed to the principle of Greater Israel, that's Eretz Israel (including Judea, Samaria and Gaza) and flatly rejected any trade off of territory in exchange for "peace" (Arab peace). Therefore, there was no way that the Maarah could have won the elections.

A political party that is not based on the faith in God, on the love of God and on the commitment to follow his commands is useless and is not worth giving it our precious vote. A vote that is not given to a serious party that respects religion, heritage, tradition and Jewish history is a wasted vote.

The participation of the Ortodox parties in the country's political life was growing. The rigidly Orthodox parties, who, in the past, shunned secular politics, have realized that the benefits of greater involvement in the political system were great and worthy as well as a very healthy development.

For many years the Orthodox parties were ignored, shoved aside, by the secular, non-religious parties. The secular left even treated them worse; in fact they despised the Orthodox and didn't want anything to do with them.

Obviously the Orthodox felt insulted. They finally realized that they couldn't afford to remain "outsiders" if they wanted to influence and be considered seriously. They finally understood that in order to influence politically and religiously they have to participate, be "inside", in the government system and take responsibilities. They can no longer stay complacent.

Therefore, this time they recruited all their voting forces. Everybody who had a voting

Right. Many were flown from abroad, to vote. The Orthodox had the highest voting rate and no wonder that they received eighteen seats in the twelfth Knesset.

Unfortunately, the Religious-Orthodox parties were strongly divided. Had they united together to a one great block they could have received several more seats.

During the election campaign it was interesting to follow the two hundred years old feud between the Hassidim (Agudat Israel, Habad) disciples of Rabbi Israel Ba'al Shem-Tov and the Mitnagdim (Degel Hatorah, Shass) disciples of Rabbi Eliyahu, the Gaon of Vilna. Unfortunately, the two parties still had some differences. Two hundred years "left overs", though, they both share the same coalition with the Likud.

In the previous elections they boycotted the polling booths decrying any contest with the Satmars, are fanatically anti-Zionist, and in this election, same as in the eleventh, the organs of state.

According to the Central Knesset Elections Committee the following were the results of the general elections taken place on November 1, 1988:

Likud –40, Maarah-39, Shass-6, NRP-5, Agudah-5, CRM-5, DFPE (Hadash)-4, Mapam-3, Tehiya-3,

Shinui (Center)-2, Moledet-2, Degel Hatorah-2, Tzomet-2, Arab Democratic-1, Progr. Peace-1,

Total- 120 Seats

From the bitter Likud-Maarah argument during the elections campaign everybody understood, without any doubt, that, the two parties, in effect, pledged no to get together again, after the poll.

From the results of these elections some Maarah activists came to realize that the changing demographic realities, in Israel, as immutable electoral facts rule out any Maarah victory in the foreseeable future, because the country is going right and religious.

From the mid 70s the left-centre parties headed by the Maarah (Mapai) Party has been constantly losing power, while the right-nationalistic block headed by the Likud has been gaining strength. This is due to the change in the sociological structure of the Israelis with the constant increase of the

Oriental-Sephardi growth. The Sephardi Jews, who felt deprived by their Ashkenazi –Maarah brethren, for years, voted for the Likud.

Also, the religious community, constantly growing in numbers, provide the right block, headed by the Likud, additional voting power to overwhelm the Maarah with its left satellites for many more years ahead.

From the results of the November 1988 elections it was obvious that the ratio of political trend is about 60:40 in favor of the Right, and that the right enjoys ideological preponderance against the Left. It seems that this will be the voting pattern in Israel for the next decades.The Likud will have the political high ground for many more years, together with its satellites in the Right and together with the Religious parties. Because they share a positive attitude towards the "Greater Israel" (Eretz Israel Hashlemah") plan as well as the "Population Displacement" ("Transfer") plan, which have become an "Unavoidable Surgery". And also because they believe that secularism should be replaced by traditional Judaism or at least strengthened by a healthy dose of traditional Judaism.

One of the main reasons, besides their unconvincing platform, that the Maarah did not win the   elections was their failure to crush the Arab uprising, the Intifadah. The Maarah held the Defense portfolio during the years 1984-1988 and did not stop the Intifadah. The Israeli voter couldn't forgive their incompetence.

The political strength of the religious orthodox parties remained constant, with very minor changes:

First Knesset-16 seats
Second Knesset-15 seats
Third Knesset-17 seats
Fourth Knesset-18 seats
Fifth Knesset-18 seats
Sixth Knesset-17 seats
Seventh Knesset-18 seats
Eighth Knesset-19 seats
Nineth Knesset-15 seats
Tenth Knesset-13 seats
Eleventh Knesset-13 seats
Twelveth Knesset- 18 seats

18 seats was the average political strength of the Religious-Orthodox parties during the last forty years. If there were changes, they were internal, by which the NRP lost to the Orthodox parties: Shass, Agudah, Degel Hatorah.

During these elections, to the twelveth Knesset, the Orthodox (Haredim) won 13 seats in the Knesset   while the NRP (Datiyim) had only five seats. This was a great victory to the Orthodox (Haredim) parties.   They never received 13 seats in the Knesset before.

Since 1981, the Likud and the Maarah have lost, each, eight Knesset seats, and the smaller parties, on the Right and on the Left have received it. This means that some of the political power moved from the center to the margins. This is the reason why the small parties, which do not represent the majority of the electorate, have such a great political influence.

The Religious-Orthodox block reached in November 1, 1988, its 1950-1960 maximum of fifteen per cent of the votes and eighteen seats in the Knesset. Yet, the size of the Observant Jewish population in Israel was somewhere between twenty and twenty five per cent. This means that some religious voters voted for Secular parties

There are many moderately religious people in Israel who belong to, or vote for, other than religious parties, because they oppose the politicization of religion, for both democratic and religious reasons, They feel misrepresented by religious parties, who they think, concentrate only on religious matters and do not deal thoroughly enough with other important issues.the Lithuanian Orthodox community in Israel. His spiritual influence over his students was immense. Many of them became heads of other Lithuanian Yeshivahs. The standard of learning in these yeshivahs was High, therefore, they became very attractive centers of learning. Many Sephardic students joined these yeshivahs, where they felt "at home". They   Rabbi Eliezer Menachem Shach headed the Lithuanian (Mitnagdim) Panevezys Yeshivah (Theological College) in Bnei Barak, Israel, many years. He was also the spiritual leader of didn't feel at home in the Agudah yeshivahs.

When these Sephardic students graduated they went to teach in other yeshivahs. Some of them even founded new yeshivahs. The Lithuanian community increased and a big Sephardic camp was formed with Rabbi Shach at their head. Rabbi Shach founded for them a new party, the Shass Party, just before the elections to the eleventh Knesset. Rabbi Shach instructed his Ashkenazi followers to vote for Shass rather than for the Agudah. The results were amazing.

In the 1984 elections Shass received 4 mandates, that's seats in the Knesset while theAguda (Agudat Israel) received only 2 seats. Shass became an important factor in the formation of the Unity Government of

1984. Ex-Chief Rabbi Ovadiah Joseph was impressed by the new Sephardic party and decided to join it and became its leader, with the blessing of its founder Rabbi Shach. Though Shass had its spiritual leader, yet, they kept consulting Rabbi Shach and receiving his advice and guidance. During all these years Rabbi Shach was also a leader to Agudat Yisrael (The Agudah). Just before the 1988 elections the Agudah made a deal with Chabad headed by Rabbi Menachem Shneorzon, known also as the famous Lubavitcher, the Rebbe from Brooklyn, New York. Rabbi Shach was against such a deal. For years he had great differences with Chabad, and, therefore, rejected the idea of running together in the elections.

Rabbi Eliezer Menachem Shach pulled out his Lithuanian followers from the Agudah and formed a new party, the Degel Hatorah.

As we have seen Shach founded two parties: Shass for the Sepharadim and Degel Hatorah for the Ashkenazim. Both parties had their roots in the Agudah. The Agudah received 5 seats in the Knesset while Degel Hatorah received only 2 seats.

The Chassidim are praying according to "Nussach" (style) Sepharad, while the Mitnagdim (Lithusnians) are praying according to "Nussach" Ashkenaz.

There is nodoubthat it was thanksto the intervention of Rabbi Menachem Shneorson, or the Lubavitcher Rebbe, on behalf of Agudat Yisrael that received five seats in the Knesset, compared with the two seats they had before.

The Lubavitcher is the most influential, charismatic, spiritual leader of the Chssidic movement of Chabad. Highly intelligent. He has several doctorates from the Sorbon (in Paris). He was admired by all who knew him. Many have visited his court: Presidents, Ministers, Scientists, Authors and other VIP's.

The Lubavitcher Rebbe lived in an extremely frugal house on 770 Eastern Parkway, in Brooklyn, New York. He hasn't left his home for the last forty years, neither has he taken a day off. His house is also the head quarters of the Chabad movement. From there he operates and controls the Interest of Chabad all over the world.

The Lubavitcher had a long "professional" conflict with Rebbi Eliezer Menachem Shach from Agudat Yisrael. Rabbi Shach requested to boycott the Chabad movement. The Agudah with a strong Chassidic majority rejected his demand. Rabbi Shach left the Agudah in anger and founded his own party, Degel Hatorah. In return, the Lubavitcher instructed his followers to support Agudat Yisrael (Agudah). It was the first time that the Lubavitcher Rebbe and Chabad got involved in the Israeli Politics.

When asked why is he not moving to Israel, the Lubavitcher Rebbe, the leader of Chabad, replied that he has to live where he can be most helpful to Judaism. Where he can have the best contacts with the World Jewry. Where he can best safeguard the interests of Chabad and the interests of Judaism. For all these reasons he can best operate from his base in New York. Also, in the US where the Jewish population is a little over six million versus five in Israel. The Rebbe lives among the majority of the nation. Besides, like many others, he believes that the ship of US Jewry is sinking, and a captain lives his ship, last.

Chabad also has a very active radio station broadcasting from New York.

It was the Lubavitcher Rebbe who brought Agudah much of its election victory and he is determined not only to ensure passage of the amendment in the Law of Return, but also prevent the return of territories at any price to the Arabs.

On November 1, 1988, that's Heshvan 20, 5749, Shass had the most impressive victory. Six seats in the Knesset. Shass is relatively new party founded by Rabbi Eliezer Menachem Shach from the Agudah and ex-Chief Rabbi Ovadiah Joseph, who up to 1983 supported the Agudat Yisrael (Agudah) Party.

All the Sepharadim, Secular, Religious or Orthodox who felt deprived and "Second Rate Citizens" in the other political parties, joined Shass enthusiastically, by the thousands. Rabbi Ovadiah joseph is a Student of Religion, an excellent Orator, highly persuasive, a man of Real-Politics and very Charismatic.

Shass is far from being a passing episode, like the Tami Party, in 1984, founded by Aharon Abu Hatzerah, nephew of the late Baba Sali, which lasted a little over one Knesset term (Four Years). Shass has extremely strong roots and backbone and is here to stay.

Unfortunately, many arrogant Ashkenazim saw the circle of their public exclusively as Ashkenazim and thus rejected any non-Ashkenazi from a position of influence and power.

For many years the prevailing Ashkenazi establishment headed by the Mapai-Maarah (Labor) Party was engaged in ostracizing Sephardis.

Against this phenomenon arose the Shass movement. It emerged from a great Sephardi awakening and from the dedication of sensitive, understanding sympathetic Ashkenazim.

This was the reply for many years of denial, disappointment and discremination by the Ashkenazi establishment.

The Ashkenazi politicians, who sort of patronized the Sephardim, were not aware at all of their silent rebellion. They were not aware also that they were losing votes to Shass. Shass became a "dominant figure" during the negotiation that was taking place before creating the new government. No government could be formed without Shass.

Many Sephardi Israelis simply cannot bring themselves to vote for the Maarah, the party they associate with "Ashkenazim Only". The party they associate with previous illtreatment and discrimination.

Shass has, since its establishment, seen itself as a full participiant in the political process of Israel. The secular Left that remained outside the government called Shass "Blackmailers", but with Shass the third biggest party in the Knesset, that line is beginning to wear thin. Because of their blind, irrational hatred of religion and Sephardi culture that characterizes the secular Ashkenazi Left parties, they will, probably, always stay small or vanish.

As a result of these elections, the enhanced bargaining power of the Orthodox parties had increased the prospect of change in the Law of Return. The Orthodox had won this power, as well as increased their political power, in a free democratic election, after they made Israel their home and became citizens, with the right to vote.

The bargaining power of the Religious Orthodox block nearly doubled in the last Knesset elections, which enabled them to demand the inclusion of the four words: "according to the Halachah" in the Law of Return, which they have waited so long. The Religious-Orthodox couldn't have made this amendment in a secular majority Knesset, or if they were outside the Cabinet.

The polarization between the two leading parties, the Likud and the Maarah increased the Haredi (Orthodox) bargaining power and their leverage. The religious parties became power brokers and king makers.

Many believed that when the Orthodox parties will acquire political power, great budget, more clout, the jealousies, competitions and differences among their various groups could increase. On the other hand, common interests might join them together into one block, "the Religious Block".

The Rabbinical Councils are a factor to be reckoned because it is they that determine the policy of the Orthodox parties (Agudah, Shass, etc.). The Rabbinical Council of sages ("Moetzet Hachachamim") is a veteran body established in 1915, long before the inception of the State of Israel, which directs the way of living of the Orthodox Jews.

The members of the Council of Sages are all noted Rabbis, chosen by the Agudah's General Assembly, but the Council may invite other Rabbis. Most of the members are Chassidic, but there are a number of non-chassidic Yeshiva Heads as well.

The secularists in Israel were completely "surprised" by the "unexpected" high rate of Haredi votes. They just didn't realize that for the last two decades, while thet were preoccupied with the acquisition of material comforts, such as, new houses, new cars, trips abroad, videos, etc., the Haredi lived modestly, frugally and enlarged their families. Their children have grown up and have reached voting age. Since most of them remained true and loyal to the Torah teachings, they have voted accordingly.

How sad and untrue is the fact that many of the Secularists see these loyal Jews as anti-Zionists, while, on the other hand, acknowledge as "Zionists" those who, for over forty years, have spurned the opportunity to settle in Israel, but do the Israelites a "favor" for holding their congresses in Jerusalem and threatening alienation from Israel if it dares make legislations on religious matters applicable in Israel, which is totally unfair.

Many Israeli Secularists have accused the Lubavitcher Rebbe, head of the Chabad movement, of interfering in Israel's election, yet, they welcomed threatening statements of Rabbi Alexander Schindler, so-called leader of the American Reform Jews.

It was sad to see the Labour and Civil Rights People bemoan the new victory of the Orthodox parties, even more than the supposed defeat to their peace hopes.

One should read the following declarations:

"Now they will force religion upon us." "I am packing my bags. Who wants to live in a religious State?" "I want to live my own life, I don't want anybody telling me how to live!"

Those very Secularists, Humanists and Left-Wingers seemed to fear more a Jewish religious state than an Arab State.

This only proves that something in their basic education was missing, and this something is religion. All studies show clearly that the loss of religious identity leads to the loss of nationalistic identity.

Many secularists were dissatisfied with the results of the elections because of the heavy Ultra-Orthodox vote. "It is not a victory when the Haredim are in position now to squeeze us dry," they said. They feared the inevitable religious coercion.

On the other hand, many other Secularists who professed themselves as non-religious declared that they accepted, indeed welcomed, a certain measure of religion in public life. "I want that when my son learns the Torah in school or at home that he should wear a kippa (head-cover, yarmulka). The increasing permissiveness is disgusting."

The election results were particularly depressing in the kibbutzim. The members of the kibbutzim were completely paralyzed. As if they just lost a member of their family. They were speechless. They just couldn't grasp it. They were in some kind of a shock. Already feeling from a succession of economic blows, they just didn't know how to handle the new situation, now that they will be further remote from the government treasury. There was a serious crisis of faith in the kibbutz movement. Since the establishment of the State, in 1948, there was always someone to pay the bill of their failure: the Government, the Histadrut, Hevrat Ha'Ovdim. Suddenly there is no- back up any more. It became more and more clear to them that they must control the treasury of the State, to cover their very heavy debts and protect their interests, not only as a matter of ideology. Suddenly they realized that they must enter the coalition with the Likud, otherwise, if they stay outside, in the opposition, they will be ruined as a party, by their debts.

The voters in Israel have decreed a virtual stalemate between the two great parties, the Likud and the Maarah. The Israeli voters have left the two great parties the choice of two options: reconstituting the National Unity Government, or going into a narrow coalition with their close allies to the Right or to the Left as well as the Religious-Orthodox parties.

The present electoral system in Israel encourages the establishment of small splinter parties that could make the formation of government quite difficult.

Speaking to the annual convention of the Israel Institute of Accountants, in Jerusalem, on November 1988, three weaks after the general elections, in Israel, Vice Premier and Foreign Minister Shimon Peres said that, now, he was convinced for the need of direct elections for the post of Prime Minister, and a sharp rise in the threshold of votes necessary for a party to gain Knesset representation, as urgently needed first steps in electoral reform.

The introduction of direct voting for the premiership would give the Prime-Minister, the power he currently lacked, while a higher vote threshold would cut the number of small parties. Thus, he said,

the voters' choices would be reflected in an effective government.

The present system, said Peres, did not allow the formation of a government that could make tough decisions. One wonders, if Shimon Peres would have won the elections, would he also criticize the present Israeli electoral system and urge an overhaul of that system. The answer is obviousss. Now that he lost the elections every thing is wrong.

Peres also criticized the the religious parties, who, he said, did not vote in the Knesset on the basis of political philosophies but rather on the basis of religious considerations.

Again, one wonders how could Peres read the minds of the religious voters. Did Mr.Peres really forget the fight after the elections of 1988? He himself led intensive negotiations with all the

religious parties, trying to form a coalition with them, with the intent to undermine Shamir, who won

the election, promising the religious parties everything, but failed?

The November 1988 elections could not have come at a worse time for the Maarah.Yitzhak Shamir had been prime minister for the last two years and had been in constant conflict with Shimon Peres. Peres was far from being popular. People "hated" Peres because his obstinacy in insisting on going to the International Conference. Then comes the Intifadah, the Palestinian uprising, and Yitzhak Rabin declares over the air, on Radio and Television, that he cannot cope with it. Thousands are thrown out of work and their Union, the Histadrut doesn't budge a finger to defend their interests. Hevrat Ha'Ovdim goes broke and so is Kupat Holim, the Sick Fund.

Inspite of all this, the Maarah came out only one Seat less than the Likud. This is something beyond comprehension. Unbelievable. This can be explained only in one way. Many of the conservative old-timers, out of habit, kept voting for the Maarah.

The secularists, members of his own party, the Maarah, have accused Peres of violating the principles of the party and the spirit of its platform. "The damage Peres did cannot be undone," they said, and added "he has supplied Mr. Shamir with what ever justification the Likud leader needed to knuckle under to Orthodox, even against his better judgement.

That the out going and future premier is not too happy to do so is plain enough. For he can readily appreciate the disastrous impact which the passage of the promised "Who is a

Jew" legislation, in whichever form is, likely to have on World Jewry."

Shimon Peres has led his party, the Maarah, to four electoral defeats: In 1977, 1981, 1984 and 1988. There must have been something in the chemistry between the majority of the electorates and between Shimon Peres, which made him vitually unelectable. There is just no chemistry between them.

True, Uzi Baram had democratized the Maarah party, and except for a few top-level nominations the rest of the members have to be elcted into office. The result of this was, that the Maarah party became more democratic than before, but it lost the elections to the Likud.

Disappointed from the results of the elections, disappointed from the Maarah's present leadership: Shimon Peres and Yitzhak Rabin, who couldn't win the election, the Maarah Party Secretary-General Uzi Baram characteristically straightforward, conceded that the Maarah will have to change its leadership before the next elections.

"There is no doubt that a change of personalities must take place," he said. "It may not happen immediately, but it will happen before the next elections. I think we'll know more in a week or two about whether it will happen in the short term."

But, Secretary-General Uzi Baram could be mistaken. Uzi Baram had very eager intentions to replace Shimon Peres as head of the Maarah Party. But Peres "wasn't born yesterday and when it comes to political survival, Peres is second to none. Inspite of his loss in the elections Peres navigated skillfully Maarah's political boat and has reasserted himself, at least temporarily, as the unrivalled leader of his party. Peres was only "a hair's breadth" from forming a coalition with the left and Religious-Orthodox parties. Members of the Maarah believed that to try and topple Peres now, will not succeed, It might succeed, may be, in some future date.

There was no doubt that the violent events in Judea, Samaria and Gaza during the eleven months prior to the elections to the Twelfth Knesset had an impact on the results of the election. Many Israelis had become more realistic and moved to the Right. There is no doubt that the Palestinian uprising was important in the Israeli voters decisions. The Israelis were already sick and tired of the continued anarchy and lawlessness, of woman and children being killed on the roads, of stones and Molotov-Cocktails. After forty years of independence they thought they deserved a little more security and peace of mind.

Like most people, the Israelis were not happy of the intervention of other nations in their internal affairs, especially when they told them how to vote, and no matter how friendly these "advisers" were.

During the November 1988 elections in Israel, the United States of America, the U.S.S.R., Egypt, Jordan and the PLO sided openly with the Maarah and even campaigned for the Maarah. If ever, the Americans, the Europeans, the President of Egypt, the King of Jordan or Arafat, expected to persuade the Israeli voters, they were totally wrong.

Right after the elections, a respectable member of the Maarah Party (Labor), ex- member of Knesset, Rabbi Menachem Hacohen, bluntly accused the Orthodox parties with the following words:

-It frightens me, as a religious Jew, to see the type of person who voted for Shass and Chabad, kisses the mezzuza, but goes to watch a football game on Shabbat,

-Their years in the government and the coalition have simply earned them money. Shabbat desecration has increased, and hatred of the religious by the secular has grown.

-They don't deal with Jewish education. In education their only achievement has been to ensure the evasion from military service.

Any way, their dovishness stems from their hartred of the State of Israel. Shach would certainly agree to give away territory: He'd give away the entire state-gladly!

-Rabbi Eliezer Shach is a dove and Rabbi Ovadiah Yossef has a record of favouring territorial concessions for the sake of peace.

-David Ben Gurion, even Menachem Begin, never visited graves, as Shimon Peres went to the Baba Sali's grave.

-There has been a steady erosion and the winners have been the anti-Zionist parties: Shass, Agudah and Degel Hatorah.

-They know who their supporters are and they will never antagonize them by going with Labor on the basis of territory for peace, just as they never come out really strongly against football games on the Shabbat.

-They would go with any body to get money for their Yeshivas.

-I will be worried even more if the Alignment (Maarah) was in position to set up an alliance with the Ultra-Orthodox, which would corrupt our society.

-I was appaled at the way Rabbi Ovadiah Yossef criss-crossed the country by helicopter with his curses and blessings. It was the most primitive appeal to superstition.

A religious Rabbi full of venom against the Orthodox! What a shame.

On November 21, 1988, that's Kislev 12, 5749 the twelfth Knesset convened for its first session. President Chaim Herzog opened the first session of the newly elected twelfth Knesset. President Herzog called on the one hundred and twenty Knesset members to cherish the dignity of the House and warned them that if they showed disrespect for their own institution, "your own prestige as members of the Knesset will be impaired, as well as the prestige of our democratic system in the eyes of the public."

The President added that Israel's democracy must not be taken for granted, "History has known many democratic regims that collapsed in times of crisis." He called on the nation to "obey the precept of tolerance" and warned that "we dare not accusing ourselves to a cheap and violent form of public and political debate characterized by slander and abusive language" Herzog said that parlimentarians dared not be oblivious to the growing concern over the future character and course of the State.

"There is concern lest we lose the Zionist content of our renewed nationhood in our ancestral land. There is concern regarding the freedom of the individual and his rights in the State. There is concern regarding the unity of the Jewish people."

In a reference to mounting anti-Arab feeling, he said: We must denounce attempts to whip up feelings against the minorities among us, without distinction between the law- abiding and the violators of the law. The injunction to respect minority rights occurs thirty-six times in the Bible," he reminded the Knesset. The founding fathers of Israel "repeatedly emphacized that the State would be judged by its relationship to its Arab-minority."

President Herzog then called on Yair Sprinzak ("Moledet"), the oldest (76 years old) member of the House, to make his declaration of loyalty and chair the session.

Yair Sprinzak, son of the late Yosef Sprinzak (Mapai), the Speaker of the first Knesset in 1948-1952, conducted the first session of the twelfth Knesset very gracefully by expounding his political philosophy. Some of the Maarah members of the Knesset, like Michael Zohar, Haim Ramon, Rafi Edri, Ariye "Lova" Eliav, Moshe Shahal and Avraham Burg, as well as all the Left parties and the Arab parties members, constantly disturbed his speech. What was to have been a festive inauguration of the newly elected legislature was marred by the deliberate, intentional, well-planned shameful disturbance of the Arab and Left-wing members of the Knesset who protested noisily. Shulamit Aloni, Yossi Sarid, Ran Cohen, Daddi Zucker, Avrum Burg, Ariye "Lova" Eliav, Abdul-Wahab Darawsha and Muhammad Miari staged a demonstrative, mini-walkout to the sides and isles of the chamber. It was clear that they set out deliberately to spoil what should have been a dignified ceremonial occasion.

The silly left-wing behavior was completely out of place.

The next step was the pledge of allegiance. The chairman MK Yair Sprinzak instructed the members of Knesset that all they should say as they were called to pledge allegiance was: "I do pledge". A hush came over the chamber as the roll call started. Three names were called by alphabetical order and it seemed that all went well. Then came the turn of Mapam's Haim "Jumas" Oron who sprang to his feet and shouted: "I pledge to keep the laws of the State of Israel and to fight against racism." He read his declaration from a prepared piece of paper. "That is not the proper form. You, Mr. MK, have not pledged allegiance," countered Sprinzak.

And thus it went on, through the CRM, Mapam, DFPE, PLP, and Arab Democratic Party lists, with each MK making his pledge to combat racism.

Then came the turn of Avraham (Avrum) Burg, the son of Joseph Burg, ex-Minister of Interior and ex-Head of the NRP. Avrum Burg, one of the two skull-capped Maarah members rose to say:"I pledge to remain faithful to the Torah which commands us to refrain from oppressing the stranger, for we our selves were strangers in Egypt!" But that formulation, too, was ruled out of order.

The roll call over, Sprinzak moved on to the next business of the House, that's the election of the Speaker.

Ronni Milo (Likud) rose to propose Dov Shilansky. There was consternation in the Maarah, and first Shachal and then Edri tried to forstall a vote. When Sprinzak asked if there were more proposals, the Maarah said they had no other candidate. As Edri again sought to delay a vote, and the House seemed to become close to ungovernable, Moshe Nissim, the Finance Minister requested permission to mount the podium. The left, he said, amid absolute silence, had shamed the Knesset. How would the country's youth judge what had happened in this session?

It was quite legal to vote for a Speaker. If Sprinzak truly respected the Knesset's honour he had no choice but to call the vote without further ado and more scandals.

At this point, Maarah's David Libai stood up to propose that Shlomo Hillel be Speaker for another term. But he was outvoted.

At first, the left-wing members of Knesset together with the Arab members of the Knesset planned to boycott the session, but then, they changed their minds and turned up to ensure their right to vote for a

Speaker. Their use of the declaration of allegiance formula for political protest statements was childish and undignified. It showed bad taste and immature politicians. They came with their "tails between their legs" begging for the right to repeat their declarations of allegiance, this time, properly. Without the pledge of allegiance they are not members of Knesset, and therefore, do not have the right to vote or to take part in the election of the new Speaker for the House. They also made it impossible for the Maarah to obtain a postponement of the vote.

Dov Shilansky of the Likud was elected Speaker of the twelfth Knesset by 64 to 55. He was supported by the entire right wing and Orthodox block after a failed last-minute attempt by the Maarah's Moshe Shachal and Rafi Edri to postpone the election of a Speaker.

Everybody agreed that the twelfth Knesset had an undignified start.

Two days later, fifty residents of the Yemin Orde religious youth Aliyah village, near Haifa, presented President Herzog with a petition signed by five hundred and thirty two pupils, immigrants from sixteen countries, who were dismayed by the MK's behavior in the Knesset.

Reading from the parchment, Ayah Brachah of Maalot said that Jewish youth were determined to change the "reprehensible norms" that had taken root in the Knesset. "Education does not end in the classroom teaching about democracy. We are watching you (MKs) and we expect something better.

You degraded our flag."

President Herzog praised the pupils for their initiative and suggested that if there were a system of direct elections, such shameful spectacles would not be repeated. Perhaps, he said, some good would eventually come of the disgrace in the Knesset.

Bet Hanassi, the President's House has received numerous calls from citizens protesting against the MKs' behavior. Herzog said he was sure the majority of the country's citizens, young and old, shared the pupils' "disgust" at the MKs' disruptions. Soon before the MKs began shouting and walking out, over a speech by Acting Speaker, Yair Sprinzak of Moledet, Herzog had advised them to honour the Knesset, if they showed disrespect for it, he warned, their "own prestige would be impaired, as would the prestige of our democratic system."

Most of the Israelis in the Knesset and at home were ashamed of the foreign dignitaries who occupied the balcony, and the whole world that were following this "circus" on television.

After the elections of November 1988, to the twelfth Knesset, Ariel (Arik) Sharon played a key role in coalition talks, prior to the formation of the new government headed by Yitzhak Shamir. Sharon had special relationship with the Orthodox (Haredi) leaders. Sharon was the most qualified person in the Likud Party to handle negotiation with the Orthodox. Sharon had also a previous experience of coalition talks, when he initiated the combination of the Gahal Party and the Liberal Party to form the Likud Party, several years ago.

The problem ahead will probably be, among others, coping with a world granting increasing recognition to the PLO, more terror and more intifadah. Bush coming to term with the Soviets, misunderstanding with the Diaspora, economic mess encouraged by the Histadrut and the Maarah, more strikes, etc. Life will not be easy for the next Premier, whoever he may be.

The Likud and the Right never defined the Religious-Orthodox parties as non-Zionist. Yet, when they were wealing and dealing with the Orthodox parties with the intention to form a narrow coalition with them, this, inspite of the fact that Yitzhak Shamir and the Likud party received the President's mandate to form the government, suddenly the Orthodox parties became "Kosher" for the Maarah, suddenly they were no longer non-Zionist.

The increasing involvement of the Orthodox parties in the Israeli politics and the affars of state will gradually bring them closer to the Secularists. The differences between the two parties will decrease, the gap will narrow and suspicion will diminish or even vanish. They will get to know each other better. Contribute to each other, influence each other. Both the Secularists and the Orthodox will benefit from it.

History sometimes repeats itself. It is quite possible that, if Yitzhak Shamir came up with a suitable offer to Yitzhak Rabin, Yitzhak Rabin and his "hawkish" supporters in the Maarah will desert the Maarah, form a new party, as the late General Moshe Dayan did, and join a coalition under the Likud, for Rabin is no less a pragmatist than Peres.

Because of the political manipulation of the Maarah, trying to steal away some Haredi (Orthodox) parties (like Agudat Yisrael, etc.) from the Likud, Shamir couldn't form his government in 21 days and needed some more time. President Herzog extended his mandate and gave Shamir 21 additioal days.

The regular Israeli citizen rightfully suspected that the long political negotiations and bargaining between the different parties trying to form a new government were no longer about ideas, but about jobs.

On Wednesday, November 30, 1988 (Kislev 21, 5749), the Maarah Bureau rejected its top leadership's (Shimon Peres and Yitzhak Rabin) bid for broad-government negotiations with the Likud. The majority of the Bureau was not prepared to sacrifice the party's identity by forming a coalition with the Likud. They preferred to stay in opposition to the Likud-Right-Religious narrow coalition and hold the option for a future political alternative open.

The President of Israel is the apolitical head of state and represents the sovereignty of the state and its mission on this earth and history. He is also responsible for the unity of the Jewish people. The President of Israel lacks executive power, which is in the hands of the prim-minister and the government.

Inspite of the fact that the President of Israel does not interfere in Political matters, President Herzog made it an exception when he requested Shimon Peres to go back to his party, the Maarah, and ask them to change their decision of November 30 and try to form a coalition with the Likud, because, that is what the Israeli voter really wanted (40:39).

President Herzog was also worried about the current situation (economy, unemployment, Arab uprsing, etc.) and believed that in order to cope with the situation the country needed badly a stable National Unity Government, like the one it had before the elections of November 1st.

Contemplating a tie, a hung Parliament (Knesset), the President decided to intervene. Therefore, it was President Herzog who revived the atmosphere of negotiations between the Likud and the Maarah, after the "compliments" they gave each other during the elections campaign.

Though the president considers himself the spokesman for Israel's higher interests, the Israelis still remember Herzog's Maarah background, and some may suspect him that he is depriving the Likud of the fruits of victory by calling for a change in the "rules".

Deputy Prime Minister David Levi was persistently for the establishment of a National-Unity

Government.Like many others Levi believed that only a broad coalition could cope with crucial problems Israel was facing. Levi was disgusted of the humiliation that the large parties have inflicted upon themselves by courting the small parties, mainly the Ultra-Orthodox (Haredi) parties.

David Levi was appointed to lead the Likud negotiation team with other parties, but when Shamir refused to commit into accepting Levi's request for the Foreign Affairs portfolio, Levi reportedly telephoned Rabbi Ovadiah Yossef, the political patron of Shass and warned him that Shamir's promises are not to be trusted.

Levi insisted that a few days earlier Shamir promised him the Foreign Ministry folio. Naturally, this scandalous incident caused a deep rift between Levi and Shamir.

It will not be the first time in history that when a large party like the Maarah loses power it breaks up into pieces never to recover again. The risk of dissolution of the Maarah Party through loss of power and going to opposition is as great as joining a coalition with the Likud, or, under the Likud. If the Maarah will decide to form a coalition government with the Likud, it will be as a result of the unprecedented interference of President Herzog, who, thus, saved the Maarah Party from degenerating on the opposition benches.

At a meeting of Maarah's "Sareinu", the forum of Maarah ministers, Defense Minister Yitzhak Rabin angrily accused a new member of the Knesset, Yossi Beilin (Maarah), for making a deal with Agudat Yisrael and signing a document with Rabbi Shmuel Halpert, MK (Agudah), by which, under certain conditions, the Agudah will be ready to back the Maarah Party. According to Rabin, the agreement with the Agudah was signeds behind the backs of the Maarah's ministers, and while Yitzhak Shamir was having his coalition talks with the endorsement of President Herzog. An underhand attempt to interfere with Shamir's coalition talks. This agreement with the Agudah was concealed from the Maarah Party Bureau, which only hours earlier had rejected Rabin's plea to go with Shamir (Likud). Beilin's agreement with the Agudah persuaded bureau members to vote against a broad government. Some of them still had the illusion that the Maarah could demand that Shimon Peres be allowed to share the premiership with Yitzhak Shamir. Another Rotation.

The description "Peres's Poodle", attached by Rabin in an early morning radio interview to MK Yossi Beilin, showed the grudge that Rabin still hold for Peres, as well as an expression of the enmity that still existed between the Maarah's two divided ideological camps, the camp of Rabin and the camp of Peres. Beilin was Peres's aid at the Prime Minister's office during the years 1984-1986 and at the Foreign Ministery during the years 1986-1988.

Rabin also detested Yossi Beilin because he represented the ideological Left wing of the party, the super doves, which prefer talks with the PLO to negotiations with the Likud.

But less than twenty four hours after Rabin's accusation of Beilin, meaning Peres, he and Peres could be seen in close conference on the proper strategies needed to win over the Central Committee. "Birds of feather stick together", both Peres and Rabin knew well that if they didn't hang together they would hang separately. They needed each other in the coalition government. They need each other in the opposition where Uzi Baram, Mota Gur and others are waiting them in the "corner".

Opposition will bring a major revolution in the Maarah, and can also spark the long awaited ideological battle between Peres and Rabin.

On December 8, 1988 (Kislev 29, 5749), the Maarah's Central Committee voted for entering negotiations with the Likud on forming a broad government, according to the proposal by Party Chairman Shimon Peres and the number 2 man in the Maarah, Defense Minister Yitzhak Rabin. This was also a vote of confidence in Peres and Rabin and nullified the Party Bureau's vote of November 30, 1988 (Kislev 21, 5749).

After the vote, Secretary-General Uzi Baram called joining a broad coalition with the Likud "running amok with no reason into a government headed by Yitzhak Shamir. The argument is not for joining or not joining the government, but between hope and despair, between accepting Maarah's certain decline and the belief that it can be an alternative.

What good did the previous National Unity Government, in the years 1986 and 1987 do? The Maarah will become a permanent satellite of the Likud, like the National Religious Party and like the General Zionists (Liberals), and we saw what became of them," Said Baram.

On the other hand, Shamir was pleased with the Maarah's decision, because it opens the way to the broad-based government that he wanted since the elections, as it will bring the country a quiet and stable economy with the minimum amounts of strikes and the cooperation of the Histadrut, the Union.

Speculators believe that it is very important for the survival of the Maarah that they grab hold of the Finance portfolio so as to save Koor, Kupat Holim, Hevrat Ha'Ovdim, Kibbutzim, from financial disaster. It is vital for the future of the Maarah that these institutions be resuscitated and preserved.

If the Maarah will eventually join the Likud in a coalition with the substantial amount of debts they (the Maarah) have to cover, it will be wise if they do not take the Treasury Folio, because, it will be obvious that they do it for party interests rather than national interests and will have to pay for it dear during the next elections, in 1992.

"The Likud Can" was the slogan of the Likud Party in the election campaign, which meant, that, the Likud can handle the political situation, the Likud can handle the outside pressure, the Likud can handle the security problems, the Likud can handle the Palestinian-Arab uprising, the Likud can crush the Arab Intifadah, the Likud can take care of the bad economy, the Likud can take care of the heavy unemployment, the Likud can take care of the problem "Who is a Jew", the Likud can take care of all these alone, without the help of the Maarah, without the support of the Labor.

The Israeli public believed, trusted the Likud promises and gave it its vote. The Likud has been given the majority. The Likud won the election. The Likud had the opportunity to carry out its promises, to carry out its policies, together with the Right block and the Religious block as partners, in a "narrow" coalition.

Finally, after so many years the Likud have become independent from the Maarah and can carry out its plans, its ideology, its platform. But instead, the Likud had suddenly, for no reason whatsoever, lost it self-confidence. The Likud have "chickened out", afraid to act alone, and sought very eagerly the partnership with the Maarah. Mr. Yitzhak Shamir, the out going Premier and the future Premier seeks to form a large coalition with the Maarah, very similar to the National Unity Government, which he presently heads with all the defects and heart brakes. This inspite of the bad experience he just had with the Maarah, for four years. Yitzhak Shamir was afraid to face the problems ahead, alone, without the Maarah on his side.

Yitzhak Shamir got the "Height Fear" which reminds of Premier Menachem Begin, when he reached power on May 1977, had the "Dayan Syndrom" when he appointed General Moshe Dayan (Maarah) Foreign Minister. Gave up the Foreign Ministry to an ex-member of the Maarah, his greatest competitors.

Shamir needed the 'broad coalition" with the Maarah so that he could withstand better the outside pressure from the Reforms and Conservatives in the U.S.A. when trying to implement the amendment of the Law of Return, that's "Who is a Jew?" and also to nutralize the Union, the Histadrut and avoid series of Labor strikes and increase in salary demands which could bring back the inflation chaos.

Likud sources said that Yitzhak Shamir was convinced that only broad government could withstand international pressure to negotiate with the PLO. Shamir believed that a narrow Right-Wing government could face constant pressure, with "the entire world" supporting the large opposition led by the Maarah. The same sources said that Shamir was also worried by the recent statements made by Rabbi Eliezer Shach, who welcomed the U.S. decision to talk to the PLO because it could help avoid blood-shed. Shamir feared that under pressure, Degel Hatorah and Shass, who consider Rabbi Shach a spiritual leader, might bolt his government and transfer their allegiance to the Maarah. Shamir was resolved to keep Shimon Peres out of the Foreign Office, where his diplomatic statements, contradicting the Likud policies would be damaging.

Shamir's main goal in working hard for National Unity Government was, to show the world that the Israeli public is united, speaks with one voice and is determined to fight the idea of an independent Palestinian-Arab state on its territories. Also to show the world that it cannot profit from the Arabs at Israel's expense.

What expedited the positive conclusion of the broad coalition negotiations between the Likud and tha Maarah was the fact that the Maarah accepted the Likud's conditions that:

1. The Maarah will not receive the Foreign Ministry and will not interfere in matters of foreign affairs.

2. Israel will resist the establishment of an additional Palestinian-Arab in the Gaza Strip and the territories between Israel and Jordan, that's Judea and Samaria or the West Bank

3. Israel will not negotiate with the PLO.

Three necessary tools with which Shamir and Arens will be able to oppose, on behalf of the two great parties, the Likud and the Maarah, any foreign policy that is dangerous to the interests of Israel. Tools with which Israel could speak outwardly, to the world, with one voice.

It was difficult to explain how a party (Maarah) that advocates negotiations with the PLO joins a government that its platform rejects any negotiations with PLO. The broad government is also based on a compromise between the Likud and the Maarah.

The Maarah didn't accept the Likud platform of a "Greater Israel" (Eretz Israel Hashlemah). On the other hand, the Likud didn't accept the Maarah platform of "Territorial Concessions". The Maarah didn't accept the Likud demand of fourty more settlements in the West Bank during the years 1988-1992 but accepted settlements in principle and agreed that the settlements are not obstacles to peace.

The common denominator rather than the dividing prevailed and brought the parties together.

During the years 1984-1988, the National Unity Government spoke with two voices, the voice of the Likud and the voice of the Maarah. Outwardly, to the whole world it looked far from unity.

After the elections of November 1988, Shamir was driving again to a National Unity Government, so that he could fight more efficiently the new PLO political offensive and the Palestinian "Declaration of Independence", with the Maarah at his side, with one voice.

After the unfortunate experience with the Maarah during the years 1984-1988, was Shamir still expecting that the Likud and the Maarah would be speaking with one voice? Was he still expecting that he and Peres, Arens, Weizmann, Sharon, Gur and Bar-Lev would be speaking with one voice? That is nothing but wishful thinking. Many Israelis are convinced that Shamir was, for one reason or another, driving the country back to another stagnant, frozen, idle government.

The Maarah's record during the four years of National Unity Government of 1984-1988 is not one to inspire confidence, nor can it justify a new Likud-Maarah partnership.

Judging from Isreal's past experience, the continuation of a so-called National Unity Government between the two major opposing parties, the Likud and the Maarah, is admittedly a bad choice. It is a formula for continued governmental paralysis. But, as some Israelis believe, that sort of bad is infinitely better than the alternative of a Likud-led coalition with the right and the religious.

On November 1, 1988, the Israelis have made their choice and the Likud, the primary beneficiary should have honoured their choice, lest it will lose face and votes in the next elections. Yet, inspite of the fact that the people have spoken and given their verdict in favour of the Likud, the democratic will of the Israeli majority is unfulfilled. Then, one should ask, what were the elections for?

When comparing with the American mentality and the results of the November 1988 elections in the U.S.A., George Walker Bush won the elections, Michael Dukakis lost the elections. George W. Bush, legally, without hesitations, became president and started to rule America. He didn't form a coalition with Dukakis. George W. Bush didn't have inferiority complex.

Same as all the Israeli governments didn't know what to do with the military victories and wasted them, so, it seems, the Likud party's will to govern is inferior to its capability to win the election.

When finally the opportunity arrived, instead of grasping it with two hands and rule the country it preferred to rehabilitate the losing Maarah, its old rival. A totally irrational attitude derived from some kind of inferiority complex towards the Maarah.

By offering the Maarah participation in his new government, Yitzhak Shamir, as a matter of fact, has raised the Maarah from the gutters and saved it from degeneration and probably total disappearance from the Israeli political map. Shamir also gave up twelve Cabinet seats, a very high price.

Shamir's Likud-Maarah coalition and its apparent commitment to national reconciliation is nothing but escape-device for a party that is hesitant to act singlemindedly, with confidence and determination, and smells of temporary ease, political sloth and a shoe that is too big for its foot.

A Likud-Nationalistic-Religious coalition could have carried out an excellent territorial-demographic-spiritual national programme and generated a new spirit in the country, but instead, Shamir preferred a broad government with the Maarah. Time will tell if the man was right or wrong.

Shamir had it all planned, long before the elections of November 1st. His national responsibility guided him to get the Maarah back into a broad coalition. He had his good reasons. His decision to bring the Maarah in reflected long-range strategy. It was far from being an opportunist tactic.

The fate of the proposed Likud-Maarah coalition hung in the balance as a divided Likud Central Committee voted in a secret ballot whether to approve the Prime Minister Shamir's proposal to bring the Maarah into his next government at the expense of the right wing and religious parties. Shamir insisted that the international situation calls for "as broad a government as possible, and argued that the Likud could find common ground with the Maarah on mutual opposition to the creation of a Palestinian-Arab state. He also added, that "although it is more comfortable to sit only with people from our camp, the national imperative compels me to make this recommendation."

Shamir referred to his sense of "National Responsibility", and threatens that if his proposal is rejected he will return his mandate to form a government, to the President.

The crowd expressed disbelief when Shamir argued that it was impossible for the Likud to form a narrow government. Committee members accused Shamir of "selling out to the Maarah", "committing party suicide", and the like.

Prime Minister Shamir's political life was at stake.

Speculators believe that even if Shamir could have formed a narrow government, it could not last for a whole term. Parlimentary crises, conflict of interests among its partners, exaggerated demands from the Maarah opposition, using its traditional tool, the Histadrut, endless labor strikes, etc. would have put an end to that government. It seems that Shamir had little choice but to take in as partners his biggest "enemies", the Maarah. It was the least of the worse. Shamir believed that, inspite of its discrepancy and defaults, the National Unity Government is a more stable government, considering the conditions and situation dictated by the results of the elections. These realistic facts became very clear to both parties, the Likud and the Maarah, and following dramatic meetings and debates of their authorized institutions they found no better way but to approve the broad coalition government.

Sharon, contradicting Shamir's decision for a broad government, argued that: "the Likud had and still has the ability to lead a government in which it is a majority, a government that can make decisions." Sharon also said that he believes that the stated goal of a broad government-presenting a unified front to the world-was not possible when "a significant part of Labour favours talking to the PLO."

From summing up the behaviour of the Israeli public during the elections it was noted that the Israelis are very politically conscientious. A little over eighty per cent of those eligible actually participated. Almost everyone who was in the country on that day, voted. There being no polling arrangements overseas, many travellers made a point of expediting their return to Israel or delaying their departure, so they can vote. Everyone regarded entering the polling booth a great responsibility and duty. The results show that the sixty-years-old state is as committed to democracy as ever and that the future of the country is everybody's business.

Fifty two days after the elections, on December 22, 1988, members of the 12th Knesset voted confidence in Yitzhak Shamir's new government of twenty eight ministers-a cabinet larger than any of its predecessors.

After long and tiring coalition negotiations as well as a stormy meeting of the Likud Party Central Committee, Israel, finally had a government, National Unity Government.

It was the grave problems facing the nation that dictated the establishment of the National Unity coalition. "The nation had to speak clearly and with one voice", said Shamir.

It had taken Shamir thirty-nine days to fulfil the mandate originally given to him by President Herzog on November 14 and extended on December 5, 1988.

On December 22, 1988, Shamir sent a communiqué formally advising the President that, in accordance with article 13b of the Basic Law: the Government, he had succeeded in his task.

In the inauguration speech of the 12th Knesset, Prime-Minister Shamir said that, Jerusalem and Washington would draw even closer during the Bush administration: "the success of Bush and his associates will be the success of all freedom-loving persons and will ensure the prosperity of the entire world."

Shamir also added that: "A Jewish and an Arab state already existed on the territory of the "Historic Land of Israel", and that there would never be a second Arab state there."

Shamir presented his cabinet to President Herzog, in the President's House, on December 22, 1988. President Herzog told Shamir that he understands that "the new government represents the desire of the majority of our people for unity and tolerance, for the closing of ranks in the face of external threats and inner divisions."

Israel's new government consisted of:

Yitzhak Shamir-Prime minister, and Minister of Labour and Social welfare (Likud)

Shimon Peres-Vice Premier and Finance Minister (Maarah)

David Levi-Deputy Premier and Housing (Likud)

Yitzhak Navon-Deputy Premier and Education and Culture (Maarah)

Yitzhak Rabin-Defence Minister (Maarah)

Rafael Edri-Without Portfolio (Maarah)

Ehud Olmert-In charge of the Arab Sector (Likud)

Moshe Arens-Foreign Affairs (Likud)

Chaim Bar-lev-Police (Maarah)

Mordechai Gur-Without Portfolio (Maarah)

Arye Deri-Interior (shass)

Ezer Weizman-Science and Development (Maarah)

Gad Ya'acobi-Communications (Maarah)

Avraham Katz-Oz-Agriculture (Maarah)

Yitzhak Modai-Economics and Planning (Likud)
Ronni Milo-Environment (Likud)
Dan Meridor-Justice (Likud)
Moshe Nissim-Without Portfolio (Likud)
Yitzhak Peretz-Immigrant Absorption (Shass)
Gideon Patt-Tourism (Likud)
Yaacov Tsur-Health (Maarah)
Moshe Katsav-Transport (Likud)
Moshe Shahal-Energy (Maarah)
Ariel Sharon-Industry and Trade (Likud)
Zevulun Hammer-Religious Affairs (NRP)

The division of ministeries between the Likud and the Maarah were as follows:

The Likud
Office of the Prime Minister
Ministry of Foreign Affairs
Ministry of Construction and Housing
Ministry of Industry and Trade
Ministry of Economics and Planning
Ministry of Justice
Ministry of Transport
Ministry of Tourism

The Maarah
Ministry of Finance
Ministry of Defence
Ministry of Education and Culture
Ministry of Communications
Ministry of Agriculture
Ministry of Health
Ministry of Police
Ministry of Energy and Infrastructure

Shamir's new government included five former generals. Hawkish Likud had one former general in the Cabinet (Ariel Sharon), while dovish Maarah had four former generals in the Cabinet (Yitzhak Rabin, Mordechai Gur, Chaim Bar-Lev and Ezer Weizman).

The Maarah had no choice but to join Shamir's government. If they stayed outside, with the debts they had, they would be ruined. Therefore, the Maarah had no choice but to consent to exchange its peace plan for a mess of economic-aid pottage for curing Histadrut industries and enterprises.

The few days of uncertainty, when it was not clear yet whether the Maarah will or will not join Shamir's government, showed exactly what would happen to the party if they stayed outside. Instead of preparing an alternative to the Likud, they quarreled with each other on internal alternatives, they were busy with internal intrigues, trying to undermine each other, which climaxed with the resignation of the Secretary General Uzi Baram, who opposed Peres's decision to join Shamir's coalition.

Apart from the extremely heavy debts and the questions of national policy the Maarah had serious reasons to prefer Shamir's government.

In this new situation the National Unity Government continues to survive. After All, a lot of people are happy with this arrangement. Peres can continue to present himself as a man of peace and talk all he likes abroad about how he is fighting for it, if only the Likud, meanwhile he needs to do nothing, concede nothing. For Peres, Unity Government is the best bargain because it assures his continued leadership of the Maarah and postpones the showdown with Yitzhak Rabin, his strongest competitor.

Yitzhak Shamir, at first, created the impression of being ready to give the Religious Party everything they demanded-to win their support to get the President to name him to form a government: then after receiving the mandate from the President to form a government Shamir did everything in his power to draw the Maarah into a broad coalition. It was his prerogative.

Shamir might have sacrificed his credibility with the Religious, but Shamir will be seventy-seven years old in the next elections, in 1992 and it is very likely that he will not run again.

Likud campaign managers were worried that the Likud might lose the next elections if the party fulfilled its agreement and promises to the religious parties, because, after all, the majority of the Likud supporters are Secularists and not Religious.

Many in Israel believed, mainly the secularists that during the coalition negotiations, the religious parties, separately and collectively, exaggerated in their demands on matters of principle, in hard cash and in ministerial seats. It was believed that their demands were far beyond what their limited strength justified. After all the four religious parties won only fifteen per cent of the vote, their stable proportion in previous votes up to the 1981 election.

"It has taken a long time," stated a secular Israeli, "but the important thing is that we have a broad government and have not given in to religious blackmail."

Certain people in Israel have accused the religious parties for extortion, blackmailing and selling their political support to those who pay more. At least everybody acknowledged that the religious parties were using these monies to maintain existing schools, building new Yeshivot, on education. With these monies they support orphanages, homes for the elderlies, philanthropic institutions, etc. So what is wrong with this?

Other parties are also doing it. That's politics. Only they do not make contributions to philanthropic institutions. They make contributions to their own pockets.

"We have been tricked and we have been cheated. The religious sector has always been discriminated against and it seems that it always will be," said an Orthodox man when he saw on television Shamir's broad coalition government. It should not surprise anyone that the religious parties which worked hard prior and during the elections for their principles have settled so soberly for their bread-and-butter, day-to-day interests. Politicians learn very quickly not to bear grudges. Politicians also learn very quickly not to count on promises given by other politicians. They know very well that after the elections, first thing to do is, to salvage whatever they could from the wreckage.

The religious parties understood that it is more efficient to sit inside than stay outside. It is a vital stake in sitting inside, so that they can watch over the religious status quo.

The religious parties also understood that since the amendment to the Law of Return has small prospect to receive a majority in this Knesset their task was, at least, to hold the big parties, the Likud and the Maarah, to their promises with regard to the Enabling Law (Hasmacha) whereby all coversions conducted abroad receive the endorsement of the Rabbinate in Israel.

The Religious parties understood that they have to join the coalition also for the sake of observing that the budgets on religious matters remain in their former levels and are not reduced.

Both the Likud and the Maarah feel more comfortable having the Religious parties inside the coalition than wandering around free, outside, cold and hungry.

It is a lie to claim that the Religious parties tried to play the two big parties, the Likud and the Maarah, off against each other. For that, the two big parties didn't need any help.

Israel that wants to save its bad "Socialitic" economy, finally realized that it could be done only by adopting a western capitalistic type of economy and by encouraging free enterprize. Therefore, one sometimes wonders if by nominating Shimon Peres as Finance minister, Shamir didn't make a terrible mistake. Shimon Peres, who was born and raised in the Socialistic school that brought complete bankruptcy to the economy of the country as well as over one hundred thousand people unemployed.

The new broad government will have to handle two important, top priority issues: the impressive PLO successful propaganda offensive in the area of foreign policy and the economic recession with the great unemployment. It will be a hindrance and obstacle to the required amendment of the Law of Return (Who is a Jew). The worse thing that the Maarah can do in the new Shamir's government is block the "Who is a Jew" amendment, that's kill it. To most Israelis this is something unforgivable.

This National Unity Government is, again, like the previous one (1984-1988), geared for paralysis, in the most critically urgent times, when full action is needed.

Speculators believe that the Unity Government was known for its political weakness because of the equal power of its two major components. But, on the other hand, this weakness caused the Government determination to behave economically in a more responsible way, which helped reduce the great inflation and put an end to the "elections' economy."

The greatest mistake of the National Unity Government was to block all settlements in Judea, Samaria and Gaza. In 1989 Israel had only 70,000 people in these territories. It could have had over 250,000.

Israel was stalled by its own democracy. Immobility in the government, total political stagnation, the momentum of settlement in Judea, Samaria and Gaza stopped completely. The elections of November 1988 produced a government of "National Unity" precisely because there was no national unity in Israel. A free, democratic society was evenly divided on matters of its own life and death, its own survival.

The 60-60 split in parliamentary support for the Likud and the Maarah is the reason why Israel is burdened with a paralysed government and a political system that doesn't function. It is the Israeli voter who has to be blamed for such a tie situation because it is the Israeli voter who is afraid to give one party a majority. By denying power from their rulers they have also denied them responsibility.

A growing number of citizens have lost all confidence in the Unity Government and view Israeli politicians and political parties as totally unreliable. Many were seriously disillusioned with the whole democratic process and declared: "We need a powerful man to come and put some order in our life."

To survive, the Maarah had to accept the inevitable. In return for continued economic aid to its hard pressed institutions and enterprisest,had to give up its foreign policy initiative teaming with Shamir,the Likud, Peres has irrevocably blurred Maarah's ideological distinction.

Ideologically the Maarah had degenerated completely. It seemed that the whole Labour movement had reached the end of the road. The Maarah is dead and living in the Unity Government.

The following is a letter to the editor of the Jerusalem Post:
Ethical Immorality

Sir-There was a time, not too long ago, when the near anarchy in Israeli electioneering practices could be viewed as quaintly characteristic of the most vibrant democracy on earth. Furtheremore, it was almost taken for granted that a candidate with even the most miniscule constituency could legitimately claim the same public financial support to mount a campaign as large party candidate.

Were we living in normal times or in a normal country, the near quarter of a million new Shekels due each candidate from the public exchequer would not raise an eyebrow. A new generation of army-age youth would accept that such expenditures were necessary to ensure those democratic practices they were soon expected to defend, thus helping to fulfil the Zionist dream.

But we neither have the luxury of considering ourselves normal nor do we live in normal times. More than ever our youth need models of moral self-scrutiny who put the public's social and economic welfare over private avarice. They are not going to find such models among the majority of our newly installed parliamentarians.

With the seating of the "new" Knesset, the large parties have successfully organized the plenum to approve the preliminary reading of a give-away bill, enriching each of the Members of Knesset by 115,000 New Israeli Shekels in retroactive funds to cover his campaign deficit. How can a treasury preaching and practicing frugality in the interest of "combating inflation", "balancing the budget", "rescuing the economy", suddenly find the resources to relieve the debts of financially crisis-ridden candidates who over-extended their legal cash campaign expense allotment?

The government has taken office amidst growing unemployment, mounting traffic and pedestrian fatalities on unimproved roads, gross official negligence of medical facilities and devaluation. The Members of Knesset glaring disdain for the public pain makes their decision to increase cash payments from 207,000 New Israeli Shekels to 320,000 New Israeli Shekels even more disgraceful. Can they afford to implement such a cavalier decision to add 20 million New Israeli Shekels to a budget already inadequate to meet social needs?

Are we naïve to still expect honour and moral examples of selflessness on the part of elected leaders to whom the young would look with pride? While high school curricula call for the teaching of citizenship and democracy, the hidden curriculum is tragically written in the halls and backrooms of the Knesset when deals like this are consummate.
RABBI SHAUL R.FEINBERG
Jerusalem, January 18, 1989.

On May 17, 1977, the Maarah Party lost their power when the Likud won the general elections. Since then it lived for twelve years with the illusion of reconquering the power. The results of the elections to the local governments and municipalities on February 28, 1989, was their final blow and showed the Maarah, the Labor, that the Likud was the real boss and had the full control over the country and its future policy. The Likud had almost a landslide. This showed that the majority in Israel is advocating the policy of the Likud and not the policy of the Maarah.

The Provisional Government of the State of Israel formed in 1948 consisted of thirteen members. The first elected Israeli government had only twelve Cabinet ministers.

Later, coalition reasons increased the number of Cabinet ministers to twenty-four in 1969 and twenty-six in 1988.

The "small" governments were much more efficient than the "big" governments and handled bigger and more important projects.

Towns like Petah Tikvah, Hedera, Ramat Gan, Ashdod, Raananah, Tveriah (Tiberias), Nahariyah, Holon, Beersheba, Hod Hasharon, Mitzpeh Ramon, Ofakim, etc. were well known form any years as Maarah bastions, were taken by the Likud, and only a few thousand votes gave Maarah another term in "Red Haifa". The only exception was Jerusalem, where popular Teddy Kollek won his sixth term. Reminding very much the late Mayor Richard Daley of Chicago. Kollek made it, as he had done it before, under his own rather than his party's (Maarah) ticket.

In the Maarah no one really believed Shimon Peres that the party did not lose the local elections. Several members in the Maarah denounced his attempt to sweep this defeat under the carpet. Responsible members in the Maarah took this defeat as a vote of no-confidense in the Maarah. Several Maarah members saw the handwriting on the wall several weaks before the election, though not imagining the full extent of the defeat. They blamed the Maarah ministers, mainly Peres and Rabin for the defeat. The cause, they believed, was entering the coalition government.

They believed that the Maarah ministers yielded to vested-interest groups, such as the Kibbutzim, the Moshavim, the Histadrut, Kupat Holim, Koor, Sollel Boneh, etc. who wanted to install Peres in the Treasury, expecting him to pay out their enormous debts.

The Maarah had reconciled itself to Likud policy, accepting the Likud's foreign affairs and defense policy in return for money.

There are members in the Maarah who believe that the Maarah sold its soul to the Likud for money. They believe that by joining Shamir's National Unity Government the Maarah denied the country an alternative and legitimized Shamir's rule and policy, and in order to avoid political disaster the Maarah must leave immediately Shamir's coalition government. They believe that the Maarah needs a great shakeup, a change in leadership.

To ignore the political meaning of the results of the 1989 municipal elections would be a great mistake for the Maarah. The Israeli citizen is very politically conscientious. Life made him a "political animal". Therefore, inspite of the fact that the elections were for the local governments there is no doubt that the Israeli voter took into consideration his political affiliation as well. This, in addition to his liking to a particular candidate in his town.

The Israeli citizen still feels that the Maarah Party is guilty for the nation's difficulties and can no longer fathom its behaviour and the personal examples of its leaders.

The Likud had another convincing victory. The Israelis, as we have seen time and again, want Likud.

The Maarah admitted that the Likud has just won a resounding vote of confidence. The results reflected a strong pro-Likud sentiment, which was sweeping the country. The voters were not only interested in garbage collection, sewage removal, and sanitation or sidewalks cleanliness. The voter was interested in ending the intifada, in getting rid of the Arabs, in the future of his children.

One should also admit that the Likud chalked up these successes despite low voter turnout. Had there been a higher turnout, its performance would have been much more impressive.

The municipal election victory deepened Likud's roots in the people. Shamir's government is strong and stands on two legs-central and local.

The results of the municipal elections with an almost landslide victory of the Likud was not accidental. It reflected the Israelis thinking, the Israelis logic. The Likud was turning into Israel's main rulling party, same as the Mapai-Maarah was for several decades.

The November 1989 election to the Histadrut had the following results:

Maarah-55%

Likud-27.5%

Mapam-9%

Joint Jewish/Arab list-4.5%

Citizens Rights Movement-4%

The Likud won the general elections on November 1, 1988 (Heshvan 21, 5749), as well as the elections to the municipalities on February 28, 1989 (Adar 23, 5749). On the other hand, the opposition, the Maarah won the elections to the Histadrut, on November 13, 1989 (Heshvan 15, 5750).

This is the direct result of general Israeli mentality that is reluctant to give away all the political power to one party, for fear of a dictatorship or tyranny. Therefore they prefer to split the power between the two main parties: the Likud and the Maarah or the Knesset and the Histadrut (The "Second Government"). This is an Israeli "Check and Balance" system.

On November 24, 1989 (Heshvan 25, 5750), Minister Mordechai Gur (Maarah) charged that Peres's lack of "Personal Appeal" had caused the party's defeat in the November 1988 general elections. Another shot in the battle to succeed Shimon Peres as chairman of the Maarah Party.

Gur spoke at the Maarah's bureau meeting and compared the November 1988 general elections defeat with the success in the November 1989 elections to the Histadrut, in which, Peres argued, the "personal support for Israel Kessar" was the reason for the Maarah's success.

"Although people obviously were aware of the problems with the Histadrut and Hevrat Haovdim, they voted Labour anyway because of their support for Kessar," Gur said.

"Another factor that contributed to our success last week was the coordination between all sections of the party and the participation of the other ministers in the campaign, "said Gur, and because this time, it was not a "one-man" campaign, like in November 1988.

"To win, we therefore need a clever campaign strategy and a credible candidate,"concluded Gur.

Shimon Peres was present at the meeting but did not respond. Haim Ramon, Maarah's Knesset faction chairman called for "real changes" in the Histadrut, warning that otherwise the 93' poll could be like the maarah's 77 Knesset election experience-a painful defeat to the Maarah.

Shimon Peres would do anything to become prime minister. Shimon Peres was "dying" to become Israel's prime minister. Shimon Peres was power edict.

The reliability, the honesty and the integrity of Mr. Shimon Peres could be illustrated in the following examples:

In April 1976 Peres declared: "If a Jew may settle in Brooklyn, N.Y. why can't he settle in Kadoum, Samaria?" A few years later he was fighting the idea of Jewish settlements in Judea, Samaria and Gaza.

All his life Peres was a typical secular (Hiloni) Jew, not once ridiculing the religious Jews. In April 1990, when he was struggling hard for the "throne" he declared that:

"In Williamsbourg, N.Y. the religious feeling of its Jewish population is fully respected and the traffic is prohibited there on Shabbat. Why can't we do it here in Israel too?"

Several other examples could be found in Yitzhak Rabin's diary, two volumes book "Pinkas Sherut" in which Mr. Shimon Peres is "crucified".

-Rabin wrote in his diary that he would never set foot in a Peres government. A year later Rabin agreed to be Peres's candidate for Defense Minister (in 1981, when he replaced Haim Bar-Lev late in the election campaign).

-Rabin's widely reported nervous breakdown as Chief-of-Staff in the Six-Day War.

-Rabin's limping three years as prime minister in 1974-1977.

-The scandal over Rabin's wife illegal bank account in the U.S., which made him step down and brought down the Maarah in 1977

-Rabin's recommendation to then-DefenseMinister Ariel Sharon that Israel "tighten" the noose around Beirut in 1981,

-Rabin's failure to foresee the intifada and supress it.

-Rabin's amazingly undiplomatic public explanations of his beatings policy in the territories.

-Rabin's castigation of the Russians for failing to prevent the hijecking of a plan to Israel, in 1988.

All these did nothing to damage his credibility in the Maarah. None of these missteps had been made to stick to Rabin by his frustrated critics.

Rabin may be an accomplished executive but he lacks vision. His analysis of events often seem superficial, Rabin can be logical but he is rarely eloquent. Rabin is never inspiring. Painfully shy and unexpressive.

Shimon Peres lead his party, the Maarah, to four defeats. The majority of the Maarah's leaders knew in their hearts that they should have replaced Peres after the November 1988 election defeat. The trouble was that they didn't happen to have an inspiring alternative. During the 16 years in which Peres and Rabin dominated the party and paralyzed with their infights, the Maarah was helplessly split and demoralized.

The late Golda Meir, Prime Minister of Israel, once defined the Maarah Party as "Tammany Hall", After thirteen years of leadership, Shimon Peres succeeded to turn the Maarah Party into a "Casino Los Vegas".

There is a substantial decline in trust to politicians. The world, in general, is fed up with lying politicians making promises they can't possibly keep. Voters are fed up with the exploitation coming from various sources: fed up with trying to live on wages that don't pay the bills, but most of all fed up with their inability to make substantial changes in the world.

6. ELECTIONS IN THE ARAB SECTOR

With the establishment of the new Islamic movement headed by Sheikh Abdullah Nimer Darwish, there will be probably an "Islamization" of the Arab-Israeli conflict.

Sheikh Abdullah Nimer Darwish from Kfar Kassem is the acknowledged leader of the Islamic movement in Israel. Their number two man is probably Sheikh Ahmad A'asi from Kfar Kara. Other leaders are: Sheikh Ahmad Azzam from Taybe and Sheikh Reeyad Salah Mahajne from Um-El-Fahem. The new Islamic movement has no commitment to Israel or to any of its political parties. It was an escape from Communism, Western and Israeli style of life.

At the start, the first steps after inception, the Islamic movement in Eretz Israel, Greater Israel, had received a moral and spiritual uplift as well as encouragement from the Ayatollah Khomeini in Iran. If there is an upsurge of Islamic fundementalism in Israel and the territories, it is due at least as much to the Isaeli influence and to the example of Jewish fundementalism as to any influence from abroad.

The Islamic movement in Eretz Israel was very impressed by the great success of the Jewish Orthodox parties in the November 1988 general elections and decided to imitate them by getting more involved in politics too. They financed their religious and political activities from local contributions as well as from money received from Jordan, Kuwait, Saudi Arabia, the World Islamic Committee, from the PLO, from Libya and from contributions from the Islamic World.

The founders of the Moslem fundementalist movemets, both in Israel proper and in Judea, Samaria and Gaza, declared that their ultimate goal was to, establish a Moslem state in the Middle East that would include the whole of Palestine. This idea of an additional Islamic state in the region penetrates slowly but constantly in the bones of most of the Arabs in the area. With time they will become more fanatic and more daring, therefore more dangerous to Israel and it does not appear that the wave of Moslem fundamentalism will disappear in the foreseeable future.

Salem Jubran, Hadash activist and deputy editor of the communist daily "Al Itihad" declared that: "The Arab population in Israel is sufficiently experienced, politically mature and responsible to choose for itself without any outside supervision or direction. We vote according to our belief and conscience in the light of our fight for equality in Israel as a national minority and in support of the Intifadah and the legitimate struggle of the Palestinian Arabs in the territories, to attain their national aspirations. As Arabs, who are citizens of the State of Israel, we are in the same boat as progressive, liberal and democratic Jews are. It is, therefore, strange to suggest that the Arab population needs anybody to tell them how to vote. It is well known that Hadash is in full solidarity with the PLO and the Palestinian-Arab people. Israeli Arabs are also concerned with internal issues, such as the government's discriminatory policies towards Arab municipalities and the fact that 12 per cent of Arab academics cannot find appropriate jobs. These topics will also play a part in the voting attitudes of Israeli Arabs, as much as the barbaric activities of the security forces in the occupied territories."

In the last Local Governments, Municipalities elections, in the Arab Sector, Sheikh Abdullah Nimer Darwish and his Islamic movement received 50,000 votes, a little over two mandates. This will probably encourage the man to try his luck again in the next elections to the Knesset. The results of these Municipal elections in the Arab Sector have shocked the leaders of the Islamic Movement and every body else in the Arab Sector as well as in Judea, Samaria and the Gaza Strip. They didn't expect a landslide, as they started to get organized very shortly before the elections.

Yet they were smart enough to avoid political discussions with the Israelis, and to leave the outlines of their larger political ambitions in the blur. But from past experience the Israelis have learned that the Arabs were not very good in hiding their ultimate goals, and sooner or later, they will reveal it.

The Israelis have lived with their "next door neighbors" for many years, they know the Arabs " by heart", "upside down and downside up" and therefore, far from being naïve. This is why it is difficult for them to believe that the Islamic Movement had peaceful political solution in mind. This is why the Israelis are vigilant and alert.

It is believed that if the new Islamic Party will be busy in local government affairs, water sewage, balancing the budget, even promoting religious matters peacefully, they will receive help from the Interior Ministry and encouragement. On the other hand, if they will get involved in fanatic anti-state or anti-Jewish activities, then the Government is likely to intervene.

The people and their newly elected leaders of the Islamic movement better realize soon that the theory that "Islam is the solution" has limited applications in Jewish Israel, The results of voting in the Arab sector in the Israeli municipal elections was disappointing and have made it clear that something new is happening in the Israeli political map, something that might endanger the so-called co-existence between the Jews and the Arabs in Israel.

The struggle for the Arab vote in Israel as from February 28, 1989 (Adar I 30, 5749) had become an internal Arab affair, with hardly anything to do with the Jewish-Zionist parties.

The Islamic fundamentalism movement received a majority in most of the Arab towns and villages in Israel and will probably, be counted as the major political force among the Israeli Arabs.

The danger is also in the fact that the new Islamic movement in the local level might eventually lead to the formation of a national-religious Arab party in time for the next Knesset elections.

It is now obvious that fundamentalism of whatever stripe, not least the Moslem variety, poses a threat to all western type democracies. It might be clever of the Israeli Government to consider the possibility of outlawing this movement on the ground of sedition.

On April 6, 1990, in a memorandum circulated in the territories by the Hamas (Islamic Resistance Movement) it was written that the Hamas would join the Palestinian National Council (PNC), only if the PLO withdraws its acceptance of partition, rejects territorial concessions and refuses to recognisze Israel. It also demanded a modification in the Palestinian National Covenant "in accordance with the faith of the Moslem Palestinian people and its glorious heritage."

The PLO's official organ, "Filastin a Thawra", accused the Hamas of playing into the hands of Israel. Arafat was afraid of the competition of Hamas, the Islamic Resistance Movement. They had a landslide in Algeria and very successful in Jordan. Their popularity was growing and it seemed that they could become an alternative to the PLO.

Arafat threatened the Hamas and on July 5, 1990 (Tamuz 12, 5750) the "filastin a Thwra" wrote the following article:

"Any break or attempt to break away from the rules and regulations of the Palestinian house will only serve the plots of the Zionist enemies and their American guardians to strike at the Arab nation as a whole and not Palestine alone."

"It is very important to remind (Hamas) that many others have tried to play the same role in the Palestinian arena. They all burned themselves to ashes."

The Hamas questioned the PLO's stated role as the sole, legitimate representative of the Palestinian Arabs.

All the Arab parties in Israel were for unification and for the establishment of an all-Arab list to run in the next Knesset elections. An Arab coalition, they believed, could create a list capable of winning enough Knesset seats to make it a power that could not be ignored, a power that could help raise or bring down governments.

7. INTERNATIONAL PEACE CONFERENCE FOR THE MIDDLE EAST

Behold, the Lord thy God hath set the land before thee: go up and possess it, as the Lord God of thy fathers hath said unto thee; fear not, neither be discouraged."

Deuteronomy 1:21

Thus saith the Lord that made thee, and formed thee from the womb, which will help thee; Fear not, O Jacob, my servant; and thou, Jesurun, whom I have chosen."

Isaiah 44:2

"Therefore fear thou not, O my servant Jacob, saith the Lord; neither be dismayed, O Israel: for, lo, I will save thee from afar, and thy seed from the land of their captivity; and Jacob shall return, and shall be in rest, and be quiet, and none shall make him afraid."

Jeremiah 30:1
Jeremiah 46:27,28

"We serve out cause for the length of our lives, a service which ends with our breath"
Lehi anthem-penned by "Yair" (Avraham Shtern, 1907-1942)

"I have stated that I totally and utterly reject Peres and consider his rise to prominence a malignant, immoral disgrace. I will rend my clothes in mourning for the State if I see him become a minister in the Israeli government."
Moshe Sharett, Personal Diary 1957-Vol. 8, p. 2301
Moshe Sharett was a former Israeli Prime minister and Minister of Foreign Affairs.

The recently suggested idea of an international Peace Conference for the Middle East does not contribute to the best interests of the State of Israel, because, some of its participants are not friendly to Israel. Some of them even donot have diplomatic relations with Israel, some are biased and far from being objective, and will, no doubt prefer to back the interests of the Arab oil producing countries, that is support the Palestinian-Arab case. Some of the participants have been, for the last several years, even openly hostile to Israel.

One also wonders what is the British or French interest to mingle or meddle in Middle Eastern affairs, except for getting cheap oil or another interest at the expense of Israeli territory.

There is no one single reason, why should Israel accept the involvement of pro-Palestinian Russia and China in this International Peace Conference.

No one, in Israel, is happy about Soviet or Chinese participation in the International Peace Conference and shaping Israel's future.

Similarly, the Israelis will not be happy if Britain or France will shape its future. The Israelis will, no doubt, prefer to shape their own future, rather than members of the UN Security Council shape it for them.

There is no one single reason why should the involvement of Britain or France in Middle Eastern affairs. It took many years to get these two countries out of the Middle East and it will be totally irrational on the part of Israel to get them back in the area. Especially after the mess they left in the Middle East.

Also, it will be unreasonable on the part of Israel to participate in a conference or in negotiations that have only one purpose: "To give", but nothing to get.

Israel should not conduct talks with the Arabs when there are so many outsiders around, outsiders with no intention to help, but with the intention to use her. Israel should only consider bilateral, face-to-face regional, direct talks with each Arab country, separately, and only if the Arabs give up the idea of receiving any territories from Israel.

What can Israel expect from the UN, which equates Zionism with racism (UN Resolution 3379)? It is naïve to think that the five members of the UN Security Council will attend the Conference without actually interfering in the negotiations and the results. There is no doubt that by going to an international conference would inevitably mean knuckling under to international pressure to negotiate the future of Judea, Samaria and Gaza with the PLO. There is no doubt that the Israeli public would support heartily any Israeli leader or party who could make a persuasive case that the Arabs were truly ready to end the conflict and to offer Israel peace in exchange of peace. There is no doubt that the international conference will not be stripped of coersive power, will be totally biased and will only satisfy the political interests of its individual members. A conference like this can only damage Israel and Israel should not dare approach such a conference. It should keep away from it as from fire.

Unfortunately for Israel, many countries in the world still consider the West Bank and the Gaza as occupied territories, and not liberated.

Israel lost billions of dollars a year in economic losses due to the Arab boycott. The Arab Boycott Office prevents companies who trade wit Israel from doing business in the Arab countries. This Arab boycott against Israel had been going on for many years, since the establishment of the State of Israel in 1948.

Economic pressures began also from the members of the Europen Market, who tried to "persuade" Israel to participate in the International Peace Conference for the Middle East. One of their several means to force Israel into tat Peace Conference was, by postponing the approval of already signed contracts with the Market. Another way to pressure Israel was, their request was to free the Arab farmers, in Judea, Samaria and Gaza Strip from Israeli control, customs, export licenses, etc. and allow then to sell their products, directly to Europe.

Yet, the European Market did approve commercial contracts with Morocco, inspite of the fact that Morocco has been fighting the "Polissario" for the control over the Sahara, for several years.

In general, the governments who are pressuring Israel to join the International Peace Conference and make concessions to the Arabs are doing it for their own heinous, egoist and cynical political objectives. The International Middle East Peace Conference has only one goal-to bite into Israeli territories and cut Israel in half or at least cut a big slice of it. The majority of the Israelis believe that an International Conference is a prescription for a national tragedy. The International Peace Conference for the Middle East will be nothing but an international umbrella for Arab blackmail and extortion, a prescription for catastrophe and self-suicide for Israel.

Everybody wants an Internationsl Conference for peace in the Middle East. Why not start first International Peace Conferences:

-For the IRA in Belfast(Ireland)?

-For the Basques in Spain?

-For the Corsicans in France?

-For the Hungarians in Transylvania?

-For the Albanians in Yugoslavia?

-For the Meskhetian Turks and Armenians in Uzbekistan?

-For the Kurds in Iraq?

And see first how it works.

Shimon Peres was running amok, for years, begging the nations to convene an International Peace Conference for the Middle East, so he could get rid of the territories. Give away Judea, Samaria and Gaza to the Arabs. The man was completely irrational, and this man was heading the Maarah Party. It is difficult to understand what makes Shimon Peres stick to his foolish formula, which can only result in a disaster, meaning, losing the Gaza Strip, losing Judea and Samaria (the West Bank), losing the Golan Heights and losing the Capital Jerusalem or part of it. That's going back to the pre-1967 lines.

One also wonders why must Shimon Peres pull Israel into a trap. The trap of the International Peace Conference.

It is believed that if Peres does not succeed with his plan he will try to topple the Unity Government and seek early elections.

Israel cannot even trust her best friend, the United States of America, which might have completely different interests, if and when, such a conference convenes. The refusal of the United States to accept the Israelis' inalienable right to Judea, Samaria and Gaza is an unfortunate fact. The refusal of the United States to accept Israel's right to Jerusalem, the Capital of Israel, is also an unfortunate fact. The refusal of the United States of America to move its Embassy from Tel-Aviv to Jerusalem, is also an unfortunate fact. This is exactly the United States' concept, this is exactly the United States attitude and this is exactly the United States' formal policy, and Israel should not ignore or underestimate it.

Israel, at such an International Conference, might find itself alone, isolated and everbody against her. Therefore, Israel should never participate in such conferences, because for Israel it means self-suicide.

The United States of America "played" neutral. Secretary of States George Shultz declared, not once, that neither he nor President Reagan, were committed to the idea of an International Peace Conference, and they hate to interfere in Israel's internal affairs, yet, everybody saw the "Peace Hop Scotching" of Robert Macfarlan, Edward Murphy and other U.S. officials, in the Middle East, which contributed substantially to the idea of the International Peace Conference. On the other hand, ex-Secretary of States, Henry Kissinger, ironically ridiculed Shimon Peres's efforts to convene an International Peace Conference for the Middle East and admitted that he had made tremendous efforts to keep the Soviets out of the Middle East, and that it is not the best interest of the United States of America or Israel to let the Soviets back into the area and allow them to have a saying in the politics of the Middle East.

The U.S. Ambassador Thomas Pickering, in a wide-ranging press conference held at the U.S. Embassy, in Tel-Aviv, on June 30th, 1987, declared that the U.S. was determined to push ahead with its effort to convene an International Peace Conference for the Middle East, but it was equally determined not to interfere in Israel's internal debate on the issue.

Pickering expressed Washington's preference for quick progress in organizing an International Conference, which would lead to direct bilateral negotiations.

The average Israeli citizen wonders why is the U.S. Government so anxious that Israel loses part of its biblical territories? Why is the U.S. Government so anxious to please the Arabs at the expense of Israel? As this will, probably, be the main result of such a conference.

The U.S. Secretary of State, George Shultz, frankly admitted that the United States is backing up Israel in matters of procedure, but once the conference is convened, Israel should not expect the United States to share the same opinion on territorial issues. In fact the U.S. has a completely different opinion than Israel on territorial matters. In general, it has been proved, that, in every territorial conflict, the United States of America always took the Arab stand.

On September 1st, 1982, when the PLO completed their retreat from Beirut, "Friendly" President Ronald Reagan expressed the U.S. policy towards the Middle East very clearly, in Burbank, California, when he said: "The United States will not support the establishment of an independent Palestinian state in the West Bank and Gaza, and will not support annexation or permanent control by Israel."

Secretary of States, George Shultz added, that such a Palestinian State could not be self- supporting.

The U.S. Secretary of State, George Shultz, admitted that the U.S. intends to submit the "Reagan Plan" before the Internationl Peace Conference and the Soviets will probably submit their "Brezniev Plan", the Europeans will probably submit thei "Venice Plan" and the Arabs their 'Fez Plan", which are not in the best interest of Israel.

In one of their meetings, in Jerusalem, when the Secretary of State, George Shultz, tried to persuade Shamir to accept an International Conference for peace in the Middle East, Shamir posed Shultz a direct question and looked him in the eyes: "Mr. Secretary, suppose we do accept an international conference, where will the U.S. stand?"

George Shultz looked Shamir in the eyes and replied:" We won't be with you. You want Jerusalem-we are against. You want Judea and Samaria-we are against. You want the Golan Heights-we are against.

Shamir then added: "And with this you want to convince us to participate in an international conference?"

Secretary Shultz declared firmly that the U.S. is against "Transfer" and that the U.S. is against "Annexation". The U.S. policy is guided, according to Shultz, by the formula: "Territories for Peace."

During the Israeli-Egyptian Peace negotiations, at Camp David, the Soviets were left out.

This time they want to be in. Therefore, this is why they proposed the International Peace Conference, by which, they intend to be reinstated, in the area, in their "proper" place, alongside with the United State of America.

The International Peace Conference and the PLO are only convenient tools, with the help of which, the Soviets intend to realize their plan. That is why, they will, probably, push the issue of the International Peace Conference and back up the PLO to the end.

Neither Israel, nor the Arabs are the main concern of the Soviets. Their main concern is, a stronger footing in the Middle East or a U.S.-Soviet "Influence Partnership" in the Middle East.

The Soviets' object is not necessarily to force an agreement between Israel and the Arabs, but to reach a U.S.-Soviet arrangement in the Middle East.

The U.S.S.R., England, France and China will never agree to form an "Umbrella" only, without being full partners in such negotiations. It is also obvious that Israel will be completely isolated around the negotiation table.

The International "Umbrella" to such a Peace Conference is dangerous to Israel, because the Soviets will never accept to play the role of statistics in such a conference. What the Soviets mean is a multi-national Peace Conference, co-chaired by the Soviets, where they can force their view and where the United States of America will not have the veto power to oppose.

In the UN Security Council the U.S. can exirt its veto power, on the other hand, in an International Conference the U.S. will not have this veto power.

There is also the possibility that what should be an Israeli-Arab face-to-face negotiation will become a U.S.-Soviet bilateral talks.

Therefore, obviously, the Soviet made International Peace Conference is not for the best interest of Israel because its aim is to bite more pieces in Israel's territories, to deprive Israel from more terrain, to force Israel to retreat to the pre-1967 borders.

The Soviets have shown lately a quickening of interest in the region. There is a diffrence in style and tone in the Soviet approach, but their anti-israeli policy hasn't changed.

Everybody in Israel is very alert to the dangers arising from having the soviets play an active role in something that should concern only the Israelis and the Arabs. It is very naïve to believe that the Soviet involvement in an International Peace Conference will be ceremonial only.

For over ten years Russia tried to revive the U.S.-Soviet sponsored Geneva Peace Conference on the Middle East, first convened in December 1973, right after the Yom Kippur War. But, both the U.S. and Israel resisted those efforts.

If anybody thinks that the Russians are also interesred to solve the Middle East dilemma of the Israeli-Arab conflict is wrong and naïve. It had been for years, in the Russian interest to have constant instability in the Middle East. They would like to see the fire burning permanently. It seemed that the Soviets' interest was to have a situation of constant tension in the Middle East, constant controlled tension. Knowing the Soviets, they won't lend a hand to something from which they won't benefit. The Soviets will not come to a conference just as a favour to the U.S. and Israel. They would insist to include their own clients: Syria and the PLO.

The United States of America told the Soviets that it would participate in such a conference only if the Soviets renew their diplomatic relations with Israel. The Soviets replied in return, that they would renew their diplomatic relations with Israel, only after Israel agrees and participates in such a conference. Israel would always welcome a renewal of ties with the Russians, provided that it was accompanied by a change of heart towards Israel and the Middle East conflict. The Soviets have been told, several times, clearly, that, unless they resume full diplomatic relations with Israel and completely change their emigration policy towards the Soviet Jews, seeking exit permit to Israel, Israel will not sit with Soviet delegates in any convention. But, the Soviets have openly declared that they will renew diplomatic relations with the State of Israel, after some progress has been achieved, meaning, only after an Israeli retreat from the Golan Heights. The Soviets have made it very clear that they will never resume diplomatic relations with Israel, as long as Israel occupies Syrian territories (the Golan Heights). Therefore, for Israel to participate in such a conference is to step right into a trap. For Israel to participate in such a conference is to commit a national suicide.

In a meeting between Israeli Foreign Minister Shimon Peres and Soviet Foreign Minister Eduard Shevardnadze, in 1987, the Russian Foreign Minister was very straightforward and clear, may be even a little threatening:"You will never reach peace without us. You must accept Soviet participation in any Middle Eastern arrangement." Shevardnadze also added that: "The only way to reach agreement is by convening an International Confrence with The PLO participation unde ther UN auspice."

In talks with American officials the Soviets insisted that:

-The right of the Palestinians to self-determination should be respected.

-The PLO must be represented in any peace talks.

-The International Conference for peace in the Middle East would not be able to impose an agreement on the negotiating parties or to veto an agreement reached by them. However, the conference plenum will be an "active" body, with the power to "assist" the sides in reaching agreement and to "recommend" solutions to them. Contrary to the U.S. proposal, that the conference receive periodical "reports" on the progress of the talks.

-In case of a deadlock in the bilateral talks, each side can unilaterally "refer"issnes dispute to the conference plenum.

-UN Security Council Resolution 242 must be amended to include recognition of the Palestinian right to self-determination.

The Soviets considered the PLO as their "Diplomatic Vehicle" into the Middle East. The Soviets had found in the <u>U.S. Secretary of State George Shultz's peace initiative a golden opportunity and an excellent vehicle to assume prominent role in the Middle East.</u>

<u>Again, as in previous years, the Arab countries proposed to introduce into the agenda the expulsion of Israel from the UN. The UN, on October 13th, 1987, voted for the expulsion of Israel from the UN. From 140 participant members, 89 voted against, 41 voted for and 10 abstained. The Soviet Union was one of the 41 who voted for the expulsion of Israel from the UN.</u>

The Israelis will be naïve to trust the Russians or deal with them. Among the nations that criticize Israel or denounce her, is obviously the Soviet Union. The Soviet Union that controls, since 1945, the end of World War II. all of Eastern Europe. The Soviet Union that controls Afghanistan, Armenia, etc. and that is strongly involved in Africa and South America. In Angola, Cuba, Nicaragua, Cambodia, etc.

Israel will be clever to leave things at standstill rather than move ahead with a Soviet involvement.

What the Soviets want is a unilateral Israeli withdrawal to the 4th of June 1967 borders.

Inspite of the fact that the Soviets were stressing the Palestinian right to "self determination" and the U.S. only spoke of "legitimate rights of the Palestinians", both the Soviets and the U.S. believed that the basis for a Middle East settlement is an Israeli withdrawal from the territories in Judea, Samaria and the Gaza Strip. The Soviet Union declared, not once, that, there would be no arrangement in the Middle East if Israel doesn't pull back to the 1967 borders and recognizes the right of self-determination of the "Palestinians".

The Soviets will, probably, be ready to make compromises if it will insure their deeper penetration in the Middle East. The Soviet backing of the PLO is conditional and subservient to their global interests. Every body knows that the Soviet definition of arrangement in the Middle East means the retreat of Israel to the pre-1967 borders and the return of the

Palestinian-Arab refugees into Israel. This means suicide for Israel and is out of the question.

Many Israelis believe that it is about time that the Israeli Government changes its silent-polite-considerate politics and starts an open, loud struggle against the U.S.S.R., using the international news media to its limit.

These same Soviets, who had a very similar experience: Once, when French Napoleon Bonaparte, and then, German Adolf Hitler, invaded and overran Russia and slaughtered Russians by the millions. Same as the Israelis, same as the Jews, they still have the nightmare, the obsession, the fear, of being surprised again by an enemy, and, therefore, made and are still making, every possible effort and sacrifice: working hard, living frugally, stealing, whatever, in order to have maximum security, thus becoming a superpower. These Soviets should be the ones to best understand the Israelis; but, unfortunately, they found that it suits better their national interest to side with the Arabs, with the Palestinians.

The Soviet Union, a Superpower, made borders modifications in the north, so that the Finish guns would not hit Leningrad. But the U.S.S.R. doesn't give a damn if the Arab guns will hit Jerusalem or Tel-Aviv, from the West Bank. The Soviet Union doesn't care a bit about the security problems of Israel, not mentioning its legal and historical rights to the West Bank, Judea, Samaria and Gaza.

Those who believe the Russian hints that Soviet participation in the International Peace Conference will render the Soviets more liberal, more linient, towards an increase of Jewish immigration from the Soviet Union, are either naive or blind. The late Soviet tactics of "loosening the chains" and "new open door" policy for the Jews of the U.S.S.R. are nothing but big lies. So the Soviets let recently two thousand Jews out of Russia, for propaganda purposes, what about the remaining three million Soviet Jews? What about the three million Jewish hostages that the Soviets are still holding? Will they be permitted to leave?

This was only a tactical change, a change in semantics. Cosmetic changes. The Soviets haven't changed really. All they did was changing violins. The recent, big hassle over a supposedly increase in Jewish immigration from Russia and the big noise over a few meetings with Israeli diplomats, is for the purpose of "blinding" the World, or, mainly, "blinding" the Americans in order to get from them more advantages. The Soviets have, partially, succeeded to form an image of compromise.

But, this is only an image to "fool" the world. But the world is not fool to swallow this "image".

Even if the Soviets and the other participating nations will agree to function as a "decorative umbrella" and remain completely silent, during the negotiations between the parties, Israel should not participate in such a conference, because it is not in the best interest of Israel to meet with the Arabs if they still insist on 'Peace for Territories" negotiations, meaning aquiring Israeli territories and establishing a Palestinian-Arab State in the West Bank. Israel should meet the Arabs only if they agree to "Peace for Peace" negotiations and with the full knowledge that they will not receive from Israel one square inch of land.

The issue, therefore, is: The whole of Eretz Israel, complete Eretz Israel versus an "Arab Peace".

The Soviets have been selling an "image" of compromise. Sometimes, quite successfully, and Shimon Peres bought it. But Shimon Peres bought nothing but a "lemon". The Soviets do not even have diplomatic relations with Israel, since October 1973, since the Yom Kipput War or the War of Atonement.

Peres is campaigning for the International Peace Conference, for fear that the "opportunity" will be "washed away", as he puts it. Peres claimed that this is a irresversible opportunity, the only chance to get peace with the Arabs. But the Soviets, Syria and the PLO declared very openly, repeatedly, that they have their unacceptable, impossible, preconditions, prior to joining the negotiation table. Therefore, how did Shimon Peres come to his conclusion is beyond comprehension. Shimon Peres hasn't learned the Arabs yet.

Foreign Minister Shimon Peres is doing a great disservice to his country, by playing into the hands of the Soviets, in advertising their "Product". Shimon Peres had no right or authority to promote the Soviet idea of an International Peace Conference for the Middle East, because the subject was discussed fully and thoroughly in the Israeli Cabinet, on May 13, 1987, and no decision were made on this subject. Therefore, as Minister of Foreign Affairs of Israel, Peres cannot, express his private, personal, political views, among the nations of the world, who might mistakingly, wrongly, legally, take it as the formal, political view of the Government of Israel.

Shimon Peres was known, in Israel, as inconsistent, unreliable and not trustworthy. He promised "no unemployment", and when he left his office as Prime Minister, Israel had over one hundred thousand people unemployed. Shimon Peres promised "no talk with the PLO," then he changed his version into "no talk with the PLO, before they accept UN Resolution 242 and 338". Shimon Peres forgot completely the PLO "famous" Charter.

From the times of the Tzars, the Russians always wanted an access to the warm waters of the Mediterranean Sea. This was always one of their interests. For many years it was only wishful thinking, but finally, during the last decade, they have realized that dream. This still does not give them the right to"legitimate interests" in the Middle East or the right to interfere or shape the future, the fate, of the countries in the area, as the Russians claim to have.

The Soviets have been dreaming for generations to have a foothold in the Middle East, which they consider a region strategically important to their national interests, and would like, therefore, to participate in the determination of the future of that region.

The Reagan Administration, and probably also the following administrations will not be so enthusiastic to let the Russians determine or influence the future of the Middle East.

The Heritage Foundation, a conservative think tank in Washington, reflecting the Republican Party's platform, portrayed Israel as America's major pointman in the Middle East:

"The chief threat to U.S. interests in the area remains the Soviet Union, which has become increasingly active in the Middle Eastern diplomacy under Mikhail Gorbachev's leadership," it said.

"Israel, America's foremost Middle Eastern ally, is threatened by radical Arab states backed by the Soviets. To deter Soviet adventurism and enhance regional stability, the U.S, should strengthen its strategic cooperation with Israel, a regional superpower with extensive experience in countering Soviet military weapons and tactics. In Israel, the U.S. has a reliable regional partner that can help stabilize the area and contain Soviet military power."

The Heritage document also offered some very specific proposals:

"Washington should integrate Israel informally and discreetly into the global anti-Soviet defense system," it said. "Joint contingency plane should be drawn up to keep Moscow and its regional allies guessing about the extent to which Israel is willing to commit itself to containing Soviet aggression in crisis".

"Washington should seek access to Israeli airbases and naval facilities. Joint naval and air exercises should be held regularly. U.S. medicine, fuel, ammunition and weapons should be pre-positioned secretly in Israel to facilitate rapid movement to the Persian Gulf or NATO's southern flank if needed."

"Military intelligence liaison and technical cooporation should be organized to promote the maximum degree of cross-pollination in the joint assessment and countering of Soviet weaponry," it continued, "Israeli military technology should be adopted were practicable, including potential Israeli contributions to the Strategic Defence Initiative. The U.S. should also push for the closest possible cooperation against terrorism and take advantage of Israeli counter-terrorist experience, intelligence and techniques."

The Mediterranean Sea is not so far from the Soviet Union. The Strait of Dardanelles (Canakkale), the Sea of Marmara, the Strait of Bosphorous, the Black Sea and the Soviet Union.

The Soviet Navy has long had a need for naval facilities to counter the U.S. Sixth Fleet in the Mediterranean. The Soviet primary strategic wartime mission was to deny the U.S. and NATO access to maritime region close to the U.S.S.R. that might be used for offensive operations against Soviet missile-launching submarine bastions or against the Soviet homeland itself.

Syria is a Soviet military client that is in a considerable state of financial indebtedness to Moscow. Increased access to military facilities appears to be the currency Syria had chosen to pay off its Soviet patron.

Speculators believe that though the Soviets and the Americans remain divided over the mechanism and methods of talks between the conflicting parties in the Middle East, yet on the substance of a Middle East settlement the two superpowers may not be far apart.

It seems that both the East and West want Israel to retreat to the pre-1967 borders, perhaps with minor modifications. This was the message conveyed by the Rogers Plan, the Brookings Plan, the Reagan Plan, the Shultz Plan and all western Europeans as well as Soviet policy statements. Suddenly, others have become "partners" of Israel's historical, legal lands, the West Bank and Gaza, or rather, in their original Biblical names: Judea, Samaria and the Gaza Strip, and use the Israeli Arab conflict over these territories to suit their own interests, just because they are strong. In all fairness, they really should not have any legal or moral right to a saying on the matter.

The Israeli Unity Government is also against transfer and annexation. So is Shamir's Likud Party and so is Peres' Maarah Party. Therefore, the

U.S. and Israel should not have any differences on this matter, so far. The conflict between Israel and the U.S. will start, if and when, the U.S. will begin demanding Israel to retreat from "The Territories", in order to please the Arabs and enable the Palestinian Arabs and Jordan to fulfil their political expectations.

A very similar scenario: The Czechs, a small peace loving nation, in central Europe, was represented in international conferences as "an obstacle to world peace, " had to lose its country and its freedom any many thousands of lives, only because the French and the British were "convinced" from recent happenings in Czechoslovakia (German population complaints of political, economic and cultural discrimination, followed by violent street riots instigated by Henlein), that keeping the Sudetenland will endanger the country. Czechoslovakia had to yield to outside pressures and give up the heavy industrialized Sudetenland to Germany (The Munich Pact of September 29, 1938-without even the presence of a Czech delegatioin), which followed later by the loss of the whole country of Czechoslovakia to the Germans and ignited the Second World War.

This is how a story of "(Territories for Peace)" came to an end.

Unfortunately, and luckilly for Israel to have two Munich precedents; the Munich Pact of 1938 and the killing of the eleven handcuffed Israeli Olympic athletes, in 1972, from which it could learn a lesson and see to it that history doesn't repeat itself.

Leo Tindeman, Belgian Foreign Minister and Chairman of the European Community was persuading the European Governments to encourage an International Peace Conference for the Middle East only because he mistakingly understood that the Israeli Government was backing its Foreign Minister on this issue. Nurturing the world with empty illusions of a quick peace in the Middle East, as Shimon Peres did, is far from being clever.

Peres's behavior caused tremendous political damages to the State of Israel.

Before the end of the Peres term in the Prime Minister's Office, and according to the Rotation Agreement between the Maarah Party and the Likud Party, several members of the Maarah Party, including Cabinet members, advised Shimon Peres to violate the Rotation Agreement. Peres knew very well that if he accepts their advice and does not hand over the Premiership to Yitzhak Shamir (Likud), he will lose face and lose credibility and will be known in the world as a man who does not keep his promise and does not honor his signature. But after fulfilling the

Rotation Agreement to the letter, thus gaining back some of his already lost credibility, Peres felt that he had to do everything to break Shamir's two years term and reenter the Premier's Office.

Shimon Peres was very anxious to become Prime Minister again. The man was "Power Hungry" and would do anything to achieve that goal. Peres's lust for power is behind the pressure for a Peace Conference. Shimon Peres requested that the Treasury, the Israel Tax payer covers the huge budget deficit and debts of the Kibbutzim and Moshavim or the Maarah (Alignment) Party will leave the Unity Government. A first ultimatum. The second Maarah ultimatum to the Likud Party was when Peres and the Maarah Party wanted to force the issue of the International Peace Conference for the Middle East.

The United States of America has made no secret of its appreciation of Peres's intensive recent weeks to reach a formal understanding with King Hussein of Jordan on the scope of an International Conference. But, there is very little chance that Jordan will join this conference without the Soviets and the PLO.

Many Israelis believe that Shimon Peres has an obsession of receiving a Nobel Prize for Peace. We have learned from the past that leaders who live with a feeling of historical purpose can bring their country to the edge of the abyss.

On June 1987, Israeli Foreign Minister Shimon Peres was again on the roads. Peres was travelling again from country to country, in Europe, campaigning for the International Peace Conference. Visiting French President Francois Miterand, Prime Minister Margaret Thatcher of England, Kantzlar Helmut Kohl of West Germany, etc., trying to convince them to agree to an International Peace Conference for the Middle East, trying to convince them to accept the Soviet Plan, fulfil a Soviet interest. When he cannot convince his own landsman, Prime Minister of Israel, Yitzhak Shamir.

Israeli foreign minister Shimon Peres kept storming the world's diplomatic corridors to drum up support for his Peace plans and International Conference. It appears that Peres was inducing foreign leaders to take sides in an international debate. Peres was constantly conniving with world'a leaders against the better interests of the State, always making the fatal mistake of ignoring Prime Minister Yitzhak Shamir's steel resolve.

It is the first time in history and in modern politics that a foreign Minister is traveling all over the world trying to get support from foreign governments against his own government. Shimon Peres is trying to force the International Peace Conference on his government, by "Hook or by Crook". Paradoxically, and much to his surprise, Peres had found his external canpaign for the International Conference, much easier than his internal campaign.

Peres runs ahead with the idea of an International Conference but each time he looks over his shoulders, he sees fewer and fewer of his Maarah colleagues following him. The distance between himself and his party grows greater each time. The time is approaching when Peres will have no one to go into battle with him. That is probably why he must paint the "conference" in rosy and unrealistic colours.

Part of his difficulties were with members of his own party, the Maarah. Many Maarah's most senior members disliked the fact that Peres embarked on his International Conference, alone, without even finding the courtesy to consult with them. Apperently, people just don't like to be overlooked, when major decisions are made. Others were worried or even insulted by the lack of proper procedures in the decision-making process. Many disagreed with Peres priorities. Many party members suspected Peres's move as part of his determination to go down in history as another Ben-Gurion.

The International Conference is a prescription for imposing a solution, which is not in the best interest of Israel and not a "window of opportunity" for peace, as the Maarah Party

Believe. By strongly advocating Israel's participation in an International Conference for Peace in the Middle East, Mr. Peres puts the fate and future of the State of Israel and its people on an international "Operating Table", which never favored Israel. To come up with such a suggestion is totally irresponsible.

Shimon Peres wants to break up the Unity Government and go to election. Shimon Peres cannot play Second Fiddle. Shimon Peres just cannot wait any longer as Minister of Foreign Affairs and believes that he has a great chance to become Prime Minister, and he just doesn't care how much these election will cost the Israeli tax payer, especially now, when Israel is suffereing from economical difficulties, and, inspite of the fact, that it is because of these economical difficulties that the Unity Government was formed by the Maarah and the Likud parties. Defense Minister, Yitzhak Rabin, in his book "Service sBook", published by Maariv, Tel-Aviv, September 1979, testifies that Shimon Peres is capable of doing things like this.

Is it worth to divide the nation over the issue? Is there any issue worth dividing Israel for?

Those who call the International Conference a "Peace Process", with the knowledge that Israel will have to give up lands, are deceiving the people of Israel.

For Israel to attend such a conference is like a lamb going to a Slaughter House, stretching its neck and asking to be butchered.

Also, there is no sense whatsoever, in wealing and dealing with King Hussein of Jordan, whose only aim is getting lands from Israel, getting the West Bank, Judea and Samaria.

An Israeli who comes up with such an idea is a masochist and completely irrational.

On November 20, 1987 (Heshvan 27, 5748), Israeli Foreign Minister, Shimon Peres, received a honorary doctorate for his efforts for peace from M.G. Verhaegen, the rector of the Free University in Brussels.

The Maarah (Alignment, Labor) Party have acquired a self inflicted complex of guilt to see themselves as occupiers and conquerors of the West Bank (Judea, Samaria and the Gaza Strip) rather than owners of the West Bank, and totally ignore the fact that the Arabs are the real imvaders, the infringers, the trespassers, that have been occupying Jewish territories, illegally, for many years. A masochistic, galutic (acquired in the Diaspora) complex of inferiority developed in the Maarah Party. A very interesting question arises: if so, how come the Maarah do not consider themselves also as conquerors of Haifa, Jaffa, Acre (Acco), Nazareth, etc.? Why only the conquerors of the West Bank?

Those who are reluctant to settle in heavily Arab populated areas, like: Shechem (Nablus), Ramallah, Hebron, Beit-Lehem, etc. are only legalizing the British Mandatory "White Paper", Land Restriction on Jews.

The majority of the Jews in Israel and in the world will never accept the thesis that there is such a place in Eretz Israel where Jews cannot settle or visit, live or tour.

The Maarah concept was: to get rid of a great part of Judea, Samaria and the Gaza Strip, with their heavy Arab population, if necessary, by means of an International Conference. The Likud, on the other hand, stuck to the "Camp David Autonomy Plan" and were against the idea of relinquishing Israeli territories to the Arabs. Speculations were, that in order to force the Likud Prime Minister, Yitzhak Shamir, to accept an International Conference for the Middle East, the Maarah decided to invite outside pressure against their Likud counterparts. Mainly, U.S. pressure.

This they did by the following way: Defense Minister Yitzhak Rabin declared on the national Israeli television that he gave order to disperse illegal Arab demonstrations and Arab riots by means of the stick, thus antagonizing the whole international community and even part of the U.S. Jewry. Meanwhile Foreign Minister Shimon Peres sent his envoy, Mr. Yossi Beilin, to Washington, to plead with the U.S. Administration for U.S. pressure against the Likud.

To justify their fight against Jewish settlement in the West Bank, as well as their desire to hand over the West Bank or part of it to the Arabs, the Maarah have been using the childish argument that this is required in order to avoid more bloodshed between Jews and Arabs. One wonders how did the Maarah (Mapai) Party avoid bloodshed between Jews and Arabs, sixty years ago? When they settled in Kibbutz Ein-Harod, in the Jezrael Valley, Degania in the Jordan Valley, in two Arab heavily populated areas. Or, when they sent out a tractor to plow the fields at Kibbutz Tel-Katzir? Were they not endangering human lives then? Why didn't they leave Kibbutz Nir-Eliyahu in the heavily Arab populated area of Kalkiliya, Jaljuliya near the Arab city of Tulkarem? Or Kibbutz Ein Gev and Ha'On near the Kineret (The Sea of Galilee), in order to avoid more bloodshed between Arabs and Jews?

The answer to those questions is, probably, because these kibbutzim were settled by the Socialist Labor parties, the Maarah, etc., while the new settlements in Judea, Samaria and the Gaza Strip were encouraged and sponsored by the Likud Party. This is part of Israeli internal politics.

For the sake of argument only, let see this scenario: Suppose that the Maarah's Party theory is accepted, the split is carried out, Judea, Samaria and the Gaza Strip are handed over to the Arabs. Pre-1967 is now without the "burden" of the Gaza strip and the West Bank, and relatively "Arab Clean", "Arab rein". A much smaller Israel, which contains only the Israeli Arabs, leftover after the War of Independence, In 1948. Those Arabs living in Haifa, Acre (Acco), Jaffa, Nazareth, or, Ramleh, Beer Shebah, Tiberias, the Galilee, etc. These "Israeli Arabs" will also grow rapidly and will outnumber the Israeli Jews and become a threat, a menace, to the Jewish State of Israel. Then, they will start asking for "equal rights". Equal rights with the Jews. Then they will ask for a Bi-National State or for another split, and this time with the very close support of the new Arab State in the West Bank, just across the border, may be also, with Soviet,

Syrian or Iranian military support. This will render life for Israel miserably unbearable. Israel will become very "skinny" after that second shrink. There will be almost nothing left over to bargain with. For Israel it will be completey insane to follow this route. Therefore, an International Peace Conference is out of the question.

Contrary to the Likud Party, the Maarah Party prefers a smaller Jewish State, with a Jewish majority rather than a big bi-national State, Israel plus the "West Bank". But, the Labor (Maarah) Party keeps forgetting that in the small Jewish State lived a big Arab minority, which is getting bigger every year, and in a very few years, with their bigger rate of birth, will become a majority and the small democratic Jewish State will simply disappear, vanish.

On October 12, 1973, on the hardest day of the Yom Kippur War, the Israeli Embassador to the United States, Mr. Simcha Dinitz met with U.S. Secretary of State, Dr. Henry Kissinger and informed the Secretary that the Israeli Government is ready to accept a cease-fire. Dr. Henry Kissinger replied: "Are you crazy? Now that Egypt and Syria have the upper hand and that their forces are deep in your territories?"

Dr. Kissinger understood very well that to start negotiations between the parties when the Arabs have the upper hand would be dangerous to Israel, in fact detrimental.

Dr. Kissinger and President Richard Nixon ordered a massive military airlift to Israel. Very shortly after the Israeli forces crossed the Suez Canal and were encircling the Egyptian Third Army, Kissinger saw to it that Israel does not defeat the Egyptian encircled Third Army, in order to enable the start of negotiations with President Anwar Sadat of Egypt.

On the other hand, Dr. Kissinger forced Israel to sign a Cease Fire with Egypt when the Israeli forces were hundred kilometers from the Egyptian Capital, Cairo and when the Egyptian Third Army was totally besieged and on the verge of collapse. That's when Israel had the upper hand. Same as then, Kissinger advised Israel not to attend an International Middle East Peace Conference or start any negotiations with the Arabs, now that the Arabs have the upper hand in the world public opinion and before the Arab uprising in Israel is crushed completely. To start negotiations with the Arabs, with the "Palestinians", now, under these conditions, is not in the best interest of Israel, and should therefore, be avoided. Where in the world is a big ethnic or national minority permitted to establish a state by territorial partition of the country that belongs to the majority? Where in the world is an ethnic or national minority permitted to attain political benefits at the expense of the majority? Inspite of the long, non-compromising terror, including the murder of Indian Prime-Minister Indirah Ghandi, India is not ready to give the seventeen million Sikhs independence or political autonomy.

Sari-Lanka will not give territories to their Tamile minority.

The three million French speaking Canadians in Quebeck will never convince the English speaking majority to let them have a "Free Quebeck", just because General Charle De Gaulle suggested it.

In Yugoslavia many believed that after Tito's death the country will be sub-divided among the Serbians, the Croates, the Slovens, the Macedonians and the Montenegrins, because they did not have a common language or a common religion. They are divided into Catholics, Pravoslavs and Moslems and they all hate each other. Not one of them received a state of his own. They all belong to Yugoslavia.

In Czechoslovakia the picture is very similar. Great hostility between the Czechs and Slovaks for generations. Yet, they prefered to live in a united Czechoslovakia.

Rumania has also a substantial Hungarian minority, mainly in the South-West, in Transilvania. But, the Rumanian President, Mr. Nicolae Ceausescu would not think of giving them, the Hungarians, political autonomy or even cultural autonomy. Yet, Mr. Ceausescu is very generous at the expense of Israel. He is ready to give Yassir Arafat and the PLO a Palestinian State, at the expense of Israel. Very wise indeed! Only the Israelis are still not that dumb, yet.

Madrid would never give the Basks political autonomy inspite of their long terror.

Iraq, Iran and Turkey are not ready to give the Kurds autonomy inspite of their long rebellions-Mustafa Barazani, etc.

In Belgium, there is a constant cultural conflict between the Flemings (Teutonic origin) and the Walloons (Celtic origin), two different ethnic groups. Yet, nobody wants to divide Belgium.

There is a long and deep hate between the English and the Scots since the times of Queen Elizabeth I and Queen Mary, yet, the English will never think of giving the Scots autonomy.

The Armenians cannot forget the Turkish slaughter against their ancestors, during World War I, and are carrying a constant terror against the Turks and the Turkish embassies all over the world, but, in vain, because the Turks will never give them back Armenia.

The population of southern Tirol, annexed to Italy, would rather return to Austria but Italy would never want to hear of it.

The Slovens minority in Austrian Corinth are long seeking cultural autonomy but Austria refuses to give it to them.

The U.S.S.R. contains fifteen different nationalities, under the strict control of the Kremlin, in Moscow. The Ukrainians hate Russians and so are the people of the Baltic States, who would like to get back their independence.

On the other hand, the population of Hong Kong is a mixture of different nationalities but are all against annexation to mainland China, but, Mrs. Margaret Thatcher, the United Kingdom, decided that they will be annexed to China in the Middle ninetees, inspite of their refusal.

Great territorial changes were made after almost every war.

Germany lost half of its land to Poland and East Germany and paid a heavy toll for Hitler's foolishness.

Poland and Czechoslovakia lost Galicia and Carpatorussia. Mexico lost in war several of its northern states that were annexed to the United States.

The Catholic Irish are fighting the British in Northern Ireland but have very little chance to see the British out.

Argentina that fought wars against England, to restore the Melvinas (Falklands) and paid a heavy toll but the British did not show the slightest inclination to leave Falkland (the Melvinas) to Argentina.

There is not a single country in the world that had to give up territories conquered in a forced war, after paying a heavy toll in human lives. There is not a single country in the world, that after a victory in a war had to give up a great chunk of its own territory (The Sinai-after the Yom Kippur War, in 1973). But this "dirty trick" is applied on Israel over and over again. No other country would accept such a treatment.

During the Jordanian occupation of Judea, Samaria and Gaza the Jordanian authorities never tried to establish a Palestinian Arab State there. They treated the Palestinian-Arabs worse than dogs. Under the Jordanians, the Palestinian-Arabs of Judea, Samaria and the Gaza Strip suffered from chronic unemployment and hunger. The Gaza Strip under Egyptan occupation received a similar treatment. The Palestinian-Arabs in the Gaza Strip couldn't leave the Gaza Strip and go find work in Egypt. In fact, they were not permitted to enter Egypt. King Hussein of Jordan didn't permit the opening of Colleges or Universities in Judea and Samaria. There was not a single University there during the Jordanian rule (1948-1967).

King Hussein was always against the idea of a Palestinian-Arab State, same as President Assad from Syria. Hussein has always been agaist the idea of annexing Judea, Samaria and the Gaza Strip to his kingdom, for fear of increasing the number of his Palestinian subjects, who might, one day, or one night, overthrow him and replace him with Yasser Arafat, that's Abu Amar. King Hussein was very careful not to sign with Israel any document for fear of being assassinated by some Moslem zealot, like his grandfather, King Abdullah or like the late President Anwar Sadat from Egypt.

This is why Hussein prefers the present situation. For him the Status Quo is the ideal solution and he will fight any one trying to change it. And all his declarations and behaviors are nothing but acting. This, in order to hide his own intentions and feelings and gain time.

Anybody. Like Shimon Peres, who comes forward with new plans for changes, only antagonizes the King and will never succeed to persuade the King.

It is also silly and unwise to nurture the idea of implementing the Camp David Administrative autonomy in Judea, Samaria and the Gaza Strip. It will never work. The Arabs will never buy it. They will never accept anything less than a Palestinian-Arab State, in the whole of Palestine, in the whole of Eretz Israel. They want "The Whole Thing". They want Jaffa, Acres (Acco), Lod, Ramleh, Haifa, Beer-Shevah, Jerusalem, etc. They will never accept the Autonomy Plan. As a matter of fact the Camp David Autonomy Plan is also not in the best interest of Israel and therefore, should be dropped immediately by Israel.

The PLO will never be satisfied with Judea, Samaria and the Gaza Strip, the PLO wants the whole land, the whole land of Israel, or the whole of Erestz Israel. The PLO wants to exterminate the State of Israel. One has only to read the PLO Charter. The PLO is Israel's enemy, Israel's dirty enemy. The PLO is a corrupt enemy, a "Blood Thirsty" enemy and all its supporters, Jews and Arabs alike, are playing into his hands.

Some Western countries conclude that the PLO had become more composed, more reasonable and less militant. True, lately, the PLO had become more "reasonable", more "composed" and less "militant". They speak with two languages, in English and in Arabic. They address the international media in English, speaking of two states, an Israeli State and a Palestinian-Arab State, living side by side, in coexistence. In Arabic they address their local audience. Telling them to keep fighting the Zionist thieves until the whole of of Palestine is freed. Until Israel, the West Bank and Gaza are back in Arab hands.

It is frightening to see how some Israelis can be so naïve as to believe that a Palestinian-PLO State will bring peace to the area. One wonders, sometimes, how can they have such a short memory, how can they forget the huge weapon stores that the Israeli army found, in Lebanon, in 1982, with which Mr. Yasser Arafat planned to exterminate Israel. Yielding to Arafat's request and hand him over Judea, Samaria and the Gaza Strip will only enable him to carry out his "Ultimate" solution for the Jews, for the Israelis.

Handing over the West Bank and Gaza to the Palestinian-Arabs, going back to the pre-1967 borders, will be disastrous to Israel, because then, the Palestinian-Arabs will in fact control Israel. Israel's industrial centers, airports, harbours, energy centers, highways, etc. will become under the range of simple, manual "Steiger" missiles, that can be carried in a hand bag or a suite case, and very easily operated, so that Israel will then have to face not stones throwers but missiles launchers.

Many Israelis believe that since the Six-Day War, since June 1967, all the Israeli governments, without exception, were guilty for fearing to Annex Judea, Samaria and the Gaza Strip and implement the Israeli law on its population, same as it did with the Golan Heights. This negligence, this wrong policy, this wrong decision, caused the Arabs and the rest of the world to consider ancient Israeli land as "territories" and the Israelis as "conquerors" or "invaders" or "trespassers". Refusal to annex Judea, Samaria and the Gaza Strip to Israel proper showed weak conviction of the natural rights of the Jews to own these territories. It meant violating the divine promise to Israel. It also meant violating the sacred Torah, it meant violating the sacred Halacha. It could only mean that the Israeli governments, since the Six-Day War, since June 1967, without exception, didn't believe in God's promise to the Jewish people. On the other hand, other Israelis believed that you do not annex territories that belong to you since time immemorial. You just take it. It is yours.

There is a general feeling that the playing figures in the Middle East arena, namely, Israel, the Arabs, are nothing but pawns in an international chess board or puppets in a puppet-show and the two Superpowers, the United State of America and the Soviet Union are the ones that are pulling the strings. The Soviet Union had shown it very bluntly in Budapest, in 1956 and later in Afghanistan. The United States had shown it very explicitly several times that it has enough ways and means to force its will on its satellites: The retreat of France, the United Kingdom and Israel from the Suez Canal in 1956. Forcing Israel to release its siege from the Third Egyptian Army in the "Yom Kippur" War, in 1973. Forcing Israel and Egypt to sign the Camp David Peace Agreement. Forcing the Israeli troops out of Beirut and later of Lebanon, in 1982. And very recently, in 1987, "convincing" Israel to scrap the "Lavi" project.

In the same manner Israel will be, probably, driven into the International Peace Conference for the Middle East, against her will.

The break of Soviet-Israeli relations, in 1967, right after the Six-Day War, was a unilateral Soviet act, which had nothing to do with Israeli-Soviet interaction and was symptomatic of the Soviet "old way" of thinking on the Israeli-Arab conflict. If Soviet "new thinking" is to be taken seriously, the reestablishment of these ties must also be a Soviet initiative.

Meanwhile, while bilateral Soviet-Israeli relations, formal or informal, in other fields can be mutually beneficial, the reestablishment of diplomatic ties is not something that Israel is desperately lacking, and it is certainly not a Soviet prize, for which Israel should pay a price.

There have been many Soviet attempts-which have continued up to the present time- to try to reach the Israeli public over the heads of the Israeli Government. All the attempts were so far unsuccessful. In 1988, whenever Soviet officials would meet with Israeli representatives, Moscow would try to portray a flexible image regarding its position on an International Middle East Peace Conference. Therefore, Mr. Shimon Peres has concluded that the Soviets have moved closer to the U.S. position and that the Kremlin's attitude toward the Israeli-Arab peace process justifies a more optimistic assessment of the basic Soviet stance.

Unfortunately, this view is not shared by Washington, which keeps reinteratic its disappointment at Moscow's attitude and insists that the U.S. and the Soviet Union remain "a long way apart" in their thinking on how to bring about Israeli-Arab peace negotiations. Washington denies that there has been any breakthrough. The Americans had taken a dimmer view of the Soviet position than Foreign Minister Peres.

Israel should be ready to face a situation, in which it will be compelled to join the International Middle East Conference by both the U.S. and the Soviet Union and should prepare itself for it,

Israel sould be prepared to confront both the Soviet Union and the United States of America, if necessary, if these insist that Israel should give up part of its territories. Territories? Never!

Israel should not be ashamed to tell the United States of America as well as the Soviet Union:

"If you pitty the Palestinian-Arabs, if you want to be "nice" to them, it is your prerogative, so long as it doesn't hurt us, the Israelis. But you cannot be generous at our expense. You both have over fifty states each. You could spare one, without even feeling its loss. We have only one state and cannot afford the luxury of handing it, or part of it, over to your Arab friends. We cannot afford the luxury of losing it."

Besides, the Arabs have already twenty-two states in the region and can easily spare one for their Palestinian-Arabs brethren, without feeling the loss of it.

Whenever the United States of America felt or believed that Israel could not handle the situation, the U.S. came up with its own initiative, its own plan:

When Israel couldn't stop immediately the "War of Attrition" in 1970-1971, the U.S. brought the "Rogers Plan" (July 1970).

When it seemed to the U.S. that Israel couldn't put an end to the war in Lebanon, in 1982, the U.S. came up with the "Reagan's Plan" (September 1982).

When the U.S. believed that Israel couldn't put an end to the "Intifadah", the Arab rebellion against Israel, in Judea, Samaria and the Gaza Strip, in December 1987, the U.S. came up with the "Shultz Plan".

Except for the Israeli Communist Party, there is no doubt whatsoever in Israel that the U.S. meant to help Israel when it came up with all these plans. Yet, one must remember that it will be Israel that will have to bear the consequences or face the results. Therefore, Israel should be allowed to decide what is its best interest, and whether it should attend the International/ Middle East Peace Conference or not. It is her own prerogative and nobody has the right to force it upon her. Not even her best friends.

8.WASHINGTON VS. JERUSALEM

Speculators believe that the United States of America offered Prime Minister Yitzhak Shamir an inducement to withdraw his opposition to an International Middle East Peace Conference. These "sweetners" were in the form of a commitment to maintain Israel's long-term military-technological edge over the Arabs. Commitment, "Morally Binding", beyond the Reagan years.

Towards March 1987, Israeli Foreign Minister Shimon Peres and King Hussein of Jordan concluded an agreement between the two countries, Israel and Jordan, and this without the knowledge of the Israeli Prime Minister Yitzhak Shamir. King Hussein of Jordan said that before he could sign such an agreement, he must have the consent of the two states bordering with Jordan, that's Syria and Iraq.

The U.S.S.R. undertook to convince the Syrian ruler, Hafez Assad, to give his consent to this agreement. The US undertook to persuade the Iraqi ruler, Saddam Hussein, to give his consent to this agreement, known as the London Agreement of April 11, 1987.

In return the Iraqis received from the U.S. very useful military information as well as the permission

to buy fifty helicopters from the U.S.

When Peres returned with his signed agreement to Jerusalem, the Prime Minister and the Cabinet rejected it because according to this agreement Israel had to give away territories. Neither the Prime Minister, nor the Cabinet ever gave Shimon Peres authorization to sign such an agreement. Foreign Minister Shimon Peres (Maarah-Mapai-Alignment) met with King Hussein from Jordan, in London, and came to an agreement with the King, on the issue of the International Middle East Peace Conference, without the approval of the Prime Minister Yitzhak Shamir or the Cabinet. Most of the Israelis described it as a scandalous affair.

The London Agreement between Shimon Peres and King Hussein worked out with the support of U.S. diplomacy, laid sufficient grounds for direct negotiations between Israel and Jordan, under the auspices of an enforcing International Conference, which could be extremely dangerous and detrimental to Israel's political interests.

When Shimon Peres, Deputy Prime Minister and Foreign Minister, realized that his idea of an international Peace Conference was rejected in Israel, he came up with another defeatist, dangerous sidea of demilitarizing the Gaza Strip, leaving it without Israeli control. One million Arabs soon, in the outskirts of Tel-Aviv, without Israeli control. A price for their terror. This is totally insane. Shimon Peres's new idea is nothing but another sacrifice of national interest to promote his personal interest.

On July 23rd, 1987, the Soviet Union warned Israel that continued development of the Jericho II missile would thrust it into the midst of the nuclear standoff between the world's superpowers.

The strongly worded warning, broadcasted on Radio Moscow's Hebrew programme, said that: the missile constituted a direct threat to the Soviet Union. The broadcast advised Israel's leaders to think long and hard about the consequences of developing the missile.

The Soviets linked their warning to their latest offer in the ongoing arms reduction talks with the U.S. in Geneva. They accused the United States of America of trying to circumvent the arms talks on short-and-medium range missiles by helping its allies, such as Israel in Asia and West Germany in Europe, to become nuclear powers.

The Russian warning came on the same day the Soviets presented a proposal to the U.S., calling for the elimination of all short-and medium-range missiles from Europe and the Asian landmass.

The Jericho II's maximum range was said to be 1,450 kilometers, which would enable it to hit some southern parts of the Soviet Union, as well as the Arab capitals as far away as Baghdad. The Soviets insist that Israel's Jericho rocket is a real threat to the U.S.S.R.

In his statement, Foreign Minister Shimon Peres flatly rejected the "Soviet Threat" against Israel and reaffirmed that Israel does not regard the USSR as an enemy and holds no hostile intentions towards the USSR. Israel's security strategy is not offensive. Peres also added that Israel is willing to stop or slow down its development of medium-range missiles if the Soviets and their Arab clients curb introduction of such missiles into the Middle East. Israel was also willing to enter into negotiations to establish a "nuclear-freeze zone in the Middle East" and is ready to enter into dialogue with all its neighbors and with the USSR, in order to reach such an agreement. Peres asserted that Israel supports wholeheartedly the two superpowers in their efforts to reach an agreement on arms control, including the removal of nuclear missiles from Europe and Asia.

Israel assured the Soviets that they have no reason for concern, because Israel doesn't look upon them as an enemy. Yet, the Soviet warning itself is ironic in view of the fact that the Soviets have been selling the Arabs long-range missiles for some years.

Therefore, it is Israel that has to be concerned and worried about the growing Arab arsenals, especially Syria's. Syria is presently developing chemical and bacteriological warheads that can be delivered by Its Soviet missiles and endanger Israel.

Moreover, Syrian Defence Minister, Mustafa Tlass admitted that the Soviets have undertaken to provide Syria with a nuclear umbrella, a claim neither denied nor acknowledged by Moscow.

The second Reagan-Gorbachev summit took place in Iceland, on October 1986.

Kremlin leader Mikhail Gorbachev declared in 1987, that the Soviet Union was ready to accept a "double zero option" eliminating Soviet and U.S. medium-range missiles from Europe and Asia. This Soviet offer can, no doubt, eliminate a key obstacle in the current negotiations between the two superpowers in Geneva on a major disarmement treaty, if the offer is sincere, in good faith and not a trick.

U.S. President Ronald Reagan had great expectations from this summit. He spoke of his "historic" meeting with the Soviet Secretary General.

"We find ourselves involved in a dramatic march of events that has captures the attention of our two peoples and the entire world," he said.

Soviet Secretary General Mikhail Gorbachev described his summit with the U.S. President Ronald Reagan, in Washington, on December 10, 1987 (Kislev 19, 5748), as "a major event in world politics, which would likely begin a 'new phase' in American-Soviet relations."

Politicians and commentators believe that Mikhail Gorbachev represents something new in the Kremlin's leadership. "Without minimizing the great political and ideological distances between us," said Gorbachev, "we want to seek and find avenues of rapprochement in the areas where this is of vital importance for our two countries and for all mankind," he said.

"The whole world is interested in seeing that happen. We can see how high the mountains of arms we have amassed are, and we are sitting atop of that all. We should try to move towards each other."

Soviet Secret General Mikhail Gorbachev's success can be attributed to his charm. He is clever, smart and polite as well as an excellent "actor". Yet, when he runs into an obstacle, he gets wild, tough and rude. He is a typical KGB man.

Inspite of the soothing tone of recent statements by Gorbachev and other Kremlin leaders on the Arab-Israeli conflict, the Reagan administration was doubtful that Moscow's approach was serious and constructive.

Peter W.Rodman, a senior staff member on the National Security Council (NSC) in the White House believed that the most recent developments in Soviet policy in the Middle East do not amount really to a significant change. Peter W. Rodman wrote in the National Interest, published in Washington, that the Soviet's readiness to expand its dialogue with Israel-including an exchange of comsular visits-is not very serious. The Soviet move was an easy substitute for full diplomatic relations with Israel.

The U.S. Administration had been aroused by the high level of Soviet naval activity throughout the Mediterranean Sea. A Sunday (August 29th, 1988) report in the New York Times said that the Soviet planned to make Latakia and Tartus in Syria, equipped to repair and maintain their Mediterranean fleet.

William O. Studeman, director of National Security Agency (NSA), in a recent report to Congress said: "It would permit longer deployments and an overall increased Soviet presence and considerable political-military volatility."

Rodman's assessment was: "The Soviet want to keep the pot boiling in the region, but, at the same time, they do not want to allow it to spill over into actual war." It is difficult to see how the Soviets can ssee an Arab-Israeli settlement as their strategic interest," he said.

It is no secret that the Soviet General Secretary is not so interested in nuclear disarmament as such, but more in securing economic advantages for the Soviet Union from the Americans. This was his real goal in this summit. There was no doubt that the latest wave of Soviet diplomatic activity in the Middle East was part of a broader effort to undermine the U.S. position in the area.

During George Shultz's visit in Jerusalem on October 1987 Prime Minister Shamir seemed to have been more ready to make concessions, though, he would not give an inch on the idea of an International Conference as a forum for peacemaking or on the idea of territories for peace. However he did not rule out a Soviet role as a co-sponsor of direct negotiations between the parties. Shamir's willingness to entertain the notion of a Soviet role in peace talks surprised many Israelis, even members of his own Likud Party.

But Shamir's sudden change in tactics has not changed his basic position that territorial compromise is out of the question and that relinquishing of territories will never be the end result of a peace process. The sooner the Arabs realize this, the sooner the Arabs will learn to accept facts, the sooner they will start thinking of other venues to fulfil their political ambitions, may be by emigrating to one of the neighbouring Arab countries. Only this will bring peace to the area.

In one of his trips to the Middle East, Secretary of State George Shultz received from ex-Secretary of State Henry Kissinger the following memorandum: "The solution that will satisfy the security claims of Israel will not satisfy the self-determination claim of the Palestinian-Arabs."

It has been standard routine in international politics that only the selected representatives of a country, that's the government, handles negotiations with a foreign government and not the opposition. This routine was always common practice in Israel too.

In order to undermine the Prime Minister, Menachem Begin (Likud), the head of the opposition, Shimon Peres (Maarah), in 1982, was handling negotiations with the U.S. Administration, the U.S. Congress and the U.S. President, behind the back of the Government of Israel and without its approval.

This, as well as other several political public expressions in the international news media were against the very best interest of the State of Israel and angered many Israelis.

On March 1988, Abba Eban (Maarah) was sent by his Party to the United States of America to handle negotiations with the Congress, the Administrtion, etc. While Prime Minister Yitzhak Shamir (Likud) was meeting with President Ronald Reagan. Something unheard of.

Again, to undermine Yitzhak Shamir's mission and the national interest of Israel and in order to sell the Maarah formula of "Territories for Peace".

To the Holy Land, to the Land of their forefathers, the Maarah call "Territories", made it negotiable and were ready to bargain on it. Are even ready to give away a great part of it, to please the Arabs.

This is nothing but breaking every ideological frame or set of values. No other democratic-coalition government system in the world would accept such standards dictated by the Maarah.

Unfortunately, Israeli Foreign Minister, Shimon Peres, succeeded, in a relatively short time:

-To cause the rebellion of the Palestinian-Arabs population in Judea, Samaria and the Gaza Strip

-To weaken the Israeli Army and the will of power of the nation so that it couldn't crush the Arab uprising.

To make the world believe that the Middle East Peace Conference is something very important, indispensable.

-To drive the European Market to boycott Israeli products.

-To disturb the peace of mind of the greatest and strongest nation on our globe, America and compel her to consider the Middle East conflict as top priority issue on its agenda.

-To dictate to her Secretary of State, George Shultz, to draft a plan that treats the Middle East crisis, not necessarily in the best interest of Israel.

-To invite outside pressure on Israel and force her to attend an International Peace Conference inspite of the fact that this conference is against Israel's will and might be dangerous to Israel.

-To draw the International News Media to focus on Israel and the Arab uprising, which was adverse publicity for Israel and detrimental to its reputation.

No doubt that the Palestinian-Arab uprising, the intifada, was encouraged by the division and conflict in the Israeli Government, between the Likud and the Maarah, over the issue of the International Conference.

During 1986 and 1987, before the Palestinian-Arab uprising started in Judea, Samaria and the Gaza Strip, three major Jewish-American organizations warned the Israeli Government of the dangers to its political standing and internal welbeing posed by maintaining the status quo in the territories. The three groups were the American Jewish Congress, the American Jewish Committee and the Union of American Hebrew Congregations (UAHC). They urged Israel not to miss the opportunity for peace offered by an International Conference.

A typical example of how the Jewish Organizations tried to intervene in the Israeli politics, in fact to dictate its policies, another fraternal pressure.

Speculations are that the U.S. administration was using the American Jewish Organizations to put pressure on Israel.

As keepers of the consensus, the leaders of the Presidents Conference take care to avoid controversial pronouncements.

The Conference Chairman, Morris Abram, said that Public airing of criticism of Israel's policies by Jewish leaders "it serves our purposes. This is not a matter of their right to do this, but of prudence. It is unwise to disagree in public with the Israeli Government's policy on matters of life and death. This can have the effect-which the critics do not intend-of creating the impression that the American Jews are divided in support of Israel in fundamental ways."

"The way is always open ", Abram said, "for American Jewish leaders to express their concerns and disagreements" to Israeli leaders in private. But disagreements, he hastened to add, "is not divorce".

However, Abram went beyond the bland tone of the concensus statement by warning Israel that "there is a danger of serious erosion" of support for Israel among the American public if "the status quo continues indefinitely". He also said the conference supports the peace initiative of U.S. Secretary of State Shultz.

Seymour Reich, the president of Bnai Brith International, expressed the dismay felt by many of the delegates at "the obvious disunity in the government and the heated debates that we have seen. If we take this back with us, then the fifty-one organizations (in the Conference) will go their own way. It will be more difficult for the conference Presidents to produce statements of consesnsus than in the past."

In London, King Hussein of Jordan and Israeli Foreign Minister Shimon Peres concluded that Itzhak Shamir, the Prime minister is the only obstacle to attaining peace. Shimon Peres was always "afraid" to "miss the last opportunity" of making "peace" with the Arabs. But, Shimon Peres was not the only one to "miss" this great opportunity."

The late Professor Chaim Weizmann, the first president of the State of Israel, "missed" the "opportunity" to make "peace" with the Arabs, when he rejected an arrangement with King Abdullah to form a Jewish-Arab Confederation, with Jerusalem as its capital, headed by King Abdullah of Jordan. Dr. Weizmann's reaction was: An Arab on the throne of King David? Never!

David Ben-Gurion, the First Prime Minister of the State of Israel also "missed" an "opportunity" to make "Peace" With the Arabs when he flatly rejected U.S. Ambassador Macdonald's advice to give away part of the Negev to Jordan and retain the Galilee.

Ben-Gurion again "missed" the "opportunity" to make "Peace" with the Arabs when he refused to meet with the Syrian dictator Hosni Zaim who claimed half of the Sea of Galilee (Kineret). Ben Gurion rightfully refused to give Syria the keys to Israel's Water Reservoir.

Moshe Sharet, the Second Prime Minister of Israel also "missed" an "opportunity" to make "Peace" with the Arabs when he refused Egyptian President Gamal Abdul Nasser's demand to a corridor to Jordan through Israel's Negev.

Levi Eshkol "missed" a "Golden Opportunity" to make "Peace " with the Arabs, when he rejected an offer made to him by King Hussein of Jordan to give away Jerusalem, Judea, Samaria and the Gaza Strip to Jordan.

Yitzhak Shamir, Prime Minister of Israel "missed" a "golden opportunity" to make "peace" with the Arabs, according to Shimon Peres, his Foreign Minister, when he rejected the "London Agreement" of

April 1987, between Shimon Peres and King Hussein of Jordan, without Shamir's knowledge or approval.

Shimon Peres and Yitzhak Rabin were prisoners of the so-called "Jordanian Option", which linked a solution of the Palestinian-Arab problem to an agreement with King Hussein. Peres had been sowing dissension among American Jews. Unity among American Jews had been eroded. It is very difficult to find another instance, where a Foreign Minister visited a country abroad and attacked his own government there.

Shimon Peres wasn't aware of, or ignored former British Prime Minister Clement Attlee's remark: " I do not criticize my government when I am abroad." The damage, which Shimon Peres did to his country, Israel, during the last decade and for trying to push the International Peace Conference plan, was irreversible, beyond repair. It looked, as if, the Foreign Minister, Shimon Peres was struggling in vain for the International Peace Conference for the Middle East. Like Don Quixote, he is fighting against windmills, a lost war. Prime Minister Shamir, nor the silent majority will ever permit Peres to take the course of such a dangerous adventure.

There is no doubt that the Maarah Party's line of going to an International Conference means losing from the start. It means the beginning of a Palestinian-Arab in Judea, Samaria and Gaza.

Mikhail Gorbachev was ridiculing the U.S. efforts to get an accepted arrangement in the Middle East:"We gave them the opportunity to act alone, but they failed."

Gorbachev felt over confident only because the U.S. gave up and decided to go along with the Soviets and agreed to convene an International Peace Conference for the Middle East.

Speculators believe that the U.S. would have never agreed to an International Conference for Peace in the Middle East together with the Soviets but changed its mind when it saw the trend, the inclination, of half of the Israeli Cabinet-Shimon Peres and his Maarah Party.

What the Soviets are after is nothing but a Soviet-American condominion in the Middle East.

In return, the Soviets promised to Israel, peace and security. Peace and security in theory. In practice it is nothing but a constant perpetual interference in every problem or conflict in the area or as the Soviets call it: "A balance of Power between Israel's security needs and the "Palestinian-Arab legitimate rights of self determination."

The American Israel Public Affairs Committee (AIPAC) has considerable influence on congressional elections campaign, which it exercises indirectly through Jewish political activists and Fund Raisers.   This is one of the main sources of its power in Washington.

If the U.S. politician expressed support for an Arab-Palestinian state or criticized Israel, in public, AIPAC would make sure that this "indiscretion" would be known in the Jewish Community. AIPAC are also ensuring that Israel continues to get a generous share of American economic and military aid and are keeping American arms that may threaten Israel out of the hands of hostile Arab states.

The American Jewish Congress (AJC) had become the first major American Jewish Organization to endorse Foreign Minister Shimon Peres's call for an International Middle East Conference. Their excuse for speaking out on the issue was: "Because the Governement of Israel is itself divided and at a deadlock over how to approach the peace process."

The AJC statement broke a tradition under which American Jewish organizations have refrained from taking public stands on issues reflecting the security of Israel and the peace process.

On September 22, 1987, Prime Minister Yitzhak Shamir blasted the AJC's statement on the International Conference and the territories, emphacizing that it was a "clear cut violation of the long-held truth" that the Jewish establishment in the U.S. does not intervene in matters, which are in dispute in Israel. The Prime Minister called on American Jewish organizations "not to take this road" and stressed that on political and security matters "Only the state of Israel has the right to decide." U.S. Jews are required to understan this," said Shamir, "and to support our struggle and our efforts."

Jew living in Hampstead Garden Suburb, West Rogers Park, Highland Park, Dollard des Ormeaux, Hillcrest, Downsview, etc. cannot monitor or ctiticize the Israeli unless they make "aliyah" and move to Israel.

The following is the Prime Minister's letter to the chairman of the Conference of Presidents of Major American Jewish Organizations, Mr. Morris Abram:

Jerusalem , October 1, 1987

Dear Morris,

As we mark the unity and the kinship of our nation on the eve of Yom Kippur, I feel compelled to address you on a matter of great concern.

Ever since the esatablishment of the State of Israel we have felt that it belongs to the whole Jewish people. We know and appreciate how actuely concerned our brethren abroad are for our well-being, and we welcome and encourage their involvement in all aspects of life. Strengthening the bonds that unite us and making all Jews feel that Israel is their home is a primary goal of our state.

But, in the 61 years of Israel's existence, all of us, here and abroad, have adhered to the principle that matters of existnce and security must be let to those who are called to shed their blood for the country. Thus and only thus has the American Jewish leadership been able to present to the world a united front on the fundamental issues of Israel's existence and help it immeasurably in its struggles. At the same time, we have maintained and will continue to maintain open channels of communication with Jewish leaders in the Diaspora and welcome their input through those channels.

The regrettable recent attempt to breach this understanding sets a dangerous precedent. There is a shock of disbelief in Israel, a pain that only a violation of a hallowed principle can cause.

In a democracy it is a duty and privilege of a political party and its leaders to try to persuade the electorate to support their position. To circumvent this process by appealing to friends abroad who do note vote in Israel would deal a blow to our sovereignty and democratic tradition. I sure you do not want it to happen.

Allowing anyone but Israel's elected government to decide on questions of Israel's security will invite and excuse intervention in life-and-death decisions by those who do not have Israel's best interests at heart.

One of the main reasons we object to an International Conference is that we believe Israel's fate must not be determined by others. Instead of acting as a sovereign state, negotiating with equals, Israel will be a nation on trial at an International Conference. Even our closest friends among the potential participants have declared they will present and support a virtually total withdrawal to the 1949 armistice boundaries-a solution the vast majority of Israelis consider a death trap. An International Conference can end in only one of the two ways: Israel's acquiescence in an unacceptable solution, or an Israeli walkout, with dire political and diplomatic consequences. I am sure you wish us neither.

Our demand for direct negotiations is irreproachable. It proved itself at Camp David and will prove itself again. But only if remain united, and muster enough faith and persistence to overcome our neighbour's intransigence and our own defeatism, shall we be able to pursue what is just and right for Israel.

I wish you a Shana Tova, and may the New Year be a year of Jewish unity. May you be inscribed in the book of life and happiness? Please share this message with your colleagues in the Conference of Presidents of Major Jewish Organizations together with my best wishes.

Yitzhak Shamir

Mr. Morris Abram's statement on the issue was: "In regard to the issue of an International Peace Conference, our position must be as follows:

"Like the people of Israel, the American Jewish Community yearns for comprehensive peace in the Middle East. We recognize that the security of the State of Israel is ultimately a matter to be decided by the Israeli people and their government, for they pay for their security with their blood and their fears. We fervently hope Israelis will find the modalities and the programme for peace and security through their democratic processes. We therefore will await the decision of the democratically constituted government of Israel on the issue of an International peace Conference."

On Wednesday, September 30th, 1987, (Tishrei 7, 5748), in an address to the Conference of Presidents of Major American Jewish Organizations (COJO)-the main umbrella group of American Jewry-Foreign Minister Shimon Peres invited the American Jewry to become actively involved in the debate over the nature of the Middle East peace-making process.

"American Jewish Organizations," Peres said, "have an absolute right to express their views publicly on the Middle East Peace process-even if those views are debatable and even in dispute, in Israel itself."

A similar remark was delivered by Shimon Peres, quite recently, to the American Jewish

Congress (AJC).

Israeli Foreign Minister Shimon Peres also added that: "The most important problem is peace, and American Jews have the right to take a stand."

U.S. Jewish leaders were as divided as the Israelis over Peres's call for American Jewry to be actively involved in the dispute over the International Peace Conference for the Middle East

Reform leader Rabbi Alexander Schindler expressed support for Peres's position and said: "I see nothing inappropriate for Peres to call on us to be involved in the peace process debate. It is our responsibility to give voice to our convictions. Peres was not the first to urge American Jews to take part on such issues. Menachem Begin often called on 'all of Israel' to become involved in the Judea, Samaria controversy.

Israel is the center of the Jewish world, but we are one people. How can the periphery be impervious to what is happening at the center? Can the lips fail to respond when the heart speaks?

I do not suggest we involve ourselves in operational details of Israeli foreign policy, for which we don't have the resources or competence. We must recognize that the final decision rests with the people of Israel who live under the gun. But it is our obligation to make our feeling known about the fundamental issue that has its impact on Israel's future and the destiny of the Jewish people."

The unity and the security of the Jewish nation in Israel and in the Diaspora are extremely important for Jewish survival. The political destiny of Israel, the center of Judaism, must be determined by the Israelis only, because they, and only they, take the risk and shed the blood.

The Diaspora role is, help, advice in private, but never criticize Israel or its government in public because this will only add more ammunition to its enemies.

If people desire to voice their criticism openly they could do it if and when they become citizens of Israel entitled to vote and participate in the public debate.

An open debate among Jews in the diaspora will bring divisiveness rather than unity and undermine Israel' credibility. It will render Israel weak and subject to political blackmail.

Most Israelis believe that the diaspora Jews have the full right to express their opinion, to comment, to advice on the different aspects of life in Israel, but not to interfere. Not only because of their great contributions to the development of Israel but also because of the mutual dependency.

Advise on every aspect of life, except defence. Not because the Israelis doubt their sincerity and honesty of their advise but because their risk is not the same as the risk of the Israelis.

The Israelis who believe in Arab transfer as well as Israelis who oppose this idea, risk their lives for their opinions. On the other hand, the diaspora Jews do not risk anything at all.

There is no doubt whatsoever of their sincere worry for the survival of the State of Israel and its Jewish population. Yet, if something does endanger the security of Israel they will be truly sorry, but will not have to pay with their lives.

This is why there must be a limit to the advice or interference of the diaspora Jews in the problems of the State of Israel.

Conservative Rabbi Arthur Hertzberg and Reform Rabbi Alexander Schindler, who are sitting quiet and safe in the United States of America, six thousand miles away from the arena of conflict, from the fire, from the rocks, had the nerves to reprimand Israel, in public, for "her mistreatment of the Palestinian Arabs."

Israeli Police who tried to force Law and Order and disperse Arab violent demonstrations, under the shower of Arab rocks, knives, sticks, Molotov-Cocktails were strongly criticized by these two gentlemen from America. Israeli police who tried to break up Arab violent demonstrations in favor of the PLO, shouting PLO slogans, raising PLO flags and burning Israeli flags, were "mistreating" the Arabs, according to these two Galut (diaspora) minded gentlemen from America. And why did they behave like this? Because the conscience of Jewish American leaders bothered them, because they knew very well that their natural and normal home should have been Israel and not the U.S.A.

Several letters of criticism and protests against the Israeli "harsh" policy, in Judea, Samaria and the Gaza Strip had been published by Jewish intellectuals abroad, mainly in the United States, emphacizing the fact that they were ashamed of the way Israel was treating the "Intifada", the Palestinian-Arab uprising in Israel, in Judea, Samaria and the Gaza Strip. They just couldn't keep their feelings to themselves and had to bring it out in public, without giving a damn if it was adverse publicity to Israel.

Intellectuals like Reform Rabbi Alexander Schindler, violonist Isaac Shtern, Comedian woody Allen, etc, all from the United States. Israel feels pitty for them, for being unable to understand the damage they caused to the State of Israel. Israel is ashamed that these Jewish Intellectuals, after two thousand years of diaspora, homelessness, prayers, tears, hope, didn't find it necessary to make "aliyah" and move to Israel. Israel is ashamed that in spite of the fact that the State of Israel exist already almost sixty years these Jewish intellectuals refuse to make Israel their permanent home. Refuse to share the fate of their people. Refuse to share the sufferings, the devotion, the sacrifices of the Israelis and instead, prefer to enjoy the fleshpot of the diaspora, the comforts of their present country. The Jews have finally, after two thousand years, redeemed the country of their forefathers and are calling back the dispersed sheep from all the diasporas, from all the four corners of the world, yet, these Jewish intellectuals prefer to "Stay Out Of It", chose to desert from Jewish responsibility. But, they are not ashamed to criticize the State of Israel by remote control, "advise" Israel from six thousand miles away, where they are safe from the Arab bullets, knives, stones, burning tires, Molotov-Cocktails, kidnappings, etc. The State of Israel is ashamed of Jewish intellectuals like these and their irrational behavior.

Several liberal U.S. Jews have expressed their feelings on the issue of the Arab uprising and the way Israel is trying to quell this "Civil Disturbance", which is nothing but another phase of the Moslem Jihad against the Jews, by saying that "there is growing pain about recent event in Judea, Samaria and the Gaza Strip, It is not monolithic, but it is broad. Therefore, U.S. Jews are increasingly concerned at the killings, at the methods of the repression."

The Israelis feel that the U.S. Jewry is not entitled to criticize Israel by remote control. Such criticism, in the media hurt the image of Israel. Israel has a lot of problems and realy doesn't need

"Back-Seat Drivers".

On January 28, 1988 (Shevat 9, 5748), Woody Allen, the American famous comedian appealed to Israel to halt its "Wrong-Headed Approach" in trying to quell the Palestinian- Arab uprising. Writing on the Op-Ed Page of the New York Times, Woody Allen said that he had to take a stand on a "situation that is quite painful and confusing."

"As a supporter of Israel, and as one who has always been outraged at the horrors inflicted on this little nation by hostile neighbours, vile terrorists and much of the world at large", he wrote, "I am appalled beyond measure by the treatment of the rioting Palestinians by the Jews."

Morton Kornreich, President of the UJA-Federation of Greater New York declared on January 1988, that the UJA-Federation had selected the neighbouring towns of Lod and Ramleh as its new Project Renewal project, in part because they contain a good sized Arab minority, which has living conditions that are realy pitiful. They live in some of the worst slums in Israel, a social cancer in the mid-section of Israel, near the airport.

It is very wrong that Israel has silently accepted the unfortunate fact that there are two separate Jewish entities. One in Israel, and the other in the Diaspora. It is very wrong that Israel has given up hope to live to see the exodus of the diaspora.

On January 21, 1988 (Shevat 2, 5748), the Soviet Union called on UN Secreary-General Peres de Cuellar to convene the UN Security Council at the foreign minister level in order to discuss setting up an International Conference for Peace in the Middle East.

In a letter published in New York on January 21, 1988, the Soviet Foreign Minister Eduard Shevardnadze referred to the "Popular Uprising" by Palestinian Arabs in the "occupied" territories, and said that there was growing support for the idea of an International Conference as the only realistic means of achieving a settlement of the Arab-Israeli conflict.

In Jerusalem, the Prime Minister's Office professed a distinct lack of enthusiam for the Soviet initiative, saying that the UN forum had "great disadvantages" because of its low standing in Israeli eyes and because the PLO, in its observer capacity in the UN, is bound to participate in any Security Council debate on the matter.

In a passionate speech that its vote on the issue next month is the key to a democratic Nicaragua and a peaceful Central America, President Ronald Reagan pulled out all the stops in a bid to persuade the Democratic-controlled Congress to pass the aid request on January 26, 1988, when the President will make his formal request to aid the Contras. "The Contras", the President said "were the only ones that stood between a peaceful Central America and chaos". The President added that: "the Contras falling apart without U.S. aid, will lead to a Communist-controlled region causing turmoil on the U.S. shores."

"It's willfully naïve to think that the Soviet Union, beset by a crisis in its own economy, would be pouring billions of dollars into a country on the other side of the world if they didn't see great opportunities there," he said. "If Congress votes down aid, we will be abandoning the only real cause for peace and freedom in Nicaragua. We will be consigning the peace process to an obscure footnote in history and handling the Soviet Union one of its greatest strategic victories since World War II," said Reagan.

"This is the moment of truth, the make-or-break vote on the freedom fighters," he said, using his preferred term for the Contras.

On January 28, 1988, Egyptian President Hosni Mubarak sent messages to both Prime Minister Yitzhak Shamir and Foreign Minister Shimon Peres.

In his letter to Shamir, Mubarak again assails the Prime Minister's opposition to the International Conference, challenging him to explain why the Conference would lead to an Arab-Palestian state and would block direct negotiations with the Arab-Palestinians.

Shamir replied immediately, in a letter to Mubarak, reiterating his previous proposals for Israeli-Egyptian-Jordanian talks.

In his letter to Peres, Mubarak wrote that: "the International Conference, which Shamir does not agree with it, is only a method for the real, direct and constructive dialogue leading to a comprehensive peace".

Jesse Jackson, leader of Black America, was campaigning for presidency of the United States of America, representing the Democratic Party. On February, 1988, in his Washington campaign headquarters, Jackson promised that as president, he would work for Israeli-Palestinian Arabs "security, recognition, and a chance at prosperity and growth," "The status quo in the territories", he insisted, "involves only false security for Israel, with no growth. That formula will not work. It leaves both very vulnerable. Israel is vulnerable in this formula; the Palestinian-Arabs are vulnerable. You simply have a formula for war, as opposed to a formula for peace."

Jackson added that the advanced U.S. arms system provided to Israel-fighter aircraft and missiles-were "essentially difunctional" in terms of oferring long-term security to Israel. "Security lies in peace, not in mutual destruction."

"We should never trade off moral authority, because from it comes every other authority, and Israel's historic strength has been that. And with each passing day-with the expulsions, with the beatings, with the locking of people in their houses, and with the occupation-Israel's strongest authority is being drained. And thus, the nation is becoming divided."

"We have interest in Israeli security and Palestinian-Arabs justice, which are inextricably bound. They are two sides of the same coin and there will not be Israeli security without Palestinian-Arab justice or a homeland or a sovereign place for the Palestinian-Arab people."

In explaining why he supported the concept of self-determination for the Palestinian-Arabs, he noted that Israel, after World War II, had itself been one of its beneficiaries.

Mr. Jackson, or rather Reverend Jackson, charged that the U.S. policy toward the Middle East during the Reagan administration has effectively collapsed."We did not build upon Camp David", he said, "We allowed it to collapse."

"Occupation is too great of a burden to bear and has no future. Occupation is too draining.

Emotionally for the Israelis, and realy for anybody. Occupation is too divisive politically, as witness the big demonstrations in Israel. Occupation is costly economically. Occupation is bloody militarily."

One of his many election campaign slogans was: "Drugs are bad, crime is messy. Don't be sad, vote for Jesse."

The Presidential candidate added that Israel and the Arab-Palestinians must be brought together, as to who would represent the Palestinian-Arabs, he said:

"The representatives of their choice, because that's what self-determination accords. They must determine their representatives and Israel must determine its representatives. Neither side can choose the other side's negotiating team."

Asked if that meant the PLO, Jackson said:"I wouldn't say PLO, I would say the representatives of the Palestinian Arabs' choice. Let's deal with the principle of self-determination, human rights and law.

"When asked to outline some specific steps he would implement to achieve that objective, he replied that he would first assure Israel of "our commitment to its security within International recognized boundaries".

While conceding that those boundaries should be open to negotiations, he added that: "it is fairly obvious that the West Bank and the Gaza Strip should be relieved of occupation."

"The idea of Palestinian-Arabs moving to Jordan is non-option. Let's deal with reality."

Reverend Jesse Jackson was very critical of the long-standing U.S. prohibition against dealing directly with the PLO.

"By giving up the right to talk, we gave up the right to act. So here we have money in the Middle East, and military in the Middle East, but not much diplomacy. We've given up the most powerful diplomatic weapon-the right to talk."

By making only indirectly-"through the back door"- with the PLO, the U.S. was missing a major opportunity to influence the PLO.

U.S. Secretary of State George Shultz stated upon his arrival in Israel, on February 25, 1988 (Adar 7, 5748), that he was carrying "a workable proposal" for a Middle East peace process and proclaimed that: "if we can work together with commitment and determination, we can make 1988 a year of peace in the region." Shultz added that given "good will, open minds and a realistic vision of what is possible, we can make strides towards our goal of a comprehensive Middle East peace." "The status quo is not a stable Option," said the Secretary.

Shamir rejected the American proposal to break the link between the talks on the interim settlement, the autonomy, and those on the final status of the territories. Shamir did not accept the International opening for peace talks as defined by the Americans; Shamir feels that the proposed American timetable is too ambitious and believes that it undermines Camp David. Yitzhak Shamir adamantly rejected the "Peace for Territories" concept that Shultz has indicated was the linchpin of the American plan. Secretary Shultz had to hear two different versions, two different answers to his question. Two concepts: The concept of the Maarah and the concept of the Likud. The Concept of Shimon Peres and the concept of Yitzhak Shamir. The formula accepted by Shimon Peres and the Maarah is "Territories for Peace", on the understanding that it does not require the cession of all the territories. On the other hand, Yitzhak Shamir, the Prime Minister's formula was "Peace for Peace" and was very clear in his declaration that the surrender of any territory of Eretz Israel is unthinkable and not under consideration.

The U.S. administration cannot come now and claim why Israel did not tell them in good time where it stood.

The U.S. Consulate-General in Jerusalem invited fifteen Palestinian-Arabs from Judea, Samaria and the Gaza Strip to meet with the U.S. Secretary of State George Shultz at the American Colony hotel in East Jerusalem.

Among the Arab leaders invited were: Bethlehem Mayor Elias Freij, former Gaza Mayor Rashad a-Shawa and the ex-Mayor of Hebron, Mustafa el-Natshe, Al-Fajr editor Hanna Siniora and Said Kanaan from Shechem (Nablus).

El-Natshe said that the Palestinian-Arabs from the territories could not meet with Secretary Shultz because such a meeting would be construed as an attempt to create an alternative Palestinian-Arab leadership in the territories.

Yasser Abed-Rabbo, who heads the PLO's Information Department, said, on February 25, 1988 (Adar 7, 5748), that: "no Palestinian-Arab personality will meet with Shultz on the trip to occupied Palestine." Any dialogue, he said, would have to be with the PLO, the sole, legitimate representative of the Palestinian-Arabs.

It is believed that the reason why the U.S. Secretary of State George Shultz arrived in the Middle East area of conflict, on February and March 1988, was, the concern to the continuity of King Hussein's regime in Jordan. If the riots, that, for some reason or other, the Israeli government didn't decide to put an end to it, yet, continue, they could spread out into Jordan and endanger the Hashemite regime and the King's seat. This, the United States of America and the Western countries will hate to accept, because it might lead to a situation in which the PLO will, eventually, control Saudi-Arabia and the Gulf Emirates and endanger the free flow of Arab oil to the West. These Arab oil countries are militarily weak and wouldn't be able to resist an outside military attack or an inside coup, backed by outside military forces, which might end up, even, with a Soviet take over.

King Hussein has been so far their guardian and that is why the West is so concerned about his welfare and future, and sometimes, at the expense of Israel. This, because Israel is economically dependent on the Unites States. It is so because of a long Israeli Government distorted economic system.

ss his visit Shultz realized, once more, that Israel is ready for a "Peace for Peace" agreement with the Arab countries but will not accept "Territories for Peace". The Arabs should realize that they couldn't get from Israel more lands. Not a single square inch.

On February 1988 (Shevat 5748), in New York, Fifty-one American Jewish organizations have issued a statement expressing identification with Israel and support for the security of Israel and for its legitimate efforts to oppose terrorism and violence. They also expressed appreciation for the Reagan administration's efforts to recharge the Middle East peace process rather than let it fade out.

Letter to the Editor of the Jerusalem Post:
Helping Our Enemies,
"Sir,- By reporting daily statements of Arab spokesmen and politicians without pointing out the lies they contain, our media serves as a mouthpiece for our enemies' propaganda.

Not onlythe foreign media, but also our own and some of our politicians have adopted the PLO terminology, talking about "occupation"without mentioning from whom we took over the "territories" and under what circumstances. They talk about "oppression" without mentioning that the oppressed Palestinian-Arabs never agreed to negotiate with us and that their declared aim is to destroy us.

Every statement by a Palestinian-Arab, like Rashad Shawa, who, according to Yehudah Litani, is a moderate, is given wide publicity. When he complains about conditions in the refugee camps, nobody reminds him of his statement on Jordanian TV that it was very clever of the Arab leaders to keep the refugees in the camps in order to keep the problem alive. Nobody asked him what he has done for the refugees when he was Mayor of Gaza or why he refused to extend municipal services to the camps when asked to do so by the civil administration of the Gaza Strip. Nobody points out the fact that the Arab States supply the PLO with vast amounts of money to buy arms and to maintain a world-wide representation in the most lavish conditions, but that they have no money to improve the living conditions of their refugees. What prompted me to write now was Yohanan Meroz's article of January 29, 1988, about Hasbarah. His article was printed, of course. However, I am very much afraid that this will remain a voice calling in the wilderness and that the media will continue to quote every "statement" by 12-year old "student" or by an old woman without paying attention to statements by residents of Gaza or Ramallah to the effect that their fight will go on until the last Jew goes back to where he came from and that Haifa is as much theirs as Ramallah is.

Tawfik Toubi keeps repeating that all the Palestinian-Arabs want is a state of their own, alongside with Israel. Nobody asked him who said so, where and when?

It is of course vital for our media to point out the disastrous results of the Likud policies, their waste of our meager resources on settlements in the West Bank and Gaza, and Shamir's obdurate refusal to participate in any positive steps towards peace. This, however, does not mean that we have to abstain from telling the truth about our enemies and point out that they have not changed their attitude towards us since the days of Haj-Amin el-Husseini."

David Smyrin
Haifa, February 26, 1988.

In his letter, Mr. David Smyrin, contradicted himself, when, on the one hand, he is blaming the Israeli media and politicians for adopting the PLO terminology of "occupation", while, on the other hand, he himself uses the PLO terminology of the "West Bank", when he should know that the "West Bank" are the old, Jewish, historical territories of Judea and Samaria.

Mr. Smyrin is totally mistaken when he thinks that settlements in Judea and Samaria are waste. Settlement in Judea and Samaria are vital to the State of Israel if it wants to keep these Jewish territories.

Mr. Smyrin is again wrong in accusing Prime Minister Yitzhak Shamir of refusing to participate in any positive steps towards peace. Prime Minister Shamir is refusing to accept the Arab concept of "Territories for Peace",because he knows very well that giving away Jewish territories will never bring peace. It will only invite blackmail.

In general, Mr. Smyrin's letter was written very well except for this part, which was not in the best interest of Israel and very damaging.

For many years it has been a custom to scare Israel and warn her from results derived from its misbehavior, behavior contrary to their wish, and the wish of those who mean "good" for her. People with "good intentions", and who always had the right answer and knew the right solution. As was the case, a few weeks prior to the Six-Day War, when Israel was warned by its "friends" that if it doesn't retreat it might lose over twenty five thousand people. Or, as was the case in a few other occasions.

Now, Israel is requested to put its trust on the British, the Russians and their friends and join the International Peace Conference for the Middle East. Otherwise, Israel might lose its friends and their friendly support and also the support of their U.S. brothers, the American Jewry.

On the other hand, there are many signs that, finally, the U.S. Jewry has undergone a certain change and finally understand that the issue is not exactly territories but the survival of the State of Israel and the Jewish people is at stake, and support Israel whole heartedly.

For years the State of Israel dealt mainly with the leaders of the diaspora, who, not once, defended our opponent, the U.S. Administration. On the other hand, recently Israel is approaching the common people, the silent majority, rather than their leaders, who are sometimes, much more understanding than its leaders.

On September 1, 1975, the United States of America and the State of Israel, had signed a diplomatic Memorandum of Agreement (MOA), at the time of the second Sinai accord. It was designed to encourage the Israeli withdrawal from the Mitla and Gidi passes and the Abu Rodeis oil fields. That Memorandum Agreement, signed by ex-Secretary of States Henry Kissinger and the Foreign Minister Yigal Allon, codified the U.S. refusal to recognize the PLO until it accepts "Israel's right to exist" and UN Security Council Resolutions 212 and 338. It has remained U.S. official policy ever since.

But, unofficially, the United States of America, was flirting with the PLO representatives ever since. Shultz highly controversial meeting in Washington on March 26, 1988 with PLO representatives in the U.S., with Palestinian-American Professor Edward Said and Ibrahim Abu-Lughod, both members of the Palestinian-Arab National Council, still very vivid. And Secretary Shultz is known to be friend of Israel. Shultz did not give up easily and kept pushing towards an International Peace Conference for the Middle East. Shultz made several declarations in public, which made very clear his stand; negotiation with the Palestinian-Arabs and "Peace for Territories", Israeli territories. The following are some of his declarations:

"The United States is for comprehensive peace achieved through negotiations."

"The people of the Middle East require peace. The situation is not improving, and the status quo remains unacceptable."

"The Palestinians-Arabs will receive their legitimate rights through negotiations in which they will participate actively. In this way, they will be able to enjoy lives of security, dignity, and freedom."

"I'm returning to the region to reaffirm our belief that a workable avenue to peace exists surely the odds against a break through are high. Pessimism and cynicism run deep. But, theUnited States ofAmerica will keep moving forward.We have a plan on the table and we willpursue it. Some have tried to say the plan won't work, but they have failed. The plan can work. It can bring negotiations. It can help achieve peace."

"If Yasser Arafat gives up terror, accepts Resolutions 242 and 338 and recognizes the State of Israel."

Foreign sources believe that with the "Westwind", with the "Aravah", with the"Luz", with the "Shafrir", with the "Mazlat", with the "Kfir", with the "Shavit II", with the "Barak", with the "Gavriel", with the "Lavi", with the "Jericho II", with the "Ofek I", "Ofek II", and with a serious pile of "Atom and Hydrogen Bombs", Israel doesn't really need Arafat's recognition.

These preconditions were introdueed by Israel in the "Memorandum of Agreement" with the United States of America, in 1975, to hold the U.S. from recognizing the PLO. Israel knew that the PLO would never accept these conditions, because it contradicts their very existence.

The Israeli public will always support heartily any Israeli party or leader who could make a persuasive case that the Arabs were truly ready to end the conflict and to offer Israel peace in exchange of peace.

Jordan was not a party in the Camp David Accord and keeps rejecting the idea of autonomy for the Palestinian-Arabs under Israeli rule, even as an interim arrangement. Yet, Jordan too considers itself bound by Resolution 242.

Anwar Sadat's precedent of receiving all the Sinai Peninsula makes it particularly difficult for King Hussein of Jordan to exchange full peace for anything less than all of the West Bank and East Jerusalem. It is assumed that King Hussein would never start direct negotiations with Israel without the legitimacy granted by an International Confernce and the consent of Yasser Arafat and the PLO.

It is also assumed that Prime Minister Yitzhak Shamir and the Likud will never agree to a procedure, which they consider dangerous and detrimental to the best interest of Israel.

It will be difficult or impossible to bridge that gap.

In his visit to the U.S. on February 23, 1988 (Adar 5, 5748) Shamir tried to abort attempts aimed at wresting Judea, Samaria and the Gaza Strip from Israel. Prime Minister Shamir rejected the U.S. plan in essence, if not in words.

Israel is asked to trust the untrustworthy. Israel is asked to give up large pieces of territory for the sake of a treaty, which the Arabs do not intend to keep.

The Palestinian-Arabs, the PLO will not live permanently in a largely sovereign Palestinian entity confined to Judea, Samaria and Gaza. They will only say that they are willing but their hidden intention is using this entity in the future as a base for further attacks aimed at taking over the whole Jewish country and probably also Jordan. Behind the words spoken for Israeli and American consumption, their secret goal remains: Today, the West Bank, Tomorrow Haifa, Ramleh, Jaffa, Jerusalem, etc.

Israel already made two "Territories for Peace" type compromises with the Palestinian-Arabs. One compromise was, by losing the whole of the Eastern Bank of the Jordan River to the Jordanian Arabs in 1921-1922. The second compromise was, by giving away the whole of Sinai to the Egyptian-Arabs in the Camp David Accord. Israel cannot make more territorial compromises without risking its survival.

On Wednesday, March 9, 1988, Senator Carl Levin, one of the initiators of the Letter signed by thirty senators calling on Israel to exchange "Territories for Peace", received the folowing letter from Israeli Prime Minister Yitzhak Shamir:

Jerusalem, March 7, 1988
"Dear Senator Levin,

I would like to refer to your letter of March 3, 1988, to Secretary of State George Shultz, which was co-signed by some of your colleagues in the U.S. Senate and was published in the media.

Your letter came as a surprise, at a crucial moment in the peace efforts that were being conducted by Secretary Shultz. We have been doing our utmost to ensure the success of these efforts, because we have sought peace relentlessly, but our Arab neighbours, except Egypt, still have to prove in deeds that they are willing to negotiate peace with us.

Although you correctly blame the Arab side for refusing until now to recognize Israel and make peace with it, we were astonished by the words of criticism you leveled at us on the formula of "Territories for Peace."

As you yourself state, Resolution 242 provided the basis for a peace settlement. Israel has accepted this resolution and implemented it in the Camp David Accords, to which Egypt and the U.S. are committed, produced an agreed formula for settling the territorial issue, and Israel made aconsiderable sacrifice to achieve agreement on this very sensitive issue.

In accordance with this formula, Israel was required to withdraw from the entire Sinai Peninsula to the International border between it and Egypt.

On the Eastern sector, President Anwar Sadat and Prime Minister Menachem Begin devised an agreed formula that would grant the Palestinian-Arabs self-rule, following which the sides would negotiate the final status of the territories in question in a vastly improved setting of coexistence and cooperation between Jordan, Israel and the Palestinian-Arabs.

In other words, the Government of Israel is committed to negotiate the ultimate disposition of Judea, Samaria (the West Bank) and Gaza in the context of the implication of the Camp David Accords.

I must add that, whereas the Sinai was uncontested Egyptian territory and therefore it was returned to Egyptian sovereignty, Judea, Samaria and Gaza were occupied militarily anf illegally by Jordan and Egypt and their status must, therefore, be determined in the peace negotiations.

I, therefore, fail to understand the reasons for your criticism, which hurts even more because it comes from friends who have Israel's security and welfare at heart.

Are we now expected to wipe away the Camp David Accords, for which we paid such a high price?

If we are going to lose faith in solemn American and Egyptian commitments under these Accords, how can we be assured of future commitments that will require us to take even further risks to our security and future?

In a few days I shall be in Washington to continue our deliberations with an Administration that has strikingly demonstrated its friendship with, and support of, Israel.

I am also looking forward to meeting with our numerous friends on Capitol Hill.

Let me assure you: nobody yearns for peace more than the people of Israel whom I have the privilege to represent.

It is the free and democratic people and government of Israel that will have to decide the issues of peace and security. It is their future and well being that is at stake and I shall endeavour to ensure them to the best of my capacity."

Sincerely

Yitzhak Shamir.

"There is no connection between friendship and political interests," Shamir told reporters, on Wednesday, March 7, 1988. "It's nice to negotiate with a friend. But, when it is a friend who strikes a blow, it hurts even more."

Following his meeting with Israeli Prime Minister Yitzhak Shamir, on March 16, 1988, in Washington, U.S. President Ronald Reagan made the following statement:

"It's been a pleasure to meet with Prime Minister Shamir again and to have this opportunity to review with him the important issue of peace in the Middle East.

We have unique relationship with Israel, a relationship of trust, friendship and shared ideals. I think we can be proud of the achievements that we've made over the last seven years in giving more substance and dimension to the strong ties between Israel and the U.S. In the reamainder of my term, we will continue to work to strengthen those ties.

The main topic of our discussion today was the search for peace in the Middle East. We have seen a new sense of urgency on the part of many in the region and a wide recognition of the reality that the status quo is unacceptable.

Our efforts have been geared toward trying to find a reasonable and practical way to make real progress. Progress that will assure the security of Israel and its neighbours and achieve the legitimate rights of the Palestinians.

The present situation is a challenge and an opportunity to move decisively to break the deadlock that has lasted for too long.

I hope we will not lose this opportunity.

Today, Prime Minister Shamir and I discussed the proposal for moving forward rapidly to peace negotiations, which, Secretary Shultz left with Israel, Jordan and Syria during his recent visit.

We believe this proposal offers alistic and achievable way to change the relationship between Israel and the Arabs. It is a concrete demonstration of my commitment to finding a solution to the Arab-Isreali conflict through a negotiation process that would begin soon.

As I told Prime Minister Shamir, the U.S. is prepared to be an active partner in the process. We hope that all the parties involved will seize this opportunity.

So, let's be clear about things: The U.S. will not slice this initiative apart and will not abandon it. And those who will say no to the U.S. plan- and the Prime Minister has not used this word-need not answer us; they need to answer to themselves and their people as to why they turned down a realistic and sensible plan to achieve negotiations. This is a time for all the parties to the conflict to make decisions for peace.

Prime Minister Shamir and I also reviewed our countries' robust and vital bilateral relationship. As you know, Israel has been designate one of our major non-NATO allies and friends. We have developed a solid basis of cooperation between our two countries. Strategic cooperation is a symbol of our converging needs and mutual commitment to ensuring that the wedge will ever be driven by us.

I want to add that Prime Minister Shamir and I both remain very concerned about the many thousands of Jews that remain in the Soviet Union and yearn to emigrate and fully express their Jewish identity. The plight of Soviet Jewry shall remain at the top of my agenda in my discussions with Secretary Gorbachev.

As I bid farewell to Prime Minister Shamir, I wish him and the people of Israel a happy 40th anniversary. Our prayer is that the anniversary will mark the beginning of an era of peace and accommodation in the Middle East."

In reply, Prime Minister Yitzhak Shamir made the following statement:

"This visit to Washington has given me the opportunity to meet again with President Reagan, Secretary of State Shultz, Secretary of Defense Carlucei and Secretary of Treasury Baker.

My colleagues and I have also met with Congressional leaders and other friends in the Congress, in the administration and in the general public.

I am indebted to the President for this kind invitation. It affords me the opportunity to discuss matters of common concern and to deepen the friendship and understanding between our two countries.

In the talks with the President and with Secretary Shultz we reviewed the state of U.S.-Israel relations and the efforts to advance peace in the Middle East.

Mr. President: We have always been in complete agreement with the principle of negotiating from a position of strength for which you have always stood.

We have stepped up efforts to seek a framework for conducting direct peace negotiations between Israel and those of its Arab neighbours who hope, would join us in the quest for peace.

Israel has welcomed the American involvement and the Secretary's efforts in this search. We have confidence in the American role, because, we share the same goal of peace-with-security for all the countries in the Middle East.

I have strong reservations concerning the proposed International Conference, which, in my view, is not conductive to peace. Some months ago, I accepted a proposal by Secretary Shultz to launch direct negotiations with the blessing of the U.S.-Soviet Summit in order to grant International legitimacy for the negotiations for those states desiring it. Unfortunately, it was rejected. Nevertheless, I shall be ready to consider a similar proposal.

Israel firmly believes that those who are prepared to live with each other in peace must learn to negotiate directly with each other.

We remain committed to the Camp David Accords, which have provided a workable, agreed framework for peace between Israel and each of its Arab neighbours.

Mr, President: These are difficult times for Israel. We shall overcome them in the best possible way, consonant with our tradition and eagerness to prevent the loss of lives.

Mr. President: On the eve of Israel's 40th anniversary, the people and the Government of

Israel are united in halling the deep friendship and the close cooperation between our two countries. This friendship has reached unprecedented levels under your leadership. We have established a strategic cooperation agreement between Israel and the U.S., a Free Trade Area agreement between our two countries and the designation of Israel as a major non-NATO ally of the U.S.

We are confident that the solid foundation of friendship between Israel and the U.S. will remain unshaken in spite of occasional differences of opinion that may arise.

I am sure that I speak for all the people of Israel and for peace-loving people everywhere when I express our gratitude for your untiring efforts to reduce tensions in the world and bring peace to our war-torn region. We will continue to do our utmost to cooperate in the search for peace. I return to Jerusalem confident that with the friendship and understanding of the U.S. government and its people, we shall succeed."

Echoing President Ronald Reagan's blunt declaration to Prime Minister Yitzhak Shamir on March 16, 1988 (Adar 27, 5748), in their meeting in Washington, Secretary of State, George Shultz said that: "the U.S. Middle East plan could not be changed or amended. The U.S. will not permit any aspect of its proposal to be eroded or compromised," said the Secretary.

In reply, Prime Minister Shamir said: "I have my position and I cannot give it up." Describing the great dangers that the International Conference would create for Israel, emphasizing his willingness to acceept only a brief U.S.-Soviet ceremonial opening for direct negotiations with the Palestinian-Arabs.

Shamir explained that although he had reservations about some of the aspects of the U.S. plan, he was not opposed to them in principle, as they were based on the Camp David Accords.

The U.S. Secretary of State George Shultz promised Shamir a "properly structured International Conference." He also promised Shamir "face-to-face" negotiations, saying that: "the U.S. opposes, and will not participate in International Conference designed to replace bilateral negotiations." Shultz added that the U.S. "will not permit the Conference to become authoritative or potentionary, or to exceed its jurisdiction."

Shultz promised that the International Conference would "sponsor" direct negotiations between Israel and the Palestinian-Arabs, which is the heart of his proposal. He also promised that the Conference plenum would not be able to impose or get agreements reached by the sides.

The U.S. administration suddenly made a U-Turn in its policy and became pro-International Conference. A complete change in its thinking. The "convening of an International Conference, including the five members of the UN Security Council, remains a vital and integral part of the U.S. initiative. Without such a conference there is simply no way that the Arabs will negotiate face-to-face with Israel," said the Americans.

When the Israelis asked the Americans why the U.S. is willingly inviting the Soviet Union and Communist China into the Middle East peace process, the Americans gave all kind of evasive, non-convincing answers.

When the Israelis asked the Americans administration to return to their old decision against International Conference or to make major changes in their peace proposal, Presiden Reagan said: "The U.S. will not slice this initiative apart and will not abandon it.

And those who will say no to the U.S. plan-and the Prime Minister has not used this word-need not answer to us. They need to answer to themselves and thair people as to why they turned down a realistic and sensible plan to achieve negotiations."

Prime Minister Shamir was very clear in his reaction when he said that the International Conference was simply unacceptable as it represents a great danger to Israel.

The U.S. administration understood very clearly that if they exert pressure on Shamir and create an open confrontation with Israel on the issue they would be pushing Israel into a corner and force Shamir to reject the U.S. plan.

Shultz's peace plan did not begin to satisfy the basic PLO demands, because it said No to Israeli sithdrawal to the so-called 1949 lines, to an Arab-Palestinian State in the territories and to the participation of the present, nonreconstructed terrorist PLO in the suggested peace Conference. That was more than enough to damn Mr. Shultz in Palestinian-Arab eyes.

Secretary Shultz had failed to narrow the existing differences between the U.S. and the Soviet Union on the Arab-Israeli conflict issue. His talks with the Soviets were not productive because the Soviets were rigid. The Soviets continued to insist on "authoritative" conference empowered to "recommend" solutions to the negotiating parties, the Israelis and the Arabs. The Soviet Union still advocates that the PLO play a direct role in the peace negotiations.

When the Western European diplomats were briefed on the U.S.-Soviet talks in Moscow by the special U.S. envoy Wat Cluverius they concluded that the Soviet reaction was relatively flexible.

Shultz's plan failed because his miscalculation on the degree of pressure which American Jews were willing to exert on any Israeli government, because his miscalculation of King Hussein's reluctance or inability to enter negotiations and because his miscalculation of the Soviet Union's willingness to accept an American peace plan and drop their support of the PLO.

Writing in the Washington Post, on March 1988, George Will noted, that, "Saigon is now Ho Chi Minh City, and Israel will be forgiven for not trusting American "guarantees" to prevent Tel-Aviv from becoming Arafatville."

On his visit to Washington, on March 1988, Israeli Prime Minister Yitzhak Shamir met with leaders of the Black Community in the U.S. Because of his tight schedule the Meeting with the black caucus was short.

Congressman Ronald Dellums said that the topics covered were: Israel's relations with South Africa, the "uprising" of the Palestinian-Arabs and finally the black Hebrews of Dimona. The American peace proposals were not raised.

Congressman Dellums said that the meeting with Shamir was "cordial" and described the Prime Minister as a very cultured man.

In a letter handed to Shamir during the meeting, the black caucus raised the issue of the "fair and equitable distribution of the U.S. foreign assistance.

In their letter, the Congressmen wrote that they were "very disappointed that Israel has not joined in the concerted international efforts to impose sanctions against the apartheit regime.

"Your policy of signing no new military contracts with South Africa is woefully," the Congressman noted. "Because of the considerable number of existing contracts that you will continue to fulfill.

The Congressmen said that one of their missions had visited the "Occupied Territories" and had been "appalled" by what they saw there. "Recalling the inhumanities of slavery in this country, having suffered the indignities of racial disrimination, black Americans recognize and identify with those who are oppressed throughout the world. We, thus, feel a growing kinship with the Palestinian Arabs," the Congressmen wrote.

"Foreign assistance has always been among the least popular programs funded by the Congress. We believe that the current state of affairs in the "Occupied Territories" as well as the disproportionate share of aid going to Israel are only likely to make a foreign aid program all the more unpopular.

"Unless these issues are seriously addressed by your government as well as our government, we feel that the relations between our two countries-as well as between Black and Jewish Americans-will become increasingly strained."

The meeting with the caucus was intended to try to improve some of the negative attitudes towards Israel, but poor planning resulted in worsening the situation.

In America Prime Minister Yitzhak Shamir had to defend his undoubtfull loyalty to Eretz Israel against U.S. administration determination to get the peace process moving and against an American and Jewish American public loyal to the U.S., which was increasingly disenchanted with Israel's continuing control of the territories.

They would have liked to see Israel comply with the U.S. interest and U.S. policy and withdraw from Judea, Samaria and Gaza. They would have liked to see Israel please their government. They didn't care too much about Israeli interest and Israeli policy.

The differences of opinion between Prime Minister Yitzhak Shamir and Foreign Minister Shimon Peres have also infected the American Jewish community, where they are being debated almost as fiercely as they are being debated in Jerusalem. Just as in Israel, there is no consensus among American Jews and supporters of Israel over issues requiring Israel to exchange land in Judea, Samaria and Gaza for peace with the Arabs.

When Shimon Peres speaks of "Territories for Peace", he means all the trritories or most of the territories.

This is actually a dramatic betrayal of the interests of our people. Americans must use every possible means to convey to Israelis that Israel is in deep jeopardy and that the occupation must end.

Israeli centrists are under the illusion that American economic and political support can be taken for granted. Conservative leaders from the American Jewish world have fostered this fantasy. The ordinary Israeli has no idea how deep American disatisfection has become or how much disatisfaction may threaten Israel's military security in the future. The only way she or he will "get it" is through a combination of public protests and private communications.

Since we can't count on Jewish leaders to convey this sense of urgency, we need to do it ourselves. Many American Jewish leaders have displayed short sightedness and cowardice in dealing with the current difficulties. The "Israel is always right" crowd, the people with moral blinders-none of these people can provide an analysis or a strategy that will speak to the American Jewish public.

A very large number of American Jews are in a state of deep personal crisis. Their identification with Judaism, Israel and the Jewish people is being fundamentally challenged. This is the moment when we need to hear a different kind of voice from the Jewish World."

Shamir achieved some important gains during his U.S. visit. He has been successful in focusing public attention on the danger of the

International Peace Conference. In fact, the chances that such a conference will work are slim. The American Jews were unsure of the wisdom of the idea of an International Conference.

Speaking at a panel discussion on world Jewry and Israel's current political crisis, sponsored by the Israel Diaspora Institute of Tel-Aviv, Simon Veil said:"I don't live here, and I don't take the risks or the responsibility for what happens, but the Diaspora cannot remain indifferent to the situation here, out of its concern for the future of Israel. We must warn Israel against the perils it faces. Even though we are not directly threatened, we are still directly involved.

In certain cases, any anti-Israeli statement, by any Jew is exploited by elements hostile to Israel, who use it as an alibi to attack Israel. Their words are being exploited by elements that wish to harm Israel. Their words are used and abused. These Jews do not think of the consequences of their actions.

On March 1988 (Adar 5748), American Jewish leaders told Israeli Government: "Israel's position in Congress has reached an unprecedented low point. Our best friends are alarmed and worried. " Even the criticism aimed at Israel during the war in Lebanon, the Pollard affair and the Irangate was "not as bad as over the present situation in the territories."

Speculators are convinced that these are nothing but more U.S. administration pressure on Israel, through the American Jewish organizations, to scare Israel and shake its self-confidence as well as put a wedge between the Maarah and the Likud.

On April 1988(Iyar 5748), Israeli writers: Yehudah Amichai, Amos Elon, Amos Oz and A.B. Yehoshuah, called on Israel to relinquish the "Occupied Territories"adding in a letter to the New York Times: " By their very silence, American Jews are massively intervening in Israeli politics and silently but effectively supporting one side in the debate, the tragically wrong side. We implore them to speak up".

"Thy destroyers and they that made these waste shall go forth from there."

Isaiah

Extremely naïve, famous Israeli writers who were ready to give away part of their fatherland in return for a piece of paper.

The Israeli Left is tremendously dangerous to its own people.

A Palestinian-Arab State, if ever created, will be a new political entity, which will contribute little to the stability of the area and the feeling of security of both Israel and Jordan, because of its international orientation will be based on Communism and the Soviets. The United States of America will not be too happy with this new state, either.

Some Israelis believe that, may be, strategically, it is very wise that the Likud is adhering to the Autonomy Plan and the Camp David Accord, yet, one must be naïve or blind not to notice that the Americans have ceased to support it and would love to meet the PLO with open arms, the minute they accept UN Resolution 242 and 338 and renounce terror. Even without changing their Charter.

In spite of the U.S. pledge not to negotiate with the PLO or PLO Representatives until such time as the PLO accepts Israel's right to exist and UN Security Council Resolutions 242 and 338 and stops terror, the United States of America carried unofficial negotiations with the PLO all the time. U.S. Secretary of State, George Shultz met with the Arab-Palestinian businessman Hassib Sabah. Watt Calabrius from the State Department met with Yasser Arafat. Robert Amse from the C.I.A. met with Hassan Salame from the "Black September", a PLO subsidiary. U.S. officials met with PLO members Hanna Siniora and Faiz Abu Rahmah. Andrew Young, U.S. Secretary at the United Nations met PLO representatives and so did U.S. diplomat Morris Draper.

There was a clear American determination to express appriciation to Shimon Peres and to strengthen him. It came in the form of the unusually blunt White House statement praising Peres and obliquely criticizing Yitzhak Shamir.

"While being steadfast in his commitment to Israeli strength and security," the White House statement said, "the Foreign Minister Peres has a vision for the future,recognizes the increasing danger of the Status Quo, and understands the negative consequences of passivity and delay in the search for a settlement. The Foreign Minister,Creative and has the courage and wisdom to say yes when real opportunity arises."

The U.S. statement, at the same time, took indirect swipe at Shamir. It said: "Those leaders who are negative, consistently reject the ideas, and fail to exploit realistic opportunities to bring about negotiations, make progress impossible. In the end they will have to answer to their own people for the suffering that will inevitably result."

The Americans, for years, have supported the right of the Palestinian-Arabs "to participate in the determination of their own future."

The Americans remained very anxious to try to achieve no more cooperative Palestinian posture. They have been trying to woo Arafat," for years.

There is no doubt that the U.S. president public declaration was addressed also to the Israeli public. What he meant really is to tell the Israeli public that Mr. Peres was a responsible leader and that Mr. Shamir was irresponsible. That Peres was a good guy and that Shamir was a bad guy. What the president meant was: "watch out you Israelis in your coming elections and do not forget who you vote for!' It meant bluntly meddling in Israel's internal affairs. It meant. U.S. deep, impolite involvement in Israeli domestic policy, which the Israeli public hate and cannot forgive.

Shultz and other U.S. officials, while prepared to signal a tilt toward Peres in the coming Israeli elections, understandably remain unenthusiastic about getting deeply involved in domestic Israeli policy. Shultz is a little more carefull than his president, Ronald Reagan. Yet, his declarations have also unvailed his intentions and U.S. The Middle East:"Peace for Territories" at the expense of the State of Israel. Israel will be out of her mind to accept such an offer.

Luckily for Israel is the fact that on May 1988, the United States and the Soviet Union were still a long way apart on the Arab-Israeli peace process.

In an interview published on July 7, 1988, in West Germany's Stern magazine, World Jewish Congress President Edgar Bronfman said that Israel should give up the Gaza Strip.

According to Mr Bronfman, the Gaza Strip is of no, or minimal value to Israel from a security point of view and has no biblical connection to the rest of Israel. An unfortunate, iresponsible, detrimental declaration. Mr. Bronfman was totally wrong, for the Gaza Strip is only half an hour drive from Tel-Aviv.

Iraq and Iran had twelve days from the time the Cease-Fire was announced until it went into effect, on August 20, 1988.

At the end of the Yom Kippur War, (October 1973), Israel had only twelve hours before the Cease-Fire with Egypt went into effect and the guns stopped roaring.

Iraq insisted on direct negotiations with Iran before signing the Cease-Fire agreement. Iran accepted this precondition.

Israel was not allowed equal opportunity. Israel was not allowed to continue the war until   the Arabs accepted direct negotiations with her.

The World public opinion and two superpowers insisted that Israel signs the Cease-Fire agreement immediately and without any preconditions.

Now Israel is forced to carry its negotiations in an International Conference, where the superpowers and the other participating parties still are able to look after their interests and not necessarily after peace.

On July 31, 1988, King Hussein from Jordan announced his disengagement from Judea, Samaria and Gaza to let the PLO take full responsibility for the Palestinian-Arab people there. By doing this King Hussein had "undone" the 1948 Jordanian occupation of Judea, Samaria and the Gaza Strip and also cancelled his 1950 decision of unification of the East and West Banks. This is his biggest retreat from territories since 1967. By doing so, as a matter of fact, the King of Jordan awarded the title to Israel, which can thus no longer be termed an "occupying" power. This also puts an end to Shimon Peres's or the Labor Party's dream of the "Jordanian Option" this side (theWest side) of the River. The Jordanian option is no longer an option, if it ever was.

Hussein's move was a bombshell. Was it a political trick, was it a nationalistic gesture or was it an act of despair? Time and History will tell. There is no doubt that Hussein's timing was influenced by the Intifada crisis, which began in the West Bank on December 9, 1987 and continued, enhanced, into April summit in Algiers.

King Hussein declared that he was severing legal and administrative ties with the West Bank in respone to PLO wishes. Some speculators believe that Hussein's move resulted from the King's fear that Israel might talk to the PLO and agree to an International Conference, which could lead to a Palestinian-Arab state. Hussein's policy has always been guided by his fear of a Palestinian-Arab state in the West Bank and his main interest has been the continuation of the present situation, that's the status quo, in which Israel has control of the West Bank.

Analysts believe that the King's step was also to prevent the intifada from spreading across the Jordan. Over sixty per cent of the residents of his kingdom are Palestinian-Arabs. This led him to sacrifice his supporters on the West Bank, along with the territory, in order to save his kingdom, Jordan.

King Hussein's move was also an additional element in his efforts to pressure the PLO and the Arab world and show them that there is no alternative to Jordanian participation in the peace process. He wanted to show the Palestinian-Arabs how much they needed him. Obviously, Israel and the U.S. have no interest in "undermining" Hussein's challenge to the

PLO and the Palestinian Arabs. The religious and political agitation inside Jordan added more fears of instability. King Hussein felt insecure.

The Intifadah in Judea, Samaria and Gaza has reawakened across the River, in Jordan, anti-Hashemite sentiments among the Palestinian-Arabs living in Jordan. Moslem fundamentalists have gained strength and courage. Naturally, it disturbed and worried him very much.

A Kuwaiti newspaper Al Kabas wrote that King Hussein made his move in fear of a Likud victory in the coming November (1988) election that could bring Ariel Sharon back to the Defence Ministry.

Jordan, thus, gave up its claim for Judea, Samaria. Therefore, it had no more claim to the territory known as the "West Bank", which makes it "Free Territories" and no longer "Occupied Territories"

The "Palstinian Problem" was "invented" by King Hussein of Jordan, and later, during the years, it became an artificial "Palestinian Entity", which is demanding now, nothing less than the whole territory of the "West Bank" and Gaza, as a start, for the establishment of a "Palestinian State". The second phase will be the whole of Israel.

King Hussein refused, for years, to permit Palestinian-Arabs, West Bankers, to settle in the West Bank or even in Jordan proper, and kept them in "Refugee Camps " and was forbidden to express them politically or establish political movements.

The West Bankers were his subordinates, whom he adopted, who later, during the years 1948-1967, became also his hostages, with which he could blackmail the rest of the Arab World as well as the WesternWorld.

It was the "Jordanian Umbrella" that prevented the Palestinian-Arabs from the West Bank, the West Bankers, to move to the other Arab countries, where they could have freed themselves from the "Refugee Camps" and start a new free life. It was King Hussein who froze this tragic situation until June 1967, when he was beaten by the Israelis and lost the West Bank.

For King Hussein Judea, Samaria and the Gaza Strip were nothing but a "Wrestling Ring" for his political struggles.

Twice, in 1970, and again in 1980, Israel warned Syria, that it would not tolerate a change in the Status Quo in Jordan. Thus, saving King Hussein from a Syrian take over.

Jordan never had sovereign rights, anyway, over the West Bank because Jordan took control of the West Bank by an aggressive action against Israel, in 1948, and therefore it is not entitled to sovereignty. This being the case and since Israel acted in self-defense, in 1967 and recaptured the West

Bank, Israel has the better, the right claim, the legal claim to sovereignty. If Jordan drops its claim on the land altogether and there is no other state claiming sovereignty, which strengthens Israel's claim.

Jordan hasn't droped its claim to the land, yet, King Hussein hasn't really yet, consummated that threat. At best, the Hashemite monarch has issued a "Declaration of Intent" only.

The Declaration will become legal only if Jordan convenes its paliament to abolish the 1950 law that unifies the East and West Banks, and alters the constitution embodying the unity principle. But so far, the King has not taken the necessary steps that would have divested him of the West Bank, that's to convene the Jordanian parliament and repeal the 1950 unity law. Therefore, the Jordanian links to the West Bank constitutionally and legally remain intact, and, if there will be any negotiations going over the territories, the negotiations will be between Jordan and Israel and not between the Palestinian-Arabs and Israel.

As a matter of fact the situation in Jordan, Samaria and the Gaza Strip or West Bank, had not changed really by his speech, as the West Bank territories before his "historical" declaration and after his "historical" declaration were and are held by Israel.

It is not only the dismissal of tens of thousands of Jordanian employees, or the refusal to renew the Jordanian passports of the inhabitants, or even the rejection of agricultural experts from the West Bank. During the first several few months the Palestinian-Arabs will be left with a vacuum that has to be filled either by Israel or by the PLO. Everybody agrees that the Jordanians disengagement will have significant impact. It will make life harder for Palestinian-Arabs.

The Jordanian measures have charged the PLO with full responsibility for dealing with the Palestinian-Arab problem. There is a sense of great expectation in the pro-PLO camp that the organization will respond effectively to Hussein's initiative and demonstrate its ability to meet the challenge, take responsibility and lead the Palestinian-Arabs in this crisis. Some advocate the establishment of a Palestinian-Arab government in exile, to highlight the Palestinian-Arabs' separate status and facilitate PLO assistance to the West Bank.

There is serious skepticism over the PLO's capacity to replace Jordan and provide the services maintained in Amman. The PLO was surprised by Hussein's move. They were not ready for such a move. They were caught with their pants down. Besides, Israel is also determined to prevent the PLO from gaining any foothold in the West Bank, which belongs to Israel.

There is, therefore, the very great possibility, that soon, Israel will expand its legislation in the West Bank, a most normal and natural reaction.

Judea, Samaria and the Gaza Strip were never recognized by the International community as part of Jordan. It was conquered and annexed by King Abdallah of Jordan between 1948 and 1950. King Hussein's declaration unsettled both Labor with its "Jordanian Option" plan and the Likud with its conflicting advocacy of "Autonomy" by some and of "Annexation" by others.

With the end of the "Jordanian Option" the Maarah, the Labor didn't have a clear and persuasive answer to the problem of the West Bank and the Palestinian-Arabs.

Many believe that the right wing demand to annex the territories would flagrantly violate Israel's international obligations, as embodied in the Camp David Accord. Israel is precluded under the Camp David Accord from doing anything that would alter the present status of the territories. Thus, if Israel were to annex the West Bank, it would be a breach of contract. That also applies to annexing any part of the West Bank, which, according to Allon's Plan, would be part of Israel.

Israel doesn't have to annex something that is her's from ancient history. Israel had received Judea, Samaria and the Gaza Strip from her forefathers Abraham, Isaac and Jacob and there isn't anything more legal than that or stronger than that. Not even the Camp David Accords. All Israel has to do is take care of the Palestinian-Arab population in these territories and transfer them across the International borders, back to the countries where they or their parents came from. Thus, Israel wouldn't do anything to alter the status of the territories, which are anyway in her hands, since June 1967.

King Hussein already established a precedent. Previously, in 1974, he made a very similar move.

"A new reality exists and Jordan must adjust to it. The West Bank is no longer Jordan and we have no place in the negotiations over its future."

This royal declaration was made in an interview with the New York Times, in November 1974, right after the Rabat summit.

Like Yasser Arafat, head of the PLO, Hussein is a world champion of survival. Therefore, neither the Rabat summit nor his own declaration prevented him from doing his utmost to preserve his share in the process of determining the future of the West Bank. He wanted his share in the spoils.

Yet, there are significant differences between the 1974 and the 1988 cut-offs. In 1974 his move did not result in further concrete steps. The king continued to pay salaries and pensions to civil servants, continued to issue Jordanian passports to the local inhabitants, considered to be Jordanians. Transferred money to the West Bank for public investments. Ministry for Occupied Territories continued to function. All these were discontinued in 1988.

Hussein expressed hope that his move will force both Israel and the PLO to reassess their attitudes towards the peace process.

Hussein's move was, may be, a golden opportunity to start moving things. Yasser Arafat is now trying to fill up the vacuum. But Israel will never let him do it.

Ariel (Arik) Sharon, Minister of Industry and Commerce came up immediately with his plan-to apply Israel law to large chunks of the West Bank and Gaza, or, in other words, to annex areas circumscribed by an expanded Allon plan. Sharon calls for a unilateral application of Israeli law to areas that, according to the consensus he sees, between the two main parties, the Likud and the Maarah, should not be surrendered even as part of a final peace. This means, the areas designated by the Allon plan with expanded perimeters, and also areas with Jewish localities, like the settlements.

This plan, Sharon believes, is something on which it is possible to forge virtual national consensus, to secure agreement between Likud and Maarah. Its purpose, Sharon adds, is to satisfy Israel's security needs in any way that "eradicates some of the dangers that have been lurking in the absence of any settlement, and in the event of an interim arrangement of another kind."

It is not only Labor's (Maarah's) proclaimed policy to part with some areas as a part of territorial compromise that is on the stake, but also the possible implementation of autonomy, as per the Camp David Accord, that holds perils, that kind of dangers that can be averted by his plan.

The late Yigal Allon, ex-Foreign Minister of Israel (Labor), showed concern about autonomy and had been insistent that if Labor went along with an autonomy plan, that it should not apply it to areas earmarked in his plan for retention by Israel. So far, Sharon was given short shrift, not only by political antagonists but also by his own Likud party, including Yitzhak Shamir. His Colleagues from the Likud Party accused him for adopting the Labor plan.

With his declaration King Hussein may have succeeded where many in the Labor Party, and some of Peres's closest advisers, have failed. He has caused Peres to break out of his mold, get rid of his obsessions, to start seeking new ways, which might replace what is often described as his worn-out, and electorally incomprehensible, "Jordanian Option","London Agreement" and "International Conference".

Labor has yet to complete its wrenching attempt to recoup from Hussein's blow. A much-needed reassessment of the party's campaign message has become urgent. Labor must have some kind of a plan for the West Bank in their platform, as the November 1988 general elections are on the threshold. Mr. Peres, or his successor, will have to come up with a new "Option".

King Hussein's decision to cut loose the West Bank seems to have buried for the foreseeable future recent initiatives aimed at reaching an agreement between Israel and a Jordanian-Palestinian delegation.

As a result of Hussein's dramatic announcement the feelings of the Palestinian-Arabs in Judea, Samaria and the Gaza Strip were mixed. Most of the Palestinian-Arabs felt abandoned, isolated and embattled. They feel the heavy burden of having to confront the challenges of the Palestinian-Arab problem alone, while the Arab nations withdrew and watch from the sidelines. They feel betrayed. Many Palestinian-Arabs felt cast adrift, threatened with the withdrawal of an infrastructure of educational, health and religious services, salaries and passports, which had become essential elements of life for an otherwise stateless population.

PLO supporters concluded that King Hussein's speech reflected a courageous reassessment of policy and recognition of the PLO's primary role in the West Bank.

By recognizing the PLO's status in the West Bank, Hussein defused a source of tension with Palestinian-Arabs that threatened to spill over into Jordan proper and erupt in its refugee camp.

Other Palestinian-Arabs expressed their feelings by saying that they were sick of being under Hussein's thumb, an Arafat leader who had mistreated the Palestinian-Arabs more than any other Arab leader (the Black September, 1970), and wished him good riddance.

Many Palestinian-Arabs, inspite of the bitterness and however betrayed, hurt and disappointed they were, they admitted that there had indeed been a real and beneficial connection with Jordan and they were angry to see it severed.

The King's influence on the Palestinian-Arab population of the West Bank and Gaza had been close to nil at the time of his declaration of separation. The Palestinian-Arabs preferred Yassir Arafat. Therefore, the King's declaration is only a final seal to an already existing situation.

A former U.S. ambassador to Jordan, Nicholas Veliotes said that King Hussein had moved "very reluctantly", but was forced into action by what the King saw as a "consistent campaign by the PLO to undermine him and to cheapen him" in the Arab World. Veliotes added that Hussein's actions were "not tactical but strategic, very carefully considered and deliberate."

U.S. officials believe that Jordan's decision was designed to further challenge the Palestinian-Arabs to come up with a concrete peace initiative.

In any case, the United States of America hasn't taken Hussein's speech seriously or rather necessarily representing his final word. The Americans believe that Hussein will be prepared to re-enter the peace process if some sort of negotiation should actually start and they point to references in his speech to his continuing commitment to the peace process and the Palestinian-Arabs cause.

King Hussein's move is considered by American experts and other analysts as simply another sophisticated step in his effort to survive. Speculators believe that Hussein's move is nothing but a tactical ploy designed to force the Palestinian-Arabs to come running back to him and plead him to return.

Inspite of the fact that Hussein is psychologically attached to the West Bank and carries a feeling of guilt for having lost it to the Israelis in 1967, yet, his advisers, it is believed, have succeeded to convince him that the effort to regain the West Bank was simply not worth the price-in terms of Jordan's own internal security and stability. His decision is final. He means it this time, for real.

King Hussein wanted to be out of the game because he was terrorized, intimidated and threatened by the PLO and he still hasn't forgotten Black September.

Hussein's fear from riots of PLO supporters, which never belonged to him, at least since June 1967.

The King's decision to wash his hands of the West Bank derives, in part, from his desire to eliminate potential problems for his country and his dynasty. This is why the King believes that the West Bank is an issue he could do without.

For the Jordanians, the other non-Palestinian Arabs, East Bankers, there is no great attachment to the West Bank or to Palestinian-Arabs in general. These Jordanians can already feel the serious demographic problem caused by the fact that two thirds of the Jordanian population in the East Bank are Palestinian-Arabs in origin. Regaininig the West Bank with its eight hundred thousands Palestinian-Arabs would merely increase the demographic dangers to Jordan and increase the headaches.

The PLO has been trying lately a new strategy. They claim that they are ready to accept all the UN Resolutions. They will be ready to accept Resolutions 242 and 338 together with Resolution 181 of November 29, 1947 (the Partition), which they rejected in 1947.

By this Yasser Arafat means turning the wheels of history back to 1947, that's the Partition borders and the return of all the Palestinian-Arabs refugees, from all the Arab and other countries, back to Jerusalem, Jaffa, Haifa, Acres, Ramleh, etc. Something that Israel can never accept.

Faisal Husseini, a Palestinian-Arab intifada leader, told a Peace Now (Shalom Achshav) meeting, on July 1988, that the uprising was more than just rocks and Molotov-Cocktails. "The Intifada", he said, "has a constructive, positive meaning. It is the construction of a Palestinian-Arab society, trying to build, under "occupation", the infra structure for a Palestinian-Arab State.

Ahdi Abdul-Hadi, head of the Palestinian Association for the Study of International Affairs, declared:"The uprising is not against Israel, but against the occupation."

Sari Nusseibeh claimed that:"It is important to emphacize that the uprising is not aimed at the destruction of Israel, but at securing freedom for the Palestinian-Arabs."

Other Palestinian-Arab intellectuals claimed that: "The intifadah is not aimed at destroying Israel, but at securing withdrawal of its army and establishing a Palestinian-Arab state, that would live in peace with its neighbors."

The message of coexistence between the two states was clearly reflected in support given by Palestinian-Arab nationalists in the West Bank to the document drafted by PLO official Bassam Abu Sharif, calling for bilateral Palestinian-Israeli talks and establishment of a Palestinian state beside Israel.

From long Israeli experience in reading between the lines, these are messages aimed at the Israeli public, divide its public opinion and also intended to win Israeli and international sympathy and defuse international suspicion of the real Palestinian-Arab aims.

It seems that King Hussein's move to disengage himself from the West Bank, and the Faisal Husseini's document-the Palestinian-Arab "declaration of independence"published a few days later, took Israel's leadership by surprise.

Husseni's declaration was also a surprise to the PLO. The Palestinian-Arabs leadership was utterly confused. Should they form a government-in-exile? Where? Will West Bankers support the PLO?

"The Palestinian-Arabs should now use the King's speech to push one step further. The time has come for us to declare our own independent state in the West Bank and to set up a transitional government made up of Palestinian-Arabs in the West Bank and Palestinian-Arabs outside."

"The PLO can turn its offices around the world into embassies, and we can turn the underground committees here into ministries for health, education, and municipal services. Having declared a state in the West Bank, we should then offer to negotiate with our neighbors-Israel and Jordan-the exact nature of relations. Jordan would have no choice but to recognize such a state."

These comments were made by Bir Zeit University philosopher, Sari Nusseibeh, to the New York Times and were published in the Times Weekly review on Sunday.

Nusseibeh's comments resemble the paper drafted by PLO official Bassam Abu Sharif, found in Faisal Husseini's office, in East Jerusalem.

This paper, or rather, this document contains the idea of declaring an independent state. It renders the uprising pragmatic and politically effective. It also gives the uprising a political initiative, a political momentum with a final goal, the establishment of another Arab state in the area, a Palestinian-Arab State at the expense of Israel with or without an International Conference. Israel must be out of its mind to allow this to happen.

The draft declaration defines itself:"This plan aims at moving the intifada from the phase of stone-throwing confrontation at the battlefront to the realm of diplomatic initiative by the Palestinian-Arab side, which will give the uprising renewed momentum toward an International Conference".

The draft explains that:"Once declared, the new Palestinian-Arab state will be accorded international respect and admiration. Internally, Israel will be divided, because voices demanding recognition of the 'newborn' will increase, especially since this newborn has come into being as the result of heroic labor pains, witnesses by everyone. The nature of the new state will confirm that it is not aggressive and that the Palestinian-Arabs do not desire the annihilation of the State of Israel. Rather, they wish to live peacefully as its neighbor."

According to professor Sari Nusseibeh from the University of Bir Zeit: "The overall idea is to put Israel in a position where it can no longer fight us back, whether on the level of street fights or on a diplomatic level."

The declaration's purpose is to win international support, create diplomatic pressure on Israel and score points in Israeli public opinion.

The Palestinian-Arabs feel that by applying constant, internal and external pressure, on a weak Israeli leadership, the Israelis will either get tired or lose control of the situation and yield to their demands.

The idea of achieving these aims through an independence declaration was apparently encouraged by an article circulated among Palestinian-Arabs and Israelis by Dr. Jerome Segal, an American Jew.

Professor Jerome Segal, a founder of the Jewish Committee for Israeli-Palestinian Arab Peace and a research scholar at the Center for Philosophy and Public Policy at the University of Maryland wrote in his article "From Uprising to Independent State," which appears to have inspired the Palestinian-Arab draft of Independence declaration seized at Faisal Husseini's research center in Jerusalem, that there is no need to wait for negotiated agreements and prior Israeli approval to establish a state. It can be declared unilaterally, same as Israel was, and then secured through diplomatic efforts.

"Once the State of Palestine is proclaimed, Palestine will be a country under foreign occupation" writes Segal, a new International situation will be created:"whereas previously Israel was occupying a territory, it is now occupying a foreign country which has declared that it is at peace." This, says Segal, will produce more pressure on Israel to withdraw. Traditional stumbling blocks such as UN Resolution 242, the PLO covenant and an international conference will have become irrelevant.

Echoes of these arguments were found in the draft declaration seized.

The draft says that Israel will be unable to fight the fledgling state, because it would win international sympathy as "the state struggling to save itself from occupation." A declaration of independence will change demands that the PLO recognize Israel to demands that the Palestinian state be recognized, says the draft.

The draft adds also that a unilateral independence declaration "will render useless all the preconditions for convening an International Conference, and who should or should not represent the Palestinian people. It will also end once and for all the American conditions for negotiating with the PLO, such as recognition of UN resolution 242 and 338."

The draft adds also that:"The occupied territories will become the occupied State of Palestine, and it will be up to the occupiers, the Israelis, to recognize or not to recognize the right of the Palestine State to exist."

The declaration, like the uprising, is a production of Palestinian-Arabs in the territories, which the PLO, outside the territories, if it chooses, can endorse and adopt as policy or reject it. The declaration of independence was planned to be made in Jerusalem even if it were not approved by the PLO.

This draft proves that there is some kind of local leadership in the territories in addition to the PLO.

Yassir Arafat would have liked to declare a Palestinian-Arab State, but Syria and Russia will not approve it. They are afraid that Arafat might sign a peace treaty with Israel and quieten the area. They want the terror, turmoil, war, in the Middle East to perpetuate forever, so they can thrive on it.

There is no doubt whatsoever that both the Likud and the Maarah want peace. Though, there is a big difference between the platforms of these two big parties. Yet, the end results are the same. The Palestinian-Arabs will not accept both platforms. The Likud is advocating autonomy for the people (not the Land) of the West Bank and Gaza, as agreed at Camp David, which the Arabs reject. On the other hand, the Maarah (Labor) is ready to give away part of the West Bank and Gaza, without Jerusalem, which the Arabs would not accept either.

The Palestinian-Arabs's representatives, Arafat and the PLO are not ready yet to recognize the State of Israel, to accept UN Resolutions 242 and 338, to stop the terror and revise their Charter.

Since King Hussein of Jordan has removed himself as a partner to any negotiation over the territories of the t Bank, since the King is out o the game, only the Palestinian-Arabs are left as potential partners to negotiations, if negotiations took place. However, the Palestinian-Arabs refuse to negotiate and refer Israel to the PLO as their "legitimate representatives", an address which both the Likud and the Maarah reject.

If, on the other hand, both the Likud and Labor reject unilateral action, in favor of negotiation, it seems that they have no choice but to confront the need to negotiate with the only partner left and the only partner that can deliver, or face an International Conference, which might be worse.

With all-Arab sanction the PLO are the "legitimate representatives of the Palestinian-Arabs People." This includes the Palestinian-Arabs living in Jordan, the East Bank Palestiians, who form a majority in the Hashemite Kingdome of Jordan. That's Eastern Palestinian-Arabs have a Palestinian-Arab majority. By withdrawing from the West Bank Hussein has in fact separated between West Palestinian-Arabs and East Palestinian-Arabs, who have strong family ties, an artificial separation, which cannot sustain. Hussein's retreat to a Jordanian "peoplehood" or a Jordanian "nation" is an illusion and is only temporary, until such time as the question arises about the legitimacy of the Hashemite claim to a separate Jordanan national identity.

If the Palestinian-Arabs self-determination and sovereignty are the issues, they cannot be satisfied by, nor limited to negotiation about, title of the West Bank and Gaza when Eastern Palestine has a Palestinian-Arab majority. This means, most probably, the beginning of endless troubles to King Hussein, from his Palestinian-Arabs, which might end up in a PLO take over.

Now that King Hussein is neutralized, Arafat will try probably to neutralize Egypt too by first introducing some strains into the Egyptian-Israeli fragile relationship and, may be, thus, nullifying the Israeli-Egyptian peace treaty. Arafat is operating very cleverly, he is an excellent strategist and one should not underestimate him. His tools are: ruse, cunning, lies, etc., which he uses shamelessly. Niccolo Machiavelli could have taken lessons from him.

It seems that King Hussein of Jordan is getting weaker and weaker when his Palestinian population is getting greater and greater. He then feels insecure and calls for help from the surrounding Arab states, mainly Saudi Arabia and Iraq. Hs arguments when shouting "wolf, wolf," are that he fears from a sudden Israeli attack and that he has the longest front line with Israel. That is Jordan's reasoning for soliciting funds, and in order to strengthen his argument, it is necessary for Jordan to show some aggressiveness towards Israel.

The following are excerpts from Vice-President George Bush's address, Wednesday, September 7, 1988 (Elul 25,5748), two months before the General elections in the U.S.A., before the International Convention of B'nai B'rith, in Baltimore, Maryland:

"This year Israel is celebrating her 60th birthday, middle age to most people but just the beginning in the life of one of the world's most creative nations. Over these years, the Israelis have shown the world how to build a new society, how to give old values a new life and the best thing I could say was that I wrote Prime-Minister Yitzhak Shamir on Israel's Independence Day: 'I want you to know that I, the president, and the American people stand with you and your country. We shall never falter or waver in our support. Israel has won a special place in America's heart and Israel has given America new perspective on history. It's perspective that only a people who know to beat the odds of history can provide.

We have got to take that long view as a nation. That's why we have pursued a policy of peace through strength of keeping our guard up but also our readiness to parley and that's how we were able to negotiate an arms-control treaty with the Soviet Union to eliminate a whole class of nuclear weapons.

In doing so, we were symbolizing the hopes of mankind, but we didn't do this as a unilateral concession, or at the expense of our security. We must never do that, and, as president, I never will do that.

Truly, the lesson for our time is that deployments work better than freezes if you want to get the Soviet Union to the table, if you want to get equitable arms reduction. That strength works better than weakness if you want to get both peace and security.

The members of B'nai B'rith know this lesson, too. Not so long ago, the Jewish people paid a horrible price for the weakness of the Western democracies. I say, never again. Never Again.

The members of B'nai B'rith-the Children of the Covenant-also know something else. Your Covenant begins with the Jewish people but doesn't stop there. You know that a good community consists of families caring for each other, not only for themselves. You know that a good nation consists of those communities extending the reach of their goodness.

I like that idea and I believe in it. I believe in an America strong and prosperous, and an America that lives by standards. An America of honourable public service. An America that takes its idealism and makes it concrete by acts of goodness. A kinder, gentler nation, a tolerant America, enriched by the contributions of many peoples and many cultures.

We may disagree in this country about many things, but we have a lot in common. Reverence for education, reverence for human life, reverence for law, reverence for the principle of separation of church and state and reverence for the duty of human kindness, to help those less fortunate.

There's another thing we share. We are concerned about the wider world, about the fate of humanity. You know as Jews, and we all know as Americans, that we must take our place in the ranks, alongside those struggling for freedom. Soviet Jews, seeking to emigrate. Ethiopian Jews seeking to find their real home. The State of Israel searching for peace. Our own freedom is diminished when theirs is diminished.

My friends, these are the hard truths of history. We should not have to relearn them.

I mentioned earlier that idealism must be translated into concrete acts. Let me take just a few minutes to discuss some very concrete acts that our administration has taken with respect to Israel and the search for peace.

Back in 1980, we had an idea and it was called "Israel-Strategic Ally." It was a simple idea and a big one. We believed that Israel was not just the object of our sympathy and out goodwill but a full-fledged partner with the United States. A partner fully capable of contributing to our security.

Well, that caused a revolution in Washington. Lots of people were aghast. We were told that our interests in the region would be jeopardized. That even the use of the expression could set off drastic diplomatic repercussions. Well they were wrong and we were right.

Even as strategic cooperation with Israel has gone forward, we have forged a stronger relationship with Egypt, Saudi Arabia, Kuwait and other Gulf states. Today, it is clear that we can have an alliance with Israel and still pursue better relations with other countries in the area. We can work constructively -with those states and not diminish our relations with Israel. This is in our interest and it is also Israel's interest.

Despite this, some people still have trouble saying the words, "Israel-Strategic Ally." Well, I don't. Israel, strategic ally. It's got a nice ring to it. The ring of hard, enduring reality.

What are the results of our efforts?

Today, the United States and Israel are engaged in joint planning on mutual threats in the Mediterranean. Eight years ago, joint planning was not even in the dictionary of U.S.-Israeli relations. Today, the United States and Israel have prepositioned supplies and are building an infrastructure to deal with emergencies. Eight years ago, a former president regarded Israel as a strategic liability-can you figure that? Not an asset to the U.S. action in the Middle East.

Today, the United States and Israel engage in joint military exercises. Eight years ago, the ships of the Sixth Fleet were often forbidden even to buy fruits and vegetables from Israel.

Today, Israel, through its own hard efforts and U.S. aid, has dropped inflation from nearly 1,000 per cent to under 20 per cent. Its economy has begun to grow again. Eight years ago, U.S. aid to Israel was thought of as a weapon, a way, to force Israel to do what it didn't want to do.

Today, we have a model free trade agreement with Israel, of benefit to both countries. Eight years ago, this idea hadn't even been discussed, much less put on the agenda for action.

Today, the United States and Israel are partners in developing new technology, whether it was drones to gather intelligence at less risk to our pilots or the new, urgent project of defence against tactical missiles, part of the Strategic Defence Initiative. Eight years ago, we could only admire Israel's technology achievements from afar, not be partners in their development.

When someone tells you that missile defence is fantasy, just think of Israel. Israelis know something about military technology and they know something about real threats. In a region where missiles are dangerously proliferating into the hands of radical regimes, where we have seen the horrors of chemical warfare, missile defence is not fantasy. It is a necessity. It is a must.

Israel undersands it is facing a threat like none it has faced before. That's why it was the first country to sign up joint Research and Development on SDI. And that's why I am proud that we are working with Israel today on the Arrow Project, an anti-tactical ballistic missile to counter this new danger.

A word on chemical weapons: You know, I have seen a few things in my time. But, I thought we had banished forever the sight of human beings tortured by chemical warfare. The sight of a mother trying desperately to shield her child against the drifting winds of death.

That's why an international effort to make sure chemical weapons are never, never used again will be at the top of my agenda as president.

Let me some it up. Eight years ago, strategic partnership with Israel was a dream of many of those who came into the Reagan-Bush administration. Today, we have translated it into reality. And this is my pledge: The American-Israeli Strategic Partnership is going to be even stronger tomorrow.

We need that partnership not least to deter a Soviet Union still building its military strength in the area. Talks to sailors and the pilots of our Sixth Fleet as they contemplate the expansion of Soviet sea power, recently reinforced by the Soviet development of a base at Tartus, in Syria. They know Israel as a friendly place and they are reassured knowing that Israel and the United States are on the same side.

The U.S.-Israel partnership is fundamental for another reason. As Foreign Minister Shimon Peres said: "Israel has never asked the United States for its soldiers, only for its diplomats and peacemakers. Our partnership holds the key to peace in the Middle East.

We all know the peace process is at a difficult stage. No one can fortell where the tragic events of recent months will lead. Yet, I believe that we can make progress toward peace if we follow these principles:

First, U.S.-Israeli cooperation is fundamental to our strategic interests. No threat, no stone thrown, is strong enough to divide us. No wedge will be driven between us.

Second, peace will be achieved through direct negotiations by the parties. It cannot be imposed. It cannot be evaded. The United States stands ready to help such a negotiation, as we have done on a bipartisan basis since the early Seventies. But, we shall not be party to a proceeding by the UN or any other international group to deny Israel's legitimacy or to force her to accept a bad deal.

Third, the purpose of negotiation is real peace. Peace for Israel. Peace for her Neigbours. That's what it is all about. We have stood together for too long through too many crises with too many lives sacrificed to settle for an armistice, or a temporary truce, or a false peace. Egypt has shown the way. It's time for others to follow.

Fourth, as George Shultz has said, the Palestinian-Arabs must be involved at every step in the negotiations. There will be no peace without them. It's their choice to help end the misery into which this region has been plunged.

As for the PLO, I will insist that it accept UN Resolution 242 recognizing Isreal's existence, abandon terrorism and change its covenant calling for Israel's destruction, before we have any discussion with that organization. I will insist not only because we have made a promise to Israel, but also because it is the right thing to do.

If the PLO cannot meet these principled conditions, then it is obviously not capable of either negotiating or delivering peace.

The stakes are just too high to be satisfied by ambiguous formulations. We need plain talk. No nonsense. No equivocations. I have made very clear that I am opposed to an independent Palestinian state for a simple reason. Such a state would be a threat to the security of Israel and of Jordan, which is crucial to any lasting settlement of the conflict. And, I would add, it would also be contrary to American interests.

Anyone who has trouble making up his mind on this issue, or who proposed to leave it open, just doesn't understand the dangers to Israel and to the United States, just doesn't understand the very real threats that continue to exist. My administration would not support the creating of any Palestinian entity that would jeoperdize Israel's security.

The creation of a Palestinian state will not lead to peace, but we must be clear on another matter too, neither will annexation of territories by Israel or their permanent control by military occupation. There has got to be another way, a better way, and that's what the peace process is all about.

I understand something about security and in a Bush administration we're not going to relax our vigilance on threats to the United States or to Israel, and I understand something about diplomacy too. That's why I pledge to you here and now that we're going to find a way to peace, we're going to keep at it. It's going to be a priority for me as president."

On October 13, 1988, Vladimir Poliakov, the Soviet Foreign Ministry official in charge of the Middle East desk, declared, that the Soviet Government believes that it was time for the PLO to recognize Israel.

"We are encouraging the Palestinian-Arabs to be as realistic and flexible as possible in their political programme," Poliakov said, in his interview with the French newspaper correspondent of "Le Quotidien."

According to the Baltimore Sun Time from November 1988 (Kislev 5749), an inter-agency group, including experts from the U.S. State Department, the U.S. Pentagon, the CIA and NASA, in discussing a coordinated approach to dissuade the Israelis from deploying its missiles.

The Livermore Laboratories, which design nuclear weapons for the U.S., calculated that the Israeli Shavit booster that carried the Ofek I satellite into orbit could transport a nuclear warhead a minimum of 3,300 miles, far enough to reach Leningrad.

Separate calculations at the Pentagon produced an estimated range for the rocket of 4,500 miles. The rocket would qualify as an ICBM, according to the definition adopted by the U.S. and Soviets in their nuclear arm control negotiations.

"We see no fundamental difference between space launch vehicles and ballistic missiles," said a U.S. expert. "They are practically interchangeable."

The American officials reacted to Arafat's announcement as "not perfect, but good enough."

President Ronald Reagan declared that: "the U.S. would certainly break off communications with the PLO if it commits terrorist actions in the future."

On December 16, 1988, the U.S. Ambassador to Israel, Thomas Pickering handed the Israeli Government a memorandum on the U.S.-PLO dialogue, it used the language that implies that "No American Administration can sustain the dialogue if terrorism continues by the PLO or any of its factions."

"Israel has to digest that fact of life," one well-placed U.S. official commented. "We know it's not easy for Israel to swallow and we know it won't come overnight."

This well-placed U.S. official wanted to teach an old people like Israel the "facts of life!"

It was very clear to Israel that the U.S. has adhered-at times reluctantly-to its 1975 commitment to Israel not to recognize the PLO.

The U.S. officials suspected that it would take some time for Israel to come to terms with the opening of an American dialogue with the PLO.

The United States leaders believed that they were cast in a more pragmatic mould and were doing a good service to Israel by entering a dialogue with the PLO, even if it was against the will of Israel. The Israelis believed that their American friends were doing a great mistake, may be irreparable.

The reasons against talking with the PLO are not subject to an executive decision. They are embodied in American law. Section 1302 (b) of the International Security and Development Cooperation Act of 1985 (Public Law 99-83) which reads: "No officer or employee of the United States government and no agent or other individual acting on behalf of the United States government shall negotiate with the Palestine Liberation Organization or any representatives thereof (except in emergency or humanitarian situations) unless and until the Palestine Liberation Organization recognizes Israel's right to exist, accepts United Nations Security Council Resolutions 242 and 338 and renounces the use of terrorism."

The law does not refer to declarations of an individual, but to the PLO as an organization. Arafat's December 14, 1988 press statement in Geneva does not reflect official PLO positions. In fact Arafat has often protested that only the Palestine National Council can change official positions, and the PLO never satisfied the conditions that would allow legal American contacts with the organization. On the contrary, as an organization, the PLO has never recognized Israel's right to exist. If it has not changed its charter, which calls for Israel's destruction, nor has it disavowed the ten resolutions of the "policy phases" adopted by the PNC in Cairo, in June 1974. Resolution states: "After the establishment of a national indipendent fighting authority or any part of the Palestinian territory that will be liberated, the Palestinian national authority will struggle to unite the confrontation countries to pave the way for the completion of the liberation of all the Palestinian territory."

All letterheads, maps and emblems of the PLO, including those on official documents submitted to the UN, show the State of Palestine as covering the whole area from the Jordan to the Mediterranean Sea. Israel, whose right to exist Arafat is presumed to recognize, does not exist on these maps.

There is no doubt whatsoever that simply by talking to the PLO would automatically imply the creation of a Palestinian State in Judea, Samaria and Gaza. There is nothing else that the PLO wants to discuss.

The Americans believed that by starting talks with the PLO they would eventually be able to control it, even tame it. The fact that the PLO didn't give a damn about its promise to stop terror had only one explanation, and that is, that the opposite happened. The PLO succeeded to tame the greatest superpower on earth. By keeping the negotiation with the PLO going, inspite of the fact that they continued their terror openly, the United States of America legitimized the PLO and terror. The Americans were naïve to believe that Yasser Arafat will abandon the idea of an International Conference were he could receive Soviet support.

It was a great mistake of the United States of America to break a long tradition of close and friendly cooperation by not even bothering to consult with Israel before making this acute decision, which was not in the best interest of Israel. This decision to start a dialogue with the Palestinians, or rather, more accurately, with the PLO was a terrible political error, stemming, probably, from failure to understand the PLO's penchant for double-talk. By meeting with Professor Edward Said of Colombia University and Ibrahim Abu Lughod of Nortwestern University, George

Shultz was effectively already accepting the PLO. The big superpower was yealding to terrorists. Shultz knew well that there was no real difference between the PLO and the PNC. Israel saw the "Writing on the Wall".

Ibrahim Abu Lughod, born in Jaffa, Israel, is the chairman of the Political Science Department at Norwestern University in Evaston, Ilinois, a northern suburb of Chicago.

Professor Lughod is also member of the Palestine National Council (PNC) speaks of four "sacred" principles on which the Palestinian Arabs cannot make any compromise and these four principles are: the right to sustain national identity, the right to an independent state within Palestine (in Israel, not in Jordan), the right to be represented by the PLO and the Right of Return.

Israel was not surprised by the dramatic U.S. decision to establish a "sustantive" dialogue with the PLO. For years, President Reagan, President-elect Bush, Secretary of States Shultz and other Americans have made clear their readiness to talk to the PLO, once America's long-standing conditions were met. In fact America was "dying" to talk with the PLO.

We have all read about the "peace" talks between Adolf Hitler and Neville Chamberlain that brought tragedy to Europe (World War II). "Peace" talks with Arafat will legitimize terror and lead to similar results, tragedy. Therefore, anybody sane should avoid it. All these men deserve is the gallows, the hanging roap.

9. PLO PROMISE TO STOP TERROR BUT THEY NEVER KEPT THEIR PROMISE

According to information received in Israel, from very responsible sources, the PLO was already on the virge of collapse, if not for the U.S., who, by very unwise, damaging declarations and certain wrong steps, which climaxed with the U.S. joininig a unilateral UN Security Council resolution denouncing Israel, encouraged the PLO to hold on and gave them more oxygen to stay alive.

The European Community (EC) also encouraged the intifada and the PLO by denouncing "the cruel oppression of a defenseless population" in the West Bank, thus turning them underdogs.

The intifada, with Western standards of what is right and what is wrong, had reversed the David and Goliath roles. The Palestinian-Arabs became the David and Israel became the Goliath. The invaders, the terrorists became the underdogs. The real owners of the Land became the "occupiers". Everything twisted and distorted.

In general, the Americans across the board believed in talking and have always been bothered by this prohibition on talking with the PLO, with Libya's Muammar Gaddafi or with Iran's Ayatollah Khomeini. "Talking is better than shooting", they said. There is no doubt that Washington's dialogue with the PLO harms any and all chances for peace and encourages violence. There is no doubt whatsoever that by talking to the PLO the U.S. is encouraging the Palestinian uprising.

Unlike the United States of America, Israel could not give backhanded recognition to a terrorist organization dedicated, for the last twenty-five years, to the destruction of the Jewish State. There is no doubt that the meeting in Stockholm between the American Jews and Yasser Arafat helped pave the way to a U.S.-PLO dialogue.

Because of the American Jewish criticism of Israel, in the open, the American government felt more freedom of action. Secretary of States George Shultz was encouraged in part to undertake his peace mission, as he had the feeling that he was not facing a monolitic American Jewish community.

The U.S.-Egyptian-Swedish plot against Israel, for convincing Arafat to accept UN Resolution 242 and renounce terror was in full cooperation and consultation with former Austrian Chancellor Bruno Kreisky. It has been the rumours that Bruno Kreisky's "fingerprints" were all over the Swedish initiative.

The following letter was published in The Jerusalem Post on January 6, 1989:

To the Editor of the Jerusalem Post,

MORAL CHARLATANISM,

Sir-Jane Fonda is still hated in the U.S.A. for her trips to negotiate in Hanoi during the Vietnam War with this country's enemies. She was an American, speaking for her own nation.

I can only imagine how Israelis must gard the five Jewish Americans who undertook to negotiate with Arafat ("call me Yasser") in Stockholm. Not party to the Israeli political discourse, not responsible for what may come of it all, they cannot enjoy very much regard for what they undertook to do. That was before the fact. Now that we see the entire charade, we only regard their action as moral charlatanism.

Nor can I locate even the remotest parallel to such action: Negotiating the affairs of a third party with that country's sworn enemy! Who has heard of such a thing? And where has it happened, beside with us Jews? I wonder how much longer the Israeli people are going to stand for the arrogance cum innocence that characterizes their Jewish American cohort: who will free you from the burden of this unwanted love?

Professor Jacob Neusner

Prividence, R.I.

On January 29, 1988, Professor Yehoshafat Harkavi, former Head of Military Intelligence, professor of International Relations at the Hebrew University in Jerusalem, wrote in The Jerusalem Post the article: "Pragmatation and the Arab Grand Design." An extremely pessimistic article, which could cause defeatism and despair in the Israeli public.

What bothered Professor Harkavi were the Demography, the Strategic Balance, the growing Arab military forces, the increasing Soviet involvement, losing the U.S. support, the "Belfastization" in the territories, the Arab terror organizations and the Israeli-Arab support of their Palestinian-Arabs brethren in Judea, Samaria and the Gaza Strip.

All these issues worry other Israelis too, and not only professor Harkavi. But others know how to take it more rationally and donot panic.

Professor Harkavi believed that if Israel does not relinquish "land for peace", "Apocalypse" is at her threshold. We have to get rid of territories," he said.

Professor Harkavi did not ask himself what would happen after Israel had made "some concessions" and relinquished some land? Will the Arabs be satisfied with it? The demographic danger will disappear? Would Jews of Israel be safer then?

His "rational" cold analysis of the situation is totally from a secular point of view and does not include any historical or religious aspects of the situation. As if the prospects of the Jews during the Egyptian's pharoes were better.

Jewish history had lived on faith. The State of Israel was built on faith, how can professor Harkavi live without faith?

According to professor Harkavi there is no hope for the Jews in Eretz Israel and insinuates that they better start a mass conversion, even into Islam.

Professor Harkavi is so naïve as to believe that for many years, the Arabs were absolutely opposed to the existence of the State of Israel, but have since moderated their political thinking and are "ready to live with a Jewish State at their side."

Harkavi also believed that the Arabs had given up their old plan of the "Grand Design" to destroy Israel, in return for political accommodations. The Arabs have never given up their "Grand Design" of eliminating Israel. The Arabs know very well that they are not strong enough to carry out their scheme and are, therefore, temporarily satisfied with political accommodations. They decided to cling to the "Salami Slices" plan of the late Tunisian President Habib Bourguiba.

Michael Lerner, an Orthodox Jew, editor of "Tikkun" (a California-based "progressive and pro-Zionist" bimonthly magazine) argued in the September 15, 1988 issue, that all the Jews in the world "are collectively guilty for Israel's aggressive policies" in Judea, Samaria and the Gaza Strip.

"The Jewish people have a great deal to repent for in light of the actions of the State of Israel in Judea, Samaria and Gaza, a state that claims to speak and act on behalf of the entire Jewish people," claimed Lerner.

While admitting that primary responsibility for the present situation lies with the Palestinian-Arabs who turned down the 1947 partition plan, the editor concluded that: "Palestinian-Arabs' rejectionism does not relieve the Jews of their responsibility for their own guilt, for their very large part in perpetuating the conflict today."

"The trouble is," continues Lerner, "that the state claims to be acting as representative of the Jewish people is today occupying land with 1.5 million Palestinian refugees from returning to their land."

Michael Lerner also blamed Israel and American Jewish leaders with failure to respond to overtures by "moderate Palestinian-Arabs" and charged that: "the Israeli government has been a major obstacle-though not the only obstacle, to be sure-to a peaceful settlement."

Obviously, article like this irritated most of the Israelis. Left or Right. To live 7000 miles away from the "fire" and write "beautiful" criticizing articles is very easy, but unfair. To be a "back seat driver" is very comfortable. Had Mr. Lerner "driven the car" himself, had Mr. Lerner lived in Israel, in the "fire" himself and served in the Israeli Defence Forces, he would have, probably, talked completely different.

Inspite of being an Orthodox Jew, it seems that Mr. Lerner doesn't know enough his background, his sources and Jewish history. Why should he? He lives in California.

When Avraham Tamir, director-general of the Foreign Ministry of Israel, came out from a meeting with U.S. Assistant Secretary of State Richard Murphy, on September 1988 (Elul, 5748), in Washington, he declared that Israel must recognize that the PLO has become the sole representative of the Palestinian Arabs in Judea, Samaria and the Gaza Strip or outside the territories and no Palestinian-Arab will dare negotiate with Israel without first receiving permission from the PLO. "Whether we like it or not" Tamir said bluntly, "the PLO is the movement of the Palestinian-Arabs".

Such a declaration from a formal Israeli official was not in the best interest of Israel and contrary to the formal policy of the Government of Israel and annoyed many Israelis. Most of the Israelis disagreed with Tamir's opinion.

While the U.S.-Egyptian-Swdish-PLO plot was going on, Israel was kept out of things very effectively.

"Whenever and wherever an international dispute remains unresolved because there is no viable diplomatic movement, then all kind of do-gooders had a tendency to step in. Over the past year, that's 1988-1989 (5748-5749), there has been just such a diplomatic vacuum in respect of the Israeli-Arab dispute. The Swedes tends to be highly visible among this army of international do-gooders."

This assessment of Sweden's highly active diplomatic posture on the Israeli-Palestinian Arabs stalemate comes from a senior Israeli Foreign Ministry official. Critics do not take seriously the Swedes as sanctimonious self-appointed supervisors of international morality.

To overcome their boring neutrality, the Swedes like, once in a while, to meddle in others' affairs, so long as things are "cold". The minute things become "hot" or dangerous; they run back to their conservative "neutrality". The world community had tasted the Swedes' "neutrality", during World War II, when they let the German army cross through their territory, and in 1988 with the deal they made with Arafat.

"We are sometimes accused rather contemptuously of assuming the role of the 'world conscience'. Swedish Premier Ingvar Carlsson put it in a recent major foreign-policy address. "We in Sweden abide by the principle of speaking up when international law is disregarded or when people are denied theit fundamental rights or oppressed, humiliated and persecuted. This ambition is sometimes confused with the idea that we believe we are more qualified then others to pass judgement and express our opinions on international matters. Apart from the fact that a little more conscience would perhaps not be out of place in world politics, this is clearly not the case. We certainly do not believe we are better than anyone else." Swedish neutrality is totally different from the Swiss type of neutrality because it is more active.

A Swedish foreign policy spokesman expressed himself on the matter:"Sweden's policy of neutrality does not imply neutrality with respect to various values and attitudes in other countries. Its standpoints are based on values reflected in Swedish democracy and not on attempts to find a middle way between conflicting international positions."

Swedish Foreign Minister Sten Anderson believes that Israel has the right to live in peace and security. Very generous of Mr.Anderson! But Mr. Anderson believes also that the Palestinian-Arabs have a right to self-determination. May be so. But not at the expense of Israel, and not in Israeli territory, that's not in Israeli Judea, Samaria and Gaza.

But Mr. Anderson also declared that if this be in the form of a PLO led Palestinian-Arab state, so be it. Israel's answer is, that if Mr. Anderson is so generous, he should transfer all the Palestinian-Arabs, including the 'Palestinian-Arab refugees' in all the Arab countries, to Sweden, which is much bigger than Israel, and let them have a "Palestinian-Arab State" in Sweden.

To interfere in a conflict like this, the Middle East conflict, without receiving the approval of both sides does not square at all with Sweden's much celebrated neutrality.

Of course Mr. Anderson can argue that all he did is to bring the U.S. and the PLO into a negotiating position. All he was doing is mediate between the U.S. and the PLO, which doesn't concern Israel. But, of course, this is not true and Mr, Anderson knows very well, because this U.S.-PLO dialogue does concern Israel very much. It concerns Israel's survival, Israel's future. Unfortunately, some people can see only the tip of their nose.

The first to confirm that the U.S. had switched positions and was about to open a dialogue with the PLO was Eugene Makhlouf, the PLO emissary to Sweden and a very good friend of Sten Anderson. Standing at the lobby of the Geneva Intercontinental Hotel, Makhlouf had just begun to tell Western reporters that the U.S.-PLO deal had been struck and suddenly, from across the packed room, a joyful becoming voice shouted "Makhlouf". Before the eyes of the startled reporters, the elegantly coiffed Sten Anderson swept across the hall and with a cry of "Congratulation" wrapped Makhlouf, the PLO emissary, in a very enthusiastic and undiplomatic bearhug.

Many of those present in the lobby were displeased by Anderson's show of emotion.

For many years Sweden's position has consistently favoured the creation of a Palestinian-Arab state in Jewish Judea, Samaria and Gaza, along side with Israel.

History repeats itself. Again, same as during the European holocaust, when the U.S. Jewry did nothing to convince President Franklin Delano Roosevelt to open the U.S. gates for Jewish refugees and let them in, one third of the world Jewry, the whole Europen Jewry, died in the German Ovens. This in spite of Emma Lazarus's poem engraved on the Statue of Liberty:

> "Give me your tired, your poor,
> Your huddled masses yearning to breathe free,
> The wretched refuse of your teeming shore.
> Send these, the homeless, and tempest-tost to me,
> I lift my lamp beside the golden door!"

The American Jewry didn't put up any opposition, any single demonstration against the U.S.-PLO dialogue. They let their government negotiate freely with a murderer, a mass murderer.

Once more the U.S. Jewry were afraid of what their gentile neighbours will say, afraid of the U.S. media reaction or may be worried about their "safety", their prosperity, their fleshpot.

This, inspite of the fact that they knew well that these U.S.-PLO talks could only end up with a U.S.-EC pressure on Israel to relinquish biblical lands, thus endangering its survival, which means, once more, ducking a chance to save Jews, this time, the Jews of Israel.

(Norman Podhoretz, Chief Editor/Israel-A Lamentation From The Future/ "Commentary", March 1989)

Mr. Norman Podhoretz wrote an excellent and thorough article in which he accused the U.S. Jewry for adhering in the false propaganda of the Liberals and the Left, both in the U.S. and in Israel, chosing the easy way and avoiding a conflict with the U.S. Administration. In his article Mr. Podhoretz also described the possible consequence of the failure of the U.S. Jews to support their brothers in Israel and compared it with the failure to support their Six million brothers during the German holocaust in Europe in the years 1939-1945.

Arafat's own reference in his speech before the UN to the right of "self-determination for six million Palestinian Arabs" and to the rights of all Palestinian Arabs "Wherever they may be to realize their sovereignty in their state," is a clear indication that Arafat has not abandoned his trategy of phases. It is also a clear indication that Arafat means a constant headache to Israel, endless troubles and no solution to the Israeli-Arab conflict. On the contrary, it is only the beginning.

Mr. Yasser Arafat wants not only to steal land from Israel, but also the Holocaust. When Arafat addressed the UN General Assembly in

November 1974, he cited six million as the number of Arab victims of Israeli aggression. In Geneva, he again used the figure of six million as the number of Palestinian Arabs entitled to self-determination. In another occasion Arafat claimed that the number of Palestinian Arab refugees were six millions (A Big Lie). Nobody knows how Arafat arrived to this figure. The man is a super crook and trying to steal from Israel and the Jews even the Holocaust. The bottom line of Arafat's impressive propaganda offensive in the area of foreign policy is crystal clear. Arafat supports the continuation of the uprising (intifada) against Israel. Arafat didn't give up "the Palestinian-Arabs Rights of Return." Arafat refused to distance himself from the PLO Charter. The outcome of these three elements is self-explanatory. To Israel it means: Never ending troubles, perpetual headache. This, in addition to loss of territories. Any Israeli government that will agree to operate under such conditions will be insane.

This little country that Arafat is so eager to have will only satisfy him and the Palestinian- Arabs temporarily, because it is too small to contain all the Palestinian-Arabs in the world, all his "Six million" refugees. Even if he now swears that that's it, and that he is not going to come up with more territorial demands in the future, and even if he accepts demilitarization, guaranteed by the UN, Israel should never be tempted to compromise, because, this "little harmless" Palestinian-Arab state can become a real military danger to Israel. It can sign military defence pacts with other countries, like Syria, Russia, Iran, etc. Which will threaten the security and even the survival of Israel. Because of the socio-economic weakness of this little Palestinian-Arab state, it can become another "Lebanon" on the border of Israel and a constant source of agitation. Which makes it more dangerous. More reasons why Israel should have nothing to do with Arafat and his PLO.

The Palestinian Liberation Organization, the PLO is far from being a liberation movement. They are nothing but terrorists, killers, assassins and murderers. This had been proven by following their behaviour during the last several years. Yet, unfortunately, they have succeeded to deceive the whole world to believe that they are really a liberal movement, even, many Israelis have fallen for it, that there is such a thing as Palestinians.

Israel must tell its friends, the Americans, that it believes that the Americans are wrong in talking to the PLO who are nothing but a bunch of terrorists. But if they have to talk to them, it is their prerogative and none of Israeli business, so long as Israel is not on their agenda and the interests of Israel are not in danger. On the other hand, by speaking to the PLO, the Americans have legitimized the concept of a Palestinian state. Israel doesn't mind even that, so long as they let them set up a "Palestinian state" somewhere else, not on Israeli territory. It will be tremendously unfair, immoral and unfriendly if the United States of America will negotiate with these terrorists Israeli land. Or may be the United States is negotiating with the PLO about giving away Pennsylvania or Illinois to the PLO? But negotiating about Israel, is Israel's business only and not American!

If the U.S. continues that dialogue with the PLO it will have to reach some kind of a compromise with the PLO because they are not in apposition to demand from the PLO unconditional surrender as the PLO has nothing tangible to deliver. This means that Israel will be asked to make the delivery. This means that the U.S.-PLO negotiations are without any shred of a doubt at the expense of Israel and totally contradictory to U.S. repeated declarations against the establishment of a Palestinian state.

The U.S. Administration has repeated several times that the United States of America is against the establishment of a "Palestinian state", yet by keeping the dialogue with the PLO they make the opposite impression.

To any sensible person it should have been clear that the U.S. resistance to the PLO is strongly influenced by Israeli determination to fight the PLO. But when George Shultz gets a cable from his Ambasador in Jerusalem Thomas Pickering that the Israelis themselves are divided on the issue and the Israeli left, including many Maarah members advocate negotiations with the PLO, no wonder that it helped decrease the U.S. conviction too. Yet, if the Israeli government was against this, Reagan and Shultz should have restrained themselves and shouldn't have crossed the Rubicon, because by recognizing Arafat and the PLO and start negotiations with them, the U.S. admits that it also recognized the PLO claim of establishing a "Palestinian state" in the West Bank, at the expense of Israel. This, inspite of the fact that the U.S.A. (Presidents: Carter, Reagan, Bush, etc.) had declared several times in the past, that it was against the creation of a Palestinian state.

No wonder that such a "friendly" step antagonized Israel. Israel should do its utmost that this will never happen.

U.S. officials, later, privately admitted that Arafat's statements at the news conference were still somewhat ambiguous, not nearly as clear as Washington would have liked or insisted previously, as Arafat had linked the acceptance of Israel's "right to exist" to the creation of the new Palestine state. The U.S. Administration could have easily continued to insist that the conditions had not been met "clearly and unambiguously."

But Reagan, constantly bothered by his inability to talk to the PLO, because of prior U.S. commitments to Israel, decided to give George Bush a farewell gift and take the heat of the announcement. So that President Bush will not have his hands tied on this matter.

The Western public opinion, without going thoroughly into the matters, without learning the problem, accused the Israelis of nay-saying, and was getting increasingly critical of Israel and sympathetic to the PLO.

U.S. Ambassador Vernon Walters' speech to the General Assembly contained no reference to Arafat's speech of the night before or of the U.S. reasons for rejecting it. Walters also adopted a tone that seemed unexpectedly critical of Israel, noting, "We must tell the parties to the Middle East conflict that their conflict is resolvable. We must tell them that we are tired of their conflict and tired of their unwillingness to make fair compromises."

If Ambassador Vernon Walters is so generous, why doesn't America make compromises to the American Indians? Take them out from their refugee camps, the Indian reservations and give them one of the fifty-one states, say, Indiana!

Why doesn't the U.S. make compromises to the American Blacks and give them also a couple of states? Say, Alabama and Louisiana!

In London, the PLO's move was hailed as a "courageous step" towards peace. Prime Minister Margaret Tatcher warmly welcomed the U.S. decision to open talks with the PLO. She added that she hoped an international conference could now be arranged.

Foreign Secretary Sir Geoffrey Howe insisted that Israel had to move quickly "towards the center, towards the common ground, for the sake of its own peace and security."

Speaking from Cairo, where he was on a six-day visit, Foreign Office Minister William Waldegrave warned Israel's leaders that: "If they miss this opportunity, it may never come again. The next war, if there ever is one in the Middle East, would be such a horrific war that it is not an option that any sensible statesman in the area can afford to risk. This is the reality that faces Israel now." The British, probably, knew best what military hardware they sold to the Arabs!

The concerted goodwill of the U.S. and the European Community would be required to take the next stage forward.

" The will for peace among the Palestinian Arabs is real," he insisted. "All Israel's friends were now hoping and praying for a positive response," said Waldegrave.

The Times of London reported on December 1988 that Britain decided to launch its own diplomatic iitiative trying to bring Israel and the PLO to the negotiating table. Britain wished to play a prominent role in the peacemaking efforts and felt that the U.S. may not move quickly enough and squander the chance for peace created by recent PLO "moderation".

Why suddenly this great British concern about Israel and its security? The British want to be generous at the expense of Israel? "Charity begins at home"! Why don't they return Northern Ireland to "Mainland Ireland" like they returned Hong Kong to Mainland China? Why don't they return the Melvinas (Falkland) to Argentina?

In 1948 they left such a mess in the Middle East, so they better "stay home" and stick their nose in their own affairs.

Out of a mixture of vanity, prejudice, ignorance and anti-Semitism, the British Foreign Office had stood against Israel ever since its foundation and even prior to that, a stand reflected in the behavior and statements of David Mellor, William Waldegrave, Ernest Bevin and many others. Speculations are that these gentlemen must have acted by the orders of their superiors, Foreign Secretary Geoffrey Howe or even Prime Minister Margaret Thatcher herself.

British Minister David Mellor should have been sent home with the reminder that the British rule ended in 1948,

An International Conference for Peace in the Middle East will automatically provide a precedent for demanding three more Iternational Cnferences:on theFalklands, on Gibraltar and on Northern Ireland. Certainly ths idea will not please Britain. Over such demands it will find itself in a minority and in a great embarrassment at the UN and in the world.

French President Francois Mitterand, on a visit at Casablanca, declared that, "recent Palestinian decisions recognizing Israel's right to exist and condemning terrorism were very important". Mitterand also added:"Thus in my eyes, the PLO has acquired respectability which certain countries denied and which France recognizes."

In Berlin, the government issued a statement welcoming the decision taken after Arafat's meeting with East German leaders. "The announcement of the United States to start direct talks with the PLO can only be beneficial to this peace process."

Italian Prime Minister Ciriaco De Mita, visiting Washington, said,"One cannot but express a positive attitude of the U.S. decision."

The Nederlands offered to upgrade contact with the PLO officials after Arafat's acceptance of Israel's right to exist. Foreign Minister Hans Van Den Broek said that the Netherlands-long considered one of Israel's closest friends in Europe-welcomed Arafat's statements. He called Washington's decision to speak to the PLO a "gratifying breakthrough" and added that Israel must now be encouraged to enter talks with the organization. Van Den Broek also told Parliament: "The expressions with respect to the PLO that we and others have demanded have now been met. We do not have to avoid political contact with the PLO when we see that such political contact will contribute to the peace process. Political contact would be at ministerial level, rather than the civil servant level contact, which the Netherlands has allowed until now. It lets the PLO keep an office in The Hague but has not accorded it diplomatic status."

Van den Broek statement made no mention of upgrading the status of the PLO office. But, he said, a committee of high-level civil servants would travel to Tunis to be briefed by the PLO.

The Belgian, Australian, Greek and Turkish governments also said that the U.S. step would advance the peace process.

The Vatican said that the U.S. decision was a sign that the force of reason was beginning to prevail and the European Parliament urged its member countries to recognize the PLO as a Palestinian government-in-exile.

In Tokyo, the Japanese government welcomed the U.S. decision as "an important step toward progress in the peace process."

The European Communty (EC) foreign ministers decided in Brussels on December 1988, to launch a diplomatic initiative, which would try to advance the convening of an International Peace Conference on the Middle East.

The U.S. initiative to start talking with the PLO encouraged averybody to tighten their embrace of the PLO.

The Vatican, and also the Italian government, feels that their policy of meeting with the PLO leadership has borne fruit. They both believe that by chosing "dialogue" over "ostracism" they have helped win PLO over to a spirit of co-operation.

Vatican concern for the fate of Catholic minorities and church interests in Islamic and Arab nations is a major influence in its politics.

The Vatican has given nothing but approval and encouragement to Arafat's moves. According to the Vatican radio, Arafat's offer of an olive branch has left Israel cold and the United States only lukewarm.   The

Vatican radio claims that this was an historic occasion that might not be repeated.

To have diplomatic ties with professional murderers, a leader of a terroristic group that kills innocent men, women and children is a scandal. Several Western countries have diplomatic ties with the PLO, and without shame.

At the UN Conference in Geneva, in 1988, Mr. Yasser Arafat received standing ovation and enthusiastic applause. Moral leaders, among them, Francois Mitterand of France and the Pope John Paul II, gave Arafat a red carpet and a royal reception.

All this is insane and beyond rational reasoning.

All Europe lauded Arafat's move. A concerted "goodwill" of the whole world to deprive Israel of its legal territories. The World just surrendered to terror.

The UN Security Council had been, and remains, the protector of terrorism. Arab terrorism, for years, the UN Security Council was unable or unwilling to act against Arab terrorism directed, mainly, at Israel.

Arafat, who was a dangerous terrorist for the last thirty years, has become a favourite. Serious American and European leaders were waiting in line to shake his hands or take a picture with him. This is something beyond comprehension.

The PLO has built an extremely well lubricated, most sophisticated propaganda sytem that addresses each of its audience in its own "language" and tells them exactly what they want to hear.

As a matter of fact, Arafat has not become more moderate. His declarations, for tactical reasons, became more moderate, in order to win friends and influence people, in order to convince the world community in the "justice" of his cause. The PLO was fabricating tactical steps to create an image of moderation.

Anybody that is expecting to get peace from Arafat should listen to Winny Uwing, president of the Scotish National Party, also member of the European Parliament, who stated that: "The only peace that Arafat could give Israel is the peace of a cemetary."

It seemed for a while that the Israelis couldn't beat the Palestinian public relation offensive or overcome their propaganda. As far as public opinion was concerned, the Israeli government was not doing enough. The Arabs, the PLO were much more ingenious, much more creative, It would be a very big mistake if Israel loses the battle over the world public opinion. But, for Israel it is not a public relation matter. For Israel it means survival, life.

Israel should not sacrifice its future or its survival for the sake of good public relations. Not even for the sake of satisfying the self-interest or the personal ambitions of some people.

Israel must not give in and pay the price by showing readiness to adopt impossible risks.

For Israel it is not a matter of just another country. Israel doesn't have another country. For the Palestinians it is just to have another country. Above the twenty-two countries, which they already have! The Israelis are fighting for survival and not just for another country. Israel is fighting for a land that belongs to her from time immemorial.

The main purpose of the PLO now, dramatic drive is to get Israel out of Judea, Samaria and the Gaza Strip, its historical land, by first undermining its Western, American and American jewish support.

The Arabs have convinced themselves that as long as the U.S. is backing Israel they will not be able to beat her. They haven't realized yet that Israel alone is strong enough to beat them all. Therefore, when they feel that there is some misunderstanding between two partners, Israel and the U.S. they believe that they have a chance to succeed by augmenting their aggression against Israel. Therefore, whenever there is some controversy between Israel and the U.S. it automatically generates tension in the Middle East, because that is the time when the Arabs feel that they could make it, they could liquidate Israel.

The Arabs have put up a campaign to undermine the U.S. support for the Jewish state. Israel is very concerned about this battle, for Israel has vested interest in this battle. The U.S. Jewry has the responsibility for the outcome of this battle.

The Arabs are also doing efforts to divide among different Jewish groups. The Jews must make certain that this will never happen. That Jews will not turn against Jews, that there will not be differences between Diaspora and Israel, Washington and Jerusalem.

On December 1988, the Soviet Union offered to restore relations with Israel as soon as efforts get under way to convene a Middle East peace conference.

"There is a unique chance today to start a political settlement in the Middle East and this chance should not be lost."

Soviet Deputy Foreign Minister Vladimir Petrovsky said in Geneva.

Petrovsky called for immediate preparations for a UN peace conference grouping the five permanent members of the Security Council and all parties involved, including Israel and the PLO.

"We consider that the process of normalization of relations should start the same day as the work for the International Conference starts" Petrovsky told reporters.

One wonders sometimes, why is "Mother Russia", suddenly, so concerned about the "freedom" and "independence" of the Palestinian Arabs only? Why is Russia not concerned also about the real freedom of Afghanistan, the BalticStates(Etonia,Latvia and Lithuania), Ukraine, Poland, Finland, Rumania, Bulgaria, Yugoslavia Czechoslavakia, Armenia, etc., etc., etc?

In Algiers, Stockholm and Geneva the PLO succeeded to convince the world that once there was a Palestinian state in Judea, Samaria and the Gaza Strip, then the Israelis came and conquered it from them, in June 1967. The World, without bothering to check the Arabs' claim thoroughly, believed the Arabs. Or, may be, because the Arabs made such a big noise, such a big fuss, that the world got tired of them and gave up. Before June 1967, when Judea, Samaria were under the control of Jordan and Gaza under the control of Egypt, the PLO claimed that Israel proper belonged to them.

This is a big lie. A Big Arab Lie. There was never in history an Arab country called Palestine. All the above mentioned territories belonged to Israel. Judea, Samaria and the Gazae Strip were never conquered by Israel. They were reconquered by Israel, they were redeemed by Israel. Israel is not a conqueror. Israel is not a colonialist.

Very important people in the U.S. and in Europe, even in Israel, believed that, if Arafat and the PLO promise to stop terror, Israel should sit down and talk with them. What about the kidnappings, killings, and murders they have committed so far? These should be forgiven? Unpunished?

The hands of Arafat and the PLO are full of blood, and even if they wash their hands with soap twice it will still be full of blood.

Israel should never negotiate with murderers.

Arafat's latest manoeuver is a change in system, not a change in goal. Reconquering Gaza and the West Bank is the first phase and than Israel, will be done in stages, using both diplomacy and terror.

Diplomacy has to convince the U.S. Administration and the American public that Judea, Samaria and Gaza belong to the so-called Palestinian Arabs, the PLO mean peace and would not endanger the State of Israel.

Terror will have to convince the Israelis to pull out from the "Palestinian territories."

Unlike the rest of the world, most of the Israelis are definitely convinced that Arafat had not genuinely been transmitted into some other species. All he did is change tactics. Change strategy. Arafat is the same murderer as he was before, and didn't change a bit.

"Can the Ethiopian change his skin,
Or the Leopard his spots?"
Jeremiah 13:23

The hysterical Israeli Left proposed to start talks with the PLO when the PLO hadn't even indicated that it wanted to talk with Israel.

The Israeli Left reaction was that Israel should recognize the "positive elements" of Arafat's offer and open a diaogue with the PLO. This means more territorial concessions and the Arab Palestinian state.

On the other hand, the Israeli right reaction was that Israel should annex the territories, declare openly that these territories are part of Israel and start a mass settlement there as well as population displacement (transfer).

The Maarah and the Israeli Left believe that by making concessions to the Arabs it will bring peace to the area. They do not understand how these relinquished territories can become a springboard and a vantage point for further Arab claims and more bloodshed.

In some religious, Orthodox circles there is a tendency to make some concessions to the Arabs and give them parts of the West Bank, parts of Judea, Samaria and the Gaza Strip, parts of their patrimonial land, for the sake of Pikuach Nefesh, that's for the sake of saving an endangered life. They unfortunately, do not understand that by doing so they will only increase the number of endangered lives. By bringing the Arabs closer to Israel's center it can only increase the number of casualties.

Ending its debate on the "Qestion of Palestine",the UN General Assembly voted overwhelmingly in favour of a resolution calling for the convening of an International Peace Conference under UN auspices, with the participation of the five permanent members of the UN Security

Council. The resolution which passed (138-2 with the U.S. and Israel opposing and Canada and Costa Rica abstaining also)

1. Demands the withdrawal of Israel from all territories occupied since 1967, including Jerusalem,
2. Guarantees Security for all states in the region, including those named in the November 1947 partition resolution,
3. Calls for resolving the problem of the Palestinian refugees in conformity with General Assembly Resolution 194, which specified the right of the refugees to Return or receive compensation, and
4. Demands the dismantling of Israeli settlements in the territories.`

The resolution notes the "expressed desire and endeavours to place the Palestinian territory occupied since 1967, including Jerusalem, under the supervision of the UN for a limited period..." and calls upon the Security Council "to consider measures needed to convene the International Peace Conference, including the establishment of a preparatory committee, and to consider guarantees agreed upon by the conference for all states in the region."

Inspite of the fact that the PLO Chief Yasser Arafat finally agreed to Israel's right to exist, further statements by him and by other PLO leaders indicate that the organization has not entirely renounced its strategy of a staged takeover of Palestine (Eretz Israel).

In Belgrade, Yugoslavia, on December 20,1988, Arafat declared: "Our decision was and has been to continue the intifada until the occupier is pushed from our territories, and until our people get a chance to enjoy their sovereignty under PLO leadership on their national soil."

Arafat's political adviser, Nabil el-Sha'ath told a University of Cairo audience that the Islamic Hamas movement, "which has been consistent in its Jihad until the complete liberation of the occupied lands, is completely supported by the PLO."

PLO No. 2 man, Salah Khalaf, told the Paris-based weekly Al-Yom-Al-Sabah, on November 28, 1988, that the meeting of the Palestinian National Council in Algiers had retained the strategy of stages adopted by the PNC in 1974:

"The PNC resolutions define the Palestinian position as adopted in the phased program fourteen years ago. The PNC session was intended to revitalize this program and to promote a mechanism that will get it moving."

In an inteview with The Times in Tunis, on December 1988, Fatah Founder Khalid al-Hassan claimed that: "Within original Israel and the occupied territories, the Palestinian-Arabs have the right to attack military targets."

Mustafa el-Zibri, a member of the PLO's executive committee and deputy leader of the "Popular Front for the Liberation of Palestne", declared in a statement, on December 1988, that "Arafat's statement, which led to PLO-U.S. talks were only Arafat's personal opinion, and they are incompetible with resolutions passed by the Palestinian National Council meeting in Algiers, a week earlier. We shall continue to exercise our legitimate right in struggling against the occupation with all means available, including armed struggle."

Neither Arafat nor any other Arab leader ever gave up the "Right of the Palestinian –Arabs to Return," according to UN Resolution 194 of December 1948. The "Right" of the Palestinian-Arabs to return to their "homes" in Eretz Israel, that's Israel proper, Judea, Samaria and the Gaza Strip, or receive compensations to those who do not wish to return.

The Palestinian-Arabs, who at the recommendation of their brethren abroad, left their "homes" and enabled the five Arab neighbouring armies to invade Israel without hurting them.

They have been waiting on suitecases for fourty years for that promised Arab victory, which will bring them back to their "homes".

Obviously, with their high rate of birth, during these Sixty years, the Palestinian-Arabs abroad, who wish to return have quadrupled? Therefore, fulfilling their right to return, according to UN Resolution 194, means the end of Israel.

The PLO's UN representative, Labib Terzi, in an article in Ha'Aretz (An Israeli Daily), from December 20, 1988, alluded to the strategy of phases when he talked about the right of the Palestinian-Arab refugees to return to their former "homes" in Israel as a "non-negotiable right-although the imp-

lementation can be discussed."

The problem of the "Right to Return" for the Palestinian-Arabs will be lingering for many years, unless the Israeli government implements the "Population Displacement" or "Transfer" plan immediately and without hesitation.

On January 1989, at the start of two days of confirmation hearings before the Senate Foreign Relations Committee, Secretary of State-designate James Baker said that the Bush Administration will "generally" continue the Middle East policies of the Reagan Administration, but will "feel free to supplement and modify those policies as the circumstances might require as we move forward." Baker also said that the new Bush Administration would support an international peace conference on the Arab-Israeli conflict provided that it was "properly structured" and would lead to direct negotiations.

James Baker strongly resisted U.S. support for Israel and made it clear that the Bush Administration would continue to oppose the creation of a Palestinian state, despite the opening of an American dialogue with the PLO.

James Baker also warned that the PLO would have to stop terrorism completely and accept more realistic political positions if it wanted its dialogue with the U.S. to succeed.

Asked by Republican Senator Rudy Boschwitz of Minnesota whether the Bush Administration would continue to accept the principle that Israel could not withdraw completely to its pre-1967 lines, Baker answered: "I have no reason to think that we would depart from it."

Baker reiterated the long-standing U.S. position calling for an exchange of Israeli-held territory on the West Bank and Gaza for peace.

Baker said that the Bush Administration would continue to support an undivided Jerusalem, but did not elaborate.

The incoming Secretary quoted President-elect George Bush as that the U.S. has "the solid consensus and the objective and means of making peace between Israel and her neighbours. These include the purpose of negotiations, which is, above all, a just and enduring peace that ensures Israeli security and satisfies the legitimate rights of the Palestinian-Arabs.

Baker added that the Bush Administration would continue to "advocate direct negotiations based on UN Resolutions 242 and 338, which include exchange of territory for peace. Realistically, Jordan must play a part in any agreement. The Palestinian-Arabs must participate in the determination of their own future."

But in rejecting an independent Palestinian state, Baker expressed support for some sort of confederation between Jordan and the West Bank.

"We have said that we believe that there will be some transitional stage required before we get to a satisfactory final outcome," he said. "What is a satisfactory final outcome is going to be determined once again, only by direct negotiations between the parties."

Baker added that he did not want to "prejudge" a final settlement.

"these are sound principles and they should guide us, he said, referring to the positions he endorsed.

Regarding to the U.S. dialogue with the Palestinian-Arabs, Baker said:"To have any value, that dialogue is going to have to, in our view, somehow contribute to the peace process. It is, I suppose, one more step toward the beginning of negotiations among the parties in the region."

"The Arab-Israeli conflict has long engaged America's attention, its resources and goodwill," Baker said. "Now President Reagan has authorized a dialogue with the PLO. Dialogues, Mr. Chairman, bring messages. And we are bringing a message to the PLO about terrorism and about the need for even more realism. Realism that makes practical progress on the ground possible."

However, Baker noted that: "the existence of the dialogue should not lead anyone to misunderstand our overall policy or to question our enduring support for the State of Israel. Nor have altered our belief that an independent Palestinian State will not be a source of stability or contribute to a just and enduring peace."

Referring to the Arab uprising, the intifada, Baker said: "Today the rocks are flying and the blood is flowing-bad blood between the Palestinians the Israelis in the areas under Israeli military administration. We are determined to build upon the achievements of our predecessors in changing that situation, which must be the foundation of secure peace. And we look forward to working with all the parties in the area to achieve it."

The second most important figures in the Bush Administration, after Secretary of State James Baker, was the new Secretary of Defence Richard Cheney, who succeeded Frank Carlucci.

Cheney was appointed secretary of defence, after Bush's first choice Senator John Tower from Texas nomination was turned down flatly by the full Senate, following a very bitter partisan debate involving Tower's alleged drinking and womanizing.

Cheney, a political conservative, continued to make clear that he still does have a positive appreciation of Israel's strategic connection to the U.S. and values Israel role in bolstering western interests in the eastern Mediterranean.

Israeli officials and American Jewish political activists have been sourrying in their efforts to size up Cheney.Will he prove to be a friend of Israel at the Pentagon?

Their assessments, based on his voting record during ten years in the Congress, are mixed. He has often voted in favour of the worldwide foreign aid package, of which Israel was the largest individual recipient, but occasionally, he had his reason to oppose it. But in explaining his opposition, he never cited the money appropriated for Israel as a reason.

On the other hand, he always voted in favour of arms sales to the Arabs.

The best guess is that he will be more supportve to Israesl than Caspar Weinberger-probably about as friendly as Frank Carlucci has been during the final year of the Reagan Administration.

Richard Cheney did speak before Aipac in 1984, a presidential election year in the U.S.

He underscored his commitment to "the growing importance of our shared strategic interests" with Israel.

"Both political parties are committed to those basic propositions," he said. "Republican and democratic presidents alike have repeatedly demonstrated their belief that the future prosperity, security and survival of Israel and the United States are inextricably interwoven."

"The determination of the United States to maintain and build on that historic relationship is not subject of partisan debate. There is no Republican or Democratic position on the security of Israel-only an American position."

In his speech, Cheney went on to urge the largely Jewish Audience to support a strong U.S. defence and a large Pentagon budget. "What is at stake," he said, "is the future commitment of the United States to maintain that military commitment-to be a strong, reliable and effective partner that future generations of Israelis can depend upon."

Cheney has visited Israel and is quite familiar with the issues of the Arab-Israeli conflict. Still, he will probably go along with the prevailing views of President Bush and Secretary of State James Baker.

U.S. Secretary of States James Baker signaled that the Administration was certainly not going to rush things in the Middle East. "There is no more intractable foreign policy problem facing us," he said.

James Baker conceded that the Soviets could play a more active diplomatic role in the Arab-Israeli peace process. The U.S. will not continue to try to shut out the Soviets.

If Israel lets the PLO take over, Judea, Samaria and the Gaza Strip and establishes a Palestinian-Arab state, their next move will be taking over Israel proper.

There is absolutely nothing to talk with the Arabs, because the minute Israel will either be seduced or forced to talk with the Palestinian-Arabs, it will mean that it has finally agreed to the establishment of a third country between Israel and Jordan.

Talks with the Palestinian-Arabs will mean searching for an arrangement of coexistence with the Arabs. On the other hand, talks with the PLO will mean negotiations with the PLO over the issue of the "Right of Return" of millions of Arab "refugees" from abroad, which will flood Eretz Israel (Israel poroper, Judea, Samaria and the Gaza Strip) with more Arabs and endanger its very existence.

Sometimes, one wonders whether the Arab inhabitants of Judea, Samaria and the Gaza Strip didn't need a homeland prior to June 1967, when the area was occupied by Jordan.

Where was the "Right of the Palestinian-Arabs" before June 1967? Before the Six-Day War, when it was recaptured by the Israelis, the original, the true owners of the land?

The PLO was not formed after 1967. The PLO was formed in 1964. The PLO was not formed in order to liberate Hebron and Nablus (Shechem) in Judea and Samaria, which were already "free", but to liberate Tel Aviv, Haifa, Jaffa, Ramleh, Lod and the Negev, and this goal is still an obsession and doesn't leave their heads and they plan to carry it out, only in phases.

In a statement broadcasted on Radio Monte Carlo's Arabic-language service, on January 1989, Arafat said:

"Any Palestinian-Arab leader who proposes an end to the Intifada exposes himself to the bullets of his own people and endangers his life. The PLO will now know how to deal with him"

Arafat's statement was apparently aimed at Bethlehem's Mayor Elias Freij, who had earlier called for one-year truce. Since Arafat's threat, Elias Freij has withdrawn his proposal.

People like: Basil Kanaan (businessman), Dr. Hatem Abu Ghazaleh (former city Councillor), Dr. Samih Taktak (Director of St. Lake's Hospital), Dr. Husam Abdel Hadi (a member of the Board of Trustees of An Najah University), Ibrahim Abdel Hadi (Chairman of the Board of the Arab Insurance Company), all five ardent PLO supporters or they will be assassinated like Zafer Al-Masri, the late Mayor of Nablus (Shechem).

During the Palestinian-Arabs' uprising (intifada) the Arabs have killed more Arabs than Jews, for "collaborating" with the Jews. They have beaten and raped the wives and daughters of those Arabs suspected to have collaborated with the Jews.

How can anybody be so naïve and trust people who behave like this, when they talk about peace? Unless he wants to deceive himself.

The Palestinian-Arabs were terrorized into supporting the uprising, the intifada. Everybody, and this includes the United States of America, is aware of Arafat's threats to anybody who doesn't toe the line.

Secretary of State George Shultz declared that the U.S. would continue to press its view that Arafat is responsible for ending terrorist activities by all factions of the PLO.

Many in Israel believe that an International Peace Conference for the Middle East means: How much more of pre-1967 land Israel should add to the Palestinian-Arab new state.

It seems that the Arab strategy was to isolate Israel and fore her to accept the dictate of the International Peace Conference.

Arafat did everything to delegitimize Israel in the eyes of the West. He considered it a major political success and an important weapon for his future struggle.

The Israeli Government expressed dismay over the readiness of the United States and Western Europe leaders to meet with Yasser Arafat, a dangerous terrorist and a murderer and to publicly advise Israel to establish contact with the PLO. The fact of the matter that the West, that is America and the European Community are asking Israel-indeed ordering Israel-to negotiate its own disappearance. "Righteous Nations" push Israel to negotiate its own destruction. One must be very naïve or even blind, not to see that territorial relinquishing ment the beginning of a national disaster for Israel.

To negotiate away whatever strategic depth Israel may still have, to an organization that plans Israel's destruction, is insane.

Not only the U.S. and the European Community put pressure on Israel to relinquish territories, but also some Jews. Israel had faced constant criticism from "beautiful" Jews abroad (outside Israel), who, with political "loyalty" and "intellectual" dishonesty urged the Jewish State to make more concessions to the Arabs, that could well spell its doom.

This irresponsible criticism was much more annoying and damaging to the State of Israel than the intifada itself. These "Criticizing Jews" who live several thousands miles away from the scene, do not care about Israel's reputation, image or survival. All they want is to impress their gentile next-door neighbours. By doing so, they not only support all those who put

Israel's existence in jeopardy but also weaken the memory of the Holocaust and strengthen the anti-Israeli and anti-Semitic feelings in the world.

For the sake of argument only, suppose that the Israeli Government accepts the proposal of the good. Naïve, liberal Jews, living 6,000 miles away from the scene, and puts an end to the occupation of Judea, Samaria and Gaza. Starts a dialogue with Arafat and his PLO and lets him have a Palestinian-Arab State. What if then Arafat signs military defense pacts with the surrounding Arab states, even with the Soviets? Israel will have to face then Syrian soldiers on her borders or even worse, Soviet soldiers on her borders. Will then these "advisers" leave America and come to Israel's defense?

What if the Arab states start an all out war against Israel, using the new Palestinian-Arab state as a springboard? And what if they decide to use chemical and biological weapon and wipe out Israel from the map? What will be the risk of these "back seet drivers"? May be, donating a few "box" for putting an ad in the New York Times saying that they have made a mistake and how sorry they were.

So, with what moral rights can they advise Israel how to defend itself?

This is not the policy of Shamir, this is the policy of Israel, of all the Jews living in Israel. Shamir was elected prime minister in a free democratic elections, Shamir is working for the best interests of Israel ands not for his personal interests.

The prime minister of Israel, Shamir, is fulfilling a mission; a historical mission, a sacred mission and all the Jews in the World must back him up. If anybody wants to criticize him, it should be in an internal family discussion, inside the house, in the family. One doesn't hang his dirty washings outside. Not in public and not over the news media.

Jewish solidarity is very important in times like these and must be cherished by all the Jews.

Therefore, there is only one way, the right way. The World Jewry must support Israel 100 per cent.

The diaspora Jews should not determine Israel's destiny. Only the Jews living in Israel can determine their destiny, their future. And, with no disrespect to the Diaspora Jews, this is the feeling of most Israelis.

For these are trial times for Israel, trial times for all the Jews in the World. Those living in Israel and those living in the diaspora. Where is the Jewish solidarity in times like these? In times like these they must be united. For United we can stand anything and anybody!

Every show of Israeli weakness brings more Arab and international pressure.

On January 1989 (Shevat 5749), Defense Minister Yitzhak Rabin suggested general elections in the West Bank so that the Palestinan-Arabs could chose their leaders with whom Israel might start direct negotiations. The Palestinian-Arabs replied that they preferred Arafat and the PLO to represent them. Free elections are a basic democratic process, which the Palestinian Arabs rejected. Rabin's offer was a personal offer, which was never discussed or approved in the Israeli Cabinet.

The Palestinian-Arabs took Rabin's "private" offer seriously and considered it a formal Israli proposal. Hassan Abdul Rahman, the unofficial representative of the PLO in Washington and Paul Ajrouny, the Long-Island based publisher of the East Jerusalem Arab newspaper Al-Fajr, expressed strong opposition to the holding of such elections, urging that they woud simply represent a ploy by Prime Minister Yitzhak Shamir and Foreign Minister Moshe Arens to perpetuate Israeli control of the "territories." Hassan Abdul Rahman also added: "that the purpose of such elections would be to try to slow the momentum now under way in the peace process." Hassan Abdul Rahman also said that:"What the PLO is trying to do is to rally as much support as possible for the idea of an International Peace Conference and to achieve peace on the basis of what was accepted at the Palestinian National Council in Algiers. We are not engaged in a public relations campaign, but rather hope to engage in discussions with whoever in Israel is ready for a dialogue. We hope to expand our dialogue with the U.S. to include substansive issues, and hope also to engage in discussions with the American Jewish Community."

Two other Palestinian Americans Rashid Khaldi of the Unversity of Chicago and Fuad Moughrabi of the University of Tennessee argued that elections could be useful in terms of providing Israel with a way to begin talking to Palestinian-Arab leaders closely linked to the PLO. The two professors emphacized, however, that the election scheme would be viable only if it was understood from the beginning that Israel was genuinely trying to find a way out of the territories and not simply looking for a device to separate the Paleestinian Arabs in the West Bank and Gaza from their brethren in the diaspora.Rabin's "private" initiative was again an unwise step, specially because it was made in public and over the international news media.

There is nothing to talk to the Arabs, the so called Palestinians before they agree to leave the country, to leave Eretz Israel For good.

On February 1989 (Shevat 5749), the U.S. State Department published an annual report on human rights, also called the Shifter Report. The report described the human rights conditions in 169 countries during the year 1988. The report concluded that Israelis were guilty of "a substantial increase in human-rights violations "While acknowledging that the Israeli Defense Forces (IDF) was often provoked by stones and fire-bombs. The report charged that soldiers frequently used gun-fire in situations that did not present mortal danger to troops, causing many avoidable deaths and injuries."

The U.S. State Department also admitted that only because Israel is a true democracy they could have gathered all this information.

The Shifter Report was nothing but a repeat of the events and statistics concrning the uprising that was already reported, time and again, by the Israeli and American news media. There was nothing in the report that was now and that had not been reported previously. The main damage caused to Israel was from the insistence of the American media to focus on the few pages devoted to Israel out of a world-encompassing list of human rights violations. Nothing unusual, because since the beginning of the Arab uprising in December 1987, the U.S. media was "after" Israel.

The Shifter Report was more contribution to the further erosion of Israel's image in American and American-Jewish eyes. Israel was a victim to journalistic scoops.

In Richard Shifter's report the human rights conditions of 169 countries were dealt with, but only the conditions in Israel was brought up by the U.S. media, and so loudly. What about the human rights conditions in the other 168 countries? Why were they not mentioned in the U.S. media? This shows, very obviously, only one thing, and that is more pressure on Israel, more pressure to force her to accept an International Peace Conference and give up more territories to the Arabs.

The U.S. report cited much worse human-rights records in Cuba, North Korea as well as in numerous other countries, but those criticisms have been almost totally overlooked, ignored by the U.S. news media.

In 1988-1989 Uzbeks have killed thousands of Armenians and nobody in the world made a comment. During the same period Uzbeks have slain thousands of Meskhetian Turks and nobody in the world commented. Even justice is selective.

The international media gave full coverage to Salman Rushdi's book. The "The Satanic Verses", which made headlines for more than a week, but remained mute to the horrors going on in Libya, Iran, Iraq, Darfour, etc.

"Amnesty" and other international Human-Rights Organizations published, and the media accepted it, that 1,000 people were killed in Iran's prisons since its cease-fire with Iraq, when the real figure was 50,000 people.

The international news media remained silent when Germany was selling the Arab countries the "Parma 150" deadly gas.

It is not very difficult to guess that the information on the human rights in the "territories", in Shifter's report, were contributed by U.S. Ambassador Thomas Pickering as a farwell present to the people of Israel, when he left the country.

This report was totally biased. Washington either failed to understand or did not want to understand the context to which the alleged abuses occurred.

The U.S. State Department report that sharply criticized Israel's "Human Rights" practices in Judea, Samaria and Gaza and the lack of balance between the report and reality.

In this report, and not for the first time, Israel is judged very unfairly and by Double Standards, and by whom? By its best friend: the United States of America.

The U.S. speaks of such lofty values as "Human Rights" as they investigated the conditions of Ketziot detention center for Arab terrorists and Arab convicted murderers and pestered Israel about deportations, etc. The conditions of Israeli prisons or detention centers in Judea, Samaria and Gaza are great compared to any other Western country, and compared to Jonathan Pollard who sits three floors underground in a cell by himself.

Therefore, the United States of America is not totally innocent. It has no right to teach Israel morals or give Israel lessons in Human Rights or teach Israel how to defend itself.

When the United States' Administration wanted Israel to give up something that Israel was reluctant to supply, because it meant bringing Israel closer to self suicide, the U.S. would appoint a Jew, an American Jew, a "landsman" to do for her this difficult task, to "pick up for her the chestnuts from the fire."

When the U.S. wanted Israel to supply water and food to the besieged Egyptian Third Army, in the Sinai, in 1973 and later to release that siege, they picked up another Jew, Dr. Henry Kissinger to do the job for them.

When they wanted Tabah returned to Egypt they picked up Mr. Abraham Sofer, also a Jew.

When the U.S. wanted to push Israel into an International Peace Conference, which will

Eventually force Israel to relinquish more territories in the West Bank and the Gaza Strip they picked up Mr. Richard Shifter.

Accusing the U.S. State Department of "Obsessive Prejudice," Israeli President Chaim Herzog hinted at a revival of anti-Semitism. "The imbalance in reporting is terrifying in its implications," he said, "because it arouses for us, the Jewish people, and specters of our past."

A few days after the report was published, Dan Shomron, Israeli Chief-of-Staff, on his visit to Washington, commented on the report with these words: "Palestinian civilians have chosen as the mean to push Israel out of the territories. The report shows that when there is an increase in the number of violent incidents ther are more people hurt."

We have been watching for decades the Civil-Rights violations in the U.S.. We all read the book and saw the movie "Roots" and we all know very well how the blacks in America were treated for years. We have been watching for years the Civil-Rights conflicts with the U.S. Police, the National Guard and the Federal Troops and saw also how the Black Demonstrations were dispersed. names like: Montgomery, Alabama (1955), Little Rock, Arkansas (1957), Birmingham, Alabama (1963), still ring the bell. People still remember the Black Civil-Rights March on Washington D.C. (1963), led by Martin Luther King, as well as Memphis, Tsennesse (1968). Not to mention the treatment received by other minorities, like: American-Indians, the Puerto-Ricans, the Mexican-Americans and the American-Japanese during World War II.

Israel never treated the Palestinian Arabs in the same way. Besides, there is a very great difference between the conflicts of the Blacks, which were fighting for their rights only and never intended to throw the White-Americans into the ocean, whereas the Palestinian Arabs want to throw out the Israelis from their biblical lands into the sea.

There is no analogy or resemblance between the way the United States of America was and is treating her law-abiding minorities and the way Israel treated and is treating the Palestinian Arabs of Judea, Samaria and the Gaza Strip, most of them, are her avowed enemies. The former is genocide and oppression. The latter is defence.

The American-Indians were proud, sovereign, autonomous nations, who were displaced, dismembered and despised by the the much-lauded American settlers and military, in quest for Greater America, in the conquest of the West, the Frontiers, from the Atlantic to the Pacific oceans. They were ridiculed, maligned as murderers in American history books, in American culture and education as well as movies. Relegated to reservations, they are now "allowed varied degrees of autonomy" on the land that was once entirely theirs.

As for America's "most prominent racial minority," the Blacks, although it acquired citizenship in 1868, until the Civil Rights Act of 1963, civil rights were not enforced in most states. Black Americans were flayed, lynched, burned and demeaned. They were denied access to public transportation, public schools, universities, lunch-counters, etc. Their churches were razed and their heritage was trampled on. Even today, many black Americans are still either infantilized ("boy") or brutalized. White and Black equality in the U.S. is still a dream and racial-motivated violence still occurs.

True the Americans of today do not like to hear this, but also the Germans hate to hear about the Holocaust against the Jews, in Europe, during World War II. Therefore, America should not be so quick in preaching Israel morals.

True, the United States of America had been, for many decades, the bastion of democracy, but it was also the native land of the Ku Klux klan, the lynch and the hydrogen bomb. It gave a shelter to many German war criminals but it closed the gates to Jewish refugees running away from the German Holocaust in Europe. It fought a great and brave war to free black slavery but it also deported and exterminated its native Indians.

Arafat's renunciation of terror has clearly caused difficulties for him and his partners. As soon as he made his declaration, in the refugee camps of Rashidiyeh, Ein-el-Hilweh and Sidon, in Lebanon, there were anti-Fatah demonstrations by the residents, expressing anger over the fact that Fatah (PLO) would stop sending its fighters on missions against the South Lebanese Army (SLA) and against Israel. Arafat had pronounced differences with his partners: Habash (PFLP), Hawatmeh (DFLP), Abu Musah, Ahmed Jibreel, Abu Nidhal, Talaat Yaakub, etc. These insisted that terror must continue.

It seems that Arafat will have to yield to these "gentlemen", otherwise, that is the end of the PLO. Arafat will have to continue his terror, even at the risk of putting an end to his dialogue with the U.S. for breaking his promise; otherwise, his own life is in danger.

On February 1989 (Shevat 5749), the IDF killed five Arab guerrillas (terrorists), who were trying to cross into Israel from southern Lebanon. They were planning to attack civilians and take hostages.

The raids on Israel's northern borders had been approved by Yasser Arafat, the Chairman of the Palestinian Liberation Organization, with whom the U.S. opened a dialogue on December 1988 on the condition that he renounces the use of terrorism. Israel proved that this condition had been bluntly violated.

On Shabbat (Adar A, 13, 5749), February 18, 1989, Shlomo Cohen, age 21, was murdered at the Zion Gate, in the Old City of Jerusalem.

On February 23, 1989, the South Lebanese Army troops killed three Palestinian terrorists in the Security Zone. The terrorists, members of the Nayef Hawatmeh's Democratic Front for the Liberation of Palestine, had set out to attac an Israeli settlement in the Galilee. The three Palestinians came from the region of Sidon in Lebanon and were intercepted near the village of Shabun. They were spotted and killed before they could fire a shot. Alongside their bodies were Soviet made Kalashnikov rifles, a considerable quantity of ammunition, dozens of hand grenades, an anti-tank missile launcher and a pair of wire cutters to get through the border fence. They were on their way to kill Jews.

It is clear that it was another severe blow to the prestige of PLO chairman Yasser Arafat. He can try to sell a "lemon" to the international news media; the fact is that his men were on a murder mission in Israel.

It is now obvious that Chairman Arafat had no control over the Palestinian organizations

in Lebanon, Syria, Iraq, etc. If he cannot control the Democratic Front, which belongs to the hardoore of the PLO, then Arafat definitely hasn't got anything to sell and he is deceiving the whole world.

On March 2, 1989 (Adar I, 25, 5749), IDF paratroopers intercepted a PLO squad, six kilometers north of the Lebanese border, killing four and wounding one. There were no Israeli casualties.

Israel's Foreign Ministry spokesman, Alon Liel said that the raid provided further proof that the PLO was both unable and unwilling to live up to their pledge to stop acts of terror.

Liel said: "The PLO continues to contravene the conditions set by the U.S. as a precondition for Washington's dialogue with the Palestinian organization."

The repeated PLO terror raids were just trying the U.S. administration patience. The PLO, Arafat, doubted that the U.S. would break off the dialogue with them. May be they had some inside information that the U.S. Administratin will not do it.

There is no doubt that there is a striking contradiction between the "peaceful" statements Arafat made in Algiers, Geneva and Stockholm and the fact that his lieutenants are doing in the field.

Interviewed at his Damascus headquarters, on March 2, 1989, Nayef Hawatmeh promised to mount more attacks against Israel, adding that Washington could not hold him responsible for Arafat's pledges.

"Statements attributed to Arafat do not represent official PLO policy. We are not committed to his stand," Hawatmeh told Reuters.

Speaking in Abu Dhabi on March 3, 1989, Arafat said that the PLO raids into Israel would continue despite the U.S. opposition. "We did not say that we will stop defending our refugee camps, towns, and cities, which are daily raided or bombarded by the Israeli army," he said. "We are also human beings and I cannot ask those in South Lebanon to stop defending their own children and women against the Israeli killings."

Arafat's heart is not sincere. He is fooling everybody. He renounced terrorism, but then, threatened Bethlehem mayor Elias Freij with death. He has not torn up, yet, the PLO Charter, which speaks explicitly about the destruction of the State of Israel. He said in Cairo, on February 1989, that he would do it after Israel tears up its Holy Bible. Arafat compared the PLO Charter with the Holy Bible.

Yasser Arafat cannot afford to give up the armed struggle and rely only and entirely on diplomatic efforts, for fear of burning his bridges and destroying the meaning and platform upon which the PLO was established. It might bring him in conflict with his splinter groups and may be even with the Arab countries around and might even endanger him physically.

Clovis Maksoud, the Arab League's UN envoy, said, on March 4, 1989, that attacks on Israeli forces in Lebanon and the "occupied territories" could not be described as terrorism.

The Palestinian Arab's hatred towards Jewish rule has turned into hatred of Jews as Jews and into an obsession to kill Jews, because they are Jews. The Palestinan Arab uprising is not only against Israel rule but also against the State of Israel, a Jewish State.

The United State of America will not be able to continue its talks with Arafat and the PLO, without losing its credibility.

An aide to Prime Minister Yitzhak Shamir said that "we hope that the American-and in their wake the rest of the Western World-are beginning to realize that Yasser Arafat cheated them. The fact that two major PLO organizations-Hawatmeh's DFLP and Habash's PFLP-are continuing, and even increasing, their acts of terror should open U.S. and everybody's eyes to the reality of Arafat and his PLO."

In a telephone call on Friday, March 3, 1989, Israeli Foreign Ministry Assistant Director General, Eithan Ben-Tzur, told Arthur Hughes at the U.S. Embassy in Tel-Aviv that Israel was concerned about the infiltration attempts, which, he said, justify an American reassessment of the decision to talk to the PLO.

Inspite of Arafat's promises in Stockholm and Geneva, terror hasn't stopped, on the contrary, it has increased. The PLO just cannot change its way of life, the reason for its existence. The PLO had learned to use force together with a more acceptable political phrasing. The PLO had adopted a different terminology but kept the same course, and all the time still sticking to their Charter, which advocates the extermination of Israel.

Because of the stubborn refusal to void or change the PLO Charter, Israel is convinced that Arafat's rejection of Israel's existence is absolute and irreconcilable and no matter what the Arabs' semantics are.

The Bush Administration will find itself in an increasingly embarrassing and untenable situation if, as it continues its dialogue with the PLO, the organization continues to engage in terrorism.

One of the points in the Iran-Contra affair that outraged the U.S. was the notion of negotiating secretly with terrorists, The Bush Administration is particularly sensitive to anything reminding the Iran-Contra scandals (Colonel Oliver North and Israeli Amiram Nir).

A couple of years later, Amiram Nir had been killed in an air crash in Southern America. Speculators believe that the CIA wanted to get rid of him, because he knew too much.

The U.S. State Department has publicly questioned Arafat's commitment to renounce terrorism because of the various attempts by PLO-affiliated groups to infiltrate into Israel from South Lebanon.

"When PLO renounced terrorism last December," a spokesman Charles Redman said, "we assumed, Mr. Arafat spoke in the name of the PLO's executive committee and its constituent groups, and that the PLO could exercise control over these constituent groups."

The most recent incidents, he added, raises "questions regarding the commitments undertaken in the name of the PLO, indeed, questions about the PLO's ability to carry out their commitments."

But Redman stopped short of describing the incidents as acts of "terror". He also refused to say that they would end the U.S.-PLO dialogue.

On Friday March 3, 1989, Redman said that the U.S. had recognized from the beginning of the dialogues with the PLO, in December 1988, that "some groups and factions, particularly those based in Damascus, were opposed to the positive evaluation in PLO attitudes toward Israel and would be trying to undermine the U.S.-PLO dialogue and block movement in the peace process."

But Redman insisted that the U.S. had stressed to the PLO from the start that the PLO leadership would have to exercise control over splinter groups.

The Americans believe that Israel must understand that a suspension of the U.S. dialogue with the PLO is out of the question. Washington was unresponsive to Jerusalem's thesis that the PLO renunciation of terrorism is sheer fraud. The Arabs have constantly insisted that their conflict with the Zionist entity is about existence and not borders. They want the Jews out of "their" area.

Inspite of the fact that the State Department's spokesman openly raised "questions" about Yasser Arafat's ability to control the Hawatmeh, Jibreel and Habash people, he did not define their actions as terrorism and neither did he warn that such actions, if repeated, might trigger a break-off of the dialogue.   The determination to continue the talks has not been affected even by the recent several terrorist attempts of "radical" PLO factions to cross into Israel from Southern Lebanon.

In order to continue the dialogue with the PLO the State Department worked hard to show that the PLO had abandoned terrorism, that the PLO disassociated itself from terrorism and ceased calling for the extermination of Israel and Israelis.

But, the fact of the matter was that all PLO groups, Arafat's Hawatmeh, Habash, Abu Nidal, Jibreel, Abu-el-Abbas, etc. continued to commit terroristic acts against Israel, inspite of everything.

In the face of all this, insisting that the PLO had kept its promise to stop terrorism was an insult to the intelligence.

The most critical public utterance on events in Judea, Samaria and the Gaza Strip came out from a serving member of the IDF, Aluf Moshe Bar-Kochbah (Brill). In an interview with The Jerusalem Post General Bar-Kochbah said that: "The IDF behaviour in the territories will leave deep deposits of hatred towards Israel among the Palestinian-Arabs, deeper even than had they lost another war. These "deposits" will affect the Palestinian-Arabs for many years, even after a possible settlement is reached."

Bar-Kochbah expressed "deep sorrow" over the killing of Palestinian-Arab "women and children" and said: "I believe that the confrontation could have been given a less extreme character." Major-General Moshe Bar-Kochbah also criticized Israel's indifference over the past decades towards the plight of the refugee camp dwellers. "We did not exhibit enough sensitivity towards the refugee camps and we were not sufficiently sensitive towards the humiliation of the workers who traveled each day to work in Israel." Bar-Kochbah was referring to the daily trial of Arab workers at Border Police and IDF roadblocks and their experiences inside Israel.

The whole country was astounded to hear something like this, even the news media. Words like these were damaging Israel's efforts to survive. It is hurting Israel's war efforts and reputation. And to come out from a Major General on the General Staff, and in a time of war. Had he been serving under Napoleon, Wellington or Blucher there is no doubt that he would have been executed. This democratic permissiveness of the Israeli system is far from being clever and is detrimental. How can Israel criticize or blame the U.S. Shifter Report on Human Rights if its own generals are talking like this?

Contacts, whether at home or abroad, by Israeli citizens with the PLO are barred by law. The reason is that the PLO is legally defined as a terrorist organization, which seeks to destroy the State of Israel. The prohibition does not, however, apply to contacts with individual Palestinian Arabs, resident of Judea, Samaria and Gaza, even if they happen to be closely linked to the PLO.

The basic policy guidelines commit the Israeli government not to negotiate with the PLO, and to oppose establishment of a Palestinian-Arab state. But they do not prohibit anyone, not even cabinet ministers, from talking with local Palestinian-Arabs, even those among them who are identified with the PLO, about ways and means of enabling them to participate in the peace process. Thus, encouraging "representatives of the Arabs of Judea, Samaria and Gaza to take part in the peace process" is, in fact, what the government of Israel undertook in the guidelines to do.

During the month of February 1989, the Palestinian Arab, Faisal Husseini and other Palestinian-Arabs activists, met with several Israeli politicians and opportunists like Amnon Rubinstein, Moshe Amirav and Avraham Poraz from Shinui. Yossi Beilin, Chaim Ramon, Nimrod Novik and Avraham (Avrum) Burg from the Maarah. Yair Tzaban from Mapam. Most of them, members of the Knesset (Parliament).

Faisal Husseini is the son of Abdul Kader Husseini, who was killed in 1948 on Mount Kastel, trying to block the road linking Tel-Aviv with Jerusalem. Faisal Husseini is also the grandchild of "the Great Mufti of Jerusalem" who cooperated with Adolf Hitler during World War II.

Faisal Husseini, Sari Nusseibeh, Ziad Abu Zayad and the other Palestinian-Arabs at these meetings are linked to the PLO, linked to the terror organizations and are part of the PLO façade, which, like their leader, Yasser Arafat, present a false picture of a supposedly respectable PLO, which has abandoned terror.

Talks like these by members of the Maarah Party is sliding towards the Left.

Finance Minister Shimon Peres supported the talks and most of the Maarah Party ministers are definitely in favour of talks like these.

On February 19, 1989 (Adar I 14, 5749), Prime Minister Yitzhak Shamir (Likud) said that the "useless and unauthorized" meetings between Israeli politicians from the Maarah and other left parties with the PLO supporters such as Faisal Husseini and his friends will only encourage PLO terrorism.

The Prime Minister's statement came as the circle of political figures and members of Knesset meeting with Husseni and his friends, all PLO representatives, widened.

Obviously, the Likud members were furious. They felt that the participants were not authorized to involve themselves in security-related affairs, which still hurt and damage the interests of the State of Israel and its reputation in the world. Talks like these are responsibility of the Prime Minister, Foreign Minister and their representatives and not the Finance Minister and his representatives

Shimon Peres truly believed that the Almighty has bestowed on him the exclusive franchise over the destiny of Israel.

Other Israeli citizens who have been violating the law forbidding contact with the PLO, a declared Israel enemy, were: Uri Avneri, Matityahu Peled, Meir Wilner, Charlie Biton, Abdel Wahab Darawshe, Toufic Ziyad, Muhammad Miari, etc. all of them were members of the Knesset.

The Attorney-General Yossef Harish, after an appeal at the Israeli Supreme Court by Tzachi Hanegbi, MK (Likud), authorized the Police to call these people in.

Sources claim that Yossef Harish was not inclined to view their parliamentary immunity as absolute. The Prime Minister's office declared that every effort should be made to launch criminal proceedings against such members of Knesset.

Criticism of the talks came even from some members of the Maarah Party. Talks like these, not by official members of the government, and in fact behind her back, are irresponsible, illegal and contributr to the PLO efforts against Israel in the international arena. Talks like these are detrimental.

Avraham (Avrum) Burg, member of the Knesset (Maarah), along with Deputy Finance Minister Yossi Beilin and other Maarah doves met also with Faisal Husseini and his Palestinian-Arab friends in a well-publicized "secret" discussion, on February 15, 1989 (Adar I, 10, 5749).

After the meeting Burg expressed himself and said that he believed that the meeting between dovish MK's like himself and leading PLO supporters from the West Bank "will create a foundation for future political talks by influencing public opinion."

But, when in this meeting, and in public, and to the news media Avraham Burg utters words like these:"The twosides found agreement on two things: both want to end the occupation and both fear the other side," Mr. Burg spoke for himself, because the majority of the Israeli citizens showed in the last elections that what Burg said was far from being true. Therefore, Mr. Burg has achieved nothing with his big mouth but damage the interest of the State of Israel and its reputation.

In no time at all, leaders of the "dovish" wing in Israeli politics were stepping on each other's foot in their rush to get to Mr. Faisal Husseini's door.

When its own political "VIP's" behaving like this, how can Israel blame or criticize the United States of America for starting a dialogue with the PLO?

The Likud suspected that these Maarah talks with Faisal Husseini were intended to legitimize the PLO and the idea of a Palestinian-Arab state, in violation of the government's basic policy guidelines. There is a bill passed in the Knesset that prohibits contact with the PLO, defined as enemy agents.

Members of the Knesset have sworn allegiance and promised to abide by the laws of the Knesset when they took office. Therefore, any Israeli citizen, member of the "Peace Now" ("Shalom Achshav") movement or member of the Knesset who defies the laws of the Knesset and or their oath should be brought to court and tried.

With the Palestinian-Arab intifada going on, to think of a "Jordanian Option" is no longer realistic. There is no non-PLO Palestinian-Arabs in the West Bank and in Gaza anymore. Most of the Palestinian-Arabs in the West Bank and in Gaza are ardent PLO supporters. Israel must face it and react accordingly.

In order to keep the State of Israel Jewish, it must have a Jewish majority. Therefore, areas with heavy Arab population should be liquidated from its Arab population rather than given away.

The demographic deficiency of Israel should never become a reason or an excuse to relinquish territories. Therefore, the Labor's platform "Territories for Peace" is a very wrong decision and a great mistake.

The Six-Day War was concluded by the following November 22, 1967 UN Resolution No. 242.

The Security Council, expressing its continuing concern with the grave situation in the Middle East, emphacizing the inadmissiblility of the acquisition of territory by war and the need to work for just and lasting peace, in which every State in the area can live in security, emphacizing further, that all member states in their acceptance of the Charter of the United Nations have undertaken a commitment to act in accordance with Article 2 of the Charter,

1) Affirms that the fulfillment of Charter principles requires the establishment of a just and lasting peace in the Middle East should include the application of both the following principles

   a) Withdrawal of Israeli armed forces from territories occupied in the recent conflict;

   b) Termination of all claims or states of belligerency and respect for an acknowledgement of the sovereignty, territorial integrity and political indipendence of every State in the area and their right to live in peace within secure and recognized boundaries free from threats or acts of force;

2) Affirms further the necessity

   a) For guaranteeing freedom of navigation through international waterways in the area;

   b) For achieving a just settlement of the refugee problem;

c) For guaranteeing the territorial inviolability and political independence of every State in the area, through measures including the establishment of demilitarized zones;

3) Requests the Secretary-General to designate a Special Representative to proceed to the Middle East and maintain contacts with the States concerned in order to promote agreement and assist efforts to achieve a peaceful and accepted settlement in accordance with the provisions and principles in this resolution;

4) Requests the Secretary-General to report to the Security Council on the progress of the efforts of the Special Representative as soon as possible.

UN Resolution 242 speaks of "boundaries" and not "the boundaries". UN Resolution 242 requires

negotiations between states and not with terrorist gangs.

In UN Resolution 242 there is no mention of a Palestinian-Arab state or self-determination for the Palestinian-Arabs. UN Resolution 242 does not prohibit Jewish settlement in Judea, Samaria and the Gaza Strip. UN Resolution 242 states clearly that any change in the conditions requires Israel's permission.

historic Land of Israel was already partitioned in 1922, when the Hashemite dynasty was established in Jordan (Trans-Jordan).

This territorial partition was meant to resolve the Palestinan-Arabs issue and should be the last one, and it is up to the Palestinian-Arabs to decide whether or not they wish the King Hussein to rule them, or Arafat. Yet, they cannot come up every week, asking for another partition.

In a letter to the Washington Post, commenting on an editorial, accusing Israel for rejecting UN Resolution 242, Eugene V. Rostow, U.S. Deputy Secretary of State (1966-1969), professor in International Law, wrote:"That this is a false accusation, because Israel, by returning the whole of Sinai to the Arabs (Egypt), had already given away over ninety per cent of the lands conquered (Redeemed) from the Arabs in 1967. Therefore, Israel had fulfilled more than required according to UN Resolution 242. Israel had already fulfilled its share. Therefore, it is wrong to believe that Israel has to give more land. It is wrong to believe that Israel has to give up the West Bank."

This whole thing is totally absurd. The Arabs believe that they could sign an international treaty at Camp David and after receiving their share, the whole of Sinai they can come back and ask for more territories? This is ridiculous!

And most unfortunate is the fact that the United States of America, the cosignor of that agreement ignores the Camp David Accord and acts as if it is no longer valid.

Israel reminded the U.S. Administration that there was no turning a blind eye to Camp David, or revoking it as outdated, because Israel, Egypt and the U.S. were fully committed to the agreements.

The State of Israel is so "BIG" in land that there is no place even to print its name "Israel" on the map. Inspite of this fact, the U.S. Administration forced Israel, in Camp David, in 1979, to give away to Egypt, the whole of the Sinai Peninsula, over half of its territory. In 1989, the U.S. Administration, again, forced Israel to give away Judea, Samaria and the Gaza Strip, to the Palestinian-Arabs, another half of the remaining land. This, after the British have already given away over half of the of Ertez Israel (Palestine) to the Jordanian Abdullah Ibn-Hussein, later, King Abdullah, in 1922.

One can realize now, how "generous" was the United States of America towards its friend, Israel, all these years, not to mention its trial to reconvene the UN General Assembly in order to cancel its vote for the Partition, on November 29, 1947.

Two states were established in pre-Mandate Palestine (Eretz Israel). One Jewish State and one Arab State (Jordan). These two states should have answered the political needs of these two nations, the Jewish nation and the Arab nation. The need for independence and the need for a country. There is no logic and no place for an additional Arab country in the area. But, if the Palestinian-Arabs want independence, they can have it. May be they deserve it, may be. But, not at the expense of Israel. Not on Israeli soil. They can go and have their independence in Syria, in Iraq, in Lebanon, in Egypt or anywhere. Not in Israel.. Syria, Lebanon, Iraq and Egypt are Arab countries, are Moslem countries. Israel is a Jewish country.

Most of the Palestinian-Arabs were and are Jordanian citizens. Most of the Jordanian citizens were and are Palestinian-Arabs. Therefore, they are all the same, and there is no difference between them. Same language, same religion and same mentality. Jordan and Palestine are analogous, identical, and any differenciation between these two concepts, Jordan and Palestine, is artificial and wrong and was invented for deceiving the whole world and shake the Israeli economy and may be also gain an additional state, at the expense of the Israelis.

The area of Eretz Israel (Palestine), including Judea, Samaria and the Gaza Strip is 26,500 square kilometers or 8000 square miles, approximately the size of the city of New York.

On the other hand, the area of Jordan, that sits on part of the National Jewish Homeland, according to the League of Nations, and that was torn away from it by force, by the unilateral decision of the British government, in 1922, is 95,000 square kilometers. Four times the size of the State of Israel.

Therefore, the so-called Palestinian-Arabs should not shed crocodiles' tears and claim that they do not have a country. Jordan can absorb them very easily. Jordan is a Palestinian-Arab State, which should answer the need for Palestinian-Arab self-determination.

Article 1 of the Palestine Liberation Organization Charter claims that:"the Palestinian people are integral part of the Arab nation."

If the Palestinians are integral part of the Arab nation, as they claim to be, the Arab nation has already twenty two countries, with a total area of fourteen million square kilometers, that is 528 times the size of Eretz Israel, which contains the State of Israel, Judea, Samaria and the Gaza Strip.

With what legal or moral justification can they steel from little Israel another "pound of flesh" in order to establish a twenty-third Arab state? And the whole world, including some of our "**B**est Friends" are not ashamed to "encourage" Israel to give away Judea, Samaria and the Gaza Strip to the so-called Palestinian?

The objective world news media never bothered to remind people that 1,200 years ago the Arab invaders came out from the Arabian peninsula, from the desert, and by the sword and fire conquered almost half of the world, and they keep doing it until this very day,

They reached the Middle East, the Near East, Turkey, Albania, Greece, Yugoslavia, Bucharest, Vienna, Budapest, France, Spain, all of the Central and Northern Africa, Indonesia, India, China, etc,

Only recently, 1987-1988, these same Arabs, the Iraqis destroyed over 5,000 Kurd villages and killed over 20,000 Kurds, innocent men, women and children, using chemical weapon.

6,000 Kurds, men, women and children were killed by Iraqi chemicals (bought from Germany) in the village of Halabja, on March 1988.

Did the international news media bother to report this? Yes, but very, very quietly, so that it won't make a big noise.

Did the objective, non-biased international news media bother to mention that these Kurds were the original settlers in the area and the Moslem invaders came much later?

Did the objective, non-biased international news media bother to mention that eight million Christian Copts are the real masters of Egypt and now they became a small minority in an ocean of Moslem invaders?

Did the objective international news media bother to mention that the Arabs have invaded all of North Africa and conquered it from its original owners, the Berbers?

Or that the Arabs have been slaughtering the Niye-Niye tribes in Sudan for years. Over 100,000 Niye-Niyes were killed so far.

And what about the Christian Biafran genocide by their neighbours, the Moslem Nigerians? Where was the International News Media then?

Yet, the objective International News Media preferred to concentrate on Israel and the intifada, the Arab uprising, which is a prelude to the invasion of Israel.

The same Arab invaders, always depriving other people from their lands, from their lives, and the whole intelligent world is siding with these "underdogs"!

And the UN was hibernating.

In 1982 the Syrians invaded Lebanon and were occupying it already for several years, bombing and shelling its capital Beirut, mainly the Christian quarters, bombing and shelling other Christian cities, like Juniye, Aleih, etc. Killing the Spanish Ambassador in Beirut and his wife, killing and wounding hundreds, mostly civilians, men, women and children, destroying whole streets, the harbors, the airfields, fuel depots, railroads, the economy, causing hundreds of big fires. Over three hundred thousand Lebanese fled from the city of Beirut, mostly Christians, many through the Israeli Ben-Gurion Airport. Fifty thousands moved south, closer to the Israeli border, where they felt safer.

The Syrians have installed artillery all over, as well as Soviet Sam-6 and Sam-12 anti-air missiles in the Lebanese Bekaa Valley.

The Syrians were carrying out slowly but surely, their old plan of "Greater Syria", yet nobody calls Syria "occupiers".

The Syrians were busy wiping out the whole Christian population in Lebanon, committing genocide, yet it did not move a bit the Christian World. Another Biafra and nobody moved a finger. Only the "Great Republic" of France sent one hospital ship to the area.

And what made this phenomenon worse was the fact that this was not news for the international media. The media hushed and shoved it under the carpet.

But what stirred the U.S. public and the European public was the "great" news of some Israeli police officer beat an Arab-Palestinian girl who was throwing rocks at him, or beat an Arab Molotov-Cocktail thrower who refused arrest. This made headlines in the U.S. as well as in Western Europe newspapers and television. What a hypocrisy!

Lebanese Christian General Michel Aoun vowed to rid Lebanon of some fourty thousand Syrian troops deployed there.

Syria has been occupying Lebanon for several years already. In 1982 U.S. President Ronald Reagan requested their withdrawal. The Syrian ignored it. President George Bush did not repeat this demand and Syria was still occupying Lebanon in 1989 and slowly destroying the capital of Beirut by constant shelling. America, the U.S. was silent. The international community was silent. The news media was silent. The world public opinion was not aware of the fact that more people were killed in Christian Beirut by the Syrians in one month than Palestinians during a year and a half of intifada.

Mr. Richard Shifter didn't mention anything on this in his report on Human Rights. On February 1989, a U.S. official declared that: "the Israelis must realize that they are becoming increasingly astranged from their most important ally and that if the rift is to be halted, they must come with serious ideas for breaking the Mideast stalemate."

The U.S. officials are by no means upset by the slow pace of the peace process.

Even Vice-President Dan Quayle underscored the need for some fresh thinking in Jerusalem. He noted that the status quo was simply unacceptable to everyone concerned. "As you know," Quayle said, "the recently formal government in Jerusalem is exploring new options, examining new initiatives to deal with this crisis. We welcome theses moves, and hope that they will lead to an atmosphere of mutual restraint."

These are nothing but "polite" pressures on Israel by the new Bush Administration expecting Israel to come up with some new plan, based on "Territories For Peace" the U.S. plan of solving the Middle East problem.

Well, this is exactly the right time for Israel to tell the U.S. and Western Europe that: "Enough is Enough". That Judea, Samaria and the Gaza Strip belong to Israel from times immemorial, and are part and parcel of Israel, and that Israel is not going to permit the establishment of another Arab state in its midst, and that Israel's plan is "Transfer" or "Population Displacement".

Two days after he addressed to the Israeli public on a video tape in a Jerusalem hotel, on February1989, Abu Eyad addressed the Arab public over the news media and told them his real meaning of what was on that tape: "We reject all the offers of direct negotiations with the Isrsaelis. We shall refuse to participate in such negotiations and oppose anybody who will try to drag us to such negotiations. We advocate only the formula of international conference and gamble on an American pressure that will convince the Israelis to participate in such conference and force a solution."

In an interview to "Almussawar" Abu Eyad declared that he is disappointed with the U.S. that is unwilling to put pressure on Israel, and, therefore, the PLO is planning as an alternative, to win over the Israeli government, to make concessions to the PLO.

Due to the absence of normal Diplomatic relations with Israel, Shevardnadze felt "unable" to include Jerusalem in the list of Middle Eastern Capitals and decided to visit on February 1989. On the other hand, he felt that he must talk to Israel's Foreign Minister Moshe Arens, urgently. Moshe Arens accepted Shevardnadze's invitation and flew to Cairo to meet with him.

At the same time, Yasser Arafat was invited to meet Shevardnadze in Cairo too. Arens' comment after the meeting was: "We achieved as much progress as we had a right to expect."

Shevardnadze's reaction to the meeting with Arens was:" the discussions were frank, very frank."

The majority of the Israeli public felt that, without formal relations with the Soviets, the Israeli Foreign Minister should have avoided from degrading himself and the State of Israel and should have stayed home.

Not only the Soviet Union offered to mediate between Israel and the PLO. Other countries and other people have offered their good services. But, the difference is that the Soviets have added to their offer threats and blackmail.

Sheverdnadze threatened Israel, when he said in Cairo, that if Israel doesn't concede to an International Conference it would have to face a possibility of a boycott by the world community, as if the Soviets had already the world community in their pocket, or as if the Soviets had already full control over the world community. He then added the threat that if Israel doesn't concede to an international conference it will probably have to face the possibility that many other countries will also refuse to talk to her and he went even as far as to mention that by refusing to talk to the PLO, Israel might face0 the danger of a nuclear confrontation. This is blackmail!

Then Shevardnad0ze declared that if Israel doesn't put an end to its policy in Judea, Samaria and the Gaza Strip and doesn't pull out from there it would be sanctioned economically by the world community.

Shevardnadze tried to scare Moshe Arens, Israeli Foreign Minister, during their meeting in Cairo, that if Israel doesn't come back to its senses it will have to face five million Arab soldiers, twenty five thousand Arab tanks and four thousand Arab plans. He also threatened Israel with an Arab population explosion and a demographic catastrophe.

Shevardnadze's conversation with Arens was flexible, polite but also tough and threatening. A real diplomat doesn't talk like this, even if he means it, every word of it. But this is not a diplomat, this ia an ordinary Russian Mujik.

After the meeting with Sevardnadze in Cairo and listening to his speech, Foreign Minister Moshe Arens made the uncharacteristically sharp comment that Shevardnadze's speech reminded him of the days of Brezhnev and even Bulganin, relations between Israel and the Soviet appeared to be backsliding. The Soviet tone was evident in threats of "isolation", "deligitimization" and "sanctions".

On February 23, 1989, in Cairo, before the ruling Egyptian National Democratic Party, Shevardnadze gave a detailed policy address on the Soviet approach to the Middle East peace process.

He bluntly stated that the price for renewing diplomatic relations with Israel would be Israel's acceptance to an International Conference and a dialogue with the PLO. That Israel needed and would receive guarantees for her own security. Dialogue could take place in different frameworks, not only in the UN, but also among groups of countries or individual states. Shevardnadze called for abandoning ideological struggles in international disputes and erasing the word "enemy" from the political lexicon. States should strive for "a balance of interests rather than a balance of strength." He called for a "glasnost" in the realm of international relations. Then he cocluded that the alternative in this region, in the Middle East, already a "Museum of Lost Civiization," would be nuclear catastrophe.

Shevardnadze didn't forget to praise the "heroic Palestinian uprising."

In a speech to Egyptian parliamentarians, Shevardnadze warned Israel that it "has no right to deny freedom of choice to the Palestinian-Arab people." Doing so, he said, "Israel is not strengthening but rather weakening both its security as a state and the legitimacy of its own self-determination."

This was an excellent opportunity to ask the Soviet Foreign Minister about the freedom of choice of the people of Latvia, Estonia, Lithuania, Poland, Czechoslovakia, Hungary, East Germany, Rumania, Bulgaria, Afghanistan, Ukraine, Mongolia, Armenia, Azerbaidzhan, Georgia, Kazakhstan, Kirghisstan, Moldavia, Tadzhikistan, Turkmen, Uzbekistan, Finland, etc,

On February 23, 1989, in Paris, Prime Minister Yitzhak Shamir said that the Soviet Union, as a world power, "can play a role" in seeking Middle East peace settlement. He emphasized, however, at a press conference, that Moscow would first have to establish "normal relations" with Israel. "Oherwise the Soviet Union will not be objectively in a position to be able to influence Israel's positions." And added "This is what we are waiting for from Moscow. I hope0 it will come."

Israel was resolved to pay no political price for the Soviet's consent to restore normal relations with Israel after a two decades of Soviet-initiated rupture. The Soviets were the ones that terminated these relations, therefore, according to Israel, they have to be the ones to renew it.

There is no doubt that the U.S. is concerned with the escalatory potential of a future Arab-Israeli war and is, therefore, interested in advancing at least a peace process. On the other hand, the Soviets have their obvious interests for interfering in this so-called peace process. For practical purposes of peace making, the Soviet motive need not perhaps matter very much or be taken seriously. But, a superpower that denies itself full diplomatic relations with one of the parties in the Middle East cannot claim to be neutral and impartial, and therefore, is automatically limiting its peacemaking role.

The Soviet Union is a superpower with very deep inferiority complex that needs constant reassurances about its global statue. Therefore, the Soviet Union's interest in the mechanism of an international peace conference can be explained by their desire for formal recognition by the U.S. and its allies that the Soviet Union is a superpowe and a force in the Middle East also. Some kind of megalomania complex. How can the Soviet Union be equal with the United States of America when it cannot feed its population and imports grains, staples and commodities from the

United States of America, and without these imports it will starve to death, because the huge arsenal of weapon that the Soviets have accumulated during the years, cannot be eaten, unlike the U.S., the U.S.S.R. is not self supporting.

An additional explanation for the Soviet interest in a conference is tied to their experience in 1970's with Henry Kissinger's diplomacy in the Middle East, which left the Soviets out, idle, impotant, and which asserted exclusive American leadership of the Israeli-Egyptian peace process.

The U.S. and Israel prefer to move at their own pace and set their own terms and conditions for Soviet participation, because there are still many fundamental differences of national interests between them and Russia.

Other motives for the launching of the Soviet government ardent diplomatic offensive in the Middle East may be: the desire to draw the attention of the Soviet public away from the domestic failures threatening the perestroika, or, may be, the fear that an aggravation in the Middle East conflict can harm the Soviet plan of renewing the U.S.-Soviet détente, founded by Dr. Henry Kissinger, and which form an important base to Gorbachev's new modern policy.

On February 23, 1988, in Tokyo, U.S. Secretary of State, James Baker spoke disparagingly of the Soviet Union's high profile performance in Cairo: "I don't think that has played a major role, quite frankly, in creating the new dynamics. I think the dynamics were there. I think that they are affected in large part by the intifada and the results that that has had on public opinion around the world, and on public opinion, frankly, within the countries in the Middle East."

This Secretary Baker said in comment to Soviet Foreign Minister Eduard Shevardnadze's visit in Cairo, on February 1989.

Secretary Baker also said that the U.S. welcomed a " limited " Soviet involvement in the Middle East process, and called on the Soviets to reestablish diplomatic relations with Israel and to reduce their support for radical Arab states, such as Syria and Libya.

Soviet Foreign Minister Eduard Shaverdnadze rejected President Bush's relegation of Moscow to a "limited role" in the Middle East peace process. Speaking to newsmen before leaving Cairo for Baghdad, he said: "The U.S. President said he was concerned about the Soviet minister's tour of the region. That is basically quite right. But in the end he made qualification that I didn't like. He said the role of the Soviet Union should be limited. That is very sad because it injects an element of rivalry. If the United States can singlehandedly resolve all the issues in the Middle East, we would welcome that. There must be a collective effort to defuse the Middle East crisis."

On the arrival in the Iraqi capital, Baghdad, on February 1989, Shevardnadze told reporters: "The prospects of a solution in the Middle East look good and more realistic, because of the PLO's peace evertures."

On February 23, 1989 (Adar I, 18, 5749), in Paris, during a lunch hosted by opposition leader Jacque Chirac, Prime Minister Yitzhak Shamir reiterated the three points he regarded as the basis of his foreign policy: "We are opposed to the creation of a Palestinian-Arab state in the heart of our country; we say 'no' to negotiations with the PLO, because the PLO is not interested in making peace with Israel; we are in favour of an exceptional effort to reach peace with the Arab world, through direct negotiations with the Arab states and with the Palestinian-Arabs living on our land."

Shamir called on "all democratic states to change their attitude towards the terrorist organizations." He added: "they should not treat their leaders and representatives as statesmen, as diplomats, as ministers. They are making a tragic mistake, paid for in blood by innocent civilians, Israelis or French, Americans, Belgians or Arabs."

Shamir said that while he would like France to be in agreement with Israel, he was compelled to recognize that there was a big difference between the two approaches. He said, however, that there was a "deep friendship and a mutual comprehension," between the two countries.

Shamir's visit to France did not appear to have narrowed the gap between the French and Israeli positions on the peace process. Prime Minister Shamir said that the French were "skeptical" about the chance of finding an alternative to the PLO as a Palestinian representative.

In their meeting in Paris, Shamir told his host, French President Francois Mitterand that:

"I have to confess that we have certain weakness towards the Arabs: We want to live with them in peace, and we do not hate them the way they hate us. May be this is our weakness. But, this weakness gives us a lot of moral strength to face the pressures. The Arabs know that Shamir is not their enemy."

U.S. Secretary of State James Baker supported a "properly structured" International Peace Conference that would result in direct talks between Israeli and Palestinian-Arab leaders. He left open whether such Palestinian-Arabs had to be formal members of the PLO.

"The Palestinian people," was how Baker defined it.

Baker also added that the new ideas should be "explored carefully, there ought to be an extensive amount of practical groundwork accomplished before we rush off to have a high-visibility conference under the television lights."

"We are concerned," he continued, "that if we act too precipitously, we might preempt promising possibilities that could surface if we adopted a more reasoned and measured approach."

Baker also added that President Bush, in Tokyo, found some important "common ground" in the views expressed by Herzog, Mubarak and Hussein. "I think all three of those leaders recognize the fact that there is a certain dynamic now in the region. There is a pre-examination on the part of a number of the major players."

This Secretary Baker said in defending the Bush Administration's "go-slow" and "easy" approach to the issue.

On Shabbat, Adar I, 27, 5749 or March 4, 1989, the IDF blocked five car convoy of the Peace Now Movement from entering Judea and Samaria to hold "peace meetings" with Palestinian-Arabs. Some of the Peace Now ("Shalom Achshav") members managed to sneek through the army roadblocks and reach Arab communities. "Peace Now" leaders and Left-wing MKs (members of the Knesset) accompanied these convoys.

One of the convoys returned to Jerusalem and its participants held a rally in a lot opposite the Old City's Damascus Gate, attended also by Palestinian-Arabs. A second convoy from Jerusalem held a rally at the entrance of Beit Sahur, near Bethlehem, where MK Deddi Zucker gave a speech, addressing to the local Palestinian-Arabs. "Peace Now" activsts distributed leaflets in Arabic outlining the movement's Platform, including its call for talks with the PLO.

A convoy from Tel-Aviv, which included MK Yair Tzaban (Mapam) infiltrated into the Arab village of Beit Sira and held there a rally and friendly discussions with the local Palestinian-Arabs, persuading them how right their cause was and how wrong was Israel.

Likud MK Sarah Doron called on "Peace Now Movement" to refrain in the future from "disturbing the peace", maintaining that the organization " represented a tiny minority of the public." Mrs. Doron accused that Peace Now or Shalom Achshav's activities "are only meant to gain media attention and in fact obstruct the IDF."

Not only did they violate the Holy Sabbath but also they are ready to give away a great part of the Jewish Promised Land in return for a piece of paper and "Arab promises", which everybody knows exactly how much it is worth. In other countries people acting like this are defined as Quislings. Their activities are very dangerous and very damaging.

They are abusing Israel's democratic regime to the extreme.

Shalom Achshav and the Israeli Left, had lost their faith, their hope, their future, and with their declarations and behaviour discouraged immigration and encouraged emogration, discouraged foreign investment and tourism, undermined Israel's deterrent influence, which is a crucial element of Israel's strategy. They were terribly pessimistic, ready to make compromises, concessions and constantly drew macabre sceneries of Israel's destruction.

It is very wrong and very unwise to ignore such demoralizing element.

Space is too short to enumerate the nasty Arab deeds against Jews in Israel:

The children in Avivim

The children in Maalot

The Sportsmen in Munich

The "Country Club" Bus

Hotel Savoy in Tel-Aviv

The various airport massacres, both in Israel and abroad

etc., etc., etc.

Yet, the Palestinian-Arabs never raised a single voice against these atrocities. Never made any demonstration. May be because they didn't have a "Shalom Achshav" movement, they didn't have a "Peace Now" movement.

And when a world known personality like Abba Eban wrote in The Jerusalem Post, on March 21, 1989, that:

"We cannot after so many centuries, change the reality that curs is a land of two faiths, two tongues, two peoples, two memories, two national identities. Dualty is intrinsic to the very texture of the land and must be integrated into any serious picture of its future."

Eban's article was very damaging, harmful, to the best interests of the State of Israel, and the people of Israel. People in Israel wonder where did an intelligent person like Abba Eban learn that the country of Israel ever belonged to two peoples? In whose Bible did he read it?

When Abba Eban was Israeli Ambassador at the UN or when he was Foreign Minister of Israel, he spoke totally different.

On March 5, 1989, the British Deputy Foreign Minister William Waldegrave was again on a week long fact finding mission in Israel, and again, as he already done before, called the continuation of Israel's occupation of Judea, Samaria and the Gaza Strip an "utter impossibility".

"My coming here only emphasizes the utter impossibility of continuing the military occupation," Waldegrave said.

One wonders when was the last time Waldegrave looked into his Old and New Testaments. It seemed that Mr. Waldegrave never knew that Judea, Samaria, the Gaza Strip and Jerusalem ever belonged to Israel. Somebody would give him a Holy Bible so he can refresh his memory. Besides, who left all this mess in 1948, if not the British? Britain should be the last one on earth to preach morals to Israel.

An irresponsible and distorted assessment of the annual Intelligence Community on the national situation was leaked out to the public on March 1989 by some dovish interested party. It is believed that one of the Maarah members in the Cabinet was responsible for this leak. The Likud ministers in the Cabinet and the Israeli public were stunned by this distorted leak.

According to the false report, "the PLO has joined the pragmatic Arab camp, which seeks a peaceful solution to the Palestinian-Arab problem and which accepts Israel's right to exist. There is no alternative to the PLO as a Palestinian-Arab partner in peace talks, and Israeli stuborness might erode Israel's friendly ties with the U.S. Therefore, the Intellignce Community recommends that the Israeli government starts a dialogue with the PLO and should be ready to relinquish some of its territories to the Palestinian-Arabs.

There is little doubt that this irresponsible, distorted and damaging report was leaked out to the public by somebody interested in a dialogue with the PLO and relinquishing territories to the Palestinians, in close comformity to the Maarah policy in the last decade.

Likud MK Michael Eitan accused the Maarah leaders for causing great damage to the national interests of Israel by leaking the report to the press, immaterial if they were distorted or not. Tehiya MK Geula Cohen demanded that the Prime Minister should take action against those responsible for the leak.

On March 8, 1989 (Adar II 5749), Aluf (reserve) Aharon Yariv, Director of the Jaffee Centre for Strategic Studies, which is attached to the University of Tel-Aviv, came out on the Israeli National Television with a report suggesting direct talk with the PLO, a long transitional period of broad autonomy to the Palestinian Arabs in Judea, Samaria and the Gaza Strip, followed, possibly, by the creation of a Palestinian state.

To come out with something volatile like this, in public, is irresponsible and damaging. This report was the fruit of nine months research, could have easily waited another week, so that the Israeli government had the chance to study its content and approve or disapprove it.

Prime Minister Yitzhak Shamir lambasted General Aharon Yariv and his conclusions on the Israeli peace options and said that: "the Israeli general is causing a weakening of Israel's position in the international arena, and the strengthening of our enemies."

The Prime Minister's spokesman, Yossi Achimeir, quoted Shamir as saying that he has heard from a French general, once, that after surrendering Sinai, Israel should not give the Arabs more territories. "And he is objective," Shamir added. "And now we hear from a general of our own who-in my opinion, cannot be objective-an opposite opinion, which is contrary to Israel's national interests."

The Prime Minister added that: "the conditions in the study for supposed agreement on negotiations with 'people connected with the PLO'- assuming that such negotiations would ever take place-are fantasy."

The JCSS's six options for peace were: The Status Quo-Autonomy-Annexation-A Palestinian State-Gaza withdrawal-Jordanian/Palestinian Federation.

All the six options suggested, comprise risks and opportunities. To attain real and comprehensive peace, in the long run, to the best of Israel's interests, the most pragmatic solution is the solution of mass deportation of Palestinians, that's population displacement or transfer.

It is not the first time that Aharon Yariv and his group have attempted to promote their political views under the guise of security expertise. He did it also previously, during the kilometer 101 cease-fire talks with the Egyptians at the end of the Yom Kippur War (the War of Atonement), on October 1973, as well as in other cases.

The JCSS's director, General Aharon Yariv, is a former IDF intelligence chief, a former Maarah Minister of Information, a political adviser to Prime Minister Golda Meir during the cease-fire talks with Egypt, at the end of the Yom Kippur War (the War of Atonement), in 1973. The man had been affiliated with the Maarah all his life, in fact member of the Maarah Party, therefore, a political figure. It was only natural that Yariv's intention was mainly to bring forward his party's interest. Therefore he cannot call his report "Israel's options for peace," a scholastic, academic research, totally objective, independent and unbiased. The fact of the matter is that his final recommendations were totally party (Maarah) oriented.

On the months of February and March 1989, President George Bush and Secretary of State James Baker requested from Mr. Yitzhak Shamir, Prime Minister of Israel. "Urgent New Ideas" and "Practical Solutions" to the Palestinian problem.

By "New Ideas" and "Practical Solutions" these two gentlemen meant nothing less than "Territories for Peace", or, in other words, a new Arab Palestinian State, in Jewish, Judea, Samaria and the Gaza Strip, through an International Peace Conference for the Middle East.

The U.S. has taken a clear position: Israel should trade territories for peace and withdraw to the pre-67 lines, with minor modifications.

This was the U.S. formal policy for many years. This means not only forgiving the Arabs for starting the wars against Israel but also rewarding them. For Israel "Territories for Peace" means national suicide.

Words like: "Washington expects Israel to come forward with new ideas on how to solve the Palestinian problem. The refusal to come out with new ideas and the lack of flexibility as opposed to Arab flexibility is a basis for potential erosion of American support to Israel."

In The New York Time and the Washington Post are clear U.S. pressure on the Israeli government to yield to PLO demand for a Palestinian state in Jewish Judea, Samaria and Gaza.

These words come directly from the U.S. Adminisration and are against the best interests of the State of Israel. Israel doesn't owe the Palestiian-Arabs anything and therefore doesn't have to come forward with new ideas to solve the Palestinians their problem. Israel has enough problems of its own, and let the Palestinian-Arabs solve their problems, they don't need the help of Isreal. Let the Palestinian-Arabs solve their problems outside the territories of Eretz Israel, that's Greater Israel, and stop being trespassers.

Why don't the Jews, like the rest of the nations, have one country of their own, without having to share it with somebody else? Somebody else who has already over twenty countries! This is totally unfair and unjust.

By demanding that Israel comes up with "new ideas" the U.S. means new ideas acceptable to the Arabs.

It is believed that the U.S. pressure on Israel to come forward with new ideas is mainly due to pressures from King Fahed of Saudi Arabia.

This is a typical example where the U.S. interests do not conform to the Israeli interests and the U.S. prefers to even, sort of, dump Israel and go alone. For one reason or another, it is the best interest of the U.S. to please King Fahed (oil, etc,),

This could only happen because the American Jewry was not doing enough, or rather, its utmost, to support Israel. Speculations are that inspite of what they publicly declared, the Bush Administration is driving for the establishment of a new Palestinian (Arab) State in Israeli Judea, Samaria and the Gaza Strip. It is believed that this is the real U.S. policy and it manipulates the European Community to operate accordingly.

What some countries want is to transfer ancient Jewish territories to the Arabs. It has become style, a new fashion. And this includes some of Israel's "Best Friends", George Bush, Margaret Thatcher, Francois Mitterand, etc. The tragedy is that they get the support and cooperation of some good, naïve, liberal Jews in Israel, in America and in Europe, who are very anxious for "peace now", at this moment, and do not care what will happen in the future.

Of course, King Hussein from Jordan and President Husni Mubarak from Egypt are extremely happy and are very active in encouraging this trend, which they hope, will lead to the formation of a new Palestinian (Arab) state and eventually to the fulfillment of their old dream, the destruction of Israel.

On March 1989, U.S. Secretary of State, James Baker, told the Congress Foreign Affairs Committee, in Washington, that if Israel is not successful in reaching a compromise with the representatives of the Palestinians, it would have eventually to deal directly with the PLO.

Baker's public declaration in Congress was a terrible mistake, a logical error, because it contradicted President Bush's policy and the spirit of his conversation with Israeli Foreign Minister Moshe Arens, in their meeting, in Washington, in which he emphasized the need of encouraging a Palestinian representation, tied to Jordan, in order to find a "No Palestinian State" solution.

Obviously, Arafat will use Baker's declaration to the best of his benefit. Now that he knows for sure that even the United States recognizes and admits that Israel will have no choice but talk to the PLO.

The Palestinians will not be encouraged by Baker's declaration to come up with representatives of their own. This puts an end to the Palestinian option and leaves only the PLO option, which Israel, hopefully, will never accept it. This means another stalemate.

On March 1989, 23 European states, East and West, along, with U.S. Secretary of State James Baker, met in Vienna for the first European Conference on international Arms limitation (CFE). The figures presented at the Conference were: for example 53,000 tanks in the Warsaw Pact versus

23,000 in NATO-a ratio considered unacceptable to Western democracies. The NATO allies had finally realized that Europe's security problem is not nuclear weapons but the unacceptable disparity in conventional weapon between the Warsaw Pact and NATO.

In terms of arms disparity, on Israel's eastern front alone more than 12.000 tanks are emplaced, compared to less than 4,000 tanks in Israel.

The strategic depth in Western Europe is some 300 miles, while "Greater Israel ", from Jordan to the Mediterranean, near Tel Aviv, was only 45 miles wide.

In terms of early warning time, NATO forces had 4 to 6 weeks, while Israel had only 2 to 3 hours.

Therefore, the Israeli-Arab arms disparity is most dangerous to Israel.

On April 1989, Arye Levin, the Israeli representative in Moscow, has been instructed to formally convey Israel's dismay at the Soviet sale long-range Sukhoi-24D bombers to Libya.

Levin's protest was identical to the official statement issued on April 6, 1989, by Foreign Ministry spokesman Alon Liel, who said that the sale was causing Israel "deep concern".

Liel expressed "surprise that the Soviet Union, which states that it seeks to relieve situations of confrontation around the world-including the Middle East-is supplying offensive weaponry to the regime of Gaddafi, who does not conceal his intentions to attack Israel."

The statement calls on Moscow to "reconsider its policy on this matter."

Foreign Minister Moshe Arens also condemned the sale, saying that it further threatens the stability in the Middle East and added that the sale does not contribute towards improved relations between Israel and the Soviet Union.

The SU-24 Fencer which the Soviet Union sold Libya and Syria is a deadly weapon, and selling weapons like this to Gaddafi or Assad does not contribute to the stabilization of the Middle East.

A country that supplies countries protecting terrorists with the most sophisticated means of aggration cannot be considered a candidate for a leading role in peacemaking.

On April 3, 1989, in Washington, President George Bush made the following statement: "I want to see the end of the occupation." How does this square with his previous several declarations of:"No Palestinian State?"

Judea, Samaria and the Gaza Strip have been Jewish since time immemorial. In 1967 the Jews have redeemed these territories from the Jordanians (Arab) invaders. Therefore calling the Israelis "occupiers" and holding to their redeemed land "occupation", is insulting, especially when it comes from a friend who believes in the Holy Bible.

One should not forget the remark made by George Bush: "we haven't backed away from historic positions on an International Conference."

President Ronald Reagan was kind and easy with Israel. The Bush Administration is different. Bush is no Reagan, Baker is no Shultz and Sanunu, an American-Arab, from Lebanese descent, the White House Chief-of-Staff, is an unknown quality.

What bothers Israel is that the two superpowers together with the European Community have turned Israel into a passive player, whom everyone worries about while they make plans for its wellbeing and decide for her how to conduct its policy, as if they didn't have any worries of their own and have already solved all their problems. This is getting ridiculous.

Steven Gray, a research scientist in the famous "Lawrence Livermore" Laboratories, in California, published, on April 1989, in "Aviation Week" that he believes that the State of Israel has the capability to send ballistic missiles with nuclear warheads to Moscow and Leningrad, in the Soviet Union.

Gray, a known expert in Jet Propulsion wrote that the Israeli "Ofek 1" was launched into 250-1150 kilometer orbit from earth, by means of the "Shavit 2" three-staged ballistic missile weighing 25,000 kilograms or 55,000 lbs. Gray added that by a slight modification, like replacing the Third stage of the "Shavit 2" by a war head, Israel could send a nuclear warhead weighing 1,100 kilograms to a distance of 5,000 kilometers. By reducing this warhead's weight to only 500 kilograms Israel could reach a distance of 8,000 kilometers and easily hit Moscow and Leningrad.

Gray could not avoid from praising the performance of Israeli "Jericho 2" ballistic missile too.

On Adar II 13, 5749 or March 20, 1989, at the Binyanei Ha'Umah, in Jerusalem, President Herzog officially opened the Prime Minister's Conference on Jewish solidarity with Israel by urging the 1,700 world Jewish leaders to "counterattack" and "regain the offensive" in the battle that is being waged in world public opinion against the State of Israel.

Prime Minister Yitzhak Shamir reaffirmed his opposition to talks with Arafat and the PLO and reminding everybody that the PLO's Covenant still denies the legitimacy of Jewish nationhood-compared the PLO to "the Hamans our people have faced in virtually every generation."

Prime Minister Yitzhak Shamir stressed that: "there is nothing we need more at this moment than unity, unity of the Jewish people and unity between Israel and the Jewish people." The Prime Minister continued, however, that "we do have a serious complaint only against these of our brethren who took it upon themselves to conduct policy on behalf of Israel, instead of Israel; to meet our enemies; to speak in our name, and to offer initiatives and political programs of their own, affecting our lives and the future of our people."

Referring to the Who is a Jew issue, Shamir reminded that it caused much anguish in the Diaspora. "It is not now on our agenda, but the problem has not been resolved yet, permanently."

Foreign Minister Moshe Arens warned against acceding to calls to "try out the PLO because there is nothing to lose." Arens added that once Israel recognizes the PLO, it would enter an irreversible path that will enable the PLO to "impose itself upon the Palestinian-Arabs in the territories, subjugate the Palestinian-Arabs who are citizens of Israel and destabilize Jordan."

Finance Minister Shimon Peres who is acting also as Deputy Prime Minister represented the theory of the Maarah and the Left parties in Israel. Peres addressing the Conference said: "difficult decisions must be made on the way to peace. Israel is strong enough for a historic compromise and does not wish to rule another people."

The Prime Minister's Conference on Jewish Solidarity gathered circa 1,700 Jewish leaders from all over the World and expressed the deep abiding ties between Israel and the Diaspora. It also reflected a broad consensus regarding Israel's needs for peace and security.

One of the main reasons for Shamir's Conference on Jewish Solidarity was to prove to President George Bush and the U.S. Congress that he enjoys the full support of the Jewish public opinion.

Speaking for Diaspora Jewry, veteran American Jewish Max Fisher strongly advised Israel not to test the unity of the Jewish people, as was the case with "Who is a Jew" issue. But, regarding issues, such as the peace process, "we have no right to crticize," Fisher said, emphasizing that "when it comes to the integrity and security of Israel, decisions must be made by the government of Israel, in which we have faith and confidence. Whatever they will decide, we will fully support."

Just as the steering committee of the Prime Minister's Conference on Jewish Solidarity was hearing Prime Minister Shamir's address, on March 20, 1989 (Adar II 13, 5749), at the Binyanei Ha'Umah, in Jerusalem, the Maarah Knesset faction chairman, Haim Ramon, issued in a press conference, in the Knesset, a stern warning to the Prime Minister, threatening the Prime Minister, that the Maarah Party will walk out of the National Unity Government if Prime Minister Shamir does not make "a move towards peace". Ramon said that:"There is no reason for the Maarah to stay on in the government, if Shamir comes back from Washington without having budged from his positions. We shall simply go over to the opposition and propose a vote of no-confidence in Shamir's government."

It is certainly not easy for Shamir to run the Israeli government with partners like these who constantly put a spoke in its wheel.

U.S. Senator Daniel Inouye (Democrat-Hawai), chairman of the powerful Appropriations Committee, on March 30, 1989, on his visit in Jerusalem said that Israel will not be able to avoid taking a political initiative for peace at this point and will eventually have to talk to its enemies, if they sincerely offer peace in return. "You can't go on all your life saying "no". You have to come up with your own initiative."

Senator Inouye added that he believed that Prime Minister Shamir does not need to be pressured to do so because "he can read the signs" and will in fact have "fruitful meetings" with President Bush and Secretary of State Baker during his coming visit to Washington.

Inouye said that neither the Administration nor the Congress would push Shamir to make even minimal concessions. They were prepared to hear any proposals the Prime Minister might make.

Inouye's view was shared by Senator Ernest Hollings (Democrat-South Carolina) and Senator Jack Garn (Republican-Utah), who were with Inouye to talk with Israeli leaders prior to Shamir's trip to the U.S.

Inouye said that he did not suggest that Israel begin talk with the PLO or any other Palestinian group yet, and said that he accepted the view of the government that "the PLO, no matter what it says, is in the minds of many of us still a terrorist organization."

Inouye also said that he considered attempted PLO attacks across the Lebanese border to be terrorist attacks, for which Yasser Arafat as chirman of the PLO is responsible. But, he added, "I am not saying that a leopard cannot change its spots."

Inouye dismissed Shamir's view that the PLO is an enemy with whom Israel can never talk. He pointed out that the U.S. fought and then made peace with both Germany and Japan.

"The image of Israel among the U.S. public has definitely suffered during the past sixteen months of the uprising," Inouye said.

Because Hawai has very few Jewish voters, Inouye's friendship for Israel has always been considered unconnected to electoral considerations.

As chairman of the Appropriation Committee, his attitude to Israel's requests for aid and grants is crucial. Inouye has opposed cuts to Israel in the past, despite cuts elsewhere and to others, and has said that Israel simply pays for its $3 billion aid package through the military intelligence it provides to the U.S.

However, Inouye refused to say, that aid would be maintained at its current level in the face of the U.S.'s huge trade deficit and defence needs. "Everything else has been cut except for Israel," he pointed out.

As for offering additional security guarantees in return for Israeli concessions on Palestinian-Arab self-rule, Inouye said, he did not see how this was possible short of becoming "Israel's puppet."

He made it clear that the U.S. needed to offer no further proof of its commitment to Israeli security.

"It's not only $3 billion," he said emphatically. "Israel is a major non-NATO ally, who votes with the U.S. at the United Nations? Let's face it, the U.S. is Israel's only friend."

Senator Inouye's friendly advice to Israel was also pressure applied on Israel to conform with U.S. policy, only in a different way. It was a "friendly" pressure. Very hurting.

The pressure on Israel was tremendous. The U.S. insisted that Israel comes up with new ideas. Both Bush and Baker have made it very clear that they will be sorely disappointed if Shamir arrives at the White House without any ideas: they wanted ideas that were not simply a rehash of worn-out old ones.

What worried Mr. James Baker was the fact that the Palestinian-Arab children didn't go to school during the Arab uprising against Israel. When the Americans were fighting in Vietnam, how many years the Vietnamese children didn't go to school?

Shamir's plan submitted to President George Bush on his visit to Washington on April 1989:

The Four Point Plan:

1. The Camp David Partners-Reconfirmation of the Commitment to Peace.
2. The Arab Countries-From a State of War to a Process of Peace.
3. A Solution to the Refugee Problem-An International Effort.
4. Free Elections in Judea, Samaria anf Gaza on the Road to Negotiations

Shamir's four-point plan is in fact Rabin's plan with some modifications and deviations from the Camp David Accord.

To adopt Defence Minister Rabin's plan was not a very clever thing to do.

To adopt "Achitophel's" advice was a very big mistake on the part of Shamir.

On his visit to the White House, on April 6, 1989 (Nissan 1, 5749), Prime Minister Yitzhak Shamir made this statement:

"In order to launch a political negotiating process, we propose a free democratic elections, free from an atmosphere of PLO violence, terror and intimidation, among the Palestinian-Arabs of Judea, Samaria and Gaza.

The purpose of such elections would be to produce a delegation to negotiate an interim period of self-governing administration."

"The aim of the elections is to bring about the establishment of a delegation which will participate in negotiations on an interun settlement, in which a self-governing administration will be set up. The interim period will serve as an essential test of cooperation and coexistence. It will be followed by negotiations on the final settlement, in which Israel will be prepared to discuss any option, which will be presented."

Shamir also said that "Israel does not want to run the lives of the Palestinian-Arabs who live in Judea, Samaria and the Gaza Strip and that is why we proposed elections to chose representatives of the Palestinian-Arabs to discuss with us a transition period of self government."

"The interim period will provide a test of coexistence and cooperation. This will be followed by negotiations on the permanent status of the areas, in which all options would be open."

The Shamir-Rabin plan was a compromise between the Likud and the Labor and the National Unity Government, and carries great and serious dangers to the security and survival of Israel.

In the proposed elections lies a great danger of creating a Palestinian-Arab entity. Any elections, even "municipal" ones, will endanger an authorized and internationally recognized Arab political entity.Therefore, it should be considered as out of the question.

The same danger lies in the idea of "Autonomy" The loss of full, or even part, control over the territories of Judea, Samaria and Gaza could become a Kiss of Death to Israel.

Every initiative which involves imposing autonomy in Judea, Samaria and Gaza or the creation of an Arab-Palestinian representation and entity must be totally rejected by the government of Israel, for it bears the danger of eventually creating a second Palestinian-Arab state in these territories, which could become suicidal to Israel.

Winding up his nine-day visit in the U.S., Yitzhak Shamir said, on April 13, 1989 (Nissan 8, 5749), in Washington, D.C., that Israel could not relinquish control of Judea, Samaria and the Gaza Strip and "survive". He then added that "A PLO state means war."

Addressing the American Society of Newspaper Editors at its national convention, in Washington, Shamir forcefully and bravely rejected the notion of Israel trading territory for peace.

"The truth is that if we withdraw, " Shamir said, "there will be a PLO state on the outskirts of Tel Aviv and Jerusalem and war."

After finishing his speech the Prime Minister was asked one especially hostile question from an editor from Wichita, Kansas, who described Israel's policies in the territories as "despicable".

In reply, Shamir coolly, but strongly, defended Israeli military behaviour in responding to what he described as "a wave of riots and terrorist attacks against our citizens."

In prepared remarks before the American Enterprise Institute, in a Washington, "think tank", Shamir rejected the notion of any Palestinian-Arab state in Judea, Samaria and Gaza.

"The slogan 'Territories for Peace' is deceptive," Shamir continued. But we do not want to run the lives of the inhabitants. We want them to have self-rule. We want them to be able to express their national aspirations through the Palestinian-Arab state on the east bank of the Jordan River. And above all, we want to end the hostility and bloodshed by negotiating with a leadership they elect to represent themselves, not with a terrorist organization based in Tunisia."

President Bush endorsed Prime Minister Yitzhak Shamir's call for Palestinian elections, in Judea, Samaria and the Gaza Strip as an initial step to revive the peace process.

"The United States believes that elections in the territories can be designed to contribute to a political process of dialogue and negotiation.

We urge Israel and the Palestinian-Arabs to arrive at a mutually acceptable formula for election, and we plan in the days and weeks ahead to work toward that end."

Bush described his meeting with Shamir as "very productive" and pledged to work closely with him to advance the peace process. "We are friends, strategic partners and allies," the President said.

"With regard to the final status issues," Bush added, " I reaffirmed to the Prime Minister that we do not support an independent Palestinian-Arab state, nor Israeli sovereignty over or permanent occupation of the West Bank and Gaza."

Prime Minister Shamir, however, rejected any steps that could lead to a Palestinian-Arab state in Judea, Samaria and Gaza, which he called "A Prescription Not For Peace But For War."

It seems that, with Shamir's Four-Point Proposal, the U.S. Administration had abandoned the idea of an International Conference and was placing its bets on Prime Minister Yitzhak Shamir's preferred Camp David Autonomy proposals.

Israel is not obliged to put Autonomy into operation, unless Jordan first signs a peace treaty with Israel. That is the clear meaning of Camp David. It is spelled out in Black and White.

The Americans were certainly sensitive enough to the realities of the Likud politics to understand that Shamir was not about to accept the principle of Territorial Compromise.

On the other hand, Shamir was aware of the need to come to terms with the U.S. Administration and the Public Opinion.

The Bush Administration was dragging Israel and Shamir, very 'cleverly' into Indirect Negotiation with the PLO, which they hoped would eventually, gradually, become Direct.

The Autonomy plan for Judea, Samaria and Gaza has no commitment to the Final Solution of these Territories. According to Camp David Accord this is Autonomy to the People, not Autonomy to the Land.

Shamir believed that the Autonomy Plan should satisfy the majority of the Arabs if they really want to Coexist with Israel. It will not give them an independent state, but besides Foreign Affairs and Defence it gives them every thing they wanted. This will only be valid if they will voluntarily stop their uprising, otherwise, it will run out of substance and the conflict will receive back its previous form.

If the elections would be carried, the same people who are now behind the wheel of the uprising, or even the leaders of the uprising against Israel, would suddenly become the legal representatives of the people of Judea, Samaria and Gaza. This means that Israel would give to the rebellious leaders a prize, and admit publicly that they have achieved success by resorting to violence, using women and children only, and by means of knives, stones and Molotov-Cocktails only, without having to shoot a single bullet.

The Autonomy Plan will only postpone a solution to the territories of Judea, Samaria and Gaza and prolonging the agony of Jews and Arabs alike. There is also the danger that it might lead to a Palestinian-Arab state. If the Autonomy Plan is realized it will give Shamir's successors a difficult start and put the people of Israel in a very difficult spot.

It is clear to every body that if these elections will take place or not depends only on the PLO. It is the PLO, which is giving the Green Light for the holding of the elections and obviously whoever is elected will be under the direction of the PLO.

Yitzhak Shamir, who, in 1979, was against the Camp David Peace Accord, signed by his colleague Menachem Begin, being under pressure from the Bush-Baker Administration, backed by part of the American Jewry, to come up with a solution to the Middle East conflict, panicked and brought up from oblivion, revived, the Camp David "Autonomy".

The PLO will agree that the Palestinian-Arabs in Judea, Samaria and Gaza participate in the elections and in the negotiations with Israel on the interim period arrangements only if Israel agrees that the PLO participates in the second phase of the negotiations on the permanent and final solution of Judea, Samaria and Gaza.

As far as the elections are concerned the PLO demands that:

-The elections will run under international supervision

-The Arab population of East Jerusalem will be permitted to participate in these elections (so that the world does not assume that the PLO recognizes the Israeli sole sovereignty over East Jerusalem).

-The intifada should not stop neither during the elections, nor during the negotiations.

-The candidates will be allowed to campaign freely, even for a sovereign Palestinian-Arab state in Judea, Samaria And Gaza.

If Shamir's 4-points proposal to the Americans meant to get some "time out" he might have been wrong, instead, it can become a "Time Bomb" and hit back Israel like a boomerang, because, it is more likely that it will lead to a maze, a labyrinth, which will end up with a Palestinian-Arab state.

Instead of the 4-points plan proposal Shamir should have told his American counterparts, frankly and openly, that Israel's proposal for peace in the area is the following:

-Eretz Israel is indivisible

-Eretz Israel belongs to the Israelis only

-Peace in the area can be achieved only by separating between the Jewish and Arab population. The Arabs should return to their original countries. The Arab Deportation is an Unavoidable Surgery.

The Transfer is the only solution.

-Israel will never agree to "Territories for Peace". Israel will only agree to give "Peace for Peace."

-Israel will not permit anybody to speculate on her land.

The Israeli proposal for "Free Elections" in Judea, Samaria and the Gaza Strip is completely unrealistic, because all the elected leaders will be either pro-PLO or PLO members, and will also instill unjustified hope and false illusion among the Palestinian-Arabs and the World Community that Israel will eventually agree to a Palestinian-Arab state.

The Israeli interpretation of the Autonomy for the Palestinian-Arab population in Judea, Samaria and Gaza was: An administrative council, elected, for self-rule, and not a legislative council that the Palestinian-Arabs demand, since that would bring a state into being before autonomy is established."

There is an enormous risk in Shamir's plan of elections and Autonomy for the Palestinian-Arab population in Judea, Samaria and Gaza, the risk that it might lead to Palestinian-Arab independence. Autonomy to the Arabs of Judea, Samaria and Gaza, the so-called "Interim Solution" would ultimately lead to the establishment of an independent Palestinian-Arab state. Therefore, Israel should "stay away" from it, like from fire.

Israel should not see itself bound by the Camp David Accord. Israel should have denounced this agreement long ago because this agreement is nothing but a prescription for the establishment of a Palestinian-Arab state in Judea, Samaris and Gaza and a disaster to Israel in a later stage. The only constitutional constraint that could prevent this from happening is Annexation and Transfer.

If the Israeli government, Likud or Labor (Maarah)-they both voted for the agreement with Egypt and the Camp David Accord-realizes the magnitude of its blunder and mistake and wishes to restore its credibility, it must distance itself from that Accord as soon as possible.

"Take heed to thyself, lest thou make a covenant with the inhabitants of the land whither thou goest, lest they be for a snare in the midst of thee." (Exodus 34:12).

By pushing the "Autonomy Option" Mr. Shamir is doing exactly the same mistake as Mr. Shimon Peres did when he pushed his famous "Jordanian Option". The "Jordanian Option" died when King Hussein of Jordan pulled himself out of the game. The "Autonomy Option" will pave the road to the new Palestinian-Arab state, detrimental to the State of Israel, same as the proposed International Conference.

Prime Minister Shamir has trapped himself in the Camp David net. He, who voted against it?

It is thanks to President Husni Mubarak of Egypt and King Hussein of Jordan that the Camp David Accords are being nullified. The insistence of Israeli Prime Minister Shamir to adhere to the Camp David Accords was a big mistake, because, the elections in Judea, Samaria and Gaza followed by interim phase of the autonomy will only strengthen the Arabs' demand for full independence, which will gain the sympathy of the whole world. Therefore, the tactical advantage of such a move is not worth the strategic harm caused, especially, when the PLO takes control over the autonomous areas.

The National Unity Government in Israel believed that the Interim Settlement is essential for the Middle East because it is realistic, pracrtical, workable and responds to the political constraints of most of the regional parties engaged in the peace effort.

Prime Minister's Shamir right wing critics suggested to annex the territories of Judea, Samaria and Gaza.

U.S. officials have made it abundantly clear that they do not view the elections and the autonomy as an end in themselves, but rather as a mean to achieving negotiations on the final status of the territories of Judea, Samaria and the Gaza Strip, which means nothing less than "Territories for Peace", or more accurately, a Palestinian-Arab state.

It is very obvious that the U.S. wants Israel to recognize what the U.S. calls "the legitimate political rights" of the Palestinian-Arabs. Israel will be ready to do it if it is not at the expense of Israel. The so-called "Legitimate Rights" of the Palestinian-Arabs could, and in fact, should, be realized across the border, in Jordan.

If the elections realizes there is very little doubt that the pro-PLO candidates would win, because there will not be other candidates, for fear of being assassinated. The PLO will not permit none-PLO candidates to take part in the elections.

It is very clear that once this "Elections-Autonomy" process starts rolling it will be very difficult, or may be impossible, to stop it. It might stop only temporarily, when the Palestinian-Arab state is established, to celebrate. The Arabs might also take "time out" to catch their breath and then will continue to try to realize their old dream to conquer Israel proper.

Once the peace process is set in motion there would be no way of avoiding a compromise. U.S. and international pressures will be tremendous, and the compromise will be at the expense of Israel. Therefore, Israel must avoid this peace process. Peace negotiations must be prevented at all cost at this stage, until the Transfer Plan is completely executed and the Arab population in Eretz Israel have been displaced, transferred to the neighbouring Arab countries, where they belong, and from where they came.

In their meeting with the U.S. Ambassador to Tunisia Robert Pelletreau, in Tunis, a delegation of PLO officials rejected the idea of the Palestinian-Arabs in the territories (Judea, Samaria and Gaza) holding elections to determine new Palestinian-Arab representatives in peace negotiations. The PLO officials claimed that only the PLO could designate the participants in talks with Israel. U.S. Ambassador to Tunisia, Mr. Pelletreau was not the first American to speak with PLO leaders. Between October 1978 and beginning of 1981, Ambassador John C. Dean to Lebanon had thirty two meetings with PLO leaders in Beirut, in spite of Carter's Administration denials that contact with the PLO ever existed. Philip Habib, U.S. special envoy, continued these negotiations with the PLO until agreement was reached and resulted in a cease-fire on the Israeli-Lebanese border.

Yasser Abed Rabo, who is heading the PLO delegation in the talks with the U.S. Ambassador in Tunis, is Hawatmeh's second-in-command. The Palestinian-Arabs claimed that their sole and only representative is the PLO. Israel, Shamir, should have replied: "Israel will never talk to terrorists and if this is your final attitude there is nothing to talk."

What the PLO is after is direct negotiation with Israel.

Bassam Shakea, former Mayor of Shechem (Nablus) declared: "It is not serious. Proposals, for elections in the territories are just tricks to prolong the Israeli occupation. The Palestinian-Arabs are now united, they want an independent state. Elections are just a tactic, a trick. Until now, we see no signs that the U.S. is ready to meet Palestinian-Arabs's conditions. They talk to the PLO, but they do not recognize it, and they reject the concept of a Palestinian-Arab state. We have did not have any clear sign of another policy."

During the British mandate, in 1920-1921, the Jewish population in Eretz Israel (Palestine) was 10% of the total population. In 1922, it became 20% and in1936-1939 it was already 30%.

In 1936 the Arabs started an uprising against the British rulers and pogroms and violent riots against the Jewish population. The Arabs wanted the British to leave the country, cancel the Balfour Declaration, which called for a Jewish Homeland in Palestine and Independence.

The Jews, though a weak minority, fought back like lions. They crushed the Arab uprising. The Jews did everything possible to maintain their rights to Eretz Israel.

In 1948, at the beginning, Israel was weak and poor, yet, it absorbed over 600,000 people, new immigrants, in three years. It then built a "National Aquaduc" ("Ha'Movil Ha'artzi"}, it dried the Chulah Lake in the Galilee, founded an excellent system of Nuclear Research, Constructed Seven new Universities, constructed several urban and rural settlements, villages, cities, kibbutzim, tens of thousands new housings, an excellent agriculture, a most modern and sophisticated industry, overcame the three figures inflation and reached full economic strength.

In 1989, a great regression, Zero immigration, no settlements, zero idustrial developments, factories were closed, the Lavi project was cancelled, the Two-Seas tunnel project linking the Mediterranean Sea to the Dead Sea in order to produce electrical energy was also cancelled, the agriculture was in the gutters, the Histadrut and its enterprises went bankrupt, Lebanon turned over to the Syrians on a golden platter, Sinai turned over to the Egyptians on a golden platter, losing the Soviet Jews to America, over 100,000 people unemployed and offering the Palestinian-Arabs full autonomy in Judea, Samaria and the Gaza Strip.

In 1989, the Jews in Eretz Israel had a majority. Between the Mediterranean Sea and the Jordan River they formed two thirds of the population. The Arabs were separated geographically in three zones (Israel, Judea, Samaria and the Gaza Strip) without territorial link. The Israelis with the independent State of Israel, with a yearly budget of 50 Billion (Milliard) Shequels (INS) (equivalent to 30 Billion U.S. Dollars), with one of the best trained army in the world and with nuclear capacity, came up with the most ridiculous idea of proposing the Arabs free elections, autonomy, which will eventually and inevitably lead to an independent Palestinian-Arab state, in Judea, Samaria and Gaza. On Israeli soil, at the expense of Israel. For those who believe in autonomy and in co-existence with the Arabs, find disturbing the prospect that extremist threats would make a mockery of whatever autonomy may be reached.

Everybody knows that Judea, Samaria and Gaza are not economically self-sufficient. Economic instability or worse appears to be the result of an independent Palestinian-Arab independent state. A Palestinian-Arab state appears to invite further instability into the Middle East, not stability.

Israeli Prime Minister Yitzhak Shamir must have been under very heavy U.S. pressure to come up with "new ideas" like these, which are far from being the best interests of Israel.

Professor Allen Weinstein from Boston published a few years ago an article in the "Washington Quarterly" describing the methods used by the U.S. Administration to embarrass Israel prior to every sensitive dialogue with Israel

Weinstein analyzed.a series of visits by Israeli prime ministers and foreign ministers in Washington. Before every one of such visit Washington leaked to the news media stories embarrassing to Israel:

-Israeli agents have smuggled out heavy waters from the U.S. Something that never happened.

-The U.S. national television interviewed Jonathan Pollard prior to Shamir's visit on April 1989.

-President Bush's unfortunate remark over the television, prior to Shamir's visit in Washington on April 1989 calling for "the end of Israeli occupation."

-etc., etc., etc.

All this is psychology. To put Israel on the defense when they came to negotiate with the U.S. Administration.

Of course the U.S. is free to say or to do anything it wishes. The U.S. is strong and powerful. But, this is not a way to treat a friend. It does not become a superpower.

Israel should not yield to false propaganda and "moral" pressure, to superficiality and hypocrisy, because if it does it might not have another chance. It will be a terrible mistake if it gambles on its survival. The Arab claim over the land of Israel is nothing but fraud.

The Likud–Maarah coalition in the National Unity Government can exist only if the parties do not try to impose their final solutions upon each other. That's if the Likud do not try to impose their "Greater Israel" policy and the Maarah do not try to impose their "Territorial Compromise" policy. Anyone who tried to impose one or the other would bring about the end of the coalition. The two parties were at odds over the nature of the permanent settlement in Judea, Samaria and the Gaza Strip, yet they both agreed on the "Interim Arrangement" which included elections and autonomy.

On his visit to Paris, on May 1989, the PLO Chairman, Yasser Arafat declared that the PLO Charter, the PLO Covenant was caduc, that's, void, null. Arafat also evoked the existence of two sovereign states, the Palestinian-Arab state and Israel, once again implying the existence of Israel. Arafat cannot abrogate the PLO Charter by a "personal declaration." According to provisions in the document, a two-thirds majority of the Palestinian-Arab National Council is required for any amendments to the Charter.

Article 33 of the PLO Charter reads:

"This Charter shall not be amnded save by (vote of) a majority of two-thirds of the total membership of the National Congress of the Palestinian Liberation Organization, taken at a special session convened for that purpose."

This document is not words written on a piece of paper or parchment. This PLO Charter, this PLO Constitution, is the Moslem ideology of hate of Jews, which is deep in their brains and veins, and, therefore, cannot be changed, not even in ten generations, not even if it gets a two-thirds majority, and any body who believes Arafat that the Charter is no longer valid, that it is caduc, is deceiving himself, is naïve.

France was the first Western country to give Yasser Arafat official reception (the red carpet). Arafat was received by President Francois Mitterand like any other head of state. In spite of the fact that Yasser Arafat didn't have a state yet.

It is amazing how French President Francois Mitterand couldn't have picked up a better day to receive Arafat at the Elysee Palace but on "Yom Ha'Shoah" or "Holocaust Day" (Nissan 27,5749-May 2nd, 1989) when the Jews commemorate the death of Six Million Innocent Jews killed by the Germans during World War II.

President Fancois Mitterand denounced the desecration of the Jewish cemetery at Carpentras and constantly denounced anti-Semitism, yet, he gave Yasser Arafat a royal reception Francois Mitterand shook the hands of an international terrorist and a murderer of Jews and even hugged him. What a hypocrite!

The important question is how can one man nullify a Charter of a large political organization? Cancel, delete the PLO Charter, all by himself, without the vote of the PLO Council, now that he is not yet a prime minister or a president? Arafat is a dictator, doing as he pleases. This means that the PLO, the organization, which Arafat is heading now is hardly a democratic body that Arafat and his friends in the U.S. and the West claim to be. In that case, using a democratic concept like "Self Determination", "The Palestinian Rights", to justify furnishing Arafat and the PLO with a state, stolen from Israel, would be obviously inappropriate.

And the great United States of America is having a dialogue with a master-terrorist, a tyrant, a dictator. Again, repeating its mistake, siding with the wrong party; Ngo Dinh Diem, Nguyen Cao Ky and Nguyen Van Thieu in Vietnam; Ferdinand Marcos in the Philippines; Fulgencio Batista, Y Zaldivar in Cuba, etc., etc. Will America ever learn? At Algiers, Stockholm Geneva and Paris Arafat went to great lengths to state that the PLO recognized Israel's right to exist and that terrorism would end.

The world applaused this well-disguised fraud, but overlooked however the fact that Arafat did not call for amending the PLO Charter, which stipulates the destruction of Israel.

The Popular Front for the Liberation of Palestine-General Command, led by Ahmed Jibreel residing in Damascus, denounced the PLO leader Yasser Arafat as a traitor and appeared to call for his death.

"We are confident that the Palestinian people will carry out the people's verdict against Arafat and all other traitors who abandon the cause of their people", said a PFLP-GC spokesman.

This comment followed Arafat's remarks in Paris that the PLO Charter was absolete.

On May 3, 1989, on Radio Monte Carlo, Yasser Arafat called on Palestinians to "carry on with the intifada until the Palestinian flag is raised in Jerusalem, the capital of the Palestinian State."

Arafat's verbal exhibition and rethoric jugglery is nothing but another exercise of deception, similar to the ones in Algiers, Stockholm and Geneva.

Arafat had been constantly using diplomatic blurring and change of tactics, deceiving everybody. Israel's greatest enemy, in our days, is Yasser Arafat. Extremely shrewd, master-lier, started a "peace assault" on Israel with the intention to shake its lines from the inside and smeer its reputation outside, among the nations, while at the same time ordered his forces to keep the terror against Israel vivid.

The PLO faced with an historic moment and obviously considered reaping all the possible political benefits from the international sympathy, resulting, probably, from the Palestinian-Arab uprising.

Defence Minister Yitzhak Rabin, once known as the man with the "Analytic Brain" didn't foresee or expect the Palestiian-Arab uprising, and when it started, underestimated its meaning and didn't even bother to cut short his visit in the U.S. and return immediately to Israel to handle this new phenomenon. Rabin analysed incorrectly the magnitude and power of the Palestinian-Arab Intifada and its side effects and publicly declared that by force the PLO will never realize any political achievements. The PLO did realize political achievements. They have declared independence. The U.S. is negotiating with them. Francois Mitterand had invited Arafat to Paris and gave him a "Royal Reception". The PLO won the sympathy of the European Community. Again Yitzhak Rabin was wrong.

On his meeting, on May 1989, in Moscow, with Soviet Foreign Minister Eduard Sheverdnadze, U.S. Secretary of State James Baker, rejected a Soviet proposal for a four countries conference, including: the U.S., the Soviet Union, Israel and the PLO. The Soviets had been doing tremendous efforts to get the U.S. full recognition of the PLO and make them equal partners in such a conference.

The European Community was very unhappy to be left out, especially Britain and France, who are permanent members of the UN, and who had high hopes to participate in an International Conference for peace in the Middle East.

In his visit to the Middle East, Soviet Foreign Minister Eduard Sheverdnadze criticized the regional arms race and called for a new political order. Sheverdnadze warned the Syrians that Coexistence, not Confrontation, would be the new Soviet policy in the Middle East. In Cairo, he even used stronger language, saying that a continued arms buildup risked turning the region into a "Museum of Lost Civilizations," and added that the ideology must be removed from the battlefield, and conflicts should be resolved according to a "Balance of Interests" rather than a "Balance of Power".

Syria was worried over Moscow's show of Middle East glasnost manifest. Yet, Syria remains the Soviet's most important client in the Middle East, and as such, must cater to her needs.

Soviet Defence Minister Dmitri Yazov's visit to Damascus intended to appease the Syrians and provide them with reassurances, probably, in the form of supply of new Sukhoi-24 offensive aircraft. In return, the Soviets would expect from Syria some political flexibility and moderation, and a promise from Hafez el-Assad that Syria will not oppose PLO Chairman Yasser Arafat's new initiatives. In short, advanced weapons in exchange for flexibility in the new peace process.

The Soviets have been trying to moderate Syria's position towards the new Middle East peace process, yet, on the other hand, there is ample proof that they have encouraged the PLO to intensify their uprising against Israel in order to use this intifada as a tool with which they believe they can dictate the terms in a Middle East settlement. The Soviet's attempt to maintain a glasnost foreign policy and also satisfy Syria's demands for a military hardware will not be easy, because the Soviets' military concessions to Hafez el-Assad undermine their efforts to moderate Syria's attitude on the Middle East peace process. By increasing the Syrian arsenal the Soviet help boost up the Syrian self-confidence, which might create a situation in which Syria might feel strong enough to undermine the peace process by a military operation against Israel, just to show the U.S. and the Soviets that Syria cannot be left out.   Syria needs Soviet weapons not only against Israel but also against Iraq. Since the end of the Iran-Iraq war Syria has been very worried about the military threat posed to her on her eastern border by the Iraqis. More than that, Iraq has been helping Lebanon's Christians to throw off the Syrian yoke. Assad is afraid to send more of his forces into Lebanon to crush the Christian uprising there, thus exposing his easten border to the Iraqis. This is why Syria needs Soviet arms: Sukhoi-24, MIG-29 interceptor fighters, latest T-72 tanks, ground-to-ground missiles, etc. The Sovists, in return, receive from Syria a naval base in the port of Tartus, one of the Russians' major Mediterranean bases in a region dominated by NATO's fleets.

The Soviets need Syria, not because of her political weight, but because of her strategic location. The Soviets would try everything to realize their old dream of a U.S.-Soviet condominium in the Middle East, and an access to the "warm" waters of the Mediterranean. Moscow would have liked the U.S. to recognize the Soviets as an equal partner, an equal superpower. Moscow would have also liked Israel to recognize the PLO. They believed they could realize it by intensifying the PLO uprising, the intifada.

The U.S. had been trying to moderate the PLO before negotiations on the "Peace Process" begin. On the other hand, the Soviets did just the opposite. They believed that only by intensifying the Palestinian uprising they could reach their mutual goals.

On May 14th, 1989, by a convincing majority of twenty Cabinet ministers versus six, the Israeli Cabinet endorsed Shamir's peace proposal. Ariel (Arik) Sharon (Likud), Yitzhak Modai (Mazevitch) (Likud), David Levi (Likud), Avner Shaky (NRP), EzerWeizman (Maarah) and Rafi Edri (Maarah) voted against Shamir's proposal.

The U.S. Administration was pleased by the Israeli Cabinet approval of the Prime Minister's proposal and undertook to pursue and promote the plan.

It was not the obligation of the Israeli National Unity Government to come up with "Peace Initiatives" because it was not Israel that broke the peace in the area. The Arabs were the ones that broke the peace by invading Israel in 1948 and spreading destruction and death in the Middle East.

This Israeli initiative could be misinterpreted. The world could think that Israel was the belligerent and is now trying to make up.

The Israeli "Peace Initiative" could be interpreted as readiness to yield to pressures which would endanger Israel's sovereignty over the mainland and heart of the country, that's over Judea, Samaria and Gaza. This readiness is nothing but the result of the constant biting of the Israeli doves and Left into the moral strength and confidence of the nation. Thus supporting Israel's worse enemies in their lie that a Palestinian-Arab entity ever existed.

The Israeli Cabinet voted over a document called: "A Peace Initiative by the Government of Israel," which included eight paragraphs and twenty sub-paragraphs.

The eight paragraphs were:

a. General.
b. Basic Premises
c. Subjects to be dealt with in the Peace Process
d. The principles Constituting the Initiatives:
   A. Stages
   B. Timetable.
e. Parties Participating in the Negotiations in Both Stages
f. Substance of Transitional Period
g. Substance of Permanent Solution
h. Details of Process for the Implementation of the Initiative

After their meeting in Tunis on May 15, 1989 (Iyar 10, 5749), the executive committee of the PLO declared that: "the Israeli peace plan approved on May 14, 1989 (Iyar 9, 5749), by the Israeli Cabinet was a "farce", because it ignored the right of the Palestiian-Arabs to an independent homeland." The committee added that: "the Israeli plan was also flawed because it did not mention Israeli withdrawal from the territories of Judea, Samaria and Gaza." The plan was addressed to Jordan and excluded by the PLO representative of the Palestinian-Arab people.

"The committee sees that this proposal does not concern the Palestinian-Arab people, because it fails to recognize their existence as a nation," said a statement issued by the fifteen-member committee of the PLO after a meeting at their Tunis headquarters. The statement continued:"The proposal by the Israeli Government expose the essence of the call for elections as being no more than a farce designed to deceive world opinion and consolidate the occupation, accompanied by an escalation of its iron-fist crackdown against the Palestinian-Arab people and the intifada."

On May 15, 1989 (Iyar 10, 5749), Defence Minister Yitzhak Rabin started promoting Israel's peace initiative in Judea, Samaria and the Gaza Strip by meeting with fifteen Palestinian-Arab public figures to explain the Government's initiative and convince the Palestinian-Arabs to accept this initiative.

Among the Palestinian-Arabs summoned to the Civil Administration office in Beit-El were Bethlehem Mayor Elias Freij, two businessmen from Nablus (Shechem), Said Kanaan and Subhi Anabtawi (who is believed to be an Islamic activist), Dr. Hatem Abu Ghazaleh, also from Shechem (Nablus), Dr. Thabet Thabet of Tulkarem (recently released from administrative detention), Attorney Jamil Tarifee of Ramallah and Muhammed Ja'abari of Hebron (considered pro-Jordanian).

Palestinian-Arabs affiliated with Left wing factions who oppose the elections were not invited, nor were persons who signed a petition by eighty prominent Palestinian-Arabs against the election proposals of the Israeli Government.

Rabin urged these Palestinian-Arabs to accept the offer and not to miss this historic chance to advance their cause. He told them that this initiative was basically for the interim period and in order to break the stalemate, yet, it is also linked to talks on the final settlement, based on UN Security Council Resolutions 242 and 338. He also told them that the initiative has received the endorsement of the United States, Britain, Spain, France, Italy, etc., etc.

U.S. Secretary of State James Baker was following the traditional U.S. policy when he wanted to "convince" Israel to help carry out the U.S. policy in the Middle East, and like his predecessors, Shultz and others, sent over "Landsmans". A "Jewish Delegation", which included Denis Ross, Richard Hass, Aron David Miller and Dan Kurtzer, all high, senior officials in the U.S. Administration, who accompanied James Baker in his recent trip to Moscow.

Six Palestinian-Arabs were scheduled to meet with the visiting State Department team, headed by Denis Ross, on May 16, 1989 (Iyar 11, 5749), in East Jerusalem, after rejecting their meeting on Sunday, May 14, 1989, with the American officials due to dissatisfaction over the guest list.

The Palestinian-Arabs attending the meeting were: Dr. Sari Nusseibeh of Bir Zeit University, Ziad Abu Zayyad, editor of the Palestinian Hebrew-language newspaper Gesher, Izzedin Aryan, head of the Red Crescent Society in Judea, Samaria And Gaza, Zahira Kamal, head of the Women's Work Committee, Ghassan al-khatib also of Bir Zeit and Dr.Zakaria al-Agha, head of the Arab Medical Society in Gaza.

The participants did not include Islamic activists or Pro-Jordanians. All the six refused to attend the Sunday meeting because the Americans have invited Dr.Mahmoud a-Zahar, a prominent backer of the Islamic Resistence Movement (Hamas) in Gaza. Hamas and the PLO have been rivals for control of the Seventeen–month-old intifada. Also they attributed their absence on Sundays to the large numbers of invitees.

The Six requested an additional "properly coordinated" meeting in which they will decide on the participants. The request was granted.

The most prominent Cabinet opponents of the Premier's Peace Plan were Ariel Sharon and Yitzhak Modai. Modai even proposed that Shamir resigns.

Minister Yitzhak Modai (Likud) charged Premier Yitzhak Shamir with betrayal of Likud principles and called for his immediate resignation, to be followed by new elections. This proposal could be realized only if the Likud's Central Committee were to turn thumbs down on Shamir's initiative, and if Shamir were to take that as an invitation to step down. Shamir already hinted that, in such an event he would resign.

On May 17, 1989 (Iyar 12, 5749), A dozen Likud Knesset members, including two Cabinet Ministers, absented themselves from the Knesset plenum rather than vote confidence in the Government's peace plan. Nevertheless, by a vote of 43 to 15, with 11 absentions, the government succeeded to receive the Knesset's endorsement to its initiative.

Mrs. Geulah Cohen from Ha'Tehiyah, who voted against Shamir's initiative commented:"Instead of coming before the House with a programme to end the Arab uprising Shamir had presented one that encouraged the uprising."

"I don't understand," said Yair Sprinzak from Moledet, also moving non-confidence. "Do the Arabs stand a chance that we will ever agree to a Palestinian-Arab state, yes or no? If no, then why not say so now? If yes, then why don't you tell us that?" The elderly ultra-right winger told Shamir, "Israel could fully permit itself to say a resounding no to any American dictate. If Shamir could not bring himself to do that, he should go home and leave the decision to the people," said Sprinzak

On May 17, 1989 (Iyar 12, 5749), Minister Ariel Sharon convened a meeting of Likud activists in his home, in East Jerusalem, to discuss the possibility of defeating Prime Minister Shamir's plan for the territories of Judea, Samaria and Gaza.

Sharon, as well as many others, believes that Shamir's plan will bring neither peace nor security. It is more likely that it could bring a new Palestinian-Arab independent state, at the expense of Israel, on Israeli soil.

Sharon, who chairs the Likud Central Committee, formally informed the Prime Minister Yitzhak Shamir of his intention to convene the Committee, sometimes in early June, to discuss the plan.

The split in the Likud party places in doubt Shamir's ability to receive the endorsement or approval of his party to the plan.

In their meeting in Sharon's home, Sharon told about thirty Likud members of the Knesset that Shamir's plan was dangerous. Sharon attacked Prime Minister Shamir for not including in his plan any mention of Jerusalem. "Over which the whole issue will be decided."

Sharon criticized Shamir for threatening with resignation should his plan be rejected by the Likud.

"We do not oppose the idea of a diplomatic initiative," Sharon said, "but we have to introduce changes and make additions. At the Committee meeting I shall demand that Shamir's plan formally incorporate pledges not to include East Jerusalem in the process, not to hold elections before the end of the intifada, not to negotiate with the PLO, in any way, and not to consider the possibility of eventual disengagement from any of Judea, Samaria and Gaza."

In a conversation with NRP (National Religious Party) leaders, Shamir charged Sharon, his party colleague, with seeking a fight with the U.S. Administration, which Shamir believed would be unwise.

Same as Shimon Peres before, with his "Jordanian Option", Shamir was totally carried away with his new initiative. It became an obsession or may be tactics.

Same as Shimon Peres did not invent the idea of an International Peace Conference for the Middle East, as it was originally a Soviet-Arab plan, so it was neither Yitzhak Shamir nor Yitzhak Rabin who came up with the idea of elections in Judea, Samaria and the Gaza Strip, but the PLO, to promote their plan of establishing a new Palestinian-Arab state.

On May 17, 1989, U.S. Secretary of State James Baker endorsed the Israeli proposal for Palestinian-Arab elections in Judea, Samaria and the Gaza Strip and called it "A Practical Mechanism" that could lead to direct Israeli-Palestinian Arab negotiations.

In a televised "Worldnet" interview with journalists in Western Europe, Baker said that Prime Minister Shamir's plan "has some potential and it gives us something to work with."

Mr. Baker was completely wrong, same as Mr. Shamir, because Shamir's plan, Shamir's initiative, was created as a result of tremendous American pressure, and one must be blind not to see or realize that it is a practical mechanism and a potential to the establishment of a new Palestinian-Arab state in Judea, Samaria and Gaza. An idea which most of the Israelis oppose categorically, and hopefully the Americans too, at least this is what the U.S. Administration is claiming. If such an Arab state is realized, the problems which it will bring along with it will be hundred times as many as the problems Israel, the U.S., the World Community is facing now.

On May 17, 1989 (Iyar 12, 5749), in a dramatic bid to rally their support in the plenum debate on an opposition non-confidence vote, Prime Minister Yitzhak Shamir told his Likud faction colleagues that: "We shall not give the Arabs one inch of our land, even if we have to negotiate for ten years. We won't give them a thing."

A dozen of them threatened to either vote against the government or to slip out of the chamber before the voting on the non-confidence motion.

"We hold the veto in our hands," Shamir told his party colleagues, "what could be better than that?"

"I shall not knuckle under to external pressure or to internal pressure," Shamir added.

To further pressure them Shamir promised them that the elections would not be prepared or conducted while the intifada was in progress. There will be no negotiations with the Arabs in an atmosphere of violence. As far as he was concerned, Shamir said, Arab residents of East Jerusalem would have no part in the process, and would neither vote nor be elected.

Shamir used words not exactly pleasing to the Americans. The U.S. Administration reacted promptly by advising Israel not to add more settlements in Judea, Samaria and the Gaza Strip.

In spite of the fact that Shamir's initiative was meant for the Palestinian Arabs of Judea, Samaria and the Gaza Strip, the United States of America was still having a dialogue with the PLO.

There is also another version for the reasons why Sharon, Modai and Levi opposed Shamir's initiative. The personal grudge left since the November 1988 elections.

Shamir deprived Sharon from the Defence Ministry and gave it to Rabin. Shamir deprived Modai from the Treasury and gave it to Peres. Shamir deprived Levi from the Foreign Ministry and gave it to Moshe Arens. And this, the three cannot forget and forgive. More than that, Shamir broke deals that Sharon and Modai made with the religious parties, on his behalf, after these elections.

Once Shamir's Peace Process gets under way, other, unexpected forces could come into play. Where the initiative leads will not necessarily be dependent on its original designers. If Shamir's Initiative, the elections in Judea, Samaria and Gaza, is ever carried out, Israel will have no alternative but to negotiate later, directly with the PLO, because the PLO will win a landslide in these elections.

Mr. Ariel Sharon, Likud Central Committee Chairman set a meeting for July 1989. The Committee will probably deal with Shamir's initiative, rejected by Sharon, Modai and Levi.

Prime Minister Shamir was taking the uproar in the Likud party over the government's peace plan very seriously and was launching an intensive lobbying effort to ensure its approval at the party's Central Committee meeting to be convened sometime in July 1989.

Yitzhak Shamir is facing this time not only the opposition of Ministers Sharon, Modai and Levi but also half of the Likud members of Knesset who are demanding changes in the plan, in order to reduce the danger of a Territorial Compromise. Shamir barely escaped defeat in the last committee meeting in December 1988, when he requested the approval to form the Unity Government. "In December we went to the Committee a little overconfident," said Shamir's spokesman. "This time, there will be some serious legwork invested in ensuring success. This time we shall do our homework better."

Shamir's basic strategy, though, will, probably, be the same. As in December 1988, Shamir indicated again that he viewed the issue as a personal vote of confidence and would resign if his plan is rejected by the members of the Committee. The move was effective in the last confrontation in the Committee, but would not have been enough without David Levi's support. Shamir will do his utmost to persuade Levi again, to change his mind and vote for the plan.

Levi's camp in the Likud has taken a beating during the past year, yet, it still constitute a quarter to a third of the Central Committee and controls the balance of power between Shamir-Arens camp and Sharon-Modai camp.

Member of Knesset Benjamin Begin, the ex-prime minister's son, accused Modai of "using a cover of ideology to obscure personal aspirations," and added, that "it is inconceivable that a Likud Minister ask a Likud prime minister to resign."

As if Mr. Begin himself did not have political aspirations. The people in Israel haven't forgotten his appearance on television a few years ago, declaring that he had a very interesting profession, as a geologist, had no political aspirations, and didn't want to become a Member of Knesset. Yet, he did become a Member of Knesset.

Sharon joined forces with the Ultra-Right MKs from the Complete Israel Front (Israel, Judea, Samaria and the Gaza Strip) also known as Eretz Israel Ha'Shlemah Front, and is demanding the formal introduction of changes in the government's plan.

Addressing to the annual conference of the American Israel Public Affairs Committee, better known as AIPAC, or Israel's Washington lobby, U.S. Secretary of State James Baker finally revealed publicly and for the first time, on Monday, May 22, 1989 (Iyar 17, 5749), the real American policy in the Middle East.Finally the U.S. had the courage to spell it out, that, as a final settlement, the U.S.policy is to support the establishment of a self-governing Palestinian-Arab entity in the territories of Judea, Samaria and the gaza Strip, which would be "acceptable" to the Palestinian-Arabs, Israel and Jordan. This means an independent Palestinian-Arab state. Thus confirming the American departure from the 1982 Reagan Plan, which envisaged a Palestinian-Arab self-government "in association with Jordan."

"We do have an idea about the reasonable middle ground to which a settlement should be directed," Baker said. "That is self-government for Palestinian-Arabs in the West Bank and Gaza in a manner acceptable to the Palestinian-Arabs, Israel and Jordan. Such a formula provides ample scope for Palestinian-Arabs to achieve their full political rights. It also provides ample protection for Israel's security."

U.S. Secretary James Baker's settlements were no policy innovations. The Israelis are far from being dumb. They saw, long ago, the "Handwriting on the Wall". The idea of territory-for-peace had, for forty years, since June 1967, been the American approach to a settlement of the Arab-Israeli conflict. Also, U.S. opposition to Israeli settlement in Judea, Samaria and Gaza, had been made clear to Israel on several earlier occasions.

Therefore, President Bush's appeasing words to balance Baker's Middle East policy is Bush's nice and soft words and the fact that he repeats, once and again, that the U.S. policy hasn't changed, means only, that the U.S. is driving towards a new Palestinian-Arab state, in Judea, Samaria and the Gaza Strip, at the expense of Israel.

U.S. Secretary of State James Baker made an unfortunate declaration when he said, that: "Israel should abandon its unrealistic dreams of Greater Israel". More U.S. pressure on Israel to accept a new Palestinian-Arab state in its midst, in Jewish Judea, Samaria and Gaza.

One of Baker's predecessors, Ex-Secretary of State Rogers learned that when outside pressure is applied on Israel, there is no more left and right. Left and Right unite and stand like a rock against this outside pressure.

Since 1948, similar pressurese were exirted on Israel, on and off, but, so far, without success. A sovereign state like Israel, would not take dictates from others and no matter who they are. Besides, Israel was never dealing with dreams, Israel was dealing with reality and what is more realistic than its survival.

James Baker controversial "evenhanded" talk at the American Israeli Committee (AIPAC) policy conference in Washington, on May 22, 1989, certainly provides the U.S. Administration's thinking on the Israel-Arab dispute. According to James Baker, the vision of a Greater Israel was unrealistic, that Israel had to forswear annexation and permanent control over Judea, Samaria and Gaza, stop settlements and reach out "to the Palestinian-Arabs as neighbours who deserve political rights." Certainly, no U.S. Administration official, since 1967, had been so blunt, so "frank", in counseling Israel how to handle its policy.

The public tone of the new administration, which started with President George Bush's public declaration of the "need to end the occupation"-is totally different from that of the outgoing Reagan's Administration.

Bush and Baker are not Reagan and Shultz. It's a completely different breed. They are far from being "vegetarians". They have led a very ugly and dirty election campaign against Michael Dukakis. They are both extremely ambitious and hate to be losers. The Bush-Baker Administration has shown itself to be the most hostile to Israel since the Eisenhower-Dulles Administration of the mid 1950's. It's "Golden Calf" is the Arab barrel of oil.

With all due respect, Israel is not a U.S. colony. Therefore, the language of Mr. James Baker is unbecoming and insulting.

Visiting Israeli Defence Minister Yitzhak Rabin openly criticized Baker for raising at this early stage the most sensitive issues that would have to be dealt with later, in this second stage of the negotiations, when the final solution is on the agenda.

According to ABC's "Good Morning America" television programme, Rabin said that the Israeli Government's call for Palestinian-Arab elections in the territories of Judea, Samaria and Gaza was "the only operative initiative" right now.

"I believe that whoever now starts to deal with the ingredients, the major issues of the ultimate solution, will not help to move ahead the start of the Peace Process," he said.

"We know that there is a wide gap between the positions of the Arabs, the Palestinian-Arabs and Israel on what should be the permanent solution," Rabin continued. "The whole idea of the initiative is to move by phases. Phase number one doesn't commit any one of the two sides to give up whatever they want to see in the permanent solution. Any dealing now with the components of the permanent solution will bring about stalmate and freeze all political activities."

Rabin was very upset by the Baker speech, regarding it as needlessly provocative. Baker tried to defend his controversial speech on the Arab-Israeli Peace Process delivered on Monday, May 22, 1989 (Iyar 17, 5749), before members of the Israeli lobby in Washington.

"I think it was a very balanced speech," he told reporters at a news briefing. "If you look at the speech in its entirely, you see that it was very balanced with respect to what we think is required of all parties. If we're going to move forward, make progress toward peace, in the Middle East. It calls on the Palestinian-Arabs, it calls on the Israelis, it calls on the Soviets and it says what we really think needs to be done."

James Baker's statement only strengthened the long suspicion of Prime Minister's Yitzhak Shamir's colleagues in the Likud party, Ariel Sharon, Yitzhak Modai And David Levi, and others. Bakers's words were strong proof of what the U.S. has in store for Israel if the government's peace plan, the Shamir- in initiative, is or is not implemented. This, in spite of the U.S. declaration that it is against the establishment of a Palestinian-Arab state on Israeli soil. Baker's declaration proves the opposite. Baker's statements will probably blow Shamir's chances of gaining approval for his plan in the Likud Central Committee, when convened on June 1989.

Minister David Levi who opposes Shamir's plan and whose support may be critical for Shamir in the Central Committee, said that Baker's statements are "very seriously worrying" and should be met by a "fitting response" on the part of Israel.

"We cannot conceivably ignore the statements, as they concern our security and future, and silence will be seen as approval," Levi said.

National Religious Party Minister Avner Shaki also opposed the plan in the Cabinet vote. Shaki commented on Bakers's statement and said that: "it constitutes a withdrawal from their (the U.S.) previous position," as they mean that the U.S. is determining a priori what the terms of the final settlement will be.

Likud MK Michael Eitan, a leader of the Eretz Israel Front, said: "that the U.S. was again using brute force to put pressure on Israel and Machiavellian methods of leaks to the presss, combined with statements such as Baker's, to leave Arens and Shamir hanging in mid-air."

Michael Eitan continued:" On one hand, they (Shamir and Arens) have proposed the plan, which I believe was excessively conciliatory, and on the other they got nothing from the U.S., which continues to represent the PLO before it represents us, instead of the other way around."

Vice-Premier Shimon Peres said that Baker's statements "show that the disagreements between the U.S. and the Likud, which appeared to have disappeared, have resurfaced. The U.S. wants to create position that both sides will be able to agree on. It is a very difficult move, but one that should be made."

Peres protested Baker's implication that "the Likud's positions were those of the Israeli Government."

The general mood of the Israelis after hearing Baker's statement calling for a ban on settlement, seemed to be one of defiance reactions in the streets, were like: "They want to ménage the entire world? Why is it their business? Or "No one tells them where to live, in Illinois or Texas or anywhere else so why do they stick their nose in our affairs? When they invaded Vietnam did anybody stop them?" others, more restrained, were equally critical of the Americans: "We gave the whole of Sinai, but shrink Israel still further? That's Suicide!" Or "Israel is so small we shouldn't forego even one square inch."

Defence Minister Yitzhak Rabin appealed to the U.S. Administration to more forcefully underline its support for the Israeli plan without sending "Mixed Signals" to the Arabs (in Casablanca).

A debate over who should represent Lebanon delayed the schedule opening of an emergency Arab summit in Casablanca, on Tuesday, May 23, 1989 (Iyar 18, 5749).

Egypt's triumphant return to the Arab League overshadowed Yasser Arafat's plan, who wanted the Palestinian-Arab issue to take center-stage at the summit.

The Lebanese seat remained empty when the formal summit opened. Egyptian President Husni Mubarak, whose country was suspended by the Arab League ten years ago because of it's peace treaty with Israel, took his seat in the conference hall alongside seventeen other Arab heads of state.

The PLO delegation to the summit requested Arab backing for its rejection of Israel's election plan for the territories.

The formal Arab reaction to the Israeli peace initiative of May 14, 1989, came a couple of weeks later in the declaration of the Arab League summit in Casablanca. It included the following policy guidelines:

"These are elements destined to bring about the liberation of the Palestinian and Arab lands, which have been occupied since 1967, from the Israelis, to enable the Palestinian-Arab people to realize its long-term national right, including its Right to Return, to self-determination and to the establishment of its independent national state, with its capital Jerusalem, under the leadership of the PLO, is sole legitimate representative, and to concentrate Arab resources in all fields, in order to obtain total strategic parity against the aggressive plan of Israel, and to retain the Arab rights."

According to British officials, the discussion between Prime Minister Shamir and British Foreign Minister sir Geoffrey Howe, in London, on May 23, 1989, "did not get anywhere, because the vital factor of territory for peace was missing." Once more, the British were very generous to speculate with Israeli territories.

British officials applauded Baker's statements and noted that Britain could not endorse Shamir's "fundamentally flawed" peace plan, because it made no provisions for "Territories for Peace" compromise or include direct talks with the PLO.

Neither Margaret Thatcher of Britain, nor Francois Mitterand of France is Israel's enemy. But, they are also not exactly Israel's lovers. They are both basically wrong in their perception of the situation in the Middle East and their understanding of the Israeli-Arab conflict. They were misled by Mr. Shimon Peres and his Maarah's policy of "Territories for Peace." For several years Shimon Peres nurtured them with a wrong concept, which was far from serving the best political interest of Israel.

To satisfy the Arabs as well as their own conscience, for hurting Israel, they can always say that they were only supporting the policy of the Maarah.

Prime Minister Shamir, in his visit to London, on May 23, 1989 (Iyar 18, 5749), dismissed as "useless" and unhelpful U.S. Secretary of State James Baker's call for Israel to grant the Palestinian-Arabs their political rights and abandon "the unrealistic vision of a Greater Israel."

Baker's demands-that Israel "forswear annexation, stop settlement activity, allow schools to reopen"-were rejected by Shamir as "details" that were "unrelated to the broader principles of his peace proposals."

"I cannot agree to what he said," Shamir told a press conference in London, "I don't think these issues, on which we differ, have anything to do with the peace initiative."

Shamir believed that Baker was addressing himself prematurely to issues that will be relevant in the second negotiation stage, the final solution to the territories of Judea, Samaria and Gaza.

"After elections had taken place and negotiations on a permanent solution were under way," Shamir said, "may be all these issues will be addressed and received, it was therefore, useless for Baker to have raised them now."

And when one says, the Secretary of State James Baker, one means President George Bush, because James Baker is only carrying out, to the letter, the Presideny's policy.

James Baker asked the Israelis to abandon their "Unrealistic" dream of the "Complete Israel" (Eretz Israel Ha'Shlemah") also called "Greater Israel". In fact Mr. Baker told the Israelis to forget about part, the greatest part, of Judea, Samaria and the Gaza Strip.

"Unrealistic" is something that looks impossible. Yet, the Jewish nation that exists already sixty centuries (5,750) is in itself an unrealistic phenomenon, a great impossible.

The Jewish nation that underwent all kinds of unrealistic processes, many times, in front of the eyes of the whole world, views dreams, wishes and visions in a completely different scale or standard.

To survive two thousand years, without a territory, without a common language, without a common economy, without physical unity, without political entity, thousands of miles far apart from each other, to constantly struggle against the pressure of assimilation, to become permanent refugees, wandering from continent to continent, from country to country and still keep your image, your unique Jewish identity; to dream, think, operate and drive all to the only one goal, the return to Zion, and then also sealize it, is in itself an unrealistic vision, an impossible task and a deviation from every natural known rule.

The very existence of the Jews in the world is a constant, continued struggle against the "unrealistic", against the "impossible" and against every rule or law by which the rest of the world abides.

Scanning through the history of mankind, we cannot find a similar example of another people, another nation, that after two thousand years of sufferings and oppressions was capable to regroup, refill its empty batteries with new energies, enough to turn back the wheels of history, restore its independence, its national conscientiousness, its ancient language, its will power to survive and even gather back its scattered sheep from the four corners of the world.

Is this not the fulfilment of an unrealistic vision? Is this not the fulfilment of the impossible?

Scanning through the history of mankind we cannot find a similar example of another people, another nation, that survived under such harsh conditions, for such a long period, with a stubborn refusal to, assimilate with its environment, lose its religion, lose its tradition, lose its identity and disappear from the surface of the earth.

Is this not the fulfilment of an unrealistic vision? Is this not the fulfilment of the impossible?

Looking back to the efforts and sacrifices invested, to the obstacles overcome, one cannot help from concluding that for the Jews nothing is impossible. It just doesn't exist.

Unlike others, for Jews, unrealistic vision is revived, it is the click that makes their hearts beat, the reactor that supplies them with vital energy.

Those who in the nineteen century dreamed of the return to Zion and the restoration of a Jewish state were certainly "irrational", "impractical". Their vision was certainly unrealistic.

It was not difficult to foresee all the negative elements, all the objective obstacles awaiting them. Not used to the hot climate during the summers, in Eretz Israel (Palestine), unable to do physical labour, reluctant to carry guns, etc. On one hand, the strong religious belief that they are the sole owners of the land, and, on the other hand, the obstinate Turkish opposition to such a heretic idea.

All these were more than enough to make anybody realize that his vision was an unrealistic plan of a nation with frivolous imagination.

Those who said then, in the nineteenth century, that the Jews are a nation and not a religious sect, that the bond of the Jews with their country is a legend, but cannot be broken, those who believed that their sufferings would supply them with the necessary political energy to realize their old dream, were considered fool, insane.

Everybody was against it. The Turks were against it, the Arabs were against it, the Pope was against it, the British were against it, the European Community was against it. Everybody rejected the idea.

All the pessimistic prophecies of all the realistic, rational, practical, sane people, came true. The Jews didn't go to Israel when they were free to do so, the country couldn't absorb all the new immigrants who poured in, the funds were not available, the Arabs resisted with arms in their hands, unemployment was sky high, a great Jewish emigration from the country, the British put every obstacle they could think of to slow down the Zionist movement, or even, eliminate its British land purchase restrictions. Jewish immigration restricted. Jewish settlement restricted. All the black prophecies did realize, as predicted, except for one thing.

Those who believed that the difficulties will force the Jews to give up their plans and that their visions will disappear were totally wrong. The unrealistic visions overcame all the obstacles. One hundred years, after modest beginnings, Eretz Israel included a Jewish state, the State of Israel. A state which contained one third of all the Jews in the world.

True, the state was full of problems,economical,social,political etc. But there was a State.

All the hopes of an ancient people that refused to die, were realized. They broke all roadblocks, they overcame all obstacles, they won and they are on the map, and up to this date they haven't given away their old vision of a "Complete Israel". They still insist on having it, and holding to it.

One wonders why U.S. Secretary of State James Baker called it "Greater Israel," as it is smaller than Belgium, Holland, Denmark, Switzerland, or even Jordan.

Yet, Eretz Israel includes the landscape in which the Jewish nation was born, its faith and character crystallized, and in which were recorded the most exalted chapters in its history.

The settlements founded until now, with the help of God, will provide strength and inspiration for the coming days. Indeed, if we continue to gain ground in this enterprise, we shall doubtless prosper with the help of God, in accordance with the efforts invested. We may then trust that gradually the idea of settlement in Eretz Israel will spread and will be embraced by the entire nation.

Anyone following the rise of the Yishuv (the Jewish population in Eretz Israel) with open eyes will realize that it enjoys Divine protection. How else could we have weathered all the storms and stresses of the hostile machineries that more than once threatened the very survival of the yishuv? Not withstanding our enemies numerical superiority sustained thrusts against the Yishuv, the ideal of Jewish national resurrection has retained its pulsating vitality. Surely, this is incontestable evidence of overt Divine Providence.

The establishment of the State of Israel on May 15, 1948 (Iyar 5, 5708), was the realization of their vision, the fulfillment of their redemption, so long waited.

The victory in the Six-Day War, on June 1967, brought them back the most important parts that were still missing: Jerusalem, Hebron, Bethlehem, Schechem, Jericho, the Dead Sea and the Jordan Valley.

If Mr. James Baker expects Israel to give away part of these territories he is totally unrealistic. Israel will, probably, never do it. Anybody who thinks he can make Israel give away part of its two thousand years vision is completely wrong and totally unrealistic.

The friendly U.S. Administration "advised" that a Jew should not settle in his own paternal land. Land restriction on Jews, in their own country!

To order a sovereign country what to do in its own land was just going a little too far.

Everybody heard of the Carter-Begin disagreement over Jewish settlement in Judea, Samaria and Gaza. When President Jimmy Carter said that the settlements were illegal, Prime Minister Menachem Begin answered: "First, that those settlements were necessary for Israel's security, hence they were legal. Also the point of view of international law as adopted by Israel's Supreme Court. Second, that even in the U.S.A. it would be inconceivable to prohibit Jews from settling in specified locations, so how could one suggest it in the Jewish ancestral homeland?"

The argument ended when President Ronald Reagan, Carter's successor in the White House, expressed the opposite opinion in his 1980 presidential campaign, that, the settlements "were not illegal."

Israel's survival is a very important factor for both the Jews of Israel and the Jews of the diaspora. Israel's survival is much much longer than any other nation living today on this planet. Much longer than the survival of the U.S.A., which is only 200 years old. This is why Israel is capable of seing beyond its present range of difficulties. Israel has always the future in its mind.

We have all seen how an isolated settlement established in remote "hostile country" without resources, without a chance to survive, have become base of power and the foundation of a state. We have also seen how the resistance of the Arabs, the intriguing and plotting of the great powers, Britain and others, were dissolved by the firm resolution of those "dreamers," or "vision cariers," who did not give up their vision just because it looked difficult or impossible. Impossibl, unrealistic, just doesn't exist in their vocabulary.

Israel will refuse and reject any proposals or restrictions, which will prevent Israelis from building their houses and raise their children, any place they please, in their paternal land, in their old country of Eretz Israel.

The Jews, the Israelis have proved it time and again that in matters of faith, belief and conviction, Israel is not afraid to go it alone, even if many believe that it is impractical or unrealistic.

The U.S. State Department was against partition and against the establishment of a Jewish state in Eretz Israel, in 1948. And, since then it has been trying to get rid of Israel. The U.S. State Department almost succeeded to choke Israel to death. It tried but did not succeed to stop President Harry Truman from recognizing Israel, but it did covince him to join the international arms embargo against Israel, then fighting for its life against five invading Arab armies.

The State Department never got tired and has not abandoned its goal and it carries on under different guises and Munich-Style "Land for Peace" schemes that all have one thing in common: they are all designed to fatally weaken and delegitimies the State of Israel.

The U.S. State Department has constantly supported the fraudulent claim of the Palestinian Arabs for a separate national identity and a second homeland (in addition to Jordan) and has opposed the right of the Jews (but not the Arabs) to live on historically Jewish land in the suburbs of Jerusalem and Tel Aviv.

The Bush-Baker Administration has been the most relentlessly hostile toward Israel of any previous American administration. George Bush and James Baker seem to be in complete accord with the policies of the U.S. State Department that have been pursued since 1948 by a pro-Arab bureaucracy whose anti-semitism is well documented in books by former presidential adviser Clark Clifford (Truman's) and by Lt. Col. Oliver North in his 1991 best seller "Under Fire."

By questioning the right of Jewish settlement in Judea, Samaria and Gaza, President George Bush has betrayed the Bible-thumping frontier spirit that made America great.

Neither Bush's reaffirmation of Israel's security rights, nor Baker's emphacize of the value of U.S.-Israel strategic partnership, could not make up with the painful fact that the passage of time had effected no revision in the basic U.S. concept of the Israeli-Arab peace. In spite of the many years elapsed, the United States of America hasn't bothered to understand what the real needs of its strategic partner were, and still sticks to its old "Even Handed" policy, which is far from being the best interest of Israel and even dangerous for her existence.

For over two decades every new U.S. administration concluded, on the advice of the State Department's Near East Affairs Bureau, that the Israeli-Arab conflict needed urgent U.S. attention, and every U.S. peace plan, in essence, a variation of the Rogers Plan.

Everybody in Israel could not understand the U.S. myopia.

Using rather blunt language, the U.S. has again warned Israel against increasing West Bank settlement activity and against deporting more Palestinian-Arabs from the territories.

During a meeting on June 2, 1989, at the State Department, Deputy Secretary Lawrence Eagleburger told Israeli Ambassador Moshe Arad that the Bush Administration strongly opposed what it regards as unnecessary provocative Israeli policies in the territories.

Mr. Lawrence Eagleburger didn't call the PLO representative demanding that the PLO stops the intifada. Again, the U.S. "Even Handed" policy". Some more pressure on Israel.

On June 29, 1989 (Sivan 26, 5749), U.S. officials admitted in Washington that they have upgraded the level of talks with the PLO in Tunis. U.S. Ambassador to Tunisia, Robert Pelletreau has held two undisclosed meetings with the PLO's second-in-command Salah Khalaf, known also as Abu Iyad and that meeting with Yasser Arafat is not ruled out.

Since the start of the U.S. dialogue with the PLO, there have been already three formal sessions between Pelletreau and his authorized PLO contact, Yasser Abed Rabbo. These formal sessions took place in Tunis on December 16, 1988, on March 22, 1989 and on June 8, 1989.

Israeli Deputy Foreign Minister Binyamin Netanyahu sharply criticized the American decision to upgrade ties with the PLO, "which will make peace remoter, instead of bringing it closer."

Netanyahu added; " We shall make the U.S. aware of our view that it could not have chosen a worse time to upgrade ties. The man whom Ambassador Pelletreau now met is the architect of the PLO's terror policies and the designer of its two-phase plan to destroy Israel.

Only on Wednesday (June 28, 1989), Abu Iyad was indicted in an Italian Court-of-Law for transferring PLO arms to the Red Brigade terror bands there. He has been behind the international terrorist movement for years. He is the terrorist leader who admits to employing declarations of peace as a tactic in the prosecution of war. Abu Iyad has been on public record in 12 interviews with the Arabic press since Algiers' declaration, as explaining the PLO plan to get Israel to withdraw from the territories as a prelude to a combined Arab assault, which would wipe out the Jewish state.

For a U.S. envoy to talk to this man and accord him status means that America is putting the Peace Process into reverse. The time has come for the U.S.to make its choice either to encourage the Arabs anxious to work for peace, or to build up men like Abu Iyad who oppose peace. It cannot be both."

Israeli Justice Dan Meridor attacked the American upgrading of the dialogue with the PLO, who defined it "a very regrettable error. It can only counterproductive, because it makes it even harder for the Arabs in the territories to take the brave step towards Israel. The closer the U.S. gets to the PLO, the further the chances of achieving a settlement."

The intervention of the Superpowers or the EC cannot bring peace to the Middle East.

Only direct negotiations between Israel and its Arab neighbours could bring a solution to the Middle East conflict. Negotiations with Arab states, not with Arab gangs, like the PLO. The U.S. could generate enough pressure to force Israel out of Judea, Samaria and the Gaza Strip. But, neither the U.S. not the U.S.S.R. could force the Arabs to maintain peace with the Jewish State. No national majority in the world would tolerate a minority, which insists on destroying its country. Arabs who chant "We shall liberate Arab Galilee with our blood and spirit," cannot claim equal right.

Ariel Sharon declared on Thursday, June 29, 1989 (Sivan 26, 5749), on Educational TV's "Erev Hadash" program that Shamir's diplomatic initiative was the most dangerous plan ever adopted by an Israeli government, worse than an International Conference.

In spite of the fact that from the Camp David Accord it is very clear that the autonomy was offered to the people of Judea, Samaria and Gaza and not to the territories, once the borders of the autonomy are defined and the zones of the elections are set, and accepted by Israel, there is a great danger it might lose its sovereignty over those areas. There is a very great danger that those areas will become the Palestinian-Arab state.

After Arafat's declaration of independence and the PLO's intention to establish a Palestinian-Arab state in Judea, Samaria and Gaza, it is very unlikely that the Palestine-Arabs or the PLO will accept less than an independent state, that's, the autonomy offered to them by the Camp David Accord and Shamir's initiative.

The three ministers: Sharon, Modai and Levi insisted that the Prime Minister's initiative should include the following four points, before they could vote for it whole heartedly:

a. The Intifada (Uprising) must stop, for elections to be held.

b. East Jerusalem Arabs will not participate in these elections.

c. Settlements in Judea, Samaria and the Gaza Strip will continue.

d. A new Palestinian-Arab state in Judea, Samaria and the Gaza Strip to be ruled out and out of the question.

Ministers Sharon, Modai and Levi wanted these four points incorporated in shamir's initiative in spite of the fact that they are part of the Likud platform.

Apart from party politics, which in itself is very natural, the three ministers, Sharon, Modai and Levi went out to kill Shamir's-Rabin "peace initiative" in order to save the national interest, because they thought, that it was very dangerous to Israel, as it leads to nothing but a Palestinian-Arab state. Shamir's initiative is an illusion. It can lead to nothing but a dialogue with the PLO and the establishment of a Palestinian-Arab state.

Shamir suspected that his three opponents, Sharon, Modai and Levi were motivated by political ambition rather than ideology. "They are not suggesting anything that is unacceptable to me," said shamir.

On July 5, 1989 (Tamuz 2, 5749), at Tel Aviv's Ganei Ha'Taarucha (Exhibition Grounds), the Likud Central Committee was convened, at the request of three prominent Likud Ministers: Ariel (Arik) Sharon, Yitzhak Modai and David Levi, to vote on the Prime Minister's political announcement, as well as on the principles demanded by the three ministers, to be incorporated in Shamir's initiative.

Prime Minister Yitzhak Shamir's announcement included the following:

-Jerusalem is the Capital of Israel

-There will be no participation of East Jerusalem Arabs in the elections to be held in Judea, Samaria and the Gaza Strip.

-There will be no negotiations with the PLO.

-There will be no elections in Judea, Samaria and Gaza so long as the Arab uprising, the intifada continues.

-There will be no negotiations as long as the Arab violence continues.

-There will be no Palestinian-Arab state in the Land of Israel.

-There will be no foreign sovereignty in any part of the Land of Israel.

-Jewish settlement in Judea, Samaria and the Gaza Strip will continue.

Sharon, Modai and Levi seemed satisfied of Shamir's announcement, which included their four principles, which they believed will neutralize some of the dangers in Shamir's initiative and hopefully will not lead to territorial compromise or to a Palestinian-Arab state.

During his speech Shamir was applauded several times by the 2,500 delegates, most notably after calling on the U.S. to stop talking to the PLO and especially after reiterating that Jerusalem would remain Israel's undivided Capital.

Only Yitzhak Modai, who led the negotiations that produced the compromising agreement with Prime Minister Yitzhak Shamir, noticed that when Shamir read the resolution, he "somehow" forgot to mention the item that contained the most important, the greatest concession: "These principles bind the representatives of the Likud in the government and in the Knesset."

Shamir, smiling, returned to the podium and read the paragraph that Sharon, Modai and Levi wanted to hear.

The Likud Central Committee approved Shamir's proposal, which included the three ministers' constraints or "iron girders" in an open vote, unanimously.

Practical as ever, Shamir accepted, though reluctantly, Sharon's constraints to his "peace initiative", thus avoiding a serious crisis, may be a split in the Likud party. By embracing his ministers' principles Shamir prevented a serious disruption of the Central Committee meeting and avoided an immediate power struggle. Shamir preferred suffering a "small" blow to his prestige rather than deepening the rift in his party.

After the voting the Likud looked more unified and stronger than ever.

The Likud decision was the result of a last-minute agreement between Prime Minister Shamir and sministers Sharon, Modai, and Levi, who during the past month have been demanding that the Central Committee be allowed to vote on qualifications to the government's plan.

The resolution adopted in the Likud Central Committee only confirmed once more the Likud's platform and ideology of "Peace for Peace" and never "Territories for Peace."

Very rarely had a political meeting such coverage in the world media.

Shamir saw no contradiction between the Likud's resolutions in the Central Committee and the government's "Peace Initiative."

The reactions to Shamir's speech and the results of the vote in the Likud Central Committee was as expected. The Right and the religious were pleased while the Maarah and the Left were appaled and infuriated.

The Likud partners in the coalition, the leaders of the Maarah believed that beyond the implications for the new distribution of power among the Likud's leaders, there was another strategically significant result to the Likud's resolution, which was, the end of the "Peace Initiative."

The Maarah sharply criticized the resolution taken by the Likud Central Committee, putting "girders" to Shamir's initiative, and even threatened to leave the National Unity Government. Their argument was that the "girders" were killing Shamir's initiative and the so-called "Peace

Process" and without a "Peace Process" there is no purpose to stay in the government.

Prime Minister Shamir was sincere when he said that: he preferred new elections, and joined in the coalition agreement, if the Maarah decides to withdraw from the government.

The polls showed that the Maarah had clearly lost popularity since the November 1988 elections while the Likud had strengthened their position by overwhelming the Maarah in the municipal elections, on February 28, 1989.

Furthermore, it is felt that the atmosphere of violence that had swept the country and the popular frustration at the inability to suppress the intifada and overcome unemployment is working to Likud's advantage. Besides, if the Maarah will leave the Unity Government over insufficient circumstances, they might be considered as deserters, which could give the Likud over 70 mandates. Unless they could convince the Israeli public that the Likud "girders" is a death warrant for the government "Peace Process". But, Shamir is much more convincing when he keeps insisting daily a very simple point, that: "Nothing had changed in the plan."

On the other hand, Shimon Peres is not sure that his party will not deny him another shot. The polls showed that if Peres led the Maarah in another General Election, the maarah would be totally beaten.

Ex-Justice Minister Chaim Tzadok, a Maarah elder statesment remarked: "Labour has to think whether it can win the next election with Shimon Peres leading the party," and other leadership contenders like Gad Yaacobi and Mordechai (Motta) Gur, have already declared that if elections will be held the party will have to reconsider its leadership.

After the Likud Central Committee meeting on July 5, 1989 (Tamuz 2, 5749), in Tel Aviv and Shamir's announcement, the Bush-Baker Administration threatened the State of Israel that if it couldn't pursue the "Peace Process" and comply with U.S. policy, the end result of which is, "Territories for Peace" or a "Palestinian State". It will have to face an International Peace Conference for the Middle East in which all its participants will be anti-Israeli.

Mr. James Baker had been running too fast with his dialogue with the PLO in Tunis, so that, now, with Prime Minuster Shamir's announcement at the Likud Central Committee in Tel Aviv on July 6, 1989, it might be found difficult to bridge between the U.S. policy in the Middle East and Israel's clear stand.

The Bush Administration and the State of Israel are pursuing totally different strategies, which could lead to great discord when the final status of Judea, Samaria and Gaza will be discussed. It is no secret that the U.S. does not see eye to eye with Israel on the issue of the permanent status of Judea, Samaria and the Gaza Strip. It never did. There were grounds to anticipate a reassessment of U.S. policy that may harm Israel's vital interests. There has been a constant "war" between the United States of America and Israel, since June 1967. The United Sates of America wanted Israel out of Judea, Samaria and Gaza, out of ancient Jewish territories, same as the U.S. wanted Israel out of Egypt, in 1973, out of Lebanon in 1982, out of Sinai in 1979 and out of Tabah in 1987. This was part of the U.S. global policy and U.S. interest in the Middle East.

By repeating time and again that the final solution for the Palestinian-Arabs in Judea, Samaria and the Gaza Strip is "Territories for Peace," the United States of America was feeding the Arabs with false pretensions and false hopes, which, in itself is a great disservice to its Arab friends as well as Israeli friends. This policy and behavior was no doubt a considerable obstacle to peace in the Middle East and further encouragement to the Arabs to pursue their intifada.

The U.S. policy of "Territories for Peace" is a total adoption of the Arab policy. That's exactly what the Arabs want, more Israeli land. The United States of America is bluntly, openly one sided and biased.   Therefore, it is no longer neutral, no longer objective. It has formed a solid opinion on the issue. Therefore, the U.S. can no longer act as a neutral arbitrator between the two parties: Israel and the Arabs. If the United States of America adopted a policy by which microscopic Israel has to shrink more, the good offices of the U.S. are no longer a benefit to Israel but a burden. Totally siding with the Arab cause and their policy of "Territories for Peace" doesn't make the U.S. an objective unbiased arbitrator. Such a go-between can only damage the interest of Israel. With no disrespect to the U.S. it will only be fair if it withdraws from mediating between the two parties. No thank you. In order to give territories to the Arabs Israel doesn't need the arbitration of the U.S.

Settlements in Judea, Samaria and the Gaza Strip are not obstacles to peace, as Jame Baker, Bush and others believe, but obstacles to the realization of the dream of Israel's enemies,

that's the establishment of an Arab-Palestinian state in Judea, Samaria and the Gaza Strip.Therefore, U.S. intervention in the settlement policy of a sovereign, democratic country is a very unfriendly act.   The issue of

Judea, Samaria and the Gaza Strip is an Israeli issue, not an American issue. The issue of Jerusalem is an Israeli issue, not an American issue. So it will be very wise if the U.S. will let Israel fight its own wars. Let Israel alone, stop interfering.

A bearded PLO terrorist shouted "Allahu Akbar" (God is Greater), seized the steering wheel of a No. 405 Jerusalem-bound Egged bus from Tel Aviv, on July 6, 1989 (Tamuz 3, 5749) and sent it crashing over a steep precipice, killing 14 passengers and injuring 27, seven of them seriously.

"This tragic incident comes to remind us that the fight against terror in our country has not ended. We will unite as a people and as one family in these difficult moments. Our hearts are with the families who have lost their loved ones," said President Chaim Herzog.

Prime Minister Yitzhak Shamir described the attack as "a new peak of madness which stems from deep hatred fed by constant incitement." Shamir called it "an awful catastrophe, the fruit of brain consumed with hate. We will find a way to deal with acts like this, to prevent them wherever possible."

Vice Premier Shimon Peres said: "From every incident we have to draw conclusions. I have no doubt that there are ways to prevent acts like this in the future."

The Ha'Tehiya Party announced: "We have no faith in the government. It has failed to deal with terror and the liquidation of the intifada, which has brought us to this terrible situation."

Members of the party's youth movement demonstrated outside the Defense Ministry headquarters in Tel Aviv, calling for the death penalty to terrorists. Placards also claimed that the Defense Minister Rabin was protecting Arabs who organize terror.

The National Religious Party (NRP) noted that the "Royal road to Jerusalem" was now stained with blood, and, more than any other party, called for "merciless blows against the messengers of terrorism everywhere and all the time."

U.S. Ambassador William Brown called the terrorist steering the Jerusalem-bound bus into abyss as: "a loathsome action and we are sickened by it. We offer our deepest condolences to the families of all the victims of this terrible tragedy."

Israel had been providing the U.S., regularly, with information regarding PLO terrorist activities. The PLO and their subsidiaries have carried out at least seventy terrorist operations inside Eretz Israel since Mr. Yasser Arafat, in his speech to the special session of the UN General

Assembly in Geneva renounced terrorism. Yet, U.S. Assistant Secretary of State John Kelly said that the State Department had no information about PLO involvement in terrorist actions against Israel. In his testimony on July 12, 1989, before the House Foreign Affairs on Europe and the Middle East, Kelly was asked by Chairman Lee Hamilton; "Do we have any evidence of PLO involvement in any of the terrorist acts that have occured inside Israel?"

"No, none that I know of," answered Kelly. He did not include even the attack on the Tel Aviv-Jerusalem bus, on July 6, 1989, as a terrorist action, which happened on July, a week ago. Mr. John Kelly was not telling the truth. Kelly lied again when he told Chairman Lee Hamilton that he was aware of the secret Israeli-PLO contacts.

Very unfortunately, the irresponsible, panic-stricken Left in Israel legitimized the Palestinian-Arab intifada while the Israeli media had inflated this legitimization.

In July 18, 1989, Minister of Interior Rabbi Ariyeh Deri (Shass) met with Egyptian President Husni Mubarak. During their conversation Israeli Minister Deri told President Mubark that for Israel Shechem and Hebron were holier than Tel Aviv and Haifa, but sometimes one amputates an arm or a leg in order to save the body, insinuating that Israel was ready to give away part of Judea, Samaria and Gaza in order to survive. A very unclever remark from an Israeli Minister and a Jewish Rabbi. Extremely damaging and not to the best interest of the State of Israel.

Israeli Minister of Interior Rabbi Ariyeh Deri was not alone with Egyptian President Husni Mubarak, former Chief Rabbi Ovadia Yossef, head of the Shass Party was with him. Rabbi Ovadia Yossef told the Egyptian President that the Jewish Halacha justifies territorial compromise if it was a matter of Pikuah Nefesh-the saving of lives.

Unfortunately, Rabbi Ovadia Yossef didn't seem to have realized that by making territorial compromises to the enemy the problem of Pikuah Nefesh will become much much worse.

In July 18, 1989, in Cairo, Egypt, Rabbi Ovadia Yossef and Rabbi Ariyeh Deri delivered to Egyptian President Husni Mibarak, a Halachaic discourse on the issue of Jews relinquishing sections of Eretz Israel in exchange for peace. Two Jewish Rabbis passing to the enemy highly classified material. This act and behavior are close to treason.

In 1979, the Chief Rabbinate of Israel stated that there was a "Severe prohibition againt transferring ownership of any of the Holy Promised

Land of Eretz Israel to foreigners. No argument of Pikuah Nefesh (the saving of lives) may revoke this ban."

On July 27, 1989 (Tamuz 24, 5749) the Chief Rabbinate again issued a Halachaic decision that the Torah forbids making territorial concessions in the land of Israel.

The Chief Rabbinate statement also recalled that in 1948, the Chief Rabbis of Israel had declared that it was a Mitzvah, a religious precept, to occupy the land of Israel and hold on to it. One, a Jew, was not allowed to withdraw "because Arab murderers were threatening bloodshed." That principle holds and applies to Judea, Samaria and Gaza, forever, the Rabbinate maintained.

Their ruling was in reaction to the statement made by Rabbi Ovadia Yossef to Egyptian President Husni Mubarak, on July 1989.

The Rabbinate also stated that it was "Surprised and Sad" that Jews had hold to a non-Jewish ruler: "By law we must hold on to Israel, but because you will kill Jews if we donot retreat, therefore, we have no choice, but to retreat."

To give away such important information to the enemy is very, very, unwise.

Immediately after the Rabbinate's ruling, Prime Minister Shamir spoke to a Rabbis gathering in Jerusalem, on July 27, 1989 (Tamuz 24, 5749) and emphacized his opposition to ceding even a "silver"of land for peace, and pledged to enhance Jewish settlements "everywhere".

"Some people are concerned that a person like me is engaged in negotiations with our enemies about settling the dispute," said Shamir. "Everything that we are doing is only for Eretz Israel and peace, and it is not true that they contradict each other."

Rejecting the U.S. idea of "Territories for Peace", Shamir said:"Peace should and can be attained without forgoing, even a silver of the pupil of our eye, the land of our forefathers, our Holy Land."

"Peace," Shamir added, "is not a monopoly of the traitors, those who surrender and yield." "Even", Shamir continued, "if Israel and its neighbours negotiate a final settlement, it will not include any territorial element, he pledged.

Two hundred Rabbis, members of a National Religious Party affiliated group, called also Hever Harabanim, applauded Shamir.

The right of the Jews to conquer Eretz Israel and hold on to it, takes priority over avoiding bloodshed.

Wars to conquer Eretz Israel should not be avoided in order to save lives, because that is what such wars are about: readiness to give one's life for one's country.

According to the Halacha it was imperative to establish the State of Israel. "The command to settle Eretz Israel includes, according to Nahmanides, coming to live in Eretz Israel, building settlements, establishing a sovereign Jewish state, having a Jewish Government, conquering the land, holding on to it and not giving it to others."

Every Israeli knows that relinquishing territories and withdrawals from territories is a sin and a potential for many more dangers of bloodshed in the future.

Jewish law requires Jews to defend forcibly their sanctified soil, and this includes Judea, Samaria and the Gaza Strip. Judea, Samaria and Gaza were always the heartland of Eretz Israel and the Halachaic status of these territories is not different than that of Tel Aviv and Haifa.

The command "you shall live by them" (Leviticus 18:5)-to which the Talmud adds:"and you shall not die by them"- is the basis for the accepted Halacha that a question of Pikuah Nefesh (danger to human life) suspends the performance of all the commandments and prohibitions except for the prohibitions on idolatery, sexual immorality and bloodshed.

Obviously, Israel might have to exert some force in order to achieve this goal, because the Arabs might apply counterforce in order not to be expelled from the land, endangering the lives of Israel's soldiers. But, unfortunately, nobody ever invented wars without casualties. The end result is worth it.

According to former Chief Ashkenazi Rabbi Shlomo Goren, one might argue that the prohibition against "giving them lodging in Eretz Israel" does not apply to the Arabs, who are not idolatrous and whose monotheistic belief is unquestionable. Rabbi Shlomo Goren said that this claim has no substance, for several reasons:

a.   According to Maimonides, in order to be permitted to live in Eretz Israel they must take upon themselves the seven Noahide laws, accepting the unity of God only is insufficient.

b.   Even if they observed these laws, today Israel could not grant them the privilege of living in Eretz Israel. As Maimonides states, a non-Jew can be accepted as a Ger Toshav only when the jubilee year laws are in effect. Today, when there is no jubilee year, there cannot be a Ger Toshav (Isurei Biah 14.6)

c.   Maimonides (M'lachim 8:11) rules that the Ger Toshav who observes the Noahide laws is considered one of the Hasidei Umot Ha'olam (a righteous gentile) and has a place in the World to Come. That is only true, though, if he keeps the laws because God commanded them in the Torah and informed us through Moses that the Sons of Noah had previously been commanded to observe them. But, not if he observes the laws because of his own logic. This proviso, noted by Maimonides, excludes the Moslems from gaining the special status.

d.   The Ra'avad differs with Maimonides and holds that even in our times Israel may grant the status of Ger Toshav. But, even he makes this contingent on the candidates's undertaking to keep the Noahide laws and on his accepting the right of the Jewish people to its land, in accordance with the Torah. The Arabs of the territories, however, had been fighting against Israel and against this right.

Nahmanides, in his comments on Maimonides'Sefer Ha'Mitzvot, takes a clear position on the question of the Holy Land. Nahmanides holds that to take possession of the Land of Israel is one of the six hundred and thirteen commandments, and that the law applies in every generation in which we have the right to conquer the land, as it states, "Behold, the Lord your God has set the Land before you: go up and possess it" (Deuteronomy 1:21).

Based on this, Nahmanides in Commandment 4, which he adds to those listed by Maimonides, writes:

"We were commanded to inherit the land that God gave to our fathers, and we are not to leave it in the hands of others. This is what he said to them: 'You shall dispossess the inhabitants of the land; and dwell therein, for I have given you the land to possess it. And you shall inherit the land" Nahmanides adds: "This is what the Sages refer to as an obligatory war."

According to Rabbi Shlomo Goren there are no grounds for discussing the retention or return of parts of Israel in terms of the question of danger. All poskim have ruled that it is incumbent on all generations to defend Jewish sovereignty over the sanctified territory of Eretz Israel, and that this commandment overrides the danger to individuals-all this conditional on unequivocal military opinion that we have the ability to carry out these commandments.

If we find that from the purely military aspect we are not in position to vanquish our enemies, then even a shaky peace treaty is preferable to defeat on the battlefield.

Israel's effort to defend Judea, Samaria and the Gaza Strip from the activities of the intifada and other hostile forces, local or foreign, whose aim is to force Israel to retreat from these regions is an obligatory war. And indeed, we find clearly in the Talmud, Sota 44b, in the name of Rava, that the war of Joshua to conquer Eretz Israel is considered by all to have been Milhemet Hova-a "duty war"- which is even higher than an obligatory war or Milhemet Mitzvah.

In an interview to Egyptian daily newspaper Al-Ahram, in Cairo, on July 27, 1989, Yasser Arafat said that he favoured Shamir's plan of elections in principle, but insisted that the elections be held under International Supervision and as part of an overall package deal based on trading land for peace. Arafat called these elections as "a good idea" but outlined four conditions:

-Partial Israeli withdrawal from the West Bank and Gaza to prepare for the elections.

-A timetable for a 27 months total pullout of Israeli troops, in stages.

-UN supervision of the elections and repatriation of Palestinian refugees as well as those deported by Israel.

-Setting a date for the declaration of an Independent Palestinian State.

Oviously, these four conditions cannot be accepted by Israel.

The Director General of the Prime Minister's Office, Mr. Yossi Ben-Aharon, in an interview with Reuters News Agency, on July 1989, severely criticized the U.S.-PLO dialogue in Tunis, Algeria. In an interview with The Jerusalem Post, on July 1989, said:

"Sooner or later the U.S.-PLO dialogue will produce results, or understanding, and we, in accordance with our policy, will have to tell the Americans: this is simply irrelevant. What you have achieved with the PLO cannot have any influence whatsoever on the situation, because we are seeking an understanding with the Arabs here, and not in Tunis.

A confrontation with the U.S. is unavoidable. We cannot ignore the fact that the U.S. is talking to a terrorist organization, which prides itself on the murder of Jews to this very day. If the Senate in Washington, found it appropriate to prohibit the Administration-or to recommend that it refrain-from talking to murderers of Americans, this is doubly true for us.

So we have a legitimate grievance, and we are entirely justified in reacting with anger and pain.

We won't stop trying to convince the U.S. that it is actually obstructing the Peace Process. There is no Arab who will treat the diplomatic process seriously as long as he believes that the real show is going on in Tunis. They see that, despite vehement Israeli protestations, the U.S. is negotiating with the PLO.

Our logic is completely opposite to the Americans. We say there is a chance for the process only if the PLO is not able to take charge of the process by remote control.

If the U.S. sincerely believes that once it gets a green light from the PLO the whole process will move to the territories, then they are living under an illusion. The other possibility is that the U.S. knows that it is now merely engaged in tactics, and that the day will come when the PLO must enter the negotiation stage.

The aims of the PLO and those of Israel are mutually exclusive and totally irreconcilable. The PLO has three targets-the first, to inject itself into the process and get international legitimization; the second, is the right of return; and the third is, Arab sovereignty over territories-and never mind now in what exact geographical borders.

And what is the purpose of the government's initiative? Negotiations with a representative delegation from the territories, autonomy and negotiations over the permanent settlement? There is absolutely no chance of finding common ground with the PLO. The legitimization of the PLO and the creation of a Palestinian State go hand in hand. Yasser Arafat wants to believe that the day will come when he will be able to disembark at some point west of the Jordan where he will have a territory to control and be received on a red carpet. This is not written in our books, and it never will be.

Thus, opposition to the PLO is necessary by definition There is no point in Israel putting the organization to the test.This is axiomatic.

Many believe that by talking to Palestinians, who proclaim themselves to be acting under the auspices of the PLO, Israel is actually holding indirect contacts with the organization. This is an inaccurate reading of reality. You have to take into account that the Arabs in Judea, Samaria and Gaza, who consider themselves to be public figures live in costant fear of terror. No matter what they really think, when they meet with Israelis they need the PLO as an insurance policy.

This is not the whole story. What the Israelis hear from the Palestinians of the territories from the PLO in Tunis. The U.S. has made this goal much harder to achieve.

Sooner or later we must tell the residents: You have two options-you can either continue with the intifada and be enslaved to the PLO, or you can sever your ties. We are not saying that it's easy, and we will help you-on the basis of your practical need to come to an arrangement with us.

There have never been elections here, and the PLO has never been elected. These residents have never had a real, free choice between these two options. I really don't know how this can be done. I must add that free choice has never existed in Arab society, in Arab society, he who has the power rules. The PLO has signaled the residents that it has the power, so they accept it. Must we also reach the conclusion that this is it, only the PLO can rule? We thus resign ourselves to the worst kind of dictatorship, if not second to Lebanon-not to mention the consequences for the security of Israel. We wouldn't be crazy to agree to it.

The question of the kind of regime that will exist in the territories and our human and economic relations with it, touches our very soul. I'm not saying that we should impose democracy on them, but by the same token why should we impose the worst kind of dictatorship?

We will not simply accept that if they say that the PLO is their representative, this is binding on us. I don't want to be patronized, I don't want to be their guardian and I don't want a Bantustan here. However, I am willing to chop off my own head in order to prevent the creation of a Bantustan.

To prevent any legitimization of the PLO Israel should not negotiate with any outside Palestinians, even if they are not PLO members, as Tunis is said to have proposed. However, I am willing to consider Palestinian Arabs who have been expelled and whom the Defence Minister might allow to return-for then they will be residents. Once you talk to outside Palestinian-Arabs, you may as well talk to the PLO. We are unable to solve the problems of outside Palestinian Arabs.

I am afraid that the PLO will once again mislead the U.S.and we will have to have another superfluous argument with the administration.

I am not saying that the government's initiative is easy to implement. It is full of mines and roadblocks. Each step has to be moderate and weighed carefully. We must forget about quick fixes. Nothing will happen without perseverance and patience.

There will only be progress when active elements-the U.S., the residents of the territories, we ourselves-understand that the dialogue will not achieve anything. We have to persuade the residents that they will not achieve anything through the PLO.

I realize that this sounds a bit far-fetched today. But it's the way, the only way that there is any hope," said Mr. Ben-Aharon.

In retaliation the Maarah Central Committee came out with its constraints to Shamir's initiative (the government's peace plan).

The Maarah's resolution of August 1989 included four constraints:

-The Arabs of East Jerusalem will be included in the elections, though they will not actually vote in Jerusalem.

-Once negotiations begin, no new settlements will be established in the territories.

-The elections will be political, aimed at choosing representatives for the negotiations.

-The government's initiative will be based on the principle of Territories for Peace.

The Maarah leaders declared that their constraints will counterweight the "dangers" of the Likud constraints.

For several years Israel had been proposing the Arabs to exchange prisoners. In spite of the fact that Israel held many more Arab prisoners, the Arabs kept rejecting Israel's proposals. The Arabs had in their hands at least three Israeli soldiers as well as several other hostages, Americans, British, French, German, Italian, etc.

In order to force the Arabs to return the Israeli prisoners, Sheikh Abdel Karim Obeid, a Hizballah top leader, along with two aides, were kidnapped from his home in Lebanon by a Israeli commando unit, early Friday, July 28, 1989 (Tamuz 29, 5749).

The Hizballah and Iran have threatened to kill the American and British hostages if the sheikh Obeid is not releasd and returned The Shi"ite Moslems threatened to execute U.S. Marine Lt.-Col.William R. Higgins, first.

There were reports several months ago that Higgins was already dead, but these reports were never confirmed.

Secret talks had been taking place about a trade of hostages for some time between Israeli and Iranian negotiators. After a meeting in London on June 1989 the negotiations were broken off because of Israeli frustration at the lack of progress.

The Israelis needed Sheikh Obeid mainly as a bargaining chip to gain the release of three Israeli soldiers taken prisoners in southern Lebanon, in 1986, as well as the release of the other hostages, American, British, French, German, Italian, etc.

Sheikh Abdel Karim Obeid had served as the Imam of Jibshit, was the chief of Shi'a cleric and was affiliated to the Hizballah movement in Lebanon. As Hizballah spiritual leader he dedicated himself to preach Jihad and venom against the Jews who control "his" Palestine and southern Lebanon.

By seizing Sheikh Obeid Israel had strengthened its bargaining position. This operation shook the Hizballah off their balance. The Israeli raid on Jibshit had brought back the forgotten hostage issue on the international agenda. The capture of Sheikh Obeid is not only the exercise of Israel's right to pre-emptive and punitive actions but also a legitimate act of self-defence. Besides, Israel doesn't forget its soldiers or its hostages in captivity. Israel had decided to undertake this breathtaking operation after three and a half years of tiring negotiations, direct or indirect, with the enemy and "after leaving no stone unturned" in the struggle for the hostages.

Once more, a brilliant performance of "Sayeret Matkal." A commando unit annexed to the General Staff.

There were few precedents before. Israel had to capture higher echelon commanders and leaders to convince the Arabs to exchange prisoners.

In 1983, a Israeli commando unit seized the nephew of Ahmed Jibreel, head of the P.F.L.P. in Beirut. Two years later Ahmed Jibreel agreed to a swap. Jibreel received back his nephew with 1,150 other Palestinian-Arabs held in Israeli prisons, in return for three Israeli POWs.

On December 1988, Israeli commando seized Jawad Kasafi, Mustafa Dirani's associate. The man believed holding one of the Israeli soldiers. When Jerusalem offered a swap, the Hizballah refused. The Israelis understood that they needed a bigger "fish" to convince the Hizballah. They chose Sheikh Obeid from Jibshit (as we have already seen before).

Until July 1989, twenty-two hostages were already executed by the Hizballah in Lebanon. Twelve were Jews, residents of the city of Beirut. The Hizballah still hold eighteen hostages, one of them is Jewish.

When Iran was begging for its survival, asking the UN to call for a cease fire and end the
war with Iraq, the UN Secretary-General should have forced the Iranian government to release all foreign hostages and prisoners, before calling for a cease-fire. An act like this could have saved the life of U.S.

Marine Corps Lt-Col. William Higgins. Lt-Col. William Higgins was on the staff of Unifil (the United Nations forces stationed in Lebanon, when he was kidnapped by the Hizballah. Unfortunately, the UN Secretary-General Javier Perez de Cuellar didn't think of it. What a terrible mistake!

Lt.-Col. William Higgins was not the first American to be tortured and executed by the Hizballah in Lebanon. William Buckley and Robert Ames, members of the CIA preceded him.

The Israeli raid on Jibshit, Lebanon, and the seizing of Sheikh Abdel Karim Obeid, surprised President George Bush and Secretary of State James Baker. The two gentlemen, suddenly realized that to head the U.S. Administration was no picnic at all. It was their first international crisis since they took office, on January 1989.

As soon as the videotape, showing Lt.-Col. Higgins hung from a rope, was broadcasted, minority leader Robert Dole took the Senate floor to make an unusually harsh assessment of Israel's actions. Senator Dole charged that Israel had "struck out alone, free-lancing," with no regard for the American hostages. Then he added that: "Perhaps a little more responsibility on the part of the Israelis would be refreshing."

Despite earlier rumblings by Bush and Baker that there was not ample coordination between the U.S. and Israel, they both, latter admitted that Israel's abduction of Sheikh Obeid had created momentum towards receiving the hostage crisis in Lebanon, which did not exist previously. Advance consultation with the U.S. would have made the U.S. an accomplice and deteriorated its relations with the Arab countries, which Israel wanted to avoid. Without allowing himself ample time for thinking or discussing the matter with the Israelis, minority leader, Senator Robert Dole, harshly criticized Israeli commando raid on Jibshit. It was an irrational outburst.

The first U.S. reaction to the Israeli operation in Jibshit was nervous, critical and disgraceful. It was, probably, a feeling of guilt, which resulted from a long U.S. negligence to try and free its hostages, which formed the psychological background for its negative reaction to the Israeli successful raid on Jibshit, Lebanon.

From following the American diplomatic and other steps it was very clear that the Americans were far from closing a deal and releasing their hostages, prior to Obeid's ubduction.

The unilateral Israeli action in Jibshit caught Washington by surprise. At first official Washington was irritated, but soon Washington calmed down when it understood that may be this was a chance to free its hostages too.

There were some strains in the U.S.-Israeli relations. This because the U.S. couldn't make up its mind whether Israel had recklessly endangered the lives of the American hostages or made a great contribution to help America and itself solve the unending hostage dilemma.

The whole world saw Higgins bound and gagged, dangling from a makeshift scafold. The U.S. public was infuriated and fulminated at the American impotence. The horrible picture of Higgins body reminded everybody that in spite of the ten years already elapsed since the capture of the U.S. hostages at the American embassy in Teheran, the United States of America still doesn't have a solution to terrorist kidnapings.

From their long experience in the area, to the Israelis, aggressiveness was much preferable than the U.S. unbudging status quo, when dealing with Arabs or Iranians. When hostages are concerned Israel cannot tolerate sitting idle and doing nothing.

The Israeli action in Jibshit dramatized the difference between the Israeli and the U.S. reaction to hostage taking. When fighting terror was concerned, Israel was always resolved while the Americans were hesitant all the way. The U.S. waiting posture was interpreted as inaction, negligence and even cowardice. Many Americans were sick already from their president's "courage of restraints."

Conservative columnist Wesley Pruden wrote in the Washington Times, on August 2,1989,the following: "The President, in the spirit of demonstrating 'resolve' the easy way, has so far screwed up only enough courage to pick on the Israelis, who he knows won't shoot back. This ought to make the old fighter pilot, a man who demonstrated against-the-odds courage in the skies over the South Pacific, blush.

Like the old woman complaining of noisy neighbours, the President and various like-minded gumbeaters arrayed around him go on and on about how the Israelis are damaging 'the Peace Process'. 'The Peace Process' is moonshine, as the President and the Arabists in the State Department, now virtually. without restraint in this Administration, know very well. There is no 'Peace Process' in the Middle East. There is only a 'Survival Process', and the Israelis, adrift in a sea of circa 400 million murderous fanatics, are hanging on to it,s best they can."

Mike Royka, Pulitzer-prize winning columnist for the Chicago Tribune, summed up the trauma felt by the American public during this hostage crisis and described the public's general feeling. Lmbasting President George Bush's suggestion to handle the situation with restraint and prudently, wrote:

"After ten years of trying to deal prudently with vicious loonies, much of America isn't feeling prudent. It is feeling that the time has come for an eye for an eye: No, that's not accurate. It's feeling that may be we should extract a hundred eyes for one tooth."

The American public is simply fed up. And if another American hostage is killed, that anger will force Bush to start military measures.

It won't matter what the prudent scholars in the Think–Tanks tell Bush," Royko said, "It won't matter what the prudent word-warriors in the State Department say: It won't matter what any of his prudent foreign policy advisers say. Bush, a politician, is going to look around and see what the millions of voters are saying and he is going to have to do more than offer prudence and words."

Republican Senator Alen Spector of Pennsylvania, from the Senate floor, pointed out that there "is an enormous question as to how much more Western civilized society can tolerate in terms of what Iran is doing. It is anintolerable situation that the most powerful nation in the history of the world stands helpless when its citizens are being held hostages," he said. "It is just an intolerable situation that we are not locating those hostages, to make a determination as to whether they can be rescued with reasonable safety."

"It is an intolerable situation when there are warrants of arrest outstanding for trrorists, such as warrants of arrest outstanding for terrorists who hijacked TWA flight 847 and that more is not being done to find the locals of those terrorists and to bring them to justice."

Senator Spector, in describing the U.S. response to terrorism as "pitiful," cited some of the failures of the past few years:

"In April 1983, the U.S. Embassy was bombed in Beirut and 16 U.S. citizens died. A few months later, in October 1983, the U.S. Marine barracks was bombed in Beirut. 241 marines lost their lives. Since 1983, four Shi'its terrorist groups are believed to have taken 12 hostages in Lebanon. We know the tragedy about TWA 847 with Robert Stathem, the naval officer who was brutally murdered. We know the incident of Achille Lauro, resulting in the death of Leon Klinghoffer, the failure of Italians to let us have Abu Abbas and the failure of Yugoslavians to extradite Abu Abbas to the U.S. We know of the killing of almost 300 innocent citizens aboard PAN AM flight 103. But the U.S. still refuses to take military action."

Republican Senator Alfonse D'Amato of New York, like several of his colleagues, with the exception of Republican Senator Bob Dole of Kansas, expressed his down-the-line admiration for Israel's own willingness to take decisive action against terrorists.

In capturing Sheikh Obeid, he said, "Israel did exactly what it should have done in taking preemptive action against terrorists.

If a nation or group sponsers terrorism, if they are promoting terrorism, then they should be at risk. And it is about time that the United States began to do more than spout rhetoric and pay lipservices. We keep saying that we are going to defend ourselves and our people, but we have been doing a pretty poor job up until now."

Sheikh Obeid's capture shook the Thatcher government much to its displeasure. Foreign Minister john Major condemned the seizure of Obeid and made efforts to convince Israel to release the Sheikh. Margaret Thatcher herself did not approve of Israel's decision. The rest of the Europeans reacted approximately the same, at least in the beginning when they first heard the news.

For more than three and a half years, in the cases of John McCarthy and Brian Keenan, and little more over three years in the case of Terry Waite, British Diplomats had been doing their utmost to release their hotages in Lebanon, but in vain.

On August 7, 1989 (Av 6, 5749), The West German government cabled Jerusalem, requesting that Israel take steps to include the two German hostages in any swap with Hizballah.

On August 6, 1989 (Av 5, 5749), Italy appealed by phone to the Foreign Ministry in Jerusalem for information on its hostage in Lebanon.

Defence Minister Rabin stated in the Knesset that he was ready to exchange all the Shiite prisoners in Israeli hands (approximately 500) in exchange for 3 Israeli soldiers and approximately 20 foreign hostages. Has he not learned yet from his previous mistake in 1985, when he acceded to the demands of Ahmad Jibreel and freed 1,150 thugs and murderers in exchange for three Israeli soldiers?

Most of the freed terrorists promptly resumed their terroristic activities and led the Palestinian-Arab intifada. Would not returning only 23 Shiite captives suffice?

To return over 500 Arabs and Iranians in return for 3 Israeli POW's (Prisoners of War) and 20 foreign hostages (American, British, French, Germans, etc.) is a lousy bargain and totally irrational, because it means, causing a bad precedent, spoiling the enemy, giving the enemy a "medal"

After Israel had used its most efficient intelligence in Lebanon to carry out perfectly executed abduction of a top Hizballah leader from deep inside hostile country, its American ally could have used its most efficient diplomatic relations to proceed towards the mutual interest of freeing the hostages.

The U.S. Administration declared that, unlike Israel, it will not bargain for the hostages or pay any "ransom" for their release-a reference to Iranian assets frozen in the U.S. since 1979.

The U.S. was ready to consider Soviet envolvement in the Middle East area on proof by Soviet deeds that Moscow was in fact applying the "New Thinking" in this region. Soviet help in obtaining the release of hostages might serve as the sort of positive that the U.S. had been seeking.

In a meeting with visiting U.S. Assistant Secretary of State John Kelly, on August 3, 1989 (Av 2, 5749), in Jerusalem, Israeli Deputy Prime Minister David Levi said that the Likud Central Committee's constraints obligate "Half the Government" and are aimed at "Averting a Loss of Control of the Process." Levi stressed that the constraints, the "Iron Girders"added to Shamir's initiative were intended to prevent a Palestinian state, to which both the Likud and the Maarah were opposed. The United States of America also claimed that it opposes a Palestinian state.

Deputy Prime Minister Levi told Assistant Secretary of State Kelly that he believed that the U.S. policies on the peace process contradict fundamental Israeli principles and might lead to "an unfortunate confrontation between true allies."

PLO Chief Yasser Arafat received the endorsement and approval for his policies from the Fatah, the largest PLO group, in Tunis, on August 7, 1989 (Av 7, 5749).

The Fatah Conference, convened after nine years, endorsed the resolutions of the Palestine National Council, which called for a Two-State solution to the Israeli-Palestinian problem.

The Conference had failed to repeat Arafat's December 1988 renunciation of terrorism, which had opened the way for the U.S.-PLO dialogue in Tunis.

The Fatah delegates in the Conference stressed the importance of the "Struggle Against Israel by all Methods," especially armed struggle. Arafat agreed that "Armed Struggle" against Israel was Ilegitimate but Not Practical Policy at the moment.

This resolution strengthened Arafat's position in the face of internal criticism that he had sometimes acted unilaterally to grant concessions to the U.S. and to Israel.

Fatah's resolution of "intensifying and escalating armed action and all formes of struggle to eliminate the Zionist Israeli occupation of our occupied Palestinian land," did not necessarily contradict the support Arafat, received to proceed with his diplomatic activities with the U.S. Arafat when pushed to the wall by the U.S. had renounced terrorism but never condemned or renounced armed struggle against Israel.

The resolution adopted at the Fatah Congress in Tunis contained "derogatory Rethoric on Israel, its tone of confrontation and violence, and its preference for unrealistic principles and solutions instead of practical ideas for peace are unhelpful," said the State Department spokeswoman Margaret Tutwiler, in a prepared statement red to reporters, in Washington, on August 10, 1989 (Av 9, 5749). Tutwiler then added that the U.S. was continuing to study the Fatah resolutions "in an effort to have a clearer understanding. We will continue our dialogue with the PLO to determine whether the PLO remains committed to the understandings of last December regarding recognition of Israel, acceptance of UN Security Council Resolutions 242 and 338, and denunciation of terrorism," she said.

The U.S. shall also "determine whether the PLO is prepared to take practical steps toward peace," said Ms. Tutuwiler.

The Fatah's resolutions in Tunis raised the question about the group's commitment to accommodation, understanding and peace," added the spokeswoman.

It is no secret that Prime Minister Yitzhak Shamir had been meeting with Palestinian Arab leaders from East Jerusalem, Judea, Samaria and Gaza, most of them were believed to be ardent supporters of the PLO, if not members.

The fact that his meetings with PLO supporter Jamil Tarifee was publicized, was far from being clever. These meeting can be, rightfully, interpreted as direct or indirect talks with the PLO, parallel to the U.S.-PLO dialogues going on in Tunis, which Israel condemned.

Talks like these, by the Prime Minister of Israel are degrading and can also be interpreted as weakness, retreat, or even worse, raising the "White Flag."

With what moral rights can Israel criticize the U.S. for its dialogue with the PLO representatives in Tunis?

Mubarak's ten-point proposal very cleverly overlooks the participation of the PLO or the establishment of a Palestinian-Arab state. Nor does it mention the "Return of the Refugees." A very clever trick to drive the

Likud into negotiations with the Palestinian-Arab representatives, the PLO.

Most probably the topic of theses negotiations would be the elections in Judea, Samaria and Gaza. The elections in the territories mean nothing less than self-determination in the short run and the establishment of a new Palestinian-Arab state in the long run.

Mubarak believed that his initiative would expedite the establishment of a Palestinian-Arab state much more than an International Conference, and hoped that these negotiations could result with a Israeli-Arab agreement, so that elections will not be necessary any more.

Egypt's Ten-Point Plan intends to push the Israeli government to recognize the PLO, in spite of its refusal to do so, as well as to push Israel to participate in an International Peace Conference for the Middle East.

By submitting its proposal, Egypt violates its signature and commitment at Camp David that clearly specifies that the negotiations should be among sovereign states and not with an organization (PLO). If Egypt will succeed with its plan, the new Palestinian-Arab state will become tangible. There was also the possibility that Egyptian President Husni Mubarak wanted to turn the negotiations, eventually, into an International Conference.

The purpose of Mubarak's Ten-Point initiative was, probably, also to drive a wedge between the U.S. and Israel as well as to split the Israeli public and government. Mubarak declared that his proposal is not a peace initiative but merely a clarification to the elections plan in the territories.

Before the matter was handed over to the government of Israel, before it was discussed in the Cabinet, Finance Minister Shimon Peres already jumped out with a statement that "Mubarak's Ten-Point proposal is a basis for negotiations with the Arabs."

As soon as the news (Mubarak's Ten-Point initiative) leaked out to the Israeli government, not even handed yet formally to the Israeli government, instead of ignoring it, the Israeli government inflated the issue out of proportion, probably, to draw away the attention of the Israeli public from the real "burning" issue of unemployment, which it did not know how to cope with.

Shimon Peres declared over the media that:

"Our goal is to reduce inflation to the levels of the countries we are dealing with. We intend to reach these levels as soon as possible. Only if we continue with our policy of budget self restrain and create tight connection between salary and productivity. Only if we could make the necessary constructive changes in the economy. Only if we all dedicate ourselves to the task and start working more and produce more, without asking the government to do the job for us, or demand from the government to perform things which it cannot. Only then we could reach our designated assignment."

Beautiful words, which mean nothing. How can an unemployed person produce more? At the lines of unemployment offices? Or while waiting in the queues of "Manpower", "ORS" or other placement offices?

Then Mr. Peres continued:

"I know that if we do not do it our economy will slide back to a heavy recession, high inflation and increased unemployment."

The Finance Minister, the Deputy Prime-Minister Shimon Peres was not aware of the fact that this had already happened. Why? Because the man was extremely "busy" with Mubarak's Ten-Point initiative. Instead of looking after the country's economical problems he was busy with foreign policy trying to do Moshe Arens' (Foreign Minister) job, as well as the Prime Minister's job.

Mr. Shimon Peres backed up from his old principle of "No dialogue with the PLO" and suddenly declared that it did not disturb him at all if part of the Palestinian-Arab delegation, which was assumed to negotiate with the Israeli delegation, will include a few PLO members, or even members that were expelled from Israel or Judea, Samaria and the Gaza District, after participating in PLO terrorist activities. Peres said:"There is no other Palestinian-Arab nation and we must talk with what we have." This means that he was ready to talk with the PLO. This sudden, surprising change in policy was not unexpected from Peres. Whoever knows Peres knows that he is capable of this.

With his shift in policy Peres had broken an old national "sacred" consensus of refusing to speak with murderers.

Tensions within the National Unity Government escalated on September 21, 1989 (Elul 21, 5749), when Defence Minister Yitzhak Rabin declared his support for Mubarak's ten-point proposal.

Addressing members of the Maarah Party Central Committee, Rabin ridiculed the Likud's opposition to President Mubarak's plan, which he considered "a great important step" for furthering the Peace Process. Rabin added that the Palestinian-Arabs should not be expected to "drop to their knees" and accept the Israeli diplomatic initiative word by word. "We must convince the Israeli people the value of the proposals," said Rabin.

Rabin brushed aside charges that agreeing to the Cairo talks was tantamount to negotiating with the PLO. We (Maarah) are willing to agree to a dialogue with a Palestinian-Arab delegation to be appointed by Mubarak and approved by us," he said. Rabin also said that the Palestinian-Arab delegation would be "composed of 100 per cent residents of the territories-as expelled Palestinian-Arabs can also be considered residents of the territories."

The fact that "One or Two" Palestinian-Arabs deportees would be included in the delegation was irrelevant. "I am not suggesting we allow them to return (to the territories), as Likud defence ministers have done in the past," he said.

Rabin warmly praised Mubarak throughout his speech said that the Egyptian leader's

"Ten-Points" constituted a conciliatory position in that they "contained no mention of the PLO, no mention of a Palestinian-Arab state or self-determination, and accepted the Israeli principle of Two-Stage settlement."

"We can't continue saying there's nothing to discuss if the Palestinian-Arabs accept elections and our Two-Stage approach to a settlement," Rabin said.

"They cannot break from the Arab and Palestinian world altogether and they need a green-or at least yellow-light from broad (from the PLO). The Mubarak plan is an acceptable means of delivering that signal."

I believe a crack has been found in the wall (preventing progress) and the Labour (Maarah) Party should do everything to convince the Government and the Israeli people, that it should be pursued.

Prime Minister Yitzhak Shamir defined the relation between the Likud and the Maarah as "Grave" because he had no intention of accepting Mubarak's "Ten-Point" proposal, which are not in the best interest of Israel. As for the possibility that this could bring down the Unity Government, sources in the Prime ministar's Office replied that:"Shamir has more important matters on his mind than continued partnership with a man like Rabin."

Shamir continued his crusade against Mubarak's prorosal, which he said: "must be rejected", because their aim was to bring about a PLO-led state in the territories, including East Jerusalem. Shamir said the Mubarak's proposal would bring the PLO into the Peace Process and require Israel to agree to an "Unacceptable Preconditions," that is "Territories for Peace."

"We want to negotiate with Arabs who want peace and who have despaired of the hope that the Intifada will bring them gains, and that the PLO in Tunis will bring them victory over the Israelis."

Shamir commanded Mubarak's attemps to promote peace; however, referring to Mubarak's direct TV appeals to the Israeli public, Shamir suggested that the Egyptian President address himself to the Israeli Government instead, "as befits proper diplomatic procedures and international relations."

Mr. Shamir's position is that Israel, having already discharged all its withdrawal obligations, according to the Camp David Accord, by evacuating the whole of Sinai, should not relinquish one square millimeter more, because it would lead to the establishment of a Palestinian-Arab state.

Maarah Minister Moshe Shahal declared that his party viewed the decision on Mubarak's proposal as "without question, the Moment of Truth." He also added that the best hope for a breakthrough in the stalemate would come if the U.S. decided to pressure the Likud to agree to terms, which, according to Moshe Shahal, "are in no way different from what the Likud itself agreed to in the Camp David Accords." Shahal was referring to the clause permitting Palestinian-Arabs from outside the territories to participate in negotiations with Israel. Mr. Shahal, like anybody else, had a right to his opinion, but to invite outside pressure and involve others in Israeli policy, is treacherous.

Mubarak's "Ten-Point" proposal did upset the Likud, but for Rabin, it was viewed as a Godsend. Rabin believes tha Mubarak's proposal will put the Palestinian-Arabs in a position where they are starting talks on the basis of a program which makes no mention of the PLO, or of a Palestinian-Arab state, or of Palestinian-Arab self-determination, or of the "Right of Return", or of an International Peace Conference.

Defence Minister Yitzhak Rabin expressed hope that the Israeli Government's proposal to hold elections in the territories of Judea, Samaria and Gaza could drive a wedge between the residents of the territories and the PLO. There is still always the risk that Rabin's hope could turn to be wishful thinking.

In order to reach elections Rabin is willing to close his eyes to the fact that the PLO will have a leading role in setting up the Palestiian-Arab delegation, which will negotiate with the Israelis. Rabin is also willing to look the other way if some of the members of the Palestinian-Arab delegation will include Palestinian-Arabs not residing in the territories.

Rabin believes that the elections will create a certain momentum, which will tip the scales in the direction of the Palestinian-Arabs leadership in the territories, at the expense of the PLO.

Unlike Rabin, Shamir is more careful and is reluctant to gamble or take risks on such an important issue.

By using Mubarak's Ten-Point Plan the United States of America, Egypt and the Maarah Party tried to drive the Likud Party into a dialogue with the PLO. Mubarak believes that "he is killing two birds with one stone," the other bird is, increased U.S. political and economical aids.

Those who advocate autonomy in the territories of Judea, Samaria and the Gaza Strip must understand that the end results of such a policy is a PLO control over these territories, in the form of a new Palestinian-Arab state. Same as the PLO found a "way" to "accept" UN Resolutions 242 and 338, it found also a "way" to "accept" President Mubarak's Ten-Point initiative, especially if it could help push Israel into a corner.

October 1989, the Shamir-Rabin National Unity Government, security wise, was a complete failure. This Government could not provide its citizens with the minimum amount of safety and security.

The Palestinian-Arab uprising, the intifada was still going on, life was unsafe. The streets and the highways were unsafe, property was unsafe, Israeli soldiers were attacked constantly; cars were burnt in Jewish neighborhoods in Jerusalem, etc.

The Israeli Government did nothing, or very little to stop this phenomenon. Both parties, the Likud and the Maarah were busy with internal struggles and personal feuds. The Government reacted like a city fire brigade, extinguishing local fires. Patching holes with no plans for the future. Both parties, the Likud and the Maarah had only one thing in mind and that is, winninig the November (1989) Histadrut (Union) elections. Whether Israel Kessar (Maarah) will be the next Secretary-General of the Histadrut or Yaakov Shamai (Likud) will replace him depends on the outcome of these elections.

The Unity Government was busy with useless, stupid, peace initiatives, which were not in the best interest of the State of Israel and even dangerous. Peace Initiatives, which can lead only to the loss of more Israeli land.

The outbursts of immoderation that disfigured President Mubarak's media appearances, was uncivilized when he commented that Israel wanted to steal Saudi Arabia's money, when he heard that Israel wanted peace with all the Arab countries, including Saudi Arabia.

While this nonchalant atmosphere prevailed and the Israeli leaders were very busy with themselves, a Syrian MIG-23 plan succeeded to penetrate Israel's airspace and land in an old bandoned airfield in Meggido, without being detected. Even the air was unsafe in Israel. The Israeli population was shocked by such complacency and negligence.

Israel is being criticized scrutinized for its handling of the Palestinian-Arab uprising, and is judged by the rules and standards existing in the West and by people who know very little about the Arabs and Islam, and some of them never met or even most, an Arab in his life.

Israel is located in one of the most volatile, most fermentable areas of the world, surrounded from all sides, except the sea on the west, by an ocean of hostile Arab population, and must deal with the most cruel terror, daily, from both within and without its borders.

Israel is located right in the Middle of a tremendously violant hostile environment, backed by twenty two other hostile Arab countries, supported by the Communist block, the Third World and even by the West, very clearly expressed at the United Nations sessions, in New York and in Geneva. Israel has also a great, dangerous, Arab Fifth Column in its midst, which is trying to destroy it from within.

Inspite of all this, Israel has been trying, since its inception, for years, to find a settlement, a treaty and peace with this environment, but in vain. With the exception of Egypt and Jordan. Inspite of the sea of hatred and the threat to its security and survival the fact is that Israel is still the only democracy in the region.

For the PLO the intifada was a complete success, as it became the focus of international

interest. Hundred of reporters flew to the Middle East from all over the world to cover it. It was displayed on the television screans all over the world, for months. It strained Israel's relationship with almost every country on the globe. It diverted the IDF from border duties and training schedules and turned it into a police task force in charge of law and order in the streets. It forced the IDF to spend millions on the intifada from an already strained defence budget. It divided the Israelis internally and invited heavy outside criticism. It succeeded to drive a wedge between Israel and the U.S. and led to the U.S.-PLO dialogue in Tunis against Israel's wish. It forced the leaders of Israel to come up with a new plan, under pressure. It led to Mubarak's Ten-Point Plan. It shook the long status quo and started a momentum towards the establishment of a new Palestinian-Arab state. It expedited talks between Israelis and Palestinian-Arabs, supporters or members of the PLO.

The PLO leaders had reasons to believe that the intifada will bring them the victory.

On November 1989 Bir Zeit University Professor Sari Nusseibeh proposed that Palestinian-Arabs announce the formation of a provisional government, whose administration would function in Judea, Samaria and the Gaza Strip. The Palestinian-Arab ministers would be members of the PLO executive committee abroad, but department heads would be drawn from the territories. This, said Nusseibeh, would be a step forward in the process of "state-creation" in progress during the intifada.

The Palestinian-Arabs have paid dear for this uprising, but they asked for it. They started it. Thousands of Palestinian-Arabs were arrested. Thousands have lost their jobs. Thousands of merchants lost substantial incomes for closing their stores during hundreds of striking days, forced upon them by the PLO. Children stayed home for several months because schools were closed, after most of the pupils were caught participating in riots. The Arabs suffered hardship, punishment, economic damages, unemployment as well as casualties. Arab gangs were hanging so called Arab collaborators in the Middle of the town square in broad day light, pulling them out from bed at night, and after raping their wives and daughters in their presence, stabbing them to death. Most of these were not collaborating with the Israelis. It was a means to settle old personal accounts. They ran into a vicious circle of a neverending cycle of violence and counter violence, which led them nowhere. It caused depression and confusion and did not lead them to a better future.

It also caused anger and frustration among the Israelis who have discounted the possibility of coexisting with them, ever. Many members of Shalom Achshav (Peace Now) learned to know them better and stopped giving them their political support. Members of other Peace Movements seemed not to know anymore what they were demonstrating about or rather what they were demonstrating for. If they ever were for Territorial Compromises they could not think whom they were supposed to compromise with. Who was their partner?

This is the result of adhereing to Arafat and his gangs. This is the price for trying to undermine another people and steal away its land.

When it saw the continuous differences between the Likud and the Maarah the Bush administration tried to play between them. With one telephone call (October 1989) to President George Bush, Prime Minister Yitzhak Shamir put an end to this "dirty" game.

Deputy Prime Minister and Finance Minister Shimon Peres (Maarah) was very angry at the U.S. Administration for not "forcing" Shamir to accept Mubarak's Ten-Point proposal.

On October 1989, U.S. Secretary of State James Baker indicated in an interview with the New York Times that if the parties in the Middle East conflict did not get "more serious" about fundamental compromises for peace, he would have no choice but to scale down his efforts to implement Israeli Prime Minister Yitzhak Shamir's election plan.

Yasser Arafat declared that: "it is increasingly clear that Shamir is reluctant to implement his own initiative."

James Baker said that he had no more intention of supporting that initiative than the Prime Minister himself. "If Shamir decided to abandon his initiative I would do the same," said Baker.

By backing up from Shamir's elections plan the United States of America will be doing Israel a great service. If the U.S. withdrew from its active role in the so-called "Peace Process," there would be no process at all and the Status Quo will remain, which is right now, in the best interest of Israel.

The only obstacle to Israel's holding Judea, Samaria and Gaza permanently is the American peace policy for the Middle East. If the U.S. only did not press Israel for withdrawal.

Bush and Baker had other worries; besides the Middle East They were very busy learning and assessing the sudden new political changes in the Communist World under Mikhail Gorbachev. Israel had every right to believe that the U.S. is not mostly interested to risk its prestige and inject itself into a losing situation in the Middle East. The U.S. had other problems, more important problems to deal with. If Israel withdrew from the "Peace Process", so would the United States.

It is most probable that the Likud will never give up its total commitment to the ideology of Eretz Israel and in no circumstances would consider relinquishing even one square inch of Judea, Samaria and the Gaza Strip, even if it means confrontation with the U.S.

On the other hand, a U.S. policy of scaling down the disengagement, as indicated by Secretary Baker, are much more likely and much more clever.

In the international conditions prevailing, the Arab-Israeli conflict does not seem to threaten the American strategic interests and therefore, the U.S. can easily withdraw its involvement in this conflict.

The United States of America came up with Baker's five-point proposal that was supposed to close up the gap between Israel's Four-Point proposal and Egypt's Ten-Point proposal.

The following is the text of U.S. Secretary of State James Baker's five-point with the changes requested by Foreign Minister Moshe Arens and Baker's responses:

1.   The U.S. understands that because Egypt and Israel have been working hard on the Peace Process, there is agreement that an Israeli delegation should conduct dialogue with a Palestinian delegation in Cairo. Arens asked to replace the clause in italics by "Palestinian Arabs residents of Judea, Samaria and Gaza." The intention was to remove the dialogue from Cairo and to rule out the participation in the Palestinian delegation of Arabs from East Jerusalem and from outside the territories. Baker refused to make any changes in this passage.

2.   The U.S. understands that Egypt cannot serve as a substitute for the Palestinians and that Egypt will consult with Palestinians on all aspects of the dialogue. Egypt will also consult with Israel and the U.S. No Changes Requested.

3.   The U.S. understands that Israel will attend the dialogue only after a satisfactory list of Palestinians has been worked out. Israel will also consult with Egypt and the U.S. Arens requested that the clause in italics in this point be changed to "has been worked out by Egypt, the U.S. and Israel"-increasing Israel's role from that of being consulted to being an active partner in making up the list. Baker rejected the proposed change, and offered Israel the option of removing the second sentence-apparently leaving open the question of Israel's exact role.

4.   The U.S. understands that the Government of Israel will come to the dialogue on the basis of its May 14th initiative. The U.S. further understands that Palestinians will come to the dialogue prepared to discuss elections and negotiations in accordance with Israel's initiative. The U.S. understands, therefore, that Palestinians would be free to raise issues that relates to their opinions on how to make elections and negotiations succeed. Arens asked to remove both references to "negotiations"-as one of the "constraints" adopted by the Likud Central Committee rules out all negotiations before "violence in the territories ceases," Baker agreed to replace "negotiations" with "the process of negotiations."

5.   In order to facilitate this process, the U.S. proposes that the Foreign Ministers of Israel, Egypt and the U.S. meet in

Washington within two weeks. No Changes Requested. When the U.S. takes an initiative, like Baker's five-point proposal, Rogers' Plan, etc., it first considers its global implication and how it will effect its relations with the Soviets. This is its top priority. Its second priority is to keep the pro-American Arab rulers, especially the monarchs of Jordan and Saudi-Arabia and the Egyptian regime in power and on the American side. That is in order to maintain the regional distribution of power and its influence on U.S. interests it must please the local Arab rulers.

In his letter to the Secretary of State, Arens writes:

These changes are minor textual modifications, but are essential to Israel and necessary in order to avoid creating a misleading impression. Any suggestion or implication that Israel meets with Palestinian-Arabs selected directly or indirectly by the PLO in Tunis flatly contradicts the spirit of the initiative.

"Accordingly, I recommend a return to your original suggestion that the Palestinian-Arab delegation be determined by Egypt, the U.S. and Israel. Each day's delay in progress towards elections is therefore a source of frustration for the Prime Minister and me, just as I know that it must be for you." Arens concludes.

The "constraints" ministers, Sharon, Modai and Levi had indications that Shamir is inclined to accept U.S. Secretary of State James Baker's revised five-point framework for Israeli-Palestinian Arabs talks and warned that any concessions by Shamir would carry heavy political price. Shamir's acceptance of Baker's framework could lead to a split in the "harderline" in the Likud by Sharon, Modai ndLevi.Sharon, Modai and Levi believe that Baker's proposal leads to negotiations with the PLO and to a new Palestinian-Arab state in Judea, Samaria and Gaza. Therefore, they opposed Baker's Five-Point proposal and are prepared to fight Shamir in the Likud Central Committee, which they were trying to convene.

The U.S. Administration did not like the two Israeli reservations to Baker's five-point framework proposal relating to the formation of the Palestinian-Arab delegation and the agenda for the dialogue. They believed that it was a diplomatic maneuver aimed at making Israel seem cooperative but stall the whole "Peace Process."

The U.S. Secretary of State James Baker did not accept Israel's two reservations and rejected its aim to make changes in his Five-Point proposal. Baker only agreed to make a few cosmetic changes, which had no substance.

Israeli formal acceptance of Baker's Five-Point proposal in principle, with only two reservations didn't seem to satisfy the Americans, and the Bush Administration's evident irritation and frustration with Israel were being manifested in different ways. Direct and indirect.

The feeling is that the great bulk of American Jewry supported Israel's stand against talking with the PLO or establishing a new Palestinian-Arab state. It seemed that they also supported the Israeli Government's position on the Peace Process guarantees.

On October 1989, the U.S. television network NBC accused the State of Israel for her nuclear ties with South Africa and for sharing with Pretoria the technology of the defunct Lavi.

In Jerusalem, on October 26, 1989, (Tishrei 27, 5750), Prime Minister of Israel, Yitzhak Shamir, denied the NBC report, called it a lie and reiterated the government's position that Israel would not be the first country to introduce nuclear power into the Middle East. The most significant effect the NBC report was its political timing, raising the possibility that it could have been intentionally leaked out to the media in order to embarrass Israel at a time when tensions are rising in the relations between Washington and Jerusalem because of difference of opinions on the subjects of the Five-Point U.S. framework for achieving Israeli-Palestinian talks and the selling of arms to Saudi-Arabia. Its policy of opposition to proliferation of missiles and nuclear weapons is well known.U.S. law is to cut support, economic and military, to countries engaged in proliferation of such weapon. This puts Israel's two billion dollars Supercomputer deal with the U.S. in jeopardy. The U.S. even hinted that it might apply the "Saymington Amendment", which forces the U.S. Government to cut every economic and military support to countries producing illegal nuclear weapon.

Spculations are that the NBC News broeadcast on October 25, 1989, of the sensational report, quoting U.S. officials as claiming that Israel had entered into a full-scale agreement with South Africa to co-produce nuclear warheads, was purposely fabricated by the U.S. Administration in order to put Israel on the defencive, as part of the diplomatic pressure on Israel to respond favourably to Secretary of State James Baker's Five-Point framework proposal.

It was very clear that the U.S. officials who leaked that report were anxious to embarrass Israel and to pressure it into making diplomatic concessions, which will later lead to territorial concessions, as they believe will happen.

Israeli officials in Washington and their American Jewish supporters were beginning to sense real confrontation with the U.S. Administration.

According to foreign sources, as of 1979, Israel became the seventh member of the "International Nuclear Club". The six other members were: The United States of America, the Soviet Union, France, Britain, China and India.

It is belived that after reassessing the political atmosphere to the area as well as the international political situation in the second half of the year 1989, it seemed to Israel that the Arabs are in no position to launch a war against Israel in the foresseable future. Syria is stuck in Lebanon and is in desperate financial straits and the Soviets are gradually distancing themselves from the military profile in Damascus. King Hussein of Jordan is doing his best to stay on the throne and alive. Iraq, after its long exhausting war with Iran needs several ears to recuperate. Egypt feels quite comfortable with the Peace with Israel.

There are very clear indications also that the PLO is losing its grip and control over the Palestinian-Arabs and the uprising. Besides, it is believed that the Palestinians themselves will tire of their own disturbances as well as of Arafat's patronage. Strategically speaking, time is indeed working in Israel's favour. Therefore, it will be totally unwise for Israel to rush now into a "Peace Process". It will be very clever to stall it.

The Bush Administration had underestimated the Israeli resolve not to get dragged into talks with the PLO.

Israel must insist that the present Territorial Status Quo, since 1967, continues, because this is its minimum security need and that the Arab claim over part of Eretz Israel is totally invalid as they can make their homeland in any of the twenty two neighbouring Arab countries.

Yitzhak Shamir's greatness was in that he did not succumb to U.S. Secretary of State James Baker's "Five Point" program, in spite of all the tremendous pressures exerted upon him by the U.S. Administration, by George Bush's Administration.

Yitzhak Shamir flatly rejected the U.S. Administration's proposals, which were nothing but PLO proposals covered with Egyptian wrapping paper.

It is believed that Secretary of State James Baker had decided to "subdue" the State of Israel because it dared reject his Five-Point proposal or rather accept it with reservations.

Same as Shultz and Reagan before, so are James Baker and George Bush as well as other U.S. policymakers, they all tried to avoid getting involved in the domestic politics of Israel. That is why, all the time, Washington wanted to work with both sides of the National Unity Government. They tried to please both the Likud and the Maarah. Baker and his aides are not only negotiating between Israel and the Arabs, but also among the various Israeli political factions themselves-not an easy task.

U.S. officials in Washington, while anxious not to get involved in any internal Israeli politics said that James Baker was determined to press for the start of an Israeli-Palestinian-Arab dialogue that would lead to elections in Judea, Samaria and the Gaza Strip. U.S. Secretary of State tried to soften Israel's resistence to his Five-Point proposal in every which way. He spoke to American Jewish leaders, several of them were either members of the Republican party or ardent supporters of the Republican party, as well as to members of the Israeli Lobby in Washington, with the intention that his massage will be transferred to Jerusalem. This conversation contained threats that the U.S. was considering the reduction of military and economic support to Israel.

James Baker was naïve if he believed that with such threats he could scare a man like Yitzhak Shamir.

It is most probable that Shamir will prefer new elections rather than give up to U.S. pressure.

Many wrongly believe that what keeps the Israeli economy running are the U.S. financial support.

In the late 80's the U.S. support to Israel included: 1.8 billion dollars military grant and 1.2 billion dollars economic aid.

The U.S. economic aid was, as a matter of fact, paying back the Israeli debts for weapon bought in the 70's. If this aid is not given to Israel, Israel will be unable to pay its debt to the U.S.

This means that all Israel is receiving from the United States of America is 1.8 billion dollars yearly military grant. This is a substantial amount of money but not critical to Israel's survival because it amounts to only five per cent to Israel's yearly budget.

This grant was given to Israel only because it is the only ally left in the Middle East after President Jimmy Carter got rid of the Shah of Iran.

Most of the defence expenses of countries such as Japan, Korea, Germany. NATO, etc. are covered by the United States of America.

The U.S. had been supporting "poor, underdeveloped countries" like Japan, Korea, Germany, NATO and others, for decades, since the end of World War II in 1945.

The U.S. military forces in these countries cost the United States hundreds of billions of dollars. Besides, the billions spent on the defence of these poor countries are hidden in the U.S. Defence budget and are part of the total U.S. defence budget.

On the other hand, the support given to the State of Israel were under disadvantageous conditions and are made public and even given the stigma of philanthropy.

U.S. Senators and Congressmen, often boast in public, quite loudly, that little Israel is getting more support than any other country. This is far from being accurate.

The greatest part of the aid to Israel was spent in the United States to support the American industry.

Israel is a loyal U.S. ally in the Middle East. May be the only one. Israel is saving for the U.S. a lot of money and receives much less in return.

Israel is a West bastion in the turbulent Middle East, watching also the American interests in the area.

Israel is supplying the United States very important information on the Soviet arms-MIGs, tanks, artillery, missiles, etc.

Israel is testing the U.S. weapon under combat conditions for free.

Israel is a terrestial aircraft carrier in the Middle East.

The United States of America had been receiving, all the time, first class, important information on classified Israeli material, research and development, global and local intelligence, etc.

To think of stopping U.S. aid to Israel is irrational, because it means to substantially increase U.S. military expense in the Middle East and probably also a deterioration of relationship with Israel.

On the other hand, the end of U.S. economic and military aid to Israel, will force the Israeli Government to cut approximately five per cent of its budget-because raising the taxes will not be accepted and will endanger the stability of the Government.

It has become standard routine and habit of the U.S. Administration, whenever Israel shows political independence, disagrees with U.S. policy or refuses to listen to U.S. dictate, to threaten Israel with "Reassesment" of its relations with Israel and/or leaks out to the media false information on the Israeli nuclear power, this in order to produce a bad image of Israel in the U.S. and the world public opinion. With friends like this Israel does not need enemies.

Israel is an independent, sovereign country and is not a satellite of the United States of America, and therefore, like any other free country in the world, is free to handle its own policy according to its best interests and without the interference of the United States of America or any one else.

People did not realize that when Prime Minister Yitzhak Shamir said that he would absolutely never, under any circumstances, negotiate with the PLO, or with its representatives, the Prime Minister was serious and meant every word he said.

Israel doesn't view and never did view the PLO as a partner to any form of settlement or negotiations. People also did not realize that when Israeli Prime Minister Yitzhak Shamir said that he would absolutely never, under any circumstance, consider the theory of "Territories for Peace" the Prime Minister really means it; and if any body is building up hopes that the Prime Minister will change his ideology, he is only losing time.

Prime Minister Shamir made it his "habit" to discuss important political matters only with Moshe Arens, the Foreign Minister (Likud), Shimon Peres, the Finance Minister (Maarah) and Yitzhak Rabin, the Defence Minister (Maarah), the "Big Four" and did not include the rest of the Cabinet as if he wanted to hide something from them, or at least, from Sharon, Modai and Levi, the "Constraints" ministers.

This is a return To Golda Meir's "Kitchen Cabinet" system, which brought disaster (the Yom Kippur War) on Israel. Ariel Sharon claimed that Shamir's behavior is against every principle of a democratic state. This was a non-constitutional forum of Shamir Arens, Peres and Rabin.

Ariel Sharon blamed Israel's diplomatic difficulties on Shamir's "halfhazard, amateurish" handling of the Peace Process.

Today, Israel possesses, finally, part of the Land of Israel, including the territories of Judea, Samaria and Gaza, which were redeemed in the Six-Day War on June 1967, yet, the danger of these territories being surrendered to the Arabs is still real.

On November 1989, the UN agency issued a declaration asserting that "acts of interference, destruction and transformation" were taking place at historical sites in Jerusalem.

Jerusalem Mayor Teddy Kollek furiously rejected this UNESCO charge that Jerusalem's cultural heritage is being "destroyed as a result of Israeli occupation" as the Arabs claim.

Mayor Teddy Kollek expressed deep disgust at UNESCO's false accusation.

"Since 1967, the cultural heritage of all peoples and all periods has been preserved without discrimination and with great dedication and, I might add, at great cost," said Mayor Kollek.

"Prior to the reunification of the city," Kollek said, "all the ancient sites were treated equally-they were equally neglected. The only exceptions were the Jewish synagogues and cemeteries, which were desecrated and destroyed. But there were no complaints from UNESCO then."

Israel, therefore, is the last country in the world that has to be reminded of the UN's double standard and hypocrisy.

During her husband's election campaign, on November 1988, Mrs. Barbara Bush repeatedly declared on the media that her husband George Bush was always friendly to Israel. Yet from very reliable Texan sources, George Bush also happened to symphathize the Arabs and the PLO.

On one hand Bush and Baker promised Shamir not to exirt pressure on Israel to negotiate with the PLO while on the other hand Bush and Baker keep "flirting" with the PLO because they believe that without the PLO the Peace Process cannot proceed. This American game is beyond Israel's comprehension. It smells deception.

The U.S. State Department had, not once, publicly announced that the U.S. policy is aimed at creating a new "political" arrangement in Judea, Samaria and Gaza-one that brings real, tangible benefits for the Palestinian-Arabs in these territories but at the same time will meet Israel's legitimate security rights.

This is not a process that is simply going to rehash former Prime Minister Menachem Begin's vision or, wishful thinking of limited self-rule for the Palestinian-Arabs in the territories. If that is what some Likud Ministers believe, they are in for a very rude awakening, a very hurting surprise. What the U.S. Administration had always in mind was something much more sweeping, because the U.S. policy is deeply committed to a real change in the territories.

This American attitude, this American policy in the Middle East, if ever carried out, can only hurt, damage, the old-long good relationship between Jews and Americans. The only ones who will benefit from such unfortunate situation will be the Arabs.

A significant number of people in America, in the Jewish and non-Jewish Communities, favour the U.S. dialogue with the PLO. Americans, by and large, believe in talking and negotiating even with terrorists. The

Americans also favour Israel's exchanging land for peace. In addition, majorities would favour the creation of some sort of Palestinian-Arab homeland or entity in Judea, Samaria and Gaza, if Israel's security could be guaranteed in the process. In short, the Americans are very generous at the expense of Israel, and so do others. The Americans could have acted totally different if they had to exchange territories in Alaska or California, with the Soviets, for the sake of peace! Most probably, its reaction would have been similar to the Israeli reaction when somebody wants to steel away part of her land.

The Americans propose that the talks on the final settlement will begin even if the talks on the interim settlement are not yet concluded. In these circumstances, is there any realistic chance for an interim settlement why should the Arabs, who have never liked the idea of an interim arrangement, negotiate it seriously?

On November 1989, Israeli Foreign Minister Moshe Arens sent letters to all foreign ministers, stating that Israel will, under no circumstance, negotiate with the PLO, because the PLO had been playing a destructive role in the Peace Process for years by terrorising the whole world.

Soviet Foreign Minister Eduard Shevardnadze reacted by sending to PLO Chairman, Yasser Arafat, a message, in which he said that Israel's peace efforts are only aimed at excluding the PLO from the negotiating process.

PLO leader Salah Khalaf (Abu Iyad) warned that the Palestinian-Arabs in Judea, Samaria and Gaza would turn to Moslem fundamentalist and radical groups if Israel continued to refuse a PLO role in the peace settlement.

In an address to the General Assembly of Jewish Federation in Cincinnati, Ohio, on November 16, 1989 (Heshvan 18, 5750), Prime Minister Yitzhak Shamir declared that: "Israel will not be pressured into commiting national suicide."

"The United States of America," said the Israeli Prime Minister, "wants to see tranquility and peace in the Middle East, and regards the ways and means to that end as secondary in importance. But for Israel every step towards that common objective is fraught with risk. One blunder can be fatal."

"Some observers have interpreted our diplomatic initiative as the result of the realization that introducing the PLO into the Peace Process is inevitable. Nothing can be further from the truth. On this issue we have differences of view with some of our American friends. There can be no bridging the gulf between Israel and the PLO."

"There are legitimate differences between Jerusalem and Washington," said the Prime Minister, "but these cannot change the very solid friendship between the two countries,"

The U.S. Administration was intelligent enough to understand the simple fact that Israel will never accept dictates from anybody. The U.S. is not a tyranny. The U.S. is a democracy. The U.S. will never force Israel or anybody else to do something against their will. This is not their system. The U.S. can persuade or convince but it will never force its will upon anybody.

On November 5, 1989, the Israeli Cabinet accepted the U.S. proposal for talks with the Palestinian-Arabs on the Shamir elections plan in Judea, Samaria and the Gaza Strip but seeked guarantees it will not be obliged to negotiate directly or indirectly with the PLO.

A group including some of the most prominent figures in American Jewish life urged Prime Minister Yitzhak Shamir, in a letter dated November 16, 1989 (Heshvan 18, 5750), not to interpret the warm reception he was likely to receive from the Council of Jewish Federations General Assembly in Cincinnati, Ohio, as evidence that American Jewry supports his determination to hold on to the territories and to resist efforts by the Bush Administration to bring about Israeli-Palestinian-Arabs negotiations.

"When you are presented to the General Assembly and all rise to greet you with every courtesy that is due the Prime Minister of Israel, we respectfully ask you this: Please do not mistake courtesy for consensus, or applause for endorsement of all the policies you pursue."

The signers of the open letter to Shamir, which was also released to the press, included leading figures in the American Jewish fundraising community, in Jewish federation life and in some of American Jewish most powerful organizations. Among the fourty one who signed the letter were: Theodore Mann, Hyman Bookbinder and Marver Bernstein.

"Israel must satisfactorily address the matter of human rights of Palestinian-Arabs in the territories, as this issue has drawn considerable attention in the U.S. Congress." said Saymour Reich, Chairman of the Conference of Presidents of Major American Jewish Organizations, at a press conference in Jerusalem, on November 23, 1989 (Heshvan 25, 5750).

"The issue of human rights is being heavily discussed in the Congress. I think Israel has to address this issue and satisfy these critics," said Reich.

The inevitable result of the debate over political, social and religious issues within Israel itself was spilling over into the American Jewish community. The Likud-Maarah conflict has reached the Jewish community in the U.S. This increased the tendency to dissent publicly from the Israeli Government's line over other controversial Israeli decisions, including the 1982 invasion to Lebanon, the promotion of the territories settlement activity, the Jonathan and Anne spy scandal, the Iran-Contra affair and the "Who is a Jew?" debate.

With each controversy there is a gradual cnipping away of some of the earlier rules of the game. What was clearly unacceptable behavior for Israel supporters a decade ago is today almost common.

Fourty-one U.S. Jewish leaders sent a letter to Shamir stating that most of the American Jews do not reject the idea of exchanging Land for Peace.

"Dear Mr. Prime Minister," they wrote, "we understand the limits of our role. Neither American Jewry, nor the U.S. Government can impose a solution or a process on you and the Israeli people. Only the Israeli people and their democraticaly-elected Government can make final judgements on these matters. But we owe you more than courtesy and expressions of respect. We owe you honesty and clarity as well, and it is in this spirit that we wrote this letter."

Since the outbreak of the intifada, on December 1987, Israel's image has been tarnished in the United States, even among Israel's best friends in Congress and the American Jewish community. Since then, there is a much greater willingness to criticize the Israeli Government on some of its actions.

Most of the diaspora Jews have become loyal to their new countries, the countries in which they have been living for generations and prefer the interest of their country rather than that of their old country, Israel. Only the Israeli is a total Jew, because only the Israeli takes full responsibility for shaping his destiny and his country's destiny. Therefore, he considers the Jews in the diaspora as partial Jews only, who have weak character and won't give up the fleshpot, the easy comfortable life in the diaspora.

On his visit to the U.S. Prime Minister Yitzhak Shamir met with the Senate Foreign Relations Committee and House Foreign Affairs Committee as well as with a group of Jewish Senators and representatives before leaving for Cincinnati, Ohio.

The Israeli Prime Minister was polite in his answers but was constantly "attacked" with questions about Israel's military involvement in Souh Africa.

The Jewish Congressmen, in particular, expressed their deep concern to the Prime Minister of Israel about the damage being done to Israel's reputation and image by maintaining military relationship with South Africa.

Shamir maintained that the stories about Israel's military link with South Africa is mainly because of the important Jewish Community that lives there.

Shamir insisted that Israel hadn't signed any new military contracts with South Africa since March 1987. but, must keep the existing contracts until they expire.

Prime Minister Shamir flatly rejected the accusation that Israel was involved in combined nuclear tests with South Africa.

On Thursday, November 30, 1989 (Kislev 2, 5750), in Rome, Soviet leader Mikhail Gorbachev flatly rejected an Italian request to renew diplomatic ties with Israel.

Soviet spokesman Gennady Gerasimov told a news conference in Rome: "We are ready for this step on condition that the Israeli Government makes steps forward in the dialogue with the Palestine Liberation Organization (PLO)."

The two issues remained to be solved by the U.S. were: the composition of the Palestinian delegates and the agenda of the dialogue. The Israelis insisted that the Palestinian delegates would include only Palestinian Arabs, inhabitants of Judea, Samaria and the Gaza Strip. The PLO, on the other hand, insisted that the Palestinian delegate will include also representatives from both inside and outside the territories, and that the PLO shall appoint them.

The U.S. told Israel that deported Palestinians who will be allowed to return to the territories should be considered "inhabitants", which assure the PLO that both inside and outside Palestinian Arabs will be included. At the same time the U.S. promised Israel that it would not be forced to negotiate with the Palestinian Arabs representatives, which it finds unacceptable.

The U.S. told Israel that the main topic in this dialogue with the Palestinian-Arabs will be the "elections" in Judea, Samaria and the Gaza Strip, but at the same time the U.S. promised Arafat that each side will also be allowed to raise other issues too.

On December 1989, the U.S. State Department announced that: "Egypt accepted Baker's five point proposal for a framework for an Israeli-Palestinian dialogue." Egypt reacted by proclaiming that it never used the word "accepted". Egypt added that it would participate in the U.S. "Peace Process" only if it will be allowed to constantly consult with the PLO leadership.

The United States of America's efforts were to reach an agreement on the Palestinian-Arab delegation issue to which Israel will agree to talk. It believed that once the talks get started they will catch momentum and will not stop until the Israeli-Arab agreement is realized. What a naïve wishful thinking!

In order to achieve this, the Bush-Baker Administration resorted to ruse, threats, lies, etc.

Somebody in the White House wanted very badly a Nobel Prize, same as Jimmy Carter.

This can be taken as a typical example of U.S. diplomacy.

The U.S. ended the war in Vietnam when Washington simply "declared victory and withdrew".

The U.S. Secretary of State James Baker seemed to be conducting the U.S. Middle East diplomacy along similar lines.

George Bush thought he could push the Jews hard as he thought that he didn't need any more the Jewish vote for his second term in 1992. On the other hand, U.S. Secretary of State James Baker wasn't sure at all that he would not need the Jewish vote in 1996.

On December 1989, U.S. President George Bush sent troops to the Panama Canal Zone, to catch Panamese President Nuriyega and bring him over to the U.S. for trial as a drug pusher.

In spite of the great cause for which the operation took place, the "Gun Boat" policy was no longer popular in the area of Gorbachev's Glasnost. Most of the Middle and South American countries severely criticized the U.S. for trying to police its neighbours.

When, on July 1989, the Israeli commando raided Sheikh Obaid's house in Lebanon, captured the Sheikh and brought him over to Israel, President George Bush reacted immediately by saying that kidnapping and militancy do not expedite peace. The U.S. even sent a six-question questionnaire asking Israel for explanations.

This U.S. action was an open admittance by the U.S. Administration that in certain specific cases, for self-defence reasons, a country is allowed to go after a criminal across the borders. Panamese President Nuriyega did not endanger the security of the U.S.

The U.S. did not give up its sovereignty over the Panama Zone in spite of the fact that Pentagon experts admitted that the Panama Zone was not essential to U.S. security.

This is an excellent lesson for Israel as far as Judea, Samaria and Gaza are concerned.

The Soviets had signaled their rejection of the most extreme Arab position, which continued to be the extermination of the "Zionist Entity" and told the Arabs that they have to give up their dreams of wiping Israel off the map.

On December 3, 1989 (Kislev 5, 5750), Egyptian Foreign Minister Ezmat Abdel-Magid summoned Israel's Ambassador Shimon Shamir in Cairo, to protest against the IDF "violence" against "innocent" Palestinian-Arabs in Judea, Samaria and Gaza.

"These Israeli practices constitute a violation of International Laws and values and a clear provocation of the feelings of all humanity." Thus interfering in the affairs of a sovereign neighbouring country.

As predicted by many Israelis, the whole of Sinai and Tabah were not enough, Egypt had some more claims to Israel.

The U.S. has been constantly defining Jewish settlemenin Judea, Samaria and Gaza as an obstacle to peace.

President Johnson laid down U.S. Anti-Israeli policy after the 1967 Six-Day War. According to President Johnson, Israel must be got to withdraw to approximately the Armistice lines of 1949. Tactics must be planned accordingly. The U.S. Middle East policy hasn't changed since.

On Saturday, March 3, 1990, in a news conference, U.S. President George Bush expressed the U.S. refusal to Jewish settlement in Jerusalem. The United States of America opposes Jewish settlements in certain suburbs and neighbourhoods of Jerusalem, the ancient Capital of Israel. The Israeli "Peace Initiative" of elections in Judea, Samaria and Gaza was turned into a U.S. proposal for negotiations over the issue of the future of Jerusalem, Israel's Capital, and the right of Jews to settle and live there. What an absurdity.

Therefore, the conclusion is, that the U.S. could no longer act as an Unbiased Arbitrator when it had already acted as a Judge.

"There are great differences in the Israeli Cabinet itself on this issue."

This was President Bush's justification for his intervention on the issue of Jerusalem, opposing Jewish settlements and new constructions in Jerusalem.

On Capitol Hill and in the American Jewish Community, however, George Bush's remark on Jerusalem has generated quite a bit of opposition.

Senator Daniel Patrick Moynihan (Democrat, New York) and Rudy Boschwitz (Republican, Minnesota), have introduced a non-binding, sense of the Congress resolution affirming that "Jerusalem was and should remain the Capital of Israel. A similar resolution had been introduced in the House of Representaives.

President George Bush tried to use the internal conflict in the Israeli Cabinet to drive Israel in a path, which would enable the U.S. President to fulfil his promises to the Egyptian President Husni Mubarak to stop Jewish settlement in Judea, Samaria and Gaza and bring an end to the Israeli occupation.

The U.S. Administration underestimated Yitzhak Shamir because it thought that it could "speak" to Shamir via the "understandings" that they have already arrived, behind his back, with Mr. Shimon Peres and Mr. Yitzhak Rabin both from the Maarah Party.

In firing Shimon Peres, Maarah Party Chairman and partner in the National Unity Government, Shamir has made his distinctive contribution to the Israeli constitutional experience.

Prime Minister Yitzhak Shamir refused to accept the mediation plan of Sephardi leader Rabbi Ovadia Yosef that would enable Israel to respond favourably to a U.S. brokered formula to advance an Israeli-Palestinian Arab dialogue. As a result of Shamir's refusal, Rabbi Ovadia Yosef instructed the Shass Party parliamentarians not to support the Government in the Knesset's non-confident vote,

Rabbi Ovadia Yosef tipped scales against Shamir.

The National Unity Government was a disaster. From its inception Shimon Peres (Maarah) didn't stop to undermine Prime Minister Yitzhak Shamir (Likud), same as he once did to ex-Prime Minister Yitzhak Rabin (Maarah), from his own party.

With the help of Rabbi Ovadia Yosef and Aryeh Deri from Shass he finally succeeded. Prime Minister Yitzhak Shamir's narrow coalition fell in a historic non-confidence vote, on March 15, 1998 (Adar 17, 5750) in the Knesset. Shamir was the first Israeli Premier to be failed in a non-confidence vote.

There was a considerable anger expressed at the way Shimon Peres appeared to have garnered the Knesset majority to topple Shamir's National Unity Government. The Israeli public just did not like it.

When Yitzhak Shamir decided to form the coalition with the Maarah, one of his main reasons was to avoid the issue of "Who is a Jew" and a possible conflict with the U.S. Jewry.

With the constant increase in the rate of assimilation, an important issue like this can be temporarily postponed but not ignored or avoided. Soon it will come back on the agenda and Shamir or his successor will have to face it. But from the lousy performance of his Maarah partners in the National Unity Government everybody believes that Shamir made a terrible mistake, which could cost him dear.

The performance of the Maarah in the National Unity Government was a complete failure.

-Defense Minister Yitzhak Rabin (Maarah) failed to crush the Arab Uprising (Intifada).

-Police Minister Chaim Bar-Lev (Maarah) failed to provide safety and security to the citizens of Israel.

-Finance Minister Shimon Peres (Maarah) failed to cope with the economy crisis and failed to find a solution to unemployment that reached a rate of ten percent.

Minister Shimon Peres' several irresponsible, defeatist, anti-Zionist declarations over the media, weakened the hearts of the people of Israel, instilled doubt in their hearts, doubt of the right of their cause, weakened the economy, injured tourism, distorted the image of Israel among the nations of the world and eroded the international relations, divided the Israeli nation, tormented the diaspora, but worse of all, encouraged the Arabs and encouraged the PLO.

Mr. Shimon Peres believed that, once in power, he would be able to produce a peace settlement with the Palestinian Arabs. Mr. Peres should have known that any concrete move towards any settlement with the Arabs without a national consensus is doomed to failure. Shimon Peres believed that he had enough backing for a narrow peace coalition. But it was nothing but wishful thinking.

The U.S. Administration had hoped that Peres would form a Government and lead it to peace with the Arabs.

With the fall of Shamir's Government the move for electoral reform gathered momentum.

On the night of April 7, 1990 (Nisan 12, 5750), tens of thousands of Israelis gathered in Kikar Malchei Israel, in Tel Aviv, to demonstrate and demand a change in the electoral system. The crowd, among whom only a small scattering of knitted kipot could be seen, represented a cross section of secular Israelis, ranging politically from right-wing Tzomet supporters to left-wing Hashomer Hatzair.

Abraham Foxman, National Director of Bnei Brith's Anti-Defamation League, declared on April, 1990 (Nisan 5750), that:

"If Israel continued to be in a paralysis, what we will see is a weakening of support, not because American Jews like Israel less, but because of a frustration over Israel's inability to act."

"I believe that the intensity of Israel's support is at a low level today," said Foxman. "Israel is going to have to get its house in order and show that it is in control of its destiny."

Foxman pointed to the fact that in the same Jerusalem hotels where a group of United Jewish Appeal leaders were asked to raise millions of dollars for the absorption of the Soviet Jews in Israel, millions of Sheqels were being bargained away as part of the coalition whealing and dealing.

"The American Jews do not want their money to go down a black hole or in the drain," added Foxman.

Massive protests, over half a million signatures and a dozen of hunger strikers only served to confirm the general cynicism and deep disappointment of the old regime. The protesters wanted new reforms in the election system in order to avoid a tie, in order to avoid chaos.

There was a growing public disgust with the entire political system and its leading actors,

the Likud and the Maarah, and a great support for a reform in the elections system. The necessity of a reform in the political system has finally struck a deep chord among a much wider stratum of the Israeli voters. A petition signed by over one hundred thousand voters, in support of such a reform was sent to President Chaim Herzog. A large number of mayors, from different cities and different parties joined the movement for a reform and supported the hunger strikers in the Knesset's Rose Garden.

On May 7, 1990, leaders of the new movement for political changes called on the thousands of demonstrators who came to Jerusalem from all over the country to support the sit-down strike outside the Knesset.

"We will not move until the Knesset acts to establish a public committee under the auspices of the President," declared Avi Kadish, whose hunger strike, during the month of April 1990 helped launch a public campaign for reform in the election system. All these people believed that the Israeli electoral system was at fault. They, as well as others, believed that the elected members must be made accountable to the voters.

In spite of the fact that a Maarah motion of no confidence toppled Shamir's National Unity Government in the Knesset, in March 1990, it failed to form a new coalition in April because of miscalculation.

In April 1990 Shamir, who previously received President Herzog's mandate to form a Government, after Shimon Peres had failed to do so, would not consider the idea of another broad coalition, as he did not trust Shimon Peres. On the other hand, Shamir feared that a narrow coalition could very easily fall apart because of the rivelry within his Likud party, between Ariel Sharon, Housing Minister, David Levi and Foreign Minister Moshe Arens.

The formation of Shamir's right-wing-national religious Government did not please the Arab population in Israel. They felt that Shamir was only a front for Ariel Sharon who is the real power. The Arab population in Israel, Judea, Samaria and Gaza feared also that Yitzhak Shamir, at most, will remain committed to the narrow conception of negotiations grounded in the Camp David Accord and the Autonomy and will reject any talks going beyond the immediate arrangements for elections in Judea, Samaria and Gaza. Other Arabs believed that a strong right-wing Government was more likely to achieve a lasting peace with the Palestinian-Arabs and Arab countries than a dovish Government.

In June 1990, when Moshe Arens became Defence Minister under Yitzhak Shamir he had to tackle with four very important problems: The Palestinian-Arab intifada, the financially hard-pressed defence industries, the defence relations with the U.S., the decision whether to extend Chief of General Staff Dan Shomron's appointment or select his successor.

It was not difficult to guess how much faith Arens had in Shomron. Naturally, he couldn't forget Dan Shomron and Air Force Commander Lt. General Avihu Binun who helped Yitzhak Rabin scrap his "baby", the Lavi, which made him resign from the Foreign Ministry.

Ami Poper, at the age of thirteen, two weeks before his Bar Mitzvah, on his way back from school, was separated by force from his kid brother and dragged into a nearby orchard by three Arabs, who raped him for four hours, six times in his behind and three times orally. When they let him go, the boy was bleeding from his behind, ran home crying and never told anybody of the event. Eight years later, on May 20, 1990, Ami, now a man of twenty one recognized his attackers in line of Arab Day workers in the slave market of Rishon Letzion. He was waiting for this day for eight years. He ran into the house, brought out his gun and showered his attackers. This was Ami Poper's personal vendetta. Finally his eight years secret was revealed.

After the killing of seven Arabs in Rishon Letzion, on May 20, 1990, the United States of America sent out presidential condolences to the bereaved families. The White House never sent out presidential condolences to the Jewish breaved families in Israel, after their loved ones were killed by the Arab terror. This discriminatory behaviour by the U.S. President against the Israelis was a shame.

There was no doubt, whatsoever, in Jerusalem that the U.S. Bush-Baker behaviour had a political meaning. It meant to push Israel to the corner and draw public criticism against Israel. It meant to apply more pressure on the Israeli Government and force her to agree to the U.S. policy of direct talks with the PLO and later, "Territorial Concessions", which is against the very best interest of the State of Israel.

The U.S. Bush-Baker Administration used every possible opportunity to embarrass the State of Israel and put it on the defence. There is very little doubt that the U.S. Administration wanted to influence the outcome of the political crisis for fear of a National Government in Israel, which will oppose to talks with the PLO on Territorial Concessions, thus breaking the great U.S. political "achievement" in the Middle East.

Bush and Baker were losing their patience and started using "Psychology" to convince the Israeli Government. This they did by trying to isolate Israel in the international arena and by threatening to cut U.S. military and economic aids to Israel.

In spite of its promise to stop terror since December 1988, the PLO carried out acts of terror. Israel kept providing the U.S. Administration, constantly, with incontrovertible evidence that the PLO was involved in terrorism and never really meant to stop it.

In order to "purify" the creep the U.S. had turned logic and morals upside down and kept its talks with the PLO going, without insisting, in fact demanding that terror be ended, as promised. "Obviously, Chairman Arafat is one of those key leaders did everything he could in recent months to promote the Peace Process." Said former U.S. President Jimmy Carter in Paris, on April 5, 1990, after meeting with Yasser Arafat for two hours.

Arafat's lies were exposed in broad day light on the Shores of Nitzanim and Gaash, when on Wedneday, May 30, 1990, (Sivan 6, 5750), on the Jewish Holiday of Shavuot, two of his terrorist boats tried to infiltrate the shores of Israel in order to mass slaughter the people on the beach and attack several hotels as well as the U.S. Embassy in Tel Aviv, this, in spite of his promise to stop terror.

On May 31, 1990 (Sivan 7, 5750), presidential spokesman Marlin Fitzwater described President George Bush as "outraged" by the coastal terrorist attack in Israel.

"President Bush condemns the terrorist attack of yesterday (May 30, 1990) and he is outraged by what appears to be a cowardly attempt to target innocent people."

In the event of a terrorist action by any element of the PLO or one or more of its members, the United States' Administration will not be able to sustain its dialogue with the PLO in Tunis or elsewhere, for a long time, and will be forced to stop it.

From the Arab raids in Gaash and Nitzanim and from other Arab militant operations against Israel one can conclude how real and stable are the moderating of her Arab radicals must be.

This Arafat's reminder is a blessing. It illustrates the true strategic proportions of Israel's situation and the many dangers involved in the establishment of a Palestinian-Arab state.

A few days before Abul Abbas attempted his beachfront attack, U.S. Under Secretary of State John Kelly was grilled by members of the House Subcommittee on Europe and the Middle East over the US-PLO dialogue. Kelly admitted that the Administration's policy was to preserve these talks even if a clearcut terrorist attack is carried out by the PLO or one of its subsidiary factions.

Abul Abbas was convicted by an Italian court, in absentia, for perpetrating the terror attack on the Italian cruise ship Achille Lauro in October 1985.

The "confession" of the Israeli Chief-of-Staff General Dan Shomron, over the Radio and television, that "the Israeli borders are not hermetically closed" will only encourage the Arabs to keep trying to infiltrate through these borders, a very unwise slip of tong.

On June 13, 1990 (Sivan 20, 5750), U.S. Secretary of State James Baker "threatened" Israel that the U.S. would cease efforts to get peace talks going unless the new Israeli Government gave a positive reply on its participation in the Cairo-based talks.

Yossi Ben-Aharon, the Director-General of the Israeli Prime Minister's Office said:"What the U.S. Administration wants is to hear a "yes" answers to a number of questions posed to Israel by the U.S. Secretary of State that would have us negotiate with the PLO appointees. This would subsequently be leading to a process with the PLO, and the accompaniying danger of a Palestinian state."

It is believed that the focus of the Washington-Jerusalem tension was precisely the issue of the Cairo talks. The U.S. Administration was trying to "force" Israel to participate in the negotiations with the PLO representatives in Cairo, against her will and her best judgement.

Israel insisted that concentrating U.S.-Israel diplomacy on the issue of the Cairo talks distorted the Israeli Peace Initiative of May 14, 1989, and therefore it should be eliminated. On the other hand, Prime Minister Shamir declared that he was ready to conduct negotiations with the Palestinian-Arabs on the issue of the West Bank elections as well as issues related to the Autonomy and the Camp David Accords.

U.S. Secretary of State James Baker's invitation to Yitzhak Shamir, over the media, asking Shamir, when his intentions for peace become serious, to give him a call, leaving Shamir the White House telephone number, was an impolite, insulting way of approach to the Prime Minister of Israel.

Once in a while the Americans do send down dictates to the Israelis and when the Israelis reject them it drives the Americans mad.

U.S. Secretary of State James Baker declared that there was no evidence that the PLO had been involved in terrorist acts since Yasser Arafat's statement in December 1988. He also said that the U.S. Administration would withhold four hundred million dollars in housing loan guarantees to Soviet Jews, unless Israel halts all new settlement in Judea, Samaria and the Gaza Strip.

Two days later come the sudden statement by the U.S. President George Bush opposing Jewish settlement in East Jerusalem. Naturally, this gave Israel very good reason to bail out of the talks planned to be taken place in Cairo, Egypt. The Israeli Government felt that the U.S. cared more for the interests of the PLO. No Israeli leader, whether from the Right or from the Left will join the negotiations table knowing that the U.S. is on the Arab side.

The Bush Administration went to Capitol Hill, on May 1990, to defend the mass murderer Yasser Arafat and define him as an honorable person who keeps his promises. Assistant Secretary of State for Near East Affairs, John H. Kelly testified that Arafat kept his word and stopped terror and that he was a real gentleman.

In his testimony before the U.S. Congress, Secretary of State Baker praised Egypt and the PLO and sharply criticized Israel on the issue of the

Middle East "Peace Process". The U.S. was supposed to be a Neutral and Unbiased Arbitrator.

James Baker became impatient, irrational and therefore unfit to act as a mediator between the conflicting parties in the Middle East.

One could notice very clearly that there was a rift with the Bush-Baker Administration and a lack of trust and that the U.S. was holding a gun to Israel's temple trying to force Israel to accept Baker's proposal.

Neither James Baker's linkage of housing loans for the Soviet Jewish immigrants to the end of all settlement activity in Judea, Samaria and the Gaza Strip nor George Bush's comment on East Jerusalem did help to build confidence among Israelis regarding American intentions in peace-making.

U.S. President George Bush would have been completely wrong had he made Egyptian President Husni Mubarak promises that he could enforce Israeli Prime Minister Yitzhak Shamir to stop Israel's settlement in Judea, Samaria and the Gaza Strip.

The settlements could have stopped temporarily because of the funds allocated for the absorption of the Soviet Jews arrived in Israel. Shamir would never make a proclamation against the rights of the Jews to settle anywhere in Eretz Israel. This is against his ideology.

Speculators believe that the United States of America fabricated the atmosphere of war in the Middle East in order to convince the European Community to intervene and "persuade" Israel to stop the settlements of Soviet Jews in Judea, Samaria and Gaza. The U.S. explained that these settlements would cause an all out Arab-Israeli war, which will hike the oil prices.

Speculations were that the U.S. policy makers believe that the U.S. will be again in need of more Arab oil and, therefore, it must improve its relations with the Arabs, please the Arabs, obviously as usual, at the expense of Israel.

That was, probably. Why President George Bush and Secretary of State James Baker were so insistent on a progress in the Middle East "Peace Process".

The voices predicting war in the Middle East came mainly from the United States of America in order to put some pressure on Israel to accept the U.S. policy of "Peace for Territories."

These U.S. voices also encouraged the Arabs to believe that by threats of war against Israel they could realize their goals.

The Bush-Baker Administration did great disservice to Israel and the World Jewry by sticking stubbornly to this policy.

Attaining peace is a very noble task shared by every Israeli, every Jew and hopefully by every human being, but, not always the end can justify the means. Steps tolerated when insuring survival cannot be morally accepted for the fulfillment of a political goal.

There is no doubt that the United States of America is eager to have peace in the Middle East. But, there are differences of opinions between the Bush-Baker Administration and Yitzhak Shamir's Government over the tactics to be used in achieving that goal. But what teases the Americans most is the fact that Shamir doesn't to follow their course.

Bush would like very much to change Israel'policy, and it justifies the use of every mean to reach that goal, provided that the U.S. Administration adheres to the international conduct norms. Every dirty trick is moral if it is accepted.

The U.S. intervention in Israel's Government formation process was part of the international conductnorm, and is unacceptable because it violates the minimal rights of a sovereign country, the State of Israel.

The U.S. Administration was so impatient that it was ready to sweep away these norms and even resort to dirty tricks in order to "bend" Israel, its so-called ally.

Even members of Shamir's opposition, who agreed whole-heartedly to the U.S. Administration's policy, found the U.S. behaviour disgusting.

The "leaking" by the U.S. Administration officials of distortions, disinformation, lies, whenever Israel does not want to abide by the U.S. dictate is totally unbecoming and is causing tensions between the two governments especially when it is connected with large sales of U.S. arms to the Arab countries, Israel's enemies.

One could clearly sense this unique, double standard attack on Israel's integrity and reputation.

It was very obvious that the introduction of the Cairo negotiations was being pushed by Egypt and by the U.S. as a means of maneuvering Yitzhak Shamir into an Israeli-PLO dialogue, against the best interests of Israel.

It was very clear that the Cairo meeting if realized would become the centerpiece of a very thinly veiled Israeli-PLO dialogue.

If the United States of America persists upon PLO participation in the Israeli-Palestinian Arab dialogue, it will be difficult for Israel to admit that U.S. is an unprejudiced mediator.

Again, the U.S. Administration intervened on behalf of Shimon Peres, trying to help him attain a majority. The U.S. Ambassador to the UN, Thomas Pickering, the former U.S. Ambassador to Israel sought connection to help garner support for Peres. This is, probably, another reason why Peres didn't succeed to attain majority. It was no secret that the Americans preferred a Maarah government in Israel.

Bush and Baker, the U.S. Administration have done a lot to erode Shamir's confidence in their reliability as friends of Israel and as honest mediators.

There is no doubt that Shamir's peace initiative was tentamount to the establishment of a PLO state in the heart of Judea, Samaria and Gaza, with East Jerusalem as its Capital.

The Bush-Baker Peace Process, a twisted form of Shamir's Peace Initiative is destructive to Israeli interest and Israel will be wise not to participate.

In 1989, and more in 1990, Israel felt very clear the immense international pressure to endorse a Palestinian-Arab state in Judea, Samaria and the Gaza Strip.

Saudi Arabia, the Arabs, the Soviets and even America's European allies were pressing hard for such a state and requested that Israel revise its position of opposition to a Palestinian-Arab state.

On June 1990 (Tamuz 5750), Israel had all the reasons to believe that the United Staes of America, the Bush-Baker Administration had an inclination to yield to international pressure and change its policy from "Territories for Peace" to the creation of a "Palestinian-Arab state", at the expense of Israel.

Therefore, Israel will be wise if it stops its participation in the "Peace Process" or at least until it gets the following guarantees: No Palestinian-Arab state in Judea, Samaria and Gaza. Israel will not be forced to negotiate with the PLO. Jerusalem will not be divided.

Immigration from the USSR will not stop. The U.S.-Israeli strategic agreement will not be discontinued.

On June 14, 1990 (Sivan 21, 5750), in Strasbourg, the European Parliament condemned Israel for what it called "bloody repression", and called for an international inquiry into human rights violations in Judea, Samaria and Gaza. It also supported the proposal to send an International Commission to the "Occupied" territories, that's Judea, Samaria and Gaza, to conduct an inquiry into human rights violations against the local Arab population.

On June 1990, the heads of 12 European states criticized the way the Israelis were handling the Arab population in Judea, Samaria and Gaza.

On June 28, 1990 (Tamuz 5, 5750), Israeli Prime Minister Yitzhak Shamir blasted the European Community Dublin summit for "Preaching Morality" to Israel, while Europeans were selling military equipment and chemicals to Libya and Iraq.

On June 20, 1990 (Sivan 27, 5750). President George Bush suspended the U.S. dialogue with the PLO in Tunis. 21 days after the PLO terrorist beach raid on the Jewish Festival of Shavuot, President George Bush announced that the U.S. suspended the dialogue with the PLO in Tunis. Israel's Prime Minister Yitzhak Shamir's reaction to this U.S. step was:

"One should see the suspension of the U.S.-PLO dialogue as an important and favourable action that we have waited for some time. The U.S. recognizes again that the PLO is engaged in terrorism."

"According to us, the PLO is an obstacle to peace in our region. After this U.S. decision, we hope it will be easier for us and the U.S. to reach common position and understanding to continue the Peace Process."

Israeli Defence Minister Moshe Arens' comment to Bush's announcement was:

"I don't think the decision of President Bush was a gesture, I think it was a demonstration that when it comes to terrorism, the principles and values that guide policy in America and Israel are the same principles, namely that we don't talk to terrorists."

It seems that the decision to suspend the dialogue with the PLO was difficult for the U.S. because the U.S. really believed that these talks could help promote the Peace Process and that is why some speculators believed that the U.S. will look for reasons to resume the talks."

At the end of two days of NATO summit in London, on July 6, 1990 (Tamuz 13, 5750), U.S. President George Bush told reporters:

"What I want to see is the Peace Process go forward. I would only to denounce the particular terrorist act but also to take some action against the person who perpetrated it.

Then I think we could certainly give rapid consideration to renewal of the dialogue. I happen to think the dialogue had been useful.

I don't think Mr.Arafat particularly agrees with that, and I'd be quite confident that Mr. Shamir doesn't, but nevertheless, that's the view of the United States."

Arafat's refusal to condemn Abul Abbas beach raid and Hani el-Hassan, Arafat's assistant's remark that justified the raid and the PLO units continuous attacks on Israel's borders are clear proofs that the PLO neither recognized Israel's right to exist nor accepted UN Resolutions 242 and 338, nor renounced the use of terrorism, as most of the countries and people in the world understand the term. It was not then, met the conditions, which would make American contacts with the organization legally permissible. It would rather seem that, unless the Palestine National Council took some drastic decisions and made some drastic changes, or the U.S. Congress repealed Section 1302 (b), the resumption of the U.S.-PLO dialogue would be violating U.S. law.

The Arabs realized that most of the African countries that discontinued their relations with Israel after the Six-Days War, on June 1967, were renewing diplomatic relations with Israel and the Arabs could do nothing about it. It also became clear to most of the Arab countries that nearly all of formerly Communist countries of Eastern Europe were renewing diplomatic relations with Israel, that Soviet Jews were arriving in Israel in massive numbers and that the USSR would no longer support any Arab military adventures against the State of Israel.

The Arabs, in their very innermost sense, are finally beginning to grasp that the nature of the Jewish link to Eretz Israel, to the Holy Land is something permanent and lasting rather than an intrusion into Arab territory. The permanence of the Israelis in the region is finally penetrating the Arabs' minds. They understand that the Jews are rooted in this region. They are not bypassers; they are here to stay forever.

1990 was a critical year for the Jewish community in the U.S. Some of its ardent supporters were not up for re-election. Others were facing serious problems with their voters and because of the erosion of support for Israel on Capitol Hill. With the tension between Israel and the U.S. Administration over the Middle East "Peace Process", the Senate becomes increasingly important. Even the usually pro-Israeli U.S. Senate was no longer safe for Israel.

The inter-Arab relations are much more complicated than the Arab-Israeli relations. Yet, it is this inter-Arab relation that caused the perpetuation of the Arab-Israeli long conflict, which constitute a major obstacle to a settlement between the parties. The inter-Arab relation forced the different Arab states to maintain a constant belligerent stand against Israel aimed at finally rooting the Israelis from the area. The Arabs believed that Israel couldn't endure a persistent Arab effort aimed to undermine Israel. No Arab leader had the courage to ignore the public Arab support for the Palestinian Arabs' cause. Such disregard would cost him his life. Typical examples were the assassinations of King Abdallah of Jordan and President Anwar Sadat of Egypt.

In a time when Israel is surrounded by unstable, dictatorial, militant Arab regimes, the minimum borders that can give Israel some security are the present borders, including Judea, Samaria, the Gaza Strip, the Golan Heights and Jerusalem, the Capital.

BIBLIOGRAPHY

1. Benjamin Netanyahu, Fighting Terrorism, Ferrar Straus Giroux (New York), Harper and Collins (Canada), 1995.
2. Benjamin Netanyahu, Terrorism-How the West Can Win, Avon, New York, 1986.
3. Chaim Herzog, Who Stands Accused? Random House, New York, 1978.
4. Chaim Herzog, the Arab- Israeli Wars, Arms and Armour Press, London, 1982.
5. Ben Hecht Perfidy, Julian Messner, USA.
6. Churba, The Politics of Defeat (America's Decline in the Middle East), Cyrco Press, 1980.
7. Alvin Rosenfeld, The Plot to Destroy Israel, The Road to Armageddon, Putnam's and Sons, New York, 1977.
8. William W. Ziff, the Rape of Palestine, Longmans, New York, 1938.
9. Ernst Frankenstein, Justice for My People, Nicholson and Watson, London, 1943.
10. Benjamin Shwadran, Middle East Oil and Great Powers, Praeger, New York, 1955.
11. Loftus and Aarons, The Secret War against The Jews, St. Martin's Press, New York, 1994.
12. Meinertzhagen, Col. Richard Henry, Notes in His Middle East Diary: 1917-1956 Cresset Press, London.
13. A. Ashtur, History of the Jews in Moslem Spain, Kiriyat Sefer, Jerusalem.
14. Samuel Katz, BattleGround, Karni Publishers, 1972, 1978, Tel Aviv.
15. Moshe Shamir, My Life With Ishmael, Maariv, 1968, Tel Aviv.

INDEX

315, 419, 423
American Jewish Congress (AJC), 105, 117, 242, 245, 247
American Jewish Organizations, 242, 245, 247, 268
American Jewish Support, 304
American Jewry, 418-19
American Jews, 265, 267-68, 292, 317, 419, 425
American Rabbis, 116
American Reform Jews, 180
American-Reform Style, 134
Ames, Aldrich, 118
Ames, Robert, 269, 395
Amichai, Yehudah, 268
Amin Al-Husseini, Haj, 32, 75
Amirav, Moshe, 324
Amman, 78, 273
Amnesty International, 64
Amster, Jules, 109
Anabtawi, Subhi, 363
Analytic Brain, 360
Anderson, Sten, 296
Androgynous, 133
Angola, 220
Anin, 34
Ankara, 88
annexation, 217, 224, 274, 341, 353
Anti-Defamation League, 425
anti-Zionist, 141, 174, 180, 184, 424
Aoun, Michel, 332
Apaches, 14
apartheit, 266
Apocalypse, 293
Appropriation Committee, 348
Arab boycott, 214
Arab Civil Rebellion, 3
Arab Democratic, 174, 186
Arab Democratic Party, 143, 169
Arab Demonstration, 75
Arab Deportation, 353
Arab Discrimination Committee (ADC), 50
Arab High Committee, 61
Arab High Committee in Palestine, 61
Arab Holocaust, 102
Arab Horse, 168
Arab intifada, 6, 65, 69, 75
Arab-Israeli, 434
Arab-Israeli conflict, 251, 309-11, 408

Arab-Israeli Peace Process, 270, 311
Arab-Israeli war, 430
Arab labor, 86
Arab League, 372
Arab Market, 77
Arab Moslem, 39
Arab Oil Community, 47
Arab-Palestinian State, 50, 94, 265
Arab Peace, 222
Arab rebellion, 38
Arab refugees, 6
Arab rein, 229
Arab riots, 229
Arabs' Revolution, 6
Arab terror, 1
Arab uprising, 6, 11, 20, 24, 35, 45, 65, 72-75, 80-81, 88, 175, 230, 241-42, 356
Arab War, 5
Arab workers, 82
Arab World, 47, 74, 77, 80, 271-72, 277
Arad, Moshe, 128, 132, 378
Arad, Ron, 68
Arad, Shmuel, 62
Arafat, Yasser (Abu Amar), 7, 46-48, 52-53, 76-77, 84-85, 233-34, 258, 274-78, 288-90, 297-303, 305-8, 312-15, 319-23, 358-61, 399-400, 427-29
Arafatville, 266
Arapahos, 14
Aravah, 258
Arb, Irit, 101
Arens, Moshe (Mishka), 49, 87-88, 111, 150, 193-94, 197, 315, 333-34, 343-44, 346, 367-68, 371, 402, 409-10, 415, 426
Argentina, 232
Armenia, 220, 231
Armenians, 215
Armistice Lines, 422
Arrow Project, 285
ARTE, 23
Aryan, Izzedin, 364
A-Shawa, Rashad, 254-55
Ashkenazi, 158, 166, 175-76, 178-79
Ashkenazim, 177-79
"Ashkenazim Only," 179
Atlanta, 130
Atom and Hydrogen Bombs, 258
Attlee, Clement, 244
Auschwitz borders, 46

Celtic, 231
Cental Intelligence Agency (CIA), 88, 99,
    101, 109, 111, 117-18, 287, 322, 395,
    441
Central America, 251
Central Knesset Elections Committee
    (CKEC), 163, 165, 167, 174
Chabad, 141, 177-78, 180, 184
Chama, 31
Chamberlain, Neville, 290
Charles XIV of Sweden, King, 65
charter, 47, 223, 269, 281, 321-22, 327,
    330, 358-59
Chassidic, 177, 180
Chassidim, 177
Check and Balance, 205
Checks, 14
Chemical and Biological Warfares, 107
Cheney, Richard, 99-100, 311
Cherbourg, 108
Cherry, 95
Cheyennes, 14
Chicago Tribune, 396
"Chickened Out," 192
Chief Rabbinate, 133
Children of the Covenant (Bnei Brith), 283
China, 100, 232, 330
Chinese, 53
Chinn, Trevor, 131
Chirac, Jacque, 337
Christian, 65, 331-32
Christian Biafrans, 331
Christian uprising, 361
Christian World, 331
Chulah Lake, 356
Citizens Rights Movement, 205
Civil Administration, 34, 363
civil disobedience, 18, 33-34
civil disorder, 29
Civil Disturbance, 250
civil rebellion, 3
civil right, 180, 319
Civil Rights Act of 1963, *319*
Clifford, Clark, 378
Clinton, Bill, 117, 119, 122
Cluverius (Calabrius), 265, 269
CNN, 23, 28
CNN, BBC, ARTE, 23, 441
coexistence, v, 20, 45, 60, 97, 163, 168,
    233, 260, 349

Cohen, Eli, 109
Cohen, Geulah, 340, 365
Cohen, Ran, 143, 185
Cohen, Shlomo, 320
collaborating, 93, 312
Columbus, Christopher, 15
Communique Number 10, *33*
Communism, 269
communist, 50, 53, 434
Communist China, 264
Communist Party, 236
Communist World, 408
"Complete Israel," 368
Complete Israel Front, 368
compromise, 48
concessions, 74, 87, 306, 333
Confederation of United Zionist, 125
Conference of Christians and Jews, 105
Conference of Presidents of Major
    American Jewish Organizations
    (COJO), 247, 418
conference plenum, 219-20
confrontation, 58
Congress, 240-42, 262, 266, 268, 310,
    343, 346-47, 418-19, 423
Congressional Committee, 108
Congressional leaders, 262
Congressmen, 266
Conservatives, 124, 126-27, 135, 149, 192
Conservative Zionist Organizations, 126
consonant, 263
constraints ministers, 410, 415
Continuing Survey, 159
Contras, 251
Conversion (Giyur), 132-34
Copts, 14, 331
Corsicans, 215
Cosmetic changes, 221
Council of Jewish Federation (CJF), 129
Council of Jewish Federations General
    Assembly, 129, 418
Council of Sages, 180
Country Club, 83, 339
"courage of restraints," 396
Court of Judges, 107
covenant, 53
Crimean Tatars, 14
"Criticizing Jews," 313
CRM, 143, 159, 174, 186
Croates, 231

Crocker, Ryan, 68
Crusaders, 72
Cuba, 220
Cuban crisis, 13
Custer, George Armstrong, 14
Czechoslovakia, 225, 231-32
Czechs, 225

D

Dacca, 29
Dakar, 29
Daley, Richard, 204
Dalkemoni, Hafez, 91
Damascus, 38
Damascus Gate, 338
D'Amato, Alfonse, 397
Darawshe, Abdul-Wahab, 143, 169
Dardanelle (Canakkale), 224
Darwish, Mahmoud, 50, 65
David, 291
David, King, 243
"Dayan Syndrome," 149
Dean, John C., 355
Declaration of Allegiance, 187
Declaration of Independence, 194
declaration of intent, 273
decorative umbrella, 222
de Cuellar, Javier Perez, 70, 395
defense establishment, 56
Defense Minister, 55-56, 58-59, 61-63, 65
Degania, 229
De Gaulle, Charle, 231
Deheisheh (Refugee Camp), 89
Dellums, Ronald, 266
De Mita, Ciriaco, 301
Democratic Front of Liberation of
    Palestine, 69
Dependencies, 16
deportation, 19, 21, 56, 70-71, 80, 92
Deri, Arye, 197, 344, 423
DFPE, 143, 174, 186
diaspora, 105, 128-29, 131, 133, 135, 145,
    268, 304, 314, 346, 377, 419, 424
Diaspora Jews, 314
Dimona, 266
Dinitz, Simcha, 111, 130, 230
Diplomatic Vehicle, 220
Dirani, Mustafa, 394
Dirty Trick, 232

Divine, 376
Dole, Robert, 395
Dollard des Ormeaux, 245
Don Quixote, 244
Doron, Sarah, 338
Double Standard, 81, 317, 416, 431
double zero option, 239
Downsview, 245
Draper, Morris, 269
Dreyfus, Alfred, 115, 120
Druz, 39
Dual Loyalty, 104
"Dual Loyalty" issue, 104
Dukakis, Michael, 155, 194, 370
Dulles, 370
Dunam, 51

E

Eagleburger, Lawrence, 378
east bank, 282
Eastern Bank, 259
Eastern Europe, 434
East German, 301
East Jerusalem, 258, 279, 352, 364-65, 367,
    380-81, 400, 403, 429-30
East Palestinians, 282
Eban, Abba, 46, 110-12, 241, 339
Eban Parliamentary Investigation
    Committee, 110
Eban's Subcommittee Report, 112
Edri, Rafael, 197
EEC, 31
Egged bus, 25, 52, 78, 83
Egypt, 232-33, 235, 270, 282, 284, 286,
    353-54
Egyptian National Democratic Party, 334
Egyptian occupation, 232
Egyptian Third Army, 230, 317
Eichmann, Adolf, 101
Eilat, 83
Eilon Moreh, 165
Ein Gev, 229
Ein-Harod, 229
Ein-Il-Hilweh, 319
Einstein, Albert, 103
Eisenhower, 370
Eitan, Michael, 340, 371
Eitan, Rafi (Refael), 166
El-Adchah, Eed, 87

Hassidim, 174
Hatechiyah, 159, 163
Hatorah, Deguel, 130, 141, 150, 174-75,
    177, 184, 193
Hawatmeh, Naief, 32, 319-21, 323, 355
hawks, 108
Hazaza, Saadi, 64
Hebrew University in Jerusalem, 119, 293
Hebron, 53, 55, 228, 312
"Height Fear," 149
Henlein, 225
Heritage Foundation, 223
Herouth, 157
Hertzberg, Rabbi Arthur, 249
Herzog, Chaim, 142, 184, 318, 385, 425,
    437
Hess, Peter, 129
Hetz, 120
Hever Harabanim, 387
Hevrat Ha'Ovdim, 139, 148, 181-82, 191,
    206
Higgins, William R., 395
High Treason, 115
Hillcrest, 245
Hillel, Shlomo, 144, 158, 186
Himmler, 32
Hiroshima, 14
Histadrut, 139, 145, 148, 150-51, 154, 157,
    162, 169, 181-82, 188, 191-92, 196,
    199, 204-6, 405
Hitler, Adolf, 32, 53, 78, 221, 290, 325
Hitnahalut, 159
Hizballah, 393-95, 398
Ho Chi Minh (Saigon), 265
Hollings, Ernest, 347
holocaust, v, 32, 102, 108-9, 115-16, 297-
    98, 314, 319
Holocaust Day, 358
Holy Bible, 321
Holy Land, 241
"Holy" Moslem War, 75
Hong Kong, 232, 301
Hopkins, John, 119
Horamshar, 38
Horowitz, Stanley, 129
Houri, Simean, 67
House, 142-44, 185-87, 197, 443
House Foreign Affairs Committee, 419
House Intelligence Committee, 99
House of Representatives, 423

Howe, Sir Geoffrey, 300, 372
Hughes, Arthur, 322
human rights, 316-17, 324, 332
Human Rights Organization, 317
Hungarians, 62, 215, 231
Hurani, Abdullah, 65
Huri, Ilia (Abu Mahar), 65
Hussein, 232-33, 271-77, 279, 281-82, 338,
    441
Hussein, King, 7, 14, 80, 226, 228, 232-33,
    237, 243-44, 254-55, 258, 265, 271-
    74, 276-77, 279, 281-82, 354
Hussein, Saddam, 53, 115, 237
Husseini, Faisal, 78, 278-80, 324-26

I

Ibn-Hussein, 329
ICBM, 287
Il Hassan, Haled, 44
Il-Najad, Ahmad, 15
Il-shark-il-awsat, 44
imam, 58
Imam of Jibshit, 394
Imbalanced, 21
Independent Palestinian State, 5, 390
India, 330
Indiana, 114, 300
Indian country, 21
Indian reservations, 70
Indians, 318-19
Indonesia, 330
Influence Partnership, 217
initiative, government's, 391
Inouye, Daniel, 347-48
Inquisition, 14
Intelligence Community, 340
Interim Arrangement, 358
Interim Settlement, 354
International Arbitration, 161
International Commission, 432
International Conference, 89, 182, 214-19,
    226-28, 237, 240, 242, 244-46, 250-
    51, 263-65, 268, 271, 305, 333-34,
    345, 401
International Effort, 349
International Law, 422
International Middle East Conference, 36,
    235, 245
international news media, 241-42

Murkos, Nimer, 42-43
Murphy, Edward, 216
Murphy, Richard, 12, 294
Museum of Lost Civilization, 360

N

Nabi Mussah, 75
Nablus (Shechem), 50, 312
Nagasaki, 14
Nahmanides, 388-89
Najab, Suleiman, 64
Najah University, 312
Narragansett, 14
NASA, 120, 287
Nasrallah, Taysir, 69
Nasser, Jamal Abdul, 50
"National Aquaduc," 356
National Committee of Arab local councils,
    42-43
National Congress of the Palestenian
    Liberation Organizations, 358
National Democratic Convention, 155
National Government, 58, 157, 427
National Guard, 318
"National Interests," 239
National Jewish Communitiy Relations
    Advisory Council Committee, 117
National Rabbinic Organizations, 117
National Religious Party (NRP), 125, 127,
    133, 143, 163-64, 166-67, 174-76,
    186, 191, 198, 362, 366, 385, 387
National Responsibility, 195
National Security Council (NSC), 239
National Sewage System, 162
National Unity Government, 38, 48, 54,
    81-83, 111, 136, 146, 148-51, 160-
    61, 189, 191-94, 196, 199, 201, 204,
    423-24
national uprising, 74
National Wars, 74
NATO, 108, 224, 344, 348, 361, 433
Navahos, 14
Navon, Yitzhak, 157, 197
Navy Intelligence, 102
Navy Laboratories, 119
Nazareth, 228-29
Nazi-collaborators, 96
NBC, 411
Nederlands, 302

Negev, 243, 312
Nerve Gas, 107
Netanyahu, Binyamin, 21, 379, 437
Neve, Yaakov, 82
"Never Again," 283
New Caledonia, 16
"new ideas," 342, 357
New Orleans, 128-29
New Thinking, 399
New Year (Shanah Tovah), 246
New York Daily News, 118
New York Times, 19, 66, 116-17, 274, 342,
    408
next door neighbor, 209
Ngo Dinh Diem, 53, 359
Nguyen Cao Ky, 359
Nguyen Van Thieu, 359
Nicaragua, 220, 251
"ninjas," 79
Nir Amiram, 322
Nir Eliyahu, 229
Nisei, 14
Nissan, 16
Nissim, Moshe, 157
Nitzanim, 427-28
Nixon, Richard, 13, 230
"Niye-Niye," 331
Noah, 389
Noahide, 388-89
Noahide laws, 388-89
Nobel Prize, 226, 421
Nof, 86, 103, 124, 257, 269, 315
Nofim, 86
Non-NATO, 262-63
North, Oliver, 322, 378
Northern Ireland, 232, 301
North Koreans, 53
North Vietnamese, 53
"Not Divorce," 242
Novak, Nimrod, 324
Nuclear Freeze Zone, 238
Nuclear Plant in Dimona, 119
nuclear reactor, 101, 108
Nurayega, 421-22
Nussach, 177
Nusseibeh, Sari, 67, 278-80, 325, 364, 367,
    400, 407

O

observant, 176
occupation, 53, 90, 252-53, 255-56
Occupied Territories, 46, 92, 159, 266, 268, 272
occupiers, 77, 291
Occupying Force, 22
Ofek i, 258, 287
Ofek II, 258
Ofra, 87
Okon, Herbert, 16
Old City of Jerusalem, 7
Olmert, Ehud, 111, 197
Olympic athletes, 225
Operating Table, 227
Oppenheimer, Robert, 103
oppression, 255
Option, 274, 276
Orde, Yemin, 144, 187
Oron, Chaim (Jumas), 143, 186
Orthodox, 124-28, 131, 133-36, 139-42, 144-45, 147, 152, 164, 173-76, 178-84, 187-89, 200, 208, 294
Orwellian charade, 68
Oslo Agreement, 90
Oz, Amos, 268
Ozirak, 101

P

Palestine, 24, 64, 95-96
Palestinian, 88-90, 92-93
Palestinian-Arab National Council, 257, 358
"Palestinian-Arab Refugees Right of Return," 308
Palestinian-Arabs, 3-7, 33-35, 37-41, 44-52, 82-88, 93-95, 171-73, 251-60, 271-74, 276-82, 294-98, 308-10, 327-30, 337-40, 363-64, 366-73
Palestinian-Arab state, 195, 222, 233, 268, 271, 278, 281, 311, 314, 365, 380-81, 400-401, 403-4, 428
Palestinian Declaration in Algeria, 161
"Palestinian Entity," 272
Palestinian Homeland, 155
Palestinian Liberation Organization (PLO), 298-99, 417-18, 420-21, 424, 427-29, 431-34

Palestinian National Council (PNC), 210, 307
Palestinian National Covenant, 210
Palestinian-PLO State, 234
Palestinian Problem, 7, 16, 18, 342
Palestinian propaganda, 76
Palestinian refugees, 89, 441
Palestinian Rights, 359
Palestinians, 61, 69, 80, 86, 90, 261
Palestinian State, 3-5, 10, 19, 35, 40, 43, 46-47, 79, 93-94, 121-22, 167-68, 299, 309-10, 340-44, 390-91, 399
Palestinian Uprise, 5, 61
Panama Canal Zone, 421
Panevezys Yeshivah, 176
Papo, Aharon, 165-66
Parliamentary Committee of Inquiry, 111
Parma 150 Poison Gas, 317
partition, 328-29
partition borders, 278
"Patients Are Running the Asylum," 97
Patt, Gideon, 198
Peace Accord, 108
peace agreement, 235
Peace Conference, 213-16, 226-27
Peace Day, 3, 39, 44
Peace for Peace, 222, 254-55, 382
"Peace for Territories," 222, 257, 270, 430
"Peace Hop Scotching," 216
"Peace Initiative," 362, 381-82, 422
Peace Movements, 407
"Peace Now" (Shalom Achshav), 278, 326, 338, 407
Peace plans, 151, 199, 378
"Peace Process," 228, 323-24, 332, 335, 337, 346, 349-51, 361-62, 370, 379, 382-83, 391, 409-12, 415-17, 421, 427
Peled, Matityahu, 325
Pelletreau, Robert, 355, 379
Pentagon, 101, 103, 119-20, 287, 310-11, 422
Pequots, 14
Peres, Shimon, 110-12, 137, 139-41, 146-48, 153-54, 181-84, 189-91, 204-7, 215-16, 222-23, 225-29, 237-38, 243-45, 247, 401-2, 423-24
Pinkas Sherut, 206

Yugoslavia, 231, 330

Z

Zabotinsky, Zeev, 159
Zaidan Abbas, Mohammed (Abul Abbas),
    64
Zaim, Hosni, 243
Zaldivar, Y, 359
Zalum, Abdul Razek, 69
Zarur, Yusuf, 34
Zeidman, Helen, 127
Zion, 107
Zion, Sidney, 118
Zionism, 94, 102, 106, 109, 167, 169, 214
Zionist, 96, 104, 145, 157, 172, 174, 184-
    85, 188, 202, 210-11, 233, 375, 400,
    422, 424
Zionist Congress, 125-26
Zionist Entity, 33, 422
Zionist Invasion, 73
Ziyad, Abu Ziyad, 325
Ziyad, Toufic, 325
Ziyada, Radwan, 69
Zohar, Micahael, 142, 185
Zucker, Daddi, 143, 185, 338
Zukerman, Pinhas, 120

Whether you are an Obama fan, or not, everyone in the US needs to know, in fact everybody in the world needs to know.

Something happened. H.R. 1388 was passed, quietly. It was not mentioned on the news. Just went by on the ticker tape at the bottom of the CNN screen.

Obama funds $ 20 M in tax payer dollars to immigrate Hamas Refugees to the USA. This is the news that didn't make the headlines.

By Executive order, President Barack Hussein Obama has ordered the expenditure of 20.3 million in "migration assistance" to the Palestinian refugees and "conflict victims" in Gaza.

The "presidential determination", which allows hundreds of thousands of Palestinians with ties to Hamas to resettle in the United States, was signed on January 27 and appeared in the Federal Register on February 4.

Few on Capitol Hill, or in the media, took note that the order provides a free ticket replete with housing and food allowances to individuals who have displayed their overwhelming support to the Islamic Resistance Movement (Hamas) in the Parliamentary election of January 2006.

Let's review ...Itemized list of some of Barack Hussein Obama's most recent actions since his inauguration.

His first call to any head of state, as president, was to Mahmoud Abbas, leader of Fatah party in the Palestinian territory.

His first one-on-one television interview with any news organization was with Al Arabia television

His first executive order was to fund/facilitate abortion (s) not just within the U.S., but within the entire world, using U.S. tax payer funds.

He was allowing hundreds of thousands of Palestinian refugees to move to, and live in, the US at American taxpayer expense.

He ordered Guantanamo Bay closed and all military trials of detainees halted.

He ordered overseas CIA interrogation centers closed.

He withdrew all charges against the masterminds behind the USS Code and the "terror Attack" on 9/11, the Twin Towers..

These important, and insightful, issues are being "lost" in the blinding bail-outs and "stimulation" packages.

If this continues, we are losing this country in a rapid pace.

AMERICA NEEDS TO KNOW!

Presidential Determination No. 2009–15 of January 27. 2009
Unexpected Urgent Refugee and Migration Needs Related To Gaza
Memorandum to the Secretary of State.

By the authority vested in me by the Constitution and the laws of the United States, including section 2(c)(1) of the Migration and Refugee Assistance Act of 1962 (the "Act"), as amended (22 u.s.c. 2601), I hereby determine, pursuant to section 2(c)(1) of the Act, that it is important to the national interest to furnish assistance under the Act in an amount not to exceed $20.3 million from the United States Emergency Refugee and Migration Assistance Fund for the purpose of

meeting unexpected and urgent refugee and migration needs, including by contributions to international, governmental and nongovernmental organizations and payment of administrative expenses of Bureau of Population, Refugees and conflict victims in Gaza.

You are authorized and directed to publish this memorandum in the Federal Register.

(Presidential Sig.)
The White House
Washington, January 27, 2009
(FR. Doc. E9-2488
Filed 2-3-09; 8:45 am)
Billing code 4710-10-P.